1897 - 1997

A Century of Bird Life in Berks County, Pennsylvania

AMERICAN GOLDFINCH
The "Distelfink" of the Pennsylvania Germans

A Century of Bird Life in Berks County, Pennsylvania

William D. Uhrich, Editor
Illustrations by Earl L. Poole
Foreword by James J. Brett

Levi W. Mengel (1868 - 1941)
Earl L. Poole (1891 - 1972)
Maurice Broun (1906 - 1979)

CONTRIBUTORS:

Robert E. Cook

Laurie J. Goodrich

Kerry A. Grim

Rudolph C. Keller

Kenneth D. Lebo

Joan E. Silagy

Matthew J. Spence

Matthew Wlasniewski

Published by the Reading Public Museum
1997

Excerpts and reproductions of articles from *American Birds* are used by permission of the National Audubon Society; from *The Auk* by permission of the American Ornithologists' Union; from the *Cassinia* by permission of the Delaware Valley Ornithological Club; from *Hawks Aloft* and the *Hawk Mountain News* by permission of the Hawk Mountain Sanctuary Association; from the *Pennsylvania German Society Journal* by permission of the Pennsylvania German Society; and from *The View from Hawk Mountain* by permission of Mary Durant.

The photograph of Levi W. Mengel is used courtesy of the Reading Public Museum, of Earl L. Poole courtesy of Dr. J. Peter Muhlenberg, and of Maurice Broun by Stanley Oliver Grierson courtesy of the Hawk Mountain Sanctuary Association.

All line drawings are used courtesy of Helen Y. Poole.
Color artwork is used by permission of The Reading Public Museum, Dr. J. Peter Muhlenberg, and Lawrence Ward.

First edition

Library of Congress Catalog Card Number: 97-68537
ISBN: 0-9654594-1-1

To Samuel C. Gundy

His knowledge and deep love of the natural world
have touched and inspired many of us, for which
we are eternally grateful.

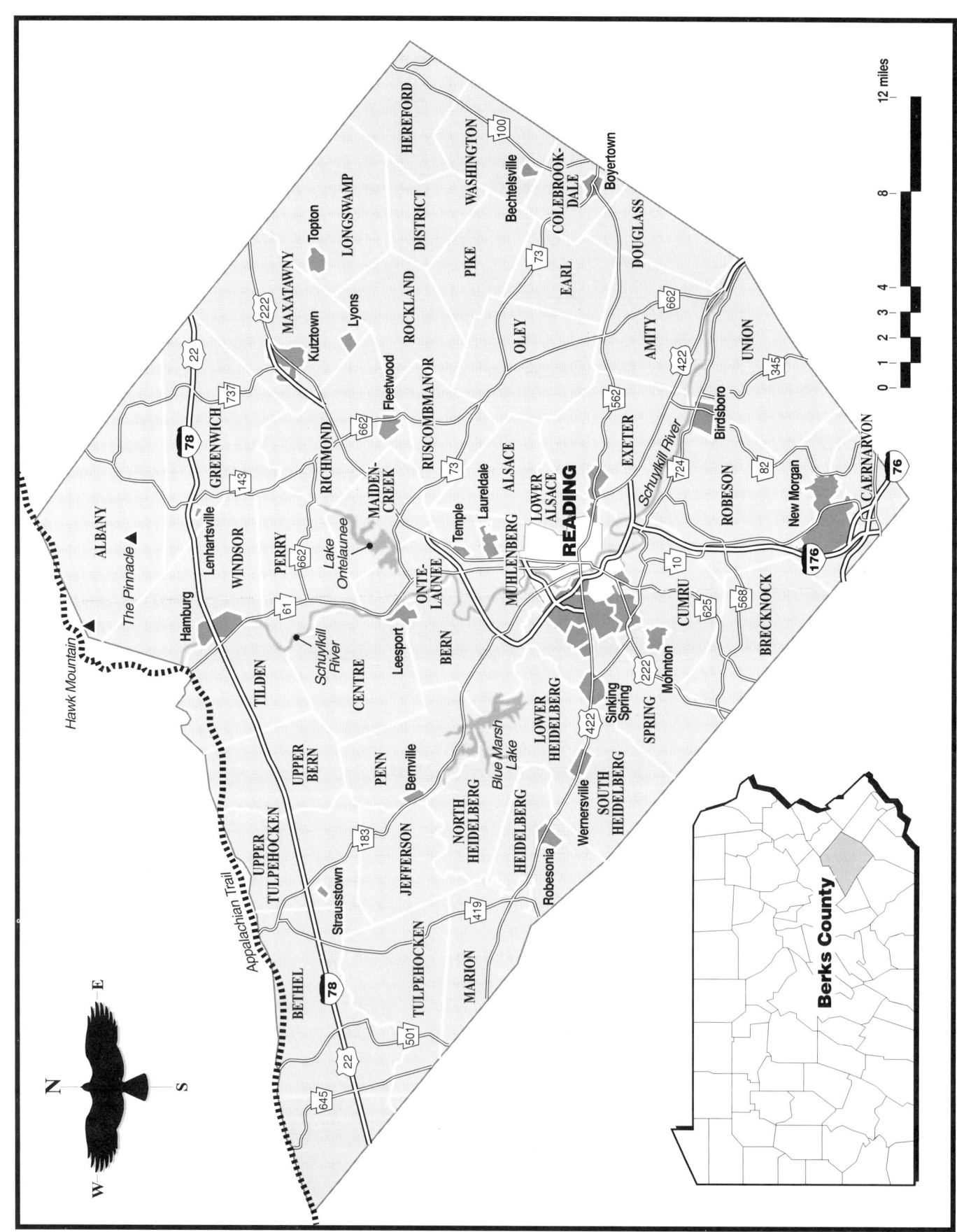

N

W E

S

Hawk Mountain ▲

Appalachian Trail

ALBANY

The Pinnacle ▲

BETHEL

UPPER TULPEHOCKEN

TULPEHOCKEN

MARION

Strausstown

JEFFERSON

UPPER BERN

PENN

Bernville

NORTH HEIDELBERG

HEIDELBERG

Robesonia

Hamburg

Lenhartsville

GREENWICH

WINDSOR

TILDEN

CENTRE

Schuylkill River

PERRY

Leesport

BERN

Lake Ontelaunee

RICHMOND

MAIDEN-CREEK

ONTE-LAUNEE

MUHLENBERG

Temple

Laureldale

ALSACE

LOWER ALSACE

READING

Blue Marsh Lake

LOWER HEIDELBERG

SOUTH HEIDELBERG

Wernersville

Sinking Spring

Mohnton

SPRING

CUMRU

MAXATAWNY

Topton

Kutztown

LONGSWAMP

Lyons

Fleetwood

ROCKLAND

DISTRICT

RUSCOMBMANOR

PIKE

OLEY

HEREFORD

WASHINGTON

Bechtelsville

EARL

COLEBROOK-DALE

Boyertown

DOUGLASS

AMITY

EXETER

Schuylkill River

Birdsboro

ROBESON

New Morgan

UNION

BRECKNOCK

CAERNARVON

12 miles

0 1 2 3 4 8

Berks County

Table of Contents

DONORS

The publication of *A Century of Bird Life in Berks County, Pennsylvania* was made possible through the grants and services contributed by the dedicated, cooperating individuals and organizations listed below.

Golden Eagle

The Reading Eagle Company
William Fox Munroe, Inc.
Helen Y. Poole
The Friends of the Reading Public Museum

Peregrine Falcon

Dr. and Mrs. Barton L. Smith
Andrew Muller and the Reading, Blue Mountain, and
Northern Railroad
Jean L. Leinbach

Egret

The Baird Ornithological Club
Samuel C. Gundy
Anthony F. Grimm
Richard J. Patrick, in memory of Ellen Patrick

Bluebird

Ruth A. Adams
Robert and Ruth Cook
Carl and Carol Drasher
Michael A. & Shirley J. Feyers
Rudolph C. Keller
Bill and Pam Munroe
J. Peter Muhlenberg M.D.
Betty A. Roughton
Wild Birds Unlimited

Golden Eagle donations denote contributions of $5,000 and above; Peregrine Falcon donations apply to contributions of $1,000; Egret donations reflect contributions between $250 and $600; Bluebird donations equal $100.

Foreword

by James J. Brett

Berks County's varied sequence of habitats - from the forested Kittatinny Mountain in the north, to the woodlands of South Mountain traversing its central part, to mixed farmland and woodlot - allows for a fairly rich diversity of bird life. The county's network of streams including the Ontelaunee Creek and Schuylkill River adds important riverine and wetland areas that enhance the richness of avian species. This diversity of habitat is equalled by a diverse group of serious students of field ornithology as well as those whose avocation for watching birds consumes much of their leisure time.

Today those ranks include the likes of Bill Uhrich, the editor of this wonderful and timely treatise on a hundred years of bird study in Berks County. Bill's dedication to this effort is worthy of much praise.

Matthew Spence of Reading, one of Berks County's leading birding enthusiasts, and Bob and Ruth Cook from Elverson have been "birding Berks" practically all of their adult lives. They, and many more, grew up under the tutelage of Dr. Earl Poole, Berks County's premiere ornithologist. Out of his efforts began an aggressive society in the Baird Ornithological Club, the birding organization named after the pre-eminent naturalist Spencer Fullerton Baird, born in 1823 in the family home on the corner of Fifth and Washington streets in Reading. Baird's distinguished career culminated in his appointment as the Secretary of the Smithsonian Institution in 1878. The Baird Club is the county's flagship birding group and continues to introduce many individuals to the joys of bird watching.

But it was radio commentator Jack Holcomb who really brought bird watching into popular vogue in the county back in the 1960s and 1970s with his radio talk show "The Bird Watching Society," which aired every day for years on WEEU. Even my mother, whose "life-list" probably amounted to no more than a half-dozen species, became a frequent caller to the show expounding on her bird feeding station in back of our home in Shillington - a station which she created by throwing out chicken and turkey carcasses and platters of left-over spaghetti. I was embarrassed to tears. But then she was the one responsible for shoving me out the door on Saturday mornings when I was not quite 12-years-old to attend the nature classes at the Reading Public Museum.

Earl Poole was, for many of us, the mentor. And before Earl, Levi Mengel, the first director of the museum, was Dr. Poole's mentor. Dr. Mengel laid much of the early groundwork for the study of birds and bird watching in Berks County.

Looking over a century of birding activities in the county, I am amazed at the strength that both the science and indeed the avocation continues to hold. Reading down the list of field naturalists during and since Earl Poole's day is an exercise in knowing some of the most ardent birders anywhere in the country. Contemporaries of Poole - the likes of such luminaries as Dr. Stanley Brunner, Maurice Broun, Alex Nagy, and Conrad Roland - were largely responsible for influencing those Berks County birders who would follow.

Certainly there are few of us whose passion for birds was not in some way influenced by Sam Gundy. Sam was on the staff at the Reading Public Museum when Dr. Poole was its director. Later, he served as director following Poole's retirement. Sam's sensitivity for the wild world was, in many ways, passed on subliminally, and you wouldn't know you were in Sam's snare perhaps until years later.

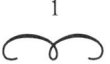

Quiet and unassuming Richard Sharadin of Kutztown, one of the most astute field birders I've ever known, did much to hone my own skills as a field observer. Fred Wetzel, who guided the education activities at Hawk Mountain in the late 1960s and whose bird art is well known, provided the spark many a young Berks Countian would take with them to the field along with binoculars and notebooks.

There are so many Berks County birders deserving recognition for their diligent time afield and in their careful keeping of records that have added much to this new treatment of the county's bird life. Anna Kendall of Leesport certainly comes to mind for her faithful observations and long-term record keeping that we have all relied upon at one time or another when writing about the birds of our area.

Earlier I mentioned the names of Spence and the Cooks, and I am quick to say that Rudy Keller, Ken Lebo, Matt Wlasniewski, Kerry Grim, and Tom Leckey, and the likes of Joan and Harold Silagy and Catherine Elwell are today the leaders of the pack. Laurie Goodrich became guardian of the collection of extensive notes that the three Hawk Mountain curators - Maurice, Alex, and I - kept up to date since 1934, and she has added her own important observations to those records since 1982. Berks is blessed with a dedicated and enthusiastic corps of birders whose observations add solid credibility to this work. Without their thousands of hours in the field, *A Century of Bird Life in Berks County* would never have been possible.

But it was Earl Poole who laid the foundation. Some of us are able to credit Dr. Poole for our own early interest in birds. I will always remember those Saturday mornings when we gathered as a group of young boys at the museum and would be taken on field trips with Gundy and Poole. Often our mornings began with Dr. Poole illustrating on the slateboard with colored chalk the birds we might see on our walk. Bill Munroe, an ardent Berks County birder and an artist in his own right, was among this group of boys whose life-long pursuit of nature, and in Bill's case art, was kindled by Earl and Sam; there are many of us.

Berks County has changed dramatically since Poole's early field excursions. In his introduction to *The Bird Life of Berks County*, Dr. Poole lamented even then that "awkward 'suburbs' are creeping into the interesting little valleys in every direction." That was almost 70 years ago. Habitat destruction is still rampant. *A Century of Bird Life in Berks County* is an important and historical document based upon thousands of hours of field observations. Used in a comparative way, it can speak to the changes in populations and numbers of birds in the last half of this century. More importantly, it can serve as a valuable conservation tool for not only students of ornithology, but for those individuals and organizations charged with protecting the future of Berks County's open spaces and, indeed, its avian species diversity.

A Century of Bird Life in Berks County, Pennsylvania
by Bill Uhrich

Fifty years have passed since Earl L. Poole published in 1947 *A Half Century of Bird Life in Berks County, Pennsylvania.* This volume at the time was the finest county bird book in Pennsylvania. However, it has not been revised since Poole wrote a small supplement in 1954. Poole dedicated his retirement years from the Reading Public Museum to the compilation of a definitive state bird book that he constantly updated until his death in 1972. His manuscript totaled almost 2,500 pages, but the sheer volume of information prevented its publication in its entirety. In 1964, the Delaware Valley Ornithological Club published a 94-page edition of his *Pennsylvania Birds.*

This abridged version did not allow for Poole's treatments of the birds contained in the unpublished manuscript. Now, in *A Century of Bird Life in Berks County* we have preserved as much of Poole's own language from that manuscript as is still applicable, including many of his unique descriptions of the birds and their times of occurrences. References in the text to his writings from 1964 indicate those from the unpublished manuscript.

Since the 1940s, there have been major changes in both the bird life and landscape in Berks County. Another vast water impoundment was created in the late 1970s at Blue Marsh, adding important habitat and preserving large areas of open space. In his introduction to the 1947 edition, Poole lamented the loss of habitat with the draining of swamps and marshes and their conversion to pasture land. Those pastures have now given rise to housing developments. Ever increasing suburban expansion, similar to that experienced throughout southeastern Pennsylvania, threatens the county's natural areas. New rounds of logging and development are fragmenting the forests and changing the face of woodlands in the northern, eastern, and southern parts of the county. All these factors have changed and will continue to change the distribution of bird life in the county.

But there have been positive changes in attitudes, too, throughout the last 50 years. The indiscriminate shooting of birds and the widespread use of dangerous pesticides were two of the most important issues during Poole's time. Now, hawks are no longer shot along the length of the Blue Mountain, as all raptors have been protected since 1972. There is a greater understanding of the effects of pesticides on the environment, and the use of the most dangerous, the organochlorides like DDT, have been banned in the United States for almost 25 years.

Public awareness of environmental issues has increased throughout the country and in Berks County during these years. Jack Holcomb's radio program, "The Bird Watching Society," on WEEU from 1965 through the 1970s energized a new generation of Berks birders. Jack still talks about birds on his "Feedback" show on WEEU. Sam Gundy wrote weekly ecology articles, "Along Nature's Trail," from 1968 to 1982 in the *Reading Eagle* and addressed many of the thornier issues such as habitat loss, pollution, and overpopulation.

Also, active participation by birders through nest box programs has resulted in the restoration in the county of Wood Ducks, American Kestrels, Barn Owls, Eastern Screech Owls, Purple Martins, Tree Swallows, and Bluebirds. Bluebirds especially have benefited, and their numbers are currently at the highest level this century after being nearly extirpated from the county in the 1960s.

Unfortunately, we are constantly faced with new difficulties such as acid rain and the effects of deforestation on the tropical wintering grounds of many of our song birds.

A Century of Bird Life in Berks County offers us an opportunity to understand the effects of all of these changes.

In 1929, the city of Reading completed a dam on the Maiden Creek, creating a reservoir to supply the water needs of its increasing population. This reservoir, Lake Ontelaunee, was then one of the largest water impoundments in the state. Poole monitored the lake from its creation and discovered new dynamics of overland waterfowl and shorebird migration through eastern Pennsylvania. Lake Ontelaunee has been observed regularly since by those who uphold Poole's record-keeping standards.

Wintering birds have been monitored consistently as well. The Reading Christmas Bird Count has been an annual event since 1911, and four other counts- Lehigh Valley, Hamburg, Elverson, and Bernville- have covered the rest of the county. Records for the Reading, Bernville, and Hamburg counts are cited in the text. The Hamburg count started during the 1965 count year, and Bernville began during the 1985 count year. Reading's 15-mile-diameter count circle lies completely within Berks, while parts of the Bernville and Hamburg count circles spill over into Lebanon and Schuylkill counties. The Elverson and Lehigh Valley counts include small areas of southern and northeastern Berks respectively, and only records from those counts that can be attributed to Berks are noted in the text.

In 1947, Poole listed 275 species of birds occurring in the county with 15 hypothetical and one extinct. Fifty years later, the Berks County list stands at 330 species with 23 hypothetical, 23 escaped or introduced, and one extinct.

The records in *A Century of Bird Life in Berks County* are current to January 4, 1997, with several exceptions. Most notably, the appearances of a Black-throated Gray Warbler until mid-February in Bern Township and of a Pink-footed Goose at a pond near Oley during March and April 1997 are included. Also detailed in the Pink-footed Goose species account by Rudy Keller is a summary of the incredible Snow Goose migration through the county during the spring of 1997.

The highest annual recorded species total in Berks is 263 found during 1995. The highlights that year included 27 species of shorebirds, three species of grosbeaks, two species of kites, and 36 species of warblers.

From 1983 to 1989, Berks birders participated in a comprehensive, state-wide, breeding bird atlasing project that resulted in the *Atlas of Breeding Birds in Pennsylvania*. Modern conservation laws and ethics no longer allow birders to collect specimens or eggs as Levi Mengel did in the last century. Nesting sites cannot be disturbed, so observational clues such as bird behavior and the presence of young are now followed to determine breeding. During the atlas years, 122 species of birds were confirmed breeding in the county out of 146 species present here during the nesting season (Brauning, 1992:17).

A Century of Bird Life in Berks County is drawn from Poole's unpublished *Pennsylvania Birds* manuscript and his field journals from 1922 to 1972, both archived at the Academy of Natural Sciences in Philadelphia, in addition to primary source records from Hawk Mountain Sanctuary and from individuals in the Baird Ornithological Club. Illustrated with Poole's extraordinary line drawings and color artwork of birds, many unpublished for over 60 years, this book introduces a new generation of birders to his artistry.

A special feature includes the Pennsylvania German bird names and bird lore. Only through the language and legends of the original settlers can we get some picture of the early status of our

Berks County birds. An article that Herbert Beck wrote for the *Auk* in 1924 introduces us to this feature, while the research into the Pennsylvania German names for birds done by William Rupp in 1946 is cited throughout the text.

Not only does this book encompass a century of bird life, but it also encompasses a century of bird *watchers*, including biographies of the three giants of Berks ornithology: Levi W. Mengel, the founder of the Reading Public Museum and the first to systematically document the bird life of the county; Earl L. Poole, the second curator of the Reading Public Museum and internationally acclaimed ornithologist and bird artist; and Maurice Broun, the first curator of Hawk Mountain Sanctuary.

Levi Mengel was profoundly influenced by Spencer Fullerton Baird, who was born in Reading in 1823 and rose to national prominence as the second secretary of the Smithsonian Institution. The two men corresponded early in Mengel's career. On December 3, 1885, Baird wrote to Mengel giving him practical advice:

"...I shall be pleased to hear of your labors from time to time, and to know that you are likely to make progress in knowledge by your efforts.

"I would not if I were you, attempt anything very ambitious, but in regard to collections would limit any special effort to gathering illustrations of the natural history and antiquities of Berks County, and limiting this even at first....

"...The collection of specimens of animals should be made in different ways. Birds may be skinned, and of necessity mounted, although keeping them in drawers is the best way to begin with. The eggs of birds, will, of course, always be an interesting addition. ...Every specimen should be labeled so that it can be identified" (Herber, 1956:69-70).

Berks Countians can be grateful that Mengel disregarded Baird's advice not to "attempt anything very ambitious," for from his exhaustive labors was built the Reading Public Museum. However, we can also be grateful that Mengel followed Baird's advice that "every specimen should be labeled so that it can be identified." Mengel's extensive collections of local bird skins and eggs with complete data still exist in the museum and form the bedrock of *A Century of Bird Life in Berks County*.

Mengel brought Earl Poole to Berks in 1915, and Poole immediately began documenting the bird life of the county. He was a bridge between the Mengel era, when the shotgun was the main tool of the ornithologist, to the modern era of the binocular. As curator of the Reading Public Museum, though, he understood the importance of specimens as a confirmation of a bird's status and maintained and expanded the extensive collection of bird skins at the museum.

Poole was one of the founders of the Baird Ornithological Club in 1922 and was a charter member of the Hawk Mountain Sanctuary Association.

His artwork has been featured in numerous publications, and he was illustrator for 40 books on various phases of natural history from Cape May, New Jersey, and Arctic Canada to Sumatra and South America, including *Bird Studies at Old Cape May*, *Birds of Malaysia*, *Birds of the Philippines*, *Birds of Colombia*, *Birds of the West Indies*, and *Birds of Colorado*.

Maurice Broun arrived in Berks in 1934 to put a halt to the hawk shooting at the newly formed Hawk Mountain Sanctuary along the northern tier of the county on the easternmost Appalachian Ridge. After stopping the shooting there, he kept daily records of the fall hawk migration and other bird life and lobbied successfully for the protection of raptors. He remained as

curator for over 30 years, and he and his successors have built the Sanctuary into an internationally respected institution. The Sanctuary's records constitute the largest continuous hawk migration database in the world, but records have also been kept there of songbird and waterfowl migration and breeding and wintering birds.

The ornithological center of Berks County during the first half of this century was located at the Reading Public Museum with its active research staff headed first by Levi Mengel, then Earl Poole and Samuel C. Gundy. However, a shift occurred in the late 1960s when Gundy left the museum. Now the center of activity resides at Hawk Mountain Sanctuary, where the staff has been actively engaged in researching the ecology of the northern Appalachian region of the Kittatinny Ridge and, of course, in the monitoring of the fall migration of hawks.

Poole, however, was aware of the hawk migration along the Blue Mountain and paid his first of many visits to the "Eckville gap" to document the migration and witness the slaughter on October 27, 1929. He writes in his journal:

"The picture on top of the mountain is one of bleak desolation, largely burnt-over scrub not over five or six feet high with a few pines, living and dead, and burnt limbs of older trees projecting alone. Twenty to 25 nimrods were stationed at strategic points along the ridge, and every time a hawk, (sharp-shin or red-tail today) drifted into sight, it sounded like a Fourth of July celebration. The birds seemed bewildered or helpless in the cross air currents that blew through the gap, and seem unable or unwilling to rise out of range, passing from 25 to 100 feet over the trees where they made easy targets."

Poole's research was published in the *Auk* in 1934 and is reproduced in the opening chapters of *A Century of Bird Life in Berks County*.

Soon after his arrival in Berks as Hawk Mountain's "warden" on September 10, 1934, Maurice Broun wasted little time in proclaiming his then-radical manifesto of hawk protection.

An article he wrote echoing the spirit of Franklin Delano Roosevelt's political "New Deal" appeared a week later in the *Reading Times* September 17, 1934, and spelled out Broun's "New Deal" for hawks. The headlines read: "Hawk Mountain to Become Sanctuary for Wild Life" and "Hawks to Get New Deal on Preserve...:"

The Emergency Conservation Committee, of New York City, has acquired control of 1,393 acres on Hawk Mountain, in Schuylkill and Berks counties. This area, automatically made a wild life sanctuary, is being posted, and during the next few weeks will be patrolled and protected from all hunting and trespassing.

For many years during this season hundreds of sportsmen have gathered on Hawk Mountain for the express purpose of killing hawks, classed as "vermin" generally. It is scarcely necessary to add that the annual killing here has aggregated many hundreds, indeed thousands, of hawk victims.

On Hawk Mountain, as elsewhere, hawks have been slaughtered indiscriminately for many years. There are but two species of hawks that are protected in Pennsylvania, namely, the osprey and sparrow hawk. Analyses of the stomachs of broad-wings have shown time and time again that this species is wholly beneficial. The red-tailed and red-shouldered hawks have also been killed in great numbers on Hawk Mountain. At least 85 percent of the red-tail's food is rodents, while about 90 percent of the red-shouldered hawk's food is harmful rodents and insects.

Sportsmanship and a spirit of fair play have always characterized the American people. But as regards the birds of prey, unfairness and blind reasoning have prevailed. Popular prejudice based upon hearsay and tradition has been the cause of unjust persecution and the destruction of thousands of birds of prey throughout the country.

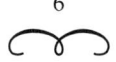

Indisputable evidence has been collected to show that hawks and owls are the farmer's best ally in preventing rodent plagues. In the United States department of agriculture year book, for 1917, it is asserted that the value of crops destroyed annually by rodents in the United States is estimated to be in excess of $150,000,000.

In taking over control of the Hawk Mountain property, the Emergency Conservation Committee desires, it announces, only to pave the way for constructive handling of wild life resources, seeing to it that the hawks get a "new deal."

Broun retired as curator at Hawk Mountain in 1966. He tells the story of the early years of the Sanctuary in his book, *Hawks Aloft*. Alexander C. Nagy of Eckville, who began working for Maurice in 1951, took over as curator and guided the Sanctuary through a challenging period of growth until his retirement in 1981. Michael Harwood in his book, *The View from Hawk Mountain*, offers us a fine portrayal of Alex. James J. Brett of Shillington started at the Mountain in 1971 and became curator after Alex retired. Jim's legacy lies in the internationalization of the Hawk Mountain mission, extending the message of raptor conservation to the Middle East, Europe, and Africa through an expanded internship program and through the promotion of Hawks Aloft Worldwide. Jim retired in 1996.

We are indeed fortunate that these pioneering ornithologists made their homes in Berks County.

We are also fortunate to have a number of public areas available in the county to pursue our birding hobby. Fourteen locations are detailed in the site guides section. There are many others in addition to these. For instance, the Baird Ornithological Club's Earl L. Poole preserve is a diversified habitat located on 54 acres along Antietam Road in Alsace Township. Natural features include a stream, several wetlands, open fields, a deciduous forest, scrub growth and brush, rocky fence rows, and a very small pond.

Monocacy Hill in Amity Township, the Daniel Boone Homestead in Exeter Township, the Conrad Weiser Homestead in Heidelberg Township, the Weiser State Forest on the Blue Mountain in Windsor and Upper Bern townships, and Rattling Run accessed from Clinton Street in Port Clinton are all natural areas open to the public.

Plus, the State Game Lands managed by the Pennsylvania Game Commission are available to the general public outside of the hunting seasons. These include State Game Land numbers 106, 110, and 80 on the Blue Mountain in Albany, Windsor, Tilden, Upper Bern, Upper Tulpehocken, and Bethel townships; 280 surrounding Blue Marsh Lake in Penn, Bern, and Lower Heidelberg townships; 274 in Spring Township; 52 in Brecknock and Caernarvon townships; 182 in Greenwich and Richmond townships; and 43 in Caernarvon and Union townships.

A book project of this magnitude involves many people, but a core group of Berks County birders ensured its success:

Robert E. Cook - Coordinator of the *Atlas of Breeding Birds in Pennsylvania* survey for Berks County, compiler of the Elverson Christmas Bird Count, past president and member of the Baird Ornithological Club, and active field observer in southern and central Berks County for the past 45 years;

Laurie J. Goodrich - Biologist at Hawk Mountain Sanctuary since 1984; compiler of the Hamburg Christmas Bird Count; participant, coordinator, and author of four species accounts for the *Atlas of Breeding Birds in Pennsylvania* survey; and author of a number of papers on raptor and songbird populations;

Kerry A. Grim - Coordinator for the North America Migration Count in Berks County, active field observer in northern Berks County since 1980, participant in the *Atlas of Breeding Birds in Pennsylvania* survey, volunteer counter for the fall migration and volunteer breeding bird census plot monitor at Hawk Mountain, and member of the Baird Ornithological Club;

Rudolph C. Keller - Compiler of quarterly bird sightings and site guide editor for *Pennsylvania Birds* and editor of *The Distelfink*, the newsletter of the Baird Ornithological Club, since 1988; past president of the Baird Ornithological Club; participant in the *Atlas of Breeding Birds in Pennsylvania* survey; monitor of breeding bird census plots for eight years and breeding bird survey routes for 25 years; and active field observer in Berks County for over 30 years;

Kenneth D. Lebo - Active field observer in southern and central Berks County since 1991, member of the Baird Ornithological Club, and traveler through all 50 states and Canadian Provinces photographing 637 species of North American birds;

Joan E. Silagy - Active field observer in western Berks County for over 30 years, member of the Baird Ornithological Club, and participant in the *Atlas of Breeding Birds in Pennsylvania* survey;

Matthew J. Spence - Retired director of science for the Reading School District, active field observer throughout Berks County for the past 45 years, participant in the *Atlas of Breeding Birds in Pennsylvania* survey, compiler of the Reading Christmas Bird Count for over 35 years, past president and member of the Baird Ornithological Club, and monitor of breeding bird survey routes for 23 years; and

Matthew Wlasniewski - Active field observer in northern Berks County since 1983, participant in the *Atlas of Breeding Birds in Pennsylvania* survey, volunteer counter for the fall migration at Hawk Mountain, coordinator of North America Migration Count in Berks, and member of the Baird Ornithological Club.

The finest experience I had in researching *A Century of Bird Life in Berks County* was meeting with this group on Sunday afternoons in Joan and Harold Silagy's home almost monthly for over two years to determine with them the status of the county's birds. The Silagys' warm hospitality was a highlight of the project.

Helen Y. Poole, Earl's widow, kindly donated the use of his line drawings to illustrate *A Century of Bird Life in Berks County*. Meeting and talking with her about the old days in Berks and about the adventures she shared with her husband were a special part of this project for me. It is with sadness that I note that Mrs. Poole passed away in the spring of 1997.

The Reading Eagle Company donated the use of a computer and support services that

made this book possible. My sincerest thanks go to William S. Flippin, president and publisher; Charles M. Gallagher, managing editor; Harry J. Deitz Jr., assistant managing editor; and J. Charles Gardner, photo department manager. Thanks also go to Richard J. Patrick for his encouragement and support.

I owe a special debt of gratitude to Bill and Pam Munroe. Without their donation of design and production work, *A Century of Bird Life in Berks County* could not have been produced. Their expertise and the skills of Theresa M. Hesser, Thomas E. Newmaster, Rachel E. Winans, and Carol D. Wohlsen, all of William Fox Munroe, Inc., are on display throughout this book. Many thanks go to Theresa for coordinating the numerous design and production aspects of this project and to Carol for helping to implement them.

Michael Feyers, science curator at the Reading Public Museum, has been an enthusiastic supporter of this book and has helped immensely with many of the details regarding fund raising and publication. Most importantly, he guided me in the research of the Reading Public Museum's ornithological collections. Thanks also go to William Kelly, Jr., and the Friends of the Reading Public Museum; Robert Metzger, director of the Reading Public Museum; and the board of directors of the Foundation for the Reading Public Museum and its chairmen, John P. Weidenhammer and Blase L. Gavlick.

Thanks for reading earlier versions of and excerpts from the manuscript go to Jim Brett, Frank and Barbara Haas, Keith Bildstein, and Donald S. Heintzelman. I especially thank Jim for writing the Foreword to this book. Laurie Goodrich and Rudy Keller critically read the entire manuscript and offered valuable suggestions. This book is much stronger because of their efforts.

The many members of the Baird Ornithological Club lent their support to this project, but former presidents Barry Pounder, Richard Matz, and Ruth Adams merit special mention. Barry organized the initial meetings to discuss the feasibility of the book project.

Frank and Barbara Haas provided me with a copy of Earl Poole's unpublished *Pennsylvania Birds* manuscript, which is central to this book. Jack Holcomb publicized the book project often on his radio program. I appreciate their help. Many thanks also go to Nancy Keeler, director of development at Hawk Mountain Sanctuary; Keith Bildstein, director of research at Hawk Mountain Sanctuary; Carol Spawn, archive librarian at the Academy of Natural Sciences in Philadelphia; Dr. Henry Tiebout of West Chester University; Robert Gray of Kutztown University; Daniel W. Brauning of the Pennsylvania Game Commission; Dr. Ned K. Johnson of the University of California; Louis Bevier of the Academy of Natural Sciences in Philadelphia; Linda M. Ingram of Nolde Forest Environmental Education Center; and Dr. Daniel Klem, Jr., of Muhlenberg College.

The important and extensive bibliography of Berks County birds was compiled with the help of Donald Heintzelman and Keith Bildstein. George M. Arentz created the map of Berks County used in the beginning of the book. Keith Fritz and Kimberly Miller coordinated the printing at the Reading Eagle Press. My sincere thanks go to them.

J. Peter Muhlenberg and Lawrence Ward provided me with a selection of Poole's color artwork from which to choose. The addition of these paintings to the book has enhanced its quality significantly.

Matt Spence has given me many important insights on the past 45 years of bird life in the county, and I am grateful for this and his dedication to precise record keeping.

Sam Gundy, director emeritus of the Reading Public Museum, offered exceptional historical

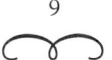

perspectives and helped keep me focused on the scientific importance of this book. His enthusiasm and his generosity saw the project through its early days.

I also thank those who supported *A Century of Bird Life in Berks County* through grants: The Friends of the Reading Public Museum, Samuel C. Gundy, Dr. Barton Smith, Jean Leinbach, Andrew Muller, Anthony Grimm, and Richard J. Patrick. Their generosity paved the way for the successful completion of the book.

Thanks also go to the American Ornithologists' Union, the Delaware Valley Ornithological Club, the National Audubon Society, the Hawk Mountain Sanctuary Association, the Berks County Historical Society, and the Pennsylvania German Society for granting us permission to reproduce historically significant articles about Berks County birds from their publications.

I express my deepest gratitude to my wife, Michele Swigart Uhrich, for her support and understanding throughout the almost four years of this project. She read the manuscripts in their many forms from a nonbirder's perspective and with a writer's eye for language and clarity. Her advice will undoubtedly make this book more accessible to novice birdwatchers.

The arrangement of birds and their common and scientific names follow the order of the sixth edition of the American Ornithologists' Union *Check-list of North American Birds* and its supplements.

Citations appear in parentheses after the date of the record. Initials of the observer are used for the second reference within the same species account. Any unattributed record dated prior to 1964 should be referenced to Earl Poole.

Following Poole's policy outlined in *A Half Century of Bird Life in Berks County*, only those species represented by local specimens, sight records of species identified by two or more competent observers, or those recently identified by a competent observer and supported by a local specimen or an old record are included in this book. Photographic records have also been accepted. A supplementary list follows the main species accounts, and records that do not meet this criteria are listed there as hypothetical. Exotic and introduced species that have been found in the wild in Berks County are also listed there.

A Century of Bird Life in Berks County is not a field guide, but a field companion. Under the heading for each species is a brief phrase indicating the relative abundance of the bird and its times of appearance to help the beginning bird watcher who may wish to annotate a field guide.

High counts for individual species are listed in the species accounts. The following terms generally apply to numbers of birds an experienced observer will find in the appropriate habitat and during the proper season in Berks County:

Abundant - 201 to 1,000 individuals per day
Very Common - 51 to 200 individuals per day
Common - 21 to 50 individuals per day
Fairly common - seven to 20 individuals per day
Uncommon - one to six individuals per day
Rare - one to six individuals per season
Casual - seven to 12 records
Accidental - one to six records

Regular - reported annually
Irregular - not reported annually

Other terms used:

Resident   -   A species that can be found year-round in appropriate habitat.
Migrant   -   A species that is found in the county on its way to and/or from its breeding areas.
Visitor   -   A species that appears in the county for purposes other than breeding or migration.
Vagrant   -   A species for which Berks County is well outside of its normal migration route, breeding range, and winter range.
Local   -   A species known to inhabit a specific and limited area or that is very scattered in its distribution.
Straggler -   An individual of a species that fails to depart from the county in the season or time period normal for that species and lingers into the following season. (Arbib, 1957:63-64; Bull, 1964:51-52)

Poole concludes in the introduction to his unpublished *Pennsylvania Birds* manuscript:

"The pressures and complexities of modern society have led many of the more esthetically and scientifically inclined to seek relaxation in a world of mild adventure, with its background the timeless world of nature, its symbols the creatures that most nearly approach our ideal of a free and unencumbered existence.

"Bird-watching as we know it today has its appeal for young and old alike, for the hardiest explorer, and for the stay-at-home whose activities are limited to the feeding station and banding trap. The display of a pair of binoculars or a spotting telescope is a letter of introduction and a guarantee of common interests.

"While few have the training, time, or opportunity to delve into the deeper problems of ornithology, those who have the native curiosity plus the capacity for accurate, incisive, and objective observation can still learn much that is not in the books and may even make valuable contributions to our present knowledge which is still fragmentary."

Now it remains for the next two generations of Berks County birders to stand on the Kittatinny Ridge, to walk the shores of the lakes and the Schuylkill River in storms and in fair weather, and even to glance over their own backyards to accumulate the data necessary to publish in 2047 *A Century and a Half of Bird Life in Berks County*. Don't hesitate to look some of us up; we may still be here watching.

Reading, Pennsylvania
June 1, 1997

A Half Century of Bird Life in Berks County, Pennsylvania
by Earl L. Poole

Introduction to the 1947 edition

The area covered by this annotated list is the County of Berks, in southeastern Pennsylvania. It is mainly in the watershed of the Schuylkill River, at its nearest point some forty-five miles above tide-water. Berks County is roughly diamond-shaped, with the long axis extending east and west, and embraces about 920 square miles. The main topographical features all run from northeast to southwest, and are, in their turn from the north-western boundary: First, the so-called "Blue Ridge," "North Mountain," or more properly, the Kittatinny Range, the crest of which forms the entire northwestern boundary line, and attains at points an elevation of almost 1700 feet. It is almost entirely forested.

Then follows the broad, rolling "Great Valley," which covers nearly half the entire area of the county and averages about 400 feet in elevation. This is a rich agricultural section, and is closely cultivated in its entirety.

Finally, in the southeastern half are the scattered South Mountains or Reading Hills, which are wooded, but interspersed here and there with rolling valleys equally as intensively cultivated as the Great Valley.

The highest points of the South Mountain system do not exceed 1280 feet in altitude; most of them are much lower. The largest valley of those in the southern hill region is that drained by the Manatawny and Monocacy Creeks, and known as the Oley Valley.

Situated both in the Carolinian and Alleghanian life zones, Berks presents many interesting examples of the overlapping ranges of birds typical of these faunas.

Of the Carolinian species, the Turkey Vulture, Louisiana Water-thrush, Worm-eating Warbler, Cardinal, Barn Owl, and Rough-winged Swallow appear to breed over the entire county wherever suitable conditions are found, while the Fish Crow is apparently absent only from the Blue Mountain region. The latter species appears to have come into the region in recent years as it was unknown to the older collectors and students.

The Blue-winged Warbler is a common breeder in the South Mountain ridges, but has not been known to nest on the Blue Mountain. Of the other Carolinian species inhabiting the county, the Carolina Wren is erratic in occurrence. A severe winter storm will often practically exterminate it throughout the area, but during its periods of greatest abundance it is quite common along the Schuylkill Valley to the southeast. It does, however, occur with some regularity along the Blue Ridge. The Kentucky Warbler is restricted to the more humid wooded valleys of the lower Schuylkill tributaries, and the Acadian Flycatcher was formerly found in the same region, although it has apparently vanished as a breeder in recent years.

The Tufted Titmouse is regularly found along practically all of the larger wooded streams.

Of the Alleghanian species the Least Flycatcher, Chestnut-sided Warbler, and Rose-breasted Grosbeak breed in suitable localities over the entire county, and the Bobolink and Wilson's Thrush have been noticed in June as far south as Monocacy and Birdsboro.

The Golden-winged Warbler is a rare breeder along the Kittatinny Ridge, while the Black-throated Green Warbler is common enough in the few remaining stands of White Pine and Hemlock that exist in the same region.

An altogether unexpected Canadian element is evidenced by the occurrence in summer along the Blue Mountains, of the Canadian, Magnolia, and Nashville Warblers, the Red-breasted Nuthatch, the Alder Flycatcher, Junco and White-throated Sparrow. A surprising zoogeographical anomaly is the occurrence together, as breeders, of the Canadian and Hooded Warblers, the latter usually considered a Carolinian species, in certain ravines in the Blue Mountain region. Both species are equally common along Rattling Run on the north slope of the Ridge.

In the present list I have endeavored to condense the results of thirty years of active field work and association with others who have been engaged in the same pleasant avocation. It has therefore been necessary to attempt to cover, in a few brief sentences, facts and experiences that could often be extended over several paragraphs or pages. My notes have attained the rather formidable bulk of five sizable volumes, and contain notations covering nearly 3000 days in the field. The length of these trips varied from a couple of hours in the morning to entire days.

In contrast to the long line of ornithologists and serious bird students who have made the adjoining Counties of Chester, Delaware, Philadelphia, Montgomery, Lancaster and others in south-eastern Pennsylvania doubtless among the most historical regions, ornithologically, in the country, Berks has received but little notice in ornithological literature. This may seem the more remarkable since it was the birthplace of several eminent men of science, many of whom, however, early sought other fields. Walter J. Hoffman and Spencer F. Baird were among the most prominent of these.

William S. Baird, a brother to the founder of the Smithsonian Institution and a former Mayor of Reading, is said to have collected some local birds many years ago. These were for some time in the possession of the Reading Society of Natural Sciences, which disbanded in 1883, when many of them came to the High School for Boys, where all the labels were carefully removed. No doubt some of Baird's specimens are now in the Reading Public Museum.

John F. Hofmann, an active student and collector of the old school, compiled a local list about 1890 and left a few very creditably mounted specimens of local birds, some of which are still in the Reading Museum, but unfortunately, without data. It is understood that all species listed by Hofmann were actually collected by him.

D. Frank Keller and B. H. Graves contributed some local data to Dr. Warren at the time of the publication of his "Birds of Pennsylvania" in 1890.

Christopher H. Shearer, the artist, collected a few of the water birds about the years 1885 - 1895 in the neighborhood of his Tuckerton studio.

The only existing collection of any size, however, is that formed by the late Dr. Levi W. Mengel between the years 1884 - 1900. Upon reexamination this collection contains a number of specimens that were incorrectly identified, but which prove to be of considerable local interest, and in some cases may constitute our only state records of such species as the Western Snowy Plover and the Greater Redpoll.

More recently, Mr. W. H. Leibelsperger of Fleetwood has taken an active interest in oology and has collected sets of some of our least known breeding species. Dr. Stanley Brunner of Krumsville has a fair series of local birds collected over a long period of years.

The present group of students living in Reading and comprising the membership of the Baird Ornithological Club, has amassed a wealth of data on the local migrations during the past few years, and the result of its work is doubtless of more interest today, since many changes have taken place during recent years in the character of the surrounding country, resulting in corresponding

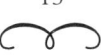

changes in the local avifauna. Certainly, some of the data from the older collections do not agree with recent experience.

In the past thirty years much of the remaining marshland has been drained and converted into pasture land; practically all of the fine large tracts of mature timber in the southern part of the country have been cut over, and the Schuylkill River has been converted by deposits of culm from the coal fields, and waste oil from the factories along its banks, to a condition little better than an open sewer.

The advent of the automobile and the improvement of roads have opened up many of the secluded spots that were formerly havens of refuge for the shyer and wilder birds, and have resulted in bungalow settlements springing up over a wide territory about Reading, while the thoughtless man with a gun has been enabled to ply his work of destruction more effectively.

Then the process of cleaning up the farms by removing the underbrush from the margins of grain fields, the cutting out of dead timber, and the close cultivation of the soil are continuing the process which the late Herman Strecker lamented so aptly, if cynically, in "It has cut me to the soul many times to see just such places burnt over, strewed with lime and plowed up to raise wheat to make bread, to keep the worthless souls in the worthless bodies of worthless beings which live and die without leaving the slightest vestige of a footprint on the sands of time."

In the immediate neighborhood of Reading the "improvements" of the past thirty years have brought about marked changes in the local distribution of birds. The "Hessian Camp," long one of the most productive spots within the city limits, has now been "developed," while the extensive and ever-productive woodland on the lower northwestern slope of Mt. Penn has suffered a like fate, and awkward suburbs are creeping into the interesting little valleys in every direction.

The draining of swamps and marshes has eliminated most of the marsh birds. Only three years ago the marsh near Elverson, which provided the last known local nesting grounds of the Swamp Sparrow and Long-billed Marsh Wren, was drained and converted into pastures.

The introduction and increase of the European Starling is largely responsible for the marked decrease of several of our native species, notably the Bluebird, Purple Martin, and Red-headed Woodpecker.

Even now, the portable saw-mill is eating into the beautiful hemlock-and-pine-clad slopes of the northern Blue Mountain region, and the day may be not far distant when the few remaining stands will be entirely replaced by the scrubby second-growth that predominates elsewhere.

Recent years have witnessed but two events that have had marked beneficial effects on the bird life of the region. One was the building of the Maiden Creek Dam (Lake Ontelaunee) in 1929, and the other the establishment in 1934 of the Hawk Mountain Sanctuary.

The first mentioned event created a body of water of some 200 acres, the largest body of still water within a radius of 50 miles of Reading. This has brought about conditions favorable to a number of species of water birds that were formerly regarded as rare or casual in the region. For the ensuing five years the water remained at a stationary level, with a series of marshy islands and mud flats at the head of the dam which formed easily the most interesting bird-hunting grounds for many miles around. In 1934, the dam breast was raised another 20 feet, and there followed a period, continuing up to 1944, during which the water has never maintained a uniform level during the summer or migration seasons, so that the various types of marsh that formerly attracted some of the more interesting marsh dwellers, were intermittently flooded and dried until anything like an

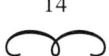

acceptable marsh habitat was out of the question. The resulting larger body of water (1080 acres) has become even more attractive to transient waterfowl, which stop off particularly during stormy weather, to rest, feed, and spend a few hours or days before continuing on their journey. There is little reason to doubt that many of these birds normally pass unobserved over our area on their migrations, since such species as cormorants, scoters, swans, brant, snow geese, gulls, and others that are not usually expected to occur inland, have been detected on a number of occasions flying high overhead at Hawk Mountain, but it is chiefly during severe storms that they are forced down to seek shelter and ride out the storm. For many years I have attempted to visit Ontelaunee during the last stage of each severe storm, for it is only at such times that many of the rarer species may be expected. A delay of a few hours after the clearing of the storm will often find all the storm-battered wanderers on their way, and the water of the lake clear of birds.

At present writing (1946) a new policy is being followed, of filling in the remaining marshes, eliminating all shallows, and maintaining a constant water-level. What effect this will ultimately have on the bird life of the area remains to be seen. Thus far it has resulted in the total elimination of shorebirds and waders and the reduction of many species of shoal-water ducks. Perhaps no conditions will quite equal the 1929 level in attractiveness to bird life, even though certain stages of the 1934-1944 levels were nearly ideal for shorebirds during the exposure of extensive mudflats and marshes for a brief period in late summer and early autumn while the water was at its lowest level.

The creation of Hawk Mountain Sanctuary has done much to attract numbers of bird students from all parts of the country to witness the fall hawk migration along the Kittatinny Ridge, which forms the northwestern boundary of the county.

With large numbers of observers stationed along the ridge daily throughout the three months of the fall migration, a mass of records has been accumulated in the past eight years, and a number of hitherto undetected species recorded. Prior to 1934, this locality formed one of the favorite points at which the local gunners gathered to slaughter the hawks that passed over during fall migration.

The writer wishes to express his obligation to Dr. David Berkheimer, Mr. Maurice Broun, Miss Anna P. Deeter, Mr. Stuart Dreibelbis, Mr. W. H. Leibelsperger, Dr. Levi W. Mengel, Mr. Harold Morris, Mr. Byron Nunemacher, and Mr. Ralph Yerger, who have generously allowed him the full use of their notes and data, also to the following for many interesting records that are included: Mr. Stanley Bright, Miss Mary Deeter, Mr. Harold Dietrich, Mr. Charles Fenstermaker, Rev. E. S. Frey, Mr. Samuel Guss, Miss Florence Hergesheimer, Mr. James Holzman, Mr. Paul Jensen, Miss Constance Kline, Mr. Richard Lawrence, Mr. Adam Leader, Mr. and Mrs. G. Henry Mengel, Mrs. John A. Nichols, Mr. Paul Martin, Mr. Oswell T. Reinhart, Mr. Conrad K. Roland, Mr. A. Lincoln Ruth, Mr. Alan G. Sternbergh, Mr. Arthur Sigman, Dr. Francis Trembley, Mr. Samuel Wishnieski, Mr. Lawrence Dillon, Mr. Francis Heine, Mr. Donald Holt, Mr. Elwood Manning, Mr. David Shaeffer and Mr. Hans Wilkens. The initials of all these observers follow the record for which they are responsible.

In the preparation of the present annotated list I have followed the policy of including only those species represented either by local specimens taken in the past 50 years, sight records of species identified by two or more competent observers, or those recently identified by a competent observer and supported by a local specimen or an old record.

All species represented by specimens taken more that fifty years ago, or sight records made by a single observer and unsupported by specimens are listed in smaller type, indicating that the inclusion of the species thus treated may be subject to some question. In this way I have sought to avoid to some extent the likelihood of error or criticism.

THE BEST BIRD LOCALITIES ABOUT READING

For bird students of comparatively little local experience, it may be well to include here a brief list of the localities that have proven most consistently productive. The letters W (winter), SP (spring), SU (summer), and F (fall) indicate the seasons when each place may prove most interesting.

W, SP, SU, F   Lake Ontelaunee, along the Maidencreek and lower Moselem Valleys. (The only region where many water birds may be expected.)

W, SP, SU, F   Hay Creek, from Birdsboro to White Bear. (A sheltered wooded valley, productive at all seasons.)

W, SP, SU, F   The Hopewell Park region. (Similar to the last.)

SU, F   The Hawk Mountain Sanctuary. (The best place to observe hawks and eagles during the fall migration.)

W, SP, F   Museum Park and the lower Wyomissing Valley. (A list of over 180 species has been made in this limited suburban park.)

SP, SU, F   Rattling Run, southeast from Port Clinton. (A favorable locality for breeding warblers.)

SP, SU, F   Northkill Gap, north of Shartlesville

SP, SU, F   The Pine Swamp, along the north base of the Pinnacle.

Many other localities near Reading are almost equally as interesting at certain seasons, or are particularly favored by a certain species, and may be covered in short walks. Such are the Carsonia Park region, the Antietam gorge at Stony Creek, Charles Evans Cemetery and the Tulpehocken Valley, along the old Union Canal towpath, especially above Charming Forge, and the lower Allegheny Creek, above Gibraltar.

Berks Ornithological Roots
by Sam Gundy

On Monday, August 8, 1887, an article in the *Reading Times* newspaper demonstrated that ornithology was then an active pursuit in Berks County. Professor D. B. Brunner of Reading (in those days public school teachers and administrators were called "Professor") had made references regarding his collection of the ornithology of Berks County. There was no reference as to the magnitude of Brunner's collection which probably consisted of study skins, mounts, and eggs:

"...Leaving the mechanical inventions alone, we come to his storehouse of natural curiosities. Under the head of ornithology we have the rare birds of the county, stuffed by the Professor himself. Nine species make up the list of chicken hawks. The only black hawk ever seen in Eastern Pennsylvania is among the collection. The long tailed, red-breasted, Harlan and other hawks are all perched in groups of dead specimens, having no terror for the farmers' poultry there. Six species of owl belong to the county. The great horned (the largest native owl) and the screech owl (the smallest) are placed by the side of the long eared, barred, barn owl and others, still appealing with their wonderful eyes as in their native state. In discoursing upon the habits and characteristics of these birds, the Professor produced specimens of bird eyes, particularly of the hawk, which are as large as a walnut. He finds they can elongate and contract them, adjusting them for the smallest mice in the field. They never fail in their catch from the highest flight...."

Levi W. Mengel was an avid collector of birds (study skins) and oological specimens (bird eggs) and had one of the most enviable bird collections in the United States. Mengel wrote a Letter to the Editor of the *Reading Times* published on August 16, 1887, responding to the statements made in the Brunner article:

Editor of the Times - Dear Sir: -

In the issue of the Times of Monday, August 8th, there appeared a statement referring to the birds contained in the collection of Prof. D. B. Brunner, of this city. It is not our purpose to discuss the merits of the Professor's collection, but only to correct several erroneous statements made in the article in reference to the Ornithology of Berks County.

The writer of the article first states that nine species make up the list of "Chicken" Hawks. We do not understand what is meant by "chicken" hawks; taken alone there are not nine species that prey on chickens found here, but taking all birds classed as hawks, we have fourteen or more species so far as known. They are named as follows: Of the Harriers, the Marsh Hawk. Of the true hawks, the Sharp-shinned, Cooper's, and the American Goshawk. Of the falcons, the American Gyrfalcon, Duck, Pigeon, and Sparrow Hawks. Of the buzzards, the Red-tailed, Red-shouldered, and the Broad-winged Buzzards; also the American Rough-legged Hawk, and the "Black" Hawk in Prof. Brunner's collection. The Fish Hawk, or Osprey, is also abundantly found here.

One of the best of American ornithologists classes the Black Hawk and the American Rough-legged Hawk as one and the same bird. If this is so, we can note several "Black" Hawks taken in the county. On the other hand, if they are separate species as described by one of our ornithologists of years back, we can again note several specimens of the "Black" Hawk taken in Eastern Pennsylvania, and indeed one of these specimens is in the city at the present time. Others have been taken by Prof. Werner, of Lehigh University. Mr. C. D. Wood, of Philadelphia, has had several, and there is no doubt but that there are other collectors who have had the good fortune to procure specimens of the "Black" Hawk taken in Eastern Pennsylvania.

The Harlan's Hawk mentioned in the paper as being found here is a very valuable accession to the

17

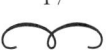

Ornithology of Berks County, as it is rarely found out of its regular districts of habitation, and being an obscure species is often confounded with the Red-shouldered Buzzard in the East and with the common American buzzard in the West.

This makes the fifteenth species of the hawks found in Berks County.

The article also stated that six species of owls belong to the county. To these we add two, making the total number of species of owls found here eight, as follows: Barn, Great Horned, Screech, American Long Eared, Short Eared, Barred, Snowy, and last, but the rarest of all, the Saw Whet Owl. All of these have been taken in the county, and at the present time are in collections in this city.

L.W.M.

While these articles were discussing publicly the subject of ornithology in this area in 1887, it is obvious that the beginning of such interest dates back to some time earlier.

In 1904, Mengel was teaching science, among other subjects, at the Boys' High School in Reading. Ornithology was one of his main interests in the field of natural history, and he already had a collection of approximately 1,600 bird study skins representing birds from most parts of North America and a considerable number from Greenland. These were kept in his home.

Relating to Berks County, Mengel had specimens of all the known resident species, including the skins, nests, and eggs. Further, he also had complete skeletons or skeletal parts and preserved stomachs containing their contents so he could become familiar with the specific foods of different species with variations according to seasons. Information labels on the bottles of stomachs included species, date collected, location, collector, and contents.

A collection of more than 4,000 eggs, mostly American, were also a part of the overall collection. As early as March 13, 1889, it was reported that Mengel had over 1,000 oological specimens. He was then collecting bird specimens, also, but there is no mention of the bird species or how many specimens he may have had.

Ornithology got an incredible boost and flourished to great heights sometime after the arrival of Earl L. Poole in 1915. For some years, Levi Mengel commuted weekly to the Academy of Natural Sciences and other museums in Philadelphia and became familiar with drawings and color works on mammals, birds, and other subjects done by Poole. Poole was an art teacher and a fine naturalist. Mengel met Poole in 1912 when Poole was working on the Academy's mammal collection in his spare time and got to know him quite well and was greatly impressed with his work.

In the spring of 1915, Carl Remment was teaching art in the Boys' High School in Reading and decided to accept a position in New York. Superintendent of Schools Charles S. Foos asked Mengel if he knew anyone who could fill the position. He immediately thought of Earl Poole, and he and Superintendent Foos journeyed to Philadelphia to meet Poole. The meeting did not take place as Poole was in Guatemala with the Rhoads Expedition of the Academy. Mengel then wrote to Poole in Guatemala City and eventually received a reply of acceptance to the offer in May.

In September, Poole was hired to "take charge of Art Education" in the Boys' High School. His success was so outstanding that he was made Supervisor of Art the following year.

The United States became involved in World War I in 1917. Poole went into the service in June 1918. The war ended on November 11, 1918, but Poole remained in France until July 1919. Poole resumed his position with the Reading Schools in 1920 and was transferred to the staff of the museum but remained supervisor of all art education. In 1924, he became assistant director of the Reading Public Museum and Art Gallery. Upon the retirement of Levi Mengel at the age of 70 in June 1939, Earl Poole was appointed acting director of the museum.

The outstanding development, scientifically and recreationally, of ornithology and bird watching in Reading and Berks County to the present, must be credited to Levi Mengel and Earl L. Poole. Mengel produced important scientific records and papers in entomology, while Poole produced three books and a number of scientific papers on local and state birds and illustrated many outstanding bird books by famous national ornithologists. Some of these books are on exotic birds.

It was my good fortune to come under the direct influence of Dr. Levi W. Mengel and Earl L. Poole, among others at the Reading Public Museum and Art Gallery, at an early age.

In my early teens, I was frequently invited to go "birding" with Poole and Byron Nunemacher. In those early years, very few people could afford binoculars. As a matter of fact, none of us young fellows ever had binoculars. We became "experts" by learning to stealthily approach birds to observe them with the unaided assistance of lenses. This became a particularly successful art based on the guidance of people like Mengel and Poole who were always willing to pass their expertise on to others.

Mengel, Poole, and others were practically idols or gods of the natural sciences to those of us who aspired to become naturalists. And while there were hundreds of us in the Reading-Berks area, only a very few of us had the incredible privilege to be so closely associated with them.

Dr. Mengel formed a small group of four of us lads in 1933 and gave us the title of "The Reading Museum Collectors." We were Irving Adams, Sam Black, Harry Gross, and I. We met with him each Saturday morning in his office for a period of about an hour. He gave us instruction, primarily regarding insects, and short talks and advice on becoming naturalists. Then he would turn us over to one of the staff members for further training in various fields of natural history and museum work: Earl Poole - bird and mammal study; Charles E. Mohr - zoology, bats, cave exploring, and mapping; Lawrence and Elizabeth Dillon - insects and botany; Herman Hornig - entomology and training to collect, care for, and work on the museum collection and our personal collections, and to prepare exhibits; Samuel Wishnieski - the skills of museum preparation in all areas of his expertise including bird and mammal study skins and mounts, casting in plaster and paraffin, trapping, etc.; and Kenneth Dearolf - cave exploring and animal life related to cave entrance creatures, mostly insects and salamanders, and the white, blind insects, crustaceans, and fish of the inner caves.

I was fortunate to have the opportunity to spend much time with Earl Poole from 1933 to 1936 when I was a student in Reading Senior High School and a member of the "Museum Collectors" group. I was invited to go on many field trips with Poole. My eyes were very keen and Poole was already having hearing loss of the higher sounds. I frequently became his "sound spotter" to locate certain birds, particularly warblers. As a result, I learned the songs, calls, and other bird sounds and behavioral traits at an early age. Because of these trips, I had exceptional opportunities to learn about variations in bird songs.

In addition to frequenting the grounds of the museum and vicinity, the best birding areas of the Tulpehocken Creek and Schuylkill River, we spent much time in the Birdsboro, Hay Creek, Hopewell Dam areas. As often as he could spare the time, Byron Nunemacher would also be on these trips. He and Poole were close friends as well as avid birders.

In those days, "bird watchers" did not have the acceptance and respect that is recognized today. Such persons were thought of, for the most part, as silly, strange persons pursuing a hobby of no value whatsoever!

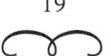

Earl Poole was, of course, very thorough and exacting in his observations and recording of what he saw. Intimate behavior and performance of birds were recorded through words and sketches.

Back in the early 1930s, I was privileged to accompany Poole and Wishnieski to collect migratory raptors at Hawk Mountain when "sportsmen" were killing thousands of them, primarily over the weekends. Most of these specimens that we prepared as study skins are in the museum collection.

Quite some years later, Dr. Poole visited me in my classroom at Reading High School where I was teaching science and asked me if I would consider being his assistant director at the museum. As you can well imagine I was very happy to accept and was officially so appointed by the board of directors. During the four years in this position, I went with Poole on collecting trips, primarily to collect small mammals - bats, rodents, shrews, rabbits, etc., and migratory birds that on foggy nights would perish by flying into tall buildings such as the Berks County Courthouse and TV towers, primarily on Route 183 on the Blue Mountain. The first state specimen of a Dickcissel for the museum collection was found at that TV tower.

As Poole's assistant, I was given much leeway in developing new exhibits and working with the public in dispensing knowledge. In this period of time working with Poole, my education was tremendously advanced in many fields all the way from art and archaeology to zoology, curatorial techniques, audio-visual education, teaching techniques with the "hands on" program in our daily class visitations of pupils from the Reading School District, and many more.

As Dr. Poole aged, he withdrew somewhat, wanting less and less to do with the public. He lost all desire to give "talks" and was mostly content within his own interests, preferring a more private life. At the time, I confess, I could not understand this. He had so much to offer, and I thought he should continue to dispense his knowledge. But we learn a lot about life as we age, and I thoroughly understand now! As one of our "birders," Charles Schaich, would say, "I now resemble that remark."

[Editor's note: The bird skins, eggs, feathers, and other related ornithological specimens survive in the Reading Public Museum Annex building. The collection was greatly increased and enhanced after Levi Mengel became the founder and first director of the Reading Public Museum and Art Gallery and by the next two directors, Earl L. Poole and Samuel C. Gundy. The collection became static when Gundy resigned in 1967 to accept a professorship in the Natural and Biological Sciences at Kutztown State College, now Kutztown University. The collection remained under his care by special arrangement until 1977.

The collection has been maintained since that time by Matthew Spence, the director of science in the Reading School District until his retirement, and Michael Feyers, the current science curator at the museum. Extinct and very rare specimens are included in the scientific collection. Among these represented by very fine specimens of skins and mounts are Passenger Pigeons, Heath Hens, Carolina Paraquets, and Ivory-billed Woodpeckers.

The important collection of mounted specimens is located in an elementary school building nearby.

The Reading Public Museum's entire ornithological collection numbers 10,837 study skins and mounted birds of 1,669 species. The oological collection contains 11,152 eggs of 2,384 sets and 549 nests.

Completely maintained by the Reading School District since the founding of the Reading Public Museum in the early 1900s, the priceless collections are now the responsibility of the Foundation for the Reading Public Museum, established September 21, 1992.]

The Baird Ornithological Club, A Historical Review
by Sam Gundy

[Editor's note: The Baird Ornithological Club meets at 7:30 p.m the second Friday of the month from October through May in the auditorium of the Reading Public Museum.]

For some time, Reading, Pennsylvania, and its neighboring communities had ardent students of ornithology. These various students were, however, freelance students, there never having been any attempt made to bring these people together. On December 20, 1919, the Reading Museum, then housed in the Reading School Administration Building at Eighth and Washington streets, for one of its free lectures to the public, brought Ernest H. Baynes of New Hampshire to Reading to lecture on "How to Attract Wild Birds." Through Earl L. Poole, then assistant director of the museum, Mr. Baynes learned that Reading had no organized bird club. That night, after his lecture, Mr. Baynes organized a bird club for Reading right from the speaker's platform. Officers were elected and other plans were made, but the club never had a meeting.

About 1921 a new and successful attempt was made to form a bird club. Mr. Harold R. Morris, one of the original members, stated that the club was named The Baird Ornithological Club. It was named for Spencer Fullerton Baird, the second secretary of the Smithsonian Institution who was born in Reading in 1823.

Very little can ever be known about the early club, for the members recalled little of the activities and most unfortunately the minutes from these early years were destroyed as a result of a house cleaning at the museum (The house cleaning was an unauthorized activity by an overzealous custodian).

When I interviewed them in 1946 about the Club, Mr. Poole and Mr. Morris both recalled that the meetings were held in the Board Room of the Administration Building about once a month. The meetings were very informal and were comprised of seven or eight persons. There were no planned programs, but general conversation of bird records usually led to chalk drawings and detailed explanations by Earl Poole. Mr. Morris stated that these talks accompanied by the drawings made while talking were very stimulating and informative. These meetings were therefore held for the purpose of gathering and compiling scientific data and for the exchange of information as to where unusual and interesting birds might be seen.

One activity carried on by the members was the building and maintaining of feeding stations.

It was most interesting for me to listen to these men unfold stories of birds and birding in excellent locations which today are large buildings or nearly barren, ornithologically speaking, "improved" parks or playgrounds.

The first record of The Baird Ornithological Club as such seems to have occurred in 1923. *Bird-Lore* first records the Club in its Christmas Census for 1923. Heretofore, all Reading observations were sent in by various individuals.

It is interesting to note that Mr. Charles E. Mohr of the Audubon Society entered the Club in 1927. (It was in 1932 or 1933, that I, as a lad, first began attending meetings. I still have my membership card for the year 1937, and a souvenir 1925 membership card given to me about 1933 by Anna Dieter because of my early interest in birds.) Charles was a zoologist on the Reading Museum Staff and a teacher of Biology at Reading Senior High School. I had the good fortune to

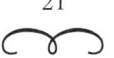

be in his Nature Study Club in the high school in 1933.

There are no available minutes of the club until 1936. From this time to date, the records are fairly complete. In spite of the fact that all the old minutes are lost, most of the interesting bird records are available in past publications by Earl Poole. Some of the most treasured minutes are those kept by the incomparable Charles Schaich. The reading of his minutes to the Club were masterpieces of hilarity and scientific data.

PAST PRESIDENTS:

Earl L. Poole . . . . .1921 to 1946
Paul Jensen 1946
Lawrence S. Dillon 1947
Samuel C. Gundy 1948
Ira Weigley 1949
Samuel C. Gundy 1950
Kenneth Dearolf 1951
Catharine A. Feick 1952
Donald Burger 1953
Charles Schaich 1954
Robert E. Cook . . . . . . .1955 to 1956
Matthew J. Spence . . . . .1957 to 1958
James Gage . . . . .1958 to 1959
Robert E. Cook . . . . . . .1960 to 1962
Matthew J. Spence . . . . .1963 to 1965
William F. Miller . . . . . .1965 to 1967
Robert E. Cook . . . . . . .1967 to 1969

William F. Miller . . . . . .1969 to 1970
Samuel C. Gundy . . . . .1970 to 1971
Gerald S. Steffy . . . . . .1971 to 1972
Robert E. Cook . . . . . .1972 to 1973
Walter W. Kelly, Jr. . . . .1973 to 1976
James Eaches . . . . .1976 to 1978
Jack Holcomb . . . . .1978 to 1981
Pam Munroe . . . . .1981 to 1983
Mike Frankhouser . . . . .1984 to 1985
Rudy Keller . . . . .1985 to 1987
Ed Barrell . . . . .1987 to 1989
Norman Smith . . . . . . .1989 to 1991
Barry Pounder . . . . . . .1991 to 1993
Richard Matz . . . . .1993 to 1995
Ruth Adams . . . . .1995 to 1997
Katrina Knight . . . . . . .1997 to 1999

Some of the earliest Baird Ornithological Club members included Earl L. Poole, Byron Nunemacher, Harold Morris, Anna Dieter, Andrew Stabolepsgy, Harold Miller, and G. Henry Mengel.

Some data I gleaned from some of my old notes from the 1930s may be of interest:

October 1936 *Meetings were held at the Reading Public Museum and Art Gallery along the Wyomissing Creek, as opposed to the earlier ones that were held at Eighth and Washington streets.*

January 1937 *The Club treasury had $61.24.*

February 1937 *A report of 30,000 Starlings that fly over McKnight's Gap at dusk and roost at Lake Antietam. B.O.C. donated $10.00 to the Emergency Conservation Committee of New York.*

March 1937 *The Club showed movies of the Audubon Camp in Maine.*

22

May 1937
Fifty persons present. Dr. Robert M. Sabler of the University of Pennsylvania gave a talk and brought his trained falcon. Paid his expenses of $2.20.

June 1937
Showed motion pictures of the Bald Eagle sanctuary on Mt. Johnson Island in the Susquehanna River. The commentator was Charles E. Mohr.

September 1937
Mohr spoke about the Pinnacle Country of northern Berks County. Ed Hill spoke about the Mt. Johnson Island.

December 1937
B.O.C. sent a unanimous protest against the newly installed bounty on the Great Horned Owls. Christmas Bird Census made for Mt. Penn, Antietam Valley and Carsonia, Lake Ontelaunee, Wyomissing, Pricetown, and Oley. New Audubon Bird Book reviewed by Earl Poole.

April 1938
Discussion of 1937 Bird Census. Talk on warblers by Poole. Club donated $10 to the Emergency Conservation Committee.

September 1938
Motion pictures "Bird Life of Florida" and "Seminole Indians."

December 1938
Sixty persons attended a talk by Maurice Broun "Five Years at Hawk Mountain."

January 1939
Discussion of 1938 Christmas Census. Kenneth Wilson offered unusual data as to the amount of food consumed by birds. Food plantings for birds was discussed.

February 1939
Travel pictures of the United States were shown by Earl K. Angstadt.

March 1939
Club gave a $10.00 donation to Hawk Mountain Sanctuary. Spring migration observations were recorded. Charles E. Mohr organized a committee to plan bird classes for the months of no regular meetings. Earl Poole spoke on "Ten Years of Bird Life at Lake Ontelaunee" illustrated by Charles Mohr (Ontelaunee Dam was opened March 14, 1929).

June 1939
Kenneth Wilson spoke on "Food Habits of Hawks and Owls."

December 1939
Plans for Christmas Census.

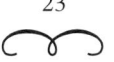

Personal Recollections of Levi W. Mengel
by Earl L. Poole

I first met "Doc" Mengel in 1912, while I was a student at the Pennsylvania Academy of Fine Arts. Like many others before and since, I was fascinated by taxidermists' workrooms, and frequently visited the shop of my old friend "Dave" McCadden, who was the taxidermist at the Academy of Natural Sciences. There, on several occasions, I met Levi Mengel, who was then a high school teacher in Reading, and vice-principal of the old Boys' High School.

Mengel seemed interested in my anatomical studies and earlier paintings and drawings. I remember that on one of his visits I was stretched out on a board suspended on trestles over a skinned lion carcass, investigating the myology of the "king of beasts;" and on another he became quite enthusiastic about a fine Indian pipe that I had found on one of my sketching expeditions to the northwest of Philadelphia. Incidentally, this pipe is now in the Reading Public Museum collection.

Levi W. Mengel at Fritz's Island - 1897

With his genuine interest in, and understanding of, striving young men, we soon found that we had many interests in common. Later, when I was appointed to the staff at the Academy, this friendship grew to a point when he suggested that I come to Reading to help him to get his museum started.

In 1915, a "break" developed while I was on a collecting expedition to Central America, and after some long-range correspondence, I came to Reading and joined the faculty of the Boys' High School. Whatever my job was at the time, I spent most of my spare time about the then embryonic museum, where, at his urging, I usually had some project under way, such as the dioramas that are still in the museum.

"Doc" was absorbed in plans for developing his pet project into something permanent and was then laying the foundations. It was then that I became aware of his many sides. He was working on his butterfly collection during every spare moment, and usually resented any intrusion. Often in passing the old building at Eighth and Washington streets late at night, I would glance up and see the lights still burning in his rooms on the third floor, where he toiled tirelessly on his butterflies, or on the other collections, whether of coins, antiquities, stamps, minerals, gem stones, or other odds and ends that fascinated him.

How, at this time, he found the time to keep up the social contacts that were so invaluable to him in the development of his museum plans, I will never know, yet he did so, attending all the School Board meetings, and dining from time to time with those people who were later to be his supporters when the going became difficult.

Many legends that have sprung up concerning his earlier activities should be "debunked," for many were under the impression that he was with Peary at the North Pole, while, as a matter of fact, he was the entomologist attached to the West Greenland Expedition that was sent to northwestern

Greenland in 1891, to make a study of the natural history of the region and establish a base for future operations. This was many years before Peary made his celebrated dash to the Pole.

Among other members of this team were: Dr. Robert N. Keely, surgeon; Benjamin Sharp, zoologist; Dr. William Hughes, physician and ornithologist; and other Philadelphia scientists who were under the direction of Dr. Angelo Heilprin, executive curator of the Academy of Natural Sciences. I was privileged to know four of the members of this expedition which was purely an Academy affair, as distinguished from the North Greenland Expedition of 1891-1892, which included Lt. Peary and the controversial Dr. Cook, and which became a separate entity after Lt. Peary left the vessel at McCormick Bay and proceeded to explore the then mysterious ice-cap that covers the interior of Greenland, a relic of the vast glacier that covered northern North America during the ice ages.

At that time Peary was chiefly concerned with the problem of exploring the unknown ice-cap, although he attempted, unsuccessfully, at the time, to attain the farthest north, a feat that he later accomplished.

The Academy party, on the other hand, was interested purely in scientific research and remained in the vicinity of their vessel, "The Kite," which was stationed successively at Godhavn on Disko Bay, Upernavik, and in McCormick Bay, where they took leave of Peary and his party and from thence returned to St. John's, Newfoundland, where they had outfitted.

Another popular misconception concerns his important collection of *Lepidoptera*, which remains in the Reading Public Museum. Many are under the impression that he personally collected many of the butterflies in his collection. As a matter of fact, his collecting was limited to Berks County and its immediate vicinity. The bulk of the collection was obtained through correspondence with collectors, both professional and amateur, in many parts of the world. In the course of this correspondence he was in contact with most of the important butterfly collectors of the period, numbering among them such celebrities as Alfred Russell Wallace; the Grand Duke Nicholas Mikailovitch Romanoff; Baron Lionel Rothschild; Adalbert Seitz, author of the monumental work, "The Macrolepidoptera of the World;" Andre Avinoff, who later became Director of the Carnegie Museum; and others.

Besides the amassing of his collections, Dr. Mengel's own scientific work was limited to his "Catalogue of the Erycinidae," 1905, about 20 descriptions of new species and forms that were published in the "Entomological News" between 1892 and 1916, and a few articles in local periodicals.

Many of the "uniques" that were received by him were sent to Dr. Henry Skinner of the Academy of Natural Sciences in Philadelphia, who described them and apparently kept them in the historic collection of the Academy of Natural Sciences, where they no doubt still remain. Concerning his attitude in permitting others to describe the new species that he had recognized, he frequently stated that he did not have the "ego itch."

From 1911 on much of Mengel's time was devoted to his plans for the museum, and his work on the butterfly collection became more of an evening avocation, which was taken up and dropped intermittently until shortly before his death, when his eyesight failed to such an extent that he was no longer able to see details of structure.

So much for two of the important incidents in his life. Of the museum and its trials and tribulations, I shall have more to write later.

Of the earlier events in his life he later wrote a series of memoirs at the insistence of some of his friends. These are much too lengthy to go into here, but there are a number of incidents that shed

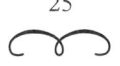

some light on his early life that may be reconstructed in part from his collecting activities and from his early writings, which were chiefly of a personal and introspective nature.

From his early childhood, he manifested a strong interest in all things scientific, and according to his own confession, was a born collector of just about everything that might be of interest.

He joined and became active in such scientific organizations as appeared in Reading from time to time, and one of the highlights of his earlier years was his meeting with Spencer F. Baird, who visited his family in Reading, and to whom he showed his collections, to be admonished with the advice to always keep data with the things that he collected. This advice he always remembered and followed throughout his life.

Other acquaintances who made a great impression on him were Dr. Walter T. Hoffman, the ethnologist, who occasionally visited in Reading; and especially Herman Strecker, a salty personality of Reading whose important collection of butterflies was the inspiration for his specialization in *Lepidoptera*.

Many other acquaintances were made through his more or less minor interest in birds, mammals, minerals, gems, Indian relics, and art and historical objects, which were continued intermittently from time to time.

Fortunately, he engaged in some business ventures that were lucrative enough to permit him to indulge in these activities. He went into the carpet business for a while, but his health made it imperative that he find some other means of livelihood; so he took over the management of the old flour mill, which still stands along the Wyomissing Creek near the museum. Here he became engaged in a wheat exporting business which was highly successful until tariff problems made the venture less lucrative, and he became a science teacher in the old Boys' High School. It was then that he became impressed with the advantage of being able to show his pupils some of the things that they were reading about in their textbooks.

I have listened to many of the tales and reminiscences of his old pupils, practically all of whom held him in high regard. There are many stories of his teaching methods that were not strictly orthodox at the time; of his interest in the boys' personal affairs; of various field trips, during one of which some of the boys rolled rocks onto the railroad from the flanks of Mt. Neversink and nearly caused serious trouble; of one student who allegedly hypnotized another in the classroom; and especially of "Doc's" fondness for the "pernicious weed," which sometimes led to embarrassing situations, and the Prince Albert can that he kept in his desk drawer as an emergency cuspidor.

At that time he caused a certain amount of amusement because of his predilection for celluloid collars, snap-on bow ties, black hat, and Congress "gators." Yet all agreed that he was an excellent teacher and "got results."

His personal interest in his better students led to his many ventures in aiding them in advancing their education, often at the cost of serious inconvenience, and as he often said later, "Only one of these boys failed to pay back the money that I loaned."

His dedication to his life work of developing a museum was responsible for many of his social contacts and it must be said that he laid his plans well. Yet, he often, in later life, spoke of himself as a "lonely old man." At one stage, one of our mutual friends, upon climbing to his fortress on the top floor of the old Administration Building, found him in a despondent mood with his head on his arm. Upon being greeted, he complained that his efforts were not appreciated, and he was thoroughly discouraged, a thought that must have occurred to him many times in his long struggle to achieve his goal.

Dr. Earl L. Poole

by J. Peter Muhlenberg, M.D.

Dr. Poole, 80, and residing in West Reading, in his years at the museum earned a national reputation as an illustrator, painter, sculptor, scientist, ornithologist, and author.

As an artist, his reproductions of birds and animals have won for him a reputation as one of the leading figures in that field; his paintings have been exhibited by the foremost art galleries and natural science academies in the commonwealth.

His pelican statue - cast into plaster before being made a bronze model - was his creative gift to the museum, that he helped to achieve a national reputation, and to the citizens of Berks County. It also is an artistic creation that ought to be seen by people who admire works of art.

...The death Sunday of Dr. Earl L. Poole left a scientific void in his adopted Berks County. His views and talents were held in the highest esteem by authorities in scientific research and endeavor, fields to which he had devoted his lifetime.

Although he stepped into big shoes when he followed Dr. Levi H. Mengel as curator of the Reading Public Museum and Art Gallery, Dr. Poole's fame, at his retirement in 1957 and at the mandatory retirement age of 65, was to outstrip that of his famed mentor.

...Genial and versatile, this cooperative and dedicated man of gentle humor, whose early spadework is mainly responsible for the Reading Planetarium that rises on the museum grounds, has been known as the board of appeals for answers to all questions pertaining to natural phenomena, from birds and bugs and earth tremors to dinosaurs, meteors, and northern lights.

Earl L. Poole

As old friends we usually had a lot to chat about. About the only thing this quiet man seemed reluctant to talk about was his own personal achievements. One had to be acquainted with them to know of his worldwide reputation.

As museum curator, Dr. Poole aimed at making the museum appealing to both children and the average citizens; as an ornithologist, he was recognized as Pennsylvania's top expert on birds; as an artist he was known internationally as one of the world's great painters of birds; as a human being who was always willing to share his scientific knowledge with others - he was loved by many - especially newspaper reporters to whom he was always most cooperative... such is the great legacy that Dr. Earl L. Poole leaves to Berks County, the commonwealth, and the world. We'll miss him greatly.

- Editorial by John Walsh in the *Reading Eagle* July 11, 1972

Born October 30, 1891, in Haddonfield, New Jersey, Earl Lincoln Poole was a son of John H. and Ida Dungan Poole, both of whom had considerable musical talent.

Poole's mother was an operatic soprano in Philadelphia, and his father was a flutist with the Philadelphia Orchestra. Earl was in the chorus of the Philadelphia Orchestra as a young boy, and this probably explains his penchant for operatic and symphonic music which persisted throughout his life. He was especially fond of Mozart.

Poole developed a keen interest in drawing at an early age. In elementary school it was found that one of the best ways to keep him out of mischief was to let him color. He had to visit the principal one time, and as a punishment he was required to paint a mural.

He attended Central High School in Philadelphia and then studied at the Pennsylvania Academy of Fine Arts and the Academy of Natural Sciences, where he had been a Jessup Scholar.

While still a resident of Philadelphia, Poole taught two years at Roman Catholic High School and a term at Public Industrial Art School. He continued his affiliation with the Academy of Natural Sciences and traveled extensively to study natural history. In 1910 he joined the Delaware Valley Ornithological Club.

It was in 1912 that Poole met Levi Mengel, the founder and first director of the Reading Public Museum, a well-known lepidopterist, and an active member of the Academy of Natural Sciences.

In 1913, at the age of 22, Poole illustrated with 14 color plates the *Birds of Virginia*. Among the many comments on his artwork was one by William Brewster, the noted Massachusetts ornithologist, who believed that "the illustrations are of unusual merit."

Mengel took a liking to Poole and admired his drawings of mammals done at the academy. Near the end of the 1914-1915 school year, the art instructor at the Reading Boy's High School announced he would not be returning. Of course, Poole came to mind as a replacement. Mengel went to Philadelphia to recruit Poole only to find he had gone to Honduras and Guatemala on the Rhoads Expedition. He sent him a letter and Poole replied affirmatively and came to Reading in September 1915 to take charge of art classes at Boy's High - teaching drawing and design - and to render incidental help with museum projects.

After only a single year of work at Reading, Poole was promoted to supervisor of art on the high school level.

From 1917 to 1918, Poole did wash drawings for his intended book *Days with the Birds*, which was never published, and yet his philosophy at that time gives us insight into his goals, as quoted in his preface:

"The constantly increasing interest in wildlife in general, but more especially in our attractive friends and neighbors, the birds, has created a demand for a nontechnical, yet scientifically accurate work, which could be used as a supplementary reader in the upper grammar grades."

Poole writes in later chapters:

"What wonderful creatures birds are! How intensely alive and full of the joy of living they seem, as when we awaken on some bright spring morning and hear the chorus of bird voices that arises from every tree and bush. It seems as though the very trees and meadows themselves were voicing their happiness at the return of springtime... yet how many of us greet these scenes with blind eyes and deaf ears, little realizing what a world of interesting neighbors we are surrounded by daily, until one day, perhaps, some brightly clad stranger crosses our path and fills us with a great desire to know his name and something of his habits.

"...How well I remember as a boy the mixed sense of delight and longing caused by the great variety of what were to me unnamed birds which seem to swarm in the woods during late April and May. How their numbers and variety bewilder and fill one with a desire to know their names and habitats; until one by one those mysteries are cleared up, and new ones are met and take their places, leading one to an endless interest in these most fascinating neighbors of the meadows and woodlands."

After serving in France during World War I, Poole was formally transferred to the museum staff in 1920 and was named assistant director of the museum in 1925.

Both he and Mengel were firm believers in visual education. Newspaper articles of the period abound with reports of his discoveries and various activities which were in addition to his work at the museum and duties as supervisor of art and included writing, illustrations on a prolific scale, and bird study on a formal basis.

He was invited to exhibit his art work at a number of prestigious exhibitions, varying in location from the Carnegie Museum to the Los Angeles Museum, and the Art Association in Harrisburg. Also featured in these exhibits were works by such artists as Frank Benson, Rex Brasher, Allan C. Brooks, Louis Agassiz Fuertes, Frances L. Jaques, Roger Tory Peterson, George Miksch Sutton, and Conrad Roland.

Poole's entry of "Harpy Eagle with Spoonbill" in the Los Angeles exhibit won him a gold medal at the San Francisco World's Fair. A reviewer of the exhibit referred to Poole as "an artist of wide versatility and finished technique."

He was one of the the founders of the Baird Ornithological Club and served as its president until the mid-1940s. In 1930, he wrote *The Bird Life of Berks County, Pennsylvania*, published by the Reading Public Museum and Art Gallery. He dedicated this volume to Dr. Levi Mengel. In 1932 he wrote *A Survey of the Mammals of Berks County*, which also was published by the museum.

After the founding of Hawk Mountain Sanctuary in 1934, Earl took an active role in promoting the association, serving on its board of directors for many years. In one of the family scrapbooks is his certificate number 3 in the sanctuary registration.

On May 9, 1939, Poole was named director of the Reading Public Museum upon Levi Mengel's retirement.

Among the books Poole illustrated are James Bond's *Birds of the West Indies*, Witmer Stone's *Bird Studies at Old Cape May*, William J. Hamilton's *The Mammals of the Eastern United States*, Richard Pough's *Audubon Bird Guide - Water Birds*, Jean Delacour's and Ernst Mayr's *Birds of the Philippines*, and R. Meyer De Schauensee's *Birds of Colombia*.

He painted covers for 25 issues of the *Pennsylvania Game News* over the years, and during 1944 and 1945, Poole did sketches of wildlife depicting 34 different species with a prevailing conservation theme that appeared in the *Reading Eagle* and the *Reading Times*.

In 1947, the museum published Poole's *A Half Century of Bird Life in Berks County, Pennsylvania*, an excellent, comprehensive regional survey. Maurice Broun said of this volume, "Almost every page bears the consummate artistry of Poole's line drawings of birds. No other county in Pennsylvania can boast a comparable work."

On June 11, 1948, at the 161st annual commencement exercises at Franklin and Marshall College in Lancaster, an Honorary Degree of Doctor of Science was bestowed upon Poole. The citation described him as an artist, scientist, teacher, and author and classified him as "one of America's leading naturalists and one of its great artists of bird and animal life."

After his retirement from the museum in 1957, Poole began work on *The Birds of Pennsylvania* and completed a 2,500-page manuscript by 1964. Unfortunately, the size of the work prevented its publication. It is currently in the archives of the Academy of Natural Sciences in Philadelphia and is used by bird scholars throughout the state. But in 1964, a condensed version entitled *Pennsylvania Birds* was published with the aid of the Delaware Valley Ornithological Club, of which Poole was a long-time member.

Albert E. Conway in the preface to this book writes of Poole: "From personal familiarity with the literature, this writer can attest to the thoroughness and accuracy of Earl Poole in this tremendous task. ...It has been the writer's privilege to have known Earl Poole since 1937. During that time he has developed a profound admiration for his competence as a scientist, for his ability to write interestingly and accurately, and for his zeal in carrying this work through to successful completion."

Maurice Broun in a tribute in the *Cassinia* writes:

Those of us who were privileged to know Earl Poole will remember him as a quiet, reserved, modest yet highly gifted personality. A field trip with Earl was an experience to be treasured. An all-round naturalist, he was extraordinarily keen and outgoing with information. And when he could drop his reserve, he was a raconteur of unusal ability. One word describes Earl Poole, and that word is versatility.

Earl attained a high degree of competence in a number of disciplines. Preeminently an ornithologist, he was also a mammalogist of distinction. He had a profound knowledge of geology and paleontology. His competence and scientific zeal were reflected in his writings, which were characterized by strict accuracy as well as fine literary style. He was a first rate administrator. In short, he excelled in anything he put his mind to. But it was as an artist that Poole was supreme.

Earl Poole's superb paintings of birds and landscapes - he was indeed prolific - hang in many art galleries and private collections. He was also an illustrator of many books. His charming illustrations and meticulous line drawings feature in such important landmark works as Witmer Stone's *Bird Studies at Old Cape May*, both editions of James Bond's *Birds of the West Indies*, and in R. Meyer de Schauensee's *Birds of Colombia*....

During his years at the Museum, Earl made a number of important contributions to scientific literature. His survey of the *Mammals of Berks County*, published by the museum in 1932, is outstanding, concise, a model of scientific thoroughness. An enormous amount of history and natural history is packed into the 74 pages of this work. For many years it was used as a textbook at Cornell University.

In 1938 a short paper, "Weights and Wing Areas in North American Birds" appeared in *The Auk*. An important and original paper showing correlation between wing-loading and flight characteristics, it is referred to perennially by students of flight dynamics.

Earl Poole's *Half Century of Bird Life in Berks County*, published by the Museum in 1947, is an excellent, comprehensive regional survey. Almost every page bears the consummate artistry of Earl's line drawings of birds. No other county in the Commonwealth can boast a comparable work....

This latter work led to the preparation of a most ambitious, definitive volume: *The Birds of Pennsylvania*. Completed in the early sixties, the huge manuscript (some 2,500 typewritten pages) was to have been published by the Academy of Natural Sciences. Perhaps the sheer bulk of this monumental work or the expense of printing it discouraged the Academy from going ahead with the project. An abridgement, in 94 pages, handsomely illustrated, was published in 1964 under the aegis of the Delaware Valley Ornithological Club. All of us are indebted to Earl Poole for his labors, for the fruition of his excellent annotated list in *Pennsylvania Birds*.

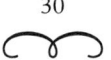

Earl was familiar with Hawk Mountain in the pre-sanctuary days when hunters dominated that area. He tried during the early thirties to halt the slaughter of birds at Hawk Mountain. He and his associates gathered up many freshly killed birds, the skins of which at the Reading Public Museum represent one of the best collections of raptorial birds in the country.

For several years Earl served as a director and treasurer of the infant Hawk Mountain Sanctuary Association, and he gave generously of his time and counsel.

Toward the end, Earl succumbed to great depression. The rampant destruction of the charming countryside of Berks County, the obliteration of favorite birding areas he knew and loved so well, the general erosion of the quality of life, the sorry mess in the world at large, all weighed upon his spirits. Those of us familiar with Earl's high standards, his quest for quality, could fully sympathize with his malaise. He died July 9, 1972, at age 80, having made signal social and cultural contributions (Broun, 1973:23-24).

Maurice Broun
by Michael Harwood

I didn't get to know Maurice Broun until I began to write *The View from Hawk Mountain* in the early 1970s, after he and his wife Irma had moved to a farm one ridge west of Hawk Mountain and he had retired as curator of the sanctuary. He was a bit leery of me at first. That was partly because he was jealous of his privacy - not so much the day-to-day, don't-drop-in-on-me-when-I'm-busy kind of privacy, but root privacy, privacy about what made him tick. And he was also leery, I think, because my book would succeed his classic about the early years of Hawk Mountain Sanctuary, *Hawks Aloft*, which the sanctuary had allowed to go temporarily out of print, a development he did not, shall I say, admire. But he was cordial and in the end irrepressible. He loved to talk about conservation, and he loved practicing the art of personal narrative.

My book was published, and I gathered that the material about him made him feel exposed and vulnerable. It was, he wrote me once, more publicity than he cared for. But in 1978, *Defenders* magazine asked me to write a profile of him. He hemmed and hawed again for a while but finally gave his consent, and for the second time he and Irma and I talked for hours with a tape-recorder running beside us. The piece was published in the October 1979 issue of *Defenders*.

Maurice died that month. The remembrance of Maurice that follows is hung on a framework constructed of parts of the book, fleshed out by what I learned through our correspondence and occasional personal encounters after the book was published, including the interview we did for the *Defenders* article.

When he entered the Hawk Mountain narrative in *The View from...*, he was 29 years old and just about to become the "warden" at the newly established sanctuary.

— Maurice Broun —

"He was already something of a Horatio Alger figure in ornithology. In later life, he didn't much like to talk about his beginnings, but his wife would a little: 'I'll have you know that this man raised himself. His mother died when he was two weeks old. His father died when he was two years old. They were people from Rumania, and they came over here, and they died of TB. He was put in a New York City orphanage, where he didn't see grass or a tree until he was taken out by a Catholic family - he was younger than seven, then. The mother became ill, and the foster father brought Maurice back to the terrible orphanage; the man who ran it was sadistic and used to beat the kids up once a week - Saturday night, they were automatically beaten with a strap. When he was ten, a Jewish family came in and took him to Boston. He ran away from his foster home when he was fifteen, and he has earned his own bread and butter since that time.'"

I hope that passage conveys a little of what still vibrates in my memory - Irma Broun's passionate telling of the story. Maurice always made a lot of Irma's seafaring antecedents on Cape

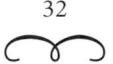

Cod. Probably to him she represented gentility and an identifiable family with a history. But she struck me as a loner, too, something of an orphan in her own right, at least in spirit. I thought she and Maurice were a uniquely matched pair, double orphans facing the world.

Neither of the Brouns would talk about why he ran away, but it may well be that birds had something to do with it.

"One spring day, in his fourteenth year, he was on his way across Boston Public Garden when he came upon a group of adults standing around under a freshly-leafed tree and staring up into it through binoculars. He stopped and tried to make out what they were looking at. One of the grownups noticed him and offered him her binoculars. With the aid of the binoculars he found a Magnolia Warbler and was instantly bird-struck. The dramatically marked warbler... was, he later wrote, 'truly the most ... beautiful thing my eyes had ever beheld.'"

So Maurice became a birdwatcher. Simple as that.

Among his acquaintances in those early days was Richard Pough, whose own career as a conservationist was to be linked with Maurice's in a very important if coincidental way. In the early 1930s, some fifteen years after they met, Pough was a central figure in the discovery and revelation of the shocking amount of hawk killing that went on at Hawk Mountain every fall. At the time he ran a photography store in Philadelphia, which was perhaps an unlikely springboard for a conservationist. Nevertheless, as encourager and counselor he played an indispensable part in the effort to have Hawk Mountain bought for a sanctuary by the Emergency Conservation Committee of New York, headed by Rosalie Edge. Pough was to go on to perform again and again such a function in conservation action- which he still does, as far as I know, well into his eighties. And the first warden of the Hawk Mountain Sanctuary, of course, turned out to be Maurice Broun, his young friend from Massachusetts.

Pough met him "... 'when Maurice was a high school student and I was at M.I.T., and he used to lead bird walks in the Boston Public Garden. I remember his going with the Brookline Bird Club on a trip to Ipswich [on the shore north of Boston] on, I think it was, New Year's Day. A bitter cold day, and Broun came along with, actually, his bare toes showing out of his shoes. We were all worried about him freezing his feet, because we walked all the way from the station out to the marsh, which was four or five miles. And the story was that his father was a Russian Jewish tailor, and they just thought this boy of theirs was nuts, and they did everything they could to discourage him, but nothing would.'"

Maurice objected energetically to something about those last three sentences when he saw them in manuscript, but he offered no amendment to improve or replace whatever it was he didn't like. His childhood was not something he wanted to uncover in public, so far as I could tell, under any circumstances. Anyway, while still in Boston English High School he rented a room and found menial jobs to support himself and his birding passion, and he published a booklet on the birds of the Boston Public Gardens. A remarkable young man. How many teenagers have you met in your life who displayed such nerve and independence while remaining on the right side of the law?

When he graduated, college was financially out of the question. He claimed in his mature years that he hadn't been much of a student, anyway. "Except I loved to read," he told me once. "...When I should be listening to algebra and so forth I'd be reading Walt Whitman's *Leaves of Grass*, something like that." He bellhopped at the Women's City Club of Boston for a couple of years until the lady who had loaned him her binoculars that spring day in the Public Gardens found him another job- an avenue into an ornithological education and a life in conservation. He went to work as an assistant to Edward Howe Forbush and John Birchard May, who were then preparing the third and last volume of Forbush's monumental *Birds of Massachusetts and Other New England States.*

Forbush first put Maurice to the task of researching the literature and writing basic species descriptions- the physical appearance of males, females, and young; measurements, molts, field marks, voice, breeding habitat and nest, range, distribution in New England, and season in Massachusetts. But Maurice was naturally literary, and Forbush eventually assigned him to write some of the chatty narrative essays, called "Haunts and Habits," that supplemented the sort of small-print sections on which Maurice had been working. The "Haunts and Habits" were what gave life and character to the great work - along with the superb Fuertes plates, of course. Maurice wrote the pieces on the Common Yellowthroat, Hermit Thrush, Black-capped Chickadee- his favorite species- and two hybrids about which little was known, Lawrence's and Brewster's warblers.

"... [H]e acquitted himself well. 'But did I read,' Maurice said, 'I never rested a second. I worked day and night, because I had to do my regular work, and then I'd go to my little cubbyhole of a room [on] Claremont Street... and I'd have all these books with me, and reports, and so on under my arm, and I'd have to wade through them, pick out the meat, and make notes, and then when I thought I had all the data I needed, then I sat right down and wrote.... I can still see myself as a young man, slaving away. I didn't take time to eat anything - I ate candy.'"

After three years of that and with Volume III nearly finished, Forbush and May pointed Maurice toward conservation work. Not only pointed him but gave him entrance velocity by convincing the garden-clubbers who were creating the Pleasant Valley Bird Sanctuary in western Massachusetts that 23-year-old Maurice Broun was just the man they needed to start up and run the place.

In the next three years he cut six miles of trails and built a nature museum for Pleasant Valley. After that he moved to the Austin Ornithological Research Station on Cape Cod, where he worked as a research associate. Then, having married the pretty and sparky Irma Penniman, he was hired by the Treadway Inns to be staff naturalist and to make nature trails and a nature center as part of Treadway layouts.

By then he had met and greatly impressed Rosalie Edge of the Emergency Conservation Committee, and when she leased Hawk Mountain in 1934 she offered him the job as warden for the fall - if he didn't charge her much. He had the Treadway job to go back to at the end of the hawk migration season, and he was as passionate a conservationist as Rosalie Edge. So he and Irma agreed to go to Hawk Mountain for room, board, and expenses.

In the next few years Maurice made important discoveries about the size and timing and weather requirements of the fall hawk migration at the mountain. Meanwhile, he and Irma (who, while he was counting the migrating hawks, often stood guard at the entrance to the trail that led to the old hawk-shooting stands) had their difficulties with the local hunters.

"... They patrolled the road to keep the hunters out, and faced down angry gunners who approached the gate, their guns casually cradled in their arms so that the muzzles pointed at Maurice's or Irma's stomach. Maurice, walking the grounds during the deer season, would hear a shotgun blast and then the whistle of a slug over his head. A Red-tailed Hawk was shot and its corpse hung as a warning from the girders of [a] bridge....

"The Brouns reacted with their own gestures. Maurice, for example, photographed the

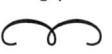

dead hawk hanging from the bridge and used it to publicize the work of the sanctuary. 'Broun was the most hated man,' said the [local] antique dealer Charley Thomas, 'if ever there was a man hated. He's lucky he's living. I pushed a gun down one day that was pointed right at his head.'"

Still, the Brouns kept the hunters out and lived to tell many tales. And that wasn't the only crucial development at the mountain in those early years.

"People - particularly young people - arrived at Hawk Mountain and were immediately attracted to the energetic and devoted Brouns. Above all, Maurice was 'a tremendous field naturalist,' in the words of Roland Clement, [whose] first job in conservation was working for Maurice at the Austin Research Station on the Cape. 'He is a wonderful naturalist, a wonderful ornithologist, a wonderful botanist, ... although his lack of formal education for years kept him from the full recognition he deserved.' Maurice assumed that any hawkwatcher would be as excited about the sanctuary as he was, and his enthusiasm was catching. He was also a natural teacher.... Tom Hanson, one of his early Hawk Mountain proteges, who [eventually] quit a successful career in business to teach science, remembers what his exposure to Maurice meant: 'Here was a person who had probably more innate knowledge concerning ornithology and botany and the other natural sciences than any other 10 or 12 people. And at that age - in my teens - I just soaked it up, just like a sponge.'

"The Brouns invited visitors in for a cup of coffee or tea and a piece of pie; put them up on rainy weekends [in the former little roadside 'hotel' down the mountain a bit from the lookout, which became both headquarters and residence for the Brouns]; gathered them around for impromptu lectures of birding talk; and in general treated them as partners in the enterprise. A family was forming, and the members of that family would find themselves, on rainy or foggy days when the hawks weren't in the air, helping Maurice string wire around the boundaries - miles of wire - or burning brush or chopping firewood or building camping shelters....

"'We actually, physically, built the place,' Tom [Hanson] said. 'In that sense, it became mine. I built it. I know all the boards there. I know the trails, because I cut them.'

"'Do you remember the time,' put in Maurice excitedly, leaning forward in his chair, with an intensity that always gives one the feeling there's a spring compressed inside him, 'we got together a lot of material and boards and built a latrine, all for under $25? And weren't we proud of it? First we had to dig a tremendous hole...'

"'In the rocks.'

"'And then we built a magnificent latrine, for less than $25.'

"'The Brouns' 'boys' would write to Mrs. Edge from overseas [during World War II]: 'There is one thing that I hope to find unchanged when this war is over, and that is Hawk Mountain. Even if the world is tearing itself apart, the hawks will continue to fly over the Sanctuary, and the days and nights will be just as peaceful and beautiful.' 'Three things with me are synonymous with Hawk Mountain,' said another, 'peace and quiet, good fellowship, and Irma Broun's apple pie.'"

The Brouns' Hawk Mountain family of friends and volunteers grew into an institution that continues today to be one of the sanctuary's distinctive characteristics. And until that family grew so large that its personal demands began to overwhelm him, it was one of the satisfying aspects of life at Hawk Mountain - though not as satisfying, I think, as the absolute privacy that settled on the place in midwinter after snow closed the road over the mountain and he and Irma could be snowbound in their little house.

A far from satisfying part of the life at Hawk Mountain was the fact that as long as Maurice was curator, and despite all his own efforts and the efforts he inspired in others, the Commonwealth of Pennsylvania resisted passing a law to protect all the hawks. What the conservationists got in 1937 was a law protecting all but the accipiters, which was meaningless, because the gunners at shooting stands off Hawk Mountain - there were a least six stands just within 30 miles of the sanctuary - could plead errors of eyesight if they were caught shooting, say, an Osprey or a Bald Eagle. The enforcement was not particularly rigorous. In 1957 the Pennsylvania legislature finally protected all hawks in the northeast corner of the state - Hawk Mountain territory - in the months of September and October; it did not pass a comprehensive protection bill until 1969, three years after Maurice retired.

"On good hawking days at the sanctuary, many of the birds of prey that sailed past were missing flight feathers or carried blood stains on their plumage, and people who loved hawks cringed at the thought of the carnage that must be going on that day farther east along the ridge. So Maurice took to leaving Hawk Mountain for a while on good hawking weekends and going to one of the shooting stands he knew about. 'You'd get a good hawking weekend shaping up,' Maurice said, 'and everybody would be calling in and saying, "How's the hawking Maurice?" and I'd say, "It looks great. You're going to have some real good hawking over the weekend." But those nights I never slept, because I knew what was happening up the ridge. It just killed me. I had no pleasure out of the hawking. You could go up to Bake Oven Knob and stand by the side of the road, facing the east, in the direction of the oncoming hawks, and there'd by half a dozen guys lined up next to you with guns, shooting these birds as fast as they came. You'd see these hawks drop in the road, you'd see them drop in the woods; there was nothing you could do about it, because they'd always make sure to shoot Sharpshins when I was there.'"

One thing I admired in Maurice was his intolerance for pseudo-conservationists. He raged about people who wouldn't put themselves on the line and join him at the hawk-shooting stands to help protect as many of the passing hawks as possible. "A lot of these so-called bird-lovers, so-called conservationists, really aren't," he said in 1978.

During that interview I asked him if he felt the battle to protect the environment was being lost. His answer, like so much he said, took me by surprise. "Ah, what a question! I'm pessimistic. I do think the environmental movement is just great, but it's come too late. I think [the future is] going to be grim. I'm not a doomsayer. I read all this stuff, and I pay attention to the doomsayers, but I look at it a little differently. Look, each generation has to adapt to the conditions they find. When I was a boy, you saw Bluebirds everywhere. They were common birds. It's very difficult to find Bluebirds now in the East - but we manage to live without them. Lots of young people, they've heard about the Bluebird, they'd like to see a Bluebird, but they're not pining about it. Take the Passenger Pigeon. Who's moaning about the Passenger Pigeon? They once filled the whole sky in clouds, in Audubon's and Wilson's time. Nobody's moaning about the Passenger Pigeon. It's gone. We've learned to live without it. All right. If I had children and grandchildren, I know damned well what [they would] face - an increasingly sterile world. But it doesn't mean the end of the world. Upcoming citizens are going to have to cope. They'll cope somehow."

Maurice could not be pigeon-holed. He wasn't good at pulling his punches, either.

He left the sanctuary he had helped build because he couldn't any longer take the crowds that became bigger each year; he couldn't take the increasing managerial demands on his time that stole from his time as a naturalist. But he wasn't at all sorry at the end that he had lived that life. With "all its heartaches," he said, "with all the sleepless nights from the hawk killing, it nevertheless was a tremendous thing for a young couple to experience. So we have no regrets."

This biography is reprinted in full from American Birds, *Vol. 43, No. 1, Spring 1989, by permission of the National Audubon Society.*

The Flying Squadron
by Charles Schaich
(from the Distelfink, *March 1954, Vol. 6, No.1)*

The "Flying Squadron" came into being in 1949 after the writer, who teaches biology and chemistry at Reading Senior High School, had seen a bird on Antietam Dam, which he had taken for a loon. My education had been premedical, so that my knowledge of natural history was limited to personal observations in the field. On learning from members of the Baird and Mengel clubs that my loon was a Double-crested Cormorant, I became a member of these organizations to seek assistance in remedying my colossal ignorance. I had never heard of a Double-crested Cormorant, much less identified one.

At this time I met Warren Kalbach on a hike over Mount Penn. He was a veteran of ten years of hiking over Mount Penn, during which time he had learned most of the land birds of the area. He was instrumental in asking Mr. Paul "Pat" Martin to accompany us on our joint ventures, knowing that Pat knew waterbirds and would conceivably be willing to join our party. Fall being upon us, Pat suggested we concentrate on Lake Ontelaunee and Hawk Mountain.

So began the adventures of the Flying Squadron, a name given us by Dr. Earl Poole. To this day the appellation has stuck - we have been joined by all active birders of the city and environs - at one time or other we have had Fox and Spence, Burger and Manning, Bressler and Shade, McIntyre and DeLuca, Nunemacher and Homan, Diener and Bertolet, to name but a few who have been our companions on our field trips to the lake.

The first thing impressed upon me by these trips was the necessity of wearing proper clothing. L.L. Bean Inc. was enriched by my purchases of woolen garments and waterproof footwear. I had no idea that birding involved such interminable waits in subfreezing temperatures. Optical equipment became important, so that I graduated from World War I binoculars to coated lens War Surplus glasses, to Navy spy glasses to tripod and finally to a 60 mm Bausch and Lomb prismatic telescope 30X.

We get out in all sorts of weather, for almost invariably, the worse the weather the better the birding. This is particularly true of Lake Ontelaunee where water birds abound. We get started at seven o'clock, reaching the dam at or before seven-thirty, so that during the winter months we see the sun rise on the lake. Once parked, we bolt from the car and, if the light is good, we scan the extensive shore-line and the surface of the lake for birds.

Often times we see deer along the shore, muskrats, and once even a wild mink. We have seen a red fox slipping on glare ice as he cut across the lake, and eagles which visit our lake with surprising frequency, have perched, wheeled, and harassed ducks before our eager eyes. Ospreys dive for their finny prey, hitting the water with a speed and a splash which seems incredible for a frail bird.

It is the ducks which intrigue me, however, for these swift water birds, together with geese and swans, exemplify to me the real wilderness. Down they slant, riding icy air currents to the equally icy waters of the lake. Gratefully they drink as they seek some sheltered cove to rest and feed before continuing on their migratory way. Oldsquaw, Scaup, Ring-necks, Redheads, Canvasbacks, Teal, Pintails, and Mergansers mix with Black, Mallards, Bald-pates [American Wigeon] and Gadwalls, and Coots, Grebes and sandpipers add their quaint presence to the scene.

We have stood transfixed as flocks of Whistling [Tundra] Swans, or skeins of geese traverse

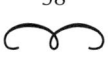

the sky over our heads. Canada Geese wing over, voicing their invincibility with thrilling yelps which stir the soul with their wild freedom. Snow Geese wing in with shrill falsetto cries, and Blue Geese blend in their hoarser calls to make a chorus of indescribable chatter. Swans seem to laugh as they fly, with overtones of wood-winds to mellow the sounds. Altogether we come away filled with awe at the privilege of seeing such wonders of nature. Beauty of the birds does not cause all of this feeling, nor the poetry of their flight, nor the music of their extended throats - some of it is the mystery of migration, the witnessing of a great natural force, the vitality and cruelty of nature and the symbol of change in seasons which move one so deeply.

The seasons change, and with them comes the birds of the arctic tundras, of treeless wastes to seek sanctuary in our land. Braving unbelievable hazards of storm, cold, blizzard, predators, gunners and exhaustion, these winged creatures bring to us at each half-year a pageant of wild life scarcely known to humans.

Rather would we see multitudes of these birds than a dozen varieties from far shores. To us they are our umbilical cord to the Far North, to virgin territories, to the unspoiled wilderness. The Flying Squadron has witnessed these things and more, and we hope to continue our activities, to enrich our lives with such sights, and to invite others to share with us this privilege to witness the passage of the birds at Lake Ontelaunee.

Charles A. Schaich	"Pilot"
Warren Kalbach	"Co-pilot"
Paul R. Martin	"Navigator"

The Pennsylvania German Names of Birds
by Herbert H. Beck

It is doubtful if there exists in the United States a more distinctive or more picturesque set of local names of birds than those current in southeastern Pennsylvania among that people of German-Swiss antecedents traditionally and broadly called the Pennsylvania Dutch; in a more limited way, by standard usage, the Pennsylvania Germans.

The language of these people, which is a fusion of South German dialects with an infusion of English, for two hundred years has persistently refused to be absorbed from its racial eddy by the strong stream of American life. It maintains itself as the dominant language of many rural regions of Berks, Lebanon, Monroe, Lehigh, Northampton and Schuylkill counties, and the northern parts of Lancaster, Montgomery, and Bucks counties. Even in the larger towns like Reading, Allentown, and Bethlehem, it is still actively used. In its sound, inflection, and flavor it is positive and dialectically detached; and this character has strongly impressed itself upon the bird names of the region.

The settlers who established this language in America came in the early eighteenth century from the German sides of Switzerland and Holland and from Swabia, Hesse, Alsace and Saxony, but mostly from the Palatinate; which was formerly an independent state made up of what is now the upper part of Bavaria and that Rhine region bounded by Baden on the east, Baden and Alsace on the south, and Alsace-Lorraine on the west. It extended north as far as the cities of Treves and Mayence. These people first broke in the rich lands of the Lehigh and the Schuylkill valleys, then pushed into the Cumberland, the Susquehanna and the Juniata valleys, thence in scattered groups into central Pennsylvania, Maryland, Virginia, and elsewhere. They were originally in greater part pioneer farmers, strong and resourceful; in mind potentially capable, but unsharpened and unextended.

A people such as this, busily occupied with the rough work of making a nation, observed only those birds of the Alleghenian and Carolinian zones which by reason of habit or character were prominent or impressive. Such species were without exception noted and named; sometimes in a way reminiscent of the European avifauna, sometimes originally and with recognition of the bird's habits or mannerisms. Thus it is that outstanding species like the Canada Goose and the Turkey Vulture have several names each in Pennsylvania German, while great families like the Warblers and the Sparrows are not noted in the language. When with the progress of American ornithology the birds of these more obscure and involved groups were differentiated, the more inquiring of the Pennsylvania "Dutch" came to know them by English or scientific names. Sometimes, though rarely, a bird is given the Pennsylvania German equivalent of its English name. Such cases are of more recent origin, and they lack the true character of the names which have come down from more ancient and less admixed sources.

Pennsylvania German has attained to grammar and dictionary only within comparatively recent years. Its vocabulary and syntax are limited. The meagre literature of the dialect, while sometimes on a basis of the German alphabet, is usually spelled phonetically. The phonetic method is used here because it is more generally readable and because it more broadly and faithfully portrays the characteristic heaviness of Pennsylvania "Dutch" as a spoken language. No consistent attempt is made to trace word origins to German sources, though they are often obvious enough and always interesting to the philologist and to the student of Germanic languages.

Berks County Overview

Courtesy of the Berks County Planning Commission

Of the provinces traversing southeastern Pennsylvania, three are important when discussing Berks County: 20 percent of Berks lies in the Piedmont Province, 60 percent in the Valley and Ridge Province, and 20 percent in the ancient Reading Prong of the New England Province. Berks County, approximately 920 square miles in size, reflects the characteristics associated with these provinces.

Berks County is roughly a diamond-shaped area. The northern boundary of the county is composed primarily of the Blue Mountain, while the southern and extreme portions of the county are composed of some lower mountains and rolling hills. The western and central portions are predominantly rolling farmland. Berks County is bordered by six other counties: Lancaster to the southwest, Lebanon to the west, Schuylkill to the north, Lehigh to the northeast, Montgomery to the east, and Chester to the southeast.

The most abundant type of land cover in Berks County is the open field. An open field can be farmland, both active and inactive, pastureland, meadows, or yards. Open fields are found throughout the county, the largest contiguous areas being north of the city of Reading and south of the Blue Mountain, and east of the city of Reading in the Oley Valley region.

The uses of open fields vary greatly and depend largely on the soils and underlying geology. One of the most common, productive, and beneficial uses is for agriculture. Given all the open field in Berks County, it is no surprise that agriculture is one of the county's top industries. Although in decline, agriculture includes everything from crop production to dairy farming.

The most prominent, contiguous area of forest cover in the county is the Blue Mountain region. The major portion of the northern boundary of the county is composed of the Blue Mountain. Second-and-third-growth deciduous trees are the most prevalent types found in this area and in the rest of Berks County. The most common deciduous species in Berks are the red maple, American beech, shagbark hickory, and white, red, black, and chestnut oaks. Coniferous species also exist in the county, an example being the eastern hemlock, which often favors stream valleys in mountainous and hilly areas. Other prominent areas of forest in the county include the South Mountain region near the boroughs of Wernersville and Robesonia, the French Creek State Park area in the southeastern portion of the county, and in the eastern-central area of the county in Earl and Pike townships.

Regions in Berks County which are covered by water are also a significant type of land cover. Berks contains two artificial lakes of appreciable size. Lake Ontelaunee, completed in 1929, is found in the northern-central portion of the county, divided between Ontelaunee and Maidencreek townships. It functions as a reservoir for water supply to the city of Reading. Blue Marsh Lake, created in 1976, is located in the central-western portion of the county. Blue Marsh functions both as a flood control project for the Tulpehocken Creek and Schuylkill River and as a source of recreation.

There are other lakes which are smaller in scale than Lake Ontelaunee and Blue Marsh: Hopewell and Scotts Run lakes in French Creek State Park, the lake in Kaercher Creek Park east of Hamburg, Antietam Lake near Reading, and Glen Morgan Lake near Morgantown. There is also an abundance of small ponds, such as those on farms, throughout the county.

A vast number of streams and springs traverse Berks County. There is also one river, the Schuylkill, which flows through the county. The Schuylkill River provides the major source of drainage in the area. The various streams drain small areas of the county, but most eventually empty into the Schuylkill, contributing to its overall flow. This river enters the county through its northern-central border and flows southward, exiting through its southeastern border.

Historically, the arrangement of land uses in Berks County was fairly uncomplicated. In general, the centers of concentrated development were the city of Reading, its urban area and the larger rural boroughs. Topographic barriers defined the limits of the city and forced development north, southeast, and west across the Schuylkill River, shaping suburban development in Muhlenberg, Cumru, Exeter, and Spring townships, along with the urban area boroughs. Development patterns were generally tied to water bodies and later to transportation routes often resulting in strip development patterns.

Today, with increased mobility and technological changes in land utilization, development patterns have changed to the point where sprawl, scatteration, and strip development are combining to blur community identity. The land use development pattern since 1973 reflects continued suburban expansion outward from Reading, in-fill development, as well as development which has leapfrogged over land close to the city of Reading to take place on rural lands beyond the present suburban areas in the direction of Philadelphia, Allentown, and Lancaster. Berks County is closely related to these cities and is feeling the impact of development pressures. Pressure for development on the eastern and southern portions of the county will most likely continue as commuting becomes easier and land near Philadelphia becomes more scarce and higher priced.

Site Guides

Hawk Mountain Sanctuary
by Jim Brett and Laurie Goodrich

Hawk Mountain Sanctuary is located on the Kittatinny Ridge in Albany Township on the northern border of Berks County. Even before the Sanctuary was established in 1934, ornithologists such as George Sutton and Earl Poole frequented the ridgetop overlooks to spot or collect hawks and other migrants. In recent years, the Kittatinny Ridge has been recognized by The Nature Conservancy as one of the most important sites for preservation of biological diversity in Berks County, and in 1996 the Kittatinny was designated as a National Audubon Society Important Bird Area for Pennsylvania.

Hawk Mountain is best known for its autumn migration of diurnal raptors. Since 1934, Hawk Mountain staff and volunteers have recorded annually an average of 20,000 hawks of 16 species from mid-August through mid-December. The Sanctuary's North Lookout provides a dramatic view of the hawks on migration, with birds passing below or at eye level on many days. Early in the fall, visitors flock to Hawk Mountain to view the Broad-winged Hawk migration. Daily counts of Broadwings usually range up to several thousand, with peak migration passing between September 10th and 20th each fall. On a rare day up to 2,000 Broadwings can be spotted in one flock. In October, the Sharp-shinned and Cooper's hawks dominate the migration stream. October is also the best time to visit to see the most number of species, as up to 13 raptor species can be seen on a good day. The North Lookout is one of the better spots in the county to see some of the rarer northern birds such as the Golden Eagle, Northern Goshawk, Bald Eagle, and Gyrfalcon. Visit the lookouts from late October through December for these late-season migrants. Another good time to sight the Bald Eagle is after a cold front in late August or early September. Northern nesting birds that regularly visit the North Lookout include Olive-sided Flycatchers in August and Snow Buntings, Evening Grosbeaks, and both species of crossbills in November and December.

Weather is key to planning your visit to view the raptor migration. The best days occur one or two days following a cold front passage. On these days, the winds gust from the northwest and hawks rocket past the rocky mountaintop. Cold fronts also tend to bring the peak counts of other birds. In September the warbler fallout in early mornings following a front can be exhilarating as the birds zip among the trees and shrubs edging the rocks. In October, flocks of Canada and Snow geese, Blue Jays, Robins, Crows, and blackbirds provide a visual contrast to the raptor flight. In November, Common Loons, Tundra Swans, and northern finches add interest to the wait between raptors.

The Sanctuary and the associated game and state forest lands provide important habitat for many forest-nesting birds. Some of the most abundant populations of forest warblers, hawks, and owls occur in these 9,000 hectares of undeveloped forest. Barred Owl, Saw-whet Owl, Sharp-shinned Hawk, Ruffed Grouse, Worm-eating Warbler, Pileated Woodpecker, Brown Creeper, and other birds depending on large forested areas can be found along the Kittatinny Ridge.

Although different times of year will yield different reasons to visit the Hawk Mountain area, mid-May through mid-June is an excellent time to visit for migrant and breeding bird activity. In the Pine Swamp area of State Game Lands 106, shrubby thickets may yield nesting White-eyed Vireo and the rare Yellow-breasted Chat. Gamelands fields provide home to the Eastern Bluebird, American Woodcock, and other field nesting species. The hemlock stands along mountain slopes and base harbor nesting Black-throated Green Warblers. Farther afield from Hawk Mountain, the farmland east of the Mountain can offer opportunities for grassland species such as the Bobolink, Grasshopper Sparrow, and others. The wetlands along the Mountain Road (running northeast along the mountain slope) can be birded from the car in early spring and provide great views of the Hooded Merganser, Wood Duck, and others.

In winter, Hawk Mountain Visitor Center feeders can offer excellent views of rarer winter birds such as the Common Redpoll and Pine Siskin. A trip can be combined with a search of the Kempton valley farmland for the occasional county rarity such as the Northern Shrike, Say's Phoebe, and Lapland Longspur, and the more dependable Horned Lark and Snow Bunting.

Fortunately, exploring the Sanctuary and nearby state lands is easy due to the numerous trails they offer. The Sanctuary trails include the famed North Lookout trail and a longer River of Rocks trail that loops through lower elevation forest and around the River of Rocks boulder field. The Sanctuary lookouts are ideal locations for watching for birds during all seasons. Breeding Broadwings soar above the canopy in summer, and Pileated Woodpeckers may be spotted taking a short-cut across the valley in any season. In recent years, Common Ravens have been regular visitors (possible nesters?) that are often spotted from the North and South lookouts. Follow Hawk Mountain's main trail for the easily accessed lookouts, and hike the Skyline Trail for a more rugged, private vista.

Dirt roads through State Game Lands 106 and the Appalachian Trail connect to Sanctuary trails, and together combine to form miles of pathways available to birders and hikers. One of the best locations for spring migration warbler watching is the Pine Swamp, located at the base of Hawk Mountain in the Eckville gamelands.

State Game Lands 106 maps can be obtained from the Game Commission Southeast Division Office in Leesport. Hawk Mountain and Appalachian Trail maps can be obtained at the Hawk Mountain Visitor Center (610-756-6961).

To reach Hawk Mountain from Reading, travel on Route 61 north past Hamburg and Port Clinton to Route 895 east. Go approximately three miles on Route 895 to Drehersville, turn right on Hawk Mountain Road, cross the Little Schuylkill River, and follow the road two miles to the top of the mountain. Enter the parking area for the Visitor Center on the right.

The Hawk Migration Along the Kittatinny Ridge in Pennsylvania
by Earl L. Poole

[Editor's note: The following article appeared in The Auk *in 1934 and represents the first detailed and comprehensive study done of the hawk migration in Berks County.]*

The Kittatinny Ridge, known locally as the "Blue Ridge," has, since time immemorial, been a favorite highway for the fall migration of certain species of birds of prey, as well as many of our smaller birds. Just why they should elect to follow this ridge is not clear to the writer, since at the locality where the following observations were made it extends from east-northeast to west-southwest, as it does for many miles in either direction. A possible explanation is the fact that, being a practically continuous ridge for many hundreds of miles, it offers a peculiar condition of continuous uplifting air-currents on the windward side in normal weather, thus aiding the typical soaring flight which is characteristic of the Hawks during migration.

My reason for entertaining this view is that during an easterly or southerly breeze the birds pass to the southeast of the crest of the ridge, while during a normal northwesterly breeze the flight follows the northwestern slope of the mountain. This rule appears to be invariable.

The point at which these observations were made is near Eckville, along the boundary line of Berks and Schuylkill counties, where a mountain road makes accessible a series of rocky prominences from which a clear view may be had of the approaching Hawks as they work their way along the ridge. Similar conditions exist, no doubt, along the entire extent of the ridge, from northern New Jersey to the Southern States.

The scene along the ridge at this point is one of bleak desolation, with a scattering of bleached skeletons of fire-mangled hemlocks and pines projecting above the new growth of the ridge.

The flight of the Hawks over this place during a heavy flight is one of the most impressive sights that one could wish to behold. Singly, or in small scattered groups, they appear from the northeast, soaring in intricate spirals, but all drifting in the same direction. Now and then a low-flying Sharp-shin, probably hoping to surprise some small prey, skims swiftly past just over the tree-tops, or an Eagle or Osprey, dwarfing even the Red-tails, circles majestically overhead. From far up the ridge they come, now flashing their white undersides toward the sun, and then disappearing for a moment as the darker backs turn sunward, but continually keeping their course along "the endless mountain," as it was known to the Indians.

The sad part of the scene, to the mind of the observer, is the scores of gunners that gather on these promontories, especially on Sundays, during the fall, and slaughter the birds wholesale and indiscriminately as they attempt to run the gantlet of the blood-thirsty mob.

The lamentable feature of this slaughter is that most of the victims are not even picked up as they fall, but allowed to decompose or serve as food for the foxes, skunks, opossums, cave-rats, mice and shrews that live in the rocks. Many of them are merely wounded and allowed to die a lingering and miserable death. One could almost condone the killing of the Sharp-shinned and Cooper's hawks, but during September hundreds of the distinctly beneficial Broad-wings are butchered in the same manner, and in October many Ospreys, Red-tailed and Red-shouldered Hawks and Eagles receive the same treatment.

On certain Sundays in October the writer has seen as many as forty cars parked along the nearby road, with considerably over a hundred gunners stationed at points of vantage along the ridge. On such days the roar of the guns is almost continuous, and resembles a Fourth-of-July celebration on a vast scale. The consensus of opinion among those who have taken part in these "Hawk shoots" over a number of years is that only a quarter as many fly past this point now as could be seen eight years ago. Little wonder!

From the information that I have been able to gather this condition has existed since 1925, although a few farmers from the immediate neighborhood have been shooting here since about 1915.

A summary of the actual observations obtained from reliable sources, along with notes made by the writer during some eighteen visits to the region, will present a composite picture of the nature of this migration during its different stages:

	Eastern Goshawk (*Astur a. atricapillus*)	Sharp-shinned Hawk (*Accipiter v. velox*)	Cooper's Hawk (*Accipiter cooperi*)	Eastern Red-tailed Hawk (*Buteo b. borealis*)	Broad-winged Hawk (*Buteo p. platypterus*)	Marsh Hawk (*Circus hudsonius*)	Osprey (*Pandion haliaetus carolinensis*)	Duck Hawk (*Falco peregrinus anatum*)	
Sept. 10 (1933)		50	2		6		1		9 A.M. to 12:30 P.M.
Sept. 22 (1932)					"2,000"		2		Report of gunners and many specimens
Sept. 25 (1932)		15	1		3	3	1		7:30 - 11 A.M.
Sept. 27 (1931)		6	1		2				9 - 11 A.M.
Oct. 1 (1933)		43	3		35	1	4		7 - 12 A.M.[1]
Oct. 3 (1931)		82	15				2		7:30 A.M. - 1 P.M.
Oct. 3 (1933)		A good flight, one Duck Hawk shot[2]					1		8:30 A.M. - 12 P.M.[3]
Oct. 5 (1930)		2	2	9			1		
Oct. 7 (1932)		50					"few"	1	Thousands flew over; 50 Sharp-shins and one Duck Hawk killed[4]
Oct. 8 (1933)		40	6	30			1		10 - 11 A.M.
Oct. 9 (1932)		120				1	50(?)		8 A.M. - 4 P.M.[3]
Oct. 11 (1931)		15	5					2	[3]
Oct. 14 (1930)		5	2	1					8:30 A.M. - 2 P.M.
Oct. 14 (1933)		10		14	1				9 -11 A.M.
Oct 16 (1932)		214	8				5		"218 picked up, shot within a week"[5]
Oct. 17 (1927)		18							Shot[6]
Oct. 17 (1931)		"A big flight today, one man shot 53"							(Conv. with gunners).
Oct. 18 (1931)		10							Shot[3]
Oct. 19 (1927)	4								[7]
Oct. 19 (1932)		6	2	1					10 -11:30 o'clock
Oct. 22 (1927)	16	90	11	32			2		[7]
Oct. 23 (1932)		15		3					
Oct. 25 (1931)		15	3	10		3			[3]
Oct. 25 (1933)		"Possibly two thousand, mostly Red-tails, with some Sharp-shins" [4]							
Oct. 27 (1929)		25		20					6 -11:30 A.M.

[1] Samuel Wishnieski.
[4] Paul Schell.
[7] Shot by A. Smith.
[2] John B. Lutz.
[5] R. H. Pough, Bird-Lore, 1932, p. 429.
[3] A. Mittower and S. Wishnieski.
[6] George M. Sutton, Wilson Bulletin, 1927, p. 84.

The migration commences about August 20 and continues on through November. It starts with a straggling movement of Sharp-shins, Cooper's and Broad-wings, and attains its full momentum by about September 10.

The large flight of Broad-wings occurs around the 20th of September, and the main flights of the other species depend to a certain extent on the weather conditions; a heavy flight being almost certain to occur during a sudden drop in temperature, accompanied by a strong northwest breeze.

The flight is usually heaviest from 9 until 11 o'clock in the morning, then there is a lull during the noon hours, and a resumption after 2 o'clock, lasting until about 4:30. From the state of the stomach contents of many of the Hawks shot, it is apparent that they feed mainly in the early morning, although food is doubtless picked up as opportunity offers during the flight. This is especially true of the Sharp-shins.

In addition a single Golden Eagle (*Aquila chrysaetos canadensis*) was shot by an unknown gunner on November 10, 1931, and seized by the game protector; a Bald Eagle (*Haliaeetus l. leucocephalus*) was seen on September 10, 1933, and another on October 1 of the same year; a Red-shouldered Hawk (*Buteo l. lineatus*) on October 14, 1930, and two on October 25, 1931; single Pigeon Hawks (*Falco c. columbarius*) on October 3, 1931, October 5, 1930, October 18 and 25, 1931, and single Sparrow Hawks (*Falco s. sparverius*) on September 27, 1931, October 8, 1933, October 14, 1930, and October 27, 1929.

Reading Public Museum,
Reading Pa.

The Hawk Migration During the Fall of 1934, Along the Kittatinny Ridge in Pennsylvania
by Maurice Broun

[Editor's note: The following account of the first fall migration study at the newly formed Hawk Mountain Sanctuary is excerpted from a 1935 issue of The Auk *and provides an overview and historical perspective of the site.]*

Until recent years the extensive fall migrations of Hawks along the Kittatinny Ridge appear to have been unknown to ornithologists. Yet each year, over a long period of time, hunters have taken a heavy toll of the migrating Hawks at a number of places along the ridge, which follows a northeast and southwest course for hundreds of miles from northern New Jersey to the southern states.

By far the most popular shooting grounds along this migratory highway were located between the villages of Eckville and Drehersville, in east-central Pennsylvania. The U.S. topographic maps give the name of "Blue Mountain" to a large section of this part of the ridge. Hunters gathered here in large numbers - as many as 150 to 200 on a Sunday, and perhaps half as many on a week day- throughout the period of Hawk migration, which extends from late August to December. Many of these men came from points a hundred miles or more distant, so attractive was this "sport" to the hunting fraternity.

The result was an appalling slaughter. The victims were rarely retrieved - merely left to rot, and if wounded, to die a lingering death, and eventually all were consumed by four-footed scavengers. It has been estimated conservatively that from 3,000 to 5,000 birds of prey were killed each fall. The number was undoubtedly much larger before the Depression. Hunters with whom I discussed the situation expressed the view that during the last two or three years less than a quarter of the numbers of Hawks went by as did ten years ago. Most of the men interviewed said that these "Hawk-shoots" had been going on for over twenty years. During the past few years they had been well advertised in local sportsmen's organizations by a couple of enterprising business men in a nearby city. Each fall these men drove a truck-load of ammunition up the mountain and made a small fortune selling their wares at much-reduced prices. Other men, equally anxious to profit, gathered and burned the used shells, in order to salvage the brass for whatever mintage they could get!

The earliest published information that we have in regard to the Hawk migrations, is found in an interesting paper by George M. Sutton, in which the author tells of a visit to the mountain (above Drehersville) on October 19 and 20, 1927. Data are presented concerning plumage differences, weights, and stomach examinations of 158 Hawks of four species, all collected in a remarkably short period of time (*Wilson Bulletin*, 1928, pp. 84-95). During the fall of 1932, R.H. Pough (*Bird-Lore*, 1932, p.429), and H.H. Collins, Jr. (*Annual Report of The Hawk and Owl Society*, Bull. No. 3, 1933, pp. 10-18), made several visits to the region, making extensive investigations into the Hawk destruction. For a very full and graphic account of the devastation, the reader is referred to Collins' article. The first definite information concerning the nature and extent of the local Hawk migrations is found in a brief, but comprehensive paper by Earl L. Poole (*The Auk*, 1934, pp. 17-20) who has been familiar with the locality for a number of years.

In the late summer of 1934, before the Hawks began to appear in appreciable numbers, this shooting paradise of the hunters was turned into an inviolate wild life sanctuary, thanks to the active interest and initiative of Mrs. C. N. Edge, of New York City. Mrs. Edge acquired control of 1393 acres of the mountain, the heart of which property held the Hawk shooting-stands. The writer was directed by Mrs. Edge to supervise the sanctuary, and as far as possible to make daily observations of the Hawk migration.

I arrived at "Hawk Mountain," as it is known to the hunters throughout the region, on September 10. Hunters were already on the grounds. The following day "no trespassing" posters went up everywhere along the steep and difficult road that led to the former shambles. Meanwhile a series of notices appeared in all the local newspapers, apprising the sportsmen and hunters of the newly established refuge and the strict prohibition of all trespassing.

The reader may easily imagine the astonishment of the local hunters, and the opposition that precipitated. The farmers of the surrounding country-side were particularly hostile. Some of them made the preposterous claim that "the Hawks even carried off young pigs," as well as poultry. The sportsmen raised the usual hue and cry that the Hawks had depleted their game. Notwithstanding the outcries of the farmers, I found large numbers of White Leghorns and other poultry roaming at large in the fields at the foot of the mountain. Rabbits, Quail, and Pheasants were very plentiful along the borders of the fields. The unusual numbers of Ruffed Grouse in these woods impressed me the most, however. Throughout September and early October they could be heard drumming almost everywhere. On October 1, I recorded 33 Grouse in different parts of the sanctuary.

My first three weeks at the sanctuary were spent in patrolling the road, fortunately the only approach, as all hunters came by automobile. From the amount of adverse discussion in the newspapers, and the rumors that circulated among the farmers in the immediate vicinity, I anticipated trouble daily. Only 53 gunners appeared at different times during this period, however most of them having heard of the sanctuary but desirous of learning for themselves the status quo. On September 27, we secured the full-time services of Robert H. Kramer, a deputy-sheriff. Henceforth I was able to spend more time making observations of the flights. From September 10 to November 1, the opening day of the hunting season, we turned away 166 Hawk-hunters, and had no serious trouble in doing so.

The greatest part of the sanctuary lies in Berks County; the western and northern borders of the tract are in Schuylkill County. A rough, dirt road traverses the mountain from Drehersville. Mounting this road a mile and a half or so to near the summit of the mountain, which is irregular and plateau-like at this point, one finds on the left a well-beaten path running northward into the rocky woods for a distance of three-quarters of a mile. The path leads to a series of sandstone promontories which jut out along the ridge and form a striking part of the rugged topography. These promontories are the vantage points from which to observe the passing Hawks. Looking up the ridge, which in this region surprisingly enough runs east-northeast to west-southwest, one is deeply impressed by the steep flanks of the mountain, and its virtually razor-back crest. Scrub-oak and black birch, showing the effects of many forest fires, form the dominant tree growth. Interspersed among these are a few hemlocks, and great tangles of rhododendron and mountain laurel. A number of fine specimens of mountain ash (*Pyrus americana*) and of mountain holly (*Ilex monticola*) have found footing among the promontories. On the whole, the scene is that of a much-scarred wilderness, withal presenting one of the most magnificent views to be had anywhere in Pennsylvania.

An explanation of the autumnal flights of Hawks along this particular ridge, the most eastern of the Appalachian Chain, may be found, as pointed out by Poole, in the unbroken character of the ridge, and more specifically in the air-currents that are generated and forced upwards by the wind striking against the steep slopes. These currents of air enable the birds to coast for mile on mile; thus they enjoy easy transit to their winter feeding grounds.

The ridge above Drehersville offers opportunities for field study of Hawks that cannot be surpassed. The reason for this is the extreme narrowness of this part of the mountain, thereby creating a focal point for the passing birds. Comparative ease of accessibility by automobile and by foot was a great point in its favor for the hunters. As the Hawks progress along the ridge and pass the promontories, alternately coasting or flapping, or circling a moment above the trees, one is keenly aware of the novelty of studying these birds from a position seldom if ever enjoyed by the average student in the field. Whereas the latter is obliged to look up to make identifications, the observer at "Hawk Mountain" frequently looks down upon the birds, or sees them come head-on, sometimes on a level with his position. It is this condition which made the Hawks such easy targets and occasioned their wholesale slaughter.

A question frequently asked is to what extent, if any, do Hawks migrate along this ridge in the spring? We are not prepared to answer. Some hunters have given me a negative view. Others have maintained that the birds straggle up the valleys. At any rate, the hunters have never manifested an interest in the mountain in the spring, although this may be ascribed to dormancy of the desire to hunt. Obviously the only definite knowledge concerning the spring migration of the Hawks will by forthcoming when ornithologists essay to visit the ridge in late March or early April.

I spent approximately 306 hours making observations from the promontories, which by the way, are some 1,506 feet in elevation. On days of particularly good flights I held a vigil of from eight to nine hours. There is an almost continuous movement, from a few straggling birds on some days to really heavy flights on others, which may however, be of but two or three hours duration. Only when the weather is rainy or very misty is there any break in the migration. Thus on October 24, a day of overcast skies during the morning, but clear weather with moderate northerly winds in the afternoon, only 10 birds were recorded: 6 Sharp-shins; 1 Red-tail and 3 Marsh Hawks. On October 31 the weather was not particularly favorable for Hawk migration; during seven and a half hours of watchful waiting 176 birds were seen: 21 Sharp-shins, 148 Red-tails, 4 Red-shoulders, 2 Marsh, and 1 Turkey Vulture. Of these, 143 passed between 10 a.m. and 1 p.m.

During the early hours of the morning a few birds may always be seen loitering over the ridge, searching for food. By 7:30 or 8 o'clock, providing the weather is favorable, the first birds fly by the promontories. An hour later the flight is well under way. In regard to the time of day the birds pass through in greatest numbers, my observations tally fairly well with those of Poole, who in past years made some eighteen visits to the region. The maximum numbers usually pass during the forenoon, and again from 2 o'clock to about 4:30 o'clock, at which hour they may be seen settling down for the night. The mid-day lull in the migration is probably explained by a feeding and resting period of which the birds avail themselves. This condition is not invariable, however, as my records show a number of days when the hour between noon and 1 o'clock proved the best of the day.

...According to Poole the earliest migrants, a few Sharp-shins and Broad-wings, arrive the latter part of August. I was able to observe no considerable flights of birds previous to September 23, owing to the close guarding that was necessary on the road. So far as I know, no large flights occurred until September 17, a day of clear, warm weather, with brisk winds from the north. I was informed by two gunners who were on the ridge a few miles away, that they saw between 1500 and

2000 small Hawks pass over during that afternoon. I gathered from their descriptions that the birds were Broad-wings, the species which is expected in large numbers during the latter part of September. Had the wind come from a southerly quarter there is no doubt I would have seen these birds from my position on the road. Invariably when the wind is in that direction the birds pass along the south side of the ridge and cross the "Kettle" - a large bowl-shaped area fronting the promontories - thus taking something of a short cut. Having crossed the Kettle the birds pass over the road, usually near the summit, and continue on over the broadening back of the mountain, which at length takes a course that is more truly northeast to southwest. A case in point is the flight of Broad-wings that we witnessed from the road on September 23. Not a Hawk of any kind was seen until early afternoon. There had been no wind during the morning, but soon after mid-day light southerly breezes sprang up. Between 3 and 3:30 o'clock we counted 427 Broad-wings pass.

Large flights depend entirely on the weather conditions. ...A cold, but not necessarily clear day, immediately after rainy weather, with strong winds from northerly quarters (preferably north-west) is most productive. For maximum number of species, I found the second week in October the best. During the nine-day period from October 7 to 15, I recorded 16 species of raptores, as many as 13 species on a single day. The greatest numbers of Hawks may be looked for after freezing temperatures and snows have settled over eastern Canada and northern New England.

...We have often heard rural folk claim that when the fire-flies are seen high in the air it is a sure token of approaching rain. I was not a little surprised to find that precipitation occurred soon after flights, during which the Hawks were seen higher than two hundred feet or so above the promontories. There were a few days when buteos and accipiters alike travelled so high in the ether as to be barely discernible. Rain of course was not necessarily local, but it was certain to fall elsewhere along the Appalachians or in New England. Thus the passage of high-flying Hawks, as influenced by atmospheric pressure or contrary winds, is succeeded by rains and falling temperatures, usually pronounced in the regions to the north, which in turn precipitate an exodus of birds of prey from those regions. ...Of course there are exceptions to every rule; the only one that is demonstrable in our case is shown for October 16 to 18, when precipitation failed to occur anywhere in the region in question. It is interesting, nevertheless, that marked meteorological changes took place in the regions adjacent in the west.

...There were relatively few days when the birds flew high, or well out of range of gun-shot. Undoubtedly during such flights many birds went by unnoticed. Bird students and conservationists may be grateful for just such migrations in the past, of all but these birds flying high were subject to the ceaseless barrage of the hunters. On the many days during my observations when the birds passed low along the ridge, from fifty to seventy-five per cent of the migrants might easily have been killed. Indeed, on some of his visits to the mountain in 1932, Collins estimated that half of the birds that went over were shot. It is quite plain, then, that if the hawks flew low invariably, certain species would long have become extinct, or nearly so, in the eastern states.

...In view of the relentless, unceasing persecution which our raptores have been universally subjected to through the years, it is amazing that large numbers may still be seen. It is particularly gratifying that we still have a fairly sound breeding stock of Red-tails, as our data seem to indicate. The rising tide of enlightened sentiment in favor of the Hawks should do much to level out the discrepancies in the laws of the different states.

Shartlesville State Game Lands 110

by Kerry Grim

State Game Lands 110 north of Shartlesville is one of the best birding areas in northern Berks County for the spring migration. During May, a birder can observe migrants returning to their more northerly breeding grounds as well as our local birds establishing their territories. A good morning of birding should produce 50 or more species, of which 14 to 18 will be warblers. Birding each weekend from late April to early June should produce 90 species of birds. A maximum number of warblers can be found by walking Northkill Road several times. By doing this you can intersect successive waves of migrant warblers as they drift northward. These waves will spread out as they ascend the mountain. Traditionally, mid-May is supposed to be the peak time for warblers. Now I find the weather to be more important than the day. A word of caution is in order, as turkey hunters will be in the woods, especially on Saturday mornings. There is no hunting on Sundays.

May mornings are often chilly and require a windbreaker and light gloves. Never pass up the opportunity to go birding in the rain. My largest warbler waves have always been associated with a warm front stalled over the area with fog or rain. On May 14, 1989, I did my entire walk in a light-to-moderate rain. Lighting was poor, and many migrants passed unidentified. However, it was my best warbler day that spring with 18 species.

From Reading, travel north on Route 61 to I-78 at Hamburg. Follow I-78 west and take Exit 8 at Shartlesville. Turn right on Mountain Road and continue straight ahead onto Forge Dam Road. Turn left at the "Y" intersection and follow Northkill Road to Parking Lot 1 on your right.

Search the trees for vireos and warblers. One or two Mourning Warblers are usually found each spring in the dense growth around the parking lot. Listen for the male's "chorry, chorry" call. Scan the treetops for Scarlet Tanagers and Rose-breasted Grosbeaks.

Between the parking lot and the intersection, follow the footpath on your left and scan the pond for Wood Ducks. They can be found here each spring, but nesting remains unconfirmed. The field adjacent to the pond is sometimes a hot spot for migrant warblers. However, you will need waterproof boots to enter this area. Several pairs of Common Yellowthroats can be found here.

Return to Northkill Road and continue to walk east. Eastern Phoebes may be nesting under the bridge, just a few feet above the stream. Blue-gray Gnatcatchers may also have their nests built by the middle of May. Carolina Wrens, Wood Thrushes, Black-and-White Warblers, Ovenbirds, Louisiana Waterthrushes, and Northern Cardinals will all be singing to advertise their territories in this area. Listen for the ruckus of a Pileated Woodpecker as it is winging its way through the woods. Cerulean Warblers can be found here each year. They will be very difficult to find and may not appear until early June. Walk to the storage shed and look for migrants along the tree line.

Retrace your steps to Parking Lot 1 and continue walking for approximately one-eighth mile. Acadian Flycatchers, Veerys, Red-eyed Vireos, Ovenbirds, Louisiana Waterthrushes, and Kentucky Warblers nest in this area. Listen for the upward spiraling songs of Swainson's Thrushes. Unfortunately, I have found a decrease of Swainson's Thrushes during the past several years.

Drive to Parking Lot 2 and walk the dirt road toward the mountain top. There will be only a handful of migrants in this area. Red-eyed Vireos, Black-and-white Warblers, and Ovenbirds are the commonest species here. Look and listen for Black-throated Green Warblers, Worm-eating Warblers, Hooded Warblers, and Canada Warblers, all of which nest here. A distant Winter Wren may be singing near the stream.

Continue walking until you come to the browse cut area at the gate. Follow this road for one-quarter mile, then backtrack. This browse cut area has become prime nesting habitat for Common Yellowthroats, as well as Chestnut-sided Warblers. Lincoln's Sparrows can be found in this area. Look for any movement near the ground, and listen for the soft, finch-like song of the male. If you do locate a Lincoln's Sparrow, watch quietly, as trying to call one closer will send it into hiding.

Walk from the gate to the top of the mountain. Ovenbirds will be the most plentiful species. Listen carefully: one will sing, then three others will respond. Look for Great-crested Flycatchers, Gray Catbirds, Chestnut-sided Warblers, Eastern Towhees, Field Sparrows, and Chipping Sparrows. Common Ravens are occasionally sighted on the mountain top.

Return to Parking Lot 2 while scanning the sky for Common Loons, Double-crested Cormorants, and migrant and local raptors. An alternative to backtracking is to follow the dirt road west for 2.3 miles, then bear left, following Sand Spring Trail for 2.0 miles, thus returning to the parking lot. I did this in 1989 and saw or heard 123 Ovenbirds! Hooded Warblers also nest here, and it is interesting to see the springs bubbling up through the sand. However, this is a rather long walk and probably should not be attempted unless you are familiar with the area or have a topographic map.

My summer would not be complete without an evening walk to hear the songs of Hermit Thrushes, which can be heard on the mountain at twilight. The summer evening chorus of Wood Thrushes on the higher parts of the mountain is also beautiful. On my return to the car I can expect to hear Whip-poor-wills, although they appear to be decreasing as their habitat, a large clear-cut area, has returned to dense forest. Listen for their calls in the area between the mountain top and the browse cut area well after sunset. A flashlight and long-sleeved shirt are necessities.

Route 183 Hawk Watch

by Joan Silagy

The Route 183 hawk watch is located on the border of Berks and Schuylkill counties. Although not the ideal hawk watching spot, due to limited visibility, it is convenient and uncrowded. Sometimes, it is very productive for viewing migrating hawks, waterfowl, and songbirds.

This site is also the former location of a television tower under which Earl Poole and Maurice Broun found many specimens of migrant songbirds killed when they struck the tower. Most of these specimens, which include Dickcissel, Connecticut Warbler, and Philadelphia Vireo, are in the Reading Public Museum collection.

Finding the hawks is fun and sometimes a real challenge. Once you learn the landmarks, it becomes much easier, and there is usually someone present on the lookout to assist you. "Over the north pole," or "over the south pole" may ring out. The reference is not to either of the earth's axes but to utility poles. You may also hear "over the double oak" or a similar statement, all of which will help you to locate the migrating hawks.

Although migration begins in early-to-mid August, with the migration of a few Bald Eagles and perhaps a few hawks, the best time to visit is between Labor Day and the first week in December.

In September there is much excitement with the Bald Eagles, Broad-winged Hawks, and American Kestrels on the move. The Northern Harriers are also passing through and will continue to do so for a few months. In October, Sharp-shinned Hawks and the other accipiters or a Common Raven will fly back and forth across the lookout. If you are lucky, a Merlin or a Peregrine Falcon may zip by. Now you see it, now you don't, because the viewing time is so short. Red-tailed and Red-shouldered hawk activity begins to pick up and by November is in full swing. By then Golden Eagles and the northern Bald Eagles are also on the move. Although the number of birds passing through will drop off considerably by the first week of December, there is still the chance of Golden Eagles, Rough-legged Hawks, and a few Red-tailed Hawks.

When hawk watching is slow, look for songbird activity. The fields and forest edges on the mountain top often abound with songbirds as the migrants stop to feed and rest. Large numbers of warblers are sometimes present and in the past, have even included the elusive Connecticut Warbler. One year a Dickcissel was found among the migrants. The fields also provide you with the opportunity to study wildflowers, butterflies, reptiles, and amphibians.

The Route 183 hawk watch is located approximately 21 miles north of Reading. Take Route 183 past Strausstown. After crossing I-78/Route 22, travel about three miles north on Route 183. As soon as Route 183 becomes two lanes, get in the left, or passing, lane. Put your left turn signal on. At the top of the hill, make a left. Parking is very limited and angle parking is advised whenever possible. If parking is unavailable, you may have to park along the shoulder on the west side of the highway. Parking is also available on the Pennsylvania Game Commission parking lot, which is located one-third of a mile south of the hawk watch on the east side of the highway. Do not park in front of the gate at the hawk watch. Walk around the gate and bear right to reach the top of the mountain where the hawk watch is located. Take a folding chair with you. No water or rest facilities are available at the lookout.

Kaercher Creek Park
by Kerry Grim

Established in 1972, Kaercher Creek Park in Hamburg is a 37-acre lake built primarily for flood control and public recreation. Bass and Muskellunge provide a challenge for the fisherman. Volleyball, quoits, and outdoor picnics are pursued during the warmer weather. The Pennsylvania Fish Commission and the Berks County Commissioners oversee park activities.

March is the best time for the birder to visit Kaercher Creek Park as this is the peak time for waterfowl. A good day will produce eight or more species of ducks, but their numbers vary greatly from year to year. A spring storm can bring an unexpected variety of birds. One day in particular, I observed five species of gulls and several White-winged Scoters. Tundra Swans are rare visitors, but Double-crested Cormorant sightings are increasing. Pied-billed Grebes are common, but Horned Grebes have alarmingly decreased.

April is a month of transition. The waterfowl have migrated, and it is too early for most songbirds. Chimney Swifts, Tree Swallows, and Eastern Bluebirds will be present. Look for migrant raptors.

May is a pleasant time to visit the park. Look for Common Loons, Ospreys, Northern Harriers, Red-tailed Hawks, and occasional Vesper, Savannah, and Grasshopper sparrows. Yellow Warblers are common nesters, and Orchard Orioles now breed here regularly. A walk through the woods, reached via the dam breast, will produce a variety of songbirds and wildflowers.

Kaercher Creek Park will never produce a bird list to compete with Blue Marsh or Lake Ontelaunee. However, there is always something unexpected happening. I've seen a Barn Owl flying over the lake at noon and a group of 10 Spotted Sandpipers feeding on the grass with Robins. Once a fledgling Yellow-billed Cuckoo remained motionless until I returned an hour later and took photos from three feet. At least one bear was seen swimming across the lake.

To get to Kaercher Creek Park, take Route 61 north and exit at Hamburg. Turn right at the second traffic light in Hamburg to State Street. Follow State Street for one mile. Turn sharply right at the park sign.

Lake Ontelaunee

by Matthew J. Spence

Since the construction of the Maiden Creek Dam in 1929, Lake Ontelaunee (which serves as the only water supply for the city of Reading) has been a magnet for birders. This 1,080-acre lake may become irresistible to those for whom exotic locations have lost their charms. The ornithological pioneers of this locality were Dr. Earl L. Poole, former director of the Reading Public Museum and Art Gallery, and Byron Nunemacher. They worked the area from the late 1920s until Poole's death in 1972.

Next on the scene came the "Flying Squadron:" Warren Kalbach, Paul (Pat) Martin, and Charles Schaich; this trio was active from 1949 to 1972. In the late 1950s throughout the 1960s, Warren Faust and Bill Miller were often found birding Ontelaunee. In the summer of 1977, Maurice Broun of Hawk Mountain fame became interested in Ontelaunee; he concentrated on the Cliff Swallow colonies at both the dam breast and the West Shore Bridge. Unfortunately, Broun's study was cut short by his death in October 1979. Recently, Rudy Keller, Dean Kendall, Ken Lebo, Barton Smith, Bill Uhrich, and Matt Wlasniewski have become frequent birders at the lake.

Of the 330 species that have been recorded in Berks County, 291 have been identified at Lake Ontelaunee. May has produced the greatest variety, but it is low in waterfowl variety. The other good months are (in order) April, September, October, November, March, and December. Without a doubt, the best time to visit the lake is after a storm, tropical or otherwise. Most outstanding sightings occur during or just after severe weather.

In over 40 years of birding here I have noticed certain trends in bird abundance.

Species that have increased are Great Blue Heron, Canada Goose, Wood Duck, Mallard, Common Merganser, Red-tailed Hawk, Ring-billed Gull, Red-bellied Woodpecker, Tree Swallow, Cliff Swallow, Northern Mockingbird, European Starling, Brown-headed Cowbird, and House Finch.

Species that have decreased are American Black Duck, Northern Pintail, Red-shouldered Hawk, Ring-necked Pheasant, Black Tern, Yellow-billed Cuckoo, Hairy Woodpecker, Alder Flycatcher (in the early 1960s both the Alder and Willow flycatchers could be heard and seen at Peters Creek), Warbling Vireo, Red-eyed Vireo, Yellow-breasted Chat, Grasshopper Sparrow, Eastern Meadowlark, Orchard Oriole, and Purple Finch.

A typical birding tour of Lake Ontelaunee would proceed as follows:

1. Drive north from Reading on Route 61, turn right (east) on Route 73, travel northeast for 0.8 mile, and park in the lot at the dam breast. This is a fine spot for observing waterfowl, herons, gulls, and other water birds, as well as the large colony of Cliff Swallows nesting under the bridge from late April to August. Walk down the dirt road that parallels the Maiden Creek below the dam. This is a good location for migrating warblers.

2. Drive east on Route 73 for 0.7 mile to a parking lot on the left side of the road. Stop here and look for waterfowl, Osprey (in migration), and Red-breasted Nuthatch (in fall, winter, and spring). On May 9, 1982, all six swallow species were seen from this point.

3. Continue to drive east on Route 73 for 0.2 mile to a fork in the road. Keep to the left, on Calcium Road, and after 0.25 mile park and walk down the old rutted road to the lake shore. This area is known as Maiden Creek Station. This is another excellent site for loons, grebes, cormorants, herons, and waterfowl. When the water is low, this becomes reasonably good shorebird territory. For years, Willow Flycatcher, Warbling Vireo, and Orchard Oriole have nested here. On November 8, 1992, an Ancient Murrelet, the first Pennsylvania record for this species, was found at this location.

4. Retrace your path back up the rutted road and drive over the small wooden bridge and turn left onto Maiden Creek Road and proceed toward Peters Creek, about one mile. This is the best all-round birding stop in the entire Ontelaunee territory. Park in the first lot on the right and explore the walled creek and the ponds. Birds to be expected include Black-crowned Night-Heron, Wood Duck, Blue-winged Teal, Common Moorhen, American Woodcock, Belted Kingfisher, Willow Flycatcher, Eastern Phoebe, Tree Swallow, Carolina Wren, Cedar Waxwing, Warbling Vireo, Yellow Warbler, Common Yellowthroat, Indigo Bunting, Field Sparrow, Swamp Sparrow, Red-winged Blackbird, Rusty Blackbird, Orchard Oriole, and American Goldfinch. Just about any migrating heron, duck, hawk, shorebird, vireo, or warbler can be spotted in the appropriate season at Peters Creek. With a bit of luck, you might spot or hear a Sora or Virginia Rail.

5. Continue to travel northeast from Peters Creek past the Campbell's Plant and the Evansville Cement Plant until you reach Molltown (about 2.2 miles). At the end of the village, turn left on Water Street and drive until you reach the intersection with Buena Vista Road. Park and walk west on the road past a chain across the path. It is only a short walk to the lake. When the water level is low in late summer and fall, this is the best place to see shorebirds. The morning light here is best. In any season it is a good general birding spot.

6. Retrace your path back out to Maiden Creek Road, turn left and continue to drive to the "Twin Churches," (1.25 mile) turning left on the road between them (Church Hill Road). Take this road to Route 662 (one mile), turn right and drive until you come to the pond at Moselem Springs Golf Club on the left (1.7 mile). Park off the road on the shoulder and scan the pond for waterfowl. This pond has been superb for Gadwall from September through April, although recent "improvements" to the area during 1996 appear to have made it less attractive for this species.

7. Turn around and go back (west) on Route 662 until you reach a bridge that crosses the Maiden Creek (2.5 miles). Stop here to do some general birding. Here nested Least Bittern, King Rail, and Prothonotary Warbler before this wetland was degraded.

8. Continue west on Route 662 for 1.1 miles, at which point Route 662 turns right. Keep going straight ahead onto Stitzel Lane until you reach a stop sign (0.6 mile). Turn left onto West Shore Drive and keep going until you reach the lake (2.2 miles). Park in the lot and take either of the two fire lanes - the south lane will take you to the lake for shorebirds and waterfowl; the east lane parallels the lake and is good for warblers and shorebirds. The Yellow-breasted Chat nested here in 1987 and 1988.

9. Continue on West Shore Drive until you reach the West Shore Bridge (1.3 mile). Park here and scan for loons, cormorants, waterfowl, gulls, and Black Tern. Yellow-throated Warbler attempted to nest here in the early 1970s. Don't forget to look for Osprey perched in the distant evergreens. Sixty yards farther west is the "trash can" parking lot. From this lookout loons, scoters, and terns often can be sighted after spring and fall storms.

10. Follow West Shore Drive to Ontelaunee Drive (2.5 miles), turn left and travel one mile to Route 73, turn left and go the 0.5 mile back to the dam breast. This stop is always worth a second look.

In the 68 years of the lake's existence, Ontelaunee has produced many exciting records. Here are some highlights:

Quantity	Species	Date
12	Leach's Storm-Petrel	August 24, 1933
1	White Ibis	July 25, 1964
1	Glossy Ibis	April 21, 1995
7	Greater White-fronted Goose	February 24, 1985
8,100	Snow Goose (white)	March 24, 1996
220	Snow Goose (blue)	March 11, 1984
1	Ross' Goose	March 24, 1995
19	Brant	November 2, 1979
18,000	Canada Goose	March 11, 1990
52	Wood Duck	October 18, 1988
1	Eurasian Wigeon	February 22, 1988
292	Black Scoter	October 23, 1977
419	Bufflehead	May 3, 1970
1	Masked Duck	June 14, 1984
1	Gyrfalcon	October 28, 1941
1	Purple Gallinule (dead)	September 18, 1983
1	American Avocet	October 15, 1995
1	Willet	August 24, 1933
1	Spotted Sandpiper	January 19, 1947
10	Whimbrel	May 25, 1930
2	Hudsonian Godwit	August 14, 1958
10	Ruddy Turnstone	June 6, 1939
4	Red Knot	August 13, 1955
1	Buff-breasted Sandpiper	August 26, 1995
1	Ruff	June 4, 1994
1	Red Phalarope	December 29, 1940
2	Little Gull	April 25, 1995
1	Mew Gull	January 2, 1992
5,130	Ring-billed Gull	December 15, 1991
1	Iceland Gull	February 28, 1991
1	Lesser Black-backed Gull	December 16, 1990
1	Glaucous Gull	October 10, 1988
2	Black-legged Kittiwake	March 31, 1991
3	Sooty Tern	August 13, 1955
1	Black Skimmer	October 16, 1954
1	Black Guillemot	April 6, 1957
1	Black-backed Woodpecker	December 30, 1964
1	Say's Phoebe	December 28, 1946
1	Western Kingbird	August 25, 1941
125,000	American Crow	December 21, 1969
1	Blue-gray Gnatcatcher	January 1, 1995
1	"Brewster's" Warbler	September 13, 1987
1	Dickcissel	October 17, 1954
1	Dark-eyed "Oregon" Junco	December 19, 1982
1	Yellow-headed Blackbird	May 11, 1984
590	Rusty Blackbird	November 3, 1995
2	Red Crossbill	August 3, 1969

Fleetwood-Lyons Farmlands
by Matt Wlasniewski

R eading area birders need not travel to the Amish farms of Lancaster County to find winter field birds to brighten the slow months of January, February, and March. The rich farms between Fleetwood and Lyons north of Reading have proven to be reliable sites for nearly 40 species year round. Ten miles north of Fairgrounds Mall on Route 222, a right turn on School Road leads to open fields broken by hedges, farm buildings, and trees.

Winter species found as early as December 15 and as late as March 8 include Horned Lark, Snow Bunting, Lapland Longspur, American Pipit, and Rough-legged Hawk. Summer species of ground birds include Killdeer, Horned Lark, Eastern Meadowlark, and Song, Field, Savannah, Grasshopper, and Vesper sparrows.

Begin the tour from either School Road at Route 222 or Oakhaven Road from the Fleetwood-Lyons Road. During winter months, snow-covered fields blotched by spread manure yield flocks of 50 to 100 Horned Larks accompanied by one or two Lapland Longspurs or Snow Buntings. During the winter of 1988, flocks of Horned Larks usually accompanied by one or two Lapland Longspurs or Snow Buntings were found feeding at the roads' edges. Be sure to pause and search the rows of corn stubble for these elusive birds. An alert ear will find them for you as you slowly drive along the roads. Check the trees and the electric towers for perching Rough-legged Hawks and other raptors. These birds also soar over the fields searching for prey. During the summer months, Northern Harriers can be found cruising the hedgerows that border many fields.

FLEETWOOD/ LYONS

The summer crops of alfalfa, corn, rye, and oats can yield sparrows that react to a warning "pssch!" Birds like the roadsides in both the summer and winter months. Check the standing pools of water during migration for American Pipits and Killdeer. Grasshopper Sparrows like to play hide-and-seek in the lush fields of alfalfa.

A scope is useful but not essential to spot winter birds, for the farmers often unwittingly cooperate by fertilizing the fields closest to the roads. The scope does aid in spotting the birds that range far afield or perch in distant trees. A word of caution about the narrow, shoulderless roads: snowplows and farm vehicles are often active, so be prepared to move and try to park as far off the road as safely as possible. A Sunday morning birding drive with a hot cup of coffee is a relaxing way to put spice in the humdrum winter months.

Blue Marsh

by Joan Silagy

One of our favorite birding spots is Blue Marsh, located about seven miles northwest of Reading off Route 183. Just mentioning Blue Marsh to some people evokes visions of boats and a crowded beach. Although this may be true at certain times of the year, it still does not describe the whole Blue Marsh project, administered by the United States Army Corps of Engineers.

In 1996, Blue Marsh was designated as a National Audubon Society Important Bird Area for Pennsylvania.

Blue Marsh encompasses 6,173 acres, of which 1,150 are under water. This means that on a hot, summer day when the beach or lake is busy with summer activities, you still have acres of open space available to you.

To reach Blue Marsh, take Route 183 north from Reading. Turn left onto County Welfare Road and bear right at the fork in the road. At the stop sign, turn right onto Palisades Road, then left into the Visitor Center. Pick up a free brochure and map. Study the map, choosing the area you'd like to bird. Before leaving the center, check the lake and surrounding area. In late winter the lake can be productive for waterfowl. In spring the trees surrounding the building are sometimes filled with migrating songbirds, and it is a good place to find the Orchard Oriole.

For your first trip, but not in summer because of the crowds, I suggest the Dry Brooks Day Use area. This will help you get a feel for the place. As you drive into the beach area, watch for Bluebirds (common), Meadowlarks, and various sparrows. From the lower parking lot, check the lake shores for herons and the dead snags for Bald Eagles and Osprey. Walk the beach and watch for Killdeer and sandpipers, and in the winter for Snow Buntings and American Pipits. Hike the Great Oak Nature Trail east of parking lot C or hike Fox Trot Trail west of the beach. Both trails are excellent for thrushes, Brown Thrasher, Eastern Towhee, vireos, and warblers.

On your next trip, try the State Hill Boat Launch area. Check the lake and hike one of the trails. Squirrel Run is a very productive trail for woodland birds. Redstart, Blue-winged Warbler, Worm-eating Warbler, Black and White Warbler, Ovenbird, Wood Thrush, Rose-breasted Grosbeak, Scarlet Tanager, White-eyed Vireo, and Veery all nest here.

It's now time to expand your horizons and move away from the lake area. You've only just begun to explore this great place. Drive north on Route 183 to Bernville and hike the levee as it follows the Northkill Creek south. Hike State Game Lands 280 on either side of Route 183. In the past some of these fields have been great wintering grounds for Northern Harriers and Short-eared Owls. Look for Long-eared and Great Horned owls in large stands of pines, but remember, these fields are open to hunting.

Put that map of the Blue Marsh project to good use and try Justa Road, Peacock Road, Skinners Road, or any of the others shown. They are all good, and it is impossible to cover the entire area in a site guide. It is by repetition and exploration that Blue Marsh reveals its ornithological treasures to you.

Western Berks in Winter
by Joan Silagy

To start this journey, we choose many different routes, but for those unacquainted with the area, it would be best to start on Route 422 west. From Sinking Spring, continue west past Wernersville. Just before you enter Robesonia, turn right onto Big Spring Road. If you passed Conrad Weiser High School, you've gone too far. This is the site of the former Big Spring Farm. Approximately 0.25 mile off Route 422 there is a beautiful pond on your right, which remains open all year. Migrants often stop by, and there is usually a large number of wintering Canada Geese. Check closely. In the past, a White-fronted Goose wintered here. Also found are Redhead, Bufflehead, Coot, American Wigeon, and Black Duck.

After checking the pond and fields on both sides of the road, turn right, travel about one block, and turn right again. This takes you back to Route 422. Take your time and check the field and stream on your right. Common Snipe are often to be found in the shallow area.

Continue west on Route 422 for about 1.4 miles to the western end of Robesonia. Turn right onto Bernville Road. Go three miles and turn right onto Milestone Road. It will be the fifth road to the right. There is a small marsh at the intersection of Bernville and Milestone roads which is well worth checking. Many Common Snipe and Killdeer winter here. In the spring, Solitary and Spotted sandpipers often join them. Parking is very limited, so please, pull off the road as far as possible and do not park or stop on Bernville Road. After checking this marsh thoroughly, return to Route 422 and proceed west.

Look for the intersection with Route 419 north and turn right. Do not bird on Route 419 as it is a busy, dangerous highway. Travel about one mile and take the very first left onto School Road. You are now in Rough-legged Hawk country. Drive slowly and check the few trees that exist for perched raptors and Red-headed Woodpeckers. Rough-legs also like to perch on the ground and often feed there, so scan the open areas with your binoculars and watch for large raptors hunting over the fields.

This is a great area to sharpen your birding skills since it is rich in raptor activity. Some winters, more raptors appear than in others. But Northern Harrier, American Kestrel, Red-tailed and Rough-legged hawks in many plumages, a few accipiters, and sometimes Bald Eagles are all attracted to this area.

The open area with its manure-covered fields is also a great place to look for Horned Lark, Snow Bunting, and Lapland Longspur. Some years, we find many Savannah Sparrow, and we always check each small stream for Common Snipe. Small brushy areas often produce White-throated and White-crowned sparrows.

You can turn left or right off School Road at any time, and you should. Any left turn will take you back to Route 422. Turn around and return to School Road or make a right onto Route 422 and take the very next right to return to School Road. If you make a right off School Road, only go about one mile before turning around and returning to School Road. The farming practices and habitat change beyond that, and you will find fewer hawks and songbirds. Make School Road your central birding point and work from there. We only go as far west as Wintersville Road. A Berks County map will help you become acquainted with this productive area.

The City of Reading
by Bill Uhrich

Many bird watchers, when considering the city of Reading, may be distracted by the prospect of finding only an abundance of House Sparrows, Starlings, and Rock Doves. But a closer look reveals a surprising diversity of bird life.

Of course, care must be taken and common sense used regarding personal safety when bird watching in the city, and it's a good idea to go with a friend.

Many habitats exist in Reading, from the barren, vacant lots to the lush greenery of Mount Penn and Neversink Mountain. The tree-lined Schuylkill River flows through the city, offering habitat for water birds and a food supply for migrating Ospreys. Chimney Swifts find homes in the abandoned smokestacks and idle chimneys, and Common Nighthawks nest on the flat roofs. Crevices in buildings have supplied nesting sites in center city for American Kestrels, attracted by an abundant prey base. At any time in downtown Reading, Turkey and Black vultures, Red-tailed, Cooper's, and Sharp-shinned hawks can be seen soaring over or darting between office buildings. Red-tailed Hawks have been seen roosting on the tops of church steeples.

Some of the most productive areas in the city during the spring and fall migrations, Pendora, Mineral Spring, and Egelman parks are connected by an abandoned switchback railroad bed. Rough-winged Swallows nest in the walls of the Rose Creek which drains Egelman reservoir, and Eastern Phoebes make their homes inside the park pavilions. Ovenbirds and Wood Thrushes are common on the hillsides during the spring and summer. Mineral Spring and Pendora parks can be accessed from either Perkiomen Avenue or Mineral Spring Road near the Lindbergh Viaduct. Egelman Park is on Hill Road. This part of Mount Penn has produced winter records of Red and White-winged crossbills and Pine Grosbeaks in earlier years, although development has reduced the habitat.

In the fall, the hawk migration can be observed along Skyline Drive near the Pagoda. Although not seen in the numbers that appear at Hawk Mountain along the Blue Mountain to the north, Broad-winged, Red-tailed, Sharp-shinned, and Cooper's hawks along with Osprey and Northern Harrier soar against the backdrop of the city. The extremely rare Swainson's Hawk has been recorded here on migration. Historically, two Golden Eagles were shot along this South Mountain flyway at Topton and in Sinking Spring. Black and Turkey vultures roost in numbers, and Red-tailed Hawks nest on the western slope of Mount Penn.

Reading Public Museum park along the Wyomissing Creek at 500 Museum Road has been the most intensely birded location in the city, thanks to former museum curators Earl Poole and Sam Gundy. The county's first record of Yellow-crowned Night-Heron was found here. A total of 186 species has been recorded in the park, including 32 species of warblers. The extremely rare Painted Bunting and Bicknell's Thrush have also been seen here. Bald Eagle, Merlin, Northern Goshawk, and Peregrine Falcon are among the raptors observed at the park over the years.

The Charles Evans Cemetery, 1119 Centre Avenue, has been a favorite spot for bird watchers since the early 1920s. The first Blue Grosbeak recorded in the county was discovered here. Encompassing 119 acres with over 7 miles of roads, the cemetery is a good place to observe the spring warbler migration. The many ornamental and native plantings throughout the cemetery spring warbler migration. The many ornamental and native plantings throughout the cemetery provide nesting habitat for a variety of birds.

Angelica Lake along Route 10 in the 18th Ward attracts gulls, waterfowl, and shorebirds in different seasons. A rare Orange-crowned Warbler was found in the park during a recent Christmas Bird Count.

The city-owned Antietam Lake just over Mount Penn in Lower Alsace Township has provided habitat for bird life throughout this century. Although not particularly attractive to waterfowl due to intensive fishing activity, the lake and its watershed have been a haven for land birds. The trails near the city's Nature Center off Hill Road are good places for spring and fall warblers. A Boreal Chickadee was recorded at Antietam and at a feeder in nearby Stony Creek Mills. The conifer plantations have drawn wintering crossbills.

From the banks of the Schuylkill River to the summit of Mount Penn, the city of Reading offers a wealth of habitat and bird life for the urban birder.

Nolde Forest Environmental Education Center
by the center staff

The Nolde Forest is located in the valley of the Angelica Creek. Historically, the area did not enjoy the development of Reading to the north and the Wyomissing Creek Valley to the west. New Holland Road was the route southern Berks County farmers used to reach Reading markets. In 1800 Philip Siedel built a "Speedwell Forge" along the Angelica. In 1815 Nicholas Yocum purchased this forge and built a second forge, "Speedwell 2," in 1835. The surrounding hills were periodically cut to produce charcoal during this period. In 1870 the forges were abandoned. Today the oldest oaks are from 100 to 125 years old, a good indication of when the woodcutters and colliers last did their work. In general the area was a quiet land of woodlots and marginal farms.

In 1904 Jacob Nolde, a Reading industrialist, began purchasing land in the area. His first purchase of 55 acres included a magnificent white pine tree among the abandoned fields, oaks, and chestnuts. One of Jacob's ambitions was to establish an estate and develop it in a manner similar to the famous forested estates of Europe. The white pine became known as "The Inspiration Pine" and still towers upward in the forest. Jacob's hope "eventually to convert a great number of acres of farmland into the most beautiful pine forest in Pennsylvania" became Nolde Forest.

Jacob began his project in 1906 when a forester was secured from Germany and a tree nursery started. In the spring of 1907, 5,000 Norway spruces purchased in Germany, along with 100 red alders and 100 Japanese larches were planted; these were followed by 50,000 pines in 1909; 105,000 in 1910; and 65,000 in 1911. The Nolde Forest by now was well underway.

In the meantime, Jacob continued to add to his landholdings. By 1912 Jacob realized the project was becoming too big to deal with on a part-time basis. In that year the estate's road system was built by Italian immigrant labor. The forester's home was also built near the Inspiration Pine as an inducement for a new forester to manage the forest. William G. Kohout was hired as that forester in the same year.

During Kohout's tenure from 1913 to 1929, over 1,400,626 conifers were planted on 310 acres in the forest. Amazingly, 90 percent of these trees survived. The trees were mainly from German and private nurseries. Although 75 percent of the trees were Norway spruce, they included white pine, Scotch pine, Douglas fir, ponderosa pine, Japanese larch, red pine, Japanese red pine, and Austrian pine. In 1916 the Pennsylvania Forestry Association held their annual meeting in Reading. The members visited the Nolde Forest to view Jacob's forest. The work at Nolde was referred to as the "Berks County Method."

Jacob died suddenly in 1916. His will stipulated that his estate be liquidated and the proceeds distributed among his wife Anna, son George, son Hans, daughter Carolyn, daughter Louise, and daughter Ella. If Jacob's hastily drawn will would have been followed, the forest would have left family hands. However, to avoid losing the forest his wife Anna purchased a two-thirds interest in the forest and daughter Ella purchased the remaining one-third interest. Son Hans was designated to manage and administer the books of the forest. Meanwhile Kohout continued his reforestation efforts.

During 1927 and 1928, Hans had the mansion constructed in the forest. The English tudor design encompassed about 10,000 square feet, with the basement about 15,000 feet. The external construction, except for two second-floor bay windows of timber and plaster, was entirely of "Fox Croft" stone from Bryn Mawr, Pennsylvania. A large tower, containing a spiral staircase, dominated the rear of the building. In addition, the landscaping included 800 rhododendron from West Virginia, and 12,000 tulip bulbs from Holland. Total cost for the mansion was $221,300.

In 1929 Kohout died. A graduate of the State Forest Academy at Mont Alto, C. Aubrey Delong was hired to manage the forest. Delong's task was different from Kohout's. Where Kohout's major task was the massive plantings, Delong's was preserving and strengthening the forest planted by Kohout.

From 1930 to 1947, 228,500 conifer trees were planted. Primarily from state nurseries, 89 percent of the trees were white pine, red pine, Norway spruce, and Douglas fir. Also planted were Scotch pine, Austrian pine, and hemlock. As the Nolde family weathered the Depression and changing economic fortunes, less and less money was allocated to manage the forest. Finally, in 1949 Delong left Nolde to start his own Christmas tree farm near Knauers.

During the period 1948 to 1966, no forester was employed to manage the Nolde Forest. From 1954 to 1964, 71,000 Norway spruces and white pines were planted mainly as underplantings in the hardwood forest. An unsuccessful pulpwood venture was tried in 1949. During the 1950s, firewood was sold to augment the forest's budget.

In 1965 Hans died. The forest and mansion were becoming more and more expensive to maintain. However, the family wished to see the forest and mansion preserved and not fall prey to real estate or commercial developers. During this time the estate was brought to the attention of Maurice K. Goddard, Secretary of the Department of Forests and Waters. After several months of study and negotiation, the property was purchased by the Commonwealth of Pennsylvania in 1966.

In 1968 the Commonwealth retained Planning Associates to prepare a feasibility study for the property. The study reaffirmed the Department's intention to develop an environmental education center at the site. The center came to fruition through a cooperative grant "An Interdisciplinary Problem Solving Approach to Environmental Education" from the U.S. Office of Education to the Bureau of State Parks and the Berks County School Board.

In 1970 the center was established as the first environmental education center in the state park system. The center serves schools, colleges, teachers, youth groups, and the general public.

The Nolde Forest Environmental Education Center encompasses 666 acres and is located in Cumru Township along Route 625.

Today approximately 213 acres of the Center are conifer plantations. Large stands of Norway spruce and white pine are present. Smaller areas of Douglas fir, Japanese larch, and red pine may be found. A mixed oak, maple, and beech forest covers 436 acres of the center. Principal tree species include red, white, black, and chestnut oak; tulip poplar; red maple; cherry; beech; black birch; and yellow birch. Field areas are extremely limited at the center. A three-acre field is main-tained near the main entrance and a quarter-acre plot at Fire Gate Five. Several older field areas have succeeded to brush and aspen, birch, and alder saplings.

Several woodland wetland areas adjoin the three small streams that traverse the center. These wetlands and adjacent areas are significant for the abundance of wildflowers found there. Skunk cabbage, trout lily, bloodroot, hepatica, and spring beauty are common to these areas.

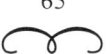

North Pond and Painted Turtle Pond are used for aquatic studies and have a variety of aquatic and emergent plants which play an important part in the aquatic food web.

Over 110 bird species have been recorded at Nolde, including the first Berks County record of a Black-backed Woodpecker and the first county record of a Bohemian Waxwing south of the Kittatinny Ridge. The first confirmed nestings in Berks of the Golden-crowned Kinglet and the Red-breasted Nuthatch have also occurred at Nolde. It is also a reliable place to see and hear Pileated Woodpecker, Great Horned and Screech owls, and Veery.

The Oley Valley
by Rudy Keller

The farmland of the Oley Valley attracts gulls and waterfowl on migration and in winter, waders in summer, and small birds of open country according to their season. Most birding can easily be done from the road.

Starting at the traffic light at the intersection of Route 73 and Friedensburg Road in Oley, take Friedensburg Road into Oley. Turn left on Main Street, then right on Water Street, drive about one mile to Stitzer Road, and turn right. Drive about 0.3 mile and scan the treetops in the woodlot across the wide field on the right. This is the site of the first recorded nesting of Great Blue Herons in Berks County. The birds are most easily seen when the trees are bare in early spring as they posture and croak while courting and refurbishing their huge stick nests. In June and early July, a telescope may be needed to clearly see the feathered young standing on their nests or clambering around the treetops as they give their repetitive food begging calls.

Continue along Stitzer Road to Jefferson Street and turn left. Starting in February, the fields along this road are a resting and feeding area for hundreds, sometimes thousands, of Ring-billed Gulls and lesser numbers of Herring Gulls on spring migration. In late winter and spring, large flocks of Canada Geese resting on the fields are sometimes sprinkled with Tundra Swans, Snow Geese, and puddle ducks. These fields are often heavily manured in winter, attracting Horned Larks, Snow Buntings, and Lapland Longspurs along with waterfowl, Killdeer, Rock and Mourning doves, American Crows, European Starlings, and sometimes Brown-headed Cowbirds wintering in nearby steer feeder barns. Look for American Pipits in spring and fall, especially in freshly plowed fields or beside rain puddles. Alfalfa fields sometimes attract migrating Bobolinks in May. Thanks to nest box placement, Tree Swallows can be seen in summer and Eastern Bluebirds almost anytime. To circle the best of these fields, continue along Jefferson Street, bear right on Mud Run Road, turn right on Bertolet Mill Road, then turn right (west) on Route 73.

Having birded the fields, follow Route 73 west to Oley, pass the Route 662 intersection and turn left on DeTurk Road. The pasture and farm pond on the left are always worth visiting. Park on the wide shoulder at the Moravian School Road intersection. Under observation for over 30 years, this small pond has attracted a remarkable variety of migrating waterfowl, including Pied-billed and Horned grebes, Double-crested Cormorants, Tundra Swans, Greater White-fronted and Snow geese, 16 species of ducks, and American Coots. Getting good looks at them is easy because the pond is so close to the road. Canada Geese and Mallards stay to nest, along with Red-tailed Hawk, Killdeer, and probably Spotted Sandpiper and Belted Kingfisher. Solitary Sandpiper and Common Snipe are regular migrants; both yellowlegs, Least and Pectoral sandpipers are rare. Great Blue Herons, Green Herons, and occasionally Black-crowned Night-Herons hunt here during the nesting season. Great, Snowy, and (rarely) Cattle egrets appear in summer as post-breeding wanderers, often staying for weeks, especially in drought years. Egrets roost at night in the trees on the small island in the pond, and Black-crowned Night-Herons are sometimes hunched there during the day. Chimney Swifts and all six of the eastern swallows come to drink, bathe, and feed. A few times, all have been present on the same visit.

By following Moravian School Road, birders can circle the Oley limestone quarry, where many Turkey and Black vultures and Red-tailed Hawks roost in late fall and winter. The birds are best seen when they soar in the afternoon. Stay on the road; entry into the quarry is strictly prohibited for safety reasons.

From the pond, continue along DeTurk Road to Route 662. The spring-fed puddle before the stop sign on the right is worth checking for Killdeer and Common Snipe in winter and other common shorebirds on migration. Cross Route 662 onto Bertolet Mill Road, then turn right onto Kauffman Road and drive about 1.5 miles to a small pond and watercress-filled spring on the right. The pond and spring often sustain ducks, Killdeer, and Common Snipe in winter when all else is frozen. The black locust grove beside the road regularly hosted nesting Red-headed Woodpeckers in the 1980s and 1990s.

Drive to Covered Bridge Road and turn right. After 0.3 miles, turn left onto Church Road, then left onto Spangsville Road. The broad fields in this area may have open country raptors like American Kestrel, Northern Harrier, and very rarely, Rough-legged Hawk. Follow Spangsville Road over the covered bridge and park on the shoulder.

With its fine bridge, old mill, and cows grazing the banks of the Manatawny Creek, this scene has probably changed little since early in the century. Besides the nostalgic beauty, it has interesting birds. Migrating Ospreys sometimes cruise the creek. Red-shouldered Hawk has wintered here, and Canada Geese, Mallards and American Black Ducks regularly do. In season Great Blue Herons, Green Herons, and Solitary Sandpipers forage along the sandbars, and Wood Ducks nest in the backwaters. Belted Kingfisher can often be heard rattling down the creek. Red-headed Woodpeckers nested here in the 1970s and 1980s and may do so again, though their nests are often taken over by European Starlings. Warbling Vireos sing all summer from the tall sycamores. Similar habitat along the Manatawny Creek can be explored by following Spangsville Road to Manatawny Road and turning right toward Route 562 or left toward Route 73.

Hay Creek and the Birdsboro Reservoir
by Ken Lebo

In September 1987, the Hay Creek flooded and eroded Route 82, closing a two-mile section of the road in Robeson Township. The road has remained closed since and has become a popular place for people to walk, jog, ride bikes, walk their dogs, fish, and bird watch. This area is one of the best birding spots in Berks County during the spring migration, and 168 species of birds have been recorded there over the years.

The north end of the closed portion is just below the borough of Birdsboro, and the south end is about five miles north of Geigertown, just past White Bear. The entrance to the Birdsboro reservoir is in the middle of this closed area.

There is a small parking lot at the north end in Birdsboro and parking beside the road at the south end.

Walking in from the south gate, listen for the Louisiana Waterthrush, Ovenbird, Acadian Flycatcher, Blue-gray Gnatcatcher, and Worm-eating Warbler. Just beyond the gate you will see where the road is eroded away. If you listen to your right, you may hear the Worm-eating Warbler and Indigo Bunting. The trees along the road are good for the Red-eyed Vireo. As you approach the gate to the Birdsboro reservoir, listen on the left for the Blue-winged Warbler, White-eyed Vireo, Northern Parula, and Cerulean Warbler. The tall trees in this area tend to be a warbler route during the spring migration.

On your right will be the gate to the Birdsboro reservoir. Walk around the gate and up the gravel road. This road goes around the reservoir. Indian Run, the stream along the road, is a good place to find the Louisiana Waterthrush and Winter Wren. The bank on the left beyond the stream is good for the Worm-eating Warbler. The gravel road will soon fork. Stay to the right and look for the Carolina Chickadee. As the road levels off by the reservoir, there is a path to the right that goes up a hill. When the path forks, stay right. You may see Hermit or Swainson's thrushes, depending on whether you are there at the end of April or mid-May respectively. This is also the best place to hear and possibly see the Pileated Woodpecker, and Hooded and Kentucky warblers in the spring and summer. This hill and the one on the other side of the reservoir are good places to encounter warbler waves.

Backtrack down the path to the gravel road and turn right toward the reservoir, which is surrounded by white pines. Instead of walking around the lake, walk across the dam. The swallows flying over the lake are Rough-winged Swallows that nest in the overflow's stone walls. The lake does not attract much waterfowl. The usual nesters are Canada Goose, Mallard, and Wood Duck. Belted Kingfishers are commonly seen diving for fish. Along the shore you may see a Spotted Sandpiper. The brush below the dam harbors Common Yellowthroat, Indigo Bunting, and Chipping Sparrow. After you reach the overflow, a small jump will get you across. The bank straight ahead usually has a pair of Worm-eating Warblers. Go back down the road. This area of the woods will have Acadian Flycatcher in mid-May. As you head down to the gate, you may encounter another wave of warblers.

Turn right on Route 82 (north) and walk toward a bridge that crosses Hay Creek at Trap Rock. This area tends to be good for Yellow-throated Vireo and Blue-winged Warbler. Before the bridge will be a gravel road to the left. Follow it as it leads you along the Hay Creek. The tall sycamore trees may have Northern Parula, Cerulean Warbler, and possibly Yellow-throated Warbler. Follow the path that takes you between the creek and a mill race. Blue-winged Warbler, White-eyed Vireo, and sometimes Northern Waterthrush can be found close along here. Take the bridge over the mill race and follow the path up to Route 82 and turn right, heading back to the south gate. By midmorning, you may see Black Vultures circling with Turkey Vultures.

Carr's Recreation Park
by Ken Lebo

Carr's Recreation Park was established in 1995, allowing public access for the first time to Glen Morgan Lake. The lake was built by Bethlehem Steel as a tailings dam for Grace Mines. Now it is more of a marsh than a lake, since it is surrounded by phragmites, and the deepest point is less than 10 feet.

In 1996 Glen Morgan Lake received the designation of a National Audubon Society Important Bird Area for Pennsylvania.

This lake has attracted many marsh birds including Virginia and King rails and Sora, American and Least bitterns, Cattle and Great egrets, Little Blue and Green herons, Pied-billed Grebe, Common Moorhen, Black-crowned Night-Heron, American Coot, Black Tern, and Marsh Wren.

Carr's Recreation Park is located on Route 10 about two miles north of Morgantown and 11 miles south of Reading just above the Pennsylvania Turnpike where Exit 22 ramps onto Route 10. Driving north from Morgantown, you will see Carr's sign on the left. Pull into the parking lot near the small office and sales building. At the sales building, you can rent a bird field guide, paddle boats, bikes, or in-line skates. There is an entrance fee to this private park.

From the entrance gate, follow the paved road which goes under Route 10 and makes a three-mile loop around the lake. Take a scope with you. The lake is large enough that some of the birds are out of range for binoculars. The dirt-bike trails also make good hiking paths for birding.

When you go under the bridge heading toward the lake, bear left. These trees are good for the Wood Thrush, Veery, and Chestnut-sided Warbler in the summer and are the best place in the park for migrating warblers in the spring.

The Stump Jumper Trail is the best woodland trail, which also goes down by Hay Creek. In the spring and summer, listen for the Acadian Flycatcher and Louisiana Waterthrush.

Next on the right is a picnic area overlook. This is the best place to scan the lake with your scope. If the lake is not frozen, there is always something to see. In the summer you will see families of Pied-billed Grebes and Wood Ducks. In the spring and fall most of the fresh water waterfowl can be seen here.

Farther down the loop, on the right, is the boat dock. You may find your closest look at Pied-billed Grebes here. In the summer you may be favored with the sight of a grebe chick riding on the back of a parent.

Next is the dam. From here you may see all five species of swallows in the spring. In the summer, you will find Tree, Barn, and Rough-winged swallows. In the evening keep an eye out for migrating shorebirds. Their observation window is from May 10 to the end of that month, and they tend to fly over the dam.

The snags are best viewed from along the dam in the morning. A Bald Eagle likes to perch on the snag throughout the year. Spring and summer often bring an Osprey with its entourage of harassing Fish Crows. Immature Double-crested Cormorants summer in this area. An immature

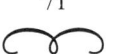

Great Cormorant spent the spring and summer of 1996 on the snags as well.

Yellow-breasted Chats and Blue-winged and Prairie warblers are regulars along the back side of the lake in the spring and summer.

You can view waterfowl in the fall and winter up close from the causeway. The three coves are each preferred by different species of waterfowl including Canvasback, Wood Duck, and American Coot.

As you turn right onto the In-line Expressway near a small picnic area, listen for Yellow-breasted Chat, Prairie Warbler, White-eyed Vireo, and Field Sparrow in the spring and summer.

Wood Ducks and Tree Swallows visit the pond on the right during spring, summer, and fall. At night you can hear rails and bitterns calling in the phragmites.

To the left of the In-line Expressway will be a very small pond that usually has a pair of Canada Geese.

Turning right onto Lakeview Boulevard, you will be walking between fields, and as you bear right, you will see thick brush on the left where a pair of Brown Thrashers hide.

Farther on the left is a pine grove where Screech Owls reside.

At the point where the In-line Expressway and Lakeview Boulevard meet, the trees are thicker, and it is more difficult to see the lake. But in the winter, without leaves on the trees, you can get the closest to the Tundra Swans. There are often more than 200 on the lake.

French Creek State Park

by the park staff

Much of the land which comprises French Creek State Park was originally acquired as part of Franklin Delano Roosevelt's Recreation Demonstration Area (RDA) Program, a program within his famous New Deal initiative during the Great Depression. The purpose of the RDA Program was to offer a temporary helping hand to state and local governments in providing labor-intensive projects, employment, training, and recreation opportunities to urban families.

To that end, RDA property was eventually transferred to the state in 1946 for further development and actual operation, as was the case with French Creek RDA.

Within the RDA program, the Federal government would buy submarginal or nonproductive land, relocating or buying out the owners. The land was then developed by Civilian Conservation Corps (CCC) or Works Project Administration (WPA) workers into a recreation area, with an emphasis on use by local, underprivileged, urban children and families.

The first purchase under the program for French Creek RDA occurred in 1935, with 4,200 acres acquired from the A. Louise Brooke estate, and a number of smaller properties from adjoining landowners. Two CCC camps were then established within the RDA in 1935 to begin the development process. The main emphasis of the CCC work was directed toward the development of roads, trails, dams, and various recreational facilities as part of the RDA project. Restoration of the historic Hopewell Village tract was also accomplished by the camps, but since the fundamental purpose was to demonstrate uses of land for the greatest public benefit, this aspect was considered secondary to recreation development.

On July 24, 1946, the United States Congress passed legislation enabling the Department of the Interior to retain 848 acres of the demonstration area to be known as Hopewell Village National Historic Site. The name was later changed to Hopewell Furnace. This encompassed the historic core of the village, surrounding farm fields, and several hundred acres of woodland to the east of the village. The remaining property was deeded to the Commonwealth of Pennsylvania and would undergo further development as French Creek State Park.

Most of French Creek State Park's cultural history can be traced to Hopewell Furnace, a prosperous iron-making community which operated from 1771 to 1883. The natural resources of the park have also been greatly influenced by the extensive furnace operations and their impacts on the surrounding forests. The original Furnace Tract, purchased by Mark Bird in 1768, comprised some 8,000 acres and included ore mines, limestone quarries, farm fields, and large forest areas of chestnut and oak which were cut to produce charcoal to fuel the iron furnace. Approximately 300 to 400 acres of forest were cleared annually and some 5,000 cords of wood were required to produce the charcoal needed for iron production. Hopewell was well known for the manufacture of high quality stoves. In addition, hammers, anvils, pots, pans, and a variety of home implements were produced throughout its operation. During the Revolutionary War, Hopewell manufactured cannon and shot for General Washington's army. Mark Bird himself served as a colonel in the Revolutionary Army and supplied arms and provisions to the U.S. Government.

The original recreational character and appearance of French Creek was the result of the facility development carried out by the CCC under the RDA program. This period saw the construction of numerous roads and trails, three organized group camps, and two earth and masonry dams which formed Hopewell and Six Penny lakes. Ironically, this period of development, which greatly benefited what was to become French Creek State Park, was detrimental to the historic preservation of Hopewell Village. Many documents and artifacts were lost or destroyed and structures removed to provide for the construction of Hopewell Dam. The early 1950s saw the completion of another earth and masonry dam which now forms Scotts Run Lake and was the site of the original head race which supplied water to the wheel and blast mechanism at the furnace two miles away.

French Creek State Park was originally covered by a forest containing a variety of mature timber of the oak-chestnut-hickory type. A study conducted in 1992 by Karl Mikan for Hopewell Furnace National Historic Site proposes that the original forested areas were dominant with oaks, American chestnut, and hickories. Maple and birch probably composed a minor portion of the forest. Periodic fire is increasingly accepted as a factor which favored this dominance of oak and hickory. This theory is supported by the presence of charcoal in the soil profiles of the area, outside of sites related to charcoal production for the iron industry. Little of the original vegetation remains in the park because of the relatively early European settlement and intensive use of the forests by early industries.

Beginning in the 1770s, the iron companies that operated Hopewell Furnace removed most of the timber for charcoal production, fuel wood, and lumber. Widespread clearcutting continued into the late 1800s until Hopewell Furnace and other furnaces in the vicinity closed. Today, the greatest proportion of the park area is forested, with most timber being second-and-third-growth hardwoods.

The majority of the wooded areas of the park is mixed oak. Two contrasting types of forests are represented: dry, rocky, upland woods, dominated by oaks and hickories; and wet, bottomland woods rich in a variety of softwood and hardwood tree species. However, most of the forests at French Creek fall into a category intermediate between these two distinct extremes. The upland woods are dominated by three oaks: chestnut oak, northern red oak, and black oak. Among these oaks, but in lesser numbers, are the mockernut hickory, pignut hickory, and American chestnut. The most prevalent trees in the park's bottomland woods are the American beech, black or yellow birch, tulip poplar, red maple, sour gum, witch hazel, iron wood, and white oak. In the intermediate forests, all of the above species will be found, along with occasional sassafras and dogwood.

Naturally occurring trees are predominately deciduous, with the exception of the coniferous red cedar and eastern hemlock. Most of the conifers found in the park have been planted, such as near old homesteads and farms. Additionally, significant numbers of white pine, red pine, and spruce were used to reforest agricultural lands after acquisition.

A large tulip poplar, located at the northern end of Scotts Run Road, is listed as the largest tree of this species in Pennsylvania's Big Trees of State Parks Program. The tree measures 140 inches in circumference, 108 feet in height, and has a crown of 84 feet in width.

As part of a vegetation study for Hopewell Furnace National Historic Site, Carl Mikan investigated a seven-acre site within French Creek State Park on the north slope of Mount Pleasure, where old-growth chestnut oaks are up to 367 years of age. The stand is located at 590 feet in elevation on a dry talus slope and abuts the western boundary of Hopewell Furnace. The greater portion of these trees began growing in a 30-year period starting in 1772. The stand is highly unusual due to its proximity to the furnace operations and otherwise extensive clear-cutting of the forests surrounding the furnace.

One of the largest acidic broadleaf swamps in southeast Pennsylvania, Pine Swamp, is located in the southwest corner of the park. Fed by Pine Creek, the swamp has sphagnum hummocks and mucky, water-filled channels which provide an ideal environment for plants such as red maple, swamp white oak, green ash, arrow-wood, and skunk cabbage. The Nature Conservancy states that the Pine Swamp is the largest wetland in Berks County. This swamp is a prime and unique example of a diverse and mixed community of flora and fauna. A lowland bog and swamp of approximately 90 acres, it is located to the west of Hopewell Lake.

The bird life of French Creek State Park is a reflection of the above habitat. Water birds can be expected at Hopewell and Scotts Run lakes during the migrations. A resident Canada Goose population has expanded beyond the lakes' ability to support it, and a control program is being considered.

French Creek continues to be a haven for both the Turkey and Black vultures, which have been found there year round.

Species Accounts

RED-THROATED LOON *Gavia stellata*
Uncommon migrant spring and fall

The Red-throated Loon is an uncommon migrant at Lake Ontelaunee, Blue Marsh Lake, and over hawk lookouts along the Kittatinny Ridge. Occasionally, a few individuals remain into the winter.

It is much less frequent in occurrence in fall than the Common Loon and even more rare in spring, so that birds in the breeding plumage are seldom seen. Ordinarily this species winters in the coastal waters and merely passes through Pennsylvania.

Most fall records are from November. An early fall date for the Red-throated Loon is September 24 (1977 - Kerry Grim at the Kernsville Dam).

Maurice Broun writes of his first sightings of the Red-throated Loon at Hawk Mountain: "Four of these birds seen early in the morning of October 8, 1939, were literally 'in a fog.' Misty lowering weather, with a raw southeast wind prevailed when the loons loomed up suddenly only a stone's throw from the lookout, coming toward us on a level with our position. They had been flying parallel with the ridge, only a few feet above the tops of the trees. A few days later, on October 15, three more Red-throated Loons flew over, rather low, but in the customary north to south direction" (Broun, 1941b:266).

December observations at Lake Ontelaunee include one on December 24, 1938 (Byron Nunemacher, Helen Y. Poole, Earl Poole); one on December 4, 1948 (E.P.); five on December 9, 1973 (Matt Spence); one on December 21, 1986; six on December 3, 1991 (Dean Kendall); and one on December 18 and 20, 1992 (D.K.). It has been recorded on the Reading Christmas Bird Count three of 86 years, the single birds appearing in 1938, 1986, and 1992.

The northward migration starts late in March or in April. Earl Poole saw one Red-throated Loon on Lake Ontelaunee March 22, 1942. Other spring records from that lake are in April and May; the latest is May 12 (1943 - E.P., five birds). The greatest number seen at any time is 14 on April 7, 1962 (E.P.).

Loons occasionally become stranded on wet highways or in fields, having mistaken these places for bodies of water. One Red-throated Loon found in a corn field at Leesport on November 6, 1926, was kept for several days in a poultry pen and offered corn by local boys. It died two days later and is now in the Reading Public Museum collection. One was discovered November 9, 1993, on Hawk Mountain Road near Kempton and was released by Laurie Goodrich and Shelby

Rudolph on Leaser Lake, Jacksonville, Lehigh County, where it remained for two days.

The Red-throated Loon was listed as occurring in the county by John F. Hofmann in 1890.

COMMON LOON *Gavia immer*
Common migrant spring and fall

A fairly common migrant on the lakes and larger ponds, the Common Loon is observed much more frequently in spring than fall. It is most often seen at Lake Ontelaunee, Blue Marsh Lake, Glen Morgan Lake, and Kaercher Creek Park, or flying over hawk lookouts along the Kittatinny Ridge during the fall migration.

The bulk of the spring migration is accomplished through April and early May. Early migrants may occur in March, and nonbreeders, mostly first-year birds, remain irregularly into June or, rarely, through the summer. Late winter records include two seen at Blue Marsh Lake January 31, 1989, and January 7, 1993 (Harold and Joan Silagy); one found at Lake Ontelaunee during an early thaw on February 19, 1949 (Earl Poole); and one there March 1, 1992 (Matt Spence, Rudy Keller).

By mid-April the Common Loon may occur on streams and ponds, even very small ones, almost anywhere, or may be heard or seen passing high overhead. The maximum observed in spring at any one time and place in Berks County is a flock of 250 on Lake Ontelaunee during a sleet storm on April 15, 1962 (E.P.). Other high counts there include over 200 seen following a heavy rain on April 29, 1958 (E.P.), and 150 observed on April 17, 1945. On April 27, 1960, Alex Nagy counted at least 240 Common Loons flying over Hawk Mountain, where 100 at a time were calling and circling over the Kettle in early morning fog.

Earl Poole took a specimen now in the Reading Public Museum collection April 27, 1922, at Bernhart's Dam in Muhlenberg Township.

The Common Loon is rarely seen after the middle of May. Belated migrants remained at Lake Ontelaunee June 7, 1958 (E.P.); June 17, 1956 (Charles Schaich); and June 20, 1993 (Ken Lebo), but from then on most of the remaining birds have been nonbreeding individuals that may remain for varying periods. One was found at Lake Ontelaunee from July 26 to September 7, 1947 (E.P.). Other late spring records include one seen at Hawk Mountain June 19, 1960 (Francis Trembley), and one at Kaercher Creek Park in Windsor Township June 18, 1986 (Kerry Grim).

The fall migration starts irregularly. An extremely early date, which might represent a summer wanderer, is one bird at Hawk Mountain August 22, 1952 (Tommy Hanson). Other early dates at Hawk Mountain are one loon September 5, 1950; one September 6, 1984; and one September 7, 1988. At Lake Ontelaunee, one bird was seen on September 16, 1956, and three were seen there on September 21, 1958 (E.P.).

Most of the fall migrants pass over Pennsylvania in late October and November. The highest number reported on any one fall day is 488 loons seen at Hawk Mountain November 13, 1977 (Jim Brett). Other high counts at Hawk Mountain include over 400 November 10, 1956 (Maurice Broun); 243 on November 23, 1995 (Steve Thorpe); and 210 November 11, 1942 (M.B., E.P.). The largest flocks that have been reported on the water in the fall consist of 29 Common Loons found on Lake Ontelaunee December 3, 1991 (Dean Kendall), 25 there October 31, 1993 (M.S.), and 20 on November 24, 1957 (Byron Nunemacher, C.S.).

Stragglers remain until late November or even into December. Late records at Lake Ontelaunee include December 8 and 22, 1946 (E.P.), and December 26, 1960 (Warren Faust).

The Pennsylvania German name for the Common Loon is "Wasserschlubber," which is the general name for all diving birds including the grebes. Sometimes "der gross Wasserschlubber" is used to distinguish this species from the smaller grebes. In Berks County, the Common Loon is also called "Der Wewwend-Voggel" from "wewwere" an almost untranslatable Pennsylvania German word which means "stirring," "shaking," "rousing," "swarming," or "bustling." The bird's voice and its restless, peculiar manners would suggest this name. The Common Loon is better known, locally, than the grebes, by its call, for its antics on water and in the air, and for its frenzied behavior when caught on land or on a body of water too small to enable it to take flight (Rupp, 1946:67 - 70).

The Common Loon has been reported on the Reading Christmas Bird Count four of 86 years, twice in the last 10. Two were found on Blue Marsh Lake for the only Bernville Christmas Bird Count record January 4, 1997.

PIED-BILLED GREBE *Podilymbus podiceps*
Common migrant spring and fall; local nester

A regular migrant, the Pied-billed Grebe may occur on almost any pond or stream of reasonable size as long as open water is available. When not wintering, it is among the first water birds to follow the retreating ice in spring, appearing on Lake Ontelaunee as early as February 20 (1954 - Earl Poole). But it often does not arrive in Berks County until late in March.

This grebe does not migrate in flocks as does the Horned Grebe, and it is unusual to find more than five or 10 present at one time. The bulk of the spring migration occurs from late March to the latter part of April, but often this bird is present well into May with occasional stragglers into June or later. Their lateness often leads to the suspicion that they are nesting nearby.

During 1937, several pairs acted as though attempting to nest on Lake Ontelaunee, but the lowering of the water level apparently caused them to leave. They were last seen May 23. A pair spent most of the summer of 1953 at Nagy's Pond near Eckville. During April 1954, Maurice Broun and Alex Nagy found a nest with eggs at Nagy's Pond. It was later destroyed by a flood, and the birds departed.

There is one nesting record at Lake Ontelaunee. Earl Poole saw two adults and five downy young on the Peters Creek pond June 26, 1968. Matt Spence saw one adult with four young on June 30.

The next Berks nesting record occurred at Glen Morgan Lake, currently the largest marsh habitat in the county. Harold and Ken Lebo recorded Pied-billed Grebes with chicks there June 28, 1995. Ken Lebo counted 78 local birds and migrants at the lake on September 28, 1995. He recorded 118 adults and immatures July 4, 1996. There were 83 grebes there September 21 and 90 on November 5, 1996.

The fall migration in Berks is a leisurely affair, and birds are present regularly from late August or early September until late November, irregularly until late December. The height of the fall movement is reached in October. This grebe is very rare after the last of December, although one individual wintered successfully at Lake Ontelaunee through 1952-1953, and others remained there until January 23 (1955) and January 26 (1957).

Other winter records include one seen on the Schuylkill River below the Kernsville Dam January 2 to 25, 1977 (Kenneth and Dorothy Grim, Kerry Grim); one at Grace Mines on January 25, 1989 (Matt Wlasniewski); and one at Blue Marsh Lake January 2, 1994 (Harold and Joan Silagy).

The Pennsylvania Germans call the Pied-billed Grebe "Wasserschlubber," a name shared with the loons. Hunters like to tell of the way this bird dives at the flash of a gun and how it disappears by swimming under water (Rupp, 1946:69). Herbert Beck gives the name "Drek Shlibber" and "Wosser Shlibber" and says that the Red-necked Grebe and the Horned Grebe, less common on the ponds and streams, share these names with the Pied-billed Grebe, from which they are not clearly distinguished (Beck, 1924: 290).

The Pied-billed Grebe has been recorded on the Reading Christmas Bird Count 27 of 86

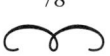

years, five of the last 10, with a high count of 11 on December 18, 1983. The peak for the Hamburg Christmas Bird Count is two on December 24, 1972. The high for the Bernville count is two on December 30, 1995.

HORNED GREBE *Podiceps auritus*
Uncommon migrant spring and fall

Numbers of migrating Horned Grebes have been declining in recent years, although it is still fairly regular, particularly on the larger bodies of water. It sometimes visits remarkably small ponds.

High numbers occasionally alight on the larger ponds during storms, as on April 29, 1929, when Earl Poole observed 250 on Lake Ontelaunee. An early spring migrant record is one seen at Lake Ontelaunee March 2, 1992 (Kevin Crilley). The latest spring record is May 15 (1937 - Earl Poole).

The single-day high counts at Lake Ontelaunee are 300 on April 28, 1958 (E.P.), and 91 after a storm on April 3, 1993 (Matt Spence).

The earliest fall observation is September 21 (1936 - Byron Nunemacher). Fall migrants reach their peak numbers late in October, November, and early December, a few remaining until driven away or stranded by a heavy freeze. There are several December records but comparatively few later than mid-November. During sudden cold spells, numbers of these birds are sometimes found stranded and unable to rise from the ice.

Single individuals wintered successfully at Lake Ontelaunee during 1931-1932 and 1937-1938. Other winter records include one February 18 and 19, 1990, at Kaercher Creek Park in Windsor Township (Matt Wlasniewski) and one at Blue Marsh Lake February 8, 1992 (Ken Lebo).

The Horned Grebe has been recorded on the Reading Christmas Bird Count 18 of 86 years, once in the last 10, with a high of five on December 27, 1970.

RED-NECKED GREBE *Podiceps grisegna*
Rare migrant spring and fall

The Red-necked Grebe is a rare and irregular migrant on the Schuylkill River, lakes, and ponds where it appears most frequently in the spring and rarely in midwinter.

Matt Spence spotted a Berks County high count of 27 at Lake Ontelaunee on April 16, 1996. The numbers had increased from six birds on March 10. This large grebe is usually seen either singly or in small groups of up to three birds.

This bird has been seen in Berks County in spring between February 26 (1930 - Earl Poole; 1994) and May 21 (1940 - E.P.).

Most of the comparatively few fall records of this grebe have occurred at Lake Ontelaunee: one October 2, 1940 (E.P.); one October 30, 1953 (E.P.); three November 11, 1991 (Dean Kendall); three November 13, 1992 (D.K.); two October 16, 1993 (Matt Spence, Matt Wlasniewski); and one November 27, 1993 (Harold Lebo). One appeared November 9, 1986, at

Blue Marsh Lake (Harold and Joan Silagy).

During the springs of 1959 and 1994, incursions of Red-necked Grebes reached most parts of Pennsylvania. In 1959, one appeared on a small pond near Morgantown on March 14 and remained there for several days (Robert Cook, E.P.). A pair in breeding plumage appeared on the Birdsboro reservoir on April 21 and remained until May 15 (E.P.). This appears to be the latest date in the state on which these birds were seen during this visitation.

In 1994, one was seen February 26 and 27 at Five Locks on the Schuylkill River below Hamburg (M.W., Rudy Keller, H. and J.S.). One was seen from March 18 to 29, four April 7, three April 9, and two April 19 at Lake Ontelaunee (M.S., Ken Lebo).

Jim Brett and Barb Lake found a Red-necked Grebe dead at the entrance to Hawk Mountain April 3, 1981.

KERMADEC PETREL *Pterodroma neglecta*
Accidental

On October 3, 1959, three days after Hurricane Gracie had spent itself in south-central Pennsylvania, John Alderman, Maurice Broun, Donald Heintzelman, and others saw a strange bird circling over the North Lookout at Hawk Mountain during the early afternoon.

Maurice Broun writes: "We were electrified when a dark bird the size of a Laughing Gull, with long, narrow wings, showing conspicuous white patches on the under wing-coverts, swept into view just below us. The bird skimmed over the tree-tops; it glided back and forth and round and about ever so gracefully, coming within 30 feet. We studied it for nearly ten minutes.... Presently the bird swerved low into the Schuylkill Valley, and vanished toward the northwest" (Broun, 1960).

Although light conditions were unfavorable, Heintzelman obtained some remarkable motion picture film. From this film Dr. Robert C. Murphy of the American Museum of Natural History and author of *Oceanic Birds of South America* identified the bird as a Kermadec Petrel, *Pterodroma neglecta*, a species which nests in the South Pacific Ocean (Heintzelman, 1961:262-267).

In a letter to Heintzelman, Dr. Murphy writes:

The short strip of motion pictures of your seabird is far more revealing than I had anticipated. It is not a Sooty Shearwater. That species has a white wing lining as conspicuous as the Black Duck's. Furthermore, your bird is not a *Puffinus* [Shearwater] of any sort. Its bill and its style of flight show that it is a member of the genus *Pterodroma*.

On geographic grounds, the most likely petrel would be *Pterodroma arminjoniana* [Herald Petrel] from the south Atlantic which has once been taken at Ithaca, New York, after a hurricane. Careful examination of the film appears, however, to rule out that species. My final conclusion is that this petrel can be nothing else than *Pterodroma neglecta* in the dark plumage phase. There is no other species that shows the conspicuous white wing patch against a generally black plumage (Heintzelman, 1961:266).

George Watson, retired Curator of Birds at the National Museum of Natural History at the Smithsonian Institution and a leading authority on seabirds, also examined the movie film and independently confirmed Murphy's identification of the petrel.

Others, however, doubtless on the basis of greater probability, considered it the related Herald Petrel *P. arminjoniana*. After comparing the best enlargements from Heintzelman's film with the large series of both species in the American Museum of Natural History, Earl Poole felt satisfied that Dr. Murphy was correct in considering it the Kermadec bird. At least 12 specimens of the dark phase of this species matched the photograph in every detail of plumage, while none of the corresponding phase of *arminjoniana* showed the strongly contrasting dark and white pattern of the primaries and rectrices which is so evident in the photographs. Only one of the numerous specimens of the latter that Poole examined showed a remote resemblance to *neglecta*.

Since the storm in question originated in the Caribbean area, it would seem that the probabilities would be in favor of the Herald Petrel, which has been found dead in New York state on one occasion as Murphy notes. However, direct comparison convinced Poole that the Hawk Mountain bird was either a typical *neglecta* in the dark phase or else an atypical specimen of *arminjoniana* which cannot be matched in the large series in the American Museum. In actual air miles the distance from Hawk Mountain to South Trinidad in the Atlantic is only slightly less than that to Mas-a-tierra off the coast of Chile, which is the home of the nearest breeding colony of the Kermadec species, and other oceanic birds have been known to cross the isthmus of Panama (Poole, unpub. man.).

According to Richard Banks of the Smithsonian Institution, the acting American Ornithologists' Union Check-list Committee chairman, this sighting will be referenced in the seventh edition of the check-list due out at the end of 1997 as the first record of Kermadec Petrel in the continental United States. The sixth edition of the check-list refers to the identification of the Hawk Mountain bird as "uncertain" (A.O.U., 1983:17) and includes the Kermadec Petrel based on a single specimen from Hawaii.

LEACH'S STORM-PETREL *Oceanodroma leucorhoa*
Accidental

A remarkable visitation of Leach's Storm-Petrels occurred after the severe northeast storm of August 23 to 24, 1933, when many were seen and others found in a weakened condition as far inland as the Susquehanna River (*c.f.* Frey, 1943). Upwards of 100 were seen on Lake Ontelaunee on August 23 during the height of the storm. On August 24, at least 12 were on Lake Ontelaunee (Earl Poole). The same day five were seen on Angelica Dam and one on the Schuylkill River nearby (Sam Wishnieski). Another was captured in a garage near Front and Walnut streets, Reading. On August 25, two that had been captured in Hamburg and West Reading were brought to the Reading Public Museum in an exhausted and starving condition. These three specimens are in the Reading Public Museum collection (Poole, 1934b:74).

GREAT CORMORANT *Phalacrocorax carbo*
Accidental

Randy Miller identified an immature Great Cormorant at Glen Morgan Lake April 28, 1996. Seen by many observers, the bird remained at the lake until July 19 (Ken Lebo) and was usually perched on one of the dead trees over the lake.

DOUBLE-CRESTED CORMORANT *Phalacrocorax auritus*
Common spring and fall migrant

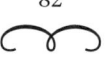

Although during the nineteenth century the Double-crested Cormorant was rather rare in Pennsylvania, in recent years it has been an increasingly common migrant and nonbreeding summer resident on large bodies of water including Lake Ontelaunee, where it was present during every month of 1993.

It has occurred more frequently in the fall than in spring, and individuals have remained for several months at a time. Most spring observations have been from mid-April to mid-June, and in the fall it can be looked for through October and early November. The Double-crested Cormorant can be expected on the larger lakes any time there is open water. One remained on the ice at Lake Ontelaunee until January 2, 1994 (Matt Spence), and was the only record for the Reading Christmas Bird Count on December 19, 1993.

The first Berks County record is of one seen at Lake Ontelaunee April 21, 1929, following a storm (Earl Poole). Thirty-five passed over Hawk Mountain on October 8, 1937 (Maurice Broun, E.P.).

In 1967, a flock of 50 Double-crested Cormorants perched on the railing around a tall gas tank near the Schuylkill River at Reading. From there individuals would fly to the river to fish. These birds were first seen on September 28, and several remained until October 1.

A high count of 103 appeared at Lake Ontelaunee April 10, 1995 (Matt Spence).

Daily high counts at the hawk lookouts along the Kittatinny Ridge include 186 on November 19, 1991, and 269 October 17, 1992, at the Route 183 hawk lookout (Robert and Anne MacClay). At Hawk Mountain Sanctuary 210 were counted October 3, 1996; 187 on September 18, 1996; 177 on September 23, 1996; and 150 on October 23, 1993.

Season high counts at the lookouts are 582 at Route 183 from September 23 to October 19, 1992, and 1,115 at Hawk Mountain during the fall of 1996.

ANHINGA *Anhinga anhinga*
Accidental

On June 1, 1996, Harold and Joan Silagy observed an Anhinga flying over their Bern Township home, viewing it for over five minutes. It had a long, snaky neck with a buffy or whitish-colored head and upper breast. The rest of the bird was dark with a long tail. It flew with slow wingbeats and soared in long, lazy circles, climbing higher and higher before heading due east. Both are familiar with the Anhinga, having seen many while birding in Florida.

AMERICAN BITTERN *Botaurus lentiginosus*
Rare spring and fall migrant

The American Bittern is a rare migrant chiefly restricted to marshy areas or the borders of sluggish streams. It is most likely to be seen from early April through May and again from late July to mid-November while occasional individuals may remain into December.

Earl Poole found it in Berks County as late as December 22 (1949). Rudy Keller recorded one in a brushy area along the Manatawny Creek at Pleasantville on the Reading Christmas Bird Count December 15, 1974, for its only count appearance.

As a spring migrant, the American Bittern has been found between March 27 (1938 -

Byron Nunemacher, David Berkheimer) and May 31 (1996 - Ken Lebo at Glen Morgan Lake).

Most recent records are of single birds found in the spring: near the Red Bridge over the Tulpehocken Creek April 11, 1992 (Matt Spence); near Shartlesville April 18, 1992 (Rudy Keller, Harold and Joan Silagy); at Peters Creek April 18, 1996 (M.S.); at Peters Creek April 21 to May 1, 1995 (Jason Horn); at Peters Creek April 22 and 24, 1990 (R.K., Matt Wlasniewski); and at Kempton April 24, 1988 (M.S.). Glen Morgan Lake near Morgantown currently has the most extensive marsh habitat in the county. Ken Lebo has recorded the American Bittern there from May 18 (1996) to May 31.

Other spring records from a marshy area along Lowland Road in Tilden Township include April 12, 1993 (M.W.); April 21, 1983 (Kerry Grim); April 25, 1982 (K.G.); and May 5, 1978 (K.G.).

On April 16, 1967, an American Bittern and a Least Bittern flushed at Peters Creek and were both in the air at the same time (M.S.).

Two American Bitterns circled a pond and flew off at Hawk Valley Farm in Albany Township July 1, 1989, and two birds flew over the same place heading northeast July 5, 1996 (R.K.).

An American Bittern, grounded by fog, was flushed from the woods up the road from the headquarters at Hawk Mountain by Perot Walker on May 14, 1960 (Broun, 1961:8).

The fall migration seems to be irregular with scattered observations in Berks ranging from July 23 (1949) to December 22 (1949 - E.P.).

There are no nesting records this century. A set of three eggs in the Levi Mengel collection was taken near Bernville May 24, 1890. The bird was on the nest before Mengel collected the eggs. A specimen dated June 5, 1887, is in the same collection.

LEAST BITTERN *Ixobrychus exilis*

Rare migrant and breeder

A secretive bird, the Least Bittern is on the Pennsylvania list of species of special concern, and most of the wetlands in which it was formerly found have been altered or destroyed.

Glen Morgan Lake near Morgantown is presently the most extensive marsh habitat in the county. Ken Lebo has recorded the Least Bittern there regularly from May 17 (1995 - three birds) to August 13 (1995 - two seen) with a high of four on May 21, 1995.

Observers in Berks County have found it present throughout the summers of 1949, 1951, and 1953 at several places in the neighborhood of Lake Ontelaunee, although no nest was found. One or more individuals had been seen about Moselem at the head of that lake practically every summer during the 1950s to the mid-1960s (Earl Poole).

Robert Cook saw one at White Bear Swamp, now drained, near Geigertown May 30, 1954, and Jim Bednarz recorded one at a pond north of Kutztown July 28, 1989.

The only records from the first half century are sightings at Moselem May 20, 1922; at Lake Ontelaunee October 3, 1929; at Lake Ontelaunee May 22, 1932; at Moselem August 11 to 18, 1935; and at the Wyomissing Creek in Shillington August 3, 1944 (E.P.).

Two specimens in the Levi Mengel collection at the Reading Public Museum were taken in Exeter May 6, 1888, and at Blue Marsh June 1, 1887.

Three sets of eggs are in the same collection. Mengel collected a set of four eggs at Blue

Marsh near Bernville from a nest built in rushes by the water May 24, 1890. He collected a set of five eggs along Willow Creek June 8, 1890, from a nest in a bush near a marshy bend in the creek, three miles or less from the mouth. Mengel secured a set of four eggs at Rockland May 23, 1899.

GREAT BLUE HERON *Ardea herodias*
Uncommon resident

The Great Blue Heron numbers have increased during the last 20 years, and the bird recently has begun breeding in Berks County. Formerly, it was most often seen as a post-breeding wanderer that became fairly common from mid-July into late autumn and occasionally wintered along spring-fed streams. In the last decade, it has regularly been seen year-round. Numbers are lowest in January and February, but even in severe winters, one or more of these hardy birds usually can be found along open streams or even stalking mice in snowy stubble fields.

During the *Atlas of Breeding Birds in Pennsylvania* survey from 1983 to 1989, the Great Blue Heron was widely reported during the breeding season in Berks, but nesting was not confirmed (Brauning, 1992:51).

Breeding was first documented April 22, 1990, when Rudy Keller discovered Great Blue Herons completing seven nests in a huge pin oak at the edge of a woodlot on Hoch Road in Oley Township. The landowner said some birds had nested deeper in the woodlot the previous year or two. The colony fledged at least 10 young, the last of which left the nest by July 4.

In subsequent years, herons were roosting at the Oley colony by mid-March, the earliest date March 13 (1994 - Rudy Keller), and nest building and repair were well under way by the end of the month. By 1994, this colony had grown to 16 nests in four trees containing a total of five downy chicks and 31 well-feathered young on June 18 (R.K.).

On July 3, 1995, Keller saw 34 large young in the nests or clambering around the treetops, and he counted 36 young on July 4, 1996.

Since the discovery of the Oley rookery, other nestings have been reported. A single nest in a tulip poplar tree in Eckville fledged two or three young in 1994 (C. J. Robertson), but the birds did not return in 1995. In 1996 small colonies of four or five nests were active along the Maiden Creek north of Lenhartsville (R.K.) and in Spring Township (Bill and Pam Munroe). Ed Barrell discovered a colony of 15 nests along old Route 22 east of Bethel on March 23, 1996.

The Great Blue Heron is most widely distributed in late summer and fall after the rookeries disperse and birds wander in from outside the county. In fall, birds regularly fly over the hawk lookouts, usually singly or in small groups. Recent single-day high counts at Hawk Mountain include 35 on September 18, 1996, and 17 on October 10, 1993.

During the early years at Hawk Mountain, fall migration totals rarely exceeded six to 10 birds. On November 11, 1951, Broun saw "three barely visible to the unaided eye, flying close together from north to south, disappear behind a cloud bank! This trio [flew] more than a mile above the lookout and easily 7,000 feet above sea level." The season high is 46 for the fall of 1996.

The Pennsylvania German name for any long-legged wading bird is "Fischroijer." The name also applies to all the herons and bitterns or any bird that feeds on fish, tadpoles, or frogs. Even the Kingfisher goes under this name (Rupp, 1946:72).

The Great Blue Heron has been recorded on the Reading Christmas Bird Count 52 of 86 years, 10 of the last 10, with a maximum of 33 on December 19, 1993. The peak for the Hamburg Christmas Bird Count is 21 on December 27, 1987. The high for the Bernville count is 49 on January 1, 1992.

GREAT EGRET *Ardea alba*

Common migrant in fall, rare in spring

Rare in spring, the Great Egret has a typical heron summer dispersal pattern and is a regular wanderer in July and August.

Around 1920, efforts to protect it in its southern breeding grounds began to succeed, and the species has since become an increasingly regular and fairly common summer visitor from late May to mid-October, and even occasionally into November.

This egret first occurred in Berks County along the Maiden Creek in 1920, returned in 1923, again in 1925 and has been seen every year since, sometimes in considerable numbers. As many as 49 have been counted along the shores of Lake Ontelaunee in a single day, September 16, 1995 (Matt Spence). Other high counts include 40 on July 26, 1936 (Earl Poole); 30 at Moselem July 6, 1949 (Charles Schaich, Paul Martin), and 25 there July 30, 1994 (Ken Lebo). On July 19, 1959, over 30 flew near the ridge at Drehersville an hour before dusk towards the North Lookout at Hawk Mountain heading southeast. On August 25, 1994, over 20 Great Egrets were feeding in Bailey's meadow in Eckville, Albany Township (Charles Nepf). Laurie Goodrich recorded one over the North Lookout September 25, 1987.

Occasionally a straggler appears in April, an early date April 6, 1992, at Peters Creek (Matt Spence). An exceptionally early arrival date is March 29, 1991, at Blue Marsh Lake (Ed Barrell). During some seasons it has not appeared until late July (July 23, 1958 - E.P.).

One Great Egret remained in the Maiden Creek south of Leesport until November 22 (1996 - Kerry Grim). In 1937 one stayed in the county until November 21 (E.P.).

The Pennsylvania German name for the Great Egret is "Der gross weiss Fishroijer," a name shared with the Snowy Egret (Rupp, 1946:73).

SNOWY EGRET *Egretta thula*

Rare fall wanderer

The Snowy Egret occurs in much the same manner as the Great Egret, except that it is rarer than either that species or the immature Little Blue Heron that reaches us during their post-breeding season wanderings.

The young Snowy Egret may sometimes pass undetected when among Little Blue Herons, which it closely resembles in size. It is generally more active than that bird while fishing and has a characteristic habit of trampling in the mud to secure food.

It visits the Lake Ontelaunee and Blue Marsh regions, sometimes remaining for a month or more. Three were seen at Lake Ontelaunee in 1954 and in August 1959.

Records earlier this century include two birds seen at Moselem from September 5 to 12, 1937, by J. Potter, Conrad K. Roland, Anna and Mary Deeter, Florence Hergesheimer, Byron Nunemacher, and Earl Poole, and one seen at the same place on August 17, 1944 (Earl Poole).

The only two spring records are three birds seen May 30, 1994, at the head of Lake Ontelaunee near Moselem (Matt Wlasniewski) and one seen from May 4 to 17, 1995, at the mud flats near Water Street at the lake (many observers).

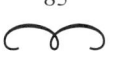

Early summer records include July 25 to 27 (1993) and July 31 (1977) at Lake Ontelaunee (Matt Spence).

One flew over the North Lookout at Hawk Mountain Sanctuary September 26, 1981 (Seth Benz).

The latest date is October 10 (1990 - Rudy Keller, one near Oley).

It was formerly reported from Berks County by John F. Hofmann in 1890. Jonas Stern of Kutztown and D. Frank Keller of Reading regarded the Snowy Egret as an occasional straggler (Warren, 1890:60).

LITTLE BLUE HERON *Egretta caerulea*
Rare fall wanderer

Visits of the Little Blue Heron in Berks County have fluctuated in frequency throughout this century.

An uncommon summer visitor from the south, it was much more regular in occurrence during the first half of this century, although not reported in 1928, 1934, and 1940.

It has since become somewhat irregular, but can be seen about suitable bodies of water during late summer and early fall. Most Lake Ontelaunee dates are between July 4 (1929, 1930) and October 7 (1956) with a high count of 35 on August 6, 1933, and August 30, 1936. Most individuals are in white immature plumage, but occasional stragglers in adult plumage have appeared at Lake Ontelaunee in spring: May 12, 1929; April 26, 1939; April 29, 1956; April 5 to 7, 1958; and April 11, 1959.

The only recent spring record is one in adult plumage May 8, 1993, at Blue Marsh Lake (Sue Wolfe, J. Hobdell, J. Metzler).

An exceptionally late date is two seen November 19, 1967, on the Schuylkill River near Reading (Robert Cook).

D. Frank Keller regarded the Little Blue Heron as an accidental visitor in Berks County (Warren, 1890:63).

TRICOLORED HERON *Egretta tricolor*
Rare straggler

The Tricolored Heron is the rarest of the southern herons that occur in eastern Pennsylvania.

"Many observers" saw one flying over Hawk Mountain on September 28, 1969 (Fred Wetzel). Joan Silagy saw one July 31, 1973, at the Dauberville Dam. Kerry Grim observed one as it flew over Kaercher Creek Park in Windsor Township, circled, and flew off May 11, 1989. The most recent record is one Silagy saw at Blue Marsh Lake September 27, 1994.

D. Frank Keller of Reading reported that the Tricolored Heron has occurred in Berks County (Warren, 1890:61).

CATTLE EGRET *Bubulcus ibis*
Rare and irregular

This newcomer to the North American avifauna has been extending its range northward and is expected to occur in Berks County from time to time.

The first Berks record is of a single Cattle Egret near Maxatawny on May 4, 1960 (C. Miller). Another bird was reported at Trexlertown, Lehigh County, on the same date. What may have been the same two birds appeared together May 13 at Eckville near Hawk Mountain, where they were photographed by Maurice Broun, Donald Heintzelman, and others. They remained in the same area until May 28 (Broun, 1961:8).

In 1964, a Cattle Egret appeared in Reading on April 20, and one arrived in Eckville on April 29. One was seen near Geigertown May 30, 1968 (Robert Cook). Another bird was found in Eckville April 20, 1979.

In 1969, one appeared along the Conestoga Creek south of Morgantown on March 20; two at Lake Ontelaunee on April 13 to 19 (Matt Spence, Warren Faust) and April 18 to 22 (Earl Poole); one at Oley August 1 to 7 (Rudy Keller); and one in Eckville November 15 (Alex Nagy).

Recent records at Lake Ontelaunee include single birds March 21, 1976, and May 7, 1978 (M.S.). The only Reading Christmas Bird Count record is of one bird December 16, 1979, that stayed at a farm near Fleetwood from the late summer until December 17, 1979 (Danny Knarr, M.S.). One was at Big Spring Farm near Robesonia May 9, 1989 (Ira Weigley, Jr.).

A Cattle Egret was seen at Blue Marsh Lake October 12, 1990, and two were in Tulpehocken Township September 14, 1991 (Harold and Joan Silagy). One was at Glen Morgan Lake April 28, 1996, and four were there on May 19, 1996 (Ken Lebo). One appeared at Water Street near Lake Ontelaunee April 29, 1996 (M.S.), and a Cattle Egret was in a Pikeville pasture September 8, 1996 (R.K., Matt Wlasniewski).

GREEN HERON *Butorides virescens*
Common breeder

A common summer resident, the Green Heron is Berks County's most abundant and most widely distributed heron. It breeds near streams, ponds, and marshes throughout the county.

This heron arrives in spring between early April and early May, although Earl Poole recorded one March 25 (1916). The majority leaves for the south before the end of September, but a few may linger well into October or rarely into December. One Green Heron was seen on the Reading Christmas Bird Count at Lake Ontelaunee December 17, 1972 (Matt Spence), for its only count record. The same bird lingered until January 1, 1973 (Walter Kelly). Another was seen there December 4, 1949 (Robert Cook).

The first Hawk Mountain record is of a bird observed by Alex Nagy on May 5, 1960 (Broun, 1961:8).

Of 12 sets of eggs in the Levi Mengel collection at the Reading Public Museum, the earliest was taken April 30 (1887), the latest June 17 (1885). Clutch sizes in the collection range from three to five eggs.

An adult accompanied by three noisily begging fledglings was at a pond near Boyertown August 5, 1971 (Rudy Keller).

The Pennsylvania German names for the Green Heron are "Scheisspok" and "Schadpok." A Berks County informant called it these names because the bird vomits freely when excited as though it were spitting at a person. The use of this name is so broad and general that it is used for any bird of mud and water (Rupp, 1946:76).

BLACK-CROWNED NIGHT-HERON *Nycticorax nycticorax*

Uncommon migrant and local breeder

The Black-crowned Night-Heron is an uncommon migrant and locally common breeder. It usually arrives in Berks County in late March or early April, the earliest date March 24 (1995 - Ken Lebo at Lake Ontelaunee).

This bird nests in rookeries, consisting of from two or three to 200 nests, and when not disturbed may occupy the same rookery for several years, although the usual tendency is to shift locations from year to year. When inaccessible islands are available, they are often used by the nesting colonies, but comparatively small woodlots and pine plantations at some distance from water may also be selected.

After arriving at their rookeries, the birds quickly begin refurbishing old nests. Despite a history of disturbance and harassment by humans, the Black-crowned Night-Heron has persisted as a breeding species in Berks, often nesting in suburban groves and shade trees.

One colony of 40 nests existed for some years in a grove of tall pines on the outskirts of the city of Reading. This rookery remained until 1959 when a road was constructed immediately adjacent to the property on which the birds nested, reducing the colony to less than a dozen pairs.

Rookeries of this heron formerly existed near Lenhartsville and at Moselem, the latter until 1904. A colony of some size nested in the pines on the Nolde Estate in Cumru Township, consisting of 75 nests in 1938. It was disturbed by local boys and raided by crows until finally abandoned in 1939.

In 1935, Earl Poole visited another rookery consisting of about 150 nests along the Schuylkill River near Douglassville. The following year the grove in which these birds nested was cut over, and the birds moved upstream. In 1943 this rookery had again moved, this time to an island near Birdsboro and had greatly diminished in size. In 1946 a colony of about 40 pairs nested on the Lake Ontelaunee refuge.

In the 1970s and early 1980s, a colony was active in tall sycamores on Park Road in Wyomissing. By the summer of 1983, all that remained were 21 old nests, probably abandoned because of home construction nearby although a neighbor said crows drove the herons off (J. L. Gilbert).

The colony moved to sycamores on residential Intervilla Avenue in West Lawn, where it grew to 20 nests in 1989 (Matt Spence). When local residents became disgusted with the nocturnal racket, the rain of dead fish, frogs, mice, and whitewash, and the habit of the young herons of walking around the yards and peering into windows, many of the sycamores were pruned to make them unattractive as nest sites. By 1993, only one nest remained active on Intervilla Avenue (Carl Williams).

Most of the birds moved to a row of Norway spruces on nearby Norman Street, where nesting first occurred in 1990 (June Brown). In 1993, about 35 young fledged out of an estimated 16 nests (J.B., C.W.). Many of these young may have been produced after early nests were lost. June Brown picked up about 40 dead chicks after severe spring storms that year and noted that some birds stayed until early October, much later than usual. With protection from the Browns, this colony was still active in 1996, when 25 to 30 young fledged, and birds had begun to nest in other trees in the neighborhood.

Each summer from 1987 to 1991, Rudy Keller saw one to three adults and as many immatures at a farm pond near Oley or flying from there toward the Manatawny Creek at dusk. These birds may have nested locally.

Levi Mengel collected 11 sets of eggs between May 16 (1884) and June 1 (1886) at Mohrsville, Monocacy Hill, Albany Township, Lenhartsville, Virginville, and Blue Marsh. Clutch sizes in the collection are either three or four eggs.

In fall, the Black-crowned Night-Heron is rarely seen after mid-October.

At the rookery in West Lawn, the only known breeding site in Berks during 1996, most birds have left by late August or early September, when the young are able to fly (J.B.).

Some birds, however, were at the rookery until early November in 1990 and early October in 1993 (J.B.). A late bird was at Lake Ontelaunee November 16, 1994 (Ken Lebo).

A pair wintered near Lake Ontelaunee in 1931-1932, and individuals remained in the Reading Public Museum park until December 11, 1936, and January 1, 1940 (Earl Poole). It has been recorded on the Reading Christmas Bird Count nine of 86 years, none of the last 10, with a maximum of three on December 21, 1969.

Away from their rookeries, adult and immature Black-crowned Night-Herons are most often seen at Lake Ontelaunee and Blue Marsh Lake in late summer and fall.

There are eight records from Hawk Mountain between 1936 and 1951, most of single birds, but on September 20, 1937, Maurice Broun saw 40 Black-crowned Night-Herons flying single file out of the north at 3:45 p.m.

The Pennsylvania German names for the Black-crowned Night-Heron are "Quackvoggel" and "Der Quack," named for its heavy "gwock" call heard at twilight (Rupp, 1946:76).

YELLOW-CROWNED NIGHT-HERON *Nycticorax violacea*
Casual

On April 29, 1954, Harriet Larrabee and Ronald Cocroft identified a single Yellow-crowned Night-Heron with some Black-crowned Night-Herons in the Reading Public Museum park. On May 8, Cocroft saw the same bird in the same area. Both observers were previously familiar with this species, having seen it on several occasions in the South.

On May 14 and 17, 1955, one was reported along Plum Creek by Dr. W. A. Weyman.

Other dates include April 21, May 5, and May 8, 1956, in Wyomissing (Elwood Manning, Earl Poole) and May 12 to 18, 1961 (two on the latter date) in the same area. Another was seen May 17, 1967, near George Kirk's Bridge along the Maiden Creek near Kempton.

On June 1, 1970, remains of a bird believed to have been killed by a bobcat were found along the lookout trail several hundred feet north of the South Lookout at Hawk Mountain Sanctuary. Fred Wetzel recovered enough parts to reconstruct an entire wing which upon comparison with specimens in the American Museum of Natural History collection proved to be the wing of an immature Yellow-crowned Night-Heron.

WHITE IBIS *Eudocimus albus*
Accidental

Helen Poole, Ursula Voge, and Earl Poole saw an immature White Ibis at the head of Lake Ontelaunee near Moselem on July 25, 1964. The bird was studied at leisure and a detailed sketch made on the spot. It was actively probing in the shallows near the head of the lake. At times its head was completely submerged, as it waded in the deeper water up to its "heels." The striking white underparts, dark brown back, and pale gray neck were set off by the pinkish basal portion of the

long curved bill. The white underwings and rump were quite conspicuous in flight. During the following two days this bird was seen by at least six other observers, including several of considerable field experience: Maurice Broun, Albert Conway, Byron Nunemacher, and Charles Schaich (Poole, 1965:37-38).

On September 16, 1967, Adele and Gene West, Theodore Hake, Frank Haas and others saw an adult White Ibis flying over the Hawk Mountain Sanctuary.

An immature White Ibis was found shot along the Schuylkill River near Birdsboro November 25, 1979. Harold and Joan Silagy tried to save the bird, but it later died.

GLOSSY IBIS *Plegadis falcinellus*
Rare

The first Berks County record of a Glossy Ibis is a bird that appeared at Lake Ontelaunee on May 22, 1959, and remained until May 24 (Byron Nunemacher, Earl Poole, Charles Schaich).

Three Glossy Ibises were feeding in a damp meadow in Albany Township April 25, 1965. The three stayed until May 5, and one remained until May 9 (many observers). A high count of 50 flew over Nagy's farm in Eckville May 23, 1973 (Margie Compton).

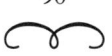

All other records follow: one at Lake Ontelaunee August 11, 1968 (C. S.); one on a wet lawn at the State School and Hospital near Hamburg in Windsor Township April 4, 1976 (Kerry Grim, Kenneth and Dorothy Grim); one that flew from the north flapping hard across the Kettle at Hawk Mountain September 4, 1976 (Dave DeReamus and K. Lewis); one that landed in fly ash at the Titus Station Generating Plant along Route 422 in Cumru Township May 2, 1977 (Kerry Grim); one that flew within 20 feet of Owl's Head near Hawk Mountain September 16, 1980 (Seth Benz, Doug Cook); four that flew over and between the North and South lookouts at Hawk Mountain heading south October 7, 1984 (Kerry Grim, Laurie Goodrich); one at Peters Creek from April 21 to 23, 1995 (Jason Horn, Ken Lebo, Bart Smith, Matt Spence); and two that appeared in a meadow on the Bernville - Robesonia Road April 14, 1996 (Harold and Joan Silagy), one there April 15 (M.S.).

WOOD STORK *Mycteria americana*
Accidental

On November 11, 1921, Dr. Stanley Brunner of Krumsville received a Wood Stork that had been found dead in Albany Township. Earl Poole saw this bird in the flesh. Since 1966, this specimen has been on display in the Pennsylvania Dutch Folk Culture Museum in Lenhartsville along with the rest of Brunner's mounted collection.

TUNDRA SWAN *Cygnus columbianus*
Regular spring and fall migrant

Formerly known as the Whistling Swan, the Tundra Swan is the largest of all the waterfowl that occurs regularly in Berks County. It is now a regular migrant during the spring and fall and is casual throughout the year.

The Tundra Swan can be seen most frequently in Berks through March and early April when many feed in the fields over the western part of the county before returning at dusk to Middle Creek Wildlife Management Area, Kleinfeltersville, Lebanon County. As many as 5,000 Tundra Swans have been recently utilizing Middle Creek as a staging area in late winter between their wintering grounds on the Chesapeake Bay and their breeding areas in the arctic.

Spring migrants have been seen in Berks between February 18 (1990 - Robert Cook, 125 at Grace Mine, Morgantown) and May 24 (1958). Spring high counts include 140 at Lake Ontelaunee April 5, 1953 (Paul Martin, Charles Schaich, Warren Kalbach) and 125 there March 16, 1971 (Matt Spence).

The only county summer record is one seen at Lake Ontelaunee June 22, 1975 (M.S.).

The fall arrival begins September 16 (1992 - Robert and Anne MacClay, four over the Route 183 hawk watch). A single individual wintered successfully at Lake Ontelaunee in 1938-1939, being present from November 12, 1938, to March 26, 1939, while another remained from November 26, 1952, to January 1, 1953 (Earl Poole). More than 100 flew over Nolde Forest January 15, 1983 (Linda Ingram). There are three January records since 1988: 23 on the Bernville Christmas Bird Count January 1, 1992; one at Lake Ontelaunee on January 17, 1993 (M.S.); and one there January 8, 1994 (Ken Lebo).

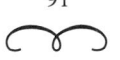

Extensive flights of swans have been noticed flying high overhead at the hawk watches along the Kittatinny Ridge, only suggesting the thousands that must pass each year on their way to and from their gathering grounds on the Chesapeake flats.

Fall high counts include 360 in three groups over Hawk Mountain November 11, 1948 (Maurice Broun); 300 at Lake Ontelaunee October 26, 1951 (E.P.); 155 at Grace Mine near Morgantown December 21, 1991 (M.S.); 208 at the Route 183 hawk watch November 13, 1992; and 400 at Glen Morgan Lake near Morgantown November 21 to 28, 1993 (Harold Lebo, K.L.).

The Tundra Swan may occur during migrations on practically all ponds of any size. In spring it has become more abundant in recent years and lingers longer.

The first record for Berks is two seen at Lake Ontelaunee March 26, 1930, during a storm accompanied by snow and high northwest winds (E.P.). On March 30, 1930, an immature bird was seen at the same place (Anna and Mary Deeter, Florence Hergesheimer, Byron Nunemacher, E.P.).

The Tundra Swan has been recorded on the Reading Christmas Bird Count six of 86 years, two of the last 10, with a maximum of 31 on December 16, 1984.

MUTE SWAN *Cygnus olor*

Uncommon resident

This European species has become wild to the extent that stray individuals or families, doubtless escaped from captivity or from areas in which they have become established, appear at irregular intervals.

One pair that escaped from a local pond has bred at Lake Ontelaunee. The first successful Berks County nesting occurred at Lake Ontelaunee April 8, 1993; one cygnet hatched May 15, 1993. The same pair nested again in 1994, and four cygnets hatched June 4, 1994 (Matt Spence).

Another pair attempted to nest at Moselem during the spring of 1993, but the nest was later abandoned. In 1992, a pair tried to nest at the Grace Mine ponds in Morgantown but were unsuccessful (Robert Cook).

A pair of Mute Swans first seen on Lake Ontelaunee on June 16, 1967, remained until July 5 at least. Sam Painsky reported them there much later.

A family of four, consisting of an adult and three young, visited Moselem Springs

December 23, 1951, and remained on Lake Ontelaunee until March 1, 1952. These were seen by many of the local observers as were two that visited the same lake from February 5 to 7, 1960.

A stray bird that appeared on Lake Ontelaunee May 12, 1929, and later remained for a week at Angelica Dam was thought to have come from a private pond near Lancaster, where it was presumed to have been raised. Another appeared on Lake Ontelaunee April 9, 1932, and still another at the same place November 17, 1940 (Byron Nunemacher, Anna Deeter). Two were reported flying over West Lawn on July 11, 1945.

The Mute Swan has appeared on the Reading Christmas Bird Count 11 of 86 years, eight of the last 10, with a maximum of five on December 18, 1994. The peak for the Hamburg Christmas Bird Count is four on December 26, 1993.

PINK-FOOTED GOOSE *Anser brachyrhynchus*
Accidental

The first Pink-footed Goose to occur in Pennsylvania appeared with about 200 Snow Geese in late March 1997 at a pond on the Gotwals farm on DeTurk Road near the intersection of Routes 73 and 662 in Oley. The bird was identified March 29 (Rudy Keller), after which it was seen by scores of observers from throughout the United States.

Many photographs taken of the bird at close range on the ground and in flight show such diagnostic field marks as the bright pink legs and feet, the very small pink and black bill, the gray upperwings contrasting with the brown head and underparts, and the bird's small size in relation to the Snow Geese.

The Pink-footed Goose and its Snow Goose flock mates were last reported April 11 (R.K.), when the restless birds were seen repeatedly taking flight, only to circle back and land on the pond. The next morning they were gone.

The Pink-footed Goose breeds in Norway, Iceland, and southeastern Greenland, migrating in winter to Denmark, Belgium, the Netherlands, Scotland, and England. There are very few North American records. Since waterfowl are often kept in aviaries, there is always the suspicion that exotic species seen in the wild are escapes. However, the Pink-footed Goose is rare in captivity. The Oley bird showed no evidence of wing clipping or leg bands often seen on captive birds, and it was capable of strong, sustained flight. These observations, plus the fact that the bird arrived and departed with migrating Snow Geese, are strong circumstantial evidence of its wild origins.

The departure of the Pink-footed Goose closed what was perhaps the longest and most remarkable goose migration ever recorded in Berks County. The Snow Goose migration alone was unprecedented in scale, with tens of thousands of birds seen all over the county from mid-February to mid-April, feeding on winter wheat and waste corn left on fields that remained free of snow. Observers scanning the white flocks documented single birds of both the blue and white forms of Ross' Goose, at least three small-race Canada Geese minimally larger than American Black Ducks, and an immature Greater White-fronted Goose.

GREATER WHITE-FRONTED GOOSE *Anser albifrons*
Casual

The first Berks County record of the Greater White-fronted Goose is five birds seen at Lake Ontelaunee April 9, 1972 (Matt Spence). All other sightings at the lake are two from April 17 to May 7, 1977; one May 7, 1978; two November 19, 1978; three March 5, 1979; one April 22, 1979; seven February 24, 1985; one February 19, 1989; and one March 22, 1989 (M.S., Matt Wlasniewski, Eric Witmer). Rudy Keller recorded one near Oley March 11, 1989. Harold and Joan Silagy and Keller observed one at Big Spring Farm near Robesonia from December 25, 1989, to February 25, 1990. The Silagys found one at Blue Marsh Lake with 300 Snow Geese April 9, 1995.

SNOW GOOSE *Chen caerulescens*

The two color morphs of the Snow Goose, the white and blue, were formerly considered two species but are now recognized as one. Early records were identified either as the Snow Goose or the Blue Goose.

In recent years, there has been a marked increase in the flights of Snow Geese in Berks County. The greatest movements now occur in March.

The most remarkable numbers were observed during the spring of 1996. On March 3, over 5,000 Snow Geese (including 35 "Blues") were feeding in fields along Old Route 22 near Hamburg (Kerry Grim, Matt Wlasniewski), and 10,000 were estimated in the same area on March 5 (Laurie Goodrich, Doug Wood). Between 8,000 and 10,000 flew over Bern Township March 16 (Ed Barrell). On March 30, as many as 50,000, about half of the huge concentration wintering at Middle Creek Wildlife Management Area in Lebanon County, were feeding in fields in western Berks (Ken Lebo). A flock of about 8,000 Snow Geese and 95 "Blue" Geese appeared at Lake Ontelaunee March 24. This tight, milling flock leap-frogged around the lower end of the lake near the dam breast all day. Besides these large numbers, much smaller flocks were seen resting and feeding in fields and farm ponds in many areas throughout the county during March (Rudy Keller).

Formerly the Snow Goose was a rare and irregular migrant in spring and fall. Individuals occasionally remain all winter at Lake Ontelaunee (Earl Poole).

The first Berks sightings were made by Maurice Broun when flocks of nine passed over Hawk Mountain on October 12, 1936, and 26 on October 30, 1938.

While watching Woodcock display at dusk at the State Hill Boat Launch area by Blue Marsh Lake on March 22, 1994, Harold and Joan Silagy and Sam and Mary Gundy saw over 1,500 white Snow Geese fly over from the southeast.

An early spring flight occurred January 13, 1992, when J. Galm and D. Gemmel counted over 800 Snow Geese at Lake Ontelaunee. The day before, only one was seen.

From March 27 to 31, 1993, over 580 white and three "Blue" Snow Geese stayed at Lake Ontelaunee (Matt Spence, K.L.). Between 400 and 500 flew over Pike Township March 16, 1991 (R.K.).

Over 220 "Blue" Geese occurred at Lake Ontelaunee from March 4 to 18, 1984 (M.S.).

A pair stopped at Lake Ontelaunee from March 24 to April 13, 1946. A single immature bird was seen there on April 23, 1949, although at the time spring records from the entire state were rare. Two Snow Geese were found grazing with Canada Geese at Lake Ontelaunee on May 24, 1967 (E.P.).

The Snow Goose is casual in summer. One was seen at Lake Ontelaunee from July 5 to July 19, 1992 (M.S.). Another was recorded from June to July 2, 1994, near Oley (R.K.).

There are numerous fall records of Snow Geese. The high season count at Hawk Mountain is 401 seen during the fall of 1995 with a daily high count of 220 on October 28, 1991. At the Route 183 hawk watch, the high season count is 135 during the fall of 1985 with a high daily count of 130 on November 15, 1985 (Robert and Anne MacClay).

On October 15, 1950, Charles Schaich, Warren Kalbach, and Donald Burger saw 170 "Blue" Geese with 30 white Snow Geese alight on the lake. All but 16 departed the same day, but 15 remained until October 21, and one stayed until December 16 (Poole, 1951b:34).

One individual that wintered at Lake Ontelaunee from late December 1959 to June 9, 1960, remained with the resident Canada Geese, feeding with them out in the valley in the early morning and returning to the lake about 11 o'clock each morning to rest.

A single bird remained on Lake Ontelaunee from November 12, 1938, until January 1, 1939. Two were seen there from February 2 to April 13, 1946.

Some winter records of "Blue" Geese from Lake Ontelaunee include one seen from October 31, 1953, to January 1, 1954; another from October 30, 1957, to January 21, 1958 (E.P.). Another stayed at Eckville from October 9 to November 19, 1960 (Alex Nagy, Maurice Broun, E.P.).

The white morph Snow Goose was recorded during the Reading Christmas Bird Count six of 86 years, three of the last 10, with maximums of two on December 16, 1979, and December 19, 1993. The blue morph has appeared on the Reading count four of 86 years, none in the last 10, with a maximum of three on December 22, 1957. With both morphs combined, the Snow Goose has appeared 10 of 86 years on the Reading count. The peak for the Hamburg Christmas Bird Count is three on December 17, 1988. The high for the Bernville count is 39 on January 4, 1987.

ROSS' GOOSE *Chen rossii*
Accidental

Ken Lebo recorded the first Berks County observation of a Ross' Goose in a flock of 600 Snow Geese at Lake Ontelaunee March 30, 1993. The flock was on the opposite side of the dam near the shore, and he went around the lake and worked his way down to the edge of the water near the flock, about 200 feet away. He observed the flock with a 30x telescope and studied each goose. The Ross' Goose stood out because of its short, stubby bill and the lack of a "grin patch." The goose was noticeably smaller than the others and had the expected black primaries with all other feathers pure white. He was familiar with the Ross' Goose from observations in Michigan.

Matt Spence identified a Ross' Goose among a flock of 200 Snow Geese, including 12 "Blue" Geese, March 24, 1995. The bird was seen until March 28 when the flock left the lake (Ken Lebo, Kerry Grim, Matt Wlasniewski).

Rudy Keller observed a Ross' Goose in a flock of about 8,000 Snow Geese and 95 "Blue" geese at Lake Ontelaunee March 25, 1996. His view of the bird was brief but definitive, showing the bird's small size (about two-thirds as big as the nearby Snow Geese); short, clean, pink bill lacking the smudge of a "grin line;" steep forehead and high rounded crown (unlike the long bill and sloping forehead of the Snows); and bright white plumage lacking the yellow head and neck stains of most of the Snow Geese. The bird quickly disappeared into the crowd when the clamorous flock rearranged itself.

BRANT *Branta bernicla*

Irregular fall migrant

The Brant is an irregular migrant in fall at the hawk lookouts along the Kittatinny Ridge, recorded there most years although not seen in 1993. Many more migrate over Berks County than land on the lakes and fields. The bulk of the migration occurs in October and November.

The first county record this century is one that visited Lake Ontelaunee after a severe storm on November 10, 1932 (Earl Poole).

The earliest fall record is 75 Brant seen flying over Hawk Mountain on October 1, 1962. High counts at Hawk Mountain include over 800 seen November 4, 1967, and another 700 to 800 seen October 13, 1974 (Alex Nagy). The late date there is November 27 (1995 - Cathy Viverette, 50 birds).

The Brant has lingered in Berks County on the following occasions: at Lake Ontelaunee from November 4 to 18, 1950; November 8, 1952, to January 4, 1953 (Charles Schaich, Paul Martin, E.P.); and November 6, 1957, to January 1, 1958 (E.P., C.S.); at Weiser Lake, West Reading, October 26 to November 15, 1960 (E.P.); and at a Spring Township field December 8 to 19, 1993 (Harold and Joan Silagy). The Brant has been recorded on the Reading Christmas Bird Count three of 83 years, the single birds in 1952, 1957, and 1993.

Spring records include two at Blue Marsh Lake March 3, 1981 (Harold and Joan Silagy); one at Oley March 9, 1993 (Ken Lebo); 12 at Hawk Mountain March 26, 1954 (Maurice Broun); 50 at Hawk Mountain March 26, 1966 (M.B.); one at Lake Ontelaunee April 8, 1990; one at Hawk Mountain April 12, 1957 (M.B.); 15 at Lake Ontelaunee May 12, 1956 (E.P.); five there on May 22, 1966 (Matt Spence); and 14 flying over Kaercher Creek Park in Windsor Township May 25, 1996 (Kerry Grim).

D. Frank Keller of Reading reported that a specimen was captured in Berks County (Warren, 1890:51).

CANADA GOOSE *Branta canadensis*
Common resident

Formerly a regular and fairly common migrant and rare winter visitor, the Canada Goose has become a permanent resident since about 1938 and has dramatically increased in numbers since the mid-1960s.

Statistics gathered by Matt Spence from the Reading Christmas Bird Count chart the increase:

1954 to 1963 - averaged 32 with a high of 66 in 1963;
1964 to 1973 - averaged 390 with a high of 814 in 1973;
1974 to 1983 - averaged 3,619 with a high of 8,110 in 1977;
1984 to 1993 - averaged 2,482 with a high of 4,663 in 1986.

The Canada Goose has been recorded on the Reading Christmas Bird Count 47 of 86 years, 10 of the last 10, with a maximum of 8,110 on January 1, 1978 (the 1977 count year). The peak for the Hamburg Christmas Bird Count is 5,569 on December 30, 1978. The high for the Bernville count is 2,463 on January 1, 1992.

High Berks County counts include 18,000 at Lake Ontelaunee March 11, 1990 (Matt Spence); 15,455 in 134 flocks over Hawk Mountain on October 14, 1969 (Richard Sharadin, Alex Nagy); and 10,000 at Blue Marsh Lake March 5, 1988 (Harold and Joan Silagy).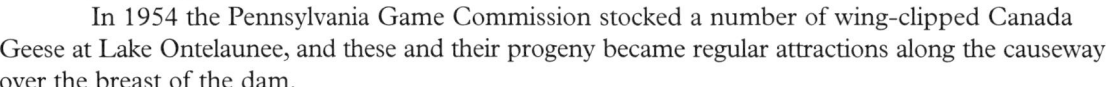

In the early part of the century, semi-tame birds spread from a few private estates in Berks, Montgomery, and Chester counties and nested about ponds and lakes in these and other adjacent counties. Since 1938 it has nested at Hopewell, Scott Run, White Bear, Reading Public Museum park, Lake Ontelaunee, and waterways throughout Berks.

In 1954 the Pennsylvania Game Commission stocked a number of wing-clipped Canada Geese at Lake Ontelaunee, and these and their progeny became regular attractions along the causeway over the breast of the dam.

Early high counts at Lake Ontelaunee include 700 on April 4, 1940. Another single flock of approximately the same number flew over this area on April 25, 1959 (Earl Poole).

Maurice Broun recorded an unusual flight of 745 of these birds that passed over Hawk Mountain on November 14, 1948, as well as an amazing movement of 9,389 during October 1961 with a peak of 5,880 on October 18. The usual peak fall counts during the last decade at the North Lookout averaged between 2,000 and 8,000 per day during early October. Recent daily highs include 6,081 on October 11, 1996, and 4,137 on September 30, 1993.

Since the mid-1960s, the Canada Goose has wintered regularly as long as open water is available. If driven out by a hard freeze, it frequently returns as soon as the first thaw produces open water. Occasional geese have wintered with the ducks that remain on the ice at Lake Ontelaunee even during the most severe winters. Three wintered in 1931, two in 1939, two in 1946, and eight in 1952.

Before the introduction of semi-domesticated stock, the Canada Goose, when not known to have wintered in the Reading area, usually appeared here in spring anywhere from January 29 (1937) to March 25 (1941), but the large flocks seldom appeared before April. Earl Poole's latest spring migration date at Lake Ontelaunee before 1939 was May 16 (1937), but since that time small flocks or family groups have been seen on ponds or flying in any direction at any time. In earlier years the fall migration started after the first week in October and continued into November, the peak numbers being observed in November.

In 1947 Earl Poole writes Canada Geese were "usually noticed as clamoring wedges and lines drift[ing] majestically overhead, heralding the changing seasons." However, by 1964 he concludes, "The message of this once-traditional herald of the changing seasons has lost much of its old thrill."

The Pennsylvania German names for the Canada Goose are "die Schnegans," or snow goose - the common name in all parts of the region, and "Wildi Gans," or wild goose. There are numerous stories and superstitions associated with the passage of the Canada Goose. For instance, a person was not supposed to count them or to point to them, for this would bring bad luck (Rupp, 1946:79).

In addition to the common Canada Goose, *B. c. canadensis*, probably two other subspecies have been reported in Pennsylvania, entirely on the evidence of sight records by experienced observers. However, it has been noted that "several races of *Branta canadensis* have been involved in numerous transplantings and releases of wild and semidomestic birds" (A.O.U., 1957:60), so that the following subspecies are to be considered hypothetical.

Interior Canada Goose *B. c. interior*

On March 3, 1959, Earl Poole saw a small goose, about one-half the bulk of the common Canada Geese that were present at the time, standing on the ice at Lake Ontelaunee.

Hutchins' Goose *B. c. hutchinsii*

The Hutchins' Goose, a diminutive edition of the Canada Goose, is rare in Berks County.

Two visited Lake Ontelaunee November 5, 1949, and remained until November 26 (Charles Schaich, Paul Martin, Earl Poole). When with Canada Geese, they were conspicuously smaller, possibly one-fourth of their bulk, with a very short bill and neck. At times they were associated with the Mallards and Black Ducks, from which they differed very slightly in size (Poole, 1951a:33-34).

Another very small Canada Goose appeared on the lake on October 12, 1952, and remained until October 19 (E.P.). One lingered at Lake Ontelaunee from April 4, 1992, until October 24, 1993 (Matt Spence).

Other recent records include one that stayed at Big Spring Farm near Robesonia from December 25, 1989, to February 25, 1990 (Harold and Joan Silagy); one in Strausstown February 22, 1989 (H. and J.S.); one at Peters Creek March 12, 1989 (M.S.); and one at Strausstown March 1, 1992 (Rudy Keller, H. and J.S.). Ken Lebo observed five small Canada Geese in a flock of 300 at Glen Morgan Lake November 20, 1994.

Occasionally, small Canada Geese have been seen flying with the flocks of common Canada Geese over Hawk Mountain in the fall: October 19, 1936; October 31, 1937; and October 21, 1940 (Maurice Broun). Other Hawk Mountain records include one on April 4, 1953; one in a flock of 57 Canada Geese on October 20, 1953; two in a flock of 39 Canada Geese October 10, 1959; and two in a flock of 67 Canada Geese October 21, 1963. Robert and Anne MacClay recorded one in a flock of over 4,700 Canada Geese at the Route 183 hawk watch September 22, 1993.

WOOD DUCK *Aix sponsa*
Common resident

The Wood Duck is a common breeding resident along wooded swamps, ponds, lakes, and larger streams including the Maiden, Pine, and Tulpehocken creeks. It winters in small numbers and is present year round as long as open water is available.

A cavity nester, the Wood Duck has been helped by the placement of man-made nest boxes. It was the most common breeding duck during 1994 at Lake Ontelaunee.

Jeffrey Schucker has maintained Wood Duck nest boxes in northern Berks County since 1990. In that first year, he erected 17 boxes, four of which attracted Wood Ducks. Out of a total of 44 eggs laid, 42 hatched. In 1996, he monitored 56 boxes which yielded 32 nests. He classified 15 of the 32 as "dump nests" with more than 15 eggs in them. A female Wood Duck will often "dump" her eggs in an existing nest. One box contained 28 eggs, 23 of which hatched. Others contained 27, 26, and 22 eggs. A total of 470 eggs in 1996 produced 346 young.

In Berks broods of downy young may appear at any time after May 5 (1934), the date on which Earl Poole had the good fortune to see 12 leave a nest along the Wyomissing Creek near Reading.

A recent high count is 75 Wood Ducks at Glen Morgan Lake September 21, 1996 (Ken Lebo).

However, during the first half of this century, the Wood Duck was one species that showed no sign of increasing. It was uncommon to rare and local as a summer resident and moderately common as a migrant. It arrived here about the middle of March, exceptionally as early as February 25 (1930), but sometimes wasn't seen before early April. There were comparatively few records later than the end of May, and these were mostly stray males. One brood, still unable to fly, was found at Lake Ontelaunee on July 20, 1949, and observed at intervals for several weeks after. Still another family appeared there on July 16, 1955, and was seen at intervals until the end of August. Arthur Sigman found a nest with nine eggs at Joanna in mid-May 1940. Observations later than January were most unusual, but there were a few: two at Moselem Springs January 18, 1947 (Earl Poole); Green Hills Lake near Reading, January 29, 1960 (E.P.); and 14, mostly paired and going through their courtship activities, at the Reading Public Museum park on February 12, 1965.

The Wood Duck was first recorded on the Reading Christmas Bird Count in 1953. This species was seen yearly from 1962 to 1978 and irregularly since. It has been recorded 25 of 86 years, four of the last 10, with a maximum of 17 on December 26, 1965. The high for the Hamburg Christmas Bird Count is two on December 27, 1987. The peak for the Bernville count is four on January 1, 1991.

There is a set of two eggs in the Levi Mengel collection taken by S. Gruber from a nest in a hollow tree at the mouth of the Sacony Creek near Virginville in 1887.

GREEN-WINGED TEAL *Anas crecca*
Common migrant spring and fall

Along the Schuylkill River, sluggish streams, and ponds this diminutive duck is a fairly common spring and fall migrant. It prefers the shallows where grasses and semi-aquatic growth afford some concealment and occasionally drops in at very small ponds that meet its requirements, but it rarely ventures out into the broader expanses of water.

It was considered common until near the close of the nineteenth century, when spring shooting began to show its effects on the duck population. Since the abolition of that practice in 1918, the Green-winged Teal has recovered some of its former abundance.

Around Lake Ontelaunee the Green-winged Teal has become a regular winter resident in varying numbers and even remains when the lake is frozen over, flying to the nearby open streams to feed.

During 1939 a trio remained about the lake throughout June, but it is doubtful whether they bred as no young was seen. Stray individuals and also pairs have appeared during the summer months, most recently at a farm pond in Shartlesville July 25, 1992 (Harold and Joan Silagy), but the first broods of the year do not arrive until the middle of August (August 14, 1938). The Green-winged Teal population gradually increases until it reaches its peak in November. Two were seen on a pond in the Kempton area December 30, 1996 (Eric Atkinson).

Small numbers remain through the winter. Recent winter records include one seen January 25, 1989, at Grace Mine near Morgantown (Matt Wlasniewski) and one at Lake Ontelaunee January 2, 1994 (Matt Spence). There is another period of maximum abundance through March and April, the last stragglers usually departing by the first week in May.

When not known to have been present throughout the summer, migrants return from August 7 (1994 - Ken Lebo) to October 18 (1931). Departure dates are between April 18 (1930) and May 14 (1972).

The maximum numbers recorded at Lake Ontelaunee are 206 on January 12, 1969 (M.S.), and 200 September 10, 1995 (M.S.).

The high for the Reading Christmas Bird Count is 129 in 1940. It was recorded on that count 55 of 86 years, five of the last 10. The high for the Hamburg Christmas Bird Count is 18 on January 4, 1971. The peak for the Bernville count is five on January 1, 1990.

Common Teal *Anas crecca crecca*
Casual

This European subspecies of the Green-winged Teal is apparently rarer than the Eurasian Wigeon and is casual in Berks County. There have been a number of records of this bird in the southeastern Pennsylvania counties since 1938, after its having previously been unrecorded.

What is probably the first state record is a drake seen on a small pond adjoining Lake Ontelaunee on February 3, 1938, by Maurice and Irma Broun, Mr. and Mrs. Edward Frey, and Earl Poole. This individual was seen at the same place on several occasions and studied carefully at close range. It was last seen on March 6, fighting with a Green-winged Teal over the attentions of a female, probably of the latter species.

Another remained with a group of Green-winged Teal at the Peters Creek pond from January 22 to March 4, 1940 (Earl Poole.). Others were seen at Lake Ontelaunee on January 17, 1942; December 4, 1943 (E.P.); November 2 and 4, 1951 (Theodore Hake, E.P.); and March 3, 1957 (C. and R. Miller).

On March 1, 1939, one was seen at very close range at Moselem in company with another that showed the distinctive characters of this species but had a faint trace of the vertical bar before the bend of the wing, characteristic of the Green-winged Teal. Upon going over a number of skins of both species, Poole was led to regard this bird as a probable hybrid. It remained until March 26.

From April 28 to May 8, 1954, Poole saw at close range another puzzling bird that may have been a hybrid or intergrade between this and the Green-winged Teal at the lower Moselem Dam. It was a typical Common Teal in all respects but had a trace of the vertical white bar of the Green-winged Teal on one side of the breast. On April 3 and 4, 1993, Matt Spence observed another possible hybrid at Peters Creek that had the vertical white bar of the Green-winged Teal and the horizontal white bar of the Common Teal.

AMERICAN BLACK DUCK *Anas rubripes*

Common migrant spring and fall

Currently a rare nester in Berks County, the American Black Duck has been declining steadily due to competition from introduced Mallards and habitat loss. Statistics from the Reading Christmas Bird Count illustrate this decline:

From 1954 to 1963: average 1,873 with a high count of 4,500 in 1955;
From 1964 to 1973: average 1,060 with a high count of 2,259 in 1967;
From 1974 to 1983: average 716 with a high count of 1,328 in 1976;
From 1984 to 1993: average 530 with a high count of 949 in 1987 (Matt Spence).

The Black Duck has appeared on the Reading count 66 of 86 years, 10 of the last 10, with a maximum of 5,003 in 1953. The high for the Hamburg count is 520 on January 2, 1967. The peak for the Bernville Christmas Bird Count is 45 on January 2, 1994.

The Black Duck is generally regarded as a common migrant in spring and fall, locally common in winter, and rare to fairly common in summer. Prior to about 1930, when the semi-domesticated Mallard started to take its place, it was the most common breeding duck of eastern Pennsylvania. Formerly, it was an abundant resident about Lake Ontelaunee and frequent on streams and marshes elsewhere throughout the county. During migrations as many as 5,000 of this species were often seen on the lake. Nests and young were found about the marshes of Peters Creek, Moselem, and similar favorable spots.

Earl Poole had seen broods of downy young along the Moselem Creek and at Lake Ontelaunee on numerous occasions since 1939. He saw the earliest brood on May 24 (1941). On June 2, 1945, he saw two broods within a few feet of each other.

On May 22, 1976, Kerry Grim chased up a pair of Black Ducks from Monk's Bog on State Game Lands 106 near Hawk Mountain Sanctuary. Maurice Broun had seen Black Ducks attempt to nest in mountain ponds, but they were never successful - probably because of raccoon predation. In 1966 Broun found a nest with eight eggs in a pond near Hawk Mountain west of Owl's Head, the last known nesting record in the county before Ken Lebo saw two Black Ducks with four ducklings at the mud flats near the head of Lake Ontelaunee on June 24, 1995.

Black Duck and Mallard hybrids also occur in Berks County, usually between October and May. A hybrid was seen at Lake Ontelaunee from March 17 to 24, 1991 (Matt Spence, Rudy Keller). The largest number of hybrids recorded is four seen feeding in a field near Oley with a mixed flock of Mallard and Black ducks January 31, 1988 (R.K.). The Black X Mallard hybrid has been recorded on the Reading Christmas Bird Count eight of 86 years, none in the last 10, with a maximum of two in 1966.

MALLARD *Anas platyrhynchos*

Common resident

The Mallard is the most common and widespread breeding duck in Berks County. While it probably nested in eastern Pennsylvania in the early part of the nineteenth century, as was stated by Audubon, it evidently became quite scarce as a breeder in later years and remained so until about the 1920s.

Levi Mengel collected four specimens: from Douglassville April 12, 1885; from the Tulpehocken Creek near Reading April 8, 1888; near Reading October 14, 1888; and near Reading

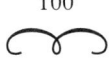

November 19, 1889.

By 1938 the Mallard became well established around Lake Ontelaunee and Moselem Creek and has bred there consistently, downy young being seen each season. These birds have lost most of the fear of man and mingle freely with the partly domesticated ducks in the Reading Public Museum park, coming and going at will.

By mid-August the local population is increased by the first migrants that come into the area until by late November upwards of 2,000 of this species may be seen at one time. The Mallard reaches maximum numbers at Lake Ontelaunee during the first 10 days of December with a high count of 5,060 on December 7, 1969 (Matt Spence). Many remain through mild winters, even resting on the ice when the lake is frozen over and going to the spring-fed streams to feed. It may be seen along the entire length of the Schuylkill River in any season.

The Mallard and more recently the semi-domesticated strain of the Canada Goose have succeeded in establishing and maintaining themselves in the middle of heavily populated areas.

A female Mallard that Maurice Broun had banded at the Nagy farm pond near Eckville on October 14, 1954, was shot in May 1959 in northern Ontario within a few miles of the Hudson Bay (Broun, 1960).

The Pennsylvania German name for the Mallard and for all wild ducks is "Wildi Ent." Since many of the ducks are mostly migratory, they were not resident long enough in the Pennsylvania German community to acquire distinctive names (Rupp, 1946:82). Herbert Beck writes that this name is used for all the edible ducks, including the three merganser species.

The Mallard has been recorded on the Reading Christmas Bird Count 65 of 86 years, 10 of the last 10, with a maximum of 3,417 on December 19, 1976. The high for the Hamburg Christmas Bird Count is 2,620 on January 1, 1970. The peak for the Bernville count is 1,459 on January 3, 1993.

NORTHERN PINTAIL *Anas acuta*

Uncommon migrant spring and fall

Once fairly common but now diminishing as a visitor to Berks County, the Northern Pintail is a spring and fall migrant on the Schuylkill River, larger ponds, and marshes, but a rare winter visitor. It is apparently more erratic in abundance than most of our ducks but at times appears in large flocks.

At Lake Ontelaunee, the Northern Pintail wintered regularly until the late 1970s, but after 1978 a general decline has occurred. Pintail high counts at Lake Ontelaunee are 548 on March 12, 1977, and 470 on February 21, 1976 (Matt Spence). Recent high numbers help illustrate the decline: 50 at Lake Ontelaunee April 1, 1989 (Rudy Keller), and 100 March 15, 1992 (Baird Ornithological Club field trip). However, numbers rebounded during 1996. Matt Spence found 510 off Water Street at Lake Ontelaunee on March 11. Rudy Keller saw 450 to 500 Pintails at Lake Ontelaunee, Oley, and Fleetwood on March 17. These exceptional numbers for recent years occurred at the same time of the record-high Snow Goose numbers recorded following a late thaw after a hard winter.

The Northern Pintail often appears during the last week in August or early September, but sometimes none is seen until the first days of October. Occasionally nonbreeders have arrived as early as July 18. It may remain in some numbers throughout the winter, often resting on the ice during the day and flying out to the spring-fed streams at dusk to feed. Ordinarily it leaves about the third week in April, but small groups or pairs sometimes remain until the latter part of May. One pair stayed until May 23 (1937 - Earl Poole).

On October 18, 1948, 532 Northern Pintails flew over the North Lookout at Hawk Mountain Sanctuary.

Occasionally, Northern Pintail X Mallard hybrids have been observed in Berks. One male seen at Lake Ontelaunee April 3, 1953, had a green crown like a Mallard with white lines up the neck like a Pintail (Charles Schaich). From October 14, 1964, to April 17, 1965, a hybrid wintered at the Reading Public Museum park (E.P.), the only Pintail X Mallard hybrid on the Reading Christmas Bird Count.

The Northern Pintail has appeared on the Reading count 55 of 86 years, five of the last 10, with a maximum of 152 on December 26, 1949. The high for the Hamburg count is 40 on December 29, 1974. The peak for the Bernville Christmas Bird Count is two birds on January 5, 1986, and January 2, 1994.

John F. Hofmann listed the Northern Pintail in 1890.

BLUE-WINGED TEAL *Anas discors*

Uncommon migrant spring and fall

A spring and fall migrant, the Blue-winged Teal is uncommon or rare in places that do not provide the marsh ponds that are its favored stopping places, but common where conditions are favorable. Peters Creek is the best location to find Blue-winged Teal in the spring.

Earl Poole saw a family of 12 downy young, evidently not more than a few days old, with their mother at Lake Ontelaunee June 30, 1930. On July 13, they were nearly full grown, and on July 27, in flight. Another family of nine was raised the same year. At least two broods were raised in 1931, and three in 1932.

On May 17, 1933, David Berkheimer showed Poole a nest containing 12 eggs at Lake Ontelaunee. On June 20, 1933, one of the local game protectors brought to the Reading Public Museum three downy young that he had found at Lake Ontelaunee after a mowing machine destroyed the nest. These died a few days later and are now in the museum collection (Poole, 1935:26).

Poole saw one or more broods of downy young at the lake at irregular intervals, although the reduction of the Peters Creek marsh in 1942 has limited the breeding habitat in Berks. Other breeding records at Lake Ontelaunee include a sighting of a hen with young July 2, 1950 (Paul Martin, Charles Schaich, Warren Kalbach); six pairs and six downy young May 10, 1953 (C.S.); and a pair sighted June 26, 1966, then with four young July 24, 1966 (Matt Spence). The most recent breeding record there is of an adult with young June 16, 1987 (M.S.).

The fall migration is under way by September with occasional early migrants appearing during the latter part of August. The earliest fall dates from Lake Ontelaunee are August 2 (1953 - C.S., eight seen), and more recently August 11 (1993 - M.S.). Katrina Knight observed a high of 60 Blue-winged Teal at Lake Ontelaunee September 19, 1996, and Matt Spence counted 38 at Peters Creek October 2, 1996. The species is last spotted during the third week in October, with a few stragglers remaining until November.

Blue-winged Teal can occasionally be seen during fall flying over the Kittatinny Ridge. At Hawk Mountain Sanctuary the early date is September 8 (1946 - 25 birds), and the latest is October 24 (1949 - 18 birds). The high count is 35 on October 18, 1948.

There are also a few winter records of Blue-winged Teal. Single individuals remained at Lake Ontelaunee until January 8, 1933, and January 1, 1940 (Earl Poole).

When not known to winter, it returns between March 8 (1939) and March 29 (1940). A recent late spring record is 30 seen at Lake Ontelaunee June 7, 1994 (M.S.).

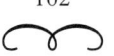

NORTHERN SHOVELER *Anas clypeata*

Uncommon migrant spring and fall

The Northern Shoveler is a rare or uncommon and irregular migrant in spring and fall. Its haunts are shallow waters and marsh pools, rarely occurring on the rivers and running streams. The Northern Shoveler usually travels in small compact bands, presumably family groups, which remain together throughout the winter.

When not wintering, the Northern Shoveler has appeared at Lake Ontelaunee as early as January 29 (1944), although during some years it does not arrive until late in March. Recent spring records are from March and April. Ordinarily it leaves by the end of April, but Earl Poole had a few May records, one as late as May 13 (1950).

During 1940 a pair was seen around the Lake Ontelaunee region until May 30, wandering in the fields some distance from the lake as though looking for a suitable nesting place fully a month after the usual departure date of the species. At this time the water level was lowered and the birds were not seen again. On August 15 of that year, after a lapse of 10 weeks, three Northern Shovelers appeared in the same area and were seen frequently for the following two weeks.

With the exception of the August 15 occurrence previously mentioned, the Northern Shoveler rarely reaches Berks County before September, September 7 (1959) being the next earliest fall record at Lake Ontelaunee. Small numbers may linger on into December or may remain through the winter as long as the strong, spring-fed streams remain open.

High counts include 30 at Moselem January 1, 1968 (Matt Spence, Warren Faust); 18 at Moselem September 13, 1969 (M.S.); and 12 at Lake Ontelaunee March 27, 1949 (Earl Poole).

On December 11, 1927, during a sleet storm, a drake Northern Shoveler joined the domesticated waterfowl on the Reading Public Museum park lake and remained with them until July 1929, becoming quite tame and contented among his adopted companions, although he was free to come and go at will (E.P.).

The Northern Shoveler has been recorded on the Reading Christmas Bird Count 22 of 86 years, twice in the last 10, with a maximum of seven on December 30, 1964. The high for the Hamburg Christmas Bird Count is 30 on January 1, 1968. The peak for the Bernville count is five on January 2, 1995.

GADWALL *Anas strepera*

Regular winter visitor

A fairly regular migrant at Lake Ontelaunee and on some of the smaller ponds throughout Berks County, the Gadwall sometimes occurs in flocks of up to 100 and remains at favorite ponds for weeks at a time. It is regular in winter at the Moselem Springs Golf Club dam.

Earlier, the Gadwall was considered a rather rare migrant and occasional winter visitor, but records have increased with the proliferation of shallow farm ponds and lakes throughout Berks County. A classic puddle duck, the Gadwall has been seen at locations such as Reeser's Dam near Leesport, Kaercher Creek

Park in Windsor Township, Green Hills Lake, and Glen Morgan Lake. The first Berks County record is of a pair identified April 23, 1929, on the Maiden Creek (Earl Poole, Byron Nunemacher).

Gadwall dates range from August 29 (1993) to May 30 (1939).

A high count of 110 was recorded at the Moselem Springs Golf Club dam January 22, 1989 (Matt Spence).

When not known to have wintered, it is among the very first migrants to arrive, putting in an appearance as early as January 16 (1960, 1962), and usually remains until the last of April.

The Gadwall has been recorded on the Reading Christmas Bird Count 36 of 86 years, eight of the last 10, with a maximum of 54 on December 16, 1984, and December 21, 1986. The high for the Hamburg Christmas Bird Count is 118 on December 17, 1988. The peak for the Bernville count is three on January 2, 1995.

EURASIAN WIGEON *Anas penelope*

Rare straggler

An extremely rare straggler, the Eurasian Wigeon usually occurs in the same places as the much commoner American Wigeon and is frequently associated with that species.

Recent records include one that stayed at a farm pond near Centerport from January 22 to April 2, 1989. Perhaps the same bird returned there the next fall and remained from November 26, 1989, to January 21, 1990. Ken Lebo recorded one at Lake Ontelaunee April 9, 1995. It was also seen at a farm pond near Centerport with a flock of American Wigeon.

One stayed at Lake Ontelaunee from January 19 to March 23, 1969 (Matt Spence).

At Lake Ontelaunee the Eurasian Wigeon wintered during the seasons of 1939-1940, 1941-42, and 1944-45, and was seen frequently at Moselem between 1939 and 1947, arriving as early as September 23 (1947) and remaining as late as May 8 (1936). On March 10, 1939, three were seen together on the Moselem Springs Dam.

The Eurasian Wigeon has been recorded on the Reading Christmas Bird Count three of 86 years, none in the last 10, with single birds on December 24, 1939; on December 28, 1947; and on December 30, 1964. Single birds were found on the Hamburg Christmas Bird Count January 2, 1966; January 1, 1968; and December 29, 1968.

AMERICAN WIGEON *Anas americana*

Common winter visitor

A common migrant and winter visitor at Lake Ontelaunee and on nearby ponds and streams, the American Wigeon is normally present from September 4 (1936) to June 25 (1967). Even during severe winters, when the lake remains frozen for months at a time, a few individuals manage to exist in the spring-fed streams nearby, returning to the frozen dam during the day to rest.

From the 1940s to the 1960s, the American Wigeon wintered regularly in numbers up to 400 at spring-fed ponds in the Lake Ontelaunee-Moselem section. A more typical wintering number in recent years is a flock of 46 that remained with a Eurasian Wigeon at a farm pond near Centerport from January 29 to April 2, 1989 (Rudy Keller).

When not wintering, the American Wigeon arrives after the middle of March, attains its maximum abundance in April, and leaves anywhere between the last week of April and the end of May. Single birds have been seen frequently during the summer about Lake Ontelaunee, but in most cases these appeared to be unmated males. A drake was observed through the summer of 1931.

The fall migration usually starts in September, sometimes with an advance-guard arriving as early as August 3 (1944). In Berks County the bulk of the American Wigeon migration is over by the first week in December. Recent December high counts are 51 on December 26, 1993, and 40 on December 27, 1992, at the Moselem Springs Golf Club dam.

The only record for Blue Marsh Lake is four seen March 3, 1988 (Harold and Joan Silagy).

On October 29, 1953, eight American Wigeon passed the North Lookout at Hawk Mountain Sanctuary, and from November 1 to 8, 1955, eight stayed at Nagy's pond in Eckville.

The American Wigeon has been noted on the Bernville Christmas Bird Count on two occasions. Because it tends to graze, 17 were found on January 3, 1993, and six on January 2, 1994, in unharvested corn fields in western Berks County.

The American Wigeon has appeared on the Reading Christmas Bird Count 57 of 86 years, six of the last 10, with a maximum of 760 on December 22, 1957. The peak for the Hamburg Christmas Bird Count is 207 on January 2, 1971.

CANVASBACK *Aythya valisineria*
Uncommon spring and fall migrant

At Lake Ontclaunee the Canvasback is fairly regular as a migrant in smaller numbers from March 3 (1951, 1956) to May 9 (1937) and again from mid-October (October 7, 1945 - Earl Poole) to early December, with an occasional single bird or two remaining on the lake or on nearby spring-fed ponds through the winter. Stragglers have been known to visit such ponds at any time during the winter and remain as long as open water is available. When forced out by a severe freeze, the Canvasback may return as soon as open holes appear in the ice. High counts at the lake include 70 on November 6, 1961, and 36 on March 27, 1994 (Matt Spence).

The Canvasback can turn up during winter at Lake Ontelaunee, Angelica, Green Hills Lake, Moselem Springs Golf Club dam, Glen Morgan Lake near Morgantown, Kaercher Creek Park in Windsor Township, and the Big Spring Farm pond near Robesonia. It is rare elsewhere. One spent the period between January 18 and February 21, 1929, on the pond in the Reading Public Museum park.

The high count at Glen Morgan Lake is 57 on December 15, 1996 (Ken Lebo).

Other December records include 14 at Glen Morgan Lake on December 6, 1994 (K.L.); two at Angelica Lake on December 23, 1990; one at Grace Mine on December 21, 1991 (M.S.); and six at Kaercher Creek Park December 29, 1986 (Kerry Grim).

January records include one on January 10, 1987, at the Moselem Springs Golf Club dam (Matt Wlasniewski), one on January 7, 1990, at Big Spring Farm (Harold and Joan Silagy), and two on January 6, 1990, at Lake Ontelaunee (Rudy Keller).

Four Canvasbacks flew over the North Lookout at Hawk Mountain Sanctuary on October 28, 1955 (Maurice Broun). Nine were counted on October 29, 1975 (Mike Heller).

The Canvasback has appeared on the Reading Christmas Bird Count 12 of 86 years, three of the last 10, with a maximum of nine on December 16, 1979. The high for the Hamburg Christmas Bird Count is three on January 2, 1977. The peak for the Bernville count is three on January 1, 1990.

REDHEAD *Aythya americana*

Uncommon spring, rare fall migrant

At Lake Ontelaunee, the Redhead is irregular and uncommon. Most of the spring occurrences have been in March or early April, although there are records as early as February 4 (1940). A pair remained on a pond near the lake from February 3 to 24, 1991 (Rudy Keller). Usually it is gone by mid-April, but in a few instances the Redhead has remained as late as May 6 (1939) and May 13 (1944). A lone female was found there July 15 (1960).

The Redhead is comparatively scarce in fall. At Lake Ontelaunee, the earliest date is October 3 (1937, 1942), but a pair appeared on a small dam at Moselem on August 28, 1947, and remained there until October 19 (Earl Poole).

The Redhead may be seen through October and usually most of November as well, with an occasional bird or two remaining through December. Winter dates at Lake Ontelaunee include two January 1, 1941; one December 4, 1943 (E.P.); and one January 4, 1986 (Matt Wlasniewski). One stayed at Glen Morgan Lake from December 6 to 8, 1994 (Ken Lebo).

The highest recent count is 36 at Blue Marsh Lake April 4, 1995 (Harold and Joan Silagy). High counts at Lake Ontelaunee include 25 on April 8, 1967 (Matt Spence); 23 on March 3, 1957 (Warren Kalbach, Charles Schaich, Paul Martin); 18 on March 26, 1949 (P. M.); and eight on November 4, 1951 (W.K., C.S., P.M.). Ten were seen at Grace Mine near Morgantown on April 7, 1993 (Ernie Schiefer).

The high count from the North Lookout at Hawk Mountain is 200 on October 13, 1974 (Jim Brett).

The Redhead has been recorded on the Reading Christmas Bird Count four of 83 years, none in the last 10, with a maximum of nine on December 16, 1973, and December 21, 1975. It has appeared once on the Bernville count, a single bird January 5, 1986. The peak for the Hamburg Christmas Bird Count is two on January 2, 1977.

RING-NECKED DUCK *Aythya collaris*

Common spring migrant

On lakes, ponds, flooded quarries, and reservoirs, the Ring-necked Duck is a common spring migrant. It is one of the hardiest of our bay ducks, and when not wintering is among the first species to arrive in spring, having appeared at Blue Marsh Lake as early as January 3 (1992 - Harold and Joan Silagy) and at Lake Ontelaunee January 4 (1986 - Matt Wlasniewski). It is most common during the latter half of March and early April, but sometimes lingers until the last of May (May 26, 1934; May 31, 1953 - Earl Poole).

Summer records include a female that remained at Lake Ontelaunee through the summer of 1960; a single bird sighted there June 10, 1972 (Matt Spence); and a male at the Berks County Agricultural Center pond in Bern Township June 30, 1989 (H. and J.S.).

It is definitely less common in fall, the first stragglers appearing in October (October 8, 1937 - E.P.). An extraordinarily early date is one at Lake Ontelaunee from September 6 to 20 (1981

- M.S.). It can be seen throughout November and generally disappears by the end of that month, although on occasions small groups have wintered at Moselem Springs Golf Club dam.

The maximum number seen at Lake Ontelaunee is 170 March 22, 1994 (M.S.). At Kaercher Creek Park in Windsor Township 110 were recorded on March 19, 1988 (Kerry Grim), and at Glen Morgan Lake 200 Ring-necked Ducks were found on December 15, 1996 (Ken Lebo).

A possible Ring-necked Duck X Scaup hybrid appeared at Peters Creek from April 7 to 13, 1994 (M.S., Harold Lebo).

The Ring-necked Duck has appeared on the Reading Christmas Bird Count 10 of 86 years, two of the last 10, with a maximum of 25 in 1938. The high for the Hamburg Christmas Bird Count is two on January 2, 1977. The peak for the Bernville count is 30 on January 4, 1987.

GREATER SCAUP *Aythya marila*

Uncommon spring migrant

The Greater Scaup is an irregular and uncommon migrant in spring on larger bodies of water throughout the county and is much less common than the Lesser Scaup.

An early spring date is a bird at Lake Ontelaunee February 20, 1988 (Matt Spence), although two males were observed along the dam breast at the lake January 30, 1938 (Earl Poole). Usual spring dates at Lake Ontelaunee range between March 17 (1990 - Rudy Keller) and June 7 (1939 - E.P.).

From March 26 to May 13, 1989, a Greater Scaup remained at a pond near Huff's Church (R.K.).

High counts at Lake Ontelaunee include 86 on April 3, 1973; 22 on April 5, 1996; 18 on April 13, 1994; and 15 on April 1, 1993 (M.S.).

A male came in to the Reading Public Museum park lake on December 21, 1936, and remained until March 1, 1937, fattening on the food provided for the park waterfowl. Another male appeared there on June 7, 1939 (E.P.).

There are comparatively few fall records. At Lake Ontelaunee 47 Greater Scaup were counted October 10, 1983 (M.S.); seven on December 7, 1992 (Dean Kendall); and four on December 19, 1989 (M.S.). A late fall date there is December 26 (1938 - E. P.).

The Greater Scaup has been recorded on the Reading Christmas Bird Count four of 86 years, once in the last 10, with a maximum of four on December 26, 1938. A single bird appeared on the Hamburg count December 29, 1984.

Levi Mengel took a specimen of the Greater Scaup near Reading on November 30, 1890.

LESSER SCAUP *Aythya affinis*

Common spring, uncommon fall migrant

At Lake Ontelaunee and Blue Marsh Lake, the Lesser Scaup is a common migrant in spring and is less common in fall.

At Lake Ontelaunee the usual spring migration begins anywhere from February 6 (1937 - Earl Poole) to April 6 (1942 - E.P.) and continues until the latter half of May, with a few stragglers remaining through June or even through the summer. In Berks County the fall migration starts anywhere from September 29 (1951 - E.P.) to October 29 (1939 - E.P.) and continues until the last of November or into mid-December.

There are also a few midwinter records, such as one at Lake Ontelaunee on January 21, 1986 (Matt Wlasniewski), and at Kaercher Creek Park in Windsor Township December 29, 1986 (Kerry Grim).

The greatest number seen on Lake Ontelaunee at one time during the spring migration is 300 on April 15, 1948, and 250 on April 6, 1957 (E.P.). Recent high counts are 75 on March 17, 1990 (Rudy Keller); 55 on April 4, 1974 (Matt Spence); and 50 on March 27, 1988 (M.W.).

The highest number recorded in fall at Lake Ontelaunee is 300 on October 23, 1937 (E.P.). A more recent high number in fall is 11 on October 12, 1992 (Kevin Crilley).

One remained on the Schuylkill River near Tuckerton from June 16 to October 2, 1923 (Stanley Bright). Another was noted near Dreibelbis July 11, 1942 (E.P.), and one at Lake Ontelaunee on June 22, 1980 (M.S.).

The Lesser Scaup has appeared on the Reading Christmas Bird Count seven of 86 years, once in the last 10, with a maximum of three on December 21, 1975, and January 1, 1978. A single bird seen January 5, 1986, is the only Bernville count record. A peak of 16 was recorded on the Hamburg Christmas Bird Count December 31, 1977.

OLDSQUAW *Clangula hyemalis*

Uncommon spring and fall migrant

The Oldsquaw is an uncommon migrant and rare winter visitor.

Essentially a deep water duck, the Oldsquaw usually prefers Lake Ontelaunee or Blue Marsh Lake where it stays as far from the shore as possible, although it has been known to land in winter on remarkably small ponds that may happen to remain unfrozen.

The Oldsquaw usually is seen in small numbers during or immediately after storms and leaves as soon as flying conditions improve. At such times, tight "rafts" of several hundred may alight for a brief rest. Such "rafts" of between 180 and 300 birds have appeared on Lake Ontelaunee, notably on April 22, 1939; April 19, 1957; and April 16, 1961 (Earl Poole, Robert Cook).

Spring dates at Lake Ontelaunee are between March 6 (1950) and May 16 (1937,1940). The earliest fall arrival date is October 22 (1938 - E.P.), and there are occurrences scattered through January and February with a high winter count of 30 at Blue Marsh Lake February 13, 1993 (Harold and Joan Silagy).

Other high counts at Lake Ontelaunee include 56 on November 2, 1986, and 45 on March 13, 1976 (Matt Spence).

An Oldsquaw stayed on a farm pond near Strausstown from November 26, 1990, to December 1, 1991 (H. and J.S.). One was recorded at a small pond in Windsor Township April 5, 1978, and one on the Kernsville Dam near Hamburg April 11, 1992 (Kerry Grim).

The Oldsquaw has been seen flying over Hawk Mountain Sanctuary during the fall migration. Records there include 130 on November 17, 1979 (K.G., Robert and Anne MacClay), and 50 on November 20, 1949 (Maurice Broun).

Levi Mengel collected a specimen at Reading October 16, 1890, and Christopher Shearer secured one at Tuckerton in November 1891.

The Oldsquaw has appeared on the Reading Christmas Bird Count two of 86 years, none in the last 10, with a maximum of five on December 22, 1935. Single birds have appeared on the Bernville Christmas Bird Count January 1, 1992, and January 2, 1994. One appeared on the Hamburg count December 31, 1977.

BLACK SCOTER *Melanitta nigra*
Rare fall migrant

The Black Scoter is a rare spring and fall migrant on the larger bodies of water. Like other scoters, it usually is a bird of stormy weather, selecting the widest expanse of water available. It alights far out from shore, and moves on with clearing skies, so that satisfactory identification is often difficult. The Black Scoter is a bird to be seen in October and November.

Early fall dates at Lake Ontelaunee are one female October 2, 1994 (Matt Wlasniewski, Ken Lebo, Matt Spence); four on October 3, 1937 (Earl Poole); and one on October 13, 1974 (M.S.).

There are fewer spring records. Late spring dates are one at Lake Ontelaunee May 22, 1942 (E.P.), and 11 on May 3, 1970 (M.S.). Three Black Scoters were reported from Kaercher Creek Park in Windsor Township on April 22, 1992 (Kerry Grim).

The high counts at Lake Ontelaunee are 292 on October 23, 1977 (M.S.), and 65 on October 20, 1974 (Robert Cook).

The Black Scoter occasionally is seen migrating over the hawk lookouts along the Kittatinny Ridge. The high count at Hawk Mountain is 70 on October 14, 1959. The most recent record is 46 on November 15, 1985.

A specimen in the Reading Public Museum collection was taken by John Giles near Reading in January 1890.

SURF SCOTER *Melanitta perspicillata*
Rare spring and fall migrant

A rare migrant in spring and fall, the Surf Scoter usually occurs in Berks County during and after storms.

Spring dates from Berks are between March 10 (1946) and May 16 (1942). In autumn it has been recorded between October 1 (1989 - Rudy Keller) and December 12 (1932 - Earl Poole), the latter a female that appeared at Weiser Lake, which was later drained and filled and is now a parking lot for the Reading Hospital and the Scottish Rites Cathedral in West Reading.

Other spring dates at Lake Ontelaunee include one on April 24, 1966; two on May 3, 1970; and three on May 2, 1971 (Matt Spence).

Recent fall dates at Lake Ontelaunee are three on October 31, 1993 (R.K., M.S., Matt Wlasniewski, Ken Lebo, Dean Kendall); three on October 23, 1977 (M.S.); and four on October 24, 1965 (M.S.).

After a severe storm October 19, 1996, two males and two females appeared at Kaercher Creek Park in Windsor Township (Kerry Grim, M.W., K.L.), and six birds occurred at Lake Ontelaunee (R.K., M.S.).

WHITE-WINGED SCOTER *Melanitta fusca*
Irregular migrant

The White-winged Scoter is an irregular migrant, only alighting during storms and moving on immediately afterward. It is comparatively the most common of the scoters seen in Berks County, but, like its relatives, usually swims well out from shore on the widest expanse of water that is available.

Spring records at Lake Ontelaunee are between April 1 (1993 - Matt Spence, four birds) and May 22 (1942 - Earl Poole). In fall it occurs from September 20 to November 24 (1991 - Matt Spence, four birds); however, there are exceptionally late records in December from Lake

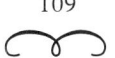

Ontelaunee: December 14, 1975 (M.S.); December 6, 1931 (E.P.); and December 3, 1991 (Dean Kendall).

Most occurrences are of singles or small groups of from three to 10 individuals, but a flock of 30 was seen at Lake Ontelaunee on April 22, 1939, and another of 28 on May 1, 1959 (E.P.). Recent high counts include 13 at Lake Ontelaunee on April 9, 1989 (Rudy Keller), and eight at Kaercher Creek Park in Windsor Township on April 22, 1977 — (Kerry Grim).

Lately, the White-winged Scoter has been a spring storm bird. Of 18 records since 1989, 10 are in April, four in May, one in October, two in November, and one in December.

Maurice Broun reported 150 flying over Hawk Mountain on October 6, 1935.

COMMON GOLDENEYE *Bucephala clangula*
Common spring and fall migrant

The Common Goldeneye is a rather common and regular migrant, less common in winter, on the larger bodies of water and the Schuylkill River and appears occasionally on small ponds and creeks as long as open water is available.

A hardy duck, the Common Goldeneye is among the last to arrive in the fall.

The earliest observation at Lake Ontelaunee is October 28 (1938 - Earl Poole). The Common Goldeneye usually leaves here around April 20, and May records are most unusual (May 6, 1934; May 7, 1922 - E.P.).

There are two summer records. A male remained on a pond near Shartlesville from June 23 to July 24, 1990 (Harold and Joan Silagy). A female Common Goldeneye was seen at Lake Ontelaunee from April 30 to July 9, 1967 (Matt Spence).

The high count is 62 seen at Lake Ontelaunee on April 2, 1972 (M.S.).

The Common Goldeneye has been recorded on the Reading Christmas Bird Count 23 of 86 years, three of the last 10, with a maximum of 19 on December 19, 1976. The high for the Hamburg Christmas Bird Count is nine on January 2, 1967. The peak for the Bernville count is four on January 2, 1995.

A specimen in the Levi Mengel collection was taken October 14, 1888.

BUFFLEHEAD *Bucephala albeola*
Common spring and fall migrant

An abundant migrant in Pennsylvania a century ago, the Bufflehead has since passed through a period of declining numbers and now seems to be a fairly regular and tolerably common migrant and an occasional winter visitor on the Schuylkill River, lakes, and ponds throughout Berks County. Stragglers can be seen in any month.

The normal spring migration occurs from the latter part of March through April, with a few remaining as late as the last week in May. Dates are between February 11 (1950) and May 25

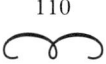

(1952 - Earl Poole). The Bufflehead is usually seen in groups of up to 50 in number, but high counts have been recorded at Lake Ontelaunee after severe storms: 419 on May 3, 1970 (Matt Spence), and 250 on April 22, 1939 (E. P.). On April 12, 1992, 70 were recorded at Kaercher Creek Park in Windsor Township (Kerry Grim).

A Bufflehead summered at Lake Ontelaunee from May 20 to August 19, 1967 (M.S.).

Fall dates at Lake Ontelaunee are from October 19 (1959) to December 9 (1950). There are also two January records: January 26, 1938, and January 3, 1954. One wintered successfully at Lake Ontelaunee in 1937-38 (E.P.); one male wintered at Big Spring Farm near Robesonia from November 16, 1991, to January 25, 1992; and another resided there from early 1989 until January 20, 1991 (Harold and Joan Silagy). The highest counts during the fall migration at Lake Ontelaunee are 116 on November 1, 1992 (Ken Lebo), and 80 on November 11, 1945 (E.P.).

Four Buffleheads flew over the North Lookout at Hawk Mountain on April 12, 1972 (Jean Litzenberger).

The Bufflehead has appeared on the Reading Christmas Bird Count 13 of 86 years, once in the last 10, with a maximum of 10 on December 21, 1975. The high for the Hamburg Christmas Bird Count is two on December 26, 1983, and December 29, 1984. The peak for the Bernville count is five on January 1, 1992.

Samuel Wishnieski collected for the Reading Public Museum an immature male Bufflehead on the Schuylkill River below Reading on the unusually early date of August 10 (1930).

The Bufflehead was listed by John F. Hofmann in 1890.

HOODED MERGANSER *Lophodytes cucullatus*

Common migrant

The Hooded Merganser was considered plentiful in Pennsylvania during the mid-nineteenth century, although it became rather rare earlier this century. Under better protection since 1922, it has regained a portion of its former abundance.

The Hooded Merganser is now a common and regular migrant and has a tendency to winter as long as favorite ponds remain unfrozen. Most migrants seem to pass through Berks County in March and April, and again in late October and November, with a few stragglers remaining until December and sometimes into January.

Most of the spring dates are between March 1 (1936, 1937) and May 28 (1937). It is most common in March with a high count of 56 at Lake Ontelaunee on March 10, 1985 (Matt Spence).

Most of the fall and winter records are between September 22 (1941) and January 14 (1939). One came to the Reading Public Museum lake on September 22, 1941, and was later joined by another. The two remained until March 8, 1942 (Earl Poole).

There are also several records of females and young during June and August, but to date no definite local breeding records are known. Lone females have visited small ponds around Reading during June on different occasions, most recently from June 4 to 25, 1978, at Lake Ontelaunee (M.S.). One was seen at Moselem Springs on August 18, 1991 (M.S.). An immature Hooded Merganser was found on a mill pond at Moselem from August 29 to September 14, 1924 (E.P.).

A male Hooded Merganser remained in a small pond along Reservoir Road in Windsor Township from August 2, 1990, to December 14, 1991 (Kerry Grim).

Two specimens in the Reading Public Museum collection were taken November 4, 1890, at Reading and October 18, 1894, at Tuckerton.

The Hooded Merganser has appeared on the Reading Christmas Bird Count 39 of 86

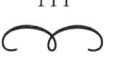

years, nine of the last 10, with a maximum of 17 in 1938. A single bird appeared on the Hamburg Christmas Bird Count December 29, 1968. The peak for the Bernville count is 10 on January 3, 1993.

COMMON MERGANSER *Mergus merganser*
Common winter visitor

The Common Merganser is a common migrant and winter resident on the larger lakes, streams, ponds, and the Schuylkill River, remaining as long as open water can be found. This is one of the few ducks whose occurrences have increased in Berks County since the middle of this century.

Single Common Mergansers have a way of appearing at unexpected times and places. At Lake Ontelaunee, nonbreeding females have been seen from mid-July (July 14, 1951; July 17, 1954) through August on occasion; in fact, the space of six weeks between May 28 and July 14 is the only period during which this species has not been noticed on the lake (Earl Poole).

Most frequently the species arrives here from the north anywhere between October 20 (1940) and November 22 (1936) and departs by the third week in April with a few stragglers staying on through May, the late date May 28 (1937).

Only during very severe winters, when the other ducks are unable to keep open holes in the ice, is it absent for a few weeks during midwinter. Often from 200 to 500 may be seen when there is an expanse of open water. High counts include over 5,000 at Blue Marsh Lake March 2, 1995 (Harold and Joan Silagy); 2,000 at Blue Marsh Lake March 13, 1993 (H. and J.S.); and 1,560 at Lake Ontelaunee on January 10, 1993 (Matt Spence).

The Common Merganser has been recorded flying over Hawk Mountain. The earliest record is September 13 and the latest is November 27 (1993). A high count of 80 was made on November 9, 1940.

It has been recorded on the Reading Christmas Bird Count 62 of 86 years, nine of the last 10, with a maximum of 503 in 1953. The high for the Hamburg Christmas Bird Count is 61 on December 26, 1993. The peak for the Bernville count is 33 on January 3, 1993.

RED-BREASTED MERGANSER *Mergus serrator*
Regular migrant in spring; uncommon in fall

The Red-breasted Merganser usually arrives at Lake Ontelaunee during the last week in March or early in April. An exceptionally early occurrence is one seen on February 21 (1953 - Earl Poole).

It is usually present in Berks County through April and the first half of May, with an occasional straggler remaining as late as June 28 (1978 - Kerry Grim at Kaercher Creek Park in Windsor Township).

During 1949 one was seen at Lake Ontelaunee on July 16 and repeatedly thereafter until September 25, and in 1940 a female appeared on August 10 (E.P.).

In fall it usually appears in smaller numbers, sometimes as early as October 20 (1935), but most observations are in November, exceptionally as late as December 5 (1953) and December 6

112

(1931). Six flew by the North Lookout at Hawk Mountain December 2, 1996 (Mark Monroe). Midwinter records include 101 on Lake Ontelaunee on January 18, 1990 (Matt Wlasniewski), and 12 at Blue Marsh Lake on December 28, 1993 (Harold and Joan Silagy).

The largest number of these mergansers on Lake Ontelaunee at any one time is 300 on November 11, 1945, but flocks of 100 or more have occurred during April storms. On March 30, 1939, a flock of 120 was seen on the lake (E.P.). The highest spring count since 1987 is 40 at Hamburg April 11, 1992 (K.G.).

The Red-breasted Merganser has appeared on the Reading Christmas Bird Count 14 of 83 years, four of the last 10, with a maximum of six on December 24, 1967.

There is a specimen in the Levi Mengel collection in the Reading Public Museum taken December 1, 1895.

RUDDY DUCK *Oxyura jamaicensis*

Uncommon migrant

The Ruddy Duck is chiefly an uncommon migrant, regularly occurring on the larger bodies of water in Berks County. At Lake Ontelaunee spring records are from March 13 (1966 - Matt Spence) to May 31. Stragglers have appeared at Glen Morgan Lake June 7 (1996 - Ken Lebo) and at Oley June 3 (1995 - Rudy Keller). Fall dates at Lake Ontelaunee are between September 25 (1988) and December 4 (1935, 1943 - Earl Poole).

Midwinter records at Lake Ontelaunee include January 9, 1994 (M.S.); January 22, 1989 (Matt Wlasniewski); and February 4, 1939 (E.P.).

As a rule, the Ruddy Duck occurs in small bands of less than a dozen, but occasionally large flocks land on the lakes. On April 22, 1939, Earl Poole found a "raft" of more than 80 on Lake Ontelaunee. Other high counts there include 66 on September 25, 1988 (M.S.); 30 on May 5, 1995 (Matt Wlasniewski); 27 on April 14, 1996 (M.S.); and 17 on September 21, 1992 (Dean Kendall). At Kaercher Creek Park in Windsor Township a high count of 28 was recorded October 19, 1983 (Kerry Grim).

Glen Morgan Lake has recently become the most attractive area in the county for the Ruddy Duck. Over 250 appeared October 27, 1995 (K.L.), and 195 occurred on November 12, 1994.

There are a few records of nonbreeding birds summering at Lake Ontelaunee (July 22 to 29, 1939; during 1957 - E.P.).

The Ruddy Duck has been recorded on the Reading Christmas Bird Count 10 of 86 years, once in the last 10, with a maximum of 20 on December 19, 1982. A single bird was recorded on the Hamburg Christmas Bird Count December 17, 1988.

MASKED DUCK *Oxyura dominica*

Accidental

Samuel McDonough discovered a Masked Duck on June 13, 1984, at the Peters Creek ponds at Lake Ontelaunee. Matt Spence confirmed the identification. This neotropical species

113

ranges to northern Mexico, and there was no indication that this bird was an escape from an aviary. Robert Cook photographed the bird June 14, and it was gone the next day.

BLACK VULTURE *Coragyps atratus*
Uncommon migrant and breeder

The Black Vulture, like the Turkey Vulture, is a southern species that has extended its range north during the past half century. By the 1980s it could be found throughout Berks County. A bird more at home in forested regions than the Turkey Vulture, the Black Vulture is a regular sight in the northern, eastern, and southern areas of the county, but it can also be found soaring over the city of Reading and its suburbs.

The first county record is one seen by Earl and Helen Poole at the Trap Rock quarry along Hay Creek on April 30, 1952. They watched under perfect light conditions for at least half an hour as it circled the quarry with a band of Turkey Vultures. The Pooles were previously well acquainted with the Black Vulture in the South.

Fred Wetzel observed Black Vultures at Hawk Mountain in August 1969, and on November 17, 1969, Richard Sharadin and Gerald and Doris Steffy saw one from Owl's Head that was seen 20 minutes later over the South Lookout by Frank Haas and J. Tobias. It has been a regular fall migrant at Hawk Mountain since 1986 with a peak count of 16 on November 20, 1991 (Doug Laye). The Black Vulture occurs there in migration between August 10 (1991 - Jeanne Tinsman) and December 21 (1995 - Steve Thorpe). The season high count is 54 during the fall of 1994. The 10-year average from 1987 to 1996 is 38.

High counts away from the ridge during the fall migration include 30 along the Schuylkill River south of Neversink Mountain November 13, 1993 (Dean Kendall); 14 at a limestone quarry near Oley November 14, 1993 (Rudy Keller); and 42 Black Vultures with 250 Turkey Vultures at the Oley quarry November 3, 1996 (R.K.).

Hawk Mountain Counts for the Black Vulture									
1934	0	1949	0	1961	0	1973	0	1985	4
1935	0	1950	0	1962	0	1974	0	1986	28
1936	0	1951	0	1963	0	1975	0	1987	30
1937	0	1952	0	1964	0	1976	0	1988	16
1938	0	1953	0	1965	0	1977	0	1989	53
1939	0	1954	0	1966	0	1978	0	1990	28
1940	0	1955	0	1967	0	1979	1	1991	43
1941	0	1956	0	1968	0	1980	0	1992	21
1942	0	1957	0	1969	0	1981	0	1993	50
1946	0	1958	0	1970	0	1982	0	1994	54
1947	0	1959	0	1971	0	1983	0	1995	43
1948	0	1960	0	1972	0	1984	0	1996	50

Note: These statistics reflect counts from the North Lookout only.

Catherine Elwell and Richard Sharadin recorded the first Black Vulture nesting in the county May 12, 1985, when an adult with young appeared on a boulder outcrop near Landis Store in District Township. Rudy Keller found two downy young in a nest at the same place July 5, 1987. Since 1988, Rich Bonnett has found nesting Black Vultures from French Creek State Park to the Birdsboro watershed. One of the nest sites has been active from 1988 to the present. Bonnett reported a nesting pair at French Creek June 1, 1989, and in late June 1990, he found a nest with two fledglings. In 1996, he monitored three nest sites at French Creek, each producing two fledged young.

There are numerous winter records from throughout the county. Over a dozen Black Vultures winter regularly in the Hopewell Furnace National Historic Site area. January records outside southern Berks include two at the Oley quarry January 24, 1988 (R.K.); 11 on the Bernville Christmas Bird Count January 1, 1989; two in Pike Township January 15, 1989 (R.K.); six on the Bernville Christmas Bird Count January 1, 1990; seven at the Oley quarry January 14, 1990 (R.K.); and three in District Township January 13, 1992 (Catherine Elwell).

The Black Vulture has been recorded on the Reading Christmas Bird Count seven of 86 years, six of the last 10, with a high count of 45 on December 18, 1994. The Hamburg Christmas Bird Count recorded single birds December 29, 1985, and December 28, 1986. The high for the Bernville count is 11 on January 1, 1989.

February records include one at Hawk Mountain February 22, 1970 (Gerald and Doris Steffey); six at Hamburg February 14, 1987 (Kerry Grim); two at Eckville February 1, 1989 (Laurie Goodrich); and one at Hawk Mountain and four at Hamburg February 17, 1990 (L.G., K.G.).

Ed Barrell reported 12 at Flying Hills March 30, 1989.

During the North American Migration Count May 14, 1994, 78 Black Vultures were recorded throughout Berks.

TURKEY VULTURE *Cathartes aura*

Common migrant and breeder

The Turkey Vulture is a well-known and common migrant and breeding summer resident. In winter it is usually rare or absent, except during mild winters when it is sometimes fairly common. Like several other southern species, the Turkey Vulture has extended its range north during this century.

Stragglers have occurred in winter along the Blue Mountain in Berks County as early as January 1 (1937) and January 24 (1943 - Earl Poole), but generally the Turkey Vulture is rare or absent in northern Berks from late November through early February. Between March 3 and 10, 1949, Maurice Broun found 155 of these birds roosting in a hemlock grove at Eckville below Hawk Mountain Sanctuary, a site that has remained active to the present time. Such roosts have become common in recent years, as the birds usually move northward in February.

On February 17, 1937, David Berkheimer and Earl Poole found about 40 Turkey Vultures roosting in a large pine tree at Hopewell Furnace National Historic Site, where a park official said they had roosted all winter. He produced a male Turkey Vulture shot on January 1 to prove his statement. This specimen is now in the Reading Public Museum collection. Turkey Vultures wintered there again in 1948-1949, and regularly since.

During the Reading Christmas Bird Count, only one Turkey Vulture was recorded between 1951 and 1981, occurring on December 21, 1975. Since 1982, it has been counted each year except 1982 and 1992, appearing 15 of 86 years, eight of the last 10 with a peak count of 66 on December 18, 1994. The Turkey Vulture was first recorded on the Hamburg Christmas Bird Count on December 29, 1984, with a high of 10. It was unseen from 1965 until 1983. The peak for the Bernville count is 24 on January 1, 1990.

Hawk Mountain Curator Alex Nagy reported an unusual incident with Turkey Vultures and a winter storm on March 4, 1971:

March 3rd brought us 10 inches of snow with an additional half-inch of ice, which proves to be a problem not only for the flora of Hawk Mountain, but also its fauna. The following morning as I returned from the school bus stop in Eckville, I passed through the white pine grove at the base of the ridge where about 30

Turkey Vultures were roosting. I noticed several unfamiliar stump-like projections on the snow-covered ground. As I got out of the car, there stood, huddled on the encrusted snow, seven Turkey Vultures partially encased in ice! They were practically immovable except for the use of their feet. Upon closer examination it was apparent what had happened. This unfortunate seven was sitting on exposed branches during the night while a light, freezing rain was falling. The rain drops rolled off the back of the birds and as it dripped off their wings it froze - much like the formation of icicles on a roof-edge. As the rain continued, the ice thickened and the perfect insulating qualities of the feathers kept the ice from melting. The ice acted as a dam along the leading edge of the primaries until finally it built up over the wings and onto the back. Come morning, as the group took off, the seven birds tumbled to the earth about 50 to 60 feet below. Fortunately their fall was broken by a two-foot snow cover. I scrambled around and finally caught them; for three of the birds I was able to remove the ice without damaging the feathers- they were immediately released. The four others were taken home in the car. Did you ever have the experience of sharing the passenger seats with four vultures? It was interesting to note that a number of other vultures must have had problems with ice. I found about a half-dozen primaries with chunks of ice on them under the trees. A light snow had fallen and I noticed some dog tracks around the roost area; however, none of the birds in the car or those released were harmed. The vultures spent the night thawing in the garage, and the following morning they were released and happy to be airborne again as they drifted eastward over the Great Valley (Nagy, 1972: 6-7).

Hawk Mountain Counts for the Turkey Vulture									
1934	80	1949	376	1961	129	1973	0	1985	0
1935	330	1950	81	1962	0	1974	0	1986	24
1936	82	1951	50	1963	178	1975	0	1987	70
1937	42	1952	31	1964	7	1976	0	1988	51
1938	60	1953	201	1965	105	1977	0	1989	203
1939	146	1954	1	1966	0	1978	0	1990	149
1940	150	1955	62	1967	3	1979	0	1991	173
1941	182	1956	1	1968	1	1980	0	1992	84
1942	83	1957	222	1969	0	1981	0	1993	88
1946	66	1958	14	1970	0	1982	0	1994	194
1947	268	1959	26	1971	0	1983	4	1995	176
1948	300	1960	5	1972	0	1984	1	1996	200

Note: These statistics reflect counts from the North Lookout only.

Assistant curator Fred Wetzel watched Turkey Vultures return to their roosts during a partial solar eclipse March 7, 1970:

The eclipse of the sun at 1:40 p.m. on the 7th provided an interesting observation of our local Turkey Vultures. During the eclipse our area was covered with light clouding, naturally screening out the deadly sun rays. We were watching from our mountaintop when at the height of the eclipse four Turkey Vultures passed low over our heads beating their wings furiously. The wind could be heard passing through their pinions. They were making a bee-line for their communal roost deep in the Kettle. As we looked around, vultures were coming from all directions. Within 20 minutes all the vultures in the area were settled for the night in the tree-tops. Although we did not have total eclipse in our area, they were completely fooled by the sudden light reduction. We watched the roost, and as the light intensified, one by one they left the area. By 2:30 all were gone (Wetzel, 1971: 4).

On August 20, 1978, Kerry Grim observed a Turkey Vulture with a blue wing marker at the Auburn Lookout on State Game Lands 110. This bird was one of 200 Turkey Vultures tagged by Sheila Gaby at Key Biscayne, Florida, during the previous winter.

There is a pronounced withdrawal southward in October and early November when flocks of considerable size sometimes use the Kittatinny flyway. Maurice Broun counted over 300 passing Hawk Mountain on November 6, 1948, sighting 126 in one flock. In this region, the Turkey Vulture becomes rare after November 20.

The season high count for the Turkey Vulture at Hawk Mountain is 376 in 1949. The earliest date there for migrants is August 12 (1965 - Alpha Reynolds, George Pyle) and the latest is December 13 (1987 - Mark Blauer). The 10-year seasonal average from 1987 to 1996 is 121. It was not counted regularly as a migrant from the mid-1960s to the mid-1980s.

The Turkey Vulture nested near the North Lookout of Hawk Mountain in 1965 on the south side and in 1979 to the west. Because of its secretive nesting habits, this vulture is difficult to confirm as a breeder, although it is found throughout Berks in the summer.

Broun and Ben Goodwin measured the flight speed of a migrating Turkey Vulture at 34 miles per hour during the fall of 1942 (Broun and Goodwin, 1943:492).

Rich Bonnett has discovered that the Turkey Vulture in southern Berks has begun nesting in abandoned barns and buildings, perhaps in response to nest site competition with Black Vultures.

Historically, nests were found in the Irish Mountains near Fleetwood May 2, 1908; at Pulpit Rock in the Blue Mountains near Lenhartsville May 5, 1907 (Levi Mengel); at Pikeville May 15, 1904, and May 8, 1907 (Walter H. Leibelsperger); and near Fritztown April 7 to May 5, 1932 (R. Seibert). Walter H. Leibelsperger collected a set of two eggs near Pikeville May 8, 1909. He noted the eggs were deposited on dry leaves under a huge stone.

Large numbers of Turkey Vultures have roosted in a quarry near Oley. Rudy Keller recorded 250 on November 3, 1996.

D. Frank Keller listed the Turkey Vulture as breeding in the Blue Mountains, and Jonas Stern of Kutztown regarded it as a rare breeder (Warren, 1890:116).

Besides the male Turkey Vulture taken at Hopewell January 1, 1937, a female, secured at Leesport November 17, 1931, is in the Reading Public Museum collection.

The Pennsylvania German name for the Turkey Vulture is "Ludervoggel." It is also an expression of disgust and contempt, usually in reference to one who leads a dissolute life. In Berks, the names "Luderaadler" and "Ooshaahne" are also used. As an example of the way in which even dialect forms can be corrupted is the name "Ohna Haahne" given the Turkey Vulture by a farmer along the Maiden Creek in Berks County, according to Raymond E. Kiebach of Reading. William Rupp never heard of any vultures being shot or trapped; rather they were left alone to do their work (Rupp, 1946:85-86).

OSPREY *Pandion haliaetus*

Fairly common migrant

A fairly common migrant, the Osprey is usually seen around lakes, larger ponds, the Schuylkill River, and smaller streams. Occasional individuals remain through the summer. This is a species whose number declined during the DDT years of the 1950s through the early 1970s.

In spring the Osprey generally arrives in Pennsylvania by the last week in March. Earl Poole's earliest arrival date at Lake Ontelaunee is March 22 (1938). Recent March records include one at the Tulpehocken Creek March 30, 1988 (Ira Weigley, Jr.); one in Bern Township March 28, 1990 (Harold and Joan Silagy); and one at Hamburg March 24, 1991 (Kerry Grim).

Two extraordinarily early dates have been recorded. Sam and Mary Gundy saw an Osprey north of Kutztown February 8, 1988, and Catherine Elwell spotted one in District Township February 20, 1992.

Most active observers around the larger lakes and the Schuylkill River see the Osprey occasionally during the summer months. No doubt these summer wanderers give rise to rumors of nesting activities in the neighborhood. During five summers - 1930, 1940, 1942, 1952, and 1954 - Poole saw single birds at almost weekly intervals at Lake Ontelaunee. His records show that during three other seasons they remained into June, and on seven occasions returned in July after having been absent for about a month. More recently since 1989, there are over a dozen June and July sightings at Lake Ontelaunee, Blue Marsh Lake, Marion Township, Lower Alsace Township, Vinemont, and Hay Creek.

D. Frank Keller listed the Osprey as breeding in Berks County (Warren, 1890:143). His record is undoubtedly an error, as neither Levi Mengel nor any of the other collectors working during that time regarded it as a nester.

Fall migrants usually arrive around the middle of August and are present until about the middle of October; Poole's latest date at Lake Ontelaunee is November 6 (1959). The early date at Hawk Mountain is July 26 (1996 - Bill Wallace), and the late record there is December 4, 1991 (Doug Laye).

Hawk Mountain Counts for the Osprey									
1934	17	1949	209	1961	287	1973	346	1985	405
1935	167	1950	309	1962	295	1974	183	1986	798
1936	200	1951	253	1963	186	1975	196	1987	669
1937	191	1952	337	1964	324	1976	314	1988	609
1938	129	1953	328	1965	452	1977	340	1989	758
1939	174	1954	320	1966	388	1978	380	1990	872
1940	91	1955	354	1967	380	1979	443	1991	606
1941	201	1956	284	1968	209	1980	364	1992	531
1942	213	1957	323	1969	338	1981	538	1993	700
1946	188	1958	324	1970	348	1982	433	1994	474
1947	215	1959	312	1971	264	1983	454	1995	468
1948	174	1960	263	1972	272	1984	579	1996	568

Note: These statistics reflect counts from the North Lookout only.

Dean Kendall sighted an extremely late Osprey near Yellow House in Oley Township December 18, 1994, for the only Reading Christmas Bird Count record.

Hawk Mountain records do not show a sharp decline from the 1950s to the 1970s in numbers of Ospreys because many of the migrants that pass there come from the interior lakes in Canada, where DDT was not widely used (Peterson, 1966:10). Coastal populations, however, were nearly wiped out by the pesticide. Hawk Mountain records have shown an increase since the 1970s.

The single-day high count at Hawk Mountain is 175 on September 23, 1989 (Phil Campbell, Patti Little). The season high count is 872 during the fall of 1990. The 10-year average from 1987 to 1996 is 648.

During the fall of 1942, Maurice Broun and Ben Goodwin recorded the flight speed of 16 migrating Ospreys. The birds averaged 41.5 miles per hour with a range between 20 and 80 miles per hour and a median of 38. The Osprey sailing along the ridge at 80 miles per hour was evidently making use of a very strong thermal, so that the bird was in reality in steep diving flight without losing altitude (Broun and Goodwin, 1943: 488, 492).

On September 28, 1981, Robert and Anne MacClay saw six Ospreys carrying fish while migrating over the Route 183 hawk watch.

The common Pennsylvania German name for the Osprey is "Fischwoi" (Rupp, 1946:94).

Three specimens are in the Reading Public Museum collection. Mengel took an Osprey June 9, 1886, in Albany Township, and he took a male at the Schuylkill River near Reading on October 16, 1890. A female was collected at Eckville October 9, 1932.

SWALLOW-TAILED KITE *Elanoides forficatus*
Accidental

On May 2, 1995, Glenn Straub from Brecknock Township, Lancaster County, near the Berks County line, contacted members of the Lancaster Bird Club to tell them that he had spotted two Swallow-tailed Kites gliding over trees on his farm. Chris Pederson from the Lancaster club confirmed the identification.

The kites drifted northeast during the next several days until the best views of them were from Chelsea Drive in Brecknock Township, Berks County. On May 27, a third Swallow-tailed Kite appeared over Chelsea Drive.

Harold and Joan Silagy observed the three Swallow-tailed Kites perched on a dead snag preening early in the morning. They watched as the kites grabbed caterpillar nests out of the tree tops, fed, and dropped the branches as they soared. One of the kites landed on a crow's nest, grabbed a nestling, took wing, and plucked and ate it in flight.

All previous sightings of kites in Pennsylvania have been of single birds. Not only were the numbers unusual, but the length of stay was also exceptional (Haas, 1995:87).

The last confirmed sighting of a Swallow-tailed Kite in the area was June 10, 1995 (Harold and Joan Silagy).

MISSISSIPPI KITE *Ictinia mississippiensis*
Accidental

On May 27, 1995, two Mississippi Kites soaring with the three Swallow-tailed Kites over Chelsea Drive in Brecknock Township, Berks County, were seen by many observers. One bird was an adult and the other an immature. Like the Swallow-tailed Kite's records, this occurrence was unprecedented in Pennsylvania in terms of numbers and length of stay. The last confirmed sighting was June 6, 1995 (Haas, 1995:87).

BALD EAGLE *Haliaeetus leucocephalus*
Uncommon migrant and winter visitor

During this century, the Bald Eagle neared extinction in the continental United States following World War II due to the widespread use of persistent organochloride pesticides such as DDT that affected the bird's reproductive system. In 1972, with the passage of the federal Endangered Species Act, the Bald Eagle was placed on the Endangered Species List. As a result of a ban on the widespread use of DDT in 1972 and in conjunction with a vigorous recovery effort, the species' population recovered. The federal government downlisted the bird in 1995 to a threatened status.

Prior to its decline, Earl Poole regarded the Bald Eagle as a fairly common visitor through-out the year at Lake Ontelaunee and in fall along the Kittatinny Ridge with records for every month

119

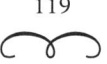

of the year. During the winter of 1938-1939, Poole found at least five immature birds wintering at Lake Ontelaunee.

The Bald Eagle has recovered sufficiently that it has again been recorded in Berks County during each month of the year. Single birds may occur anywhere south of the Kittatinny Ridge outside the fall migration, but most records are from Lake Ontelaunee, Glen Morgan Lake, and Blue Marsh Lake. The majority of sightings occurs from January to April and during August and September.

The Bald Eagle's status in Berks must be looked at in context of the pre-DDT and post-DDT years. The migration records at Hawk Mountain illustrate the decline and recovery.

The peak one-day count of Bald Eagles at the North Lookout in the first half century is 45 adults and three immatures September 4, 1950 (Maurice Broun). The season count peaked during the fall of 1950 with 116 birds - 23 immatures and 93 adults.

Maurice Broun commented on the steady decline in the number of young Bald Eagles that passed each year during the late 1940s: "Immature birds have averaged fifty-nine per cent of the Bald Eagles that were counted from 1934 to 1939. In recent years, however, there has been a sharp decline of immatures to thirty-seven per cent" (Broun, 1949a:165).

The drop in the number of immature Bald Eagles almost certainly reflected nesting failures due to eggshell thinning, a consequence of high levels of persistent pesticides accumulated in the female. The weight of the brooding adult crushed the weakened eggs.

Poole writes in 1964: "...other recent reports of unsuccessful nestings in many parts of its range would seem to indicate that the Bald Eagle, our national bird, is in imminent danger of following the Whooping Crane and the California Condor on the road to possible extinction."

The ratio of immatures to adults continued to decline at Hawk Mountain until it reached its lowest point during the early 1970s. Only one immature Bald Eagle was seen during the fall of 1969 compared to 29 adults. In both 1971 and 1972, only two immatures were recorded each year. The lowest total numbers were recorded in 1974 when three immatures and 10 adults were seen.

After the widespread use of DDT was banned in the United States in 1972 and after intensive reintroduction programs, the number of Bald Eagles slowly increased until a noticeable recovery occurred in the early 1980s. During the fall of 1982, immature Bald Eagles outnumbered adults at Hawk Mountain for the first time since 1936.

New York State pioneered reintroduction efforts during the 1980s. On December 11, 1988, Matt Spence found an immature Bald Eagle wing-tagged with the number 32 perched near the dam breast at Lake Ontelaunee. According to Peter E. Nye of the New York State Department of Environmental Conservation (DEC), this eagle was one of 16 relocated during 1988 by the department as part of its efforts to restore the Bald Eagle in New York State. During the previous 13 years a total of 198 translocated Bald Eagles had been released. Bald Eagle number 32 was originally taken as a nestling from southeast Alaska in July 1988 and brought to the DEC hacking site on the Alcove Reservoir near Albany, New York. The last contact with the bird at the hack site was October 31. On November 8, eagle number 32 was sighted on the Erie Canal near Cohoes, New York. The bird remained on the canal for one week before moving on. The next contact with the eagle was Spence's at Lake Ontelaunee. After that sighting, number 32 was not seen again; however, the tag was not permanently affixed to the wing and could have fallen off.

Robert and Ruth Cook saw a wing-tagged immature Bald Eagle at Joanna September 2 and 3, 1987. It had been released during the second week of August at Albany, New York.

Despite protection efforts during this time, the Bald Eagle was still targeted by lawless gunners. On December 7, 1982, an immature Bald Eagle was found shot near Rehrersburg and was taken to the Willow Creek Animal Hospital by Phil Haas of the Hawk Mountain Sanctuary staff. Dr. William P. Czajkowski X-rayed the bird and found a gunshot wound to one wing, which was amputated on

December 14. Seth Benz transported the eagle to Hawk Mountain on December 23. It was transferred on December 31 from Hawk Mountain to the University of Maine in Orono where it had been banded and tagged as a wild nestling. No arrest was made.

The post-DDT season high count at Hawk Mountain occurred during the fall of 1995 when 136 Bald Eagles, 80 immatures and 56 adults, passed the North Lookout. The single-day peaks are 11 on September 18, 1996 (Laurie Goodrich, Bill Wallace), and nine the next day, September 19 (L.G., Beth Garland). The early date for an adult Bald Eagle is July 19 (1995 - Ron Homa), and the late date is January 13 (1997 - Steve Thorpe). For an immature, the early date is August 6 (1948 - Tommy Hanson), and the late date is January 8 (1997 - S.T.). The 10-year seasonal average from 1987 to 1996 is 77.

The Bald Eagle has appeared on the Reading Christmas Bird Count nine of 86 years, once in the last 10, with a maximum of three on December 26, 1938, and December 24, 1939. Four records on the Hamburg Christmas Bird Count are of single birds on December 29, 1984; December 27, 1987; December 26, 1993; and December 31, 1995. A high of three was found on the Bernville count January 2, 1995.

Hawk Mountain Counts for the Bald Eagle

	T	U	I	A		T	U	I	A		T	U	I	A
1934	23	2	17	4	1961	40	0	9	31	1985	37	1	15	21
1935	65	6	14	45	1962	35	0	9	26	1986	56	0	28	28
1936	73	0	43	30	1963	21	0	7	14	1987	65	2	37	26
1937	31	0	15	16	1964	27	0	6	21	1988	57	2	33	22
1938	37	0	15	22	1965	36	1	8	27	1989	62	0	33	29
1939	64	1	28	35	1966	25	0	6	19	1990	76	4	46	26
1940	38	0	8	30	1967	30	0	6	24	1991	70	0	30	40
1941	50	2	12	36	1968	41	0	10	31	1992	91	1	52	38
1942	70	3	33	34	1969	30	0	1	29	1993	81	4	35	42
1946	39	0	9	30	1970	25	0	5	20	1994	82	1	34	47
1947	89	1	22	66	1971	14	0	2	12	1995	136	0	80	56
1948	79	2	16	61	1972	14	1	2	11	1996	120	1	55	64
	T	U	I	A		T	U	I	A					
1949	84	0	24	60	1973	17	1	7	9					
1950	116	0	23	93	1974	13	0	3	10					
1951	87	0	17	70	1975	19	0	4	15					
1952	91	0	14	77	1976	18	1	4	13					
1953	59	0	17	42	1977	19	0	7	12					
1954	65	4	11	50	1978	27	0	6	21					
1955	88	2	24	62	1979	16	0	8	8					
1956	53	1	13	39	1980	22	0	11	11					
1957	39	0	3	36	1981	28	1	13	14					
1958	41	0	7	34	1982	33	0	21	12					
1959	45	1	13	32	1983	24	0	10	14					
1960	23	0	1	22	1984	41	1	21	19					

Note: These statistics reflect counts from the North Lookout only.

U - Undetermined Age

I - Immature

A - Adult

T - Total

Seth Benz reported a pair of eagles playing tag over the North Lookout on November 14, 1981:

> ...precisely at 2:30, two huge, flat silhouettes appeared beyond Number Five. They were visible to the naked eye, and at that distance they could only be eagles. Bringing binoculars into focus confirmed it- two eagles, wingtip to wingtip! Furthermore, it was soon apparent that they differed. Making their way toward the handful of awestruck observers on North was an immature Golden Eagle, matching wingbeats stroke for stroke with an immature Bald. All at once they rolled and clasped talons, each momentarily suspended upside down high above the forest canopy. Then each loosed one talon but still clutched tightly with the other, and they flailed at each other with powerful wings. They separated. The Golden lifted up above the Bald, dipped slightly and with long primaries gently tapped the Bald Eagle between the shoulders. As quickly the Bald, in a half roll, made contact with the Golden's underside. Again they separated. The Golden circled, moving southwest toward Hemlock Heights. The Bald went low to the north side. At 3:10, 40 minutes after the initial spotting, both birds were out of view (Benz, 1982a: 20).

On September 28, 1985, an immature Bald Eagle snatched a Sharp-shinned Hawk that had been harassing it and carried the bird past the North Lookout at Hawk Mountain before dropping it (J. George, Cathy Viverette).

Broun and Ben Goodwin measured the flight speed of two migrating Bald Eagles during the fall of 1942 at 36 and 44 miles per hour (Broun and Goodwin, 1943:492).

Ken and Karin Lebo watched two Bald Eagles at Glen Morgan Lake separate a Ring-billed Gull from a flock of several hundred and chase it for approximately five minutes on December 3, 1994. When the gull went down to the water and flew back up, one of the eagles grabbed it in flight. Both eagles flew back to a snag and ate the bird. Ken Lebo also reported Bald Eagle predation on American Coots at Glen Morgan Lake. He first saw a dead coot draped on the eagle's favorite snag on December 23, 1995. He later saw the eagle eat a coot, and once watched the eagle swoop down to stand on the ice at the water's edge as the mob of coots huddled at the far end of the open water, then only about 25 feet across.

Lebo has found the Bald Eagle at Glen Morgan Lake throughout the year. Spring and summer records include occurrences from April 1 through September 9, 1995, and from May 3 to June 29, 1996.

John F. Hofmann listed the Bald Eagle in 1890. An immature shot near Adamstown in 1921 and an immature female shot near Mohnton April 22, 1940, are in the Reading Public Museum collection.

The southern *H. l. leucocephalus* and the northern *H. l. alascanus* races pass through Berks on migration. The former moves north following its breeding season in Florida during the winter, spending the summer months farther north of the county.

Observations at Hawk Mountain suggest that the earlier southbound migrants in late August and September appear to be the much smaller southern race and that the November birds are the larger northern race (*cf* Broley, 1947:3-20).

The common Pennsylvania German name for both the Bald and the Golden eagles is "der Aadler." (Rupp, 1946:91) William Rupp writes of a northern European folk-tale that appeared in at least one colonial primer: "It is the story of how the birds gathered to elect a king, how the eagle in his turn soared higher than any other bird, and how the little wren, perched on the eagle's back, at the last moment rose a bit higher than the eagle, thus winning the royal title for himself" (Rupp, 1946:93).

NORTHERN HARRIER *Circus cyaneus*
Common migrant

The Northern Harrier is a common migrant from mid-March to mid-May and from late August through November, less common to rare in winter, and uncommon as a nonbreeding summer resident in Berks County. Numbers fluctuate, and the Harrier can be locally common in winter in response to high meadow vole populations.

Earl Poole had records of the Northern Harrier for every month of the year. In 1932, 1934, and 1950, he saw the bird frequently during the nesting season around Lake Ontelaunee, although there are no recent June, July, or August records there. From 1932 until the mid-1960s, it was seen at intervals through nearly every winter in the Lake Ontelaunee area. Because of the maturing of the

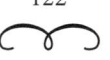

conifer growth on the watershed from 1965 to the present, Matt Spence has only six winter records from there. The Northern Harrier is now more frequently seen during the winter at Blue Marsh.

There are no confirmed nesting records for the Northern Harrier this century, although Jim Olmes saw a female with three young during August 1983 in Windsor Township. The birds remained until December. Earl Poole knew of no definite nestings, but Walter H. Leibelsperger had a nest described to him by a farmer in the Pine Swamp in Albany Township in 1913, and Herbert Diehl found a pair present through the summer of 1939 in a boggy section of the State Game Lands 110 on top of the Blue Mountain above Shartlesville. He was under the impression that they were breeding.

Levi Mengel collected three sets of eggs now in the Reading Public Museum collection: a set of four eggs among bushes along the Tulpehocken Creek May 12, 1886; a set of three eggs from a nest made of hay and dried grass on the ground along the Antietam Creek May 13, 1888; and a set of three eggs from a nest in some brush at Moselem May 17, 1889.

Recent summer records of nonbreeding birds include one female near Lenhartsville June 24, 1988, its fifth summer there (Kerry Grim); one female near Justa Road near Blue Marsh from May 21 to June 11, 1989 (Matt Spence); one male in Tilden Township June 17, 1989 (K.G.); and one female near Albany June 27, 1996 (Rudy Keller).

At Hawk Mountain, Maurice Broun observed that the Northern Harrier is prone to disregard the ridge in its migration: "Many drift in from the north, cross the ridge at right angles to the regular line of flight, then continue south over the broad hump of the mountain" (Broun, 1949a:165).

Broun notes that immatures make up nearly all of the August and September migrants. Both male and female as well as immatures come in varying numbers during October, while late in the migration the males outnumber the others.

During the fall of 1942, Broun and Ben Goodwin measured the flight speed of four Northern Harriers in migration. Their speeds ranged from 21 to 38 miles per hour with an average of 28.7 (Broun and Goodwin, 1943:492).

The early migration date at Hawk Mountain is August 1 (1996 - Bill Wallace), and the late date is December 29 (1994 - Steve Thorpe). Alex Nagy recorded a single-day peak of 36 on September 30, 1953. The season high is 475 in 1980. The 10-year average from 1987 to 1996 is 296. During the spring migration count, Jim Olmes observed a high of 10 on April 5, 1985.

The Northern Harrier has been recorded on the Reading Christmas Bird Count 47 of 86 years, seven of the last 10, with a maximum of eight on December 16, 1990. The peak for the Hamburg Christmas Bird Count is 50 on December 29, 1985. The high for the Bernville count is 21 on January 1, 1986. During the winter of 1985-1986, the rodent populations were high, resulting in larger numbers of wintering Harriers.

Hawk Mountain Counts for the Northern Harrier									
1934	89	1949	209	1961	261	1973	177	1985	368
1935	126	1950	213	1962	182	1974	163	1986	304
1936	141	1951	214	1963	175	1975	267	1987	356
1937	152	1952	312	1964	185	1976	248	1988	306
1938	184	1953	252	1965	182	1977	288	1989	401
1939	270	1954	158	1966	160	1978	183	1990	318
1940	161	1955	224	1967	147	1979	235	1991	197
1941	251	1956	136	1968	240	1980	475	1992	162
1942	107	1957	192	1969	221	1981	280	1993	355
1946	169	1958	201	1970	249	1982	293	1994	296
1947	176	1959	252	1971	136	1983	318	1995	272
1948	185	1960	229	1972	154	1984	317	1996	131

Note: These statistics reflect counts from the North Lookout only.

Five specimens are in the Reading Public Museum collection. Levi Mengel collected three: a male in Albany Township June 4, 1886; one near Reading September 9, 1887; and a male at Bowers April 18, 1890. A male was shot near Geigertown in Robeson Township July 27, 1933, and a female was shot near West Lawn November 10, 1940.

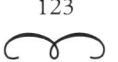

The Pennsylvania German name for the Northern Harrier is "der schloossweiss Woi," or "Schloosswoi," meaning a hawk showing white "like hail," describing the rump patch. Thomas Brendle's informants in Lehigh County told him, "This hawk does not eat pigeons or chickens. It was eaten by older people, as hawks were used for food in the long past" (Rupp, 1946:93).

SHARP-SHINNED HAWK *Accipiter striatus*

Very common to abundant migrant

A fairly common migrant in late March and April and a very common to abundant migrant in September and October, the Sharp-shinned Hawk is uncommon to rare in winter, although it is becoming more commonly seen at that season because of increased bird feeding. Sharp-shins are opportunistic and will prey on birds coming to feeders, both in the city and in the county. Wintering birds may remain until the end of March or early April.

A rare nester along the Kittatinny Ridge in northern Berks County, the Sharp-shinned Hawk breeds in extensive, unbroken woodland, especially those containing conifers, which it prefers as nesting sites. It may also breed in eastern Berks along the Oley hills and in southern Berks near the Hopewell region.

Walter Leibelsperger and Levi Mengel found 18 nests in Berks. These contained full sets of eggs between May 15 (1886, 1924) and June 7 (1910). The nests were placed in tall pines and oaks. The clutch sizes in the collected sets are three or four eggs. From 1929 until the mid-1960s, Earl Poole knew of only two occupied nests. Kerry Grim found recently fledged young during the summers between 1982 and 1994 at Kaercher Creek Park in Windsor Township, State Game Lands 106 and 110, and the Hamburg reservoir. Harold and Joan Silagy, Rudy Keller, and Grim found four fledglings at State Game Lands 110 in late July 1996. A nest Grim found in Kaercher Creek Park in 1982 was taken over by Great Horned Owls the next year.

The best places in Berks to observe the Sharp-shinned Hawk is at Hawk Mountain and at the Route 183 hawk watch, where it is one of the commoner species during the fall migration. From the second week in September, and often earlier, these small accipiters zoom along the ridge on their way to their wintering grounds; at first a few scattered individuals, and then, on good flight days, a steady stream. By October they are in full retreat, and with favorable winds, as many as 2,475 Sharp-shinned Hawks have been counted in a single day. After October there is a gradual slackening in the flight, but late-comers continue to drift by until well past the middle of November.

In 1930, Poole writes: "One of the most remarkable local ornithological phenomena is the migration of Sharp-shinned and other hawks along the Blue Ridge, forming the northwestern county line. During September and October Sharp-shins literally swarm along the ridge on certain days, and are shot by the thousands every fall in Albany Township."

On October 17, 1931, one gunner reported to Poole: "A big flight today, one man shot 53."

Since 1970, the Sharp-shinned Hawk has been a protected species.

The early fall migration date at Hawk Mountain for the Sharp-shinned Hawk is July 26 (1996 - Bill Wallace) and the late date is December 29 (1994 - Steve Thorpe). The single-day high is 2,475 on October 8, 1979 (Seth Benz). The season high count occurred in 1977 with a total of 10,612. The 10-year average from 1987 to 1996 is 6,758.

Maurice Broun writes "nearly all of the first-comers are birds of the year," and "early October brings a gradual transition from immature to adult birds, and after mid-October immatures are seen infrequently" (Broun, 1949a:157).

Broun and Ben Goodwin measured the flight speed of 37 migrating Sharp-shinned Hawks during the fall of 1942. The speeds ranged from 16 to 60 miles per hour with an average of 30.0 and a median of 26. A Sharpshin, flapping continuously in no wind, was timed at 34 miles per hour (Broun and Goodwin, 1943:488, 492).

Trends of the fall counts at Hawk Mountain show that numbers of Sharp-shinned Hawks were low during the 1960s but rebounded when DDT was banned in Canada in 1966. Counts from 1990 through 1996 have shown a decline of 20 to 30 percent.

The spring migration occurs in March and April. The spring hawk watch high count at Hawk Mountain is 58 on April 18, 1984 (Jim Olmes).

George M. Sutton examined 113 Sharp-shinned Hawks that were shot from October 17 to 22, 1927, at what is now Hawk Mountain. There were 20 females and 93 males. Fifty-one of the Sharpshin stomachs were empty. In the other 62 stomachs were found the remains of 12 Song Sparrows, nine Yellow-rumped Warblers, six Northern Juncos, five Golden-crowned Kinglets, five Hermit Thrushes, three Tree Sparrows, three Fox Sparrows, three Blackpoll Warblers, three Robins, two Downy Woodpeckers, two Eastern Towhees, two Winter Wrens, two Brown Creepers, two Ruby-crowned Kinglets, one Horned Lark, one Rusty Blackbird, one American Goldfinch, one Henslow's Sparrow, one White-throated Sparrow, one Cape May Warbler, one Chickadee, and one Swainson's Thrush. Sutton remarked that the most interesting of these prey species was the Henslow's Sparrow, not only because it is rare in Pennsylvania, but because it is a very retiring species of the open fields which the Sharpshin would not be expected to normally catch (Sutton, 1928b:86-87).

Hawk Mountain Counts for the Sharp-shinned Hawk									
1934	1703	1949	2963	1961	1723	1973	3347	1985	5766
1935	4168	1950	3674	1962	2181	1974	4477	1986	9239
1936	4406	1951	3008	1963	1518	1975	5354	1987	6776
1937	4791	1952	3566	1964	1259	1976	5376	1988	6714
1938	3105	1953	2791	1965	3103	1977	10612	1989	9832
1939	8620	1954	3183	1966	2883	1978	6826	1990	8127
1940	2406	1955	4709	1967	2330	1979	10306	1991	5678
1941	3908	1956	2048	1968	2253	1980	8319	1992	4629
1942	3200	1957	2662	1969	2670	1981	9464	1993	5449
1946	2382	1958	1752	1970	1906	1982	4541	1994	4929
1947	1726	1959	2825	1971	2135	1983	6517	1995	6217
1948	1650	1960	2233	1972	2233	1984	3796	1996	4470

Note: These statistics reflect counts from the North Lookout only.

From 1931 to 1937, Samuel Wishnieski of the Reading Public Museum examined the stomach contents of Sharp-shinned Hawks collected throughout Berks. Most were birds picked up dead near the shooting stands at Eckville, now Hawk Mountain, during October 1931 and 1932. Of 35 stomachs examined, 12 were empty and 23 contained songbirds. He found no poultry or mammal in any stomach. Prey included Goldfinch, Brown Creeper, Ruby-crowned Kinglet, Junco, House Sparrow, Starling, and an unidentified warbler species.

There are 17 specimens in the Reading Public Museum collection. Eight males and four females were shot at Eckville or Albany Township in the fall between September 27 (1931) and October 27 (1929). Levi Mengel collected a female at Pricetown April 12, 1886, and a male at Boyertown September 3, 1892. The others are a female shot at Shalter Dam in Cumru Township October 12, 1930; a female shot in Tilden Township November 12, 1932; and a female shot at Hopewell January 22, 1937. The stomach of the Hopewell bird contained one Starling.

The Pennsylvania German name for the Sharp-shinned Hawk and all the accipiter species is "Schdoosswoi" or "Schtoosswoi." Another name from Berks for the Sharp-shinned Hawk is "Dauwehabbich" (Rupp, 1946:87-88).

The Sharp-shinned Hawk has appeared on the Reading Christmas Bird Count 48 of 86 years, 10 of the last 10, with a maximum of 13 on December 18, 1994. Rarely seen on the Hamburg Christmas Bird Count before 1973, the Sharpshin peak for that count is 19 on December 29, 1985. The high for the Bernville count is 12 on January 3, 1988.

COOPER'S HAWK *Accipiter cooperii*

Uncommon resident; common migrant

A common migrant in fall along the Kittatinny Ridge, the Cooper's Hawk throughout the rest of Berks County is a regular but uncommon migrant, a local breeder, and uncommon resident. Seen in spring from late March to mid-May, the Cooper's Hawk is most frequent in fall from late September through October.

Not a deep woods bird, the Cooper's Hawk has nested within the city limits of Reading as well as in small wood lots and near openings of contiguous forests throughout the county. The Cooper's Hawk is more tolerant of forest fragmentation than is the Sharp-shinned Hawk. Confirmed nestings have occurred along the Kittatinny Ridge, the woodlands of eastern Berks, on the Topton Mountain, in Bern Township, at Blue Marsh, and in the city of Reading.

Of 34 sets of Cooper's Hawk eggs taken in Berks County between 1887 and 1918, the earliest was collected on April 26 (1908) and the latest on May 30 (1896, 1898). Unlike the nests of the Sharp-shinned Hawk which are generally in coniferous trees, the majority of Cooper's Hawks nests have been in deciduous trees, particularly oaks, sassafras, buttonwood, and formerly, chestnut trees. Levi Mengel also found nests in tall pines. Nests were placed in the trees 35 feet or higher.

On retrieving a set of four eggs from a Cooper's Hawk nest near Bernville on April 30, 1887, Mengel remarked: "In obtaining this nest of eggs, I fell from the tree on stepping on a dead branch. It took me two hours in the second attempt to reach the nest. One of my most exhaustive climbs."

Hawk Mountain Counts for the Cooper's Hawk									
1934	262	1949	174	1961	104	1973	81	1985	291
1935	526	1950	271	1962	77	1974	150	1986	569
1936	461	1951	235	1963	74	1975	126	1987	590
1937	489	1952	308	1964	61	1976	109	1988	459
1938	204	1953	155	1965	100	1977	231	1989	786
1939	587	1954	190	1966	82	1978	153	1990	642
1940	166	1955	281	1967	76	1979	336	1991	578
1941	416	1956	122	1968	145	1980	374	1992	663
1942	292	1957	200	1969	111	1981	756	1993	562
1946	214	1958	180	1970	105	1982	302	1994	573
1947	128	1959	180	1971	69	1983	352	1995	643
1948	203	1960	123	1972	114	1984	171	1996	537

Note: These statistics reflect counts from the North Lookout only.

On June 29, 1924, Earl Poole climbed to a Cooper's Hawk nest in a white pine near Eckville on the Blue Mountain and found four fledglings in the nest. These promptly fluttered out of the nest as his head appeared above the rim. He believed they were probably about ready to leave at the time.

Poole, writing in 1964, states that after the American Kestrel, the Cooper's was Berks County's commonest breeding hawk. This is no longer true today, as the Red-tailed Hawk and the American Kestrel have become the most common breeding hawks in Berks.

During the fall migration along the Kittatinny Ridge, the ratio earlier this century was about one Cooper's to 12 Sharp-shinned by actual count. However, this may be due in part to the more northern range of the Sharpshin. More recently, the ratio has been one to 10.

At Hawk Mountain, the early date for the migrant Cooper's Hawk is August 6 (1983 - Mark Blauer) and the late date is December 20 (1992 - Steve Thorpe). The single-day peak is 204 on October 8, 1981 (Jim Brett). The season high count is 786 in 1989. The 10-year average from 1987 to 1996 is 606.

During the fall of 1942, Maurice Broun and Ben Goodwin recorded the flight speeds of 12 migrating Cooper's Hawks, ranging from 21 to 55 miles per hour with an average of 29.3 and a median of 26 (Broun and Goodwin, 1943:492).

The high count for the spring migration at Hawk Mountain is five on April 27, 1984 (Jim Olmes).

The Cooper's Hawk has appeared on the Reading Christmas Bird Count 56 of 86 years, nine of the last 10, with a maximum of eight on December 26, 1938. The peak for the Hamburg Christmas Bird Count is 10 on December 27, 1992. The high for the Bernville count is nine on January 3, 1993.

George M. Sutton examined 11 Cooper's Hawks that were shot from October 17 to 22, 1927, at what is now Hawk Mountain. All 11 were adult birds, seven males and four females. Four of the stomachs were empty. Of the others, one contained the hind quarters of a gray squirrel, two held Song Sparrows, two contained American Robins, one held the head and breast of a Bobwhite, and one held a Fox Sparrow. Both the gray squirrel and the Bobwhite had been captured by female Sharpshins (Sutton, 1928b:90).

There are 13 specimens taken from throughout the county in the Reading Public Museum collection. Levi Mengel took a male and a female Cooper's Hawk at Monocacy Hill April 4, 1888. He collected a female at Mount Penn April 7, 1891. Sam Wishnieski collected two downy young from a nest near Morgantown June 8, 1932.

The Pennsylvania German name for the Cooper's Hawk is "der gross Schdoosswoi " to distinguish it from the smaller Sharp-shinned Hawk. Also, general names heard in Berks for any hawk are "Habbich," "Habbicht," "Haabicht," "Hawicht," "Haawich," and "Hoppich" (Rupp, 1946:89).

NORTHERN GOSHAWK *Accipiter gentilis*

Rare and irregular

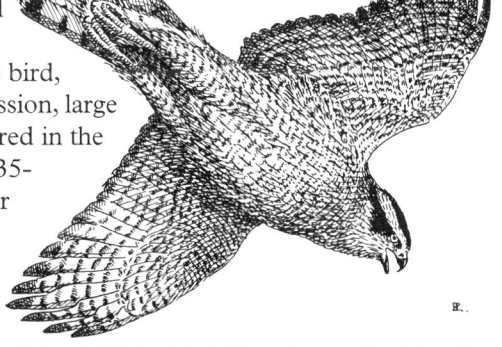

Over most of Berks County, the Northern Goshawk is a rare and irregular winter visitor. Higher numbers occur along the Kittatinny Ridge during the fall migration.

Normally the Goshawk is considered quite a rare bird, but periodically, and often for two or three years in succession, large numbers invade Pennsylvania. Such invasions have occurred in the fall and winter of 1926-1927, 1927-1928, 1934-1935, 1935-1936, 1945-1946, 1954-1955, and 1972-1973, with minor flights in 1936 and 1937.

Fall flights of over 100 Goshawks have occurred at Hawk Mountain in 1934, 1935, 1936, 1965, 1968, 1969, 1972, 1973, 1975, 1981, 1982, 1983, 1986, and 1993. The highest season totals were compiled during the fall of 1972 with 347 and the fall of 1973 with 307.

During other years comparatively few birds are seen. The lowest season total at Hawk Mountain is three in 1953. From 1934 to 1991, the mean seasonal count at Hawk Mountain has been 70. The 10-year average from 1987 to 1996 is 68.

At Hawk Mountain the earliest migration date is August 16 (1988 - Bruce Williams) and the late date is December 26 (1992 - Steve Thorpe). In good flight years as many as 64 and 51 Goshawks have passed Hawk Mountain on single days on November 10, 1973 (Jim Brett), and on November 24, 1935 (Maurice Broun).

During the fall of 1942, Maurice Broun and Ben Goodwin measured the flight speed of a migrating Goshawk at 38 miles per hour (Broun and Goodwin, 1943:492).

During the winter of 1968-1969, a Goshawk wintered at Hawk Mountain (Alex Nagy, Richard Sharadin).

The Northern Goshawk has appeared on the Reading Christmas Bird Count 12 of 86 years, two of the last 10, with a maximum of three on December 27, 1970. The peak for the Hamburg Christmas Bird Count is three on January 1, 1970, and December 31, 1977. A single Goshawk appeared on the Bernville count January 5, 1986.

D. Frank Keller rated the Northern Goshawk as a rare winter visitor (Warren, 1890:125).

During the spring hawk watch at Hawk Mountain, single Goshawks were recorded March 21, 1985 (Jim Olmes), and April 14, 1987 (Laurie Goodrich).

On April 25, 1996, Matt Spence observed an adult Goshawk bathing in Indian Run below the Birdsboro reservoir. It flew up into a tree about 30 feet from him, and he had a great view of the bird as it shook off the water. Spence noted that the prominent white eye stripe was easily seen. The latest recent spring date is April 27 (1994 - Cathy Viverette in Eckville).

However, Levi Mengel took a female Northern Goshawk in Albany Township June 17, 1886. This specimen is in the Reading Public Museum collection.

There is one nesting record. During the spring of 1980 Jim Brett and Seth Benz discovered a nest in a yellow birch tree on the east side of Hawk Mountain. The female was extremely aggressive, raking the

Hawk Mountain Counts for the Northern Goshawk									
1934	116	1949	7	1961	83	1973	307	1985	50
1935	241	1950	6	1962	34	1974	61	1986	106
1936	177	1951	21	1963	26	1975	136	1987	57
1937	48	1952	7	1964	17	1976	62	1988	50
1938	9	1953	3	1965	102	1977	85	1989	27
1939	26	1954	90	1966	22	1978	58	1990	88
1940	11	1955	40	1967	25	1979	68	1991	54
1941	21	1956	7	1968	182	1980	83	1992	43
1942	9	1957	82	1969	124	1981	138	1993	110
1946	32	1958	18	1970	75	1982	140	1994	34
1947	5	1959	25	1971	33	1983	129	1995	120
1948	14	1960	11	1972	347	1984	59	1996	42

Note: These statistics reflect counts from the North Lookout only.

scalps of both Brett and Benz on different occasions that summer. She and her mate raised two young, but the following year Great Horned Owls used the nest (Weidensaul, 1992a:18).

Twenty adult Goshawks, four males and 16 females, were shot between October 17 and 22, 1927, at what is now Hawk Mountain and were examined by George M. Sutton. Sixteen of the birds were shot on October 22. Ten of the stomachs were empty. Four of these stomachs were of birds shot early in the morning, apparently before they had had opportunity to capture food. Two stomachs held Ruffed Grouse, one held a gray squirrel, one contained a red squirrel, two held chipmunks, and one contained an adult White Leghorn Chicken (Sutton, 1928b:92).

There are nine specimens, four males and five females, in the Reading Public Museum collection. All - except the June bird taken by Mengel - were shot in the fall between October 27 (1936) and November 28 (1934) in Dauberville, Schubert's Gap, Spies Church, Exeter Township, Boyertown, and Oley.

RED-SHOULDERED HAWK *Buteo lineatus*

Uncommon migrant and winter visitor

Chiefly a bird of wooded river bottoms and swampy woodland areas, the Red-shouldered Hawk is less conspicuous than the Red-tailed Hawk, and in its woodland haunts it is more often heard than seen.

An uncommon winter visitor, the Red-shouldered Hawk usually disappears about the third week in April, but there are enough scattered records through late May, June, and August to leave a strong suspicion that it may still nest in Berks County.

The only recent breeding record is of an adult with an immature giving food begging calls from early August through September 1988 near Huff's Church. At least three birds were present during this time (Rudy Keller).

Earl Poole saw pairs or single birds during the breeding season in likely places throughout Berks during 1934, 1938, 1940, 1947, 1949, and 1962 and believed they were nesting nearby, although no nest has been found during this century.

Levi Mengel collected a set of four eggs in Albany Township May 3, 1886, from a nest of great size in the fork of an oak 40 feet from the ground. S.S. Gruber collected a set from a nest in a hemlock near Evansville May 29, 1897.

At Lake Ontelaunee, the Redshoulder is present from September 25 (1983 - Matt Spence) to April 16 (1978 - M.S.).

As a migrant the Red-shouldered Hawk is uncommon in most areas, possibly more frequently seen in spring away from the Kittatinny Ridge than in fall. Like the other Buteos, it "rides" the ridges during the fall migration. The fall flight commences in October, occasionally late in September, and continues well into November. The earliest date for a migrant Red-shouldered Hawk there is August 18 (1984 - Mark Blauer) and the latest is December 26 (1996 - Steve Thorpe).

The single-day high count is 148 on October 19, 1958 (Maurice Broun, Fred Mears). Maurice Broun observed a flight of 110 Red-shoulders on October 24, 1956. The season high is 468 in 1958. The 10-year average from 1987 to 1996 is 280.

Broun and Ben Goodwin measured the flight speeds of seven migrating Red-shouldered Hawks during the fall of 1942. They ranged from 18 to 34 miles per hour with an average of 28.3 and a median of 31 (Broun and Goodwin, 1943:492).

Hawk Mountain Counts for the Red-shouldered Hawk									
1934	–	1949	284	1961	311	1973	116	1985	203
1935	–	1950	346	1962	271	1974	182	1986	175
1936	159	1951	379	1963	198	1975	205	1987	351
1937	160	1952	348	1964	217	1976	167	1988	365
1938	143	1953	179	1965	300	1977	266	1989	260
1939	308	1954	311	1966	197	1978	163	1990	328
1940	149	1955	425	1967	140	1979	234	1991	168
1941	197	1956	284	1968	273	1980	349	1992	243
1942	123	1957	220	1969	186	1981	250	1993	248
1946	236	1958	468	1970	130	1982	320	1994	260
1947	238	1959	341	1971	87	1983	451	1995	402
1948	262	1960	331	1972	123	1984	208	1996	310

Note: These statistics reflect counts from the North Lookout only.

The bulk of the spring movement takes place in March and early April. On March 10, 1986, Catherine Elwell found six Red-shouldered Hawks at State Game Lands 182 in Greenwich Township.

Rudy Keller writes of migrating Red-shouldered Hawks moving through Pike Township on February 7, 1970:

"I saw a Red-shouldered Hawk fly out of a tree and begin spiraling in the warming forenoon air. Noted all field marks except the red shoulders. When the bird was well up above the field still spiraling, a second bird sailed into view straight at the first one, until both banked and grabbed for each other's talons. They separated, gaining more altitiude, and repeated the game. Then a third bird soared in, but didn't join in the play. A bit later it sailed off out of sight. The first pair continued their raptorial game, finally disappearing into the sun."

Spring observations at Hawk Mountain have been meager, but on March 20, 1954, 25 flew past within two hours. More recently, Jim Olmes counted 18 on March 20, 1984.

The Red-shouldered Hawk has appeared on the Reading Christmas Bird Count 48 of 86 years, six of the last 10, with a maximum of five on December 22, 1957. Single birds have been found on the Bernville count January 5, 1986; January 1, 1990; January 1, 1992; and January 2, 1995. The peak for the Hamburg Christmas Bird Count is four on January 1, 1970.

There are seven specimens - three males, three females, and an unsexed bird - in the Reading Public Museum collection. Levi Mengel collected a female in Albany Township May 14, 1885; one along the Schuylkill River above Reading November 17, 1888; and a male near Reading March 6, 1892. The stomach of a female collected February 7, 1937, in "Berks County" contained two meadow mice. The other specimens are a male shot on Mount Penn March 6, 1933; a male shot near Shillington November 20, 1933; and a female shot near Eckville October 25, 1936.

BROAD-WINGED HAWK *Buteo platypterus*

Fairly common breeder; abundant fall migrant

In spring the Broad-winged Hawk usually arrives in numbers in Berks County with considerable regularity around mid-April, but during exceptional years a few individuals return several weeks earlier, and occasional single birds have been reported much earlier.

Extremely early dates are March 4 (1996 - Catherine Elwell) at Lake Ontelaunee, March 8 (1995 - Ken Lebo) at Glen Morgan Lake, and March 12 (1961 - Charles Schaich) near Moselem.

The earliest specimen that Earl Poole saw was taken by Charles Berck near Fleetwood on March 29, 1927. Late winter and early spring observations of the Broadwing must be regarded with caution because it and the Red-shouldered Hawk are easily confused.

When the migrant Broadwings arrive in spring they sometimes do so in loose bands of up to 15 or 20 in number that wheel and circle in intricate patterns but drift slowly northward somewhat like the fall bands that make the reverse journey. Maurice Broun reported a flight of 500 passing over Hawk Mountain on April 22, 1957. Jim Olmes counted 501 on April 27, 1984. Kerry Grim saw 380 over Hamburg April 19, 1995.

After its arrival the Broadwing evidently loses no time selecting a nesting place and proceeding with the business of laying its eggs. Levi Mengel collected a set of four eggs in Albany Township on April 30, 1886, and noted: "Nest in pine tree - 30 feet from ground - Large, bulky, well-lined and lousy." Walter Leibelsperger collected 11 sets of eggs around Fleetwood and Moselem between May 8 (1902) and May 30 (1886).

S.D. Green and Poole found an occupied nest at Monocacy Hill on May 26, 1917, and Edward Hill photographed one on Mount Penn, within the city limits of Reading, during June 1942.

Currently, the Broadwing nests regularly in larger woodlands with streams in eastern, southern, and northern Berks County. The Broadwing in Berks is a less common breeder now than in the early 1960s due to the breaking up of forests. This hawk is sensitive to forest fragmentation.

Donald Heintzelman and Alex Nagy recorded an unusual incident of apparent nest cannibalism involving Broad-winged Hawks. On July 20, 1958, they climbed to a hawk's nest located about 65 feet above the ground in a white pine tree along the base of the Kittatinny Ridge about three miles northeast of Hawk Mountain in Albany Township. They discovered two apparently healthy nestlings, each about three weeks old. On July 27, they revisited the nest and found one well-developed nestling standing beside its dead nest mate. The dead nestling was completely decapitated and appeared to have died recently, although the cause of death could not be determined. Heintzelman and Nagy concluded that the victim's head served as food for the surviving nestling (Heintzelman, 1966a:307).

The fall migration of the Broad-winged Hawk at Hawk Mountain and other points along the long ridges of Pennsylvania is one of the ornithological sensations of the year. The big flight usually occurs during the third week in September, and several thousand hawks are often seen on one day.

The fall migration at Hawk Mountain starts with a few stragglers during early August, the early date August 1 (1996 - Bill Wallace), and gathers momentum until the big flight develops as weather conditions are favorable after which it drops off gradually. The last Broadwings are usually gone by the middle of October, although Broun saw single birds as late as October 22, 1941; October 30, 1960; and November 1, 1946. John Bachman recorded an extremely late Broadwing November 17, 1984.

During the fall of 1942, Broun and Ben Goodwin measured the flight speeds of eight migrating Broad-winged Hawks. The speeds ranged from 20 to 40 miles per hour with an average of 31.7 and a median of 32 (Broun and Goodwin, 1943:492).

The season high count at Hawk Mountain is 29,519 in 1978. The 10-year average from 1987 to 1996 is 7,428. The lowest fall count occurred during 1996, when only 1,809 Broadwings were recorded as unfavorable winds pushed the birds away from the ridge.

The single-day peak is 21,448 on September 14, 1978. This total was compiled from observations at the North and South lookouts and the Owl's Head firetower. The count that day from only the North Lookout is 11,349. Jim Brett writes about the record day:

Thursday 14 September 1978. I limped to the lookout with a pulled muscle in my leg. Broadwings were already on the move, and Charlie Gant, "Broadwing Charlie," was prancing excitedly around the rocks. Oh-oh. I had told two fellows in the headquarters that the day wouldn't be very good - they might as well go home. Most of the regulars seemed to feel the same way. They weren't here. We had only 35 people on North and South Lookouts combined. But the weather was a classic set-up for a big Broadwing day - wind east-northeast at about 8 miles an hour, sky becoming overcast with small patches of blue. The numbers of Broadwings began to mount. Meanwhile, Brad Owens called from Bethlehem to tell us that 1,500 Broadwings had passed over his house the night before and 1,500 more in the morning. By 11 each lookout had recorded more than 1,000 hawks. Then a very large kettle developed over Broad Mountain to the north, containing well over a thousand birds, and in that hour before noon we counted 8,547 Broadwings! By now we had three points covered: Curator Alex Nagy had gone out to the Owl's Head firetower, to count there. The sky was filled from horizon to horizon and from below treeline to the zenith with birds. The two-way radios were hot, and everyone was feeling exhaustion and exhilaration. On North Lookout, Bruce Williams, Charlie Gant, Warner Berthoff, and Fred Casey kept their eyes peeled to the north. After noon, the hourly counts were never less than 2,000, until 4, when the flight slowed and sheets were tallied. The old daily record of 11,000, set in 1948, had been shattered shortly after noon, and the final tally was nearly twice that - 21,448. During the 11-to-noon hour, Alex said with amazement, he had been surrounded by birds as they thermaled around his station above the treetops. They were so close he could hear the air passing over their wings (Brett, 1984c: 54-55).

Maurice Broun writes about the previous high count of 11,392 Broadwings:

Thursday, September 16, 1948

And now for the miracle day, when the sky was literally darkened by Broadwings, giving us a glimpse of the way it must have been any mid-September day a couple of centuries ago. Some sixth sense forewarned me of this flight! John and Grace Prest, of Wilmington, Delaware, were visiting the Sanctuary. They had a week on their hands, enjoying excellent birding with us. I said to the Prests, "Better hang around until Thursday - that's the big day." They hesitated, but departed at last to visit some relatives in New Jersey. You can imagine their chagrin when later they heard all about it.

The morning looked hopeless for good hawking. A dull, sullen sky, and a fresh easterly wind - the worst possible wind for a flight - chilled us in body and spirit. But not for long! At exactly 8 o'clock an adult Bald Eagle circled above Schaumboch's, followed by 50 Broadwings, on both sides of the ridge, and at moderate elevations, many of the birds so close we could have hit them with stones. There was nothing remarkable the first two hours - only 1,396 Broadwings, and a sprinkling of Ospreys and Sharpshins. An additional 1,371 Broadwings were tallied in the next hour. But soon after 11 o'clock, a swirling mass of Broadwings boiled over the mountain, and they soon filled the southern sky in a seemingly interminable, densely straggling line, moving rapidly. My 18-power binocular revealed a level sheet of moving birds as far to the south as I could see. It was impossible to count, and I found myself making estimates, for the first time in all my years at Hawk Mountain. My tally for that last hour of the morning was 7,587 plus broad-wings. My companions on the Lookout, making independent counts, found my figures extremely conservative. Many more birds went by. The handful of observers who were present are not likely to see such a sight again. In the more than 7,200 hours that I have watched birds atop Hawk Mountain, there has never been anything remotely comparable to this avalanche of hawks. In that one hour before high noon, we saw more Broadwings than we usually see in an entire season. Only a thousand odd hawks passed the rest of the day; and the day's count was 11,392 plus hawks. This historic migration was witnessed by Donald Bieber and Walter Listman, both of Rochester, New York, Theodore Hake of York, Pennsylvania, Mabel and Ralph Lutz of Philadelphia, and my wife. Apparently the Broadwings had been pent-up somewhere along the ridge. But why? During the five days prior to this mass exodus, the weather had been favorable for migration, and indeed the collective Broadwing count for September 11th to 15th was 1,530 birds. In any event the birds moved south in a body on this fabulous September 16th. At noon of this same day, George Pyle observed 1,500 plus Broadwings over Riegelsville, along the Delaware River, and about 18 miles south of the nearest part of the ridge. In the days following the 16th we recorded only 1,140 Broadwings (Broun, 1949a:185-186).

Hawk Mountain Counts for the Broad-winged Hawk									
1934	-	1949	9579	1961	8642	1973	6404	1985	3415
1935	-	1950	5305	1962	8254	1974	9146	1986	13996
1936	6990	1951	10997	1963	9791	1975	10390	1987	8409
1937	4343	1952	12603	1964	10180	1976	8461	1988	5944
1938	10754	1953	7247	1965	9235	1977	13009	1989	7504
1939	5736	1954	5956	1966	10110	1978	29519	1990	4656
1940	3159	1955	9542	1967	8000	1979	11173	1991	5858
1941	5170	1956	8734	1968	14041	1980	10141	1992	10661
1942	4362	1957	8935	1969	8515	1981	8660	1993	3592
1946	2866	1958	8880	1970	9153	1982	7163	1994	3513
1947	6664	1959	5301	1971	5603	1983	6922	1995	10077
1948	15026	1960	11107	1972	8131	1984	13619	1996	1809

Note: These statistics reflect counts from the North Lookout only.

During years of exceptionally mild Septembers comparatively few hawks ride the updrafts along the ridge but drift straight southward across the mountains, often at great heights. On October 5, 1969, glider pilot Barney Johnston was aloft over Kutztown and observed a kettle of 2,500 Broadwings and another of 3,000 only 300 yards apart, although no Broadwings were seen that day over Hawk Mountain (Nagy, 1970:9). Catherine Elwell and Richard Sharadin recorded 8,297 Broadwings near Kutztown September 21, 1975.

Many migrating Broadwings also follow the South Mountain and Reading Prong. On September 22, 1939, Ira Weigley, Sr., saw more than 500 Broadwings over Bernhart's valley in

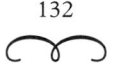

Reading (Broun, 1949a:149). Between September 15 and 18, 1995, observers counted 3,454 birds migrating along the South Mountain. Rudy Keller saw over 2,000 in seven towering kettles pass the Trout Run reservoir near Boyertown in about 30 minutes just after noon on September 16.

Kerry Grim sighted a partial albino Broad-winged Hawk at the Hamburg reservoir August 13, 1979, noting a dark eye and faint tail banding on the bird. There are many records of light-colored Broad-winged Hawks during migration at Hawk Mountain and at the Route 183 hawk watch. For instance, Richard Sharadin observed an immature partial albino at the North Lookout September 5, 1967.

There are 14 specimens - nine males, three females, and two unsexed birds - in the Reading Public Museum collection. Levi Mengel collected two males at Moselem on April 19, 1884. Nine were shot in the fall near Eckville between September 7 (1937) and October 3 (1931). Four of these were shot there on September 18, 1932, and two on September 7, 1937. The others are an unsexed and undated bird taken in "Berks County" by John F. Hofmann, an unsexed bird from Bernhart's Dam in 1932, and a female from Millmont April 24, 1937.

SWAINSON'S HAWK *Buteo swainsoni*
Very rare

There are 13 records for this western species at Hawk Mountain. Fred Wetzel observed a Swainson's Hawk over the North Lookout on October 22, 1969, the first Berks County record. Two Swainson's Hawks were recorded there during each of the 1982 and 1987 fall seasons. A dark morph bird passed the North Lookout on September 23, 1993.

The early date at Hawk Mountain is September 9 (1982 - Jim Brett), and the late date is November 22 (1981 - John Bachman).

Robert and Anne MacClay observed a Swainson's Hawk at the Route 183 lookout October 9, 1993. They found a light adult Swainson's Hawk August 13, 1996, at the lookout in the rain. The bird was sitting on a wire about 200 feet to the north. Robert MacClay writes that it was "vigorously trying to wipe off the water with its feet. It seemed very annoyed, but maybe it was enjoying the bath as it kept wiping all over, even putting out its wing and rubbing underneath."

Away from the Kittatinny Ridge, Matt Spence saw a Swainson's Hawk north of Morgantown on October 6, 1990, and Joan Silagy found one at Blue Marsh October 3, 1993. Doug Wood recorded one September 15, 1995, in a flock of 30 Broad-winged Hawks over Skyline Drive in Reading.

Hawk Mountain Counts for the Swainson's Hawk

1934	0	1949	0	1961	0	1973	0	1985	1
1935	0	1950	0	1962	0	1974	0	1986	0
1936	0	1951	0	1963	0	1975	0	1987	2
1937	0	1952	0	1964	0	1976	0	1988	1
1938	0	1953	0	1965	0	1977	1	1989	0
1939	0	1954	0	1966	0	1978	0	1990	1
1940	0	1955	0	1967	0	1979	1	1991	0
1941	0	1956	0	1968	0	1980	0	1992	0
1942	0	1957	0	1969	1	1981	1	1993	1
1946	0	1958	0	1970	0	1982	2	1994	0
1947	0	1959	0	1971	0	1983	0	1995	0
1948	0	1960	0	1972	0	1984	1	1996	0

Note: These statistics reflect counts from the North Lookout only.

RED-TAILED HAWK *Buteo jamaicensis*

Fairly common resident; occasionally abundant fall migrant

No other hawk has responded as well to protection and has adapted itself as well to man during the past 25 years in Berks County as has the Red-tailed Hawk.

In 1964, Earl Poole considered the Redtail rare and local in summer and fairly common in winter and during migrations in Berks. Poole had not seen the Redtail earlier than August 1 (1942), nor later than May 25 (1940).

It is now a fairly common resident and one of the most common hawks in Berks County.

The nesting requirements of the Redtail are not as strict as those of the Broad-winged Hawk. The Redtail will nest in smaller woodlots and woods edges near open fields throughout the county. Robert Cook found the first confirmed nesting Red-tailed Hawks in the county this century near French Creek State Park in May 1975. Since then, the nesting population has grown.

In southern Berks, Rich Bonnett found 11 active nests in mid-April 1990. He has found that most of the Redtails nest in red or white oaks and in shagbark hickory trees. He found two nests in sycamores, but a Great Horned Owl occupied one, and neither of the Redtails were seen the next season.

The Redtail was noticed in Berks near Hawk Mountain throughout the nesting seasons of 1946, 1947, 1949, 1951, and 1954 (a pair present during the two latter seasons) by Maurice Broun and Alex Nagy. Stray individuals were found elsewhere in Berks on several occasions in summer. But no nests were found.

Levi Mengel took a set of four eggs in Albany Township May 11, 1886. The nest, located in a tall oak, was roughly made, two feet or more in diameter, and nearly two feet deep.

The Red-tailed Hawk is most common in Berks as a migrant, reaching its peak numbers during the fall migration at Hawk Mountain toward the end of October and early November. On October 24, 1939, Maurice Broun reported a record flight of 1,144.

One of the highest seasonal counts of 5,426 Red-tailed Hawks was made during the fall of 1934, the first year of the establishment of the sanctuary. The season high is 6,208 in 1939. The 10-year average from 1987 to 1996 is 3,901. At no time between 1941 and 1978 did the total for the year reach 4,000. The number of migrants for 1956 was down to 1,525, the lowest ever, prompting Earl Poole to lament, "the future of the species looks very dark, indeed."

However, beginning in the late 1960s, an upward trend in Red-tailed Hawk populations occurred in the county. In the following chart, Matt Spence examines Christmas Bird Count statistics from southeastern Pennsylvania and Berks regarding the abundance of the Red-tailed Hawk. In southeastern Pennsylvania, the number of Redtails per party hour rose from .16 in 1960 to .72 in 1995. The biggest jump occurred during the 1970s. In the Reading count, the number per party hour in 1960 was .10 and increased to .99 in 1995. The years from the late 1980s to the mid-1990s saw the biggest rise. The population increase in Berks apparently occurred later than the increase in the rest of southeastern Pennsylvania.

Early and late migration dates at Hawk Mountain are a result of observer effort as Redtails are seen throughout the official count period of August 15 to December 15. The early date is August 2 (1959 - Maurice Broun), and the late date is January 12 (1997 - Bill Wallace).

DATE	NUMBER OF S.E. PA COUNTS	PARTY HOURS	NUMBER OF REDTAILS	BIRDS PER PARTY HOUR	AVERAGE BIRDS PER COUNT	RANGE OF NUMBERS COUNTED	READING PARTY HOURS	READING REDTAILS	READING BIRDS PER PARTY HOUR	ALLENTOWN/ LEHIGH VALLEY	BERNVILLE	HAMBURG	ELVERSON	MID-QUARTILES	REDTAIL HIGH COUNTS
										(Birds per Party Hour)					
1960	14	625	99	.16	7	1-21	79	8	.10	.17	-	-	.25	.17 .06	21 West Chester
1965	16	924	124	.13	8	1-24	65	15	.23	.07	-	.06	.20	.14 .07	24 Glenolden
1970	17	1,391	443	.32	26	4-68	128	40	.31	.25	-	.61	.41	.42 .20	68 West Chester
1975	17	1,890	672	.36	40	12-79	111	29	.26	.49	-	1.05	.29	.44 .28	79 Bethlehem-Easton
1980	19	2,056	848	.41	45	6-91	125	38	.30	.59	-	.52	.65	.53 .28	91 So. Lancaster Co.
1985	22	2,558	1,682	.66	76	7-207	127	62	.49	1.04	1.06	1.13	.70	.86 .49	207 Hamburg
1990	22	2,609	1,869	.72	85	12-179	115	74	.64	.83	1.41	1.05	.81	.83 .52	179 Upper Bucks
1995	22	2,496	1,805	.72	82	8-183	117	116	.99	1.13	1.41	.77	.56	.89 .53	183 Upper Bucks

Occasionally, large concentrations of wintering Red-tailed Hawks, attracted by waste products, occur at poultry processing plants and pig farms in western and northwestern Berks. Rudy Keller and Harold and Joan Silagy counted over 100 Redtails near a poultry farm in Upper Bern Township January 27, 1991. They found between 40 and 50 Redtails near a Jefferson Township pig farm March 30, 1990.

Poole writes in 1930: "During the winter it is the common large hawk of the open meadow country, where it is often a conspicuous object in the winter landscape, owing its comparative abundance to its hard-earned ability to correctly judge the range of the ever-ready shotgun."

Poole also writes in 1964: "It seems remarkable that such a conspicuous bird of prey has managed to hold its own as well as it has in the face of the multitude of gunners that swarm over the fields in November, looking for anything large enough to offer a tempting target. To some uninformed farmers and many 'sportsmen,' it is still one of the species that are collectively alluded to as 'chicken-hawks,' in spite of the fact that all of the food studies have resulted in a 'beneficial' rating for this handsome, distinctively American species."

The Red-tailed Hawk has appeared on the Reading Christmas Bird Count 76 of 86 years, 10 of the last 10, with a maximum of 116 on December 17, 1995. The high for the Hamburg Christmas Bird Count is 207 on December 29, 1985. The peak for the Bernville Count is 135 on January 2, 1994.

Because of natural variability in the population, Red-tailed Hawks appear in a variety of plumages and in some extreme forms. Kerry Grim observed a totally black Red-tailed Hawk at Kaercher Creek Park in Windsor Township February 21, 1976.

Periodically, albino Red-tailed Hawks pass over Hawk Mountain during the fall migration. Fred Wetzel writes about a partially albino Red-tailed Hawk sighted there in 1970: "In the gray afternoon of November 7th, a large white bird circling over number four caused much confusion at the Lookout. The bird soon revealed itself to be a partial albino Red-tailed Hawk, and as the bird drew closer, one could see a normally red tail as well as dark primaries and secondaries on an otherwise chalk-white bird. Its symmetrical patterning and unusual color combination made it an intriguing and spectacular sight" (Wetzel, 1971:13).

Kerry Grim first observed a partially albino, female Red-tailed Hawk, all white except for the back of the head and a few red tail feathers, near Lenhartsville in Windsor Township during November 1982. Grim kept track of the hawk monthly and noticed that she was bigger than her mate when the two birds perched side by side. He also saw her during several seasons incubating on her nest. Richard Phillips, the farmer on whose land she resided, said she would follow him when he was plowing, presumably seeking meadow voles. She remained a year-round resident until suffering a wing injury. On November 19, 1987, Phillips found the injured bird and took her to Hawk Mountain Sanctuary. She was then taken to Dr. Lee Simpson for surgery. After extensive rehabilitation at Hawk Mountain, the bird was returned to the farm March 10, 1988. Jim Brett writes: "What was most remarkable about the release occurred within minutes after Trica Oshant hoisted the bird into the air. With good strength, the Redtail - a female - gained altitude even though buffeted by a stiff wind and flew above a small rise in the landscape and disappeared over a field of corn stubble. We raced for the truck and headed north on the farm road to a lower area where we found the bird atop a utility pole. To our utter astonishment the white bird had been approached by a normal-colored Redtail who mounted the white bird and copulated." Grim last saw her February 23, 1992. During March 1992, he visited the area and found two normal-colored Redtails together in the same tree.

Grim recorded an albino Redtail near Krumsville December 15, 1989, and Spence found one at the same place March 25, 1992.

On October 21, 1972, Hawk Mountain Sanctuary volunteers C. J. and Sue Robertson placed an aluminum band numbered 0877-17127 on the leg of a migrating Red-tailed Hawk at a banding station north of Hawk Mountain. Len Soucy of the Raptor Trust in Millington, New Jersey, trapped Redtail 0877-17127 nearly 60 miles upridge from the Sanctuary on November 12, 1994. In adult plumage when the Robertsons banded it 22 years earlier, this hawk must have hatched no later than the spring of 1971. Its age, therefore, had to be at least 23 years and five months at recapture, making it the oldest Redtail ever banded. It surpassed the National Biological Service's previous record for Redtail longevity - an adult banded in Wisconsin in 1963 and recovered dead in Iowa in 1983 - by almost two years. According to Soucy, the bird was still in good shape when recaptured and re-released (Bildstein, 1995a:22).

Hawk Mountain Counts for the Red-tailed Hawk

1934	5426	1949	2749	1961	2566	1973	3098	1985	2895
1935	3214	1950	2667	1962	2772	1974	3658	1986	3305
1936	3162	1951	2307	1963	3402	1975	2880	1987	4215
1937	4932	1952	2754	1964	2626	1976	3694	1988	4687
1938	2228	1953	2051	1965	3297	1977	3504	1989	3710
1939	6208	1954	2070	1966	2126	1978	2852	1990	3785
1940	4725	1955	3764	1967	1854	1979	4175	1991	2970
1941	4698	1956	1525	1968	3765	1980	5715	1992	3288
1942	2378	1957	2730	1969	3366	1981	3939	1993	3744
1946	2306	1958	2951	1970	2503	1982	5025	1994	4434
1947	1680	1959	1904	1971	1781	1983	3954	1995	4854
1948	2343	1960	2200	1972	3463	1984	3157	1996	2735

Note: These statistics reflect counts from the North Lookout only.

Broun and Ben Goodwin recorded the flight speeds of 54 migrating Red-tailed Hawks during the fall of 1942. The speeds ranged from 20 to 40 miles per hour with an average of 29 and a median of 28 (Broun and Goodwin, 1943:492).

George M. Sutton examined 32 Red-tailed Hawks shot between October 17 and 22, 1927, at what is now Hawk Mountain. Three of the birds were immatures. Twelve stomachs were empty. In the 20 stomachs which held food were 11 field mice, four short-tailed shrews, three red-backed mice, three chipmunks, three small garter snakes, two red squirrels, one Winter Wren, one Song Sparrow, one Hermit Thrush, one gray squirrel, one brown rat, one half-grown White Leghorn Chicken, one large grasshopper, two crickets, and one large beetle of the family *Elateridae*. Seven of these stomachs held only one item, and the others had a variety in each (Sutton, 1928b:93-94).

There are 26 specimens taken from throughout Berks in the Reading Public Museum collection. Levi Mengel collected a male in Albany Township May 14, 1885; a female in Bethel June 28, 1885; and a female in Lenhartsville April 16, 1886.

Excluding Mengel's specimens, Redtails in the museum collection were taken between October 15 (1926) and March 20 (1936). The stomach of a male shot November 6, 1941, in "Berks County" contained one Cooper's Hawk. Analyzed stomach contents of other Redtails in the collection include one meadow mouse in a male shot at Farr Nursery in Wyomissing November 27, 1933; a meadow mouse and a chicken in a female shot in Bern Township November 10, 1930; two meadow mice in a male shot in "Berks County" November 16, 1932; three meadow mice in a male shot at Bernville March 20, 1936; one pheasant in a female shot October 29, 1932, and in a female shot December 28, 1932, both at Maidencreek; and a chicken in an unsexed bird shot at Tuckerton October 15, 1926. Poole noted that a Redtail shot at Angelica December 11, 1952, "shows some of the characters of the western Redtail." Seven specimens of Red-tailed Hawks in the collection appear to be of the dark, northern race, *B. j. abieticola.*

Krider's Red-tailed Hawk *Buteo jamaicensis kriderii*

At Hawk Mountain on October 12, 1959, Earl Poole had an excellent view, from above, of a very pale Buteo with a pale "pinkish" tail which was the exact counterpart of specimens of this subspecies, including some of Krider's own collecting, that he had been examining to find a typical specimen that would serve to illustrate this race. It was either *kriderii* or an extremely pale color phase of the eastern Redtail, which he was unable to match in any of the available eastern collections. Maurice Broun also noted this bird.

Robert MacClay saw a very pale Redtail he believed to be a Krider's adult at Route 183 on November 12, 1987. He described it as extremely light with distinctive Krider's features including a bright head, lack of belly band, and pinkish tail. It sailed slowly overhead at a distance of 125 feet.

Western Red-tailed Hawk *Buteo jamaicensis calurus*

An individual typical of this western race of the Red-tailed Hawk was captured, photographed, and banded by C. J. Robertson near Hawk Mountain on October 17, 1959. Dr. W.R. Spofford recognized this bird as *B. j. calurus.*

Rudy Keller and Harold and Joan Silagy described a dark morph bird, probably a Western Red-tailed Hawk, found near Marion Drive off School Road in Marion Township during the Bernville Christmas Bird Count January 1, 1989: a broad blackish-brown belly band; rufous throat and breast meeting the belly band in a broad "V," like a vest; face dusky rufous; undertail coverts rufous; underside of tail barred black on rufous-white; back and hindneck and top of head blackish-brown with rufous highlights.

The Pennsylvania German name for the Red-tailed Hawk and all the Buteos is "Hinkelwoi," or chicken hawk. William Rupp writes:

The Sharp-shinned goes after small birds, the Cooper after larger birds, game and poultry; and the larger hawks get all the blame. The above name was applied loosely to all large hawks and the result was something of which our people can only be ashamed. The farmer saw a Red-tail, or a Red-shouldered hawk, sailing in wide circles above him and uttering his screaming call. Meanwhile a shrewd, low-flying accipiter slipped by and stormed into the poultry yard or after the pigeons. The average person did not see that the damage had been done by a smaller hawk of a different color; and if it was a female accipiter, it was still easier to assume that a bird like the high-flying hawk had done the dirty work. So, a hawk was a hawk, and the farmer declared war against his friend. The large hawk became the 'hen hawk,' a slow-flying, easy target, whose slaughter was as continual as it was unfortunate, while the smaller, more difficult target got away (Rupp, 1946: 90).

Rupp summarizes the Pennsylvania German names for the hawks:

"Woi" is a general name for all hawks; the plural is 'die Woi.' In the counties west of Lehigh, "Habbich," "Habbicht," "Haabich," "Haabicht," "Hoppich," "Hawich," and "Hawicht" are also heard. The writer never heard these names in Lehigh County; a number of other persons have said the same thing. The names "Hinkelwoi" and "Hinkelhabbich" were applied, usually, to all large hawks, beginning, approximately, with the female Cooper's. The smaller hawks, beginning with the male Cooper's, and the small falcons, went by

the name of "Schdoosswoi," "Dauwewoi," or some form of these two. "Hinkelwoi," as applied to the large hawks, is for the most part an unjust and undeserved name, and should be used for the rare Goshawk and the accipiters.

In this instance the dialect names are not as well chosen as in some others. Some reflect no keen powers of observation; rather, they seem to be the result of snap judgments arrived at, perhaps, in anger. Hawk did some damage in the barnyard and that was enough for any Pennsylvania German farmer; the war was on from there, and no time was taken to give the friends of the open fields the names they deserved. Even the law has not yet succeeded in wholly changing the farmer's attitude toward the large hawks, and a hawk is still just a hawk when many a "Dutchman" goes for his gun.

Old hunters used to say that it was impossible to kill a hawk by shooting at its breast, the feathers being so thick and compact as to prevent the penetration of the shot. To kill a hawk, it was said that the hunter had to fire from the side or from the rear. They were shot anyway, and their pathetic bodies were nailed up on the side of a barn or shed to keep other hawks away from the barnyard fowl and from the pigeons. Sometimes they were put up simply as trophies of the hunt, and there would be rivalry in the neighborhood as to who could nail up the largest hawk or the greatest number of "birds of prey" - "Raabveggel." For one reason or another, the carcasses were never taken down; left to hang until decomposed, the feathers and bones finally came down of their own accord.

...The eaves of the house, unlit by the light of the sun, were places where, in ancient belief, the protective house spirits dwelt. The eaves are the boundaries of the house; thus far and no farther can the evil spirits come. The belief goes back to the time when some protective symbol was mounted on the roof of the house. We still have these protective symbols. It is a frequent sight to see the carcass of a hawk, crow, or owl hanging or nailed to the side of a farm building. The reason for this custom is that the other birds of prey will be frightened away by the sight, and this undoubtedly is the present day motive for the custom. Our Teutonic ancestors, however, nailed birds, wings of birds, or carved figures of birds on their barns and sheds to frighten away pestilence and disease (Rupp, 1946:95-97).

ROUGH-LEGGED HAWK *Buteo lagopus*
Rare migrant and winter visitor

Throughout this century, the number of Rough-legged Hawks migrating through and wintering in Berks County has always been low. There are occasional winters, however, when it occurs in some numbers, such as 1934-1935, 1949-1950, 1959-1960, 1970-1971, and 1986-1987. Roughleg counts can be tied to the abundance of meadow voles.

Nesting far to the north, the Rough-legged Hawk rarely arrives in Berks before the last of October or in November, although it has been seen at Hawk Mountain as early as October 1 (1987 - Jim Brett).

It winters regularly near the large, open fields of western Berks in Marion Township and in the fields near Kutztown, Fleetwood, and Lyons from December to early March. Rudy Keller and Harold and Joan Silagy found 20 Roughlegs in Marion Township January 4, 1987.

Individuals on three occasions have remained at Lake Ontelaunee until May, the latest May 5 (1935 - Earl Poole). During the winter of 1935 the meadow voles were particularly abundant and did a great deal of damage to the trees. A Roughleg wintered near Hawk Mountain until May 5, 1983.

Not one Roughleg was counted at Hawk Mountain Sanctuary in 1938, 1942, 1946, 1947, 1951, and 1955. The season average from 1987 to 1996 has been

12, making it the rarest of those hawks which occur with any regularity there.

The late date for the migrant Roughleg at Hawk Mountain is January 4 (1996 - Steven Thorpe). The single-day peak is seven on November 11, 1961 (Maurice Broun, Darwin Palmer). The season high count is 31 in 1961.

Jim Olmes recorded single Rough-legged Hawks during the spring migration count at Hawk Mountain on March 20, 1984, and April 2, 1984.

Earl Poole writes in 1964: "Being large and comparatively unsuspicious, it is a tempting mark for the 'trigger-happy' nimrods who are too obstinately ignorant to realize that it is one of our most beneficial birds of prey. In 1934 I examined the stomach contents of several Rough-legged Hawks that had been shot by a hawk-hating Deputy Game Protector on the Ontelaunee watershed and found that they consisted entirely of the remains of meadow mice."

There are six specimens - five males and one female- in the Reading Public Museum collection. The stomach of a male from Evansville November 18, 1933, contained one white-footed mouse, and the stomach of another male from Maidencreek January 3, 1935, contained two *microtus* species. A male near Kutztown was "caught in a trap" on January 8, 1947. The other Roughlegs in the collection are a male from Yellow House November 3, 1934; a female from Blue Marsh January 15, 1935; and a male from Flying Hill January 20, 1935.

Hawk Mountain Counts for the Rough-legged Hawk									
1934	17	1949	16	1961	31	1973	8	1985	12
1935	6	1950	2	1962	7	1974	17	1986	11
1936	9	1951	0	1963	6	1975	9	1987	22
1937	4	1952	9	1964	14	1976	13	1988	14
1938	0	1953	2	1965	4	1977	17	1989	12
1939	8	1954	3	1966	3	1978	7	1990	21
1940	4	1955	0	1967	5	1979	14	1991	9
1941	2	1956	10	1968	5	1980	23	1992	4
1942	0	1957	7	1969	18	1981	18	1993	6
1946	0	1958	1	1970	10	1982	17	1994	9
1947	0	1959	10	1971	7	1983	14	1995	10
1948	9	1960	25	1972	6	1984	5	1996	3

Note: These statistics reflect counts from the North Lookout only.

The Rough-legged Hawk has appeared on the Reading Christmas Bird Count 33 of 86 years, eight of the last 10, with a maximum of 10 on December 27, 1970. The peak for the Hamburg Christmas Bird Count is nine on December 28, 1980. The high for the Bernville count is 28 on January 4, 1987.

GOLDEN EAGLE *Aquila chrysaetos*
Regular uncommon migrant, rare winter visitor

In 1930, Earl Poole regarded the Golden Eagle as a very rare straggler in late fall, but intensive observations by Maurice Broun and others at Hawk Mountain since 1934 have shown that this fine bird is a regular fall migrant and a rare winter visitor in Berks County. Individual Golden Eagles have spent the entire winters of 1938-1939, 1939-1940, 1942-1943, 1972-1973, and 1974-1975 at Lake Ontelaunee. Two wintered until March 6 near Eckville in the winter of 1959-1960 (Maurice Broun, Alex Nagy), at least one remaining in the same area throughout the winters of 1960-1961 and 1961-1962.

Recent winter records include single birds near Kempton February 9, 1988 (Laurie Goodrich); in Albany Township February 8 and 9, 1989 (L.G.); and near Steinsville, Lehigh County, at the Berks County line, January 24, 1992 (Cathy Viverette).

As many as 14 a day and 100 in one season (1995) have been counted from Hawk Mountain's North Lookout, but during poor years there have been as few as 12 (1966) tallied. The 10-year seasonal average from 1987 to 1996 is 70.

The fall migration lasts from late September, occasionally as early as September 2 (1957 - M.B., an adult) and casually, August 4 (1972 - Frank Haas, an immature), to January 8 (1997 - Steve Thorpe, an immature).

Hawk Mountain Counts for the Golden Eagle

	T	U	I	A		T	U	I	A		T	U	I	A
1934	35	5	16	14	1961	48	3	12	33	1985	58	1	37	20
1935	62	0	18	44	1962	37	0	14	23	1986	43	2	34	7
1936	53	0	18	35	1963	23	0	6	17	1987	98	2	72	24
1937	71	1	24	46	1964	24	0	6	18	1988	66	6	44	16
1938	31	1	11	19	1965	34	1	11	22	1989	45	3	27	15
1939	83	4	28	51	1966	12	1	4	7	1990	77	4	43	30
1940	72	0	15	57	1967	30	2	11	17	1991	58	2	37	19
1941	55	3	14	38	1968	27	1	10	16	1992	56	4	32	20
1942	35	0	14	21	1969	22	2	4	16	1993	70	6	40	24
1946	68	0	14	51	1970	15	1	9	5	1994	88	4	44	40
1947	33	1	8	24	1971	23	0	12	11	1995	100	5	64	31
1948	41	1	6	34	1972	33	0	20	13	1996	87	4	54	29

	T	U	I	A		T	U	I	A
1949	47	0	20	27	1973	46	2	21	23
1950	65	0	18	47	1974	27	1	15	11
1951	55	0	8	47	1975	27	1	9	17
1952	81	0	20	61	1976	40	1	22	17
1953	30	0	10	20	1977	28	2	17	9
1954	40	0	14	26	1978	28	2	20	6
1955	57	1	10	46	1979	33	7	15	11
1956	42	0	13	29	1980	63	2	35	26
1957	37	0	12	25	1981	52	4	22	26
1958	39	1	8	30	1982	53	1	24	28
1959	31	1	7	23	1983	56	4	36	16
1960	23	1	8	14	1984	36	0	21	15

Note: These statistics reflect counts from the North Lookout only.

U - Undetermined Age

I - Immature

A - Adult

T - Total

Laurie Goodrich writes about the single-day high count of 14 at Hawk Mountain on November 12, 1987:

Five inches of snow and a brisk northwest wind greeted Jim Brett and intern Jane Kidd as they climbed to the summit on November 12, following a harsh storm. A flock of 25 Pine Grosbeaks landed in a lookout hemlock and began another record day. The first Golden Eagle arrived at 10:20 a.m. skimming Number Four before heading south along the ridge. One after another, the eagles continued. At 1:55 p.m., an adult Golden Eagle tied the single-day record at Hawk Mountain, 13, recorded November 5, 1946, by Maurice Broun. At 2:20 p.m. an immature Golden coursed low past the small frozen group of jubilant hawkwatchers, bringing the daily total to 14. Another Hawk Mountain record etched into the books (Goodrich, 1988: 33).

The single-day record of 14 Golden Eagles was matched at the North Lookout on October 28, 1996 (Beth Garland).

During the fall of 1942, Broun and Ben Goodwin measured the flight speeds of two migrating Golden Eagles at 28 and 32 miles per hour (Broun and Goodwin, 1943:492).

A Golden Eagle preyed upon a Red-shouldered Hawk as they passed the North Lookout on November 1, 1946. Maurice Broun writes:

Imagine, if you can, lying on your back and gazing with me into the zenith through a pair of 7 X 50 glasses. We see in the field of the binocular a large dark bird, and a small hawk, neither clearly identifiable. We wonder how many hawks have been missed, flying at that incredible height above the Lookout. We switched to the greater reach of an eighteen-power binocular and find that the big bird is an adult Golden Eagle, its satellite still indeterminate. The smaller bird is making desultory passes at the eagle. Suddenly the eagle thrusts forward, executes an Immelman turn as effortlessly as a fly landing on a ceiling, and grabs the smaller hawk, which puts up a feeble, momentary, struggle. The eagle, with set wings, hurtles earthwards at terrific speed, and, still clutching its prey, disappears into the densely wooded flank of the ridge. The wings of the smaller hawk are fully outstretched during the meteoric descent, and we note the ruddy breast of the Red-shouldered Hawk. It is all over in a matter of seconds! (Broun, 1949a:194)

In the years Golden Eagles wintered at Lake Ontelaunee, individuals were seen repeatedly from December 26, 1938, to April 7, 1939; from January 7 to March 9, 1940; from December 27, 1942, to April 23, 1943; from November 29, 1943, to April 22, 1944; and from December 9, 1944, to March 21, 1945. On several occasions they were accompanied by a Bald Eagle, roosting on adjacent trees and living in a state of mutual tolerance. More recent winter records from Lake Ontelaunee include single birds November 30, 1969; December 17, 1972; and from December 8 to 15, 1974 (Matt Spence). The Golden Eagle has appeared on the Reading Christmas Bird Count seven of 86 years, all records of single birds previously cited. The peak for the Hamburg Christmas Bird Count is two on January 1, 1970.

Robert Cook recorded a Golden Eagle January 1, 1946, near Morgantown. In December 1948, a Golden Eagle lingered near Morgantown until it was wounded by a farmer, kept in a chicken coop, and then taken to the Norristown Zoo. It was ultimately stolen from the zoo.

Late spring dates include May 29, 1977, when Kerry Grim saw one migrating over State Game Lands 106 near Eckville; May 8, 1974, when Kenneth and Dorothy Grim found one feeding on a road-killed groundhog in Albany Township; and May 3, 1953, at Hawk Mountain (Maurice Broun). Jim Olmes recorded a single Golden Eagle on April 27, 1984, during the Hawk Mountain spring migration count.

A Golden Eagle summered near Hawk Mountain in 1968. Michael Harwood writes of the occurrence:

One June day a few years ago, Alex [Nagy] happened to notice, from his car, a troop of crows harassing a vulture. There was something wrong with that picture, and a mile or so farther on he remembered what it was: crows wouldn't be pestering a vulture in June. He swung the car around and went back to look. The "vulture" was a male Golden Eagle, an individual so old that its hackles had turned from gold to gray. It was not much of a hunter any longer. Alex's father used to see it beating back and forth over his farm, and, occasionally, it tried to hunt there. One day, it was after Ring-necked Pheasants feeding in a cornfield. "The eagle would come down," Alex says, "and he'd fly between the corn rows - he'd fold his wings - trying to drive these pheasants out into the open. And after he did drive a couple out, he'd stoop at them and he'd miss, and he'd go up again, and stoop at them, and miss." His father said afterward he felt so sorry for the eagle he had considered getting a shotgun and shooting one of the pheasants for him.

The elder Nagy was also raising sheep at the time, and hunger made the eagle brave enough to make a pass at one of the lambs, while the farmer looked on. No damage was done....

Much of the time, the old eagle was reduced to eating carrion like a vulture, particularly road kills - which doubtless gave a number of motorists something of a start. The first time Alex's wife Arlene saw the eagle, it was blocking her way down the state road, its three-foot wings spread threateningly in defense of its meal....

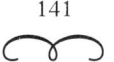

After it had been around the neighborhood for two years, the Hawk Mountain staff tried several times to trap it.... But the eagle wasn't caught that summer; the hawking season began at the sanctuary - eliminating any free time for trapping expeditions - and that fall a man hunting crows at a nearby lake shot the eagle (Harwood, 1973:176-180).

Two local specimens in the Reading Public Museum collection were taken from gunners by the game protectors at Eckville November 10, 1931, and in the Blue Mountains above Shartlesville October 21, 1936. On December 17, 1963, two deer hunters found a mature male Golden Eagle shot dead with a shotgun near Sinking Spring. Sam Gundy picked up the bird for the museum collection.

A fine adult specimen, shot at Brandywine Hill near Topton October 25, 1920, was in the library at the Kutztown State Teacher's College, now Kutztown University, until 1944. In that year the natural history collections were transferred to what is now West Chester University. In January 1997 Dr. Henry Tiebout at West Chester confirmed that according to the university's records, the specimen was received but apparently was later destroyed due to damage.

John F. Hofmann listed the Golden Eagle in 1890.

AMERICAN KESTREL *Falco sparverius*
Fairly common resident

A permanent resident, the American Kestrel is a fairly common bird of prey in open country throughout Berks County, most often seen perching on wires and poles or hovering over fields searching for prey.

In March and April, and again from late August to mid-November, there is an evident increase in the number of American Kestrels moving through the county.

During winter Kestrels often visit the heart of Reading to prey on the House Sparrows. In 1918 a pair nested in the steeple of Trinity Lutheran Church, 527 Washington Street.

On June 9, 1994, two American Kestrel nestlings fell from a nest near the Berks County Courthouse at Reed and Washington streets in Reading. Berks County Sheriff's Deputies Christopher Billman and Alan Baumener found one of the fledglings, placed it in a box, and delivered it to Charles Lincoln, a Pennsylvania Game Commission wildlife conservation specialist, at the commission's office near Leesport. Another courthouse employee, Elizabeth Adames, picked up the other Kestrel and had a friend drive her and the bird to the Game Commission office. Lincoln delivered the two birds to Hawk Mountain Sanctuary (*Reading Eagle* and *Reading Times*, June 10, 1994, p. B1). The birds were fostered into local nest boxes near the Sanctuary by C. J. Robertson and successfully fledged.

The American Kestrel responds to man-made nest boxes placed in the proper habitat. In 1995, more than 250 nest boxes within a 25-mile radius of Hawk Mountain Sanctuary were home to more than 110 pairs of American Kestrels and Eastern Screech-Owls. A total of 97 were occupied by Kestrels, which averaged 4.7 eggs and 3.1 fledglings per nesting pair for a total of 303 young.

During the 1950s, Alex Nagy maintained about a half-dozen nest boxes on his parents' 300-acre farm in Albany Township that were used by one or two pairs of falcons each year. In 1961, nine boxes held five pairs of Kestrels that raised 25 young. By the end of the 1986 nesting season, Kestrel boxes totaled 29. In March 1987, Victor Apanius, a graduate student, erected an additional 120 boxes (Bildstein, 1996a:22).

According to Hawk Mountain records, the average egg-laying dates for American Kestrels using Hawk Mountain Sanctuary nest boxes are as follows: 48 pairs - May 2, 1992; 74 pairs - May 3, 1993; 64 pairs - April 28, 1994; 79 pairs - April 23, 1995; and 68 pairs - May 6, 1996.

The average numbers of eggs laid and chicks fledged in more than 200 Hawk Mountain nest boxes are as follows: 86 pairs averaged 4.47 eggs and fledged 1.91 young in 1992; 90 pairs averaged 4.71 eggs and fledged 3.21 young in 1993; 72 pairs averaged 4.57 eggs and fledged 3.35

young in 1994; 97 pairs averaged 4.72 eggs and fledged 3.12 young in 1995; and 90 pairs averaged 4.42 eggs and fledged 2.54 young in 1996 (Bildstein, 1996b).

A Kestrel nested in a Wood Duck box maintained by Jeffrey Schucker in Albany Township in 1994, producing five eggs.

Six sets of eggs in the Levi Mengel Collection were taken from April 30 (1894) to May 22 (1900). Four of the nests were in hollow trees. Mengel found one clutch of four eggs in Albany Township May 14, 1886, "...in a hemlock tree in a nest which was in all probability that of a Crow." He took another set of five eggs from an old Crow's nest in a pine tree south of Birdsboro May 2, 1890.

Egg dates from nest boxes studied in Albany Township by Donald Heintzelman and Nagy from 1959 to 1963 range from April 15 (1961) to July 4 (1959). The latter date is extremely late and may be the result of a second nesting attempt. The mean period of incubation, in days, for eight marked eggs from two [Kestrel] clutches studied on the Nagy farm in 1960 was 30.9 days. (Heintzelman and Nagy, 1968).

Heintzelman also studied the spring and summer food habits of the Kestrels on Nagy's farm in Albany Township from 1960 to 1963, based on examinations of pellets and prey remains. Among insects taken were the Short-horned Grasshopper (*Acrididae*), Periodical Cicada (*Magicicada septendecim*), Libellulid Dragonfly (*Libellulidae*), Beetles (*Coleoptera*), and Ground Beetles (*Carabidae*). Bird species included *Passeriformes* species, *Icteridae* species, Eastern Meadowlark, Common Grackle, Cowbird, *Fringillidae* species, Cardinal, and Grasshopper Sparrow. Mammals taken were Short-tailed Shrew, *Microtinae* species, Meadow Mouse, and Meadow Jumping Mouse. An unusual reptilian prey item Heintzelman found was a Five-lined Skink. He concludes: "...the [Kestrels] which I studied restricted their predation to a few species of animals, in comparison with the wide variety of food items known to form the diet of the species in North America. This illustrates the importance of seasonal and geographical conditions in dictating the diet of this falcon. In Albany Township, *Mircrotinae* (probably *Microtus pennsylvanicus*) were the principal animals taken. *Icteridae* and *Carabidae* appeared less frequently. In 1962, the Periodical Cicada formed only 16.5 per cent of the [Kestrel] diet, although present locally in great abundance. The falcons did not penetrate the forest to exert great predation pressure on the cicadas" (Heintzelman, 1964a).

During this study in Albany Township, Heintzelman photographed in May 1959 a female Kestrel capturing aerial prey, probably a *Lepidoptera* species. On two other occasions he observed a Kestrel capturing prey in flight at Bake Oven Knob in Lehigh County. The Kestrel rarely captures prey which is aloft and seems to be a more efficient predator on slower moving animals (Heintzelman, 1966b).

Heintzelman and Nagy trapped an adult male Kestrel with an unusual tail. The six left rectrices were normal in length but appeared worn. The six right rectrices, however, were about half the length of those on the left side. Evidently all six right rectrices had been pulled simultaneously and were growing back into place. After banding and releasing the bird, they noticed it had little or no difficulty in flying or maneuvering normally (Heintzelman, 1962:204-205).

There are nine specimens- six males and three females - in the Reading Public Museum collection. Mengel collected a female at Virginville April 25, 1884; a female at Pricetown April 29, 1885; a female April 16, 1886; and a male at Slate Hill April 18, 1887. The stomach of a male collected in Wyomissing April 24, 1937, contained one garter snake, and the stomach of a male collected at Beckersville November 7, 1936, contained a meadow mouse and grasshoppers. Other Kestrels in the museum collection are a male from Esterly January 10, 1933; a male from Hamburg December 9, 1933; and a male from Robeson Township November 24, 1935.

Hawk Mountain Counts for the American Kestrel									
1934	11	1949	339	1961	464	1973	479	1985	383
1935	121	1950	234	1962	456	1974	434	1986	455
1936	100	1951	247	1963	260	1975	487	1987	577
1937	141	1952	219	1964	235	1976	413	1988	634
1938	87	1953	220	1965	391	1977	705	1989	839
1939	184	1954	174	1966	539	1978	370	1990	726
1940	60	1955	264	1967	554	1979	544	1991	632
1941	196	1956	204	1968	592	1980	529	1992	546
1942	113	1957	174	1969	537	1981	708	1993	646
1946	99	1958	217	1970	409	1982	400	1994	688
1947	116	1959	281	1971	365	1983	461	1995	655
1948	145	1960	221	1972	393	1984	331	1996	367

Note: These statistics reflect counts from the North Lookout only.

The American Kestrel occurs during the fall migration at Hawk Mountain from July 26 (1996 - Bill Wallace) to November 25 (1968 - Alex Nagy; 1978 - John Bachman, Jim Brett, Seth Benz). The single-day high count is 168 on September 3, 1987 (Jim Brett). The season high is 839 in 1989. The 10-year average from 1987 to 1996 is 640.

Maurice Broun and Ben Goodwin measured the speeds of four migrating Kestrels during the fall of 1942. The speeds ranged from 22 to 36 miles per hour with an average of 26.2 (Broun and Goodwin, 1943:492).

During the spring migration at Hawk Mountain, Jim Olmes recorded a high of eight on April 17, 1984.

The American Kestrel has appeared on the Reading Christmas Bird Count 83 of 86 years, 10 of the last 10, with a maximum of 62 on December 21, 1980. The high for the Hamburg Christmas Bird Count is 128 on December 29, 1991. The peak for the Bernville count is 83 on January 3, 1993.

MERLIN *Falco columbarius*
Very rare spring, regular but uncommon fall migrant

A regular but uncommon migrant in fall, the Merlin is rare in spring and very rare or casual in winter.

Winter sight records of this species are accepted with caution, as Sharp-shinned Hawks and American Kestrels have frequently been misidentified as this rarer bird, which normally winters from the Gulf States to northern South America. A specimen in the Reading Public Museum collection was taken at Wyomissing on January 3, 1886. Matt Spence saw one February 16, 1948, near Green Hills. Ken Lebo found a Merlin March 4, 1995, in the Fleetwood-Lyons area, and Laurie Goodrich reported one near Kempton February 16, 1996.

The Merlin has appeared on the Reading Christmas Bird Count December 22, 1957, and December 26, 1960.

There are many fall observations from Hawk Mountain, where the Merlin is seen more often than elsewhere. Seasonal counts have fluctuated widely from a low of seven in 1972 to a high of 168 in 1995. The 10-year average from 1987 to 1996 is 94. The single-day high count is 34 on October 22, 1989 (Mark Blauer). The extreme dates are from July 26 (1996 - Bill Wallace) to December 10 (1995 - Steve Thorpe), the bulk of the flight taking place in October. A male specimen in the Reading Public Museum collection was taken in Eckville October 18, 1932.

During the fall of 1942, Maurice Broun and and Ben Goodwin recorded the flight speed of a migrating Merlin at 28 miles per hour (Broun and Goodwin, 1943:492).

Earl Poole writes in his journal of a Merlin preying on shorebirds at the recently flooded Lake Ontelaunee on October 3, 1929:

On my first arrival, the small marsh near the road was alive with sandpipers which were constantly circling about in flocks. There were 25 White-rumps in one flock, and others were scattered with the Red-backs [Dunlins] and Semipalmated Sandpipers. They were easily picked out in flight. While watching one of the flocks that had just settled in the drift along the high water mark in the flooded area, a Pigeon Hawk [Merlin] dropped among the flock, reached out his talons, and gripped one of the poor Semipalmateds, flying off with its hapless victim screaming in terror as it bore him off.

Hawk Mountain Counts for the Merlin									
1934	9	1949	24	1961	13	1973	13	1985	36
1935	19	1950	44	1962	20	1974	10	1986	78
1936	34	1951	15	1963	26	1975	19	1987	51
1937	10	1952	47	1964	10	1976	20	1988	49
1938	12	1953	11	1965	20	1977	27	1989	157
1939	43	1954	22	1966	21	1978	16	1990	144
1940	11	1955	23	1967	16	1979	52	1991	90
1941	34	1956	10	1968	13	1980	29	1992	73
1942	17	1957	21	1969	27	1981	47	1993	80
1946	20	1958	19	1970	15	1982	20	1994	54
1947	10	1959	17	1971	12	1983	21	1995	168
1948	19	1960	25	1972	7	1984	21	1996	127

Note: These statistics reflect counts from the North Lookout only.

It is rare in spring. Poole had but five records between April 2 (1933) and May 10 (1936). Kerry Grim found a Merlin perched in a tree along the Schuylkill River in Tilden Township near Hamburg on April 16, 1978. Grim saw one flying at the Shartlesville State Game Lands 110 on May 5, 1990, and found a male perched inside a tree line there on May 20, 1996. On April 14, 1991, Matt Spence, Bart Smith, and Rudy Keller observed a Merlin by the dam breast at Lake Ontelaunee. Laurie Goodrich recorded a Merlin on April 23, 1994, during the spring migration count at Hawk Mountain, and Bill Wallace and Eric Atkinson saw a brown Merlin from the North Lookout April 28, 1996. Two birds in the Reading Public Museum collection were taken in April. Levi Mengel collected a male April 1, 1888, in Albany Township, and another was taken "about April 1924" in Wyomissing. Poole notes in his journal that a female Merlin was shot at the Janssen estate in Wyomissing on April 13, 1929.

The Merlin, or Pigeon Hawk, is not the so-called "Pigeon Hawk" of the Pennsylvania Germans. The names "Dauwedieb" and "Dauwehabbich," and the general name of "Schdoosswoi," and nearly all of the other names used for the accipiters have been given to this species. William Rupp states that this bird is an enemy of all small birds, but it is highly doubtful that any of the names given were based on accurate identification of the species. Most of them, it seems, were intended for the accipiters and the Kestrel, with which this small falcon may be readily confused (Rupp, 1946:94 - 95).

PEREGRINE FALCON *Falco peregrinus*
Rare migrant and winter visitor

Like the Bald Eagle, the Peregrine Falcon suffered the negative effects of persistent organochloride pesticides including DDT, and its numbers plummeted from 1946 to 1972 until nearly the entire eastern population was eliminated. The pesticides caused reproductive failure by eggshell thinning, and the weight of the incubating adult would crush the eggs.

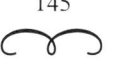

The Peregrine Falcon in Berks County has always been a rare migrant and winter visitor most frequently seen at Hawk Mountain and Lake Ontelaunee. The earliest fall record is July 2 (1942 - Earl Poole), and the latest spring observation is May 18 (1992 - Rudy Keller in Pike Township).

Earl Poole's local Berks records cover every month except June and indicate a slight increase in numbers during March, which probably represents the northbound migration. The fall migration evidently starts about mid-September with a period of comparative abundance during October.

Poole writes in his journal of his first visit to the recently flooded Lake Ontelaunee on March 31, 1929:

Our last stop was at the new Maidencreek Dam, where we [Poole and Byron Nunemacher] had the thrill of seeing about 100 ducks... all bunched on the water and apparently satisfied to stay there. The reason later became evident. I had been watching the group of Scaups, when they flew. At about that time two Black Ducks detached themselves from a flying flock and started down toward the water. Suddenly as I had my glasses on them, a fine male Duck Hawk [Peregrine Falcon] appeared from nowhere and swooped. I saw him stretch out one leg, turn over, and make a grab for one of the Blacks, which dodged, and both hit the water in a hurry. The hawk started to soar in short circles, getting higher and higher. All this time as I watched it a flock of hundreds of Pipits was continuously passing over, looking through the glasses like black stars against the sky. The consciousness that there was still a flock of 70 unidentified ducks just upstream made me forget the Peregrine after a few minutes, and I failed to watch him further.

This was a red-letter day for Berks.

Later the same year on September 19, Poole writes in his journal of the flight of another Peregrine Falcon at Lake Ontelaunee:

This morning an adult Tiercel made an attack on a group of Yellowlegs, but could not get them to rise from the grassy marsh. Later it circled overhead, alternately flapping and soaring in a leisurely manner. As it drifted to the south, I noticed it quickening its pace, flapping rapidly and steadily now and gaining altitude until it was invisible to the naked eye. I kept my glasses on it, however, and saw it start on an inclined plane increasing its speed and setting its wings in a long swoop until it disappeared behind a rise. The length of the "stoop" must have been at least 3/8th of a mile. What happened at the bottom of the glide I could not see, but it had apparently started for its mark fully a mile away.

Even though this is one of the rarest species to be seen along the Kittatinny Ridge, more Peregrine Falcons are seen during the fall at Hawk Mountain than anywhere else in Berks. The early fall migration date there is August 2 (1959 - Maurice Broun), and the late date is December 2 (1957 - M.B.). The greatest number seen seasonally during the pre-DDT years is 45 in 1941. The high count after DDT was banned in 1972 is 51 in 1989. The 10-year average from 1987 to 1996 is 36.

On October 3, 1993, a Peregrine Falcon captured a Sharp-shinned Hawk in flight near the North Lookout: "A Peregrine was steaming down the ridge, diving on a flock of Crows. As it neared the Lookout, a bold Sharpie rocketed out of the treetops and shot straight at the falcon to harass it. The Peregrine flipped sideways and in a lightning moment, executed a brutal 'snap,' latching onto the smaller hawk. Slowed by the weight of its prize, the falcon struggled across the valley to settle momentarily at Three Quarters Lookout" (Viverette, 1994a:14).

The single-day high count is 11 on October 7, 1937, when Maurice Broun watched nine adult males and two adult females pass the North Lookout, most of which came in pairs after 2 p.m.

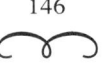

During the fall of 1942, Broun and Ben Goodwin measured the flight speeds of three migrating Peregrine Falcons. The speeds ranged from 28 to 32 miles per hour with an average of 30 (Broun and Goodwin, 1943:492).

On October 27, 1950, Robert Cook observed a Peregrine Falcon feeding on Rock Doves at Penn Square in Reading.

Recent fall sightings away from the ridge include one at Nolde Forest October 1, 1987 (Mike Slater, Scott Schreiber); one immature at Lake Ontelaunee September 26, 1993 (Matt Spence); and one at Lake Ontelaunee October 27, 1993 (M.S.).

As part of the Peregrine Falcon reintroduction program, the Pennsylvania Game Commission placed nestling Peregrine Falcons at several sites in Reading from 1993 to 1995. Todd Morgan of Birdsboro oversaw the project.

In 1993, a male and female Peregrine were "hacked" from the top of the Berks County Services Center at Reed and Court streets. Hacking is the process whereby immature birds are gradually released into the wild. The male soon disappeared, but the female survived the summer. She was found dead, however, in Maine in 1995.

In 1994 three falcons, two males and one female, were hacked from atop the Eisenhower Apartments at Ninth and Franklin streets. The Services Center was not used in 1994 because of logistical problems encountered during hacking, according to Daniel Brauning, wildlife biologist for the Pennsylvania Game Commission. The Eisenhower Apartments provided a lower building than the Services Center with numerous perches and less reflective glass. The birds were banded on June 15, when they were placed in the hack box. The box was scheduled to be opened on June 20, but apparently it was opened prematurely by maintenance personnel on June 18. All three birds fledged that evening. The males were observed on the neighboring apartment building the next day, and the female was detected nearby with a radio telemetry signal, but was not observed. All three birds were observed on various buildings within three blocks of the Eisenhower Apartments for the following seven weeks. They spent some time on the Services Center, the tallest building in the area. They returned to the hack site daily to feed until August 3, when the birds were last seen. Food continued to be placed on the site and was used until August 16, when birds were last believed to use the hack facility. The female from that group made it to Toronto, Ontario, where she was found nesting the following year on a 12-story building. Canadian Fish and Wildlife officials documented two young, three weeks old, on June 14, 1995. This represents the first nesting activity of a Peregrine Falcon hacked in the recent state-wide program. Brauning believes it is unlikely that a one-year-old falcon would nest successfully, and she may have taken over the care of young produced by an adult falcon. She returned to the area in 1996 and nested again.

In 1995 five falcons were hacked from the Eisenhower Apartments at Ninth and Franklin streets. On June 3, three birds that were taken from a nest on the Walt Whitman Bridge in Philadelphia were placed in a hack box on top of the apartment building. On June 14 the last two males, younger than the other birds, were placed in the box, which was opened on June 15. The

Hawk Mountain Counts for the Peregrine Falcon									
1934	19	1949	35	1961	20	1973	9	1985	12
1935	14	1950	33	1962	30	1974	7	1986	25
1936	36	1951	22	1963	21	1975	6	1987	31
1937	41	1952	34	1964	19	1976	8	1988	15
1938	24	1953	13	1965	13	1977	11	1989	51
1939	37	1954	28	1966	22	1978	9	1990	48
1940	25	1955	35	1967	16	1979	14	1991	44
1941	45	1956	16	1968	12	1980	9	1992	41
1942	36	1957	15	1969	17	1981	20	1993	50
1946	26	1958	23	1970	17	1982	6	1994	24
1947	18	1959	35	1971	9	1983	8	1995	28
1948	33	1960	18	1972	6	1984	8	1996	39

Note: These statistics reflect counts from the North Lookout only.

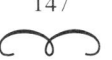

older birds came out of the box within a day. One flew and the others stayed with the younger two. In the following days the oldest bird started flying well. The youngest female hit the ground twice but later started to fly well after being returned to the box. The two youngest males disappeared on June 18 and were never seen again. It was rumored that they were taken by local residents and ended up in a cockfight. The three oldest birds hacked out without incident and by July 21 there were no more signs of the birds.

The Peregrine Falcon has appeared on the Reading Christmas Bird Count six of 86 years, none in the last 10. All records are of single birds.

An immature male Peregrine Falcon in the Reading Public Museum collection taken at what is now Hawk Mountain on October 6, 1929, by Lester Leinbach matches specimens of the very dark northwestern race, *F. p. pealei*. Its cere, eyes, and feet were greenish yellow, and its stomach contained one Pectoral Sandpiper. Another male taken at Eckville October 3, 1933, by S. Lutz is also in the collection. Its stomach contained one warbler species.

GYRFALCON *Falco rusticolus*
Casual migrant

All three color morphs - the white, gray, and black - of the Gyrfalcon have occurred in Berks County.

Maurice Broun observed a white Gyrfalcon *F. r. candicans* at Hawk Mountain on November 2, 1934. Rosalie Edge, Mrs. M. H. Edey, and Broun saw a dark morph Gryrfalcon *F. r. obsoletus* at Hawk Mountain on October 12, 1934. Broun saw another dark morph bird from the road on October 16, 1934, that is not included on the North Lookout counts. He saw another dark bird October 16, 1936. Broun recorded a dark morph Gyrfalcon September 15, 1940, and writes: "The Black Gyrfalcon was indeed a surprise, considering the incredible date, September 15th, when after the passage of nearly three hundred hawks, it was seen late in the day by George Pyle and myself. The bird was carefully identified and studied with 18x glasses." Bob and Clinton Miller observed one in the dark plumage over Hawk Mountain on February 22, 1953. Ned Smith and Jim Brett observed a dark morph Gyrfalcon fly over the North Lookout November 2, 1975.

Laurie Goodrich writes about the most recent Gyrfalcon sighting at Hawk Mountain on November 10, 1988:

...blustery south winds foretold impending rain. The thick haze obscured the view beyond Owl's Head and the East Rocks. The first bird of the day was an immature Bald Eagle gliding through the thick gray mist - an omen of good things to come. After a wait, a second raptor - a Redtail - emerged at eye level. As I watched it approach, I noticed a distant Redtail-sized speck approaching on the same path. I swung my binoculars back to the close Redtail to determine its age. Within seconds the distant speck overtook the Redtail and dove on it from behind. The Redtail veered toward the forest and the new arrival careened toward the Lookout. It passed so close that it had to bank belly-up to go around the trees behind the Lookout. In seconds it flapped out of sight. With its long pointed wings and massive brown-streaked body, there was no mistaking its identity - an immature Gyrfalcon! Among the rarest of our migrant raptors, Gyrfalcons have only been sighted at Hawk Mountain lookouts on five other occasions since 1934! Although only 71 more hawks were sighted before a steady rain ended the count, it was the most exciting day of the season for me (Goodrich, 1989a:30).

Hawk Mountain Counts for the Gyrfalcon									
1934	2	1949	0	1961	0	1973	0	1985	0
1935	0	1950	0	1962	0	1974	0	1986	0
1936	1	1951	0	1963	0	1975	1	1987	0
1937	0	1952	0	1964	0	1976	0	1988	1
1938	0	1953	0	1965	0	1977	0	1989	0
1939	0	1954	0	1966	0	1978	0	1990	0
1940	1	1955	0	1967	0	1979	0	1991	0
1941	0	1956	0	1968	0	1980	0	1992	0
1942	0	1957	0	1969	0	1981	0	1993	0
1946	0	1958	0	1970	0	1982	0	1994	0
1947	0	1959	0	1971	0	1983	0	1995	0
1948	0	1960	0	1972	0	1984	0	1996	0

Note: These statistics reflect counts from the North Lookout only.

"Probable" light Gyrfalcons were observed at the Route 183 hawk watch October 10 (Dean Kendall) and November 13, 1993 (Pat Santee, Ann Marie Liebner). Robert and Anne MacClay recorded a dark bird October 16 and a light bird November 27, 1982, at Route 183. The most recent record there is of a light bird October 28, 1996, seen by the MacClays and Harold Silagy. Robert MacClay writes: "It flipped and showed all white. As it came toward us it looked like a large, white Peregrine. Other Gyrs I saw appeared first more Goshawk-like. But it turned and showed us top and bottom as it passed... all white, no brown flecks even, nice dark wing tips."

Earl Poole saw a light gray individual at Lake Ontelaunee on October 28, 1941. An immature female Peregrine Falcon was near at the time, and this bird was definitely larger and grayer in color, contrasting with the buffy and brownish tones of the Peregrine.

Some sight records of the lighter Gyrfalcons are apparently misidentifications of either pale adult male Northern Harriers or Peregrine Falcons.

An unsexed (probably female) specimen in the first-year plumage of the white phase was taken near Mountain Inn, Carbon County, on November 11, 1928, by Samuel Kerns of Slatington, from whom it was acquired by the Reading Public Museum (Poole, 1933a: 97-98).

RING-NECKED PHEASANT *Phasianus colchicus*
Resident

Introduced in the state by the Pennsylvania Game Commission in 1915, the Ring-necked Pheasant is the most commonly hunted game bird in Berks County. In previous years, it was abundant in many parts of the county, particularly on the Lake Ontelaunee watershed, which served as a center of distribution for much of the surrounding country.

However, with increasing suburbanization and cleaner farming practices that reduce the amount of edge and other "rough" habitat, the Ring-necked Pheasant has become less common throughout the county, its decline most dramatically pronounced during the 1980s. Currently, there is only a small, viable wild population, and most birds seen are stocked each fall by the game commission.

Numbers of Ring-necked Pheasants on the Hamburg Christmas Bird Count set national bird count records for 1969, 1970, and 1973. During those years 1,468 were counted January 1, 1970; 1,232 on January 2, 1971; and 812 on December 23, 1973. After the 1981 count year, numbers have not broken 100 on the Hamburg count. A low of 10 was recorded December 17, 1988.

The first Reading Christmas Bird Count record is of one bird in 1926. The Ring-necked Pheasant has appeared 69 of 86 years, 10 of the last 10, with a maximum of 934 on December 31, 1961. After 1981, no more than 100 have been recorded during any year. The peak for the Bernville count is 36 on January 4, 1987, and December 30, 1995. The Bernville count began January 5, 1986.

Earl Poole writes in 1964: "At present it is our most popular game bird, and should be able to stand the tremendous hunting pressure indefinitely, with regular restocking." However, the loss of habitat has been the most important factor in the decline of this bird in Berks.

Nests with full sets of eggs have been found anywhere from the first week in May to mid-July, the latter date probably representing a second nesting.

RUFFED GROUSE *Bonasa umbellus*

Fairly common resident

The Ruffed Grouse, Pennsylvania's State Bird, is a fairly common resident in the mountainous districts and heavy woodlands of northern, eastern, and southern Berks County. It has been found sparingly this century as close to Reading as Mount Penn, Deer Path Hill, Guldin Hill, and Flying Hill.

This species is subject to periods of fluctuation, and may be comparatively rare for several seasons, then return to a period of comparative abundance.

Maurice Broun writes: "In the winter the grouse come to feast on the buds of the poplar trees or on the sumac, visible from our kitchen window. We have watched as many as four grouse in one tree, feasting with patrician decorum. Grouse have been abundant on our mountain, but the deadly ice storms of the winter of 1948 depleted their numbers as effectively as though the birds had been caught in the grip of an epidemic plague" (Broun, 1949a:130).

This bird is more often heard than seen, its drumming carrying long distances.

The Ruffed Grouse has appeared on the Reading Christmas Bird Count 48 of 86 years, nine of the last 10, with a maximum of nine on December 16, 1979. The peak for the Hamburg Christmas Bird Count is 42 on December 28, 1986. The high for the Bernville count is four on January 4, 1987.

Three sets of eggs in the Levi Mengel collection were taken at Moselem May 17, 1887; at Blue Marsh May 24, 1890; and at Monocacy May 28, 1887. Another set was taken near Topton May 6, 1906. Clutch sizes in these sets average 12 to 13 eggs.

The Pennsylvania German names for the Ruffed Grouse in Berks County include "Fassant" and "Fersant." All names for the grouse are based on the European names for the pheasant. Calvin S. Stump of Maxatawny reports the name "Buschfersant" in speaking of the grouse that were very abundant in the Pine Swamp near Eckville at the foot of the Blue Mountain. He also reports the name "die Globber," derived from their drumming, in the Allemangel section of Albany Township. W. W. Kemp of Alburtis gives the name "es Buschhinkel" for a wild pheasant. Raymond E. Kiebach of Reading reports that the grouse was spoken of as "en Fersant," rarely as "Baerrickfersant," until the Ring-necked Pheasant came and took the former name. After that, "Baerrickfersant" was more generally applied to the grouse (Rupp, 1946:98-100).

William Rupp writes, "The Rev. Michael Schlatter in his 'Journal' tells how on November 2, 1750, he left the home of Pastor George Michael Weiss in Goshenhoppen and went 'to the so-called flying mountains in Oly [sic] - which are so called on account of the multitude of wild Indian chickens which abound there' (Henry Harbaugh, *The Life of Rev. Michael Schlatter*, Philadelphia, 1857).

"Dr. Henry Harbaugh adds the note that 'prairie-hens, which still abound in the western prairie, were abundant at an early day along the south side of the Blue Mountains.' This may be a reference to the now extinct 'heath hen' (*Tympanuchus cupido*) which is said to have been a common bird from Massachusetts to Virginia until the early part of the last century. Or was Schlatter thinking of the ruffed grouse? ... Obviously some of the pioneers were not always sure of what they were seeing, whether grouse or quail or heath hen!" (Rupp, 1946:101)

WILD TURKEY *Meleagris gallopavo*

Increasingly common resident

Although the Wild Turkey was extirpated from most of the southeastern part of Pennsylvania during the nineteenth century, a few flocks persisted in isolated forest areas, such as the Kittatinny Ridge, until programs of restocking with farm-raised birds came into effect. Since 1918 it has been re-established and restocked periodically in many sections from which it had been absent for a century or more.

Currently, the Wild Turkey has become increasingly common, nesting in woodlands throughout Berks County. Flocks of between 20 and 50 Wild Turkeys have come to feeders during winter in eastern Berks County during the 1990s. Catherine Elwell counted 48 Wild Turkeys in District Township March 11, 1995. Jim Brett saw 128 on Hamm's Hill in Albany Township August 16, 1996.

It has appeared recently on Mount Penn and on Neversink Mountain. On April 2, 1992, a Wild Turkey stopped traffic in the 1300 and 1400 blocks of Cotton Street in Reading, strutting down the middle of the street. Concerned residents herded the bird up South 14th Street and back onto Neversink Mountain (*Reading Times* and *Reading Eagle*, April 3, 1993, p. B1).

Earl Poole spoke with older residents of Albany Township in northern Berks who insisted that a few Wild Turkeys remained on the Pinnacle region of Berks County until the practice of stocking came into effect. They were there in 1890, and to Poole's personal knowledge had been there continuously since 1921.

The Wild Turkey was listed by John F. Hofman in 1890. D. Frank Keller reported it as breeding sparingly in the Blue Mountains (Warren, 1890:109).

In 1921 Daniel Hollenbach, who lived near Strausstown, spoke of killing one each year near there, and six or seven were shot during the season of 1923 and 1924. On May 23, 1926, Poole saw a hen near Eckville that acted as though it had young nearby.

It has also been seen at frequent intervals on and about the Hawk Mountain Sanctuary. Maurice Broun writes: "I shall never forget a certain quiet afternoon in late October, 1936, when I was alone on duty. A subdued rustle in the low growth in back of me, at one of the lower promontories, caused me to turn round very slowly, in time to see four wild turkeys emerge from the undergrowth and run stealthily over the rocks. I had fine views of the birds. They saw me and flew over to the nearest rock-pile, where three of them scurried away, while the fourth volplaned into the 'kettle,' a beautiful sight" (Broun, 1949a:197).

A specimen in the Reading Public Museum was taken at Eckville November 12, 1932.

The Wild Turkey first appeared on the Reading Christmas Bird Count in 1984 and has been seen seven of 86 years, six of the last 10, with a high of 21 on December 19, 1993. The high for the Hamburg Christmas Bird Count is 83 on December 31, 1989. The peak for the Bernville count is 11 on January 2, 1995, its first appearance on that count.

The Pennsylvania German names for the Wild Turkey are "der wild Welschhaahne" for the male and "es wild Welschhinkel" for the female. The plural is "die wilde Welschhinkel" (Rupp, 1946:110).

NORTHERN BOBWHITE *Colinus virginianus*

Rare resident

It is not known if a viable wild population of the Northern Bobwhite still exists in Berks County. Most recent observations are of tame releases or escapes.

Throughout this century, the Northern Bobwhite was subject to pronounced fluctuations in population but was generally rare. Earl Poole last considered it abundant in 1929. Severe winters, overshooting, the abandonment of the old practice of maintaining marginal strips along fence rows, and the mistaken assumption that southern stock could replace the shot-out coveys of native birds, all have contributed to the precarious situation of the Northern Bobwhite.

Extremely cold, snowy winters, such as those of 1917–1918 and 1934–1935, reduced the local population to such a point that several years were required to recover any degree of the Northern Bobwhite's abundance. Deep snow prevents the bird from finding food.

To offset the declines, numerous efforts have been made by the Pennsylvania Game Commission, private individuals, and sportsmen's organizations to introduce birds from the western and southern states, as well as Mexico, without success, as the less hardy southern birds are unable to stand our severe winters. What effect these birds may have had on the native population through cross-breeding was the subject of some controversy. As far as Berks County was concerned, Poole could see no difference between the Northern Bobwhites shot during his time and those collected 80 years previously. If any interbreeding had occurred, it was negligible.

The Northern Bobwhite has appeared on the Reading Christmas Bird Count 38 of 86 years, none in the last 10, with a maximum of 49 in 1928. The last Reading count record is 13 on December 21, 1980. It was recorded during two of 32 years on the Hamburg Christmas Bird Count: 18 on January 1, 1970, and seven on January 2, 1966.

Levi Mengel took sets of from nine to 15 eggs between May 17 (1887) and June 14 (1890).

The Pennsylvania German names heard along the Blue Mountain in northern Berks County for the Bobwhite are "Badrisesl" and "Badries" (Rupp, 1946:106-107).

KING RAIL *Rallus elegans*

Very rare migrant

The highly secretive King Rail is a very rare migrant and occasional summer resident in extensive marshy areas. There are no recent nesting records.

Levi Mengel, who found a nest and 10 eggs at Blue Marsh June 8, 1900, noted, "The nest of dry grass [was] on [the] ground in tuft of timothy in hay field on slope 50 yards from marsh, which was flooded."

An adult was seen in a marsh at the head of Lake Ontelaunee on several occasions between June 15 and July 20, 1930, and until October 4 (Anna and Mary Deeter, Earl Poole, Florence Hergesheimer). During the following summer, Earl Poole saw another one at the same place on August 9 and September 13, 1931. Two young accompanied by an adult were seen frequently there between July 17 and September 11, 1932. When first noticed these young rails were unable to fly (Poole, 1935:28).

Lester Leinbach captured a specimen now in the Reading Public Museum collection at Egelman's reservoir on Mount Penn October 1, 1934. Arthur Sigman found one dead in a steel trap near Elverson on January 7, 1937.

Robert Cook saw one in a meadow near Geigertown March 30, 1949. On May 11, 16, and 30, 1958, Charles Schaich,

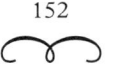

Matt Spence, and Poole saw a King Rail in a marsh at the head of Lake Ontelaunee. Schaich found two in the same place on June 23.

These were the last records reported in Berks County until Ken Lebo heard a King Rail calling at Glen Morgan Lake near Morgantown May 19, 1996. That location currently has the most extensive marsh habitat in the county.

D. Frank Keller listed the King Rail as a straggler (Warrren, 1890:68).

VIRGINIA RAIL *Rallus limicola*
Rare migrant and nester

The Virginia Rail's secretive habits and confinement to marshy areas cause it to be overlooked unless a special search is made for it and its distinctive calls are known. It evidently became scarcer year after year as the marshy meadows were drained or filled in, although it apparently does not require such wet marshes as the Sora does.

By 1947, Earl Poole had 62 observations between April 19 (1939) and October 5 (1930). Charles Schaich saw one at Lake Ontelaunee April 12 (1953) and one there on December 15 (1957). Two specimens in the Reading Public Museum collection were taken at Lake Ontelaunee on November 27, 1930, and at Hopewell on December 25, 1936.

Levi Mengel found it nesting in Exeter Township May 24, 1903, a clutch of 11 eggs in a nest of dry, reedy stems. Walter H. Leibelsperger found it nesting at Moselem on two occasions. Sets taken June 1, 1918, and June 7, 1921, are in the museum collection.

Poole saw a Virginia Rail carrying nesting material at Moselem July 7, 1929. He found downy young in the Reading Public Museum park July 12, 1931, and at Peters Creek August 9 and 12, 1936, and on July 22 and August 1, 1939.

One record from Hawk Mountain is of a badly mangled bird, evidently killed by a car, that Maurice Broun picked up on the road one-third of a mile uphill from Schaumboch's on May 28, 1951. A drizzle in the early morning apparently grounded the bird.

A Virginia Rail found on Neversink Mountain with both legs broken was brought to Joan Silagy for possible rehabilitation on September 27, 1971, but it died several days later.

Recent observations include one at Peters Creek on April 22, 1992, and two there four days later on April 26 (Matt Spence). One called in a marshy pasture near Virginville May 28, 1995 (Rudy Keller).

Ken Lebo has found the Virginia Rail at Glen Morgan Lake from May 17 (1995, two birds) to July 24 (1996) with a high of four rails May 31, 1996.

D. Frank Keller regarded the Virginia Rail in Berks County as an uncommon summer visitor (Warren, 1890:70).

SORA *Porzana carolina*
Rare

Like the other rails, the Sora is rare. This, together with its secretive nature and nocturnal habits, makes it difficult to detect. The draining of marshes during this century has reduced its habitat.

Earl Poole's earliest observation is April 30 (1939) and the latest is October 19 (1932). Seth Benz and Catherine Elwell found a Sora in the Hahn Mountain meadow in Albany Township November 1, 1982.

Most recent records are from May. Matt Spence recorded Soras at Peters Creek on the following dates: May 12, 1959; May 10, 1970; May 12, 1974; and May 9, 1976. Kerry Grim found one in a marsh along Lowland Road in Tilden Township May 18, 1978.

Ken Lebo has recorded the Sora at Glen Morgan Lake from May 4 (1996, six birds) to July 5 (1996, two birds).

Stanley Bright and Earl Poole watched a Sora carrying nesting material at Moselem Springs May 20, 1922. Charles Schaich saw one immature at Lake Ontelaunee September 5 and 7, 1953. In 1957 a family of three birds of the year was observed almost daily from July 16 to 23 at Moselem (Earl Poole).

On September 12, 1970, an immature Sora was found dead atop a snag at the North Lookout at Hawk Mountain. The bird was apparently left by a predator.

Levi Mengel took a set of 13 eggs at Virginville near a mill dam May 30, 1896. D. Frank Keller listed it as a breeder (Warren, 1890:71).

PURPLE GALLINULE *Porphyrula martinica*
Accidental

Matt Spence found a Purple Gallinule dead on Ontelaunee Drive near Peters Creek September 18, 1983. The body was crushed, but the bird's wings and a photograph of the bird are now in the Reading Public Museum collection.

COMMON MOORHEN *Gallinula chloropus*
Rare and local

The Common Moorhen is a rather rare and irregular migrant in marshes and shallow sloughs.

It has nested in Berks County. Matt Spence saw a young bird with its parent June 26, 1960. On July 20, 1971, Earl Poole saw two adults and four young at Lake Ontelaunee. Spence saw two adults and three young September 12, 1971, at Peters Creek. The late date at Peters Creek that year is November 6 (Matt Spence).

The most recently recorded nesting occurred at Glen Morgan Lake near Morgantown. Ken Lebo saw two adults there May 9, 1995. On July 2, he and Matt Wlasniewski recorded two adults and six young. On July 30, there were one adult and five young at the lake. A pair bred in 1996, raising two young (Ken Lebo).

In the Ontelaunee-Moselem area and elsewhere in Berks County, the Common Moorhen is a rather rare migrant in spring, having been recorded between April 10 (found dead) and June 6 (1979 - Kerry Grim at Lowland Road in Tilden Township).

Individuals have been seen during the summer on several occasions. Byron Nunemacher and Earl Rollman saw one at Moselem on July 14, 1928. Bill Munroe found one at Gring's Mill along the Union Canal July 11, 1989.

It is quite rare in autumn as a migrant, seen between September 28 (1929) and October 23 (1932).

An immature Common Moorhen flew into a window at Conrad Weiser High School in Robesonia October 7, 1979 (Lester Breininger).

AMERICAN COOT *Fulica americana*

Fairly common migrant; rare and local nester

The American Coot is a fairly common migrant and a rare and local breeder on sluggish streams, lakes, and ponds, occasionally wintering as long as open water is available. There are records for every month of the year, but it is most common during the migrations, particularly in the fall.

There are two nesting records. In 1968, the American Coot was recorded during every month. Warren Faust found a nest May 18, 1968, at Peters Creek and saw two pairs and 16 young throughout July. Harold Lebo recorded an adult with five young at Glen Morgan Lake July 8, 1995.

Single birds remained on Lake Ontelaunee throughout the summers of 1930, 1939, and 1957, and a pair was seen in a likely breeding area on June 3, 1956, but no nests or young were found. N. Musser saw a pair at Elverson from June 9 to July 10, 1957.

When not wintering, the American Coot has arrived at Lake Ontelaunee as early as March 7 (1954) and except for summering individuals was last seen in spring on May 28 (1961).

The earliest fall arrival date is September 15 (1929). The fall departure is very irregular, anywhere from November 5 (1940) to the freeze-up, often in January. During exceptionally mild winters, a small flock may remain through the winter, as in 1939–1940, 1948-1949, and 1955-1956.

An American Coot was photographed in a hemlock just below the North Lookout at Hawk Mountain Sanctuary by Peter C. Doyle and Dr. Carlos Benevides on September 25, 1965. The day before, the Lookout was shrouded in fog, and the bird, lost in the mists, apparently dropped to the Lookout and then into the hemlock where it remained, perhaps injured, until it was photographed, after which it disappeared into the woods, probably never to emerge (Broun, 1966:11).

Ken Lebo counted over 200 Coots at Glen Morgan Lake November 11, 1995, and November 16 and December 15, 1996.

The American Coot has appeared on the Reading Christmas Bird Count 37 of 86 years, 10 of the last 10, with a maximum of 138 on December 18, 1983. The peak for the Hamburg Christmas Bird Count is five on December 28, 1975. The high for the Bernville count is four on January 5, 1986.

Herbert Beck gives the Pennsylvania German name "Shdink Ent" for the Coot. He says it is so called on account of its foul odor on being drawn. It is sometimes shot when mistaken for a game duck (Rupp, 1946:113).

SANDHILL CRANE *Grus canadensis*

Casual

The first Berks County record of a Sandhill Crane occurred April 28, 1963. Fred Blacker, fire warden on duty at the Port Clinton fire tower near Hawk Mountain, reported a huge, slow-flying bird passing in a northerly direction and at close range at 6:30 p.m. His detailed description given to Maurice Broun fits only the Sandhill Crane.

On April 26, 1969, Chris Martin saw one from the South Lookout at Hawk Mountain Sanctuary (Alex Nagy). Fred Wetzel observed one from the North Lookout October 17, 1970. Seth Benz recorded single birds at the North Lookout October 11, 1978, and October 13, 1980.

A Sandhill Crane remained at Blue Marsh Lake from August 24 to October 9, 1983 (Joan Silagy, many observers).

One flew over the Route 183 hawk watch December 2, 1985 (Robert and Anne MacClay). Harold and Joan Silagy saw single birds from the Route 183 lookout on August 29 and September 1, 1992, then one at Blue Marsh Lake the same day, September 1.

Howard S. Huenecke reported five flying over Bally May 16, 1992. A retired wildlife biologist, Huenecke has seen thousands of these birds in North and South Dakota.

Matt Spence spotted a Sandhill Crane flying over the closed portion of Route 82 along Hay Creek near Birdsboro May 7, 1995. Harold Lebo saw one flying near Plowville November 17, 1996.

BLACK-BELLIED PLOVER *Pluvialis squatarola*
Uncommon migrant

Unrecorded before 1929, the Black-bellied Plover usually occurs on extensive mud flats during migrations, more frequently in fall than in spring. It is more regular in its occurrence than the American Golden-Plover, with which it is sometimes confused.

Earl Poole saw it seven times at Lake Ontelaunee in spring between May 5 (1935) and June 6 (1939) and on 44 occasions in fall between August 18 (1929) and November 13 (1932). Charles Schaich has a later record, November 17 (1957). Dean Kendall saw two at Blue Marsh Lake October 23, 1991.

Poole never saw more than six individuals in Berks County at any one time (October 12 to 28, 1938), but on the night of May 29, 1933, following a violent thunderstorm, he heard many Black-bellied Plovers calling over the city of Reading at about 10:30 p.m., as they apparently flew back and forth, confused by the city lights.

There are three records from Hawk Mountain. One flew north over the North Lookout September 16, 1950 (Maurice Broun). One was observed October 15, 1955 (M.B.), and 14 flew past October 14, 1959, following the passage of five Golden-Plovers (M.B.).

Robert and Anne MacClay saw 19 fly down the center of the ridge at the Route 183 hawk watch September 8, 1983.

Ken Lebo and Rick Wiltraut found 23 Black-bellied Plovers on the mud flats off Water Street at Lake Ontelaunee August 17, 1994. Only two remained the next day (Matt Wlasniewski).

D. Frank Keller listed it as a straggler (Warren, 1890:98).

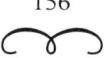

AMERICAN GOLDEN-PLOVER *Pluvialis dominicus*
Uncommon fall migrant

The American Golden-Plover was unreported for many years prior to 1929, but since the creation of Lake Ontelaunee it has been recorded in the immediate neighborhood and is seen with some frequency at this site whenever the receding waters leave broad mud flats exposed.

Earl Poole had 28 observations between August 13 (1957) and November 20 (1932).

Matt Spence recorded a high count of 37 American Golden-Plovers at Lake Ontelaunee October 12, 1963, a year when the lake level was extremely low. From one to 22 were seen there continuously from August 13 to October 16, 1957, by dozens of observers.

The American Golden-Plover has been seen flying over Hawk Mountain between September 7 (1952 - Maurice Broun, a flock of nine) and October 14 (1959 - M.B., five birds).

Robert Cook saw three on the mud flats off Water Street at Lake Ontelaunee September 14, 1980. The number increased to nine by September 21. More recently, Spence saw four on August 18, 1991, and Ken Lebo found four on the same mud flats on September 10, 1994. Matt Wlasniewski recorded six in a rain pool on a field in the Fleetwood-Lyons area October 29, 1996, with American Pipits and Killdeer.

Joan Silagy recorded one at the Reading Airport August 24, 1986.

The American Golden-Plover was listed by John F. Hofmann in 1890.

SNOWY PLOVER *Charadrius alexandrinus*
Accidental

Earl Poole examined a specimen in the Reading Public Museum originally labeled "Piping Plover (*Charadrius melodus*)" taken near "The Pinnacle," June 29, 1886, by Levi Mengel and identified it as a Snowy Plover. He referred it to the southern race, *C. a. tenuirostris* .

There are no records this century.

WILSON'S PLOVER *Charadrius wilsonia*
Accidental

Levi Mengel took two male Wilson's Plovers in the Pricetown Hills September 26, 1886, and he collected one female at Fritz's Island August 2, 1888. These three specimens are in the Reading Public Museum collection.

In the *Supplement to A Half Century of Bird Life in Berks County, Pennsylvania*, published in 1954, Earl Poole writes for the Wilson's Plover: "Casual. One seen at Lake Ontelaunee on August 28, 1953, by Dr. Perry Kendig and Clinton Miller is the first local record since 1888." However, in his unpublished manuscript of *Pennyslvania Birds* in 1964, he cites the above specimen records and two other state sight records, excluding this Lake Ontelaunee record.

John F. Hofmann listed the Wilson's Plover in 1890.

SEMIPALMATED PLOVER *Charadrius semipalmatus*
Fairly common migrant

The Semipalmated Plover is a fairly common migrant in spring and fall wherever beaches or mud flats are exposed during the migrations. It appears regularly at Lake Ontelaunee but is rare elsewhere.

At Lake Ontelaunee spring dates are between May 7 (1944) and June 18 (1939), and fall dates are from July 12 (1938) to October 24 (1957).

The earliest Berks County date is May 1 (1977 - Kerry Grim at Kaercher Creek Park in Windsor Township).

Charles Schaich recorded over 50 birds when the water level was low at Lake Ontelaunee on September 1, 1957.

Levi Mengel collected four Semipalmated Plovers now in the Reading Public Museum collection at Yost's Island October 4, 1888; at the Tulpehocken Creek September 16, 1889; at Fritztown September 9, 1890; and at Neversink September 26, 1892.

KILLDEER *Charadrius vociferous*
Very common migrant; common summer breeder

A very common migrant and common summer resident in open country over most of Berks County, the Killdeer winters here in smaller numbers.

When not wintering, the Killdeer is one of the earliest migrants to arrive, frequently putting in an appearance in February, making bona fide migrants difficult to determine. It is almost always common by mid-March in Berks and remains in numbers until late October or early November, usually leaving a few stragglers or small flocks to winter about springy meadows.

When not known to have wintered, it has arrived from February 7 (1926) to March 20 (1920) and departs, usually, from October 14 (1923) to December 27 (1936). Early fall migrants at Hawk Mountain include three birds September 24, 1958; two on October 7, 1939; and one October 12, 1984.

Nesting dates from 26 sets averaging four eggs each in the Reading Public Museum collection range from April 24 (1890) to June 1 (1887), although Sam Gundy photographed a nest near Stony Creek Mills in which three newly hatched young had just emerged and a sterile egg remained on April 12 (1957).

High Killdeer counts in fall are 163 in Marion Township November 15, 1992 (Rudy Keller, Harold and Joan Silagy), and 154 at Lake Ontelaunee November 4, 1994 (Ken Lebo).

The Killdeer has appeared on the Reading Christmas Bird Count 56 of 86 years, nine of the last 10, with a maximum of 106 on December 16, 1973. The peak for the Hamburg Christmas Bird Count is 48 on December 27, 1987. The high for the Bernville count is 31 on January 3, 1988.

The Pennsylvania German name for the Killdeer is "der Gillerie," derived from its call. Arthur D. Graeff reports the name "Gillrie" from western Berks County. Calvin Stump also reports the name "der Reggevoggel" for this species and all the plovers (Rupp, 1946:113-116).

AMERICAN AVOCET *Recurvirostra americana*
Accidental

Bob and Clinton Miller of Allentown saw an American Avocet on Sunday, September 11, 1947, flying low, north to south, just in front of the North Lookout at Hawk Mountain as heavy mists hung over the ridge. On September 20, 1947, one appeared at Lake Ontelaunee near Maiden Creek Station and remained until October 25, being observed during that period by hundreds of bird watchers. At least one sequence of motion picture film was made of this bird by W.W. Lukens.

An American Avocet appeared briefly October 31, 1953, in the same spot, and was observed by J. H. Arnett, Earl Poole, and others, but was apparently disturbed by the thousands of crows that were roosting nearby and left on the same day.

An Avocet frequented the lake from September 16 to 25, 1957, and was also seen by dozens of interested visitors near the cement bridge along West Shore Drive.

Ken Lebo found an American Avocet on extensive mud flats off Water Street at Lake Ontelaunee October 14, 1995. The bird stayed until October 20. A photograph of the bird appeared in the *Reading Times* and *Reading Eagle* October 18 (p. B1).

GREATER YELLOWLEGS *Tringa melanoleuca*
Common migrant

The Greater Yellowlegs is a fairly common migrant both in spring and fall on beaches, mud flats, and shallows. It occurs less frequently than the Lesser Yellowlegs on the smaller bodies of water.

Spring dates at Lake Ontelaunee range from March 23 (1930, 1933) to June 2 (1929). Fall dates are July 19 (1942) to November 14 (1993). A pair spent the entire summer of 1930, and a single bird was present on June 22, 1939. The largest flock noticed there was 20, seen on August 21, 1954 (Earl Poole).

When conditions are favorable, as in 1930, individuals may be present throughout the summer. Whether these are nonbreeders or north-and-south-bound migrants that meet on their respective journeys, Earl Poole believed, is problematical.

Maurice Broun counted a single-day peak of over 25 Greater Yellowlegs flying past the North Lookout at Hawk Mountain on September 27, 1953. Hawk Mountain fall records range from August 23 (1986) through October 25 (1959).

Levi Mengel collected a Greater Yellowlegs at Moselem November 27, 1885, and Christopher Shearer secured one near Tuckerton October 14, 1890. These specimens are in the Reading Public Museum collection.

Rudy Keller and Jim Cook recorded a Greater Yellowlegs at Hopewell Lake during the Elverson Christmas Bird Count December 14, 1974.

LESSER YELLOWLEGS *Tringa flavipes*

Common migrant

The Lesser Yellowlegs is a rather common migrant, occurring in the same situations and under the same conditions as the Greater Yellowlegs, but is usually much commoner than the latter and in the fall can occur in flocks of considerable size. Earl Poole recorded over 100 at Lake Ontelaunee on September 4, 1933.

At times smaller flocks will remain in a favored spot for weeks at a time during the fall migration.

This species and the Greater Yellowlegs sometimes occur together, and the difference in size between the larger females and smaller males of each species causes a considerable amount of confusion among bird watchers. Doubtless, many species identifications should be qualified with "probably."

Spring dates at Lake Ontelaunee run from March 12 (1933) to May 31 (1936). There is one June record: June 22, 1940 (E.P.).

Fall dates range from July 6 (1930, 1954) to November 24 (1957). Maurice Broun recorded a single-day fall high count of over 30 over Hawk Mountain on September 21, 1962.

SOLITARY SANDPIPER *Tringa solitaria*

Common migrant

The Solitary Sandpiper is a common migrant, spring and fall, at streams, lakes, and ponds. This sandpiper can occur almost anywhere in Berks County where there is standing water. A Solitary Sandpiper appeared at the pond near Schaumboch's on Hawk Mountain September 19, 1964.

It is one of the first migrants to start southward in the summer. During some seasons less than six weeks elapse between the time the last northbound migrant leaves and the first southbound bird returns. It occasionally is seen in the county as early as July 4 (1930, 1932).

Spring dates include April 21 (1923) to May 30 (1932). An unusually early observation is March 25, 1928 (Earl Poole).

Fall dates range from July 4 (1930, 1932) to October 19 (1917). Alex Nagy recorded a single bird at Hawk Mountain on July 9, 1966. An extreme date is November 2, 1961 (E.P.).

Levi Mengel collected specimens now in the Reading Public Museum at Greenawald, Albany Township, April 22, 1887; near Reading September 11, 1890, and September 27, 1895; and at Yost's Island October 4, 1888.

A BALD EAGLE ROBS AN OSPREY

LONG-EARED OWL

WINTER BIRDS
Clockwise from top: Northern Cardinal, American Tree Sparrow,
Ruby-crowned Kinglet, Winter Wren, Carolina Wren, and Golden-crowned Kinglet

MARSH BIRDS
Clockwise from top: Belted Kingfisher, Black-crowned Night-Heron,
Green Heron, American Bittern, and Great Blue Heron

RUFFED GROUSE
Pennsylvania's State Bird

BLACKBURNIAN WARBLERS

BLACK-AND-WHITE WARBLER

COMMON YELLOWTHROATS

WOOD THRUSH

OSPREY AT LAKE ONTELAUNEE

RED-HEADED WOODPECKERS

WILLET *Catoptrophorus semipalmatus*
Accidental

Anna and Mary Deeter and Earl Poole observed a Willet under very favorable conditions, both at rest and in flight, at Lake Ontelaunee following a severe storm on August 24, 1933.

Doug Cook, Dick Morton, and Seth Benz saw four Willets from the South Lookout at Hawk Mountain September 20, 1980. The birds were grouped flying along the ridge toward the North Lookout but between the lookouts over the Kettle. The wing pattern was unmistakable, and the observers had an exceptional view for over 300 yards as the Willets crossed in front. Cook heard several call in flight.

SPOTTED SANDPIPER *Actitis macularia*
Common

The Spotted Sandpiper is a common summer nester at all fair-sized streams and farm ponds.

Early arrivals appear during the first week in April, and a late fall date at Lake Ontelaunee is October 23 (1959).

G. Henry Mengel reported a straggler at Wyomissing November 21, 1925. There are two winter records: one below the overflow of Lake Ontelaunee on January 19, 1947 (David Berkheimer, Byron Nunemacher), and one near Kutztown February 7, 1984 (Catherine Elwell).

A pair bred in the Reading Public Museum park in 1929, three young coming off the nest June 6 (Earl Poole). There are numerous nesting records from throughout Berks County.

Six sets of eggs in the Reading Public Museum collection were taken in Berks County between May 12 (1904 - S. Gruber, four eggs near Evansville) and June 13 (1905 - Walter H. Leibelsperger, three eggs "far advanced" near Auburn).

Levi Mengel secured six specimens between May 15 (1886) and October 20 (1895) near Reading, at Fritz's Island, at Tuckerton, in Bethel Township, and in Albany Township.

The common Pennsylvania German names for all sandpipers in Berks County are "die Schnepp" and "die Wasserschnepp" (Rupp, 1946:120). Herbert Beck says that the name of "Schnepp" is used "for the Wilson's [Common] Snipe, Greater Yellowlegs, [Lesser] Yellowlegs, Solitary Sandpiper, Spotted Sandpiper, and other less common species of wet meadow or mudbank" (Beck, 1924:291).

UPLAND SANDPIPER *Bartramia longicauda*
Rare

The Upland Sandpiper is now a rare migrant in Berks County.

The last breeding season record is one seen by Matt Brett June 9 and by Jeanne Tinsman June 19, 1989, in Albany Township.

Earlier this century, it was an uncommon to fairly common migrant and summer nesting resident in open, flat areas. For nesting it requires broad, ungrazed pastures, airports, or grass fields.

Until 1900 it was considered a common summer resident over the greater part of southeastern Pennsylvania, according to Earl Poole. He writes in 1947:

"The Upland Sandpiper is an uncommon summer resident in the Oley and Great Valleys. Elsewhere a regular transient, its rolling call being frequently heard over Reading at night during the last weeks of July and early August. This lovely bird is steadily diminishing in numbers with us, and its spirit-like whinny, once as much a part of our rolling summer landscape as the waving grainfields and fleecy clouds, is less frequently heard each year."

He adds in 1964, "Now one may travel for miles over apparently ideal habitat in May without hearing the strangely thrilling 'song' of this, the loveliest of our shorebirds."

Poole's earliest spring arrival date is April 6 (1929). The latest fall date is September 26 (1889 - Levi Mengel, specimen collected at Monocacy).

The Upland Sandpiper previously nested during the 1940s and 1950s at the Daniel Boone Homestead in Amity Township (Earl Poole).

Recent records are from Albany Township and include one seen May 16, 1988, along Hawk Mountain Road (Catherine Elwell); one seen from May 24 to June 13, 1987 (Kerry Grim); one on May 3, 1986 (Laurie Goodrich); one heard calling May 1, 1982 (Seth Benz); and one August 28, 1981 (Kerry Grim).

The first Hawk Mountain record is October 19, 1969 (Nagy, 1970). More recently, Ken Lebo identified three Upland Sandpipers flying southwest along the ridge at the North Lookout October 8, 1995.

Robert and Ruth Cook saw five at the Reading Regional Airport September 6, 1981.

Levi Mengel collected an Upland Sandpiper in Bethel Township May 1, 1885, and along the Tulpehocken Creek August 7, 1889. Poole found one dead at the dam breast at Lake Ontelaunee June 19, 1936. Three sets of eggs in the Reading Public Museum were taken on the Wyomissing Creek May 4, 1890 (L.M.); in Tuckerton May 4, 1893 (L.M.); and at Fritz's Island on July 1, 1886 (John Hofmann).

Walter Leibelsperger found a nest with a complete set of eggs at Windsor Castle on May 11, 1914, and another near Fleetwood on May 28, 1907. Poole saw recently hatched young near Walnuttown on June 6, 1920.

The common Pennsylvania German name for the Upland Sandpiper is "es Feldhinkel." William Rupp once heard a farmer in Berks County call an Upland Sandpiper, perching on a fence post at the far end of a stubble field, a "prairie chicken." Rupp writes in 1946:

"This is a shy bird of the upland pastures. It was once a common and popular game bird, but it is now very rare. In late summer, after the harvest, hunters would ride out in to the stubble fields, on horseback and in wagons, to approach these birds more closely and to get better shots at them. The birds, after feeding in the fields, would be so fat and plump that they burst when they landed on the ground after being shot.... When landing on their perch, usually a post or stump, they would stretch their wings high over their backs, then slowly let them fall and gently fold them. This, said an old hunter, was a good field mark, and their spirited whistle of 'whip-whip-whee-ee-ee-ou-u' was a sound never to be forgotten" (Rupp, 1946:119).

WHIMBREL *Numenius phaeopus*

Rare

Earl Poole identified a flock of 10 Whimbrels, led by a Black-bellied Plover, that circled rather low over the marshes at Lake Ontelaunee on May 25, 1930, just after a storm. They then continued on toward the north without alighting.

A single bird was seen under very satisfactory conditions at the same place by Helen and Earl Poole on May 24, 1942.

Rick Wiltraut saw a Whimbrel on the mud flats near Water Street at Lake Ontelaunee July 23, 1994.

While waiting for the Swallow-tailed Kites to appear at the Straub farm in Brecknock Township, Lancaster County, May 23, 1995, Ken Lebo and about 15 others saw three flocks of Whimbrels totaling 270 birds flying from Lancaster County into Berks. The birds were identified by size, shape, silhouette, and their V-shaped flock pattern.

HUDSONIAN GODWIT *Limosa haemastica*

Accidental

During Hurricane Connie August 13, 1955, Earl Poole and Carl Stohler found two Hudsonian Godwits on an island in Lake Ontelaunee. They saw them at close range at rest and in flight. One remained until the following day and was seen by R. Diener, Warren Kalbach, Paul Martin, Byron Nunnemacher, and Charles Schaich.

Bart Smith and Matt Spence saw a Hudsonian Godwit October 1, 1989, at Moselem.

RUDDY TURNSTONE *Arenaria interpres*

Rare migrant

A rather rare migrant, the Ruddy Turnstone occurs on mud flats at Lake Ontelaunee, particularly after severe storms.

Earl Poole had seven sightings at the lake including a flock of 10 June 6, 1939, and two after Hurricane Connie on August 13, 1955. Matt Spence and Bob Cook saw an immature Ruddy Turnstone at the Water Street mud flats September 15, 1963. Rick Wiltraut reported a single bird picking bark from a log at the mud flats on the early fall date of July 15, 1994 (Wiltraut, 1994:144). Ken Lebo found three there May 14, 1995.

On October 16, 1969, a Ruddy Turnstone approached the North Lookout at Hawk

163

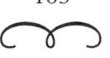

Mountain from the north, passed low over the rocks within 100 feet and went south along the escarpment (Fred Wetzel).

A specimen in the Reading Public Museum collection was taken by Christopher M. Shearer at Tuckerton September 30, 1889.

RED KNOT *Calidris canutus*
Accidental

A Red Knot seen by Earl Poole on the mud flats at the head of Lake Ontelaunee on September 16, 1953, apparently is the first local record since the nineteenth century. He saw this bird at a distance of 30 feet with good glasses and under perfect light conditions, and he was previously well acquainted with the species in life. Poole noted the distinctive lacey gray back pattern, whitish rump (shorter than the gray back of the Dowitcher), and the distinctive, throaty "woit" call, given when it flew.

On August 13, 1955, following Hurricane Connie, five Red Knots appeared at Lake Ontelaunee (Earl Poole, Carl Stohler).

John Hofmann listed the Red Knot in 1890.

SANDERLING *Calidris alba*
Uncommon fall migrant

An uncommon migrant in fall and rare in spring, the Sanderling is almost invariably observed during or after severe storms and is rarely seen on two successive days.

Earl Poole had two spring records: June 6, 1939, and June 5, 1941. Between April 28 and May 2, 1995, Joan Silagy recorded one Sanderling on the State Hill Boat Launch parking lot at Blue Marsh Lake.

At Glen Morgan Lake on the evening of May 31, 1996, Ken Lebo saw about 500 small shorebirds pass fairly low over the lake in V-shaped flocks. Based on size, prominent wing stripes, and white underparts, he thought they were probably Sanderlings.

Fall records range from July 22 (1994) to October 12 (1943). High counts of five were seen at Lake Ontelaunee after a severe northeast storm on August 24, 1933 (E.P.), and on July 22, 1994 (Ken Lebo, Rick Wiltraut).

Sanderlings were reported from Angelica Lake on September 11, 1921 (E.P.), and September 4, 1922 (G. Henry Mengel).

There is a specimen in the Levi Mengel collection at the Reading Public Museum taken at Greenawald, Albany Township, on April 22, 1887.

SEMIPALMATED SANDPIPER *Calidris pusilla*
Common migrant

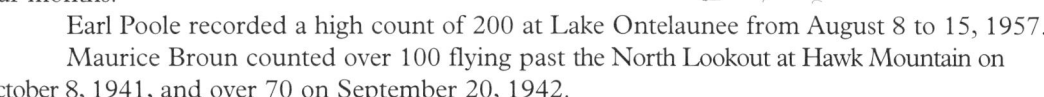

The Semipalmated Sandpiper is a fairly common migrant at Lake Ontelaunee, where 100 or more are sometimes seen after fall storms. It is rather rare elsewhere, having been found on a farm pond near Shartlesville and at the Oley Quarry (Rudy Keller).

This is an abundant shorebird on the mud flats during the late summer and fall. It is irregular in spring and passes through Berks County within a few weeks, while the fall migration may extend over nearly four months.

Earl Poole recorded a high count of 200 at Lake Ontelaunee from August 8 to 15, 1957.

Maurice Broun counted over 100 flying past the North Lookout at Hawk Mountain on October 8, 1941, and over 70 on September 20, 1942.

Spring dates at Lake Ontelaunee extend from May 11 (1930) to June 18 (1939). Fall records are from July 10 (1954) to October 30 (1934).

Levi Mengel collected specimens at Yost's Island October 4, 1888; along the Tulpehocken Creek September 16, 1889; at Fritztown September 9, 1890; and at Neversink September 26, 1892.

WESTERN SANDPIPER *Calidris mauri*
Rare fall migrant

A rare migrant in fall and very rare in spring, the Western Sandpiper occurs in the same manner as, and often with, the Semipalmated Sandpiper.

Earl Poole believed bird watchers can expect a certain percentage of error in identification because some female Semipalmated Sandpipers have longer bills than the males of the Western, and other supposed field characters cannot be depended on.

Poole had two spring observations: May 28, 1933, and June 5, 1939.

Eight fall records this century range from August 7 (1993 - Matt Spence) to September 12 (1965 - M.S.). Ken Lebo and Matt Wlasniewski found three Western Sandpipers on the mud flats near Water Street at Lake Ontelaunee August 12, 1994.

LEAST SANDPIPER *Calidris minutilla*
Common migrant

The Least Sandpiper is a fairly common and regular spring and fall migrant on mud flats, flooded meadows, and the shores of the Schuylkill River, lakes, and ponds.

This bird has been found every year at Lake Ontelaunee since its flooding in 1929, its numbers varying with the water level, but never more than 50 at a time. In spring it appears between April 29 (1956) and June 6 (1939), and in fall between July 6 (1930) and October 25 (1994 - Ken Lebo).

Six Least Sandpipers quickly flew by the North Lookout at Hawk Mountain on the south side of the ridge September 26, 1980 (Robert MacClay, August Mirabella).

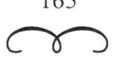

There are five local specimens in the Levi Mengel collection at the Reading Public Museum from Bernville April 30, 1887; Lenhartsville May 1, 1887; Greenawald, Albany Township, August 27, 1889; White Bear Station, Robeson Township, May 2, 1890; and Bernville September 6, 1890.

WHITE-RUMPED SANDPIPER *Calidris fuscicollis*

Uncommon migrant

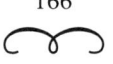

The White-rumped Sandpiper is an uncommon migrant occurring more often in fall than in spring, especially when mud flats and bare beaches are exposed. It usually appears singly or in small groups. Earl Poole recorded a flock of 30 at Lake Ontelaunee on October 3, 1929, following a hurricane.

Spring records range from May 7 (1944) to June 5 (1939). Fall dates are from August 3 (1943) to an extreme date of November 24 (1957 - Byron Nunemacher, Charles Schaich).

Sue Meitzler found a White-rumped Sandpiper dead on the road by the Kempton Community Center on October 25, 1989. Stan Senner identified the bird and sent it to the Academy of Natural Sciences in Philadelphia.

Two specimens in the Levi Mengel collection were taken locally on August 11, 1892, and October 17, 1899. D. Frank Keller noted that one of these sandpipers was taken in Berks County (Warren, 1890:85).

BAIRD'S SANDPIPER *Calidris bairdii*

Rare fall migrant

The main migration route of the Baird's Sandpiper is in the Mississippi Valley, along which it appears to pass hurriedly in spring on the way to its arctic breeding grounds. In the fall it pursues a more leisurely, and sometimes a more indirect route, so that a few individuals appear in Berks County with some regularity.

At Lake Ontelaunee the Baird's Sandpiper has been recorded between August 1 (1966 - Matt Spence) and November 2 (1961 - Earl Poole). It appears at the lake during years of low water when extensive beaches and mud islands are exposed. High counts are seven on August 24 to 26, 1944 (E.P.); seven on August 26, 1995 (Ken Lebo); and six on September 17, 1994 (K.L.).

Rudy Keller recorded a juvenal Baird's Sandpiper September 10, 1988, at a quarry in Oley.

Ken Lebo recorded the only spring record at Lake Ontelaunee May 23, 1995.

The Baird's Sandpiper was named for Spencer Fullerton Baird, the second secretary of the Smithsonian Institution, who was born in Reading in 1823. He served the Smithsonian beginning in 1850 and was named secretary in 1878. He died at Wood's Hole, Massachusetts, in 1887.

PECTORAL SANDPIPER *Calidris melanotos*

Rare spring, common fall migrant

The Pectoral Sandpiper is rare or absent in spring but generally rather common in fall at Lake Ontelaunee. The occurrence of this species, as of most of the other shorebirds, depends largely on the prevalence of extensive mud flats during the period of migration.

Spring records date from March 25 (1933) to May 24 (1938), and fall sightings are from July 13 (1940) to November 10 (1929). An extremely early fall date is June 29, 1930 (Earl Poole). Earl Poole recorded a high count of 80 over the lower meadows at Lake Ontelaunee on August 15, 1929, after a storm.

There are two records at Hawk Mountain. Maurice Broun saw six Pectoral Sandpipers flying below the North Lookout heading northwest on September 22, 1954, and two over the lookout on October 18, 1959.

Levi Mengel collected specimens at Lenhartsville May 15, 1884; at Douglassville November 22, 1889; and at the Wyomissing Creek near Reading September 24, 1890. Poole collected one at Lake Ontelaunee October 1, 1933. These specimens are in the Reading Public Museum collection.

DUNLIN *Calidris alpina*
Uncommon migrant

At Lake Ontelaunee, where its appearance depends upon the water level, the Dunlin is almost certain to be present in numbers in the fall, and to a lesser degree, during the spring migration whenever mud flats are exposed.

It is one of the hardiest of our shorebirds and is among the latest to move southward in fall.

The Dunlin appears in spring between April 23 (1995 - Matt Spence, Bart Smith at Water Street mud flats) and June 1 (1930) and in fall between August 24 (1938) and November 21 (1935). Earl Poole recorded a high count of 30 at Lake Ontelaunee on October 24, 1957. Levi Mengel collected a specimen in Berks County on the early fall date of August 3, 1887. He collected another in Maidencreek Township April 25, 1900.

The Dunlin has been seen flying over Hawk Mountain at least three times: a flock of 13 on October 17, 1942 (J.C. Tracy, Earl Poole); 300 on October 3, 1952 (Maurice Broun); and 18 on September 20, 1977 (Kerry Grim). Jim Olmes saw one bird in Drehersville, just over the county line in Schuylkill County, on May 26, 1986.

A most unusual observation was a Dunlin seen under excellent conditions at Lake Ontelaunee on December 27, 1942 (Arthur Sigman, E.P.), for its only Reading Christmas Bird Count record.

STILT SANDPIPER *Calidris himantopus*
Uncommon fall migrant

The Stilt Sandpiper frequents fresh water pools and muddy shallows margining mud flats and is often associated with Lesser Yellowlegs, Pectoral Sandpipers, and the smaller species that pass through at the same time. Where conditions are to its liking, this sandpiper is quite regular in occurrence, although it rarely appears in Berks County in flocks of any size.

However, Rick Wiltraut discovered a flock of 25 at the Water Street mud flats at Lake Ontelaunee on September 22, 1994.

Fall dates at Lake Ontelaunee range from July 16 (1955) to October 24 (1954), from single individuals to eight on September 25, 1954 (Earl Poole); 10 on August 26, 1957 (E.P.); and 12 on August 12, 1964 (E.P.).

John Hofmann listed the Stilt Sandpiper in 1890.

BUFF-BREASTED SANDPIPER *Tryngites subruficollis*
Accidental fall migrant

The Buff-breasted Sandpiper has a normal migration route far to the west of Berks County.

Robert Cook, Ira Weigley, and Matt Spence found one on the mud flats at the head of Lake Ontelaunee on September 6, 1958. Spence recorded another at the Water Street mud flats at the lake September 7, 1966. Dean Kendall saw two there the next day. He had an excellent view from less than 100 feet.

Harold and Ken Lebo found a Buff-breasted Sandpiper at Lake Ontelaunee August 26 and 27, 1995. Because of drought conditions, the water level of the lake was extremely low and therefore attractive to migrating shorebirds.

RUFF *Philomachus pugnax*
Accidental

Earl Poole recorded a female Ruff, or Reeve, October 14, 1965, on the mud flats near Water Street at Lake Ontelaunee.

Ken Lebo found a Reeve with a flock of 10 White-rumped Sandpipers at the same location June 4, 1994. It was gone the next day.

SHORT-BILLED DOWITCHER *Limnodromus griseus*
Rare fall migrant

A rare and irregular migrant, the Short-billed Dowitcher is typically a bird of the coastal salt marshes but is seen in late summer and early fall at Lake Ontelaunee and Moselem during periods of low water.

Earl Poole reported one bird in spring from May 3 to 19 and June 1, 1930.

The Short-billed Dowitcher occurs between July 12 and October 5 (1932). Poole recorded a high count of six on September 2 to 4, 1944, but Rick Wiltraut counted 44 on the mud flats near Water Street at Lake Ontelaunee on July 23, 1994.

COMMON SNIPE *Gallinago gallinago*
Fairly common migrant

A fairly common migrant and local winter resident at marshy meadows and spring heads during mild winters, the Common Snipe remained in Berks County until mid-January during eight winters between 1916 and 1940, and spent the entire winter of 1933–34.

It is sometimes difficult to distinguish early arrivals from wintering birds. What may have been early arrivals have turned up in the county as early as February 7 (1926), February 10 (1935), and February 25 (1923 - Earl Poole).

The bulk of the migration occurs in April, but quite a few stragglers may remain through

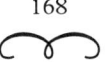

May, and one individual remained at Lake Ontelaunee until June 8, 1930 (E.P.). Levi Mengel collected a specimen at the Pinnacle June 29, 1886.

The fall migration begins in August, although one appeared at Lake Ontelaunee with Short-billed Dowitchers on July 18, 1957 (E.P.).

Maurice Broun saw one Common Snipe on the road by the gate at Hawk Mountain November 7, 1935, and one at the North Lookout on October 27, 1940. John Bachman recorded a Common Snipe flying low over the North Lookout on November 17, 1984.

Harold and Joan Silagy reported a high count of over 100 Common Snipe in a wet meadow off Route 419 in Marion Township December 15, 1985.

The general Pennsylvania German name for the Common Snipe, American Woodcock, and any small, long-legged wading birds except the herons is "die Schnepp" (Rupp, 1946:117).

The Common Snipe has been recorded on the Reading Christmas Bird Count 29 of 86 years, five of the last 10, with a high count of 16 on December 20, 1981. The high for the Hamburg Christmas Bird Count is 15 on December 23, 1973. The peak for the Bernville Christmas Bird Count is 56 on both January 5, 1986, and January 4, 1987.

AMERICAN WOODCOCK *Scolopax minor*
Regular migrant, local breeder

Formerly an abundant and fairly regular migrant and common summer resident in alder swamps, moist woodlands, and near springheads, the American Woodcock by the mid-1960s was reduced to a remnant of its former abundance.

While there are a number of indefinite references to wintering birds from Berks, it is probable that very few of these can survive our usual winters. This bird arrives before the last snows are over and often has to endure late storms. Dean Kendall heard one calling at Leesport from March 16 to 18, 1993, despite a 6-degree temperature and 15 inches of snow.

The earliest arrival date is February 5 (1993 - Matt Spence at Antietam). Other February records include birds at Joanna February 18, 1976 (Robert Cook); at Reading February 21, 1971 (Joan Silagy); at Pike Township February 22, 1992, and two there February 24, 1991 (Rudy Keller); and seven at Blue Marsh February 22, 1995, and six there February 26, 1996 (J.S.). Reliable places in Berks to see and hear Woodcock display in spring are the State Hill Boat Launch at Blue Marsh Lake and the Bailey's Creek area of Lake Ontelaunee. The best time is probably late March at dusk.

During the *Atlas of Breeding Birds in Pennsylvania* survey from 1983 to 1989, the Woodcock was noted as a probable breeder in the extreme corners of Berks, absent throughout the center of the county (Brauning, 1992:143).

Rudy Keller notes that the American Woodcock nested at his farm in Pike Township from 1967 when the fields were abandoned to 1990 when they became so overgrown that the birds were no longer attracted to them. This bird doesn't need swamps and wet woods for nesting but will nest in dry, early successional fields.

Levi Mengel collected a set of three eggs in Flannery's Woods near Douglassville April 30, 1895, and Walter H. Leibelsperger collected a set of four near Fleetwood on April 15, 1929.

Rich Bonnett flushed an American Woodcock from a nest with eggs at Lake Ontelaunee on April 30, 1989. Earl Poole also flushed it several times during the breeding season in the vicinity of Moselem. Maurice Broun flushed one from the orchard at Hawk Mountain on June 25, 1950.

On October 28, 1993, Darryl Leh walked a brushy, forested floodplain near Lobachsville and flushed at least 25 American Woodcocks, allowing for repeat sightings (*fide* R.K.).

The latest fall record is November 26 (1991 - R.K. at the Route 183 hawk watch). Other November dates are at Hawk Mountain November 11, 1950 (Albert Conway), and November 18, 1991 (Laurie Goodrich); near Mortgantown November 15, 1953 (R.C.); and at Pike Township November 11, 1971, and November 7, 1972 (R.K.).

The American Woodcock has been recorded on the Reading Christmas Bird Count three times in 86 years, none in the last 10, with a high count of four on December 24, 1933. The peak for the Hamburg Christmas Bird Count is three on January 1, 1970.

WILSON'S PHALAROPE *Phalaropus tricolor*

Casual

A full-plumaged female appeared on a mud flat with a flock of Least Sandpipers at Peters Creek on May 9, 1940, and by a curious coincidence, a male was seen on the same flat on May 17, 1941 (Earl Poole). One was seen at the mud flats off Water Street at Lake Ontelaunee May 15, 1995 (Ken Lebo).

On September 2 and 4, 1944, Poole saw another Wilson's Phalarope on the extensive flats at the head of the lake, and on October 22, 1944, Q. Kramer (*ms.*) found one at Moselem Springs. In August 1955 D. Cutler reported another Wilson's Phalarope at Lake Ontelaunee (*Audubon Field Notes.* Feb. 1956). Two were found in the same place on September 5 and 6, 1958 (E.P., Ira Weigley, Robert Cook), and one on July 29, 1962 (Warren Kalbach, Paul Martin, Byron Nunemacher, E.P.).

RED-NECKED PHALAROPE *Phalaropus lobatus*

Rare spring and fall migrant

The Red-necked Phalarope has occurred in Berks County more often than either of the other phalaropes, but is still far from common. It has appeared at Lake Ontelaunee following heavy rains.

Two spring records are April 22, 1937 (Earl Poole), and May 25, 1940 (E.P.). Fall records range from August 8 (1965 - E.P.) to October 3 (1929). A high count at the lake is five, following Hurricane Connie on August 13, 1955.

A specimen in the Reading Public Museum was taken at Tuckerton on April 20, 1890, by Christopher H. Shearer.

RED PHALAROPE *Phalaropus fulicaria*
Accidental

The first Berks County sighting of a Red Phalarope occurred on November 10, 1932. Earl Poole saw three birds on the dam at Lake Ontelaunee during a severe storm accompanied by high easterly winds.

On December 29, 1940, after two days of rain, Poole saw one under excellent conditions at the same place. He watched it at leisure as it turned in the water and apparently picked up small objects from the surface. He noted the distinctive white crown, compact form, and other characteristics.

Kerry Grim, L. Romanoff, and M. Schappel observed a Red Phalarope feeding on insects September 27, 1991, on the lake at Kaercher Creek Park in Windsor Township from a distance of 20 feet under good lighting conditions just before sunset. It was gone the next morning.

The Red Phalarope is more likely to alight in deep water than either of the other phalaropes. The Wilson's seems more typically a wader in shallows and mud flats, and the Red-necked a swimmer or wader.

LAUGHING GULL *Larus atricilla*
Casual late summer and fall

The Laughing Gull usually occurs at Lake Ontelaunee in the late summer or fall between August 4 (1991 - Bart Smith, Matt Spence) and November 26 (1950 - Earl Poole). Most occurrences follow storms accompanied by strong easterly winds.

After the great storm of August 24, 1933, Earl Poole counted at least 10 on the lake. The only spring observation at Lake Ontelaunee is one seen at close range on April 7, 1957 (E.P.), following a storm which also brought several oceanic birds inland. Matt Spence identified one at Lake Ontelaunee June 28, 1969.

It has been recorded in spring at Kaercher Creek Park in Windsor Township April 3, 1991; April 27, 1977 (Kerry Grim); and April 30, 1991 (Kenneth and Dorothy Grim).

During the late 1980s and early 1990s when uncovered garbage at a pig farm in Strausstown attracted tens of thousands of gulls during the winter, the Laughing Gull was recorded several times in the county. Robert Cook found an immature bird during the Bernville Christmas Bird Count January 1, 1992, and Spence saw one at Lake Ontelaunee January 3, 1992. Before these invasions, Spence and Warren Faust found one at Lake Ontelaunee on January 2, 1960.

LITTLE GULL *Larus minutus*
Accidental

Jason Horn and Ken Lebo identified one adult Little Gull in full breeding plumage and one in winter plumage with 90 Bonaparte's Gulls April 25, 1995, at Lake Ontelaunee.

BONAPARTE'S GULL *Larus philadelphia*

Common spring migrant

A regular and fairly common migrant along the Schuylkill River and on larger ponds and lakes in spring, the Bonaparte's Gull is irregular in fall, occasional in winter, and rare in summer.

Since 1922 it has appeared in spring between March 20 (1957 - Earl Poole) and May 16 (1940 - E.P.). The majority of records since 1988 are in April.

Occasionally, large flocks of Bonaparte's Gulls are reported in Berks County. The high count is 90 at Lake Ontelaunee on April 23, 1995 (Jason Horn, Ken Lebo). Other flocks include 75 at Blue Marsh Lake April 4, 1995 (Harold and Joan Silagy), and 70 at Lake Ontelaunee April 11, 1952 (E.P.).

Alex Nagy recorded five on his pond in Eckville, Albany Township, on April 24, 1966.

Stragglers have appeared at Lake Ontelaunee June 9, 1957, and August 3, 1952 (E.P.).

In fall the Bonaparte's Gull occurs between October 2 (1920 - E.P.) and November 26 (1953). Christopher Shearer collected a Bonaparte's Gull at Reading on August 30, 1891, and John F. Hofmann secured one at Reading on September 22, 1886.

December dates at Lake Ontelaunee include December 26, 1938 (E.P.); December 13, 1953 (E.P.); and December 12 and 13, 1994 (Ken Lebo, Dean Kendall).

January records include a flock of 55 at Lake Ontelaunee January 15, 1972 (Matt Spence); at Blue Marsh January 7, 1992 (D.K.); at Lake Ontelaunee January 15, 1992 (D.K.); and a flock of 14 at Lake Ontelaunee January 4, 1995 (K.L.).

At Hawk Mountain, Maurice Broun counted 60 Bonaparte's Gulls at the North Lookout November 5, 1954; 38 on May 7, 1955; and four on October 30, 1955. Anne "Babe" Webster recorded one on November 15, 1986. Mark Monroe counted 30 on November 12, 1996.

The Bonaparte's Gull has been recorded on the Reading Christmas Bird Count twice in 86 years, single birds on December 26, 1938, and December 27, 1970.

MEW GULL *Larus canus canus*

Accidental

On January 2, 1992, Jonathan Heller, David Rich, and Harold Morrin identified a bird of the European Common Gull race of the Mew Gull at Lake Ontelaunee among thousands of Ring-billed and Herring gulls. The gull was seen and photographed by many observers at Blue Marsh Lake the next day and from January 5 to 13. This sighting is the first Pennsylvania record for this species (Rich et al, 1992:7).

To most observers it appeared slightly smaller than many of the Ring-billed Gulls present. The head was more rounded and the crown peaked slightly just behind the eye. The head and neck were heavily streaked with brownish-gray, particularly on the nape. Most of the markings on the neck and breast were brownish-gray crescents on the feather edges. The coarseness of the markings indicated that the bird was still in full basic plumage. The rest of the underparts were pure white. The character which made the bird immediately obvious in a flock of Ring-billed Gulls was the mantle color. This was a noticeably darker gray than in Ring-billed and Herring gulls, approaching a pale Laughing Gull in shade. The bill was noticeably shorter and thinner than that of a Ring-billed Gull, and the eyes were noticeably larger in relation to the size of the head. The irises were very dark (Kwater, 1992:8-9).

RING-BILLED GULL *Larus delawarensis*

Abundant migrant and winter visitor

The Ring-billed Gull is an abundant migrant at Lake Ontelaunee, Blue Marsh Lake, and the Schuylkill River. It is common on freshly plowed farm fields in spring and at landfills during winter. There are records for every month of the year, although the majority of sightings are from March through May.

In fall, this gull appears in numbers during October and November.

The early date at Hawk Mountain is August 20 (1949) and the late date is December 20 (1996). The single-day peak there is 805 birds December 11, 1995.

The Ring-billed Gull has significantly increased in number in Berks County over the past 40 years. Earl Poole considered it as only a tolerably common migrant. At Lake Ontelaunee, for instance, on November 7, 1959, there was a high count of 71 in one flock and on October 15, 1961, a high count of 86 in one flock.

Previously, only a few remained over the winter, but with the increase of landfills in the county the Ring-billed Gull has become a winter resident. Extremely high counts were made during the years the pig farm in Strausstown operated. The farmer stockpiled trucked-in garbage in the open, attracting tens of thousands of gulls. During the Bernville Christmas Bird Count January 3, 1993, a high count of 13,728 of these gulls was made. The high for the Hamburg Christmas Count is 1,935 on December 29, 1984, when a landfill operated in the count circle. It has been recorded on the Reading Christmas Bird Count 32 of 86 years, 10 of the last 10 years, with a high count of 5,948 on December 15, 1991.

Nonbreeders and immature birds are seen at irregular intervals during the summer.

A specimen in the Reading Public Museum was taken on the Sacony Creek near Kutztown in April 1904 by Walter H. Leibelsperger.

There are no Pennsylvania German dialect names for the gulls or terns except the general terms "Seeveggel" and "Wasserveggel" (Rupp, 1946:122).

HERRING GULL *Larus argentatus*

Common migrant

A tolerably common migrant and less frequent winter visitor, the Herring Gull may occur at any season.

It is most abundant during the migratory periods, from late February through May and from September to early December, and is then likely to appear on lakes and ponds anywhere. Nonbreeders and immature birds occasionally linger around the larger bodies of water throughout the summer.

Migrants occur between August 24 (1933) and June 8 (1922 - Earl Poole). One individual remained at Lake Ontelaunee from July 26 to September 5, 1941, and Poole saw another there throughout the summer of 1942.

The early fall date at Hawk Mountain is September 15 (1985), and the late date is December 2 (1996). Maurice Broun counted a single-day high of 60 flying past the North Lookout on October 31, 1946.

During the early 1990s when the pig farm in Strausstown operated, the number of Herring Gulls increased in the county.

The Herring Gull has been recorded on the Reading Christmas Bird Count 51 of 86 years, 10 of the last 10, with a maximum of 1,176 on December 20, 1992. The high for the Bernville count is 662 on January 3, 1993. The peak for the Hamburg Christmas Bird Count is 553 on January 1, 1983.

Levi Mengel collected a specimen at Reading September 20, 1886.

ICELAND GULL *Larus glaucoides*
Rare winter visitor

The Iceland Gull first appeared in Berks County with the influx of gulls attracted to the pig farm in Strausstown during the late 1980s and early 1990s.

Matt Spence recorded the first county sighting of this gull, in first-winter plumage, at Lake Ontelaunee February 19, 1989.

Ernie Schiefer found another Iceland Gull, also in first-winter plumage, at Lake Ontelaunee February 28, 1991, for the second county record. Rudy Keller observed the bird March 2 (Keller, 1991c:23).

This gull was a rare but regular winter visitor in 1992, 1993, and 1994. Sightings declined, though, when the pig farm ceased operations in 1995. Ken Lebo found one at Glen Morgan Lake from January 1 to March 8, 1995.

Most records are from December and January, dates ranging from December 1 (1992 - Harold and Joan Silagy) to April 18 (1992 - J.S., Rudy Keller; 1996 - Matt Spence, a bird in second-winter plumage at Lake Ontelaunee).

The high count is five at Blue Marsh Lake January 5 and 7, 1992 (Ed Kwater, Dean Kendall). There were four gulls in first-winter plumage and one gull in third-winter plumage.

The Iceland Gull has been recorded on the Reading Christmas Bird Count twice in 86 years with a high count of two on December 18, 1994. The high for the Bernville count is three on January 3, 1993.

LESSER BLACK-BACKED GULL *Larus fuscus*
Rare winter visitor

Since 1990, the Lesser Black-backed Gull has been a rare but regular winter visitor to Berks County. Bart Smith and Matt Spence sighted one adult for the first county record at Lake Ontelaunee December 16, 1990, during the Reading Christmas Bird Count.

This gull has been found from October 29 (1995 - Matt Spence at Lake Ontelaunee) to April 2 (1992 - Harold and Joan Silagy) but is usually seen November through January.

Ed Kwater recorded a high count of four at Blue Marsh and Strausstown January 5, 1992. He found two birds in adult plumage and two in third-winter plumage.

There is one Hawk Mountain record. Jonathan Heller and Harold Morrin identified a Lesser Black-backed Gull flying past the North Lookout November 16, 1992.

Dean Kendall saw one perched on a dumpster at the Fairgrounds Square Mall in Muhlenberg Township December 27, 1993.

The Lesser Black-backed Gull has appeared on the Reading Christmas Bird Count twice in 86 years, both occurrences in the last 10 years with a high count of two on December 20, 1992. The high for the Bernville count is two on January 1, 1992.

GLAUCOUS GULL *Larus hyperboreus*
Casual winter visitor

The first Berks County record of the Glaucous Gull is an individual in the second-winter plumage which appeared at Lake Ontelaunee on March 5, 1961, and remained there until March 7. During that time it was studied under favorable conditions by Robert Cook, E. Gage, M. York, Matt Spence, and Earl Poole.

The Glaucous Gull then went unreported in Berks until the gull invasions of the late 1980s and early 1990s. The dates for this gull during the invasion years ranged from December 17 (1991 - Rudy Keller and Dean Kendall, two in first-winter plumage at Lake Ontelaunee) and February 10 (1988 - Matt Spence, an adult at Lake Ontelaunee).

A high count of four Glaucous Gulls was sighted by Ed Kwater and Dean Kendall at Blue Marsh and Strausstown January 5, 1992. They recorded two in first-winter plumage, one in third-winter plumage, and one adult.

The Glaucous Gull has appeared once on the Reading Christmas Bird Count, a single bird on December 21, 1986. It appeared twice on the Bernville count, single birds on January 1, 1992, and January 3, 1993.

GREAT BLACK-BACKED GULL *Larus marinus*
Regular winter visitor

Earl Poole saw two immature Great Black-backed Gulls on Lake Ontelaunee March 6, 1965, for the first Berks County record. Formerly, this large gull was considered only casual in southeastern Pennsylvania, but its numbers have been increasing as it expands its winter range.

Now, the Great Black-backed Gull is a regular winter visitor to Berks County and can be seen at the larger lakes or in migration from November 26 (1978 - Seth Benz, Michael Root at Hawk Mountain) until April 18 (1992 - Rudy Keller, Harold and Joan Silagy).

An exceptionally early date is September 17, 1991, one immature at Hawk Mountain (Laurie Goodrich).

High counts are 22 at Glen Morgan Lake near Morgantown January 1, 1995 (Ken Lebo), and 15 at Blue Marsh Lake March 7, 1993 (H. and J.S.).

The Great Black-backed Gull has been recorded on the Reading Christmas Bird Count five of 86 years, four of the last 10, with a maximum of eight on December 18, 1994. The high for the Bernville count is 10 on January 3, 1993. There are two Hamburg Christmas Bird Count records: single birds December 29, 1984, and December 26, 1993.

BLACK-LEGGED KITTIWAKE *Rissa tridactyla*

Accidental

Earl Poole saw a Black-legged Kittiwake at Lake Ontelaunee on November 17, 1935, during a severe northeast storm.

Matt Spence and Rudy Keller recorded two adults at Lake Ontelaunee March 31, 1991. They saw the birds at Maiden Creek Station and noted the tern-like flight, the birds dipping down to the water and bouncing right back up. They also noticed the gray mantles and black wingtips; the black of the first primary extending up the wings; white heads; dark eyes; and fairly small, pale bills (Keller, 1991d:23).

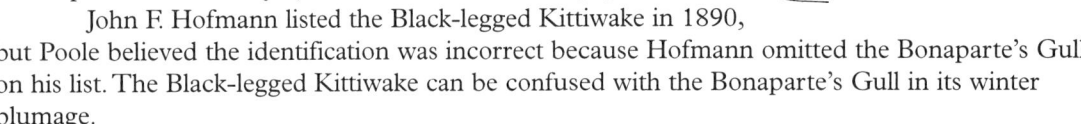

Ernie Schiefer identified two Black-legged Kittiwakes in first-winter plumage November 12, 1991, at Blue Marsh Lake. He saw them first out on the lake with Ring-billed Gulls. They took off and flew to the beach at the swimming area. He was able to pick up with a 22X scope the black band on the white, slightly forked tails; black half-collars; black bills; black spots behind the eyes; and no white on the wingtips.

John F. Hofmann listed the Black-legged Kittiwake in 1890, but Poole believed the identification was incorrect because Hofmann omitted the Bonaparte's Gull on his list. The Black-legged Kittiwake can be confused with the Bonaparte's Gull in its winter plumage.

SABINE'S GULL *Xema sabini*

Accidental

Kerry Grim and Dan Niven identified a Sabine's Gull September 17, 1987, as it flew within 200 feet of the North Lookout at Hawk Mountain. They observed the bird in direct sun as it flew below eye level and noted the white triangular wing patch, gray wings, grayish head, and forked tail.

CASPIAN TERN *Sterna caspia*

Uncommon migrant

Most records of Caspian Terns are from Lake Ontelaunee, usually after storms, and comprise from one to 13 individuals.

At Lake Ontelaunee it is observed regularly, either during spring or fall. Spring records range from April 3 (1982 - Matt Spence) to June 16 (1957 - Earl Poole). Fall dates are August 7 (1993, 1994 - M.S.) to October 3 (1939 - E.P.). The bird that appeared on the lake from June 8 to 16, 1957, was already assuming the white-streaked crown of the post-nuptial plumage, and Earl Poole believed it may have been a nonbreeding casual.

There are two July records. Poole reported one Caspian Tern at Lake Ontelaunee July 11, 1966, and Matt Spence saw one there July 16, 1995.

The greatest number present in Berks County

on any single day is 13 at Lake Ontelaunee on September 5, 1935 (E.P.).

Robert Cook recorded a Caspian Tern at Hopewell Lake April 25, 1962. Kerry Grim saw one at Kaercher Creek Park in Windsor Township September 15, 1978, and Matt Wlasniewski saw two birds over Hamburg May 2, 1993.

ROSEATE TERN *Sterna dougallii*
Accidental

A specimen in the Levi Mengel collection at the Reading Public Museum was taken by Christopher H. Shearer on the Schuylkill River near Tuckerton August 17, 1895.

COMMON TERN *Sterna hirundo*
Uncommon migrant

An uncommon migrant along the larger lakes and streams, the Common Tern appears in spring between April 17 (1954 - Earl Poole) and June 13 (1951- E.P., a flock of 20) and in fall from July 10 (1994 - Matt Spence) to October 19 (1932). The high count is 30 on May 4, 1940 (E.P.), and on September 5, 1935 (E.P.) at Lake Ontelaunee.

Robert Cook identified a Common Tern at Hopewell Lake April 25, 1954.

Single Common Terns have been recorded at Hawk Mountain on three occasions. Tommy Hanson saw one with two Herring Gulls August 3, 1948, flying low during an east wind. The tern was calling as it flew. Ronald Cocroft saw one over the North Lookout August 28, 1954. On September 1, 1987, Laurie Goodrich saw one in winter plumage around 8:05 a.m. flying southeast to north in front of the North Lookout. It flew out away from the ridge over the Christmas tree farms.

There are five local specimens in the Reading Public Museum, four taken along the Schuylkill River by Christopher Shearer in September in the 1890s (September 1893; two on September 22, 1894; and one September 30, 1894), and one at Wyomissing on October 4, 1927.

John F. Hofmann listed the Common Tern in 1890. D. Frank Keller regarded it as an accidental visitor (Warren, 1890:20).

FORSTER'S TERN *Sterna forsteri*
Rare fall migrant

Most records of Forster's Tern have been in the fall when this species is most easily distinguished from the Common Tern. Matt Spence, however, has three spring records at Lake Ontelaunee: one April 19 and May 26, 1995, and six April 16, 1996.

Earl Poole saw one at the head of Lake Ontelaunee on August 17, 1930, for the first county record this century. The distinctive head markings, silvery primaries, and harsh call were carefully checked as the bird "hawked" over the marshes and mud flats, not over the water as the Common Terns are apt to do. This bird was under observation for fully an hour. Poole was previously well acquainted with this species.

Following Hurricane Hazel on October 16 and 17, 1954, two Forster's Terns were seen at Lake Ontelaunee by D. Cutler, Ronald Cocroft, Charles Schaich, and Poole. Another appeared at Lake Ontelaunee during and after Hurricane Connie August 13 and 14, 1955 (Charles Schaich, Earl Poole, Paul Martin).

Kerry Grim observed a Forster's Tern at Kaercher Creek Park in Windsor Township October 19, 1996, after a storm. Spence and Rudy Keller saw two on the same day at Lake Ontelaunee.

John F. Hofmann listed the Forster's Tern in 1890.

LEAST TERN *Sterna antillarum*
Accidental

Earl Poole observed a Least Tern at Lake Ontelaunee following a severe northeaster and hurricane on August 24, 1933.

On August 13 and 14, 1955, Hurricane Connie brought numbers of Least Terns as far west as the Susquehanna River (Hake, 1955:77–79). Poole saw eight on Lake Ontelaunee.

The only recent record is one seen by Kerry Grim at Kaercher Creek Park in Windsor Township June 1, 1977.

John F. Hofmann listed the Least Tern in 1890. D. Frank Keller regarded it as an accidental visitor (Warren, 1890:22).

A specimen taken on the Schuylkill River near Tuckerton by Christopher Shearer August 11, 1892, is in the Reading Public Museum collection.

SOOTY TERN *Sterna fuscata*
Accidental

During Hurricane Connie on August 13, 1955, three of these striking birds appeared on Lake Ontelaunee where they were seen at close range by Carl Stohler, Charles Wharton, and Earl Poole. By the following morning, the birds had left.

On September 7, 1996, the day after Hurricane Fran brushed Berks County, Ken Lebo spotted two large terns at 8:15 a.m. while he was driving north on I-176 in Cumru Township. He pulled over and tried to identify them through binoculars. All he could see were the dark upper wings as they were flying toward the Schuylkill River, so he exited and drove to the bridge over the Schuylkill River at Gibraltar. He heard terns calling and looked up the river as they were about to fly over. He identified the first as an adult Sooty Tern and noted the dark upper wing; the white under wing, belly, and forehead; the black line running through the eye; and the black bill. He also noticed the deeply forked tail. The second bird was completely dark and also had a deeply forked tail and was the same size and shape as the adult Sooty Tern. He watched them as they flew down the river, both having a slow, steady wing beat (Pulcinella, 1996.139).

BLACK TERN *Chlidonias niger*

Uncommon migrant

The Black Tern was formerly a fairly regular migrant in spring and fall along the larger streams and lakes, but the numbers of sightings have declined.

At Lake Ontelaunee the earliest arrival date for this species is April 21 (1955 - Earl Poole). Most records are from May.

There are three June records of the Black Tern at Lake Ontelaunee: June 1, 1930; June 5, 1941; and four on June 14, 1951 (E.P.). Two July records are July 7, 1956 (E.P.), and July 10, 1994 (Matt Wlasniewski).

The earliest fall record is July 31 to August 2 (1920 - E.P. at Angelica Lake). The latest dates are September 29 and 30 (1996 - Matt Spence, Bart Smith, Ernie Schiefer) and September 25 (1921 - G. Henry Mengel at Angelica Lake).

The high count is five at Lake Ontelaunee May 7, 1989 (Matt Spence).

Levi Mengel collected one on the Schuylkill River near Tuckerton on August 12, 1892.

BLACK SKIMMER *Rynchops nigra*

Accidental

A Black Skimmer appeared at Lake Ontelaunee on October 16, 1954, blown in by Hurricane Hazel which passed directly over Reading the night before. This bird was identified independently by David Cutler, Charles Schaich, and Earl Poole. By the following morning it had departed.

DOVEKIE *Alle alle*

Accidental

In November 1932 there was a remarkable influx of these little "sea doves" throughout eastern Pennsylvania, following a violent easterly storm which left many stranded around Philadelphia and as far inland as Birdsboro and Pottstown. The westernmost record was one found, much emaciated, on a small pond near Birdsboro on November 19 by Lester Leinbach and brought to the Reading Public Museum where it died. It was later mounted and placed on exhibition (Earl Poole).

After a storm October 30, 1973, Doris Steffey and Joan Silagy released a Dovekie on a farm pond in Pikeville, Pike Township, after it was found by an unidentified woman who kept it in a tub in her kitchen. It died shortly thereafter. The specimen was sent to the Academy of Natural Sciences in Philadelphia.

THICK-BILLED MURRE *Uria lomvia*

Accidental

On December 4, 1950, Terry Bingaman brought a living but much emaciated Thick-billed Murre to the Reading Public Museum. Unable to fly, it had been picked up on Holland Street in Shillington and is now in the museum collection (Poole, 1951c:34).

BLACK GUILLEMOT *Cepphus grylle*

Accidental

On April 6, 1957, after two days and nights of rain accompanied by easterly winds, a Black Guillemot in winter plumage appeared on Lake Ontelaunee along with 25 other species of waterfowl. This guillemot was associated with a band of Buffleheads, and Earl Poole had it under observation with a 25X telescope at close range for the better part of an hour. The flank feathers were drawn over the wings so that the bird appeared largely of a dirty whitish color, and it was not until it raised a bright red, webbed foot to scratch its neck that Poole felt completely satisfied with the identity of the bird. He later checked with skins in the Academy of Natural Sciences in Philadelphia to verifiy his observation.

ANCIENT MURRELET *Synthliboramphus antiquus*

Accidental

Matt Spence discovered an Ancient Murrelet at Lake Ontelaunee November 8, 1992, for the first Pennsylvania record of this bird. Spence, Harold Lebo, and Matt Wlasniewski noted the light-colored bill and the marked distinction between the head and back of the bird. The white throat patch and a dark eye were visible. Eric Witmer photographed the bird. It was gone the next day (Wlasniewski, 1992:143).

ROCK DOVE *Columba livia*
Abundant resident

The abundant and well-known "pigeon" of our cities is the descendant of domestic stock that has become feral and lives at tall buildings, bridges, quarries, and barns everywhere. It maintains its existence in public parks and squares to the delight of the children but often to the dismay of public officials.

The Rock Dove was not counted on the Reading Christmas Bird Count before 1973 because of its introduced status. Since then, it has been recorded every year with a maximum of 3,722 on December 19, 1976. The high for the Hamburg Christmas Bird Count is 2,309 on December 28, 1986. The peak for the Bernville count is 2,011 on January 4, 1987.

The Pennsylvania German name for the domestic pigeon is "die Daub." The male is "der Daubert" and the squab is "en yungi Daub" (Rupp, 1946:123).

MOURNING DOVE *Zenaida macroura*
Abundant resident

Earlier this century, Earl Poole found the Mourning Dove abundant in summer but uncommon in winter. However, with the help of bird feeders and automated farming machinery that leaves more waste corn in the fields, it has thrived during the winter months with large flocks of several hundred birds gathering in stubble fields in the Great Valley.

In Berks County the Mourning Dove can be heard calling on fine days as early as January 30 (1960 - E.P.). By the second week in March, its cooing is heard throughout the countryside.

The Mourning Dove nests early, and the first nests are commonly put together in evergreens. During the blizzard on March 13, 1993, Kerry Grim found a Mourning Dove on a nest, and one dove successfully fledged. Poole found nests from April 22 (1951-in an old robin's nest) to August 1 (1924), and saw young, evidently just out of the nest, as late as September 30 (1951).

Maurice Broun writes of a late nesting: "In September, 1941, a pair of mourning doves nested belatedly at the very crest of the Lookout, successfully rearing two young in a chestnut oak over which many an Accipiter zoomed by. And scores of people passed within a few feet of the nest, which I disclosed to no one, until at length the two young doves, for whose safety I was so concerned, 'took off' to see the world, on September 13. Could there have been a more fitting symbol of peace at Hawk Mountain!" (Broun, 1949a:197-198)

Levi Mengel collected 11 sets of eggs between May 10 (1901) and May 30 (1887).

Fall migration data apparently does not exist beyond the fact that some doves leave by late October or November, leaving behind the birds that remain over the winter.

The Mourning Dove has appeared on the Reading Christmas Bird Count 59 of 86 years, 10 of the last 10, with a maximum of 2,339 on December 22, 1996. The 1953 count was the last one without a Mourning Dove. The high count for the Hamburg Christmas Bird Count is 3,296 on December 28, 1986. The peak for the Bernville count is 1,475 on January 4, 1987.

In Berks, the Pennsylvania German name for the Mourning Dove is "der Reggevoggel." William Rupp writes:

"The sweet, tender love-song of the male, given with such depth of feeling, sometimes quite mournful and then again as light and spirited as the spring itself, has probably earned this name for the bird. The call is often confused with that of the cuckoo, and a number of persons have told the writer that 'Reggevoggel' meant the 'rain dove - the cuckoo!'" (Rupp, 1946:124).

MONK PARAKEET *Myiopsitta monachus*

Escape

This cage bird has nested twice in the wild in Berks County. The first nesting was sometime prior to 1972, a pair and their conspicuous stick nest seen in Molltown (Matt Spence). A second nesting occurred August 10, 1972, on a telephone pole near Schuylkill Avenue and West Windsor Street in Reading (M.S.).

The most recent record is two seen in Temple July 30, 1991 (M.S.).

There are two Reading Christmas Bird Count records: one on River Road on December 17, 1972, and one on Neversink Mountain on December 15, 1974.

On September 18, 1988, a Monk Parakeet flew by the North Lookout at Hawk Mountain at eye level and called out as it passed the owl decoy (Laurie Goodrich).

BLACK-BILLED CUCKOO *Coccyzus erythropthalmus*

Uncommon migrant; rare breeder

The Black-billed Cuckoo is an uncommon migrant and rare summer breeder in second growth as well as deeply forested areas, varying considerably in numbers from year to year. The abundance of both cuckoo species in summer depends largely upon the prevalence of the various larvae upon which they feed, such as gypsy moths, tent caterpillars, and fall cankerworms.

It arrives at about the same time as the Yellow-billed Cuckoo, the earliest arrival date May 2 (1945 - Earl Poole; 1994 - Catherine Elwell).

Apparently this cuckoo does not lose much time in going about the business of nesting. Eight sets of eggs from Berks County in the Levi Mengel and Walter Leibelsperger collections were found between May 24 (1890) and July 4 (1909). Clutch sizes in the collected sets range from four to five eggs.

Rich Bonnett photographed a nest with three young at French Creek State Park in June 1994. Rudy Keller observed a Black-billed Cuckoo chick incapable of flight perched near its nest in Pike Township June 4, 1970.

Both cuckoos become comparatively quiet and secretive toward the close of summer, so there are few fall migration dates. Earl Poole had two unusually late observations in Berks: October 14 (1922) and October 26 (1957).

YELLOW-BILLED CUCKOO *Coccyzus americanus*

Uncommon summer breeder

The Yellow-billed Cuckoo can be a variably common breeder, depending on the abundance of caterpillar prey species. A very secretive bird, it is more often heard than seen, arriving after April 29 (1959 - Earl Poole). Both cuckoo species often sing at night.

Complete sets of eggs have been found as early as May 19 (1895 - Levi Mengel collection), and Poole saw a nest containing three young about a week old as late as August 23 (1922). Clutch sizes in collected sets range from five to seven eggs.

Jim Brett found a nest with two young June 15, 1981, in Albany Township.

The Yellow-billed Cuckoo is very erratic in its departure, disappearing in late August

(August 28, 1928, 1947 - E.P.) or remaining as late as October 16 (1959 - E.P.). Maurice Broun observed a Yellow-billed Cuckoo at the North Lookout of Hawk Mountain October 13, 1959. An exceptionally late date is November 20 (1971 - Robert Cook).

This is easily the commoner of the two cuckoos occurring in Berks County.

The Pennsylvania German name for the Yellow-billed Cuckoo is "der Reggevoggel." William Rupp writes, "This bird is known far and wide as the 'rainbird' or 'rain-dove.' The call of this bird is a sign and summons!" Rupp also lists "der Kucku," probably just a dialect form of the English name (Rupp, 1946:138).

BARN OWL *Tyto alba*
Uncommon resident

Uncommon but declining in Berks County, the Barn Owl is secretive and easily overlooked. Changing agricultural practices plus increased development pressures are affecting the populations of these owls.

Some Barn Owls remain throughout the year and may breed at any season. Others appear to be migratory, leaving in the fall and returning in late February or some time during March.

A pair that nested regularly for many years during mid-century in a barn near Kempton left in the fall and did not return until late February or March. In 1957 one of the pair definitely made its first appearance on March 27 (Earl Poole). Maurice Broun banded a nestling at the Kempton site on June 10, 1953, that was recovered at Key West, Florida, the following December, having flown 1,140 miles in the meantime.

Other pairs in Berks stay in their nesting "dens" throughout the year and may be found breeding at all seasons. A nest at Montello in Spring Township that Poole visited May 26, 1921, contained two fresh eggs, although a brood of young had already been raised in the same cavity. During the summer of 1926 a family occupied the belfry of St. Mark's Reformed Church in the City of Reading, much to the annoyance of the neighbors, who were kept awake by the rasping nocturnal calls of the birds. A large sycamore cut down near Evansville October 10, 1926, contained two young, one able to fly and the other approximately three weeks old, while a nest in the same neighborhood contained two healthy young on January 12, 1927 (Poole, 1930b:84). Four young, unable to fly, were found in a deserted pigeon loft in Wyomissing during the first week in December 1942. On November 28, 1956, in answer to a call from near West Reading, Poole found a young Barn Owl that had just left its nest but was incapable of protracted flight. Rich Bonnett monitored a pair in a box in an abandoned silo in the Oley Valley that were incubating six eggs February 28, 1990, and fledged four young on May 10.

The Barn Owl in Berks has nested in hollow trees, barns, deserted houses, church steeples, in a fire alarm tower, under a bridge, in a hole in a quarry, and in the dam breast at Blue Marsh Lake. The Barn owl has more recently accepted nest boxes as breeding sites.

At a farm in Lenhartsville, from one to two pairs of Barn Owls have nested annually from 1979 to 1995. In 1995, one pair nested in a chimney and another in an owl box. The owls usually remain into the winter.

Recent Barn Owl nestings have been recorded in Lenhartsville, Hamburg, Kutztown, Reading, Blue Marsh, Rehrersburg, Oley, and the Daniel Boone Homestead. Six in one nest fledged at the homestead in mid-May 1991 and were banded by Alan Gehret (R.B.). Three young

fledged at the homestead in 1996, and a pair in Rehrersburg fledged four young the same year (R.B.)

Six nests in the Reading Public Museum were taken locally between April 11 (1905, 1907) and May 12 (1914), but as noted before, eggs or young may be found at any season. Levi Mengel took a set of six eggs April 29, 1885, from a nest "in a triangle, just under the eaves of the barn of the Pricetown Hotel. There were a number of mice and squirrel remains in or near the nest."

D. Frank Keller listed the Barn Owl as occasional and a possible breeder (Warren, 1890:145).

On January 30, 1939, Poole collected 25 Barn Owl pellets at Gibraltar. He analyzed the pellets and found they contained the remains of 44 meadow voles, four shrews, one mole, two rats, and two white-footed mice.

The Barn Owl high for the Hamburg Christmas Bird Count is 11 on December 23, 1973, but it has not been recorded since 1978. It has appeared on the Reading Christmas Bird Count 18 of 86 years, four of the last 10, with a maximum of seven on December 24, 1967.

The general name for all owls in the Pennsylvania German is "die Eil." "Die Scheiereil" is a name heard not too commonly in Berks for the Barn Owl. Screech-Owls are sometimes found in barns and sheds, and then they are given this name (Rupp, 1946:143).

EASTERN SCREECH-OWL *Otus asio*

Common resident

The Eastern Screech-Owl is the commonest and most familiar owl in settled areas and frequently makes itself at home in the suburbs and in towns. In heavy forests it appears to be less common, its numbers controlled by the larger owls, which prey upon it at times.

Earl Poole writes in 1947, "Screech-Owls are frequently seen in and about Reading, where they take toll among the roosting sparrows at night and spend the day in some old tree or convenient crevice."

Poole believed that the gray form is slightly more abundant than the red in Berks County.

The Screech-Owl has recently adapted to using nest boxes as natural tree cavity sites have declined. Five nestlings and the parent bird were banded in a Wood Duck box at the Daniel Boone Homestead May 24, 1989 (Rich Bonnett), and five young fledged from the same box June 14, 1990 (R.B.). In northern Berks County, Screech-Owls have nested and fledglings have been banded in American Kestrel boxes monitored by Bob and Sue Robertson from 1990 to 1995. Nest initiation usually occurred in late March or early April. Screech-Owls have also nested in Wood Duck boxes maintained by Jeffrey Schucker in Albany Township. In 1990, two gray Screech-Owls raised nine young in these boxes. In 1993, two gray owls each laid four eggs, and one red owl laid five eggs. In 1994, there were one red owl with four young and one red owl with five eggs.

Poole saw young just out of the nest on July 1 (1916).

Local sets of eggs in the Levi Mengel Collection at the Reading Public Museum were taken between April 4 (1888) and May 19 (1895). Clutch sizes in the collected sets range from four to five eggs. Six nests were found in holes in apple trees and one in a pear tree.

The Screech-Owl population declines during hard winters when heavy snow cover protects the small mammals it preys upon. There has been an increase in Screech-Owl mortality during winter along roads as owls have been struck by cars while hunting.

Maurice Broun notes a gray Screech-Owl spent the winter in a box in the lower shelters at Hawk Mountain but died of starvation under the porch at Schaumboch's during a severe storm March 1, 1963.

The high Screech-Owl count for the Hamburg Christmas Bird Count is 67 on December 29, 1985. It has appeared on the Reading Christmas Bird Count 52 of 86 years, 10 of the last 10, with a maximum of 39 on December 22, 1968. The peak for the Bernville count is 46 on January 1, 1989.

The most prominent of the many Pennsylvania German names given for the Screech-Owl is "es Schteekeizel." One name suggested by the fact that these little owls sometimes lived in the stone piles and stone fences near orchards and woodlots is "die Schteeeil" or "Schdee-eil." Also "Nachteil" is the general name applied specifically to this bird because it is the most prominent (Rupp, 1946:145-147).

GREAT HORNED OWL *Bubo virginianus*
Uncommon resident

In 1930, Earl Poole considered the Great Horned Owl a rather rare and local resident. Since then, it has steadily increased in Berks County as the woodlands matured and the shooting of these owls was outlawed. A significant increase occurred during the 1970s and 1980s, but since then their population has leveled off.

Poole's writings indicate the scarcity of this bird during the opening decades of this century. On September 1, 1921, while trapping Allegheny cave rats on the Pinnacle in Albany Township, he heard one Great Horned Owl call repeatedly through the night. On a later trip to the same place on September 23 and 24, 1922, he heard one or two at intervals through the night, one approaching to within a few feet of his camp. He suspected that they habitually hunted these rats which were then quite common in the crevices.

A. Ericksen and Poole heard one hooting on Mount Penn on the night of February 4, 1925. Walter H. Leibelsperger saw a young Great Horned Owl in some heavy woodland in Oley Township on April 18, 1908, and a hollow tree felled in the same place April 20, 1913, contained a young owl and the bodies of two rabbits.

During the middle of this century, the Blue Mountain - especially that section which traverses Albany Township, the wider portion of the Reading hills, and the region between Flying Hill and Hopewell -sometimes spoken of as "the forest," seemed to harbor more Great Horned Owls than any other part of the county.

The earliest breeding bird, the Great Horned Owl lays eggs early in February or occasionally late in January. It can be heard calling in early winter. Joan Silagy found a nesting Great Horned Owl incubating eggs in Bern Township January 20, 1986. On April 15, the young were out of the nest. Laurie Goodrich found an owl on a nest near Kempton February 19, 1988.

Levi Mengel took a pair of half-incubated eggs from an old hawk's nest in Albany Township April 1, 1888, and Poole saw young fully capable of flight and apparently on their own in the hills near Reading on April 30 and May 1, 1929. Poole saw practically full-grown young at Rattling Run on July 1, 1950, except that their "horns" were not fully developed.

A study of the food habits of the Great Horned Owl based on over 15,000 owl pellets gathered and dissected by Judy Wink between 1960 and 1986 shows the great diversity in the bird's diet. The sample pellets came from territories in 17 counties across the state, but about 80 percent were from southeastern Pennsylvania. The pellets contained the undigested remains of 2,606 different prey items, representing 35 species of mammals and birds. The Norway rat, white-footed mouse, and eastern cottontail rabbit, combined, accounted for nearly 60 percent of all the prey. The Ring-necked Pheasant comprised 3.3 percent, and the Ruffed Grouse, 3 percent. When the estimated weights of prey taken by the Great Horned Owl are considered, the Virginia opossum, eastern cottontail, and the Norway rat account for more than 70 percent of the owl's diet (Wink et al, 1988:25-30).

The Pennsylvania Model Hawk Law enacted in 1970 protected all raptors except the Great Horned Owl. An amendment to the 1936 wildlife treaty between the United States and Mexico ratified March 10, 1972, offered protection to all hawks and owls.

The Great Horned Owl has appeared on the Reading Christmas Bird Count 38 of 86 years, 10 of the last 10, with a maximum of 34 on December 16, 1984; December 18, 1994; and December 17, 1995. Its first appearance on the count was in 1942. The peak for the Hamburg Christmas Bird Count is 75 on December 27, 1987. The high for the Bernville count is 57 on January 1, 1992.

The Pennsylvania German names for the Great Horned Owl are "die gross Eil" and "die gross Nachteil" (Rupp, 1946:147).

SNOWY OWL *Nyctea scandiaca*
Rare winter visitor

Now protected, the large and striking Snowy Owl is a rare and irregular winter visitor to Berks County, occurring when prey populations in the north collapse.

While it probably appears somewhere in Pennsylvania nearly every winter, there are some years in which considerable numbers are reported, such as the winter of 1926–1927, when George M. Sutton writes that 204 were reported shot and 39 others seen in the state. During that season the first one was shot on October 20 at Phillipsburg, Centre County. But the great wave occurred in November, when Snowy Owls were taken in all parts of the state, but principally in the southeastern and western counties. Nineteen were killed in Bucks County alone. The latest one recorded during that year was at Sugar Grove, Warren County, on March 8, 1927 (Sutton, 1927:35-41).

Earl Poole doubted whether any Snowy Owls survived to return to their original habitat.

During November 1926, at least seven were shot in Berks County at Lyons November 12 by Charles W. Smith; at Kutztown November 15 by Robert Schlenker; near Kutztown November 18 by Frank Wiltrot; near Fleetwood November 20 by Peter Strunk; near Shartlesville "Late November" by Adam Hiester; near Adamstown "November" by George Michael of Reading; and near Kutztown "Late November" by Howard Dietrich.

A male in the Reading Public Museum collection was shot on the Blue Mountain near Strausstown November 18, 1937, by Carmen Civitos.

In 1945 there was another extensive invasion when observations were made at Hopewell November 27 by Albert Bachman; Glenside December 5 by K. Chubb; and near Moselem December 10 by A. R. Bachman. During the same season at least three were shot in Berks County at Fleetwood R. #1 November 27 by Chester Meals; at West Lawn December 1 by Arthur Stauler; and at Hamburg R. #1 December 11 by Raymond Althouse.

The earliest arrival record in Berks is of one that remained about a limestone quarry in Sinking Spring from October 23 to November 16, 1941 (J. Hendel, E.P.). Another appeared in a quarry near Limekiln and stayed from December 1972 through January 1973 (Robert Cook).

Between February 21 and 28, 1954, many bird watchers from Reading and Allentown saw a Snowy Owl in Monterey, Maxatawny Township (E.P.).

On January 18, 1967, Robert Gustan, the manager of Pomeroy's at Sixth and Penn streets in Reading, found a Snowy Owl dead on the roof of the store while showing workmen where to make repairs. This owl was first seen in November 1966 and ranged between the city and the suburbs. In December, it stayed in the area of State Hill Road near Wyomissing (*Reading Times*, January 20, 1967). Sam Gundy retrieved the bird for the Reading Public Museum collection.

Other Berks sightings include an immature owl on the Nagy Farm in Eckville January 25, 1975 (Alex Nagy, Seth Benz); one at Blue Marsh December 1, 1986 (Harold and Joan Silagy); and one in Laurel Run Park in Muhlenberg Township during late January and early February 1992 (Carl and Carolyn Drasher).

A Snowy Owl first seen November 27, 1996, in Muhlenberg and Ontelaunee townships along the Fifth Street highway was found in a weakened condition December 4 in a parking lot at one of the shopping centers. Pennsylvania Game Commission officials Dan Lynch and Cheryl A.

Trewella captured the bird and transported it to raptor rehabilitator Hope Anwyll in Mount Bethel, Northampton County. The owl was severely emaciated and dehydrated and died the following day.

John F. Hofmann listed in 1890 the Snowy Owl as occurring locally.

The Pennsylvania German name for the Snowy Owl is "die Weisseil." Another name used is "die Schnee-eil," simply "the snow owl" (Rupp, 1946:147).

NORTHERN HAWK OWL *Surnia ulula*
Accidental

Levi Mengel collected a Northern Hawk Owl in Albany Township January 26, 1887. This specimen is in the Reading Public Museum collection.

BARRED OWL *Strix varia*
Rare resident

The Barred Owl is a rare resident in the mature, unbroken woodlands of the Kittatinny Ridge. It is partial to dense woods, particularly near streams or swamps either at high or low elevations, and usually occurs as a rather rare and irregular winter visitor in other areas of Berks County. It has been regular and territorial at Hawk Mountain since 1985.

There were two confirmed breeding records in northern Berks County during the *Atlas of Breeding Birds in Pennsylvania* survey from 1983 to 1989 (Brauning, 1992:161).

Carl Hess saw fledged Barred Owl young June 30, 1986, a mile north of the Port Clinton fire tower. This area lies within Berks County, a mile from the Schuylkill County border at the head of a ravine close to the mountain top.

Rich Bonnett heard two adults and one or two young giving begging calls at French Creek State Park June 1, 1991, in the pine swamp near the headquarters.

Joanne Kintner reported a Barred Owl near Bechtelsville from July 3 to 10, 1988. It sat on a wire and flew to fields across the road to hunt. She found it dead on the 10th, apparently struck by a car. Joan Silagy, Dean Kendall, and Ernie Schiefer recorded a Barred Owl at the Berks Campus of Penn State University in Spring Township from December 1 to 11, 1993. Bill and Pam Munroe heard one intermittently at State Game Lands 274 in Spring Township from September 11, 1994, to April 26, 1996. Rudy Keller heard one in District and Pike townships from April 3, 1995, to August 25, 1996.

A single bird flushed at Flying Hill December 7, 1924, is Earl Poole's only local observation. Byron Nunemacher and Calvin Stott saw one along the Schuylkill River at Seyfert on December 28, 1924.

Levi Mengel took an egg at Douglassville April 10, 1888, from a nest in an elm tree 45 feet from the ground. He secured a specimen in Albany Township May 16, 1885. Both are in the Reading Public Museum collection.

The Barred Owl appeared on the Reading Christmas Bird Count five of 86 years, three of the last 10. Single birds were recorded on all five occasions, the last December 18, 1994. A peak count of three was found on the Hamburg Christmas Bird Count December 27, 1987. Four birds were reported at Rattling Run during the Hamburg count week in 1994.

LONG-EARED OWL *Asio otus*

Rare winter visitor

Formerly a rare and local breeding resident, the Long-eared Owl is now a rare visitor seen from December to March when it roosts in evergreen groves, often in bands of considerable size. There are no recent nesting records.

It decreased in numbers, largely due to its being mistaken for the Great Horned Owl. Many had been turned in to the State Game Commission for the bounty offered for that species earlier this century, and nearly all of the dozen or more local roosts that Earl Poole had known over 40 years had been abandoned because of repeated disturbance. He examined many quarts of pellets from under its roosts and determined its prey consists almost entirely of mice, rats, and shrews.

Most recent observations are in the fall and winter, but there are scattered records throughout the year. Seth Benz found a Long-eared Owl July 7, 1974, on a farm in Eckville.

Long-eared Owls have roosted near Blue Marsh Lake. Harold and Joan Silagy discovered between 11 and 13 owls in a tangled, overgrown orchard in Penn Township from January 15 to March 19, 1989. Eight owls roosted in Jefferson Township between January 5 and February 8, 1987 (H. and J.S.). Barry Pounder recorded three there April 3, 1987.

Between three and five Long-eared Owls roosted in shrubbery at a residential development in Whitfield during March 1994, photographed on March 7 (Bill Uhrich).

Nine sets of eggs in the Reading Public Museum were taken in various parts of Berks County, the earliest April 4 (1911 - S. Gruber), and the latest May 17 (1889 - Levi Mengel). Levi Mengel took a set of six eggs near Virginville May 17, 1889, from a hollow buttonwood tree 20 feet from the ground. He took a set of five eggs in Bethel Township April 30, 1885, from a nest in a hollow chestnut stump at least 20 feet from the ground.

Walter H. Leibelsperger found it breeding at Virginville April 7, 1907; near Pricetown April 16, 1911; and near Perryville April 13, 1911.

On May 4, 1932, Poole saw three young just out of the nest near Shartlesville. On June 4, he saw two young accompanied by a parent.

During 1934 Byron Nunemacher and Poole saw a nest in the hills above Fleetwood on which one of the parents was setting on April 22, while the mate roosted in a nearby scrub pine. On May 13, the young had left the nest and were perched in the nest tree.

In 1938 a pair nested in jack pines on the Nolde estate in Cumru Township and remained in the grove until June 17, according to C. A. DeLong, the forester. Jim Brett and Terry Bingaman found a nest with three young accompanied by both parents in June 1953 at Dives Hill, south of Shillington. They found two young in the same area in June 1954. On May 18, 1955, Dr. Weiman showed Poole a family group that had come from a nest in a thick growth of spruces on the former Berks County Sanatorium grounds in Bern Township.

There are eight fall records at Hawk Mountain ranging from October 3 (1951) to November 14 (1949). During 1942, two Long-eared Owls were present during most of the fall. Maurice Broun heard one calling from the escarpment above the shelters on October 29, 1949. One owl wintered from February to March 1986 (Stan Senner, Jim Brett).

The Long-eared Owl has appeared on the Reading Christmas Bird Count 16 of 86 years, twice in the last 10, with a maximum of 12 on December 30, 1964. The high for the Hamburg Christmas Bird Count is 13 on December 28, 1986. The peak for the Bernville count is eight on January 1, 1990.

SHORT-EARED OWL *Asio flammeus*
Rare migrant and rare winter resident

The Short-eared Owl is a rather rare migrant and a rare winter resident. The winter vole population determines the frequency of sightings.

The fields around Blue Marsh Lake have been the most reliable place in Berks County recently to see the Short-eared Owl. Harold and Joan Silagy recorded five January 10, 1986; two from March 27 to April 8, 1993; and two near Bright School Road January 15, 1995.

The wintering period ranges from November 7 (1935) to April 29 (1885 - Levi Mengel).

Earl Poole flushed 15 in one group at Lake Ontelaunee on April 19, 1935. The most recent high count is nine January 18, 1989, near Blue Marsh Lake (Harold and Joan Silagy).

Levi Mengel took a clutch of eggs attributed to this species at Slate Hill near Shillington on April 18, 1887, but Poole questioned whether these eggs were correctly identified.

Through May, June, and July 1932, Poole saw a Short-eared Owl on a number of occasions flying over the meadows at the head of Lake Ontelaunee in broad daylight and at dusk. He saw three flying over the meadows at 10 a.m. July 10, 1932. He saw one at the same place on July 27, 1929, and three on July 14, 1935. At least one remained until August 18. During 1935 the dam level was raised and the marshy meadows were flooded. No Short-eared Owl has been seen there during the breeding season since then.

While usually found roosting in marshes and weed-grown meadows, during the winter of 1926–1927 a small flock of four or five congregated in the evergreen trees of the Charles Evans Cemetery in Reading, after the manner of Long-eared Owls (Anna Deeter, Earl Rollman, Byron Nunemacher, E.P.). During the late winter of 1960–1961, a group of four roosted both in a weedy field and in evergreens at Muhlenberg Park, a suburb of Reading. They remained there at least until March 29 (E.P.).

The Short-eared Owl has been recorded in migration during the day at Hawk Mountain in both spring and fall. On April 20, 1961, Alex Nagy saw one flying southwest to northeast over the headquarters. Scott Weidensaul flushed one from the Cobble April 21, 1995. Dr. Richard Clark recorded a Short-eared Owl flying past the South Lookout October 14, 1972, and Doug Cook sighted one there October 21, 1978. One perched in an oak tree near Owl's Head December 16, 1980. Laurie Goodrich saw one fly past the North Lookout at 10:30 a.m. November 8, 1990. She spotted a Short-eared Owl soaring high over Number Five on October 24, 1995. It dropped down and passed low in front of the lookout to the south and circled over the Kettle, appearing to want to perch on the lookout. It then dove into the trees behind the lookout and perched on rocks near the trail. It took off for the south after circling a few more times in the Kettle.

Specimens in the Levi Mengel collection were taken in Pricetown April 28, 1885, and in Bethel Township April 29, 1885. Two other specimens in the Reading Public Museum were shot by gunners at Kirbyville November 23, 1925, and near Host on November 25 of the same year.

Jonas Stern of Kutztown and D. Frank Keller of Reading mentioned the Short-eared Owl as a winter visitor (Warren, 1890:149).

The Short-eared Owl has been recorded on the Reading Christmas Bird Count twice in 86 years, single birds on December 26, 1960, and December 31, 1961. One owl was recorded on the Hamburg Christmas Bird Count January 3, 1982.

Calvin Stump of Maxatawny gives the Short-eared Owl the Pennsylvania German names "die Feldeil" or "die gross Feldeil." Stump recalled that these birds were found in the tall grass of pasture land in Maxatawny Township, and that a number of them were flushed during several summers (Rupp, 1946:148).

NORTHERN SAW-WHET OWL *Aegolius acadicus*
Uncommon resident

The Northern Saw-whet Owl is an uncommon local breeding resident and regular fall migrant along the Kittatinny Ridge. It is present year-round in Berks County, usually in low numbers. However, this owl is sometimes more common during fall and winter. The migration occurs during October and November.

During October 1981, Seth Benz counted 18 Northern Saw-whet Owls on an evening walk at Hawk Mountain Sanctuary and adjacent State Game Lands. Apparently they were attracted to the abundance of flying squirrels.

The Northern Saw-whet Owl is a breeding summer resident found in, but not restricted to, the Kittatinny Ridge in cool mountain ravines and mountain-top cliff-sides where large stands of hemlocks dominate.

Breeding records include five young at the South Lookout at Hawk Mountain Sanctuary June 20, 1981 (Seth Benz), and two adults and fledglings in Bern Township June 25, 1982. Laurie Goodrich recorded Northern Saw-whet Owls near the River of Rocks throughout the summer of 1987 and in June 1988.

Kerry Grim observed recently fledged young at the Hamburg reservoir July 11, 1985, in a Hemlock grove at an elevation of 1,240 feet. An adult was perched nearby and called nonstop for more than 20 minutes, offering no protection for its young.

Usually this little owl is found dozing during the day, perched low in some dense evergreen or in a tangle of Japanese honeysuckle, but on November 23, 1919, John Eshelman and Earl Poole saw one with a white-footed mouse that it had evidently just caught before noon in a cedar grove near Beckersville. This was the first of Poole's five observations of this small owl in Berks County.

This owl is probably more common than numbers indicate. Its call has little carrying power. To complicate matters, the Eastern Screech-Owl sometimes will do a perfect imitation of a Saw-whet.

On April 30, 1922, Poole found an adult Northern Saw-whet Owl roosting within four feet of the ground in a clump of young hemlocks at Eckville. From the pellets scattered about and the liberal sprinkling of lime on the ground below, this bird had evidently been using the roosting place for some time, and the date is well within the nesting period of the species. Levi Mengel collected a Northern Saw-whet Owl about 20 miles west of this point along the Blue Mountain in Bethel Township on April 20, 1885.

Rudy Keller observed an aggressive and vocal Northern Saw-whet Owl in District Township from February 27 to March 12, 1970. As he stood at his front door imitating its call one evening, it swooped at him out of the darkness, looking for the rival owl. It called almost every night, and Keller studied it several times by flashlight.

During the late fall and winter between 1976 and 1980, Seth Benz and Michael Root "tooted" birds up from the eastern boundary of Hawk Mountain Sanctuary. On November 17, 1985, a Northern Saw-whet Owl roosted in a hemlock by the front door of the Visitor Center at Hawk Mountain, where it slept while visitors came by in droves to see it. It flew off at dusk (Laurie Goodrich).

Maurice Broun and many observers at the North Lookout on October 15, 1960, witnessed 30 to 40 kinglets gang up on a Northern Saw-whet Owl.

There are other records from earlier this century. Walter Leibelsperger recorded one in Albany Township November 12, 1913. Byron Nunemacher heard and saw one November 16, 1921, at Antietam. Nunemacher and Poole found the remains of one that had been recently killed by some larger bird of prey at Moselem on December 25, 1926. Poole saw one sleeping in a scrub pine in the Hessian Camp within the city of Reading on January 30, 1920.

The Northern Saw-whet Owl has been recorded on the Reading Christmas Bird Count three of 86 years, single birds on December 16, 1990; December 19, 1993; and December 18, 1994. The peak for the Hamburg Christmas Bird Count is seven on December 29, 1985.

COMMON NIGHTHAWK *Chordeiles minor*

Locally common summer resident

A common migrant and locally common summer resident, the Common Nighthawk is most numerous in towns and the city of Reading where it nests on flat, gravel roofs. It is one of the few native birds that have made themselves at home in densely populated areas. Like most of the neotropical migrants, though, the Common Nighthawk has experienced population fluctuations throughout this century.

An early arrival in Reading is April 27 (1957- E.P. *fide* Byron Nunemacher), but the Common Nighthawk usually arrives by the second week of May.

Early in the century, Richard Harlow found the Common Nighthawk more common in parts of Berks County than elsewhere in the state (Harlow, 1918:28). The 69 sets of eggs in the Reading Public Museum collected in the county by Levi Mengel, Walter Leibelsperger, and others prior to 1914, would seem to lend credence to this belief. The nesting dates from these sets are between May 27 (1899) and July 30 (1903). Sets collected by Mengel all contain two eggs and were collected from the ground or on cinder banks. During this century it has nested on slag roofs in the heart of the city of Reading. While it is most active in the early morning and at dusk, it frequently hunts at midday, and Earl Poole did not think it unusual to see one perched for hours throughout the day on the crossarm of a telegraph pole on a busy street.

During August these birds gather in loose bands, which increase in size as the month progresses until they sometimes reach into the hundreds. These flocks appear to move aimlessly about the country for a while, but finally, during the last week of August or early in September, they move definitely and swiftly to the south, leaving a few stragglers which may remain into October. Matt Spence saw 190 Common Nighthawks over Reading August 25, 1993, and Ernie Schiefer saw over 100 there September 4, 1992.

The Common Nighthawk can be seen in migration at Hawk Mountain Sanctuary. Between 5:15 and 7 p.m. August 30, 1950, Tommy Hanson witnessed a flight of 2,179 Nighthawks over the North Lookout before rain terminated the flight. On August 28, 1955, Maurice Broun recorded 1,400 birds there, 865 before 10 a.m. Recent high counts at Hawk Mountain are 26 on September 3, 1987, and 22 on August 29, 1983.

In Berks it is last seen anywhere from August 8 (1926) to October 10 (1996 - North Lookout at Hawk Mountain). Most years, the Common Nighthawk is gone by the second week in September.

The Pennsylvania Germans refer to the Common Nighthawk as "der Wibberwill." In Berks, "der Schwupp" is a dialect version of the English word "swoop," a reference to its flight style. Another name from Berks is "Lufthengscht" or "air stallion" (Rupp, 1946:151-154).

CHUCK-WILL'S-WIDOW *Caprimulgus carolinensis*
Accidental vagrant

Kerry Grim heard a Chuck-will's-widow call from a Virginia (scrub) pine woods in Hamburg June 11, 1984. Phil Haas and Ron Ramsey heard another call near the Port Clinton Fire Tower May 18, 1986.

While he was painting his house on Bloody Spring Road near Strausstown at 3:30 p.m June 15, 1996, Chuck Cravotta "...heard a Chuck-will's-widow calling from its roost at an overgrown field edge approximately 50 yards southeast of my front door. The bird called softly repeating its namesake about six times in succession, paused for several minutes, and then resumed the calls. I was unable to make a visual confirmation before the calls ceased."

WHIP-POOR-WILL *Caprimulgus vociferus*
Locally uncommon

The Whip-poor-will is an uncommon summer resident in extensive second-growth woodlands, particularly around clearings, in northern and southern Berks County. It was a regular breeding bird during the 1950s and 1960s, but its numbers have decreased in recent years. In 1930 and 1947, Earl Poole considered it a common summer resident in heavily wooded, hilly regions of the county. It is occasionally found elsewhere during migrations.

At State Game Lands 110 near Shartlesville, Kerry Grim recorded it as a summer resident from the mid-1980s until 1991. Laurie Goodrich and Jim Giacomo found one in May and June 1995 on the ridge top of State Game Lands 106 in Eckville. Tom Leckey reported one calling in the River of Rocks area at Hawk Mountain June 20, 1988. Rich Bonnett heard two Whip-poor-wills call until the end of August near Birdsboro in 1990 and two calling all summer near French Creek State Park in 1991. Harold and Joan Silagy heard one in Bern Township May 7, 1987, and in Tulpehocken Township June 1, 1991.

The earliest arrival date is April 4 (1989 - Rudy Keller in Pike Township). At Hawk Mountain, Maurice Broun found the Whip-Poor-Will on April 14 (1963) and April 15 (1947, 1960).

Broun heard a Whip-poor-will give 1,091 consecutive calls at the lower shelters at Hawk Mountain on April 26, 1958.

The Whip-poor-will leaves by the last of September, but a few may remain into October. Some late dates are October 3 (1942 - Maurice Broun) and October 13 (1953 - found dead, Robert Cook). Poole believed that fall dates are probably not representative since these birds call irregularly at this season and migrants must have occurred more frequently than his few records indicated.

Eight sets of eggs taken by Levi Mengel between May 22 (1884) and July 10 (1894) are in the Reading Public Museum collection. These collected sets from nests on the ground contain one or two eggs.

The Pennsylvania German name is "der Wibberwill," a very common and popular name, based on the bird's clear call (Rupp, 1946:150).

According to Jim Brett, Elmer Rauch of Kempton claims the Whip-poor-will says in the dialect: "Ei quick weik will, Ei quick weik will, Ei quick weik will," or "I get who I want."

William Rupp writes: "Generally our people heard the Whip-poor-will and saw the Nighthawk. The name and call of the former were therefore attributed to the latter whose habits rendered it more conspicuous, and both birds were frequently considered to be the same species" (Rupp, 1946:150).

Another name for the bird is "der Reggevoggel." Rupp says, "When the bird's call was heard on a warm evening in spring, it was said that the weather would change during the night and that a warm, slow rain ('en Landregge') would set in the next day" (Rupp, 1946:150).

CHIMNEY SWIFT *Chaetura pelagica*
Abundant migrant and summer resident

An abundant migrant and summer resident throughout Berks County, the Chimney Swift is well known in both city and country as an inhabitant of unused chimneys. It also nests on occasion in sheds, attics, and dark barns. There are no known recent records of its nesting in hollow trees, its original habitat. In late summer and early fall it sometimes roosts in numbers in abandoned smokestacks.

An early date in Reading is April 12 (1924 - Earl Poole), but it usually arrives by the third week in April. Kerry Grim counted 500 Chimney Swifts at the Schuylkill River in Reading May 6, 1978.

Maurice Broun kept records of Chimney Swift pairs that nested at Schaumboch's at Hawk Mountain Sanctuary from the 1930s into the 1950s. On July 18, 1951, a pair was feeding young who took their initial flight the next day. On August 9 and 10, a family of eight was cruising and feeding around the house. In 1955, a family of young was fed in the nest through late August until September 3. The pair was gone on September 11. In 1961, young birds left the nest by July 24.

Fall departure dates vary widely from year to year. At Reading Poole failed to see it some years after September 21, but quite often it lingered on until October. A lone bird seen on October 19 (1919) is his latest record. Hawk Mountain dates from the North Lookout range from early August through October 17 (1996).

Joan Silagy and Rudy Keller counted 250 at Blue Marsh Lake September 7, 1992. A high count of 102 Chimney Swifts was recorded at Hawk Mountain September 8, 1992.

Nine sets of eggs in the Reading Public Museum were taken between June 9 (1896) and July 10 (1897). Levi Mengel found nests with clutch sizes of from two to four eggs in an old corn crib, in a fireplace of an old outhouse, on the wall of a deserted furnace, on the side of an old building, and on the side of a wagon shed's wall.

The most common Pennsylvania German name heard in Berks County for the Chimney Swift is "die Scharnschteeschwallem." Another is "die Russ-schwalm," meaning "soot swallow." One Berks informant also applied the names for the Nighthawk to the Chimney Swift. Swifts have even been referred to as "Schpeckmeis," or bats, due to their manner of flight (Rupp, 1946:157).

RUBY-THROATED HUMMINGBIRD *Archilochus colubris*

Fairly common summer resident

A fairly common migrant and summer resident, the Ruby-throated Hummingbird is most widely distributed in late August and September and nests in extensive woodlands as well as near cultivated areas.

Observations have increased recently with the popularity of feeders and landscaping for the Hummingbird. Favorite flowers are quince, columbine, bee balm, scarlet sage, and jewel weed. When blossoms are no longer available, it has been seen capturing insects on the wing.

The earliest arrival date for Reading is April 19 (1941 - Byron Nunemacher). Local sets of eggs in the Reading Public Museum collection have been taken between June 9 (1892) and July 5 (1890). The clutch size of all the sets is two eggs. Levi Mengel took a nest at 620 Penn Street, Reading, on August 1, 1892, the day that two young left the nest.

The Hummingbird is most in evidence throughout the summer and into September, when it visits gardens and feeders in numbers, often making itself conspicuous by its constant bickering.

The Ruby-throated Hummingbird uses the Kittatinny Ridge during migration. The high season total at Hawk Mountain in recent years is 128 in 1996.

Observers at Hawk Mountain have determined that there are two peaks to the migration. Maurice Broun found that locally breeding males at Hawk Mountain depart before the females and immatures, usually by late August. In 1955 he noted that the males had left by August 27, but the females were at his feeders until September 11. Similarly, in 1957 he noted that females were present until September 16, long after the departure of the local males (Willimont, 1988:486).

Single-day peak counts at Hawk Mountain are 45 on September 3, 1975 (Jim Brett), and 39 on August 29, 1967 (Richard Sharadin). The earliest migrant there was recorded on August 2 (1983) and the latest September 29 (1953, 1956 - Maurice Broun).

Rudy Keller found one feeding on *salvia* flowers in District Township October 18, 1972.

Earl Poole writes in 1964 of a hummingbird found numbed from the cold near Pricetown some years before. It was kept alive by a resident until well into late December but finally escaped.

The Ruby-throated Hummingbird has several colorful names in the Pennsylvania German. "Der Schnarrvoggel," referring to its halting and jerking movements, is a name used throughout the region. Another form is "es Schnarrveggli." "Der Blummeriecher" means the little bird that smells the flowers (Rupp, 1946:158-160).

BELTED KINGFISHER *Ceryle alcyon*

Common summer resident

A common summer resident, the Belted Kingfisher breeds wherever high vertical cut banks are available and reasonably pure, unpolluted streams afford an adequate supply of food.

It winters in reduced numbers. Earl Poole failed to find it during January and February only once - in 1925. It arrived that year on March 7.

Its departure in fall is irregular and may take place anywhere from October 14 (1923) to January 1 (1937). Fall dates at Hawk Mountain's North Lookout include September 26, 1988; September 14, 1990; and September 21, 1992.

Dates on eight sets of eggs in the Levi Mengel collection range from May 19 (1895) to June 15 (1890). He found the nests in banks along the Schuylkill River and the Tulpehocken Creek, seven to eight feet into the bank. Clutch sizes in these sets are from four to six eggs.

The Belted Kingfisher has been recorded on the Reading Christmas Bird Count 75 of 86 years, 10 of the last 10, with a maximum of 25 on December 20, 1992. The high for the Hamburg Christmas Bird Count is 27 on December 29, 1984. The peak for the Bernville count is 20 on January 1, 1992.

The Pennsylvania Germans refer to this bird as "der Fishroijer," the same name applied to the herons and bitterns. Raymond E. Kiebach offers the name "der Fischfresser," meaning "fish glutton." The most common name is probably the dialect form of the English, "Kingfisha" (Rupp, 1946:160-161).

RED-HEADED WOODPECKER *Melanerpes erythrocephalus*
Rare and local

An increasingly rare and local summer resident in the Oley and Great valleys, the Red-headed Woodpecker nests in scattered groves and shade trees in farm country and can be seen migrating in fall along the Kittatinny Ridge. Immature birds winter erratically in favorable places.

A cavity nester, the Red-headed Woodpecker has declined in Berks County since the introduction of the European Starling in the beginning of this century. The Red-headed Woodpecker, like the Northern Flicker, is a terrestrial feeder and during winter will feed on corn from the fields.

When not wintering locally, the Red-headed Woodpecker arrives in Berks during the latter half of April or early in May. The earliest arrival date around Reading is April 21 (1929). Maurice Broun saw an adult flying up the road by Schaumboch's at Hawk Mountain on April 16, 1953.

Most of these woodpeckers leave by the last days of September, and it is in this month that the migrants pass through. A few remain into October, but departure dates are uncertain because of the occasional wintering individuals. During the winter of 1918-1919 one wintered in Carsonia Park and was seen repeatedly until March 16 (Anna Deeter). Another was observed at Wyomissing January 17, 1921 (G. Henry Mengel), and one was found near Blandon throughout the winter of 1928 - 1929 (A.D., Earl Poole).

Earl Poole's departure dates in Berks County up to 1941, before the Red-headed Woodpecker became extremely local, are from September 7 (1930) to November 3 (1939).

Hawk Mountain records show peak counts in late September and early October with a late date of November 7 (1993). Fall migration counts have fluctuated. The season high is 63 during the fall of 1977 (*American Birds*, 32(2):187), a number which may be an anomaly. Numbers have decreased slightly from the early 1980s when from five to 27 birds were recorded seasonally to the early 1990s when from three to seven birds were counted. Three birds were recorded during the fall of 1996. Single-day peaks include seven on September 7, 1985; five on October 22, 1984; and four on September 21, 1960, and September 19, 1983. An additional spring record there is May 11, 1989.

Levi Mengel collected four sets of eggs from May 30 (1890) to June 20 (1895) in Blandon, Virginville, Mount Penn, and near Birdsboro. One set has three eggs, one has four, and two have five.

The Red-headed Woodpecker has been recorded on the Reading Christmas Bird Count 20 of 86 years, four of the last 10, with a maximum of five on January 1, 1978. The peak for the Hamburg Christmas Bird Count is four on December 26, 1983, and December 29, 1985. The high for the Bernville count is two on January 5, 1986.

Pennsylvania German names for the Red-headed Woodpecker include "der Rotkopp" and "der rotkeppich Woodpicker." Rev. Alfred J. Herman of Maxatawny Township referred to this bird as "der Globber." Calvin Stump reports that these birds are said to have been very abundant at the old Herman homestead in Maxatawny. The Blue Jays were also plentiful there, and Pastor Herman is said to have called them "birds of paradise." The general names like "Woodpicker" and "Schpecht" would also apply to the Red-headed Woodpecker (Rupp, 1946:168).

William Rupp writes: "These colorful birds once were a familiar sight. You saw them on the oaks and chestnuts, on the old rail fences and on posts, and in the tall, old apple and cherry trees in the orchard. Great numbers of them were shot, probably because of their destructive habits, for they were not eaten as were the Flickers. The passing of the old trees and fence posts has deprived them of breeding places and their numbers have been greatly reduced" (Rupp, 1946:169-170).

RED-BELLIED WOODPECKER *Melanerpes carolinus*
Fairly common resident

The Red-bellied Woodpecker, like the Mockingbird and Tufted Titmouse, is a southern species which has greatly expanded its range north during the latter half of this century. Its numbers have increased to where it is now the third commonest woodpecker in Berks County after the Downy and the Northern Flicker.

During the first half of this century, however, Earl Poole regarded the Red-bellied Woodpecker as a rare visitor but probably more frequent in the nineteenth century, based on specimens collected by Levi Mengel in Bethel Township May 17, 1885; along the Wyomissing Creek July 1, 1885; and at Monocacy Hill November 16, 1890. Samuel Wishnieski collected a Red-bellied Woodpecker near Friedensburg January 10, 1930.

Mengel collected a set of six eggs June 5, 1898, from a cavity 12 inches deep in a dead stump nine feet from the ground in DeWee's Woods in Muhlenberg Township.

Poole writes that stragglers had been reported as far north as Hawk Mountain from April 26 to May 2, 1954. Since 1985, the Red-bellied Woodpecker has been seen regularly there in small numbers during fall from three to 21 (1987) annually, with a peak count of 10 on October 2, 1987. It first nested at Hawk Mountain in 1967.

A vocal bird, the Red-bellied Woodpecker is more tolerant of humans and can reside in smaller woodlots than the Hairy Woodpecker.

The Red-bellied Woodpecker was first recorded on the Reading Christmas Bird Count in 1961 and has been seen each year since with a maximum of 91 on December 19, 1993. The Hamburg Christmas Bird Count recorded a peak of 101 birds on December 27, 1992. The high for the Bernville count is 70 on January 1, 1992.

It was listed by John F. Hofmann in 1890.

YELLOW-BELLIED SAPSUCKER *Sphyrapicus varius*
Fairly common migrant

The Yellow-bellied Sapsucker is a fairly common migrant and regular winter resident in Berks County.

Spring migration dates range from March 23 (1948) to May 21 (1928). The March 23rd Sapsucker arrived at Schaumboch's on Hawk Mountain and stayed for 23 days, feeding on persimmons (Maurice Broun). A more recent late spring date is May 10 (1964 - Matt Spence at Shillington).

The early fall date is September 13 (1941 - M.B.) at Hawk Mountain. Since there are many winter records, it is practically impossible in most cases to separate actual departure dates, although there is usually a marked reduction in the number of Sapsuckers present by the middle of October. The late date for migrants at Hawk Mountain is October 29 (1995). In recent years, between one and seven Yellow-bellied Sapsuckers have been recorded there during each fall season.

Nearly all of Earl Poole's winter records are from the Schuylkill River below Reading.

In the wooded hills of eastern Berks, the Yellow-bellied Sapsucker can be found wintering in most years, arriving in late September or October and departing in April. The bird is easily overlooked unless its quiet tapping or occasional mewing call is heard. During the coldest weather, it will eat fruit but rarely comes to feeders (Rudy Keller).

D. Frank Keller of Reading listed the Yellow-bellied Sapsucker as a migrant (Warren, 1890:169).

The Yellow-bellied Sapsucker has appeared on the Reading Christmas Bird Count 45 of 86 years, 10 of the last 10, with a maximum of 15 on December 18, 1983. The peak on the Hamburg Christmas Bird Count is 21 on December 27, 1992. The high for the Bernville count is five on January 3, 1988, and January 1, 1992.

DOWNY WOODPECKER *Picoides pubescens*
Common resident

The most common and vocal of Berks County's woodpeckers, the Downy Woodpecker is a common resident, more visible and familiar in winter when it comes to feeding stations.

A later nester than the Hairy Woodpecker, the Downy often brings its young to feeders for suet. Levi Mengel took a set of two eggs at Willow Creek June 15, 1895, and a set of six eggs at Antietam June 11, 1901.

The Downy Woodpecker has appeared on the Reading Christmas Bird Count 85 of 86 years, unrecorded only during the first count in 1911, with a maximum of 223 on December 27, 1970. For Reading, the count of Downy Woodpeckers has dropped 20 percent in recent years. Between 1977 and 1986, the count averaged 137, but between 1987 and 1996, it averaged 112. The high count for the Hamburg Christmas Bird Count is 305 on December 29, 1985. The peak for the Bernville count is 166 on January 3, 1988.

The Pennsylvania Germans in Berks County call the Downy Woodpecker "der scheckich Woodpicker," the spotted woodpecker - a name which also applies to the Hairy. "Der schiwwerich Woodpicker," the gray-spotted woodpecker, is another name which applies to both the Downy and the Hairy woodpeckers (Rupp, 1946:170-171).

197

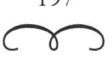

HAIRY WOODPECKER *Picoides villosus*
Fairly Common Resident

A fairly common resident, the Hairy Woodpecker is more frequently seen in winter. Earl Poole believed that in the first half of this century, the Hairy Woodpecker was about one-seventh as abundant as the Downy.

During the breeding seasons this woodpecker retires to the deeper woodland, where it is more often heard than seen. Poole found it breeding at Grill, Monocacy Hill, Mohnton, Mount Penn, near Strausstown, and well up on the side of the Blue Mountain at Pulpit Rock, where one was feeding well-grown young on June 16, 1917.

Because the Hairy Woodpecker needs larger woodlands for breeding, it is susceptible to disturbance from forest fragmentation. The numbers in mature forests appear to be stable but are decreasing in fragmented areas where the Red-bellied Woodpecker, more of an edge-habitat bird, seems to be displacing it.

The Hairy Woodpecker has been recorded on the Reading Christmas Bird Count 70 of 86 years, 10 of the last 10, with a maximum of 41 on December 15, 1974. Like the Downy, the Hairy Woodpecker has shown a drop of about 25 percent on recent counts. From 1977 to 1986, the Hairy numbers on the Reading count averaged 24, while from 1987 to 1996, the numbers averaged 18. The high for the Hamburg Christmas Bird Count is 41 on December 26, 1983. Averages on the Hamburg count are not decreasing. The peak for the Bernville count is 18 on January 2, 1994.

There is the potential to mistake an immature Hairy Woodpecker with yellow markings for the Three-toed Woodpecker. Male and female Hairy Woodpeckers with yellow on their heads remained throughout the summer of 1991 at Hawk Mountain (Keller, 1991e:78).

A set of four eggs in the Levi Mengel collection at the Reading Public Museum was taken from a nest in a hollow tree along the Wyomissing Creek June 2, 1892.

BLACK-BACKED WOODPECKER *Picoides arcticus*
Casual

On November 1, 1953, Samuel Wishnieski of the Reading Public Museum staff reported seeing a female Black-backed Woodpecker on the Nolde estate near Reading. This bird was flaking bark off a sickly red pine tree and allowed him to approach within 10 feet, giving him an opportunity to observe closely all the details of its plumage. Later he checked with skins in the museum collection. The bird could not be found on the following day.

Nevin Musser and Clair Mast reported a male Black-backed Woodpecker on the watershed at Lake Ontelaunee on March 3, 1956. Earl Poole was unable to find this bird later on the same day, but he did see it at very close range near the same spot on March 10. It was absurdly tame at the time and allowed him to watch it at leisure as it worked within three feet of the ground on a dead pine, peeling off bark and then drilling small holes for borers. He was able to note every detail: approximate size of a Hairy Woodpecker, solid black back, white cheek marks and throat, barred breast, white bars on primaries and white outer tail feathers. The yellow crown patch was somewhat smaller than usual and may have indicated a young male (Poole, 1958:22).

Warren Kalbach reported one at Moselem on December 3, 1961.

On October 26, 1974, Richard Sharadin, Catherine Elwell, and Tom Clauser saw a Black-backed Woodpecker within 30 yards of the South Lookout at Hawk Mountain around 8:05 a.m. It appeared to land a short distance north of the lookout, but they were unable to relocate it. The bird called several times in flight. At 8:30 a.m. on November 2 of the same year, Elwell saw possibly the same bird on a dead red pine west of Schaumboch's orchard. She saw the yellow cap as it flew. This record is incorrectly listed under the Three-toed Woodpecker in Merill Wood's *Birds of Pennsylvania* (Wood, 1979:75).

There are three records of Black-backed Woodpeckers on the Reading Christmas Bird Count. On December 30, 1964, Warren Faust, Charles Schaich, Warren Kalbach, and Matt Spence found a female near the dam breast at Lake Ontelaunee. June Archambault reported that from December 4, 1974, to January 4, 1975, a Black-backed Woodpecker visited a feeder in her yard near Pine Avenue in Birdsboro. Joan Silagy and Doris Steffey identified the bird on the former date. The bird was included on the Reading Count December 14, 1974. George Kershner recorded one at Antietam Lake December 21, 1980.

NORTHERN FLICKER *Colaptes auratus*

Common summer resident

A common summer resident, the Northern Flicker is regular during mild winters but sometimes remains in sheltered places during severe winters, as in 1924-1925, 1994-1995, and 1995-1996. It arrives in numbers in Berks County during the second week of March.

Although its fall movements depend largely upon the food supply, the Northern Flicker is not a bird that comes to feeders. Bands of various sizes often wander about until December, gradually disappearing until only the few wintering individuals are left.

In eastern Berks, there is a mass movement of Flickers in late September through mid-October with loose flocks widespread in fields and forest edges. Small numbers remain through the winter (Rudy Keller).

At Hawk Mountain, Maurice Broun recorded large fall flights along the ridge during the 1950s with many dates of 100 or more birds. The peak flight occurred October 6, 1954, when over 350 Flickers passed the North Lookout. Much smaller numbers have been recorded recently as Northern Flicker movements over the North Lookout have declined, perhaps due to the milder winters which allow the bird to stay closer to its summer territories. The recent fall season high count of 72 was recorded during 1991 with 15 seen on October 13.

Broun recorded a spring flight at Hawk Mountain of over 100 Flickers on April 6, 1955.

The Northern Flicker has appeared on the Reading Christmas Bird Count 72 of 86 years, 10 of the last 10, with a maximum of 78 on December 19, 1993. The last Reading count when a Northern Flicker went unrecorded was in 1934. The Hamburg Christmas Bird Count recorded a high of 103 on December 28, 1986. The peak for the Bernville count is 70 on January 3, 1993.

Eggs in the Levi Mengel collection at the Reading Public Museum were taken from May 17 (1888) to June 18 (1890). Clutch sizes in these sets range from five to 15 eggs.

A very common name for the Northern Flicker throughout the Pennsylvania German region is "des Gehlschpect." "Der Grieschpecht" is another name used which is derived from the German "Grunspecht," the largest of the European green woodpeckers that resemble the Flicker in shape and habit but not in color. Raymond E. Kiebach of Reading reports that "Grieschpecht" is the name for a young Flicker that has not left its nest, or for one that has just left the nest and still is unable to fly. This name was used in the Host section of Berks County and also in lower Berks and upper Montgomery counties from where his parents had come. He gives the usual "Gehlschpecht" for the adult Flicker, also "Schpecht" for any flicker or woodpecker. Another name is the dialect form of the English "Woodpicker," a common general name for all the woodpeckers (Rupp, 1946:163-164).

William Rupp writes that the lack of a good name for the woodpecker family has been explained by saying that the Northern Flicker once was an important game bird and therefore got specific names, while all the others of lesser importance were passed by. He explains:

There was a time when many Flickers were shot for food, and the young were watched and trapped in the nests just before they were ready to take wing. "Gehlschbecht-bodboi" was a particular delicacy, and the birds are said to have had a better taste than squabs. [Raymond E.] Hollenbach writes, "I remember very well that my father liked to shoot these birds, which was not much of a sport, because the flickers congregated in the gum trees, the fruit of which they ate, and all one had to do was to sit and wait for them." Another has said that lots of them were shot in the fall when they were after "Gummebeere." [Calvin] Stump has told us of a valley in Albany Township, Berks County, which contained many old gum trees in which the Flickers nested and to which they came in large flocks in the fall to feed on the berries. Hunters would lie in wait on both sides of the valley and fire into the trees, with each shot bringing down a few Flickers. He also recalls that the tongues of the Flickers were removed, dried and kept in a small box for use as "charms." It was an old belief, he says, that if you put a Flicker's tongue in your mouth and then kissed a child or a young person, the one kissed would have a kind disposition ever after (Rupp, 1946:165-166).

PILEATED WOODPECKER *Dryocopus pileatus*
Uncommon resident

During the beginning of this century, Earl Poole considered the Pileated Woodpecker a rare and local resident in the Blue Mountain region, but as the forests matured during the past half century, this woodpecker has become more common and nests regularly along the Blue Mountain, Nolde Forest, Hay Creek, French Creek, Mount Penn, and the wooded ridges of eastern and southern Berks County.

On May 28, 1922, Poole had an excellent view of one of these fine birds along the base of the Blue Mountain in Albany Township after the bird had been supposedly extirpated from the county for at least 25 years. According to residents of the area, the Pileated Woodpecker was unknown in that section. On November 17, 1924, two were shot by a squatter under the pretext that they were "after his chickens!" However, a few were still seen in the vicinity until 1938 (E.P.).

According to Jacob Degler, who lived along the mountain near Strausstown, Pileated Woodpeckers bred near his home in 1933, and remained in that neighborhood at least until 1935. Byron Nunemacher and Poole saw one near there on April 14, 1928.

Several pairs nest on or adjacent to the Hawk Mountain Sanctuary in northern Berks, yet unless they happen to be calling or drumming, particularly during the early morning hours, they are comparatively rarely seen. Poole heard two calling and one working on what he believed to be a nest near the Sanctuary on April 30, 1939.

Poole writes in 1964: "Rarely indeed could one hope to witness a spectacle such as Maurice Broun and I were privileged to watch on the morning of September 4, 1957, at the lookout, with four Pileated Woodpeckers playing what appeared to be a grotesque game of 'tag' with a Sharp-shinned Hawk among the stark skeletons of dead pines on the top of the ridge."

It is probable that individuals wander a great deal during the course of the year; certainly for such a seemingly conspicuous bird it is comparatively seldom seen, even by those who spend

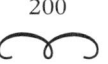

much time looking for it. This is due, in a measure, to its habit of feeding well down in the trunks of dead trees, or even on the ground, where it can swiftly slip out of sight upon the slightest suspicion of danger.

The Pileated Woodpecker has been recorded on the Reading Christmas Bird Count 23 of 86 years, seven of the last 10, with a maximum of four on December 22, 1963. The high for the Hamburg Christmas Bird Count is 11 on December 28, 1986. The peak for the Bernville count is two on December 30, 1995.

A mounted specimen in the Reading Public Museum was taken in Albany Township about 1890 by John Hofmann. D. Frank Keller of Reading reported it as very rare (Warren, 1890:171).

OLIVE-SIDED FLYCATCHER *Contopus borealis*

Rare spring and fall migrant

A rare migrant, the Olive-sided Flycatcher occurs in both spring and fall. During the migrations, it perches on the tops of the tallest dead trees available, usually on some wooded hillside, where it can look over a wide expanse of country.

At Hawk Mountain Sanctuary and elsewhere along the Blue Mountain it is observed more frequently in the fall than at any other place.

Several birds may be seen on favorable days during late August and early September. Byron Nunemacher, Earl Rollman, and Earl Poole saw three Olive-sided Flycatchers September 5, 1926, at Moselem. On August 27, 1988, Laurie Goodrich found three at the North Lookout.

Donald Heintzelman recorded the duration of feeding flights of Olive-sided Flycatchers at the North Lookout at Hawk Mountain August 25, 1962. Of 14 flights observed, the minimum time was 1.6 seconds and the maximum was 7.6 seconds with the mean of 4.86 seconds. He also notes, "intra-specific strife appeared to develop between two Olive-sided Flycatchers when one bird attempted to land in the same tree already occupied by the other bird. The approaching bird was driven away by the bird already on the perch. It landed on another tree about 200 feet to the east" (Heintzelman, 1964b:37).

The early fall date is August 3 (1963 - Alex Nagy at Hawk Mountain; 1965 - Matt Spence at Antietam Lake), and the late fall dates are October 1 (1962 - Maurice Broun at Hawk Mountain; 1995 - Jack Holcomb at Charles Evans Cemetery, Reading) and October 23 (1992 - Cathy Viverette at the North Lookout, Hawk Mountain).

Poole collected a specimen now in the Reading Public Museum at Moselem on August 15, 1927.

Irregular in spring, it appears from May 6 (1956, 1962 - Earl Poole) to June 3 (1928, 1945 - E.P.). The earliest spring date at Hawk Mountain is May 9 (1970).

EASTERN WOOD-PEWEE *Contopus virens*
Common migrant and summer nester

A common migrant and summer resident in woodlands throughout Berks County, the Eastern Wood-Pewee is among the latest species to arrive in the spring, rarely reaching the county before the second week in May. The Pewee is one of the characteristic voices of the summer woodlands.

An early arrival date is April 25 (1962 - Maurice Broun in the lower camping shelters at Hawk Mountain). The Pewee has arrived as late as May 21 (1920, 1934 - Earl Poole).

Levi Mengel took 11 sets of eggs between June 1 (1893) and July 4 (1895). Clutch sizes in the collected sets range from two to five eggs. The Pewee is a frequent victim of the Cowbird. Four sets contain Cowbird's eggs.

Joan Silagy found a Pewee feeding fledglings at Blue Marsh on September 6, 1988, a late date for nesting.

Maurice Broun recorded over 35 Pewees at Hawk Mountain on September 3, 1960.

Departure dates range from late August to early October, the late date October 9 (1964 - E.P.).

The Pennsylvania Germans in Berks County call the Eastern Wood-Pewee "der Buschbiwwi." William Rupp writes: "This is the bird whose 'sad, sweet call' of 'pee-a-wee' is heard in the woods through the long and hot summer's day. When all nature seems to be holding its breath, this lone voice can be heard in the tree-tops, the singer unseen" (Rupp, 1946:176).

YELLOW-BELLIED FLYCATCHER *Empidonax flaviventris*
Rare spring and fall migrant

A rare and erratic migrant in both spring and fall, the Yellow-bellied Flycatcher is frequently overlooked because of its late arrival in spring and its retiring habits.

In Berks County, it is usually found in dense woods and boggy places, where it keeps well concealed and is most often located by its sweet, plaintive call, which suggests that of the Wood-Pewee but pitched higher and slurred into one syllable.

During some years it may be missed entirely, yet on certain days in late May it may be quite common in favored woodlands. On May 30, 1924, Earl Poole saw at least a dozen and heard several others during a morning's walk along the woodland paths at the northern end of Mount Penn.

Levi Mengel took a specimen May 22, 1887, and Poole collected one May 22, 1920.

A remarkably late spring record is a bird that struck a television tower on Route 183 at the Berks-Schuylkill County line on June 8, 1953. It is now in the Reading Public Museum collection, and there is a still later spring specimen in the same collection, a male taken by Levi Mengel in Albany Township on June 12, 1886.

Migration dates in Berks County for spring are May 8 (1932) to June 12 (1886 - Levi Mengel specimen) and for fall are August 16 (1971 - Rudy Keller in District Township) to September 21 (1933 - Earl Poole; 1995 - Dean Kendall at Leesport). Maurice Broun reported one from Hawk Mountain on the extremely late date of October 10 (1942).

The Yellow-bellied Flycatcher is more likely to call during the fall than any of the other *Empidonax* species.

ACADIAN FLYCATCHER *Empidonax virescens*

Fairly common but local nester

Now fairly common but local, the Acadian Flycatcher nests at Hawk Mountain Sanctuary, Hay Creek, Rattling Run, the Northkill Creek, and along the Pine Creek in District and Albany townships. This flycatcher appears to have expanded its range in Berks County from the south during the latter part of this century as the woodlands matured.

Earl Poole found the Acadian Flycatcher through the 1960s an uncommon to rare migrant and a rather rare and local summer resident.

Prior to 1900 it was probably a rare summer resident, although no nests from the county were collected.

Earlier this century, the Acadian Flycatcher was known to have nested only up the Schuylkill Valley at least as far as Hay Creek, near Birdsboro, where G. Henry Mengel found it present June 24, 1917; June 23, 1918; June 12, 1921; and June 22, 1922.

Poole discovered a nest with eggs there on June 1, 1947, and later watched the progress of the brood until June 21. On June 10, 1950, he found a nest containing two eggs along Indian Run, the stream that drains the Birdsboro reservoir. On June 21 this nest had been overturned by a storm, but he found a new one, just completed, along a mill race 200 yards from the first.

Poole observed a pair under conditions that indicated nesting, although he did not see a nest, near the mouth of Rattling Run at Port Clinton, Schuylkill County, on June 21, 1961, and again in the same place in 1962.

A local specimen taken June 12, 1884, and another taken May 28, 1883, are in the Reading Public Museum.

The Acadian Flycatcher arrives in Berks County during the first two weeks of May, the early date April 28 (1996 - Kerry Grim at Shartlesville). The late date is September 15 (1942 - Maurice Broun at Hawk Mountain).

The difficulty of identifying the five small flycatchers of the genus *Empidonax* in life unless they happen to be singing is well known, and sight records, especially in the fall, are to be accepted with reserve.

ALDER FLYCATCHER *Empidonax alnorum*
WILLOW FLYCATCHER *Empidonax traillii*

The records for the Alder Flycatcher and the Willow Flycatcher were combined until 1973 under the name Traill's Flycatcher (*Empidonax trailli trailli*). Ultimately the research of Robert C. Stein led to the separation of the Alder Flycatcher, which has a call of "fee-bee-oh" or "wee-bee-oh," from the Willow Flycatcher, which has a call of "fitz-bew" (*Auk*, 1973, 90:411-419).

During the 1950s and 1960s, Robert Cook and Matt Spence heard the distinctive call of the Alder Flycatcher and saw this bird at Lake Ontelaunee during late spring and early summer under conditions which would indicate breeding. Spence's last Lake Ontelaunee record for this flycatcher is July 10, 1966.

Since the 1960s, the Alder Flycatcher has become quite rare in Berks County. Its breeding range seems to have contracted to the more northern counties in Pennsylvania.

Kerry Grim and Maurice Broun heard one on June 3, 1979, near the New Bethel Union Church in Albany Township. Ken Lebo heard one calling on June 2, 1994, near Moselem.

There were no Berks County records for the Alder Flycatcher on the *Atlas of Breeding Birds in Pennsylvania* survey from 1983 to 1989 (Brauning, 1992:203). No fall observations have been reported.

Most of the Traill's Flycatcher records probably can be referred to the Willow Flycatcher rather than to the Alder.

Anna and Mary Deeter and Earl Poole found a singing male Traill's Flycatcher present in the Pine Swamp along the upper Pine Creek in Albany Township of northern Berks County on June 13 and 21, 1925, and it seemed quite likely that there was a nest nearby.

In 1949 Poole found one of these flycatchers at Lake Ontelaunee throughout the breeding season, and it had been present in increasing numbers in subsequent seasons. No occupied nests were found in the area, but on August 6, 1953, Poole saw the adults feeding two short-tailed young that were scarcely able to fly, and on August 4, 1974, Spence saw an adult carrying food at Peters Creek.

The Willow Flycatcher is one of the latest species to arrive on its breeding grounds, but there are some early records: at Geigertown May 1, 1994 (Ken Lebo); at Lake Ontelaunee May 10, 1964 (Matt Spence); and at Peters Creek May 12, 1991 (Matt Wlasniewski).

Since it is one of the very latest migrants in spring, it is inclined to keep within the dense foliage of alder swamps and is comparatively rare away from its nesting areas. A regular summer resident at Lake Ontelaunee, the Willow [Traill's] Flycatcher arrives between May 12 (1956 - Earl Poole) and May 30 (1950 - E.P.).

Fall dates are even scarcer, and there is a strong possibility that some of these may be questionable since the small flycatchers of the genus *Empidonax* are notoriously difficult to identify unless they happen to be singing. Last-seen fall dates at Lake Ontelaunee are between August 30 (1936 - E.P.) and September 30 (1953 - E.P.). Rudy Keller observed a Willow Flycatcher in Pike Township September 7, 1992.

The Willow and Alder Flycatchers cannot be safely separated in the field by sight alone. Therefore, the calls must be heard for identification: "fee-bee-oh" for the Alder and "fitz-bew" for the Willow.

John F. Hofmann listed the Traill's Flycatcher in 1890.

LEAST FLYCATCHER *Empidonax minimus*
Rare migrant

Once a fairly common nester, the Least Flycatcher is now only a rare migrant in Berks County, its southern range expansion apparently halted.

The last confirmed nesting occurred along the Sacony Creek at State Game Lands 182 in Greenwich Township May 12, 1986 (Catherine Elwell). Kerry Grim recorded a singing male atop the Blue Mountain at Shartlesville State Game Lands 110 from May 19 to June 2, 1990. Apparently it failed to attract a mate and departed.

Illustrating this decline, Matt Spence's records from mid-May at Hay Creek show from 1963 to 1971 the Least Flycatcher was present each year; from 1972 to 1987 it was present nine of 16 years; and from 1988 to 1995, it was not present at all.

Earl Poole up to the mid-1960s found the Least Flycatcher abundant during the spring migrations and a fairly common summer resident, nesting over the entire county.

It arrives in Berks during the first week of May, the early dates April 22 (1916 - Earl Poole) and April 25 (1993 - Kerry Grim at State Game Lands 110).

Poole found it undoubtedly nesting at Gouglersville, Plow Church, Birdsboro, Hopewell, Strausstown, Rittenhouse Gap, Greenawald, Eckville, and Temple. Two sets of eggs taken at Fleetwood May 29, 1904, and June 21, 1906, are in the Reading Public Museum collection.

Poole saw a Least Flycatcher on a completed nest at White Bear as early as May 17, 1947, and another feeding nearly full-fledged young at Birdsboro on June 9, 1917.

Poole writes in 1964: "This little flycatcher has adapted itself admirably to changing conditions, and is just as much at home in orchards and in rural districts generally as in open woodlands and thickets in which they presumably nested before the settling of the land."

Aside from the maturing of the woodlands in the county, there is no good explanation for the Least Flycatcher's apparent range contraction and decline in Berks.

As with all of the small flycatchers, the identification of fall individuals is often a perplexing matter, since the birds are not singing, and autumn plumages are somewhat different from those of spring. Poole's late date is October 5 (1935). Dean Kendall finds the Least Flycatcher more common in fall at Leesport, some birds giving a "weece" call at that time. Kendall's recent late date is September 23 (1995). Fall records at Hawk Mountain range from August 4 (1946 - Maurice Broun) to September 6 (1989 - Anne "Babe" Webster).

The Pennsylvania German name for the Least Flycatcher is "Busch Biwwi," but William Rupp believes that this is probably a case of mistaken identification. He writes: "The bird prefers our lawns and orchards and his strong, business-like 'chebec, chebec,' is a prominent call that cannot easily be confused with that of the other flycatchers. He is a little fellow but he can speak for himself, even it it does sound as though he had the hiccups" (Rupp, 1946:175).

DUSKY FLYCATCHER *Empidonax oberholseri*
Accidental

Edwin Bieber found a freshly killed flycatcher on the seat of his pick-up truck parked inside a shed near Kutz's Bridge, Kutztown R.D. 3, on December 25, 1969. He gave the bird to Richard Sharadin, who brought it to Alex Nagy at Hawk Mountain Sanctuary for identification. Sharadin said that the bird was in great shape and clearly had died only recently. Fred Wetzel prepared a study skin of the bird. His examination of the carcass showed the crop and stomach to be empty, but the bird did not appear to be emaciated even though the weather for the five days preceding the find was characterized by cold temperatures and heavy snows.

The specimen was later sent to Dr. Ned K. Johnson, curator of birds and professor of zoology at the University of California at Berkeley, who identified it as a Dusky Flycatcher. He writes on October 7, 1970: "This one looks to me like *Empidonax oberholseri*, both from the standpoint of general coloration and wing shape. ...I am fairly certain that your bird is an immature, that is, it was hatched perhaps six months prior to having been found dead, and I also think it is very likely a female. ...This assumption is based on wing shape, which in your bird is closest to the pattern shown by immature females. ...All other measurements are appropriate for *oberholseri* as well. In coloration including pale lower mandible, it matches winter immatures from Mexico."

Chandler Robbins of the United States Fish and Wildlife Service reports in a letter to Wetzel dated December 17, 1970, that this is the first record of this species from east of the Mississippi River and perhaps the first east of the states in which the species breeds. The Dusky Flycatcher breeds from the southern Yukon and northwestern and central British Columbia south to southern California. It winters from southeastern Arizona through western Mexico as far south as Guerrero and Oaxaca.

Unfortunately, the specimen was misplaced and, as of this writing, could not be located.

Coincidentally, on December 23, 1966, Donald Heintzelman collected a Hammond's Flycatcher (*Empidonax hammondii*) near Schnecksville, Lehigh County, for the first Pennsylvania record of this western *Empidonax* species (Heintzelman, 1968:512). This location is less than 20 miles from where the Dusky Flycatcher was found.

These two records indicate that there can be a late autumn or early winter movement of some western flycatchers to the eastern United States.

EASTERN PHOEBE *Sayornis phoebe*

Fairly common migrant and nester

A fairly common migrant and summer resident, the Eastern Phoebe is also occasional in winter, although there are few records of birds that survived the entire winter.

Earl Poole found one apparently settled for the winter in a honeysuckle thicket along the Tulpehocken Creek near Van Reed's Paper Mill on December 18, 1920, and what he assumed to be the same one in the same place on the following February 26. It appeared to be subsisting on Japanese honeysuckle berries and other small fruits. He also found one at Moselem on January 1 and 9, 1955.

The Eastern Phoebe usually arrives in Berks County during mid-to-late March, the early dates March 5 (1921) and March 6 (1992 - Barry Pounder at the Red Bridge over the Tulpehocken Creek in Bern Township).

Complete sets of eggs in the Reading Public Museum collection have been found from May 24 (1903) to June 25 (1894). Clutch sizes in these sets range from four to six eggs, and eight sets contain a Cowbird's egg. This bird often produces two broods a summer.

A Phoebe nested in the Hall of the Mountain King at Hawk Mountain and fledged five young on June 4, 1988. A second clutch was laid by June 23.

The Eastern Phoebe population dwindles in September, but a few stay well into October, with stragglers remaining until Christmas, or even later.

It has appeared on the Reading Christmas Bird Count 10 of 86 years, three of the last 10, with a maximum of two on December 24, 1950; December 23, 1956; and December 15, 1974. Single birds have been recorded during nine of 31 years on the Hamburg Christmas Bird Count. It has appeared twice on the Bernville count, single birds January 1, 1990, and January 1, 1991.

The Pennsylvania German name for the Phoebe is "der Biwwi." William Rupp writes, "He is the voice of spring and it was said that when you heard his call and when you had seen two or three Barn Swallows together, then it was time to take your shoes off and go bare-footed" (Rupp, 1946:174-175).

SAY'S PHOEBE *Sayornis saya*

Accidental

Sam and Mary Gundy found a Say's Phoebe during the Reading Christmas Bird Count under very favorable conditions at Lake Ontelaunee on December 22, 1946. James Holzman, Ralph Yerger, and Earl Poole also saw the bird. Poole was previously well acquainted with this species, having seen it in several places in the West. Upon returning, members of the party checked their observations with skins from the Reading Public Museum collection. David Shaeffer saw the same bird at the same place on December 28. This occurrence is the first state record for the species.

From April 1 to May 8, 1975, Barb Lake and Alex Nagy recorded one at the Miller farm near Kempton. Franklin and Barbara Haas observed the bird April 5 and noted the bird was in excellent plumage, with the rusty belly and long, dark tail evident (Haas, 1975:39).

Tom Leckey and Jim Brett found a Say's Phoebe at the Hawk Valley Farm near Hahn Mountain in Albany Township December 29, 1985. It stayed until mid-January 1986.

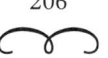

On December 27, 1987, Dan Klem and Peter Saenger recorded one in Albany Township in a wet area near a farm off Philadelphia Pike. It was found until January 2, 1988.

From January 4 to 9, 1993, Leckey found another Say's Phoebe at a farm east of Hawk Mountain.

Leckey and Brett found one again December 26, 1993, at a farm in Albany Township.

The birds previously listed were recorded on the Hamburg Christmas Bird Count on December 29, 1985; December 27, 1987; and December 26, 1993.

GREAT CRESTED FLYCATCHER *Myiarchus crinitus*
Common breeder

A common summer resident throughout the county, the Great Crested Flycatcher usually arrives from the south during the first week of May. Early arrival dates include April 19 (1987 - Catherine Elwell at State Game Lands 182 near Kutztown) and April 23 (1959 - Maurice Broun at Hawk Mountain).

This is the only locally nesting flycatcher that uses a tree cavity or nesting box. Eggs taken from May 30 (1896) to September 16 (1893) are in the Reading Public Museum collection, the latter a remarkably late date. Clutch sizes in these sets range from three to five eggs.

Occasionally this flycatcher leaves by the last of August, but usually a few remain until well into September, a late date September 25 (1956 - Earl Poole).

Ed and Sarah Barrell found an extraordinarily late Great Crested Flycatcher during the Bernville Christmas Bird Count January 1, 1992. The bird was seen by Dean Kendall, Ernie Schiefer, and Doris and Gerald Steffy until January 6. It was located in a mature pine grove off Penn-Bern Road adjacent to Blue Marsh Lake. Kendall observed the bird January 5 and wrote a detailed description which separated it from western *Myiarchus* species flycatchers, such as the Ash-throated, which stray east at times late in the year. Kendall heard it give its "wheep!" call notes and saw it perched and flycatching. This documentation confirmed it as the first winter (January to February) record of this species in the northeastern United States.

WESTERN KINGBIRD *Tyrannus verticalis*
Accidental

Earl and Helen Poole observed from a distance of 50 feet a Western Kingbird at rest and in flight on September 18, 1938, at Lake Ontelaunee. Both were thoroughly familiar with the species in its normal habitat in the West. This, like the following occurrence, followed a severe storm with northeasterly winds.

Earl Poole saw another one at Lake Ontelaunee August 25, 1941, following a storm. This was also a most satisfactory observation, and the bird performed in characteristic fashion, calling frequently.

Alex Nagy reported a Western Kingbird at Eckville on November 26, 1950.

From October 10 to 16, 1986, Harold and Joan Silagy observed a Western Kingbird at Blue Marsh Lake. Franklin Haas photographed the bird.

EASTERN KINGBIRD *Tyrannus tyrannus*
Common migrant and breeder

The familiar Eastern Kingbird is a common migrant and summer resident, generally distributed in hedgerows and shade trees in agricultural areas and especially attracted to old apple orchards. It usually arrives during the first week of May, early dates April 23 (1957 - Maurice Broun at Hawk Mountain) and April 24 (1992 - Matt Wlasniewski in Hamburg).

By early August the Eastern Kingbird becomes more in evidence, and the local population is augmented by young and migrants starting to move south. The actual time of leaving varies greatly from year to year. Some years Earl Poole had not seen it after August 15, while in others it did not leave until well into September. Poole's latest departure date in Berks County is September 20 (1931), although Don Gamble reported one at Lake Ontelaunee on October 9, 1951.

Local sets of eggs in the Reading Public Museum collection range from May 19 (1890) to June 25 (1895). Clutch sizes in these sets are from two to five eggs. Seven sets were taken from apple trees in orchards.

The Pennsylvania German name for the Kingbird is "der Iemefresser," or "bee eater." William Rupp writes: "The large hawks have suffered under the name 'Hinkelwoi' and this bird under the name of 'bee martin' and others like it. Bees are but a small portion of his diet, for he is a flycatcher first of all and cannot help it if a bee crosses his path now and then as he sallies forth from the topmost branch of an apple tree." Another name heard in Berks County is "der Iemevoggel," or "bee-bird" (Rupp, 1946:172-173).

HORNED LARK *Eremophila alpestris*
Rare breeder and common winter visitor

Two races of the Horned Lark occur in Berks County.

The Northern Horned Lark, *E. a. alpestris*, is a common but irregular migrant and winter visitor in the broad valleys and agricultural lands where it is the predominant wintering form. It can occur in flocks numbering several hundred birds.

The race *E. a. praticola*, formerly called the Prairie Horned Lark, is a rare breeder in the county.

Prior to 1888 the paler Prairie Horned Lark was unknown as a breeding bird in Pennsylvania. It spread from the west into the southeastern counties, first appearing in Berks County in the early 1920s. It nests sparingly over the wide expanses of cultivated or pasture land, on golf courses, and airports.

On July 4, 1923, Byron Nunemacher and Henry Stott saw one Prairie Horned Lark near New Bethel Church in Albany Township. On July 22 of the same year a flock of about 25, mostly young of the year, was seen in a stubble field near Mountain, Albany Township, for the first Berks County breeding record (Byron Nunemacher, Earl Poole, J. Hendel).

It was seen under conditions that suggest nesting at Albany Township May 6, 1934; near Fleetwood March 31 to April 21, 1935, and April 22, 1939; and at Windsor Castle, May 26, 1935 (E.P.).

James Holzman and Ralph Yerger found a nest on the fairway of the Rich Maiden Golf Course near Lake Ontelaunee in the spring of 1938. Paul Martin and Earl Poole found it at the Reading Regional Airport throughout the springs of 1942, 1944, and 1946.

The Prairie Horned Lark is an early nester. Poole saw adults feeding well-grown young near Fleetwood as early as May 7 (1960).

More recently, Kerry Grim found 10 Horned Larks, some of which were birds of the year, in Windsor Township July 23, 1993.

After the nesting season the family groups wander over the stubble fields. In October and November these are often joined by the somewhat larger Northern Horned Larks, so that individuals of both races can be seen in the same flock.

Early fall dates for the Horned Lark at Hawk Mountain include August 26 (1985 - one bird) and September 1 (1940 - Maurice Broun; 1941 - M.B., two birds).

The Northern Horned Lark usually arrives from the north in November, occasionally as early as October 19 (1924 - E.P.), or rarely may not appear until mid-December, and very rarely, apparently does not reach Berks County at all.

During some years these larks pass through this region by early January and do not again appear until well into February and March, with a few flocks remaining into April.

In spring just before its departure, flocks of hundreds swirl over the freshly plowed fields, singing and indulging in the jealous bickerings incidental to courtship. Its flight song, reminiscent of the famed European Skylark, can be heard at these times.

The largest flock that Poole saw locally was one of more than 500 on March 31, 1935.

The latest date is April 13 (1919 - E.P.), although Levi Mengel took specimens of the Northern Horned Lark in Albany Township April 19, 1887; in Tuckerton April 26, 1893; and in Lenhartsville May 1, 1887. Other local specimens in the Reading Public Museum collection taken by Mengel include one at Monocacy Hill April 5, 1888, and one on Mount Penn April 7, 1892. Poole took a specimen October 29, 1921.

Some of the wintering flocks include varying numbers of the native Prairie Horned Larks, but many consist exclusively of the Northern Horned Larks, or may contain one or more Lapland Longspurs or Snow Buntings.

The Horned Lark has appeared on the Reading Christmas Bird Count 53 of 86 years, nine of the last 10, with a maximum of 633 on December 20, 1992. The peak for the Hamburg Christmas Bird Count is 1,527 on December 26, 1990. The high for the Bernville count is 2,847 on January 4, 1987.

The Pennsylvania German name for the Horned Lark is "die Laerrich," named for the European Skylark and used in a general way for all the lark-like birds including the Meadowlark and Pipit (Rupp, 1946:176).

PURPLE MARTIN *Progne subis*

Locally common breeder

The Purple Martin is a fairly common but local summer resident, rarely seen away from its nesting colonies. Its presence as a nester depends entirely on the sympathetic attitude of local people to provide and maintain suitable nesting places, either houses or gourds. The Purple Martin has long since abandoned its former habit of nesting in hollow trees, and competition with the House Sparrow and the Starling along with a lack of housing has probably been responsible for a decline in the Martin population.

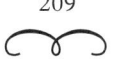

Many thriving colonies of 40 or 50 years disappeared by the 1960s. During the middle of this century, Earl Poole believed that apathy on the part of the rural population in maintaining Martin houses contributed to the decline. He estimated one-eighth of the former Martin population of a half century earlier existed by 1964.

For 35 years at the beginning of this century, William Grim maintained a colony of more than a hundred pairs in Hamburg. Colonies near the following places were active during the 1940s: Angelica, Bechtelsville, Earlville, Elverson, Hamburg, Fleetwood, Kempton, Kutztown, Lenhartsville, Plowville, Robesonia, Wernersville, and Womelsdorf. One colony existed in Gibraltar from the 1940s to the 1960s.

The Purple Martin Conservation Association was founded in 1986 at the Edinboro University of Pennsylvania to study Martin ecology. Since that time, at least two dozen Purple Martin colonies from Berks County have been registered with the organization.

Kenneth Miller of Mohrsville has maintained a colony of over 40 pairs since the mid-1970s. Other colonies have been re-established in Centerport, the Fleetwood-Lyons area, and Hamburg.

The Purple Martin usually arrives from its wintering grounds in Brazil by the second week in April, an early date March 23 (1984 - Kerry Grim at Hamburg).

Levi Mengel collected a set of fresh eggs at Elverson June 1, 1894.

It leaves its nesting grounds early, and most have gone long before the last week in August, although a few migrants from farther north trickle through until well into September. An early date for fall migrants at Hawk Mountain is July 2 (1958 - Maurice Broun, two at the North Lookout). The late date there is September 21 (1952 - M.B., four birds; 1956 - M.B., one bird).

The Pennsylvania German name for the Purple Martin is "die gross Schwalm." "Die gross Hausschwalm" is another name because they like to be near dwellings and also because they will breed in the gourds, boxes, and apartments that are put up for them. William Rupp writes:

"The martins were looked upon with equal respect [with the Barn Swallow] and, as [Peter] Kalm noted two centuries ago, people were anxious to have them near so that they might alarm the poultry by their anxious notes when hawks and crows approached, and so that they, by their influence, might protect the houses against the evil spirits even as the swallow protected the barn. Hence the fine little 'martin houses,' the pride of local craftsmen, which were set up on poles in the yard or attached to the side of the shed near the village store or tavern" (Rupp, 1946:179-181).

TREE SWALLOW *Tachycineta bicolor*

Common migrant and breeder

Uncommon until the 1960s, the Tree Swallow has benefited from Eastern Bluebird nest boxes which provide it with nesting sites. It is now a common migrant and breeder, abundant at Lake Ontelaunee and Blue Marsh Lake.

As recently as 1977, Matt Spence did not find the Tree Swallow nesting at Lake Ontelaunee.

As a migrant during the first half of this century, the Tree Swallow was usually common to abundant in spring and irregular in fall. It nested locally around the larger bodies of water, particularly where woodpecker-worked stubs projected above the water, furnishing nesting places.

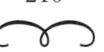

Earl Poole noted young recently out of the nest in Albany Township on June 15, 1953. He found the Tree Swallow throughout the breeding seasons of 1951, 1955, 1956, and 1957 at Lake Ontelaunee. In 1950, a pair nested at Nagy's Pond near Eckville (Maurice Broun, Alex Nagy).

The Tree Swallow is usually the first of the swallows to appear in the spring, arriving during the first week of April. The early date is March 17 (1990 - Rudy Keller, four at Lake Ontelaunee).

Between 1983 and 1992, Dean A. Boyer maintained nearly 160 Bluebird houses in a trail that stretched from State Hill at Blue Marsh Lake in Bern Township through Bernville to Cross Keys. In that time 2,527 Tree Swallows were fledged by nesting birds in those houses.

On September 27, 1992, Matt Spence observed nearly 2,000 Tree Swallows at Lake Ontelaunee, and Matt Wlasniewski found the same number there October 22, 1995. The latest date from the lake is November 5 (1995 - Matt Spence, Matt Wlasniewski).

The late fall records from Hawk Mountain are October 27 (1996 - nine birds) and November 12 (1994). The high count there is an estimated 1,200 on October 10, 1996.

NORTHERN ROUGH-WINGED SWALLOW *Stelgidopteryx serripennis*
Common migrant and breeder

A common migrant and summer resident, the Northern Rough-winged Swallow breeds locally along water courses and in cut banks throughout Berks County.

It first appears in the county by the second week of April, an early date March 30 (1994 - Matt Spence at Lake Ontelaunee).

The Northern Rough-winged Swallow utilizes quite a wide variety of locations for its nest. Stone walls of canal locks and bridges, riprapping, drain pipes, and the deserted nests of the Belted Kingfisher are among the places chosen.

Four sets of eggs taken at Fleetwood May 31, 1908; Kutztown June 17, 1906; Moselem Springs June 16, 1907; and Virginville May 26, 1914, are in the Walter H. Leibelsperger collection at the Reading Public Museum.

The Northern Rough-winged Swallow does not remain long after the young are able to care for themselves, and its numbers dwindle rapidly during the latter half of July. Earl Poole seldom saw it near its nesting places after the third week in July, and his latest date at Lake Ontelaunee is August 7 (1948), although Maurice Broun saw two at Hawk Mountain September 4 (1947).

More recent late dates include September 30 (1995 - Ken Lebo, three at Lake Ontelaunee), October 18 (1992 - Joan Silagy near Robesonia), and October 24 (1994 - Matt Wlasniewski at Lake Ontelaunee).

The Pennsylvania German name is "Cave Schwolm," referring to its nesting places in holes or "caves" along the banks of streams (Rupp, 1946:178).

BANK SWALLOW *Riparia riparia*
Rare migrant; locally common breeder

The Bank Swallow is currently a locally common nester in Berks County at desilting basins along the Schuylkill River, which provide the high cut banks this swallow prefers.

The most active colony is at the Kernsville Dam in Tilden Township, which has supported as many as 100 nests during 1981 (Kerry Grim). The early arrival date at this nesting site is April 12 (1995 - Kerry Grim) and the latest departure date from there is August 15 (1996 - M.W.).

Earl Poole never found a nest in Berks County in 43 years of active field work, although Walter H. Leibelsperger collected a set of eggs near Fleetwood on May 22, 1902. Earlier this century, Poole regarded the Bank Swallow only as a rare migrant. During two seasons, 1929 and 1945, small numbers remained until June 2.

As a migrant, it usually arrives during the first week of May.

The Bank Swallow raises only one brood. By mid-July the families have left the nesting places and gather along the larger water courses, where they eventually form into large flocks, sometimes with other species, before starting on their southward journey.

Southbound migrants appear at Lake Ontelaunee as early as July 12 (1936 - Earl Poole), July 14 (1974 - Matt Spence), and July 17 (1966 - M.S.). Matt Spence counted 210 Bank Swallows at Lake Ontelaunee on August 30, 1992.

Rudy Keller found between 200 and 300 in Bern Township August 23, 1992, and 50 at a pond near Oley August 26, 1989.

Late dates are September 14 (1984 - two birds at Hawk Mountain) and September 17 (1996 - Katrina Knight, three birds at Lake Ontelaunee).

The Pennsylvania German name for the Bank Swallow is "Sandbenk Schwalm," describing its favorite nesting place. "Schwalm" is a name which refers to all members of the swallow family (Rupp, 1946:177-178).

CLIFF SWALLOW *Hirundo pyrrhonota*
Uncommon migrant and locally common breeder

During the past 25 years, the Cliff Swallow has increased as a breeding bird in Berks County after a 50-year period of relative scarcity.

Earl Poole found at midcentury that there were usually several colonies in the neighborhood of Eckville, although they had diminished in numbers over the years, and a much smaller colony had persisted near Seyfert.

The Cliff Swallow was evidently much more abundant in the county during the beginning of this century, as Levi Mengel found nests at Bernville, Stouchsburg, Fleetwood, Kutztown, Bethel, Albany Township, and along the Wyomissing Creek from May 29 (1884) to June 27 (1886). Clutch sizes of these sets range from four to six eggs, and four nests contain Cowbird's eggs.

Mengel described a nest he collected near Bern Church June 19, 1890: "Flask shaped of mud lined with feathers under eaves of old outhouse."

Maurice Broun saw young still in the nest in northern Berks as late as August 8 (1947).

One colony was established on a barn near Elverson around 1914 and was still active through the mid-1980s (Robert Cook). According to Roy Trexler, conservation education assistant at the Pennsylvania Game Commission, the farmer told him that the first pair had nested under the barn shed in 1913. At that time they attached their nests to a suspended wagon bed. The birds returned each year and numbered more than 100 in 1949. Their nests ran practically the entire length of the barn (*Pennsylvania Game News*, February 1950: p. 13).

Cliff Swallows still nest on barns in the Oley Valley (Rudy Keller).

The Cliff Swallow arrives by the last week in April, the early date April 5 (1936 - Earl Poole).

Most of the Cliff Swallows leave by the end of August, but during some years they remain in numbers well into September. In 1929 Poole saw them regularly at Lake Ontelaunee until September 28.

Late dates at Hawk Mountain include 11 birds seen from the North Lookout October 12, 1955, and three flying from south to north over the lookout on October 25, 1956 (Alex Nagy).

On May 15, 1977, Matt Spence saw 50 Cliff Swallows disturbed by a swimming groundhog at the dam breast of Lake Ontelaunee.

At Hopewell Furnace National Historic Site, Barn Swallows can be found nesting on the inside of the barn while Cliff Swallows nest on the outside.

Kerry Grim has occasionally found Cliff Swallows nesting under bridges at larger streams such as at the Maiden Creek in Lenhartsville and the Schuylkill River in Hamburg.

Spence found evidence of the first nesting of Cliff Swallows under the bridge at the Lake Ontelaunee dam breast on May 7, 1966. Broun elaborates on the status of Cliff Swallows at the lake in an article published in the *Cassinia*:

Cliff Swallows at Lake Ontelaunee: Those of us concerned for the welfare of birds have been distressed by the continuing decline of many bird populations. The Cliff Swallow in particular has suffered greatly from changing times. In his *Pennsylvania Birds* (1964) Earl L. Poole recorded the bird's status in the Commonwealth as "uncommon transient and breeding resident, gradually retreating from populous areas." In an earlier work, *A Half Century of Bird Life in Berks County, Pennsylvania*, (1947) Poole gives the status of the Cliff Swallow as "a rather rare and local summer resident and uncommon transient."

The Cliff Swallow was actually a common bird, well distributed throughout the Northeast around the turn of the century. Its decline, in large measure, can be attributed to the disappearance of the old-fashioned unpainted barns which were favorite nest sites; farmers who simply would not tolerate the nests; interference by House Sparrows and small boys with B-B guns; rain storms which demolish the nests, or excessively dry conditions which cause the nests to fall.

The good news is that the Cliff Swallow has found a haven in the Great Valley of Berks County. And the focus for the bird's dynamic, and indeed dramatic increase, is the two massive, concrete bridges of Lake Ontelaunee. Hidden from view, the birds attach their adobe homes to the under surfaces of the broadly arching bridges. Here the nests are completely protected from prowling mammals, meddlesome men and all the adversities previously mentioned. The cool, perpetually sunless nest sites preclude excessive drying and consequent falling of the nests. And the birds have the blessings of the City of Reading!

During the past season I made a number of visits to the Lake, about 300 feet above sea level and embracing roughly 1,000 acres. Great was my surprise, on May 16, to see hundreds of the swallows darting low over the water, as far as one could see, enjoying the abundant insect resources of the area. A few birds were actively engaged in nest building, gathering mud from rain puddles below the spillway.

All of this was enormously exciting and encouraging to me, in view of the scarcity of Cliff Swallows in recent years. In the early 1950s I knew of a few colonies along both sides of the Blue Mountain. I well remember a colony of over 100 birds that had become established at a large barn in Drehersville in 1952. Two larger colonies appeared to be flourishing on old barns near New Ringgold. Then the birds disappeared.

According to Matthew J. Spence of Reading, who has devoted much time to field studies of birds at Lake Ontelaunee since the early 1960s, a few Cliff Swallows appeared at the Lake in late April of 1966. Five pairs built nests, apparently for the first time. In late July as many as 40 birds including young were noted. Many of these lingered well into August.

Almost comparable results were obtained from 1967 to 1969. On July 4, 1970, Spence saw about 100 birds at the dam - the first real upsurge in the population. No specific counts are available since 1970, though Spence has recorded Cliff Swallows at the dam through August, and sporadically as late as September 15, 1974. The lack of specific counts is understandable, as we shall see.

My interest - and frustration - was heightened with each visit I made to the Lake, for I found that it was impossible to make a reliable count or to determine what was going on. To gauge the extent of nest building and activity in general, one had to use a boat! And so I contacted Daniel Kennedy, who is in charge of the Reading Water Works, and this young man graciously arranged to pilot me in a motor boat to both bridges so that an examination could be made of the entire under surfaces, the many cornices and overhanging abutments to which the nests were attached in rows.

On July 13, under the main bridge (530 feet in length) at the spillway, and over which rumbles the continuous heavy traffic of Rte. 73, we found a thriving community of birds tending 132 nests with young. All but six nests were located on the north side of the bridge. Less than two miles to the north, the smaller Lake Shore bridge, carrying very little traffic, had its complement of 50 nests, and here at least 55 young birds were testing their wings or resting on the south-facing overhang. Hence the 1977 breeding population of Cliff Swallows at Lake Ontelaunee was at least 364 birds, based on 182 active nests - possibly the largest colony of Cliff Swallows in the Commonwealth!

It should be noted that very few of the nests were gourd-shaped, as they are at all exposed situations. At Lake Ontelaunee the nests are so ideally sheltered and protected that many completed, active nests were simply cup-shaped.

Checking the swallows on July 30, I was surprised to find not a single swallow at the dam. Only six pairs of adults were tending young in nests under the Lake Shore bridge. Why the extraordinarily early departure? Curiously, despite the protracted tropical heat of the summer of 1977, Barn and Tree swallows at my farm made similar premature departures.

It gives me great pleasure to report this sanguine turn of events in the fortunes of these charming birds. May their fecundity and good fortune continue; and may their sanctuary bridges endure! My sincere thanks to Daniel Kennedy without whose help this inquiry would have aborted; and to Matthew J. Spence for the generous use of his notes (Broun, 1979a:47).

The Pennsylvania Germans in Berks County commonly refer to the Cliff Swallow as "die Dreckschwalm." William Rupp notes, "A number of persons noted that the Barn Swallow enters its open, mud nest from the top, while the Cliff Swallow enters its enclosed, bottle-shaped nest through a 'spout' at the top or side." "Die Scheierschwalm" is rarely used for this species although its nests may be found in rows beneath the eaves of a barn or shed (Rupp, 1946:178-179).

BARN SWALLOW *Hirundo rustica*
Abundant migrant and breeder

The Barn Swallow is an abundant migrant and summer resident in farming districts throughout Berks County, nesting in barns and sheds throughout the region.

It usually arrives in the county around the middle of April, the early dates March 25 (1990 - Matt Spence, two birds at Lake Ontelaunee) and March 31 (1929 - Earl Poole).

Levi Mengel collected a set of five eggs in Robesonia June 19, 1884, and a set of two eggs in Albany Township June 16, 1885.

During July and early August the Barn Swallows start to flock in the neighborhood of the larger ponds and streams.

Maurice Broun writes:

"Barn Swallows are the curtain raisers of the great fall migrations at Hawk Mountain. We see these birds, joined by Purple Martins and other swallows, all apparently migrating, in early summer.... Hundreds, often many thousands of the fleeting, graceful birds sweep low over the Sanctuary woods, in a rather narrow line of flight, every evening in July and early August. Tommy Hanson and I counted almost fifty thousand swallows during July evenings of 1948. These remarkable flights had us mystified until, one evening in 1949, we discovered the swallows' roosting area, at Deer Lake, just three and a half miles to the southwest. There, every July evening, an aggregation of at least fifteen thousand swallows fills the air like an enormous swarm of bees" (Broun, 1949a:199).

The peak flight at Hawk Mountain is 3,483 Barn Swallows on July 30, 1951 (Maurice Broun).

Most of the Barn Swallows leave by mid-September, but stragglers continue to pass through up to the end of September, and there are even a few October records. The late dates are October 26 (1980 - Matt Spence at Peters Creek) and October 27 (1993 - Harold Lebo at Lake Ontelaunee). The latest date at Hawk Mountain is October 13 (1952 - M.B.).

The Pennsylvania Germans in Berks County call the Barn Swallow "die Scheierschwalm." William Rupp elaborates:

"The Barn Swallows are the ones usually referred to in the lore of our people. When new barns and sheds were erected, carpenters would take great pride in the 'swallow holes' which they cut into the 'weather-boarding' that covered the gable ends of these buildings. Done in a variety of designs, usually in the shape of a kind of star, they were called 'Schwalmelecher - so dass die

Schwalme nei un raus kenne!' A swallow's nest in a building was regarded as sure protection against the fury of the elements, and everything possible was done to encourage the swallows' annual return to their old resting place. Their coming and going was a sign of the changing of the seasons, and their abundance on the homestead was a mark of pride and sure prosperity" (Rupp, 1946:178-181).

BLUE JAY *Cyanocitta cristata*
Abundant migrant; common resident

A common permanent resident throughout Berks County, the Blue Jay is usually most conspicuous and noisiest in the fall, most secretive during the nesting season, and least abundant in winter.

There is a definite migrational movement in May and again from late September to the end of October. This is one of the species that uses the Pennsylvania ridges as an aerial pathway during the fall migration, and on certain days it is the most abundant migrant along the Blue Mountain. It is one of the few passerines that migrate during the day.

Maurice Broun writes:

At Hawk Mountain, Pennsylvania, and along the adjacent ridges, the Blue Jay occurs in migration from the third week in September until mid-October. The jays may be seen in loose flocks, or in orderly processions, on either side of the ridge, and at any elevation, in numbers varying from twelve to three hundred or more birds. I have noticed each season that jays are on the move by 7 a.m., but by midafternoon their flights terminate. As a rule, the birds keep just above the treetops, and seldom is there much fuss or noise; indeed, observers at the lookout must be keenly alert to detect each passing group of jays. At times, an entire group will alight on the trees for a moment of rest.... Prior to the fall of 1939, I have recorded inconsequential numbers of Blue Jays, with the exception of 603 birds counted on September 26, 1935.

During a sixteen-day period beginning September 24, 1939, I made an approximate count of 7,350 Blue Jays. Doubtless many jays slipped by uncounted. The majority of the birds passed through in a constant stream, regardless of the weather conditions, from September 30 to October 6. The peak of the migration came on October 1, a day of alternating rain and mist, with raw northerly winds; at least 1,535 birds passed the lookout, even during the rain, in groups of from 100 to 350. Again on October 3, despite obliterating mists during the forenoon, and fresh easterly winds all day, I counted several large flocks at various parts of the Sanctuary, and the far from complete count for the day was 1,250 birds... (Broun, 1941a:262).

During a four-week period beginning September 15, 1965, over 55,000 Blue Jays migrated over Hawk Mountain (Broun, 1966:12). From September 11 to October 30, 1957, over 42,000 were tallied. More recent counts during the same time period number from 300 to 2000 jays: 336 in 1992; 1,889 in 1993; 396 in 1994; 2,017 in 1995; and 182 in 1996.

The first wintering Blue Jays at Hawk Mountain were recorded during the season of 1959-1960.

Spring flights at Hawk Mountain occur from late February to late May, with peak flights from late April to early May. On May 3 and 11, 1956, Broun counted 40 Blue Jays, and on May 14 he counted over 100.

Levi Mengel collected 16 sets of eggs from May 10 (1885) to June 16 (1893). Clutch sizes in the collection range from one to six eggs.

The Blue Jay has appeared on the Reading Christmas Bird Count 78 of 86 years, 10 of the last 10, with a maximum of 537 on December 17, 1995. The peak for the Hamburg Christmas Bird Count is 695 on December 29, 1985. The high for the Bernville count is 388 on December 30, 1995.

Pennsylvania Germans in Berks County refer to the Blue Jay as "der Haerrevoggel" and "der Guthaerr." William Rupp speculates that "Haerrevoggel" comes from the German word for the European jay. Herbert Beck believes that the name "Guthaerr" comes from the German word meaning "landlord" because of his rich garb and officiousness. Other names include "der Blokopp" or "blue-head." Raymond E. Kiebach of Reading reports the name "der Greisch-schpecht" because of the bird's screaming and the noise a company of them can make when they are up to some mischief (Rupp, 1946:185).

AMERICAN CROW *Corvus brachyrhynchos*
Common resident

A common permanent resident throughout Berks County, the American Crow is fairly evenly distributed as a nester in open woodlands.

The Crow nests early. Levi Mengel collected a set of eggs on April 1 (1882). There are 54 sets taken in all parts of the county in the Reading Public Museum collection. Clutch sizes in these sets range from four to seven eggs. Mengel secured a set of five eggs April 15, 1885, near White Bear Station and counted 57 nests in the area.

In winter American Crows congregate at night in roosts of considerable size. Seidel's Hill in Bern Township was the site of a large roost for many years during the early 1900s (Earl Poole, 1947).

From the 1950s to 1975, Lake Ontelaunee was the site of an enormous roost, one of the greatest ornithological spectacles in Berks County. A maximum of 125,000 American Crows was estimated on December 21, 1969.

Rudy Keller describes the sight of the crows leaving the roost during predawn hours as "black ghosts against a red sky."

The pressure of organized crow-shooting "sportsmen" drove Crows from place to place during midcentury. They chanced to select a protected area at the Lake Ontelaunee watershed and were able to continue roosting unmolested for almost 20 years.

However, during the heyday at the Lake Ontelaunee roost in the late 1960s and early 1970s, the Pennsylvania Game Commission organized a number of Sunday winter Crow shoots. Hunters came from near and far to slaughter the birds roosting in the watershed pine trees. Later in the morning, when the birds flew from the roost, gunners lined the adjacent roads and killed many of the flying birds. Quite a number of other protected birds were accidentally dispatched during the shoots, including a Rough-legged Hawk (Matt Spence).

In the late 1970s, a large roost existed at a landfill near Lenhartsville. On the Hamburg Christmas Bird Count December 30, 1978, Warren Faust estimated the roost contained 50,000 Crows.

The fall migration for the American Crow at Hawk Mountain ranges from August 30 (1995) to December 30 (1995). The single-day peak is over 4,000 on November 2, 1946 (Maurice Broun), and the season high is 13,665 in 1937.

During the fall of 1942, Maurice Broun and Ben Goodwin measured the flight speeds of 15 migrating Crows. The speeds ranged from 17 to 35 miles per hour with a mean of 26 and a median of 27 (Broun and Goodwin, 1943:492).

A. Ericksen and Earl Poole saw a complete albino American Crow several times in August 1924 near Bernhart's reservoir. Matt Spence found an albino Crow near Lake Ontelaunee on January 2, 1960. A partial albino was recorded at Hawk Mountain September 16, 1994 (Betsy Daub).

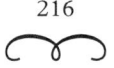

The American Crow is one of three birds recorded on all of the Reading Christmas Bird Counts with a maximum of 125,000 on December 21, 1969. The high for the Bernville count is 1,622 on December 30, 1995.

The Pennsylvania German name for the Crow is "die Grabb," a word derived from the bird's call. William Rupp writes:

"Our crow has not had a good reputation. Its destruction of the eggs and nestlings of smaller birds, its raids on hens' nests in the poultry yard and orchard, and its destruction of newly planted corn and the ripening ear have given it a bad name. A crow would be shot and nailed on a tree or post to frighten the rest of the flock, and sometimes it took its place with a hawk or an owl on the gable of a barn. Great numbers are shot sometimes, when loose companies are wandering over the countryside or when a long line heads for the roosting places, and are left to lie where they fall. Nests of spoiled hens' eggs, injected with poison, would be set out as lures and many crows would be taken that way; or nests of eggs would be set in small bowers of brush along a fence, with a trap placed in the one entrance to the nest, and crows would be trapped that way. Their call and the manner of their flight have been connected with the weather" (Rupp, 1946:189-190).

If, in winter, the Crows congregate and scream and caw on the "summer side" (south side) of the hills, it indicates rain; if on the "winter side" (north side) it indicates snow. If the Crows call before seven o'clock on a rainy morning, it will be clear by noon (Rupp, 1946:244).

FISH CROW *Corvus ossifragus*
Locally common breeder

Like a number of other southern birds, the Fish Crow apparently has increased and expanded its range into Berks County during the past century. Since none of the older egg collectors mentioned the Fish Crow, and no sets are among the rather large series of Crow eggs taken in the county between 1884 and 1910, Earl Poole believed that this southern species has only recently been extending its range from the lower river valleys.

The first set of Fish Crow eggs actually collected in Berks was taken along the Wyomissing Creek on May 12, 1933, by Sam Wishnieski. Since that time Fish Crows have nested each year along the Wyomissing Creek.

In the Schuylkill Valley, at least as far up that river as Leesport, Moselem, and Lake Ontelaunee, this crow is a permanent resident in small numbers. A few often roosted among the hordes of American Crows that resorted to the Lake Ontelaunee refuge area in winter during midcentury.

The Fish Crow is easily overlooked if not calling. Noncalling Fish Crows are nearly impossible to separate from the more common American Crow.

A fairly common but local summer resident, the Fish Crow winters in small numbers in the flocks of the American Crow, although they do not appear to associate during the summer.

During late winter and early spring, Fish Crows pass overhead in the early morning in pairs or small groups, giving their nasal calls, but are seldom heard during the rest of the day.

There is a noticeable influx of the Fish Crow from the south, beginning sometimes during the third week in February and continuing into April. Usually it straggles up the valleys in small bands; but on April 20, 1958, Poole saw a compact flock of from 25 to 30 individuals flying up the Schuylkill River at Reading. Rudy Keller and Harold and Joan Silagy more recently saw and heard over 100 Fish Crows moving north in small flocks April 18, 1992, in western Berks.

H. Beechert took a specimen at Seidel's Hill on April 3, 1924, and Sam Wishniewski took another at Millmont on April 5, 1930.

The Fish Crow as a nester may be moving into northern Berks County. Keller found a territorial pair on a breeding bird census plot near Albany during 1990 and 1991. Kerry Grim saw one engaged in nest building at Hamburg April 27, 1996.

It usually becomes scarce after September.

During the Bernville Christmas Count December 30, 1995, Keller counted 353 calling Fish Crows flying into the count circle before dawn. He saw many of these birds feeding in manured fields later in the day. The previous high for the Bernville count was 18 on January 2, 1994. A high of 369 was recorded on January 4, 1997. The Fish Crow has appeared on the Reading Christmas Bird Count 54 of 86 years, seven of the last 10, with a maximum of 22 on December 16, 1984. The peak for the Hamburg count is 94 on December 31, 1977.

COMMON RAVEN *Corvus corax*

Uncommon migrant

An uncommon migrant along the Kittatinny Ridge, the Common Raven is being sighted with increasing frequency. However, there are no confirmed Raven records in Berks County south of the Blue Mountain.

D. Frank Keller listed the Raven as a very rare straggler in Berks (Warren, 1890:202).

The first record this century is of single birds seen by Maurice Broun at Hawk Mountain October 14 and November 2, 1934. The season high count at Hawk Mountain is 70 in 1994, with peak flights of seven Ravens November 7 and 9, 1994.

The Common Raven has been recorded annually in fall at the Route 183 hawk watch since regular observations began in 1982. The single-day high count there is 15 birds October 18, 1993 (Robert and Anne MacClay), but usually between one and six birds are seen there at any one time.

The extreme dates for fall observations along the Kittatinny Ridge range between August 19 (1995 at Hawk Mountain) and December 29 (1994 at Hawk Mountain; 1995 - Steve Thorpe at Hawk Mountain).

A single Common Raven appeared on the Hamburg Christmas Bird Count December 27, 1987.

Although there are no breeding records in the county, the Common Raven has appeared during the spring and summer. Conrad Roland saw one on April 16, 1945, at Hawk Mountain. Broun recorded single birds May 11, 1952, and July 4, 1963. Broun writes of this first summer record at Hawk Mountain: "On July 4, 1963, at 9 a.m., I flushed a Raven from a rocky outcrop deep in the woods in the south sector of the Sanctuary. The bird had been resting there. It circled the area silently and within 25 feet of me, exhibiting its rudder-shaped tail and enormous black bill" (Broun, 1964). A nonbreeding pair found near Owl's Head on March 15, 1985, stayed all summer. On June 18, 1995, Matt Wlasniewski saw a Raven flying east from Hawk Mountain. Since 1993, Common Ravens have been noted regularly in early summer near the Port Clinton Fire Tower (Laurie Goodrich, Cathy Viverette).

Kerry Grim noted one Raven remained near a dead deer pit from May 26 to June 26, 1986, at State Game Lands 110 near Shartlesville. He found a pair perched in a tree line near a different pit on May 6, 1990.

BLACK-CAPPED CHICKADEE *Parus atricapillus*

Common resident

The familiar Black-capped Chickadee is a common permanent resident in Berks County, widely distributed in winter and during the migrations.

In late September and October there is usually an increase in the number of Chickadees throughout the county, due in part to the resident birds moving into the more populous areas from

the deeper woodlands and partly to a southward movement of birds from farther north.

Occasionally this movement fails to materialize and there is a lack of Chickadees throughout an entire winter; or as sometimes happens, a normal number of birds will be present up to early January and then disappear for the balance of the winter.

However, in recent years wintering populations of the Black-capped Chickadee have stabilized, the birds remaining due to feeding stations and milder winters.

Earlier this century, it bred regularly in the Pine Swamp in Albany Township and throughout the wooded portions of the county. Now it has moved into the suburbs and will nest in wren houses.

In southern Berks County, the Black-capped Chickadee overlaps the range of the Carolina Chickadee, and the two interbreed. According to research conducted by Frank B. Gill for the *Atlas of Breeding Birds in Pennsylvania*, the two species hybridize extensively in the low hills between Boyertown and Kutztown. Gill writes:

"Both species occur together with hybrids in a band less than 13 miles wide between Pottstown and Kutztown. The hybrid zone in this part of southern Berks County is centered in the vicinity of Earlsville and Pikesville, with little introgression of Carolina genes to Fredericksville or Kutztown. Atlas records may include some misidentifications from areas of overlap because of the inherent difficulty of visually differentiating the Carolina Chickadee from the Black-capped Chickadee, and because either species may sing the other's song" (Brauning, 1992:240).

Gill has stated that the area between the two species can be viewed as a "sink." The two chickadee populations come into contact, interbreed, but the young either fail to breed or breed very poorly, so that the interbred population increases neither in size nor area. DNA analysis has shown that the two species are not as closely related as they appear in plumage.

Earl Poole found the Black-capped Chickadee nesting in heavily wooded valleys and swamps in southern Berks County, where he saw their nests and watched their nesting activities from April 25 to June 2, 1954, and again through May 1956.

Maurice Broun received a banding return in 1962 of a juvenal he banded in July 1954.

Broun noted a major migration of Black-capped Chickadees during the fall of 1957, when he saw over 25 on September 13. The movement continued until November 17, the heaviest flights in October.

Between 1954 and 1966, wintering Black-capped Chickadee numbers fluctuated widely. In January 1954 Broun noticed a drop in wintering chickadees, and a low of 16 wintered at Schaumboch's during January and February 1961.

Reading Christmas Bird Count records during this period illustrate the disparity:

1954 - 188	1959 - 177	1964 - 181
1955 - 213	1960 - 62	1965 - 356
1956 - 66	1961 - 374	1966 - 144
1957 - 232	1962 - 167	
1958 - 60	1963 - 636	

The Black-capped Chickadee has appeared on the Reading count 83 of 86 years, 10 of the last 10, with a maximum of 732 on December 21, 1975. The peak for the Hamburg Christmas Bird Count is 726 on December 31, 1995. The high for the Bernville count is 344 on December 30, 1995.

The Pennsylvania Germans call the Black-capped Chickadee by a dialect version of the English name, "der Tschickedie." Another name is "der Wintervoggel," or winter bird. William Rupp explains:

"The new arrivals of late February, March, and April were generally known as 'die Friehyaahrsveggel,' - such as the song sparrows, whip-poor-wills, robins, and bluebirds. The arrivals of the late spring were called 'die Summerveggel,' - such as the swallows, orioles, chipping sparrows, and goldfinches. Those that stayed until early fall, like the goldfinches and some of the field sparrows, and the arrivals of early fall, like the field larks and the juncos, were called 'die Schpotyaahrsveggel.' The common winter residents, like the downy woodpeckers, the bluejays, titmice, chickadees, nuthatches and cardinals, were called 'die Winterveggel.' Of these, 'Summerveggel' was the most prominent name, for these birds were most numerous and prominent. Other general names, applied in all seasons were 'Buschveggel,' 'Raabveggel,' 'Wasserveggel.' Various families were given characteristic names of this type, based on color, mannerism or habitat" (Rupp, 1946:190).

CAROLINA CHICKADEE *Parus carolinensis*

Common resident

A common resident in southern and eastern Berks County, the Carolina Chickadee here reaches its northernmost limits in eastern Pennsylvania. It hybridizes with the similar Black-capped Chickadee in areas where the two ranges overlap.

The Carolina Chickadee appears to have spread farther north during this century, although Levi Mengel took a specimen at Mount Penn on April 7, 1891, and at Klapperthal near Reading April 15, 1892.

Earl Poole had not found the Carolina Chickadee in Berks by 1930 and regarded it as accidental in 1947, believing that its occurrence resulted from random wandering after the breeding season. He saw and heard two in the Reading Public Museum park on December 28, 1938, and had an excellent observation of one at Moselem on September 20, 1941. He had several good winter observations at West Reading, a typical Carolina Chickadee visiting his feeder almost daily during January and February 1958 and another during the winter of 1959-1960.

Alex Nagy saw one on several occasions at Owl's Head at Hawk Mountain during December 1969. A Chickadee singing the Carolina's song was heard outside the Common Room in May 1986 (R. Ramsey). One appeared at the North Lookout October 6, 1995 (Phil Campbell).

Now the Carolina Chickadee breeds in southern and eastern Berks, nesting confirmed during the *Atlas of Breeding Birds in Pennsylvania* survey from 1983 to 1989 (Brauning, 1992:241). Harold and Joan Silagy found it in Bern Township during June 1996.

The first record for the Carolina Chickadee on the Reading Christmas Bird Count occurred on December 23, 1962, near Lobachsville. It has appeared 23 of 86 years, seven of the last 10, with a maximum of 13 on December 19, 1976. Single birds have been recorded December 29, 1985, and December 26, 1993, on the Hamburg Christmas Bird Count. The Carolina Chickadee has appeared once on the Bernville count on January 3, 1993.

BOREAL CHICKADEE *Parus hudsonicus*

Accidental

The Boreal Chickadee is an accidental winter visitor in Berks County, the first recorded at Hawk Mountain November 13, 1954 (Charles Price, John Miller, Ken Wright).

On January 2, 1960, a Boreal Chickadee appeared at a feeding station maintained by Anna Leinbach at Stony Creek Mills and remained until January 12. During that time Byron Nunemacher and Earl Poole watched it from a distance of five feet. Leinbach also secured some excellent color slides. On January 15, Charles Schaich saw possibly the same bird at Antietam Lake, about a half-mile distant.

Two Boreal Chickadees were recorded in Berks during the winter of 1969-1970. Joe Taylor found one on the Escarpment Trail at Hawk Mountain October 31, 1969, and Dean Kendall saw one near Kindt's Corner at Lake Ontelaunee December 21, 1969, for the only Reading Christmas Bird Count record. One was recorded in Schuylkill County on the Hamburg Christmas Bird Count January 1, 1970.

Catherine Elwell, Marcia Bachman, and Jim Olmes observed a Boreal Chickadee on Bald Overlook at Hawk Mountain on October 31, 1983.

TUFTED TITMOUSE *Parus bicolor*
Common resident

A common resident, the Tufted Titmouse has expanded its range north this century and now breeds throughout Berks County.

In 1930, Earl Poole listed it as a rather rare and local resident. A small colony lived along the Upper Tulpehocken Creek near Blue Marsh until the winter of 1922, and a pair evidently nested near White Bear in 1922, although Poole could not find the nest. Stragglers appeared at intervals over the southern half of the county, but the only areas where he saw it consistently were at Hopewell, White Bear, and Birdsboro.

By 1947, Poole noted that the Tufted Titmouse varied in abundance but was usually fairly common along the larger streams. In 1946, it was as common locally as Poole had known it to be in the previous 25 years. The bird apparently moved north along the Schuylkill River and its tributaries before dispersing through the county.

Maurice Broun considered the Tufted Titmouse erratic and irregular during the early years at Hawk Mountain, the first record of a single bird October 26, 1938. It was first recorded at the Hawk Mountain feeders on December 9, 1954 (Maurice Broun), and has been seen every year since. Broun recorded the first successful nesting on April 29, 1957. At least three young and the adults appeared at the feeders through July.

On the Reading Christmas Bird Count, Tufted Titmouse numbers exceeded 100 for the first time in 1960 when 144 were counted. It has appeared 73 of 86 years, 10 of the last 10, with a maximum of 299 on December 22, 1996. It was first recorded on the count in 1919.

The peak for the Hamburg Christmas Bird Count is 407 on December 27, 1992. The high for the Bernville count is 201 on December 30, 1995.

This bird is one of "die Winterveggel," but the Pennsylvania Germans have no specific dialect name for it (Rupp, 1946:191).

RED-BREASTED NUTHATCH *Sitta canadensis*
Erratic migrant

The Red-breasted Nuthatch is one of the most unpredictable and erratic birds whose movements appear to defy any attempt at explanation.

In Berks County during many years it is rare or absent. In some years it does not appear until late September or even in October, occasionally not at all. Although there are records for each month of the year, it is least likely to be seen in June and July.

The most reliable places to see this nuthatch are among the mature spruces and pines at Kindt's Corner at Lake Ontelaunee and at Nolde Forest in Cumru Township. It is attracted to

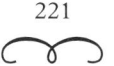

the man-made habitat of conifer plantations.

There is one confirmed nesting record of the Red-breasted Nuthatch in Berks. Frank and Barbara Haas recorded fledged young at Nolde Forest while conducting the *Atlas of Breeding Birds in Pennsylvania* survey on July 7, 1985. They recorded several pairs on June 15, 1985. This species nests in Pennsylvania wherever the micro-habitat of extensive stands of spruces exists. Although it hasn't been looked for since the atlas project, it probably still can be found breeding here.

It has been observed in the Blue Mountain region during the nesting season. Walter H. Leibelsperger found it on a spur of the ridge on June 6, 1907. Francis Trembley saw one during the last week in June 1941. Maurice Broun recorded it from June 8 to July 5, 1954; June 14, 26, and 30 1957; and June 21, 1961.

Peter Saenger found it in Henningsville, Longswamp Township, June 22 and 30, 1985. He also recorded it that year on August 19, 28, and 29. Rudy Keller found the Red-breasted Nuthatch in Pike Township June 30, 1990; June 24, 1993; and June 27, 1996. Kerry Grim saw it at State Game Land 110 June 27, 1993.

There are also several July records. Broun saw a Red-breasted Nuthatch July 7 and 12, 1951. Matt Spence recorded it in the Reading Public Museum park July 4, 1983; at Nolde Forest July 25, 1981; and at Peters Creek July 22, 1990. Keller recorded it in Pike Township July 3 and 23, 1993. Dean Kendall saw one at Leesport July 5 and 6, 1993, and Grim found it in Hamburg July 9, 1994.

Earl Poole saw it at Lake Ontelaunee July 14, 1957. By August 13 it had become abundant among the pines on the Lake Ontelaunee watershed and remained so through the entire fall and into midwinter, its toy horn-like calls heard everywhere throughout the entire season. Invasion years of this nuthatch occurred in 1951, 1957, 1989, and 1990, when it appeared in August and stayed throughout the winter.

The fall migration peak of the Red-breasted Nuthatch at Hawk Mountain occurred during 1957 when 222 were counted. The daily high count there is 40 on September 10, 1961 (Maurice Broun).

Its spring movements are equally erratic, but there is usually a perceptible movement in late April or the first half of May. Poole's latest spring migration date when there was no suspicion of the bird's nesting was May 22 (1917). More recently, Harold Lebo recorded one in Plowville May 18 to 25, 1993.

Levi Mengel collected specimens of the Red-breasted Nuthatch in Stouchsburg June 12, 1884; in Bethel Township May 31, 1885; and at Blue Marsh June 2, 1887.

With the exception of the invasion years when unusual numbers of the Red-breasted Nuthatch appear in June and early July, the early fall arrival date in the county is August 26 (1921 - E.P.).

The Red-breasted Nuthatch has appeared on the Reading Christmas Bird Count 55 of 86 years, nine of the last 10, with a maximum of 52 on December 18, 1983. The peak for the Hamburg Christmas Bird Count is 39 on January 3, 1982. The high for the Bernville count is eight on January 3, 1988.

WHITE-BREASTED NUTHATCH *Sitta carolinensis*
Fairly common resident

A fairly common resident in wooded areas, the White-breasted Nuthatch is more frequently seen in winter when it forages in the more open country and comes to feeders.

In Berks County, where this nuthatch is fairly common throughout the year, it becomes secretive during the nesting season from April to June. Earl Poole had only one June record during 45 years of field work in the county.

Maurice Broun recorded his first summer occurrence of a White-breasted Nuthatch at Hawk Mountain on the morning of July 6, 1959, at Schaumboch's. He found one at the North Lookout June 15, 1960, and one at Schaumboch's on July 12, 1961.

Poole found family groups consisting of parents and young as early as May 29 (1921 - at Maidencreek).

Periodically, unusually large migrations of White-breasted Nuthatches have been observed at Hawk Mountain. On October 8, 1935, Broun counted 12 migrants at the North Lookout. During the fall of 1951, he recorded 156 at the lookout during September with as many as 25 on two different days. He saw 128 in October with high counts of 28 on October 1; 12 on October 4; 15 on October 6; and 12 on October 14.

After recording only one bird during the fall of 1956 on October 5, Broun counted 133 during September 1957 and 88 in October with birds "all over the mountain" during November and December. Over 10 were at the feeders through December 1957.

Broun notes another migration during the fall of 1959, counting over 100 at the North Lookout from September 19 to October 6, with a high of over 36 on October 5.

Another extraordinary White-breasted Nuthatch migration was observed farther east of Hawk Mountain along the Kittatinny Ridge in Lehigh County at Bake Oven Knob during the fall of 1968. Donald Heintzelman and Robert MacClay counted 297 that fall, whereas from 1961 through 1967, only 53 were recorded, and during the autumn of 1969, 22 were counted. On September 4, 1968, they observed eight birds that began the migration that continued until October 24. The heaviest flight occurred September 17 when 80 were counted. Other exceptional flights that fall included 29 on September 15, 22 on September 29, and 20 on September 21 (Heintzelman and MacClay, 1971:129).

The White-breasted Nuthatch has appeared on the Reading Christmas Bird Count 83 of 86 years, 10 of the last 10, with a maximum of 160 on December 17, 1995. The high for the Hamburg Christmas Bird Count is 264 on December 31, 1995. The peak for the Bernville count is 136 on December 30, 1995.

The Pennsylvania Germans call the White-breasted Nuthatch "Nusspicker," a name which can also apply to the Downy Woodpecker (Rupp, 1946:191).

BROWN-HEADED NUTHATCH *Sitta pusilla*
Accidental

Levi Mengel collected a Brown-headed Nuthatch, a bird of the southern pinelands, at Boyertown on September 6, 1894. This specimen is in the Reading Public Museum collection.

BROWN CREEPER *Certhia americana*
Fairly common winter visitor

In Berks County the Brown Creeper is a rather common migrant and winter visitor.

A rare summer resident, the Brown Creeper is found during the breeding season in swampy and heavily wooded areas. The first Berks nesting record is of two adults feeding young at Antietam Lake June 26, 1964 (Matt Spence). It was confirmed nesting in southern Berks during the *Atlas of Breeding Birds in Pennsylvania* survey from 1983 to 1989 (Brauning, 1992:249). One territorial pair was recorded on the Hawk Mountain Sanctuary breeding bird census plot at the River of Rocks in 1984 (Laurie Goodrich). Three singing males were at Rattling Run in June and July 1994 (Kerry Grim, Rudy Keller).

Fall migrants usually reach the county during September and October but occasionally do

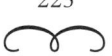

not put in an appearance until well into November or, as happens every few years, may be rare or absent all winter. Some early arrival dates in the county are August 20 (1963 - M.S.) and September 4 (1954 - Earl Poole).

Sightings at the North Lookout at Hawk Mountain range from September 19 (1984) to December 6 (1952). The single-day peak there is six on October 7, 1936 (Maurice Broun).

The Brown Creeper has appeared on the Reading Christmas Bird Count 75 of 86 years, 10 of the last 10, with a maximum of 27 on December 26, 1949. The peak for the Hamburg Christmas Bird Count is 44 on December 29, 1985. The high for the Bernville count is 15 on January 1, 1989.

It was regularly found on the Hawk Mountain winter bird census plots from 1983 to 1988 and in 1995 and 1996.

Migrants leave by the third week of April, the latest spring departure date May 6 (1955 - E.P.).

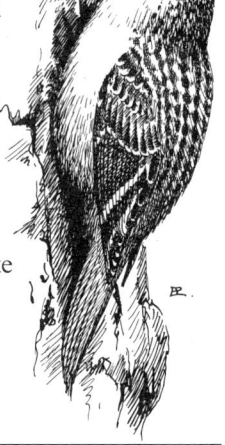

CAROLINA WREN *Thryothorus ludovicianus*

Common resident

Carolina Wren numbers fluctuate in Berks County depending on the severity or the mildness of the winter weather. Widespread throughout the county, it is one of the most persistent singers, its spirited carol heard throughout the year.

At least five times this century, Carolina Wren numbers rose until severe winter weather decimated the populations.

During the winter of 1917-1918, the Carolina Wren was practically exterminated in the county and was then not recorded for three or four years (Earl Poole). Again in the winter of 1932-1933, it was nearly wiped out and took several years to recover. From 1944 it made a strong comeback and was fairly common until the heavy snows of February 16 and March 21, 1958, again decimated its numbers.

The population crashed during the frigid and snowy winters of the late 1970s. On the Reading Christmas Bird Count in 1977, 16 were recorded; in 1978, not one was recorded; and in 1979, three were counted.

Because of the mild winters in the 1980s, the Carolina Wren reached new highs in its populations, only to crash during the severe winters of 1993-1994 and 1995-1996. Christmas count data from this period illustrates the effects of these winters. After a record 146 Carolina Wrens were found during the Reading Christmas Bird Count on December 20, 1992, only 27 were recorded on the 1994 count. A high of 127 was recorded on the Hamburg Christmas Bird Count on December 30, 1990, but only 14 appeared on the 1994 count. A peak of 121 occurred on the Bernville count January 3, 1993, but for the count on January 2, 1995, only five were tallied. It has appeared on the Reading count 57 of 86 years, 10 of the last 10.

Like the House Wren, the Carolina Wren will nest in unusual places. Arthur Schultz described a nest that was built in a pile of iron shavings in one of the buildings of the Reading Bone Fertilizer plant near Neversink (Poole, 1947:86).

BEWICK'S WREN *Thryomanes bewickii*
Accidental

An accidental visitor from the South, the Bewick's Wren has occurred three times in Berks County, all in Albany Township.

Maurice Broun found one September 30, 1934, at the entrance to Hawk Mountain Sanctuary. Broun saw and heard one singing near Schaumboch's at the Sanctuary on April 12 and 13, 1947. Broun, Jay Schnell, and Joel Abramson saw one along the Pine Creek in Eckville on May 20, 1951.

HOUSE WREN *Troglodytes aedon*
Common breeder

The House Wren is a very common migrant and summer resident throughout Berks County.

It arrives during the third week of April, an early date April 14 (1922, 1929 - Earl Poole).

Levi Mengel took 13 sets of eggs in the county between May 21 (1885) and June 20 (1890). Clutch sizes in these sets range from six to eight eggs. Two or three nestings are not unusual. Besides nest boxes, the House Wren nests in unusual places wherever there is a small cavity available including the pockets of clothing left outside and tin cans.

The House Wren leaves in fall usually by the first week in October, a late date November 20 (1991 - Ed Barrell at Blue Marsh).

There is one Reading Christmas Bird Count record. Dean Kendall found a House Wren at Lake Ontelaunee December 16, 1979. On the Hamburg Christmas Bird Count, single birds were recorded December 26, 1971; December 30, 1990; and December 27, 1992.

The Pennsylvania Germans call the House Wren "der Zaahschlipper" or "der Zaunschlibber," variations of the German name for the common European wren (Rupp, 1946:192).

WINTER WREN *Troglodytes troglodytes*
Fairly common migrant and winter visitor

A fairly common migrant and irregular winter visitor, the Winter Wren has nested at least once in Berks County.

Kerry Grim found an adult feeding fledged young August 20, 1979, near the Auburn Lookout on State Game Lands 110 (Grim, 1992:146).

The Winter Wren prefers ravines and rock outcroppings for nesting and has appeared during the breeding season at different areas of the county. It is irregular in summer at Shartlesville and Eckville State Game Lands 106 and is found most summers at the Hamburg reservoir.

Maurice Broun, Alex Nagy, and Conrad Roland found two Winter Wrens at the "Ice Cave" on the Hawk Mountain Sanctuary from June 29 to July 11, 1955. The male sang during this time and remained in the same area. Apparently no effort was made to find a nest. On July 8, Broun writes that the song had a bubbling quality and was "the longest song of any of the local birds." It was found during the breeding season at Hawk Mountain from 1955 through 1961, when Broun heard a singing male in the same area in June (Broun, 1962). On May 21, 1971, Fred Wetzel heard two Winter Wrens singing along the escarpment trail. During the summer of 1990, four Winter Wrens sang from May through June in the River of Rocks at Hawk Mountain (Laurie Goodrich).

Singing males have been found near Hay Creek, where a hillside stream empties into the Birdsboro reservoir. Ken Lebo and Matt Spence heard one singing there from April 9 until the end of June 1992. One sang at the same place from May 1 to 8, 1993.

Catherine Elwell heard one singing in District Township May 23, 1993.

The Winter Wren starts to move south during September, although the migration usually does not attain its full momentum until October. The early arrival date is August 20 (1995 - Matt Wlasniewski at Hawk Mountain). Broun banded one at Hawk Mountain on August 29, 1954.

The Winter Wren is most frequently seen in October and April. Kerry Grim found a fall high count of 13 at Shartlesville State Game Lands 110 October 12, 1996, and a spring high of nine there April 17, 1995.

Earl Poole noted that the Winter Wren was rare or unnoticed during the winters of 1919-1920 and 1920-1921, but more common during the winters of 1922-1923, 1932-1933, and 1938-1939.

In District Township at the headwaters of the Oysterville Creek, Rudy Keller has found one or two birds each year until late January. Two were here during the entire winter of 1970-1971. One spent the winter of 1994-1995 roosting every night in a Phoebe nest in his garage. He last saw it about mid-March, when the Phoebe returned.

It has appeared on the Reading Christmas Bird Count 72 of 86 years, 10 of the last 10, with a maximum of 12 on December 26, 1938. It recently went unrecorded during severe winter weather in 1978, 1981, and 1986. The peak for the Hamburg Christmas Bird Count is nine on December 27, 1987. It was last unrecorded in 1978. The peak for the Bernville Count is five on January 2, 1994.

SEDGE WREN *Cistothorus platensis*

Very rare

There are no recent records for the Sedge Wren in Berks County.

Earl Poole found the Sedge Wren in marshy meadows and on islands at the head of Lake Ontelaunee. On August 6, 1933, he saw one carrying food to one of the unlined nests, and on July 24, 1936, another one was carrying nesting material. He saw several in the same area during the late summer of 1941, but none has appeared there since.

Spring records at the lake include May 21, 1931; May 11, 1940; and May 17, 1941. Fall observations are between July 16 (1939) and October 17 (1932), most about Lake Ontelaunee, where it was fairly regular during fall until the marshes were destroyed.

The only local Sedge Wren specimen in the Reading Public Museum collection was found at Fifth and Laurel Streets, Reading, by Robert Morris on September 24, 1944.

MARSH WREN *Cistothorus palustris*
Rare

A locally distributed migrant, the Marsh Wren nested irregularly in the smaller marshes in Berks County where it is also a rare migrant, particularly in late summer and fall. There are no recent nesting records, however.

Several small marshes in Berks harbored nesting Marsh Wrens from time to time. Earl Poole knew of one breeding colony in a marsh at the village of Kenneys in Caernarvon Township until it was drained and converted into pasture in 1943. The wrens have not been seen there since.

A few marshes near Moselem have been inhabited at irregular intervals, nests seen in June and July 1955 (Earl Poole). Byron Nunemacher and Earl Rollman found several pairs summering there during 1928.

Matt Spence recorded a Marsh Wren on August 7, 1960, at Peters Creek.

The species is so local that few representative migration dates are available. The earliest arrival date in Berks County is April 21 (1995 - Robert Gray and Kutztown University biology class at Peters Creek). This bird stayed at Peters Creek until April 30 (Jason Horn).

Ken Lebo recorded a Marsh Wren May 4, 1995, at Glen Morgan Lake near Morgantown.

The Marsh Wren appears to disperse from its breeding marshes quite early, and may appear in places in which it had not previously been found during that season as early as July 5 (1957 - E.P.) and July 16 (1948 - E.P), both at Lake Ontelaunee.

The fall migration peaks in September, with a few stragglers remaining until mid-October. Spence found single birds September 10, 1956, and September 17, 1957, both at Peters Creek. Anne "Babe" Webster, Mark Blauer, and Kerry Grim found a Marsh Wren in a cattail marsh near the Visitor Center at Hawk Mountain in the rain September 19, 1987.

The late fall departure date from Lake Ontelaunee is October 23 (1932 - E.P.). Arthur Sigman reported one wintering at Kenneys in Caernarvon Township before 1943, but the exact dates are lost.

GOLDEN-CROWNED KINGLET *Regulus satrapa*
Common migrant and winter visitor

The smallest of the passerines, the Golden-crowned Kinglet is a common migrant and usually a fairly common winter visitor in Berks County.

It has adapted to conifer plantations in Berks. The only confirmed nesting in the county was recorded at Nolde Forest in Cumru Township by Frank and Barbara Haas during the *Atlas of Breeding Birds in Pennsylvania* survey on July 7, 1985. They found several pairs earlier on June 15, 1985. Like the Red-breasted Nuthatch, this species will nest wherever a micro-habitat of extensive stands of spruces exists.

From July 16 to 30, 1988, Rudy Keller found a singing male Golden-crowned Kinglet closely accompanied by two or three female or immature birds foraging high in mature Norway spruces at the bottom of Spook Lane near Oley. On June 29, 1990, Jean Patton watched a male repeatedly carry white feathers high into a Norway spruce in her yard in Lobachsville. She could not find a nest in the dense foliage.

Dorothy and Oliver Smith found a Golden-crowned Kinglet in the pines along Route 73 at Lake Ontelaunee July 30, 1960.

The bulk of the fall migration takes place during October, an early date September 2 (1991 - Rudy Keller in Pike Township). Foraging Golden-crowned Kinglets have been recorded at the North Lookout at Hawk Mountain, highs of over 75 counted on October 10, 1987, and October 9, 1988. Kerry Grim found 40 Golden-crowned Kinglets at Shartlesville October 13, 1996. Occasionally a considerable number are present through November.

Like many winter visitors, the Golden-crowned Kinglet is somewhat erratic in its occurrence and may be present in numbers through some winters and rare or absent during others. But it can usually be found during winter in coniferous woodlands in the county.

The Golden-crowned Kinglet has appeared on the Reading Christmas Bird Count 78 of 86 years, 10 of the last 10, with a maximum of 159 on December 26, 1938. The peak for the Hamburg Christmas Bird Count is 143 on December 27, 1987. The high for the Bernville count is 34 on January 2, 1995.

It stays in Berks through the second week of April when the migration tends to peak. The late date for migrants is May 11 (1986 - Matt Spence at Green Hills).

RUBY-CROWNED KINGLET *Regulus calendula*
Common migrant; uncommon winter visitor

The Ruby-crowned Kinglet is a common migrant in both spring and fall, occasionally remaining into the winter.

During the spring migration, it is most common from about mid-April to the second week in May. Migrants have been seen from March 8 (1939 - Earl Poole) to May 19 (1917 - E.P.). On April 18, 1992, Rudy Keller and Harold and Joan Silagy counted over 100 Ruby-crowned Kinglets in western Berks County.

In the fall the Ruby-crowned Kinglet does not usually appear until around the third week in September, although Maurice Broun had early observations at Hawk Mountain on August 15 (two birds) and 22, 1950; August 25, 1952; and August 23, 1958.

Kerry Grim counted 47 Ruby-crowned Kinglets at Shartlesville October 12, 1996.

The Ruby-crowned Kinglet leaves in October, but there are numerous November and December records. During some years birds remain through the winter but do so much less commonly than the Golden-crowned Kinglet.

It has appeared on the Reading Christmas Bird Count 55 of 86 years, 10 of the last 10, with a maximum of 36 on December 19, 1976. The peak for the Hamburg Christmas Bird count is 21 on January 1, 1995. The high for the Bernville count is eight on January 2, 1995.

BLUE-GRAY GNATCATCHER *Polioptila caerulea*
Fairly common breeder

The Blue-gray Gnatcatcher, rare during the first half century, has expanded its range from the south during the past 50 years until it is now a fairly common breeding bird throughout Berks County.

In 1930, Earl Poole regarded it as a rare straggler. The first record this century is one seen near Pleasantville April 25, 1920 (G. Henry Mengel).

It was listed as occurring in Berks by John F. Hofmann in 1890, and may have been more common then. Levi Mengel collected Blue-gray Gnatcatchers in Albany Township June 16 and 17, 1886; at Blue Marsh May 30, 1887; in Caernarvon Township June 4, 1888; and in Bethel Township June 18, 1888.

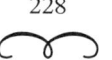

Poole still considered it a rare straggler in 1947, although he observed a nest at Trap Rock along Hay Creek from May 12 to 30, 1946. On May 19, the nest contained two eggs, and he saw another pair of Gnatcatchers about a half-mile away. On June 16, four young left the nest. The Trap Rock nest was later collected and is in the Reading Public Museum.

It has since become a regular breeder at Hay Creek, nests observed every year since 1946, one as early as April 29 (1962 - Earl Poole).

On May 6 and 19, 1951, Poole saw one occupied nest near Joanna. In 1955 Conrad Roland found a nesting pair along the Pine Creek in Albany Township. Sam Gundy found another nest at Shillington in June 1955.

It now nests in moist woods near water throughout Berks County.

The Blue-gray Gnatcatcher arrives in the county during mid-April, the early date April 10 (1988 - Matt Wlasniewski at Peters Creek). In fall it moves through during August and September, the late dates September 28 (1957 - Hawk Mountain), September 29 (1996 - Dean Kendall at Leesport), and October 9 (1994 - Matt Spence at Lake Ontelaunee).

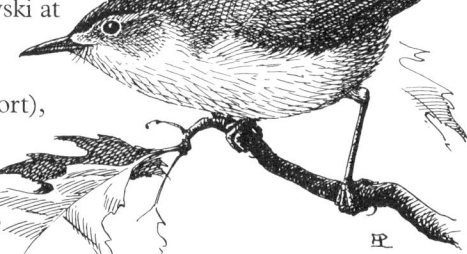

Matt Spence found a Blue-gray Gnatcatcher at Peters Creek near Lake Ontelaunee January 1, 1995, for the only Berks winter record. Matt Wlasniewski saw the bird there the next day.

EASTERN BLUEBIRD *Sialia sialis*
Common migrant and breeder

The Eastern Bluebird had undergone a gradual decline this century after the introduction of the European Starling, which drove the bird from its nesting cavities, until it almost disappeared by the early 1960s.

In 1960, Earl Poole noted that the Eastern Bluebird population had reached an all-time low, and many observers over the greater part of the eastern counties failed to find any nestings in their area. In 1964 he writes: "The arrival of the House Sparrow and the European Starling, together with a succession of late winter snows, have accelerated the disappearance of this favorite harbinger of spring, until it is now reduced to a sad remnant of its former abundance."

Because of the efforts of individuals and groups to reintroduce the Bluebird through a nest box program, numbers of the bird in Berks County are currently at the highest level this century.

The Eastern Bluebird is now common as a migrant and breeder and uncommon in winter.

Where the Bluebird doesn't winter, it usually arrives during the first week of March, the earliest date February 14 (1954 - Earl Poole).

Dean A. Boyer kept records from 1983 to 1992 on almost 160 Bluebird houses he maintains from the State Hill area of Blue Marsh Lake through Bernville to Cross Keys. During that time, 2,932 young successfully fledged from the boxes.

He found that Berks Bluebirds usually have two clutches and rarely three or one. The first eggs are laid in the third week of April and as late as mid-May. Incubation lasts 12 days, and then nestlings fledge after 18 days. The fledging date for the first clutch usually occurs in mid-to-late June.

After five days, the female begins a second clutch, which appears in early-to-mid July. Those birds fledge in mid-to-late August. The size of the first clutch averages five or six eggs, the second clutch four or five eggs. Clutches range from single eggs to nine, an extraordinarily large number.

On May 14, 1988, Boyer checked his Bluebird boxes and found one with nine young Bluebirds about 12 days old. He built a larger box to accommodate the birds, and watched as two females and one male attended the brood. All nine young fledged. He replaced the larger box with the original, and in late July it contained a second brood of five ready to fledge (Boyer, 1989:15-16).

Thirteen sets of eggs in the Levi Mengel collection at the Reading Public Museum were taken between April 25 (1884) and May 15 (1887). Clutch sizes in these sets range from three to six eggs.

The fall departure of the Eastern Bluebird consists of a gradual withdrawal following the main migratory movement in October and the first half of November. The single-day high count of migrating Bluebirds at Hawk Mountain is 128 on October 23, 1991 (Doug Laye). The late date at the North Lookout is November 27 (1996 - Beth Garland, one bird).

The few wandering groups that remain to spend the winter seek some sheltered spot that promises an adequate supply of food.

Reading Christmas Bird Count records reflect the low numbers of Bluebirds during midcentury. From 1959 to 1981, there were only five years when Bluebirds were found: one in 1961, one in 1962, six in 1964, four in 1970, and 18 in 1976. Since 1982, the Bluebird has been recorded each year. It has been found on the count 51 of 86 years, 10 of the last 10, with a maximum of 94 on December 18, 1994. The peak for the Hamburg Christmas Bird Count is 265 on December 27, 1992. The high for the Bernville count is 243 on January 4, 1997.

Matt Spence photographed a leucistic Eastern Bluebird on Mount Penn April 13, 1991. The photo appeared in *Pennsylvania Birds* (5:78).

"Der Blovoggel" is the Pennsylvania German name for the Bluebird. When William Rupp asked persons about dialect bird names they invariably began naming them this way: "Amschel" (Robin), "Grabb" (Crow), and "Blovoggel." Rupp says, "With so few persons knowing many dialect or English names [for the birds], ... the above three would always be among those named" (Rupp, 1946:206-207).

TOWNSEND'S SOLITAIRE *Myadestes townsendi*
Accidental

At 7:45 a.m. on October 15, 1989, Jeff Bouton and Harry Fink watched an adult Townsend's Solitaire fly out of the woods and perch on a snag at the right of the North Lookout at Hawk Mountain. There was heavy fog in the valley, but it was bright and clear at the lookout. It remained on the snag for two minutes before flying back into the woods to the west. Bouton observed the bird through 8.5X binoculars and a spotting scope. He had previously seen the species in Colorado. He noted the Robin size, erect posture, uniformly gray body, white outer tail feathers, dark eye, white eyering, and buffy wing patches.

VEERY *Catharus fuscescens*
Uncommon breeder and migrant

The Veery has expanded its breeding range in Berks County during the second half of this century. It currently nests uncommonly throughout Berks County in moist, mature woodlands at places such as Nolde Forest, Shartlesville, Hay Creek, Glen Morgan Lake, and French Creek State Park.

It has been present every summer from 1967 along the headwaters of the Oysterville, Swamp, Perkiomen, and Pine creeks in District and Pike townships (Rudy Keller). The Veery has also been found nesting during the *Atlas of Breeding Birds in Pennsylvania* survey from 1983 to

1989 in woods in eastern and western Berks (Brauning, 1992:267).

In 1930, Earl Poole had not found the Veery breeding in the county although G. Henry Mengel and he heard one singing its hauntingly beautiful song at Birdsboro on June 2 and 9, 1917. By 1947, Poole noted that it may have bred occasionally. Arthur Sigman and Robert Cook found a nest from which the young had just flown on June 18, 1950, in the former Sixpenny Creek picnic area in French Creek State Park in southeastern Berks.

Kerry Grim has recently found the Veery nesting near the Port Clinton fire tower, where it shares the same ridge habitat with the Hermit Thrush.

Levi Mengel took sets of four eggs now in the Reading Public Museum collection at Pricetown June 19, 1887, and in Caernarvon Township June 4, 1888.

An uncommon spring and fall migrant, the Veery departs by the middle of September. It arrives in spring during the second week of May, early dates April 22 (1995 - Kerry Grim at State Game Lands 110) and April 28 (1956 - Earl Poole). Except for occasional call notes, the Veery falls silent in July after the nesting season and stays hidden in dense undergrowth, making it difficult to locate. The latest fall date is September 28 (1972 - R.K. in District Township). The latest Hawk Mountain record is September 9 (1995 - Jack and Helen Holcomb).

GRAY-CHEEKED THRUSH *Catharus minimus*
Rare migrant

The Gray-cheeked Thrush is a migrant of varying abundance in spring but is usually rare or often undetected in the fall. The difficulty in identifying the bird may be one reason for the lack of definite records.

On May 11, 1975, Matt Spence and Robert Cook observed an extraordinary fallout of over 50 Gray-cheeked Thrushes along Indian Run near the Birdsboro reservoir.

The Gray-cheeked is the latest of the thrushes to reach Berks County in the spring, the earliest date this century May 6 (1954 - Earl Poole). Levi Mengel took a specimen at White Bear on May 2, 1890. The late spring date is June 10 (1971 - Rudy Keller in Pike Township).

Maurice Broun found three in song at the Lower Shelters at Hawk Mountain May 17, 1961.

The Gray-cheeked Thrush is rare in fall. Anna Kendall has five fall records in Leesport as early as September 5 (1984) and as late at October 16 (1965). Fall Hawk Mountain records include October 6, 1959; September 21 to 26, 1962 (one or two feeding on fruit of black gum at the North Lookout - Maurice Broun); September 25, 1987; September 25, 1993; and September 15 and 20, 1996.

E. Newkirk found a dead Gray-cheeked Thrush, now in the museum collection, near the Reading Public Museum on September 20, 1926.

BICKNELL'S THRUSH *Catharus bicknelli*
Accidental migrant

Few experienced observers are willing to record observations of this small edition of the Gray-cheeked Thrush because it is so difficult to identify. Previously regarded as a subspecies of the Gray-cheeked Thrush, it was elevated to full species status by the American Ornithologists' Union in 1995.

Earl Poole found a dead male under a television tower on the Blue Mountain near Bethel on September 20, 1955. It is now in the Reading Public Museum collection.

Harriet Larrabee and Poole saw one in the Reading Public Museum park on May 1, 1957.

It was so small that Poole believed it could only have been a Bicknell's Thrush.

On April 30, 1995, Kerry Grim saw three "possible" Bicknell's Thrushes at Shartlesville. He noted that they seemed very small.

Matt Spence identified a Bicknell's Thrush near Water Street at Lake Ontelaunee May 19, 1996.

SWAINSON'S THRUSH *Catharus ustulatus*

Uncommon migrant

The Swainson's Thrush is an uncommon migrant whose numbers appear to have diminished during the last decade.

In 1947, Earl Poole regarded it as common in spring and irregular in fall.

The Swainson's Thrush arrives later in spring than the other thrushes, the migration taking place almost entirely in May although April dates have been reported. Identifications should be checked carefully because Hermit Thrushes are sometimes confused with this bird.

Early arrival dates include April 18 (1962 - Alex Nagy at Hawk Mountain) and April 28 (1953 - Earl Poole). On May 23, 1986, large numbers of Swainson's Thrushes were found along the trails at Hawk Mountain with many more reported flying over. The late spring date is June 6 (1996 - Catherine Elwell in District Township).

The fall migration starts rather early. Anna Kendall observed one at Leesport August 30, 1991. Maurice Broun banded a Swainson's Thrush at Hawk Mountain on September 3, 1958, and Earl Poole found one at Reading on September 8, 1958. Most of the migrants pass through Berks County during the latter part of September with a few stragglers remaining into October. The late date is October 25 (1991 - Laurie Goodrich at Hawk Mountain's North Lookout).

Migrants can often be heard at night in spring and especially in September after the passage of a cold front. On September 27, 1970, Rudy Keller counted 410 call notes of Swainson's Thrushes as they migrated overhead between 10:45 and 11 p.m. in Pike Township. He writes: "There was a songbird flight of great magnitude last night after the rains. It was the heaviest of the fall to date... and it continued heavily throughout the evening and night. Joan Silagy reported a flight so heavy at Reading that she heard it indoors. Mrs. [Anna] Kendall reported huge numbers of birds in the woods near Eckville at dawn the next morning."

The Swainson's Thrush can be reliably identified by its high-pitched, rather sibilant "heep" note, although the other thrushes sound like each other or give calls resembling those of the Rose-breasted Grosbeak or the Scarlet Tanager. Since the 1970 flight, the best Keller heard in recent years occurred in 1993. He listened to between 30 and 50 call notes of the Swainson's Thursh in the predawn darkness on September 19. Dean Kendall heard between 48 and 60 calls about 11 p.m. in Leesport the previous night. At first light on September 30, Keller heard 20 to 30 Swainson's calls as they flew low over the treetops of Pike Township.

There are three winter records. One was recorded on the Hamburg Christmas Bird Count December 29, 1974. Alex Nagy found a Swainson's Thrush feeding on autumn olive January 8, 1977, at Hawk Mountain. Sam Gundy observed one in Wyomissing December 17, 1978, for the only Reading Christmas Bird Count record.

HERMIT THRUSH *Catharus guttatus*

Fairly common migrant; local breeder

Throughout Berks County, the Hermit Thrush is a fairly common spring and fall migrant and a locally common nester in cool forests on the Blue Mountains, principally above elevations of 1400 feet.

It has increased as a breeder since the first nesting this century was recorded in 1980, a pair Alex Nagy found June 26 and 27 along the River of Rocks at Hawk Mountain. Kerry Grim and Laurie Goodrich have found that the largest nesting population currently occurs on the mountaintop between Hawk Mountain and the Port Clinton fire tower. It has nested regularly there since 1986.

During the nineteenth century, the resident thrushes were frequently confused. Levi Mengel collected sets of eggs in Berks County which were identified doubtfully as those of the Hermit Thrush. Earl Poole believed that one set of four eggs Mengel took in Bethel Township May 27, 1885, was correctly identified.

Occasional stragglers brave Berks County winters in sheltered places where there is a supply of berries in places like Nolde Forest, Kindt's Corner at Lake Ontelaunee, and the Five Locks area along the Schuylkill River below Hamburg. Poole found the Hermit Thrush wintering successfully in sheltered places around Reading 14 of 40 years and felt confident that it could have been found during other years if the nearly impenetrable tangles of greenbrier and honeysuckle that it frequents had been searched.

The Hermit Thrush has appeared on the Reading Christmas Bird Count 48 of 86 years, 10 of the last 10, with a maximum of 22 on December 17, 1995. The peak for the Hamburg Christmas Bird Count is 22 on December 27, 1992. The high for the Bernville count is 10 on January 1, 1992.

A Hermit Thrush that spent the winter of 1994-1995 near a conifer grove in District Township was last seen April 20, 1995 (Rudy Keller).

Because of wintering individuals, migration dates are difficult to determine in Berks, and the first spring arrivals usually appear during the first week of April. During years in which this thrush was not known to have wintered, it has arrived as early as March 4 (1934, 1944 - Earl Poole). Most of the Hermit Thrushes pass through in April although a few nonbreeders remain well into May, the latest date May 18 (1960 - E.P.).

The Hermit Thrush can be fairly common in the latter half of April. It rarely sings on migration but moves quietly through the woods in small, loose flocks. Rudy Keller counted 18 in Pike Township April 25, 1967.

The main southward migratory movement takes place in October. The earliest fall arrival date at Hawk Mountain is September 3 (1941 - Maurice Broun) and at Leesport is September 14 (1982 - Anna Kendall).

WOOD THRUSH *Hylocichla mustelina*

Common migrant, summer breeder

The Wood Thrush is a common migrant and nester throughout the wooded portions of Berks County.

It arrives with fair regularity during the latter part of April, the early dates April 15 (1996 - Sue Guers at Hawk Mountain) and April 21 (1992 - Rudy Keller).

Thirty-one sets of eggs from Berks County in the Reading Public Museum collection were found between May 19 (1887, 1888, 1890) and June 16 (1886). Clutch sizes in these sets range from three to five eggs. The Wood Thrush nests low in the understory.

Recent research conducted from 1990 to 1994 by Dr. Margaret Brittingham of Penn State University and Laurie Goodrich at Hawk Mountain has shown that although there are higher nest densities in fragmented forest areas of northern Berks, there is lower nesting success compared to the contiguous forests of the Blue Mountain. Nest predation in the fragmented forests is the main problem. Of 171 nests studied in 1990 and 1991, a 76 percent successful nesting rate was found in contiguous forests while there was only a 43 percent success rate in forest patches. Only 19 percent of the nests in large areas of forest were preyed on compared to 56 percent on small. Brood parasitism by the Brown-headed Cowbird differed between the large and small areas of forest, as 4 percent and 13 percent of the nests were parasitized, respectively. The probability of nest success increased as the size of the forest increased. On four occasions, Common Grackles were observed preying on Wood Thrush nests (Hoover, 1992b:1-2).

The Wood Thrush leaves Berks before the last of September and is decidedly uncommon in October. Earl Poole's departure dates range from September 8 (1929, 1935) to October 20 (1960). A late date from Hawk Mountain is October 30 (1947 - Maurice Broun).

There are two Reading Christmas Bird Count records. An apparently healthy individual remained about Poole's feeding station at West Reading from December 28, 1952, to January 2, 1953, and was seen daily at close range during that time by several experienced observers including Sam Gundy and Byron Nunemacher, who were aware of the novelty of the observation. The second record is one seen December 15, 1974.

The Pennsylvania German name for the Wood Thrush is "die Buschamschel" because it is related to the Robin and because the thrushes and the immature Robins resemble each other. The bird's habitat suggests this form of the name (Rupp, 1946: 204).

AMERICAN ROBIN *Turdus migratorius*

Abundant migrant and breeder

So well has the American Robin adapted itself to human activities that it is now probably the most abundant and most generally distributed of all the resident birds. It nests in every part of Berks County, and while it is most familiar in suburban areas where shade trees and well-kept lawns provide conditions most to its liking, it also frequents town and country, woodland and cultivated areas alike.

In winter it usually is present in varying numbers in sheltered areas that offer cover and a plentiful supply of the small fruits which form the bulk of its winter diet. At this season it is regular and not uncommon. Because of its comparative shyness and retiring habits during the winter, it is much less conspicuous than in summer and is seldom seen unless searched for.

It remains in one area as long as the food supply lasts. By mid-February there is often an influx of birds that have wintered a little to the south of here. These pioneers are often forced back by late snows and may not return for two or three weeks. The irregularity of these late winter movements makes it impossible to determine the date of the main migratory movement. During some years the American Robin does not reach Berks County in numbers until March 22, as it did in 1931.

Thirteen sets of eggs in the Reading Public Museum collection were taken between May 18 (1885) and June 10 (1888). Clutch sizes in these sets range from two to six eggs.

Fall migration dates from most areas mean little, since the movements of the southbound flocks depend on the weather conditions and on the local crop of berries. Usually the American Robin population dwindles imperceptibly during the latter part of October and early November, leaving smaller bands to spend the winter.

Large numbers of migrating Robins have been recorded at Hawk Mountain. Maurice Broun counted over 3,000 Robins October 18, 1955, and over 1,000 the next day. On October 13, 1959, he tallied over 1,500 Robins. On November 1, 1993, over 2,500 Robins were counted migrating over the North Lookout (Barry Peifer).

The American Robin has appeared on the Reading Christmas Bird Count 68 of 86 years, the last 43 years in a row. During the count December 22, 1985, Robert Cook and Ed Barrell found a roost near Gibraltar that contained over 10,843 Robins. The peak for the Hamburg Christmas Bird Count is 580 on December 31, 1989. The high for the Bernville count is 342 on January 5, 1986.

Matt Spence collected an albino Robin along Friedensburg Road April 5, 1959. The specimen is in the Reading Public Museum collection.

Earl Poole saw a highly colored individual which he felt certain belonged to the far northern black-backed race, *T. m. nigrideus*, at Moselem on February 16, 1957. The head, throat, and upper back appeared to be entirely black and the breast of a much deeper red than in the other American Robins that were present at the time. That race doubtlessly occurs in Berks both during migrations and in winter.

The Pennsylvania German name for the Robin is "die Amschel." William Rupp says that no other bird is as well and as widely known in Pennsylvania German lands as this universal favorite. It is always known by this one dialect name, based on the German "Amsel," the name for the European blackbird. Rupp also writes:

"They say that there was a time when many Robins were killed for food, but, as with the Flickers, good laws put an end to the unhappy practice. A good friend and a reliable informant, who must remain anonymous, has told us that the first flesh which he was given as a child was Robin's flesh, - so that he would have a voice like a Robin. He tells us that Robins were not killed at any other time by the members of his family. What is more, he confesses to the shooting of two Robins in his lifetime, so that the first meat which his two daughters would eat might be that of the Robin, - 'so dass sie singe kenne wie die Amschel!'" (Rupp, 1946:201-203)

VARIED THRUSH *Ixoreus naevius*

Accidental

The first Berks County sighting of a Varied Thrush occurred in December 1995 when an adult male was seen and photographed at a feeder near Boyertown for approximately one week prior to the heavy snow of December 19, according to Robert Davidheiser, a friend of the bird's "hosts."

The second county sighting occurred February 4, 1996, when Catherine Elwell identified a male in a yard near Lobachsville. Access was restricted by the homeowners, wishing to retain privacy,

to about 20 birders who had excellent views when it came to feed on crab apples a few feet from a window. It left with milder weather on February 28. Many photos and a videotape were taken.

Although these two locations are only about 10 miles apart, the photos show that the Boyertown bird had a darker breastband, a darker gray cap, and a deeper orange breast than the other male, so most likely two birds were seen.

GRAY CATBIRD *Dumetella carolinensis*
Common migrant and breeder

The Gray Catbird is a common migrant and widespread breeder throughout Berks County. There are numerous records up to the first few days of January, but there are very few observations of Gray Catbirds that have survived an entire winter.

When the really cold weather sets in, the Gray Catbird usually disappears. However, Joseph Malek banded a Gray Catbird that survived the winter of 1959-1960 near his home at McKnight's Gap in Alsace Township, being seen as late as March 6. It had learned to subsist on sunflower seeds! One bird remained in Pike Township from October 1994 to January 7, 1995 (Rudy Keller). One was observed in Gibraltar January 5, 1924 (Earl Poole), and at Blue Marsh Lake January 15, 1993 (Ernie Schiefer). Another Gray Catbird visited a feeder in Wyomissing on February 22, 1968 (Peter Muhlenberg).

In Berks the Gray Catbird puts in an appearance anywhere from April 17 (1954 - E.P.) to May 6 (1927, 1928, 1934), usually arriving by the end of April. An extremely early arrival date is March 11 (1996 - Matt Spence at Lake Ontelaunee).

There are 45 sets of eggs taken locally in the Reading Public Museum collection that range from May 14 (1886) to June 28 (1885). Clutch sizes in these sets are from three to six eggs.

Matt Spence and Bart Smith observed a Catbird chasing a Ruby-throated Hummingbird for about 90 seconds at Peters Creek on September 9, 1990. They were sure the Catbird viewed the Hummingbird as food.

Most of the Gray Catbirds leave by mid-October, but the few stragglers left behind make it difficult to estimate the time of bulk departure.

It has appeared on the Reading Christmas Bird Count 29 of 86 years, five of the last 10, with a maximum of six on December 16, 1984. It has been tallied on the Hamburg Christmas Bird Count 10 of 32 years with a high of two on December 26, 1983, and December 27, 1992. The peak for the Bernville count is four on January 1, 1992. The Catbird was found on all three counts in 1996.

The Pennsylvania German names for the Catbird are "der Schpottvoggel" - a name for any "mocking" bird, and "der Katzevoggel" (Rupp, 1946:98-199).

NORTHERN MOCKINGBIRD *Mimus polyglottos*
Common resident

The Northern Mockingbird has dramatically extended its range from the south during this century and is now a common resident throughout Berks County.

In 1930 Earl Poole considered it a rare straggler, the first observation in Berks County this century made at Cedar Top in Cumru Township on June 1, 1919, by G. Henry Mengel.

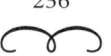

On May 9, 1937, Poole found the first nest at Wyomissing Park, where it has since nested regularly.

By 1947, Poole regarded the Mockingbird as a rare and local resident. He visited a nest near Lorane in Exeter Township on June 24, 1957, that contained four eggs, said to have been the second set for that season.

The Northern Mockingbird had become well established in Berks by 1958 and has nested near Kempton in the extreme northern part of the county, finding welcome sanctuary in the hedges of multiflora rose planted as cover for wildlife. By 1961 it had become so common in suburban areas that one or more could be found during a brief stroll at any season.

The ability of the Mockingbird to mimic bird vocalizations as well as other sounds is extraordinary. On June 29, 1962, Donald Heintzelman saw a Mockingbird perched on a tree about 100 feet east of an active Kestrel nest on Alex Nagy's farm in Albany Township and was startled to hear the bird briefly, but quite perfectly, imitate the "klee klee klee" defense call of the Kestrel. The falcon ignored the Mockingbird's vocalization (Heintzelman, 1963a).

There are three North Lookout records for the Northern Mockingbird at Hawk Mountain: November 3, 1958; October 19, 1987; and September 2, 1996.

It first appeared on the Reading Christmas Bird Count in 1935 and has been recorded on every count since 1955. The maximum is 192 on December 15, 1974. The peak for the Hamburg Christmas Bird Count is 177 on December 29, 1985. The high for the Bernville count is 130 on January 1, 1992.

John F. Hofmann listed the Northern Mockingbird in 1890. The Reading Public Museum contains a specimen taken in Albany Township by Levi Mengel on June 2, 1888.

"Der Schpottvoggel" is a general name heard throughout the Pennsylvania German region for a "mocking" bird (Rupp, 1946:197).

BROWN THRASHER *Toxostoma rufum*

Uncommon migrant and summer breeder

The Brown Thrasher is an uncommon migrant and summer resident over the greater part of Berks County, occurring in scrub growth even at higher altitudes.

Since it sings less frequently during the nesting season and is extremely secretive compared to its relatives - the Gray Catbird and Northern Mockingbird, it is often overlooked.

The Brown Thrasher usually reaches Berks County in mid-April but occasionally arrives as early as April 9 (1995 - Ken Lebo at Lake Ontelaunee).

There are 36 local sets of eggs in the Reading Public Museum collection taken from May 17 (1888) to June 16 (1885, 1887, 1888). Clutch sizes in these sets range from three to five eggs.

Most of the Brown Thrashers leave Berks by the end of September, but a few remain well into October and some may attempt to winter. One remained in the Reading Public Museum park from January 30, 1943, to February 10, 1944 (Earl Poole). Another was found in Pike Township from

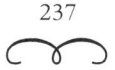

November 21 to December 2, 1968 (Rudy Keller).

The Brown Thrasher has appeared on the Reading Christmas Bird Count eight of 86 years, twice in the last 10, first counted in 1971. The maximum is two on December 19, 1971, and December 16, 1979. Single birds were recorded on the Hamburg Christmas Bird Count on January 1, 1968, and January 2, 1983.

The Pennsylvania Germans call the Brown Thrasher "der Schpottvoggel." In Berks County, the name "der Drescher" has also been used. This is the German name for a thrasher or thresher, and this dialect name is probably only a translation of the English (Rupp, 1946:199-200).

AMERICAN PIPIT *Anthus rubescens*
Regular migrant

During the spring and fall migrations, the American Pipit is partial to beaches, mud flats, and the shores of lakes and ponds and also occurs commonly on freshly plowed fields in eastern and western Berks County and in the Oley Valley.

The American Pipit is regular but about equally common in spring from March 13 (1959 - Earl Poole) to May 12 (1935 - E.P.) and in fall from September 22 (1935 - E.P.) to November 26 (1950 - E.P.).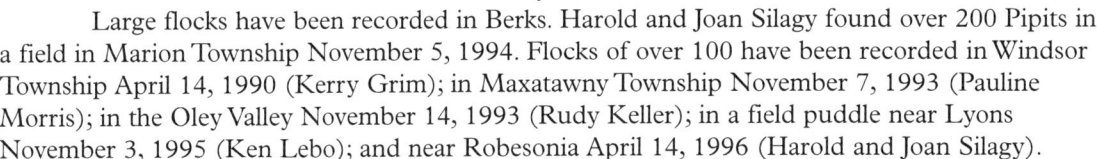

Migrants have been counted during most years over Hawk Mountain between September 9 (1936) and December 4 (1990). The single-day peak is 30 on October 13, 1935, and October 29, 1952 (Maurice Broun).

Earl Poole recorded small, winter flocks at Blue Marsh February 26, 1922; at Fritz's Island February 15, 1931; and at Lake Ontelaunee January 15, 1938. Bernie Morris saw 15 in Maxatawny Township February 13, 1993, and Ernie Schiefer found five near Robesonia two days later.

Large flocks have been recorded in Berks. Harold and Joan Silagy found over 200 Pipits in a field in Marion Township November 5, 1994. Flocks of over 100 have been recorded in Windsor Township April 14, 1990 (Kerry Grim); in Maxatawny Township November 7, 1993 (Pauline Morris); in the Oley Valley November 14, 1993 (Rudy Keller); in a field puddle near Lyons November 3, 1995 (Ken Lebo); and near Robesonia April 14, 1996 (Harold and Joan Silagy).

The American Pipit has appeared on the Reading Christmas Bird Count five of 86 years, twice in the last 10, with a maximum of eight on December 31, 1961. Single birds have been counted twice on the Hamburg Christmas Bird Count on December 23, 1973, and January 1, 1995. It has appeared once on the Bernville count, 24 seen January 3, 1993.

Levi Mengel took a specimen at Antietam April 26, 1888.

BOHEMIAN WAXWING *Bombycilla garrulus*
Accidental

Nearly all Berks County sightings of the Bohemian Waxwing have occurred at the North Lookout of Hawk Mountain or in Eckville at the base of the Blue Mountain.

The first Berks County record is one seen November 9, 1975, by Gordon Meade and Jim Brett.

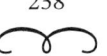

Two sightings occurred in 1980. Seth Benz saw one November 3, and he and Allen Metz found one November 17.

Mary Bailey saw a Bohemian Waxwing in a flock of Cedar Waxwings in Eckville on January 5, 1989.

On November 9, 1993, Laurie Goodrich saw one with five Cedar Waxwings calling and circling the North Lookout at 8:50 a.m. She said the Bohemian had a "flatter, louder, buzzier trill" than the Cedar Waxwings and was "larger, grayer, more robust looking" with a small area of white in the wings and a gray belly, while the Cedar Waxwings had yellow bellies. At the lookout the next morning, Cathy Viverette heard a loud "tzeet tzeet" that sounded "stronger, louder" than the Cedar Waxwing call and saw a lone Waxwing silhouetted at the top of a tree but was unable to focus her binoculars on it before it flew away. There were several sightings of Bohemian Waxwings throughout Pennsylvania that year.

Tom Leckey identified a Bohemian Waxwing among a flock of 40 Cedar Waxwings near the sawmill at Nolde Forest in Cumru Township January 6, 1996.

CEDAR WAXWING *Bombycilla cedrorum*

Common migrant; regular breeder

The Cedar Waxwing is an erratic but usually fairly common permanent resident, sometimes common and seen during practically every week in the year, or occasionally absent from a given area for many months.

It is frequently absent or rare in winter, its presence at that season usually depending on the prevalence of the various kinds of berries on which it feeds.

The Cedar Waxwing nests throughout Berks County, commonly in old orchards and shade trees. It is also a late nester. Maurice Broun found a pair building a nest in an apple tree at Schaumboch's at Hawk Mountain on August 6, 1951. Birds were incubating August 30. A pair nested in late September 1985 at the Aspen Cut Campground at Hawk Mountain.

Levi Mengel collected five sets of eggs in Albany Township from June 10 (1886) to June 19 (1888). Clutch sizes in these sets range from three to five eggs. Walter Leibelsperger collected a set at Fleetwood June 10, 1905, and at Walnuttown on July 5, 1907.

The peak count for fall migrants at Hawk Mountain is 593 on September 11, 1996 (Beth Garland).

One of the tamer birds, the Cedar Waxwing will often fly-catch. On September 13, 1962, Donald Heintzelman and Alex Nagy observed a flock of 25 Cedar Waxwings in the trees behind the North Lookout at Hawk Mountain. Shortly before noon a mass of winged ants (*Formicidae*) boiled over the lookout and clustered around the top of a tree near the birds. Almost immediately the Waxwings began darting after the insects in flycatcher fashion, plucking the insects from the air and returning to their perch to eat them (Heintzelman, 1963b:37).

The Cedar Waxwing will also get "tipsy" after eating fermented fruits.

Usually it is most abundant in September, or again it may be recorded more often in January, depending on the crop of edible fruits.

It has been recorded on the Reading Christmas Bird Count 59 of 86 years, 10 of the last 10, with a maximum of 435 on December 19, 1982. The peak for the Hamburg Christmas Bird Count is 569 on December 29, 1985. The high for the Bernville count is 455 on January 4, 1997.

The Pennsylvania Germans call the Cedar Waxwing "Der Kaerschevoggel," or cherry bird, because of its fondness for fruit and berries (Rupp, 1946:208).

NORTHERN SHRIKE *Lanius excubitor*
Rare winter visitor

A rare and irregular winter visitor, the Northern Shrike has appeared in Berks County in unusual numbers during invasion years.

The first extensive invasion of Northern Shrikes to reach Berks this century was during the winter of 1921-1922, when Byron Nunemacher found the first one on October 30, 1921. Earl Poole saw one a week later on November 6. From then until March 29, 1922, Poole recorded the Northern Shrike on 11 occasions, seeing two birds on two different dates.

Often several years elapse between observations of this bird. In the winter of 1925-1926, Poole had three observations of Northern Shrikes in different areas.

The most recent invasion of Northern Shrikes in Berks occurred during the winter of 1995-1996. At least three and possibly four individuals were recorded. Laurie Goodrich saw an immature at the North Lookout at Hawk Mountain on December 5 and 6. At least one, but probably two adults frequented the area around Eckville November 15 and from December 2 to 31 (Tom Leckey, Arlene Koch). Another Northern Shrike appeared at Blue Marsh Lake on December 30 for the only Bernville Christmas Bird Count record (Norman Reifsnyder).

Due to heavy snows in January 1996, birders lost sight of all these Shrikes except one. Kerry Grim, Catherine Elwell, and Matt Wlasniewski found an adult near Eckville February 18 and 19, and Eric Atkinson last reported this bird on March 21.

The Northern Shrike has appeared in Berks from October 30 (1921 - Byron Nunemacher) to April 11 (1973 - Kenneth and Dorothy Grim and Ethel Fink in Albany Township).

An adult female specimen in the Reading Public Museum collection was taken by Levi Mengel at Flying Hill on September 16, 1887. Poole suspected that there may have been an error in labeling this specimen, as the date seems improbable. Mengel took two other specimens, one in Bethel Township March 5, 1886, and another along the Schuylkill River below Reading on November 7, 1886.

It has appeared on the Reading Christmas Bird Count three of 86 years, single birds on December 27, 1959; on December 21, 1969; and on December 19, 1976. Records on the Hamburg Christmas Bird Count are of individuals seen on December 24, 1972; January 2, 1977; December 28, 1980; January 3, 1982; and December 31, 1995.

In Berks County, the Northern Shrike is more inclined to frequent partly wooded, brushy country, rather than the wide open agricultural lands inhabited by the Loggerhead Shrike, with which it is often confused. It is also a bolder, more aggressive bird. On November 1, 1925, Nunemacher and Poole saw one annoying a Black-crowned Night-Heron, and on another occasion Poole saw one fly almost straight into the air to attack an American Tree Sparrow that was flying at least a hundred feet overhead.

The Northern Shrike has been recorded frequently at Hawk Mountain. The first record there is one Maurice Broun observed January 22, 1956. He saw it on the top-most twig of a tall oak at the east end of the orchard at Schaumboch's against a gray sky at 7:20 a.m. The bird stayed only a few minutes. Broun noted that it had the Evening Grosbeaks so demoralized, for they flew round and round the place and would not drop down to the feeders. The Shrike flew down the mountain towards the east. On February 28, possibly the same bird reappeared in the lilacs at Schaumboch's at 12:45 p.m. Broun remarked, "Chickadees unconcerned."

On January 30, 1969, Mickey Mutchler observed an immature Northern Shrike fly down to the feeders at the Visitor Center, grab a Goldfinch, flip it over, bite its throat, and fly off with the bird. This all occurred within a few seconds. Over 20 Goldfinches were feeding on the ground.

A Northern Shrike was found at Hawk Mountain throughout the winter of 1978-1979. Barb Lake and Seth Benz recorded one near the feeders December 10 and 11, and on December 26 George and Verdi Silfies saw an adult along the fire tower road. Benz found one on February 6,

1979. One was recorded at the Visitor Center feeders from January 9 to February 1, 1982, and an immature was recorded from the North Lookout in November 1991. On October 31, 1996, an adult flew by the North Lookout (Laurie Goodrich, Dave Hollenback).

The Northern Shrike has even been seen within the city of Reading. One chased feeder birds at Joan Silagy's home on Meade Street December 1 and 2, 1974.

On at least three occasions, a Northern Shrike was heard singing. During the Elverson Christmas Bird Count on January 1, 1966, Robert Cook and Matt Spence found one in song at Joanna Furnace; on the Reading Christmas Bird Count December 19, 1976, Bart Smith and Spence found one singing at Peters Creek; and on the Elverson count December 23, 1995, Rudy Keller heard and saw an immature bird singing.

LOGGERHEAD SHRIKE *Lanius ludovicianus*
Very rare migrant

There are no recent Berks County records for the rapidly declining Loggerhead Shrike, the last sighted during the Reading Christmas Bird Count on December 16, 1979.

It was previously a rather rare and irregular migrant in spring and fall.

On at least one occasion an individual wintered in Albany Township from September 7, 1936, to April 11, 1937. During that time it was seen by many of the local observers.

After the breeding season the Loggerhead Shrike is very erratic and irregular in its movements, and there are numerous August records at some distance from its breeding grounds. Byron Nunemacher and Earl Poole had eight August records in Berks, the earliest August 23 (1941). The late fall date outside of Christmas count records is November 28 (1965 - Matt Spence at Peters Creek).

There was a perceptible spring movement between March 27 (1943,1954 - Earl Poole) and April 22 (1939 - E.P.).

Levi Mengel collected a Loggerhead Shrike now in the Reading Public Museum at Virginville March 18, 1887.

The Loggerhead Shrike has been recorded on the Reading Christmas Bird Count four of 86 years, single birds in 1943; December 24, 1967; December 22, 1968; and December 16, 1979. Three records on the Hamburg Christmas Bird Count are of two birds December 26, 1971, and single birds December 23, 1973, and December 29, 1974.

EUROPEAN STARLING *Sturnus vulgaris*
Abundant resident

Originally introduced from Europe into Central Park in New York City during the 1890s, the European Starling is now one of Berks County's most abundant birds, nesting in summer and roosting in winter in the city of Reading, villages, and farm buildings and competing with several native birds for nesting cavities in old trees and nesting boxes. Such species as the Red-headed Woodpecker, Eastern Bluebird, and Purple Martin seem to have suffered most from its aggressive action.

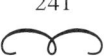

The first published reference to the appearance of the European Starling in Pennsylvania is the report of a pair that raised a brood of young on the property of Dr. W. H. Ridge at Trevose, Bucks County, in the spring of 1904 (*Auk*,1908:221).

By 1915 the European Starling reached Reading.

William Rupp writes that the Starling was first seen in Maxatawny Township about the year 1920, and was called "die neie Veggel fer die Schpatze ausdreiwe" by the Pennsylvania Germans there. "Schtarling," the dialect version of the English name, is the most prevalent throughout the region (Rupp, 1946:208-209).

It first appeared on the Reading Christmas Bird Count on December 23, 1917, when 34 birds were counted. It has been recorded 79 of 86 years, 10 of the last 10, with a maximum of 40,000 on December 24, 1939. The peak for the Hamburg Christmas Bird Count is 15,903 on December 29, 1974. The high for the Bernville count is 15,685 on January 4, 1987.

Earl Poole believed that the young European Starlings, at least, are partially migratory, and they are often seen in mixed flocks with Common Grackles and Red-winged Blackbirds from mid-June on through the winter, although the great majority of adults appear to be resident.

Migrants are seen passing Hawk Mountain Sanctuary regularly, although counts are not always recorded. The single-day peak at the North Lookout is 235 on November 12, 1991.

During the winters of 1936-1937 to 1939-1940, at least 30,000 European Starlings roosted in the pines near Antietam Lake just east of Reading, along with thousands of Grackles, Brown-headed Cowbirds, and a scattering of Red-winged Blackbirds, but they have since adapted to the taller buildings in Reading for their roosting places as they have done in many other towns throughout the county.

A macromutation of a Starling with an unfeathered head and long, decurved bill was obtained for the Kutztown University Museum Collection by a student who observed the bird at a feeder in Greenwich Township sometime in the early 1980s. The fledged Starling probably remained near its nesting area and fed on bread from around the feeder. An attempt to maintain the bird as a live specimen failed, the bird dying a few days after capture. The university had the bird mounted by a local taxidermist, and it is on display in the Boehm Science Building on the university campus (Robert Gray).

WHITE-EYED VIREO *Vireo griseus*

Uncommon migrant and local summer resident

Because of its preference for dense, swampy thickets, the White-eyed Vireo is heard far more often than it is seen. An uncommon and local summer resident, it apparently fluctuates in numbers. During the summer of 1925 none was observed, although Earl Poole visited all its usual haunts. By 1946, it seemed to have recovered its former abundance.

An uncommon spring migrant, the White-eyed Vireo arrives during the last week in April, the early date April 22 (1995 - Matt Wlasniewski at Hay Creek).

This vireo is present in Berks County each year throughout the breeding season under conditions that indicate nesting in at least four areas, mostly to the south of Reading. Swamps at White Bear, Douglassville, Elverson, and Gouglersville usually harbor one or more pair each season. According to the *Atlas of Breeding Birds in Pennsylvania* survey taken from 1983 to 1989, the White-eyed Vireo is more likely to be found nesting in southern Berks County than it is in northern or western Berks County (Brauning, 1992:289). It is common at Glen Morgan Lake (Ken Lebo) and at several locations around Blue Marsh (Joan Silagy).

In northern Berks County, the White-eyed Vireo is uncommon. Most of Kerry Grim's records are of singing males in nonbreeding habitat where they could not be relocated. During the 1980s, White-eyed Vireos appeared to be territorial at Eckville State Game Lands 106 and at the Five Locks area near Shoemakersville. Laurie Goodrich heard this vireo at Eckville on July 10, 1995, and Rudy Keller heard singing males near Albany in May and June 1992 and 1996.

During the migrations it may appear in unlikely places such as parks and suburban areas.

Local birds disappear during July and few fall records exist. Recent late dates include September 27 (1989 - J.S. in Bern Township) and September 26 (1993 - Matt Spence at Moselem). Earl Poole's latest observation is September 21 (1941 - at the Reading Public Museum park). Fall records from Hawk Mountain range from August 24 to September 16.

Two sets of eggs taken by Walter H. Leibelsperger near Bowers June 23, 1907, and near Fleetwood May 30, 1911, are in the Reading Public Museum collection.

SOLITARY VIREO *Vireo solitarius*
Common migrant and rare nester

The Solitary Vireo is a comparatively hardy species. In addition to being the earliest vireo to arrive in spring, it is the last to leave in fall, remaining behind after most of the warblers have left. Individuals sometimes remain into November.

The earliest spring arrival date is April 9 (1922 - Earl Poole; 1971 - Anna Kendall at Leesport), and the latest spring departure date is May 23 (1926 - E.P.).

The Solitary Vireo is also a rare nester along the Kittatinny Ridge. Harriet Larrabee found adults with young at the Blue Mountain near Hamburg in June 1954. Earl Poole found a singing male near Eckville on June 3, 1934. A singing Solitary Vireo was heard at Hawk Mountain near the River of Rocks and on the north slope in June 1996.

During the *Atlas of Breeding Birds in Pennsylvania* survey from 1983 to 1989, the Solitary Vireo was not found nesting in Berks County (Brauning, 1992:291). However, Rudy Keller and Joan Silagy found adults feeding young at Rattling Run July 4, 1993, in two different locations. One nesting occurred in Berks County, the other in Schuylkill County. A year later, several pairs were established there (Kerry Grim, R.K.) with late spring records at Shartlesville State Game Lands 110 (K.G.). This apparent southern expansion of its range coincides with a population increase as noted in United States Fish and Wildlife Service breeding bird survey routes in Pennsylvania from 1966 to 1989.

An early fall arrival date from areas to the south of, or otherwise removed from, the nesting areas is September 6 (1954 - Joseph Malek; 1968 - A.K). Late dates include November 3, 1996, at Lake Ontelaunee (Matt Spence, Bart Smith) and at Hawk Mountain Sanctuary November 13 to 16, 1960, and November 7, 1996.

Alex Nagy found a Solitary Vireo dead on the highway at Moselem Springs December 7, 1973.

Robert Heise identified an extremely late Solitary Vireo among evergreen and deciduous trees near the Fleetwood reservoir December 22, 1996, for its only Reading Christmas Bird Count record.

YELLOW-THROATED VIREO *Vireo flavifrons*
Uncommon and local summer resident

A fairly common migrant in spring but an uncommon and local summer resident, the Yellow-throated Vireo is seldom observed after June and is rather rare in fall.

In Berks County this vireo sometimes arrives as early as April 24 (1992 - Catherine Elwell at Baldy Hill, District Township) and April 25 (1954 - Earl Poole). Occasionally it is not recorded until May 20 (1929 - E.P.) but usually appears during the first part of May.

A favorite area, in which Earl Poole never failed to find several pairs of Yellow-throated Vireos during the nesting season, is the wooded valley of Hay Creek between Birdsboro and White Bear. He writes in 1964: "In some other places they may be present one year and absent the next, but here, where tall trees flank the stream for several miles, the contralto song of the Yellow-throated Vireo has been one of the characteristic sounds throughout May and June."

Ken Lebo reports the Yellow-throated Vireo still can be heard singing into July along the Hay Creek from the Birdsboro reservoir to Joanna Furnace. It is also found regularly at Hopewell Furnace National Historic Site.

Bart Smith and Matt Spence saw a singing male and a second adult bird, possibly a female, at Maiden Creek Station on June 16, 1996. Kerry Grim regularly notes Yellow-throated Vireos in northern Berks County during June and July but has found no evidence of nesting. Spence, however, observed a pair, one of which was carrying nesting material, at the Hamburg reservoir June 23, 1996. Rudy Keller found one adult feeding a quietly begging fledgling in District Township August 18, 1996.

Levi Mengel took a nest with a full set of four eggs in Lenhartsville June 17, 1887, and Poole saw young, just out of the nest, on June 18, 1929, in the Reading Public Museum park. During the *Atlas of Breeding Birds in Pennsylvania* survey from 1983 to 1989, the Yellow-throated Vireo was confirmed nesting in southern Berks County (Brauning, 1992:293).

By the end of June the Yellow-throated Vireo usually has stopped singing and becomes exceedingly hard to find, frequenting as it does, the dense foliage of tall trees.

Late summer and fall records are few and far between. Anna Kendall's range for 30 years of observation at Leesport is August 21 (1972) to October 4 (1988). Poole's latest date in Berks is September 17 (1935). Matt Wlasniewski recorded a late Yellow-throated Vireo at Hawk Mountain's North Lookout October 12, 1996.

WARBLING VIREO *Vireo gilvus*
Uncommon migrant and summer breeder

The Warbling Vireo is an uncommon migrant and summer resident of somewhat spotty distribution.

In spring the Warbling Vireo arrives as a rule a little before its Red-eyed relative. At West Reading, where Earl Poole found the Warbling Vireo regularly inhabiting the double rows of tall sycamores, it has arrived anywhere from April 26 (1925, 1939, 1945) to May 17 (1924, 1926). At Hawk Mountain, the early arrival date is April 21 (1974 - Catherine Elwell).

The Warbling Vireo is uncommon to rare away from its breeding sites. It is a local nester, found among tall trees near streams such as the Maiden Creek near Lenhartsville, the Manatawny Creek near Spangsville, Stony Run in northern Berks County, and the Tulpehocken Creek near the Red

Bridge at the Berks County Heritage Center and Gring's Mill. Matt Spence has found it nesting at Maiden Creek Station at Lake Ontelaunee each year since 1956. It does not occur where there is extensive woodland such as the Blue Mountains. The Warbling Vireo tends to be found at the same location from year to year.

It is very difficult to observe among tall treetops. Undoubtedly, this bird would be undetected if it were not for the male's distinctive song.

An early departure date from Reading is September 25 (1962 - E.P.). Anna Kendall's range of fall dates at Leesport is August 1 (1988) to September 24 (1972).

An extremely late date is November 12, 1967, at Hawk Mountain. Richard Sharadin and Alex Nagy saw a Warbling Vireo sitting atop a spicebush behind Schaumboch's. The chilled bird sat for a few minutes then departed (Nagy, 1968:27).

The Reading Public Museum contains a set of eggs collected by C. Zell at Moselem Springs on June 2, 1908.

PHILADELPHIA VIREO *Vireo philadelphicus*
Rare migrant

The Philadelphia Vireo is a rare and irregular migrant in both spring and fall.

Earl Poole notes that in eastern Pennsylvania the Philadelphia Vireo was very rare or unknown in spring prior to 1935. Since 1935 this vireo has been observed more frequently in spring in the eastern counties. However, there is always a possibility of misidentifying the female Warbling Vireo having a yellowish wash on its breast for a Philadelphia Vireo.

The early spring date in Berks County is May 9 (1994 - Catherine Elwell at Baldy Hill, District Township). The late spring date is May 24 (1970, 1972 - Anna Kendall).

During the fall, the Philadelphia Vireo is regular, but rare. Most records are in September. Anna Kendall's range of dates at Leesport is August 12 (1970) to October 11 (1965). Poole's fall dates are August 25 (1956) to October 10 (1954 - specimen).

Poole's first Berks County observation occurred September 18, 1927, at Moselem, where he studied one intermittently for over an hour, during which he checked every detail carefully. The Warbling and Red-eyed vireos and the Tennessee Warbler were all present, and at no time could he confuse the four.

The early fall date at Hawk Mountain is August 24 (1951- Maurice Broun; 1989 - Jeanne Tinsman). Maurice Broun observed four Philadelphia Vireos at the North Lookout on September 16, 1951, and saw three there on September 19, 1934. The late date at the North Lookout is October 9, 1979 (Mike Tove).

Two local specimens are in the Reading Public Museum collection. Both were collected after they collided with a television tower on top of the Blue Mountain in Bethel Township on October 10, 1954 (Alex Nagy, E.P.), and September 20, 1955 (Sam Wishnieski, J. O'Leary).

RED-EYED VIREO *Vireo olivaceous*
Common migrant and breeder

The Red-eyed Vireo is a common migrant in both spring and fall and a nesting summer resident in woodlands throughout Berks County.

It rarely reaches us before the first week in May, yet over the years there have been a number of April records, the earliest recent record April 27 (1995 - Ken Lebo at Joanna Furnace). Some April records are surprisingly early and subject to doubt because of some similarity of song between the Red-eyed and Solitary vireos. However, Maurice Broun and Fred Wetzel observed an extremely

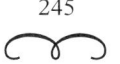

early Red-eyed-Vireo at Hawk Mountain March 20, 1966.

The neatly built, cup-shaped nests of the Red-eyed Vireo are models of avian architecture and are usually found from four to 14 feet about the ground. It nests commonly throughout the Blue Mountain and along Rattling Run.

During June 1955, Broun recorded over 130 pairs of Red-eyed Vireos along the southern boundary of Hawk Mountain Sanctuary and in 1951 found over 80 pairs.

On Hawk Mountain Sanctuary breeding bird census plots, nesting densities are usually two times higher on the lower elevation slope forest than on the ridge-top forest (Laurie Goodrich).

The fall migration usually takes place around the middle of September, and Red-eyed Vireos are seldom seen after the third or fourth week of that month. There are several October sightings and two November records: November 5, 1960, at Hawk Mountain (Maurice Broun), and November 18, 1952, at Wyomissing (Conrad Roland).

The latest date, though, is one reported from Antietam Lake by Dr. George Kershner during the Reading Christmas Bird Count December 21, 1975.

On September 22, 1946, Broun saw three Red-eyed Vireos, two Solitary Vireos, and one Philadelphia Vireo all feeding together in one mountain holly bush on the North Lookout at Hawk Mountain (Broun, 1949a:201).

The Reading Public Museum collection contains 10 sets of eggs taken June 10 (1885) to June 20 (1887). Three contain Cowbird's eggs. Clutch sizes in these sets range from two to five eggs.

The Pennsylvania German name in Berks for the Red-eyed Vireo is "der Preddicher," a translation of the English "the Preacher," a name commonly given to this bird because of its emphatic and repetitive song (Rupp, 1946:209).

BLUE-WINGED WARBLER *Vermivora pinus*

Rather common but local summer resident

Throughout the Piedmont province of southeastern Pennsylvania, the Blue-winged Warbler is a locally common migrant and nesting summer resident, building its nests on the ground in old weedy fields with a scattering of young trees and shrubs and along the edges of woodlands.

The Blue-winged Warbler rarely arrives in Berks County before the first week in May. There are a few April dates, the earliest at Hawk Mountain April 18, 1964 (*Audubon Field Notes*, 18:442). Other April sightings include single birds at Green Hills Lake April 21, 1994 (Ken Lebo); Pike Township April 22, 1995 (Rudy Keller); Lake Ontelaunee April 25, 1996 (Matt Spence); Reading Public Museum park April 27 and 28, 1953 (Earl Poole); and at Baldy Hill in District Township April 27, 1994 (Catherine Elwell).

Earl Poole found it in June under conditions indicating probable breeding on Mount Penn, at Birdsboro, Hopewell, White Bear, Monocacy, Adamstown, Gouglersville, Rittenhouse Gap, and in the Blue Mountain region.

The Blue-winged Warbler also nests rather commonly throughout the Reading Hills, where nests have been found at New Jerusalem (July 3, 1910 - Walter Leibelsperger) with numerous observations of this bird during the nesting season at many points in the hills south and east. Nest building is often well under way before the middle of May, although Poole found a nest with the young ready to fly as early as June 4 (1957) at Ridgewood, a few miles south of Reading.

Fall departure takes place early, usually by the third week of August. Anna Kendall's arrival - departure range of migrants at Leesport is July 28 (1979) to September 23 (1994).

Poole's latest observation is September 7 (1925), although Maurice Broun has reported it at Hawk Mountain on September 23, November 8 and 13, 1936.

On the Blue Mountain during the first half of this century, the Blue-winged Warbler was rare both as a migrant and summer resident, although Byron Nunemacher reported one there above Shartlesville on June 12, 1927. Poole writes in 1964: "North of the Appalachian Valley, the Blue-winged Warbler is quite rare. ...I have encountered it only twice on the Blue Mountain in many years of exploration."

Now the nesting range of this warbler has expanded to include disturbed areas along the mountain in northern Berks, with confirmed breeding records there during the *Atlas of Breeding Birds in Pennsylvania* survey from 1983 to 1989 (Brauning, 1992:299).

Rudy Keller and Joanne Kintner saw a Blue-winged Warbler sing only the Golden-winged Warbler song dozens of times for 20 minutes at Trout Run reservoir in Earl Township May 13, 1995. Matt Spence and Bill Uhrich found a Blue-winged singing like a Golden-winged at Glen Morgan Lake May 16 and 18, 1995.

GOLDEN-WINGED WARBLER *Vermivora chrysoptera*

Rare migrant

Formerly an uncommon migrant and a rare summer resident in the Blue Mountain, the Golden-winged Warbler is now a rare migrant in Berks County.

Earl Poole believed this species was undoubtedly more regular during the first half century, but its fondness for dense, scrubby thickets and an early fall migration caused it to be overlooked: "It is sufficiently scarce to elude the average bird student two years out of three, unless he is fortunate enough to be in the field frequently during the first two weeks in May when this species is passing through."

The early spring date in Berks is April 28 (1942 - Maurice Broun at Hawk Mountain; 1984 - Kerry Grim at Hamburg; 1991 - K.G. at Shartlesville).

According to records kept during the *Atlas of Breeding Birds in Pennsylvania* survey from 1983 to 1989, the Golden-winged Warbler showed a decline as a nesting species throughout the state, replaced by the Blue-winged Warbler. Wherever found, its presence as a breeding species is governed to a considerable extent by the presence of brushy second growth. There were no nesting records in Berks County during the atlas project (Brauning, 1992:301).

Poole found the Golden-winged Warbler under conditions that would seem to indicate breeding along the length of the Blue Mountain at several areas in the neighborhood of Hawk Mountain, at Northkill Gap, and rather commonly along the broad top of that mountain, at least as far as Route 183, where he found it in June on each visit from 1927 to 1954.

Kerry Grim reports summer records at Eckville State Game Lands 106 as recently as 1984 (June 23).

Because of its early departure for the south and the dense foliage it frequents at that season, the Golden-winged Warbler is rarely detected in the fall; consequently, there are very few fall migration records. Catherine Elwell reported two early migrants at Baldy Hill, District Township, on July 14, 1993. It passes through Berks between August 3 (1925 - E.P.) and September 11 (1971 - Anna Kendall at Leesport; 1993 - Rudy Keller in Pike Township). Mark Monroe recorded one bird behind the Hawk Mountain Sanctuary Visitor Center August 18, 1996.

Brewster's Warbler and Lawrence's Warbler *Vermivora pinus x chrysoptera*

The various hybrids between the Blue-winged and Golden-winged warblers that were formerly recognized as the Lawrence's Warbler, *V. lawrencei*, and the Brewster's Warbler, *V. leucobronchialis*, are not recognized in the fourth, fifth, or sixth editions of the American Ornithologists' Union Check-list, but are always interesting because of their rarity.

The Lawrence's Warbler is the recessive form, and should be the less frequently seen of the two, but there are also a variety of plumages intermediate between these two typical forms and also between these and the parent species, due to the interbreeding.

Earl Poole recorded a Brewster's Warbler at Moselem August 21, 1932; Matt Spence sighted one at Antietam Lake August 10, 1965; Catherine Elwell found a Brewster's Warbler at State Game Lands 182 in Greenwich Township May 14, 1984; Laurie Goodrich and Tom Leckey discovered one in the Pine Swamp near Eckville May 9 and 13, 1988; Anna Kendall had two sightings at Leesport on August 18, 1979, and August 25, 1992; and Matt Wlasniewski found a male singing like a Blue-winged Warbler at Peters Creek May 11, 1995. Mark Monroe recorded a Brewster's Warbler in Schaumboch's yard at Hawk Mountain on September 10, 1996.

Maurice Broun found a male Brewster's Warbler mated with a female Golden-winged Warbler and evidently nesting on the north side of the Blue Mountain in Schuylkill County close to Hawk Mountain Sanctuary along the railroad tracks near the Little Schuylkill River in 1953 and again in 1962 and 1963.

Sightings of Brewster's Warblers in the future will most likely be even less common as Golden-winged Warbler populations decrease.

There are two Berks County records of Lawrence's Warbler.

Poole saw a Lawrence's Warbler associated with a Golden-winged Warbler at Bernhart's reservoir in Muhlenberg Township on August 19, 1921.

Scott Dearolf heard and saw a male Lawrence's Warbler in typical plumage on several occasions near Angelica between May 10 and 24, 1958. This bird had apparently established a territory near a Blue-winged Warbler, both singing in competition for the two weeks this bird remained in the area. The Blue-winged remained after the latter date, but the hybrid disappeared. Dearolf described the song of the individual as similar to that of the Blue-winged Warbler rather than of the Golden-winged.

TENNESSEE WARBLER *Vermivora peregrina*
Erratic spring and fall migrant

A spring and fall migrant in Berks County, the Tennessee Warbler appears erratically during both seasons.

It is usually uncommon, or sometimes seemingly absent during the spring migrations, but common to very abundant for a short period during the fall migrations, especially in 1923, 1935, and 1942 (Earl Poole).

Occasionally it is very rare or entirely absent in the fall, and during certain years such as 1929, 1935, and during the late 1970s, has been definitely common in spring. Matt Spence found 50 Tennessee Warblers on Mount Penn May 19, 1978. Kerry Grim heard singing Tennessee Warblers during May from 1978 to 1982 at their peak numbers tending to drown out the songs of other warblers along the Blue Mountain. But by the mid-1980s to the mid-1990s, Grim had recorded only a few each spring.

Earl Poole noted in 1947 that there were seven years when he failed to find the Tennessee Warbler in both spring and fall.

During the spring migration the Tennessee Warbler seldom reaches Berks County before May, peaking during the second week. Catherine Elwell saw an extremely early Tennessee Warbler near Kutztown April 8, 1985. The late spring date is June 2 (1973 - Anna Kendall at Leesport).

The fall migration dates range from August 13 (1979 - A.K. at Leesport) to October 21 (1955 - E.P.). Dean Kendall saw an extemely late Tennesse Warbler in Leesport November 2, 1978.

Peak flights at the North Lookout at Hawk Mountain include 10 on September 7, 1988, and September 16, 1995, and nine on September 25, 1983.

Two local specimens in the Reading Public Museum collection were both taken by Levi Mengel in Bethel Township May 18, 1886.

ORANGE-CROWNED WARBLER *Vermivora celata*
Casual spring, rare fall migrant

The Orange-crowned Warbler is a casual migrant in spring, rare in fall, and a very rare and irregular winter visitor.

Spring records include one at Peters Creek April 8, 1990 (Matt Spence, Bart Smith), and one in the Reading Public Museum park May 5, 1934 (Earl Poole). Spring sightings at Hawk Mountain include one from May 13 to 15, 1955 (Maurice Broun); May 14, 1981 (Alex Nagy); May 15, 1947 (M.B.); and one at Schaumboch's May 30, 1985 (Laurie Goodrich).

The Orange-crowned Warbler occurs in fall during the latter half of September through October.

Extreme dates are from August 24 (1951 - Tommy Hanson at Hawk Mountain) well into the winter: Birdsboro December 3, 1933 (Anna Deeter); on the Reading Christmas Bird Count December 16, 1979; at Angelica Lake on the Reading count December 18, 1994 (Harold Lebo); at Moselem on the Reading count December 23, 1934 (Byron Nunemacher); at Moselem on the Reading count December 27, 1931 (B.N., E.P.); southwest of Lenhartsville January 1, 1995, for the only Hamburg Christmas Bird Count record (Rudy Keller); at Birdsboro January 17, 1932 (B.N., E.P.); and the Reading Public Museum park January 24, 1934 (F. Cassel, E.P.).

Levi Mengel took a specimen near Douglassville on October 22, 1889.

NASHVILLE WARBLER *Vermivora ruficapilla*
Uncommon spring migrant; fairly common fall migrant

Somewhat erratic and apparently subject to fluctuations in numbers, the Nashville Warbler is an uncommon spring and fairly common fall migrant.

It has nested several times along the Blue Mountain in northern Berks County.

The early spring arrival date is April 23 (1946 - Maurice Broun at Hawk Mountain). In areas where it is not known to nest, the Nashville Warbler is rarely seen later than May 9 (1933 - Earl Poole) or, more recently, May 29 (1994 - Kerry Grim at State Game Lands 110).

Between 1884 and 1895, Levi Mengel collected several Nashville Warblers in Berks County where it has not been found in June this century: Stouchsburg June 12, 1884; Blue Marsh June 1, 1887; Neversink Station June 10, 1888; and Klapperthal June 17, 1889.

He collected other specimens June 18, 1895, and June 20, 1885, in the Blue Mountain region of Bethel Township, where the Nashville Warbler might possibly be found nesting today. Matt Spence heard a singing male along Route 501 near Pilger's Ruh on June 27, 1996.

Earl Poole saw and heard several individuals in June on the flat top of the Blue Mountain at Northkill Gap June 27, 1925, and June 12, 1927. On June 3, 1928, Poole and Byron Nunemacher heard two or three Nashville Warblers along Rattling Run near Port Clinton. Maurice Broun saw a female carrying food during June 1947 on the southern boundary at Hawk Mountain.

More recently, Kerry Grim found adults feeding fledged young south of Hawk Mountain

Sanctuary on State Game Lands 106 on July 16, 1977, and July 8, 1984. Also on July 8, 1984, Grim found adults feeding fledged young one-half mile north of the Port Clinton Fire Tower.

As a nesting species, the Nashville Warbler is partial to sphagnum bogs and marshy mountain clearings, although Grim's observations of nesting Nashville Warblers have occurred at higher elevations of the mountain along wooded roads in fairly dry, deciduous woods.

During 1993, Grim unsuccessfully attempted to relocate the Nashville Warbler where it had nested previously. It may continue to nest in northern Berks County, although this area is its extreme southern limit.

The fall migration starts in August with a gradual fanning out from its breeding grounds but attains full momentum in September with stragglers into October. Anna Kendall's early fall arrival date at Leesport is August 16 (1977). At Hawk Mountain, the Nashville Warbler has appeared as early as August 17 (1948) and August 21 (1951, 1958). On the 1951 date, Tommy Hanson heard a singing male, and in 1958, Maurice Broun saw a female with three young.

The late date of October 26 (1996 - Dean Kendall at Leesport) presents a general idea of the withdrawal of the Nashville Warbler towards its winter range in the tropics.

NORTHERN PARULA *Parula americana*

Uncommon spring, fairly common fall migrant

As a migrant, the Northern Parula is regular, both in spring and fall.

In spring it frequently arrives with the first wave of warblers. There are a number of April records, the earliest April 20 (1995 - Ken Lebo, three at Hay Creek).

A strangely erratic summer resident, the Northern Parula may breed locally in a variety of habitats.

The Northern Parula has appeared in June in rather widely separated areas of Berks County. Along Hay Creek near Birdsboro, birds were noticed singing on June 30 and July 7, 1946 (Anna and Mary Deeter); June 1 and 8, 1947 (A.D., M.D., Harold Morris, Earl Poole); June 5 and 6, 1954 (Ira Weigley, E.P.); June 7, 1980 (Matt Spence); July 2, 1992 (M.S.); and July 14, 1994 (M.S.). No effort was made to find a nest in the maze of white pines, hemlocks, and spruces.

A.C. Vaurie and Conrad K. Roland reported a Northern Parula singing along the Pine Creek near Albany on June 30 and July 2, 1944, but again no nest was found. Alex Nagy and Donald Heintzelman observed a pair at Rattling Run July 4, 1966.

Formerly a regular summer resident at Shartlesville, the Northern Parula has not been seen there after 1984 except in migration. A male was on territory at the bottom of Spook Lane near Oley in June and July from 1988 to 1990 (Rudy Keller). Another held a territory along Stony Run near Kempton in June 1989 (R.K.). It was a summer resident along the Maiden Creek during June 1990 (Kerry Grim). Joan and Harold Silagy heard singing males at Blue Marsh June 15, 1996, and a singing male was heard throughout June 1996 at Hawk Mountain.

The Northern Parula seems to disappear completely after the nesting season and does not appear again until the last few days in August, the bulk of the migration occurring around the middle of September.

The earliest fall dates are August 27 (1995 - Steve Thorpe at Hawk Mountain's North Lookout) and August 29 (1940 - E.P.), and the latest is November 2 (1978 - Anna Kendall at Leesport).

YELLOW WARBLER *Dendroica petechia*
Common migrant and summer resident

The Yellow Warbler is one of the earlier warblers to arrive in Pennsylvania, usually reaching Berks County during late April. The earliest spring arrival date is April 19 (1975 - Catherine Elwell at Yamadall Valley, Greenwich Township; 1992 - Barry Pounder at the Red Bridge over the Tulpehocken Creek).

A common and widespread breeder throughout Berks County, the Yellow Warbler prefers fairly open country, willow and alder thickets near streams, dense shrubs such as multiflora rose, or shade trees and orchards, rather than heavily wooded regions.

Levi Mengel found a set of fresh eggs in Bethel Township June 2, 1885.

After the nesting season, the Yellow Warbler disperses over the surrounding country and is commonly seen until late in August when it gradually withdraws to the south, a few migrants being noted into September. Dates when the Yellow Warbler has been last seen in Berks range from August 6 (1953 - E.P.) to October 9 (1973 - Anna Kendall).

The Yellow Warbler is rare and irregular in the Blue Mountain during the migrations. At Hawk Mountain's North Lookout, this warbler is recorded irregularly during the fall.

The Pennsylvania Germans call the Yellow Warbler "der glee Gehlvoggel," the little yellow bird. William Rupp notes that as a family the warblers are known only in the mass, generally seen during migration as they fill the tree tops on a spring morning. Herbert Beck says they are generally called "Finke," from the German name for finches (Rupp, 1946:210).

CHESTNUT-SIDED WARBLER *Dendroica pensylvanica*
Fairly common migrant; uncommon breeder

Formerly an abundant breeder in the Blue Mountain, the Chestnut-sided Warbler now nests in low numbers there along scrubby edge habitat, usually at the higher elevations, particularly at State Game Lands 110 at Shartlesville and Auburn Lookout Road (Kerry Grim). During 1939, it was a common nesting species at Hawk Mountain, but now due to the maturing of the forests, it has decreased and probably no longer nests there.

Nesting was not restricted to northern Berks County, however. Earl Poole had found it under conditions that indicated breeding in the Hopewell Hills and throughout the South Mountain region. According to the *Atlas of Breeding Birds in Pennsylvania* survey from 1983 to 1989, the Chestnut-sided Warbler is a confirmed nester throughout southern Berks County (Brauning, 1992:311), and Ken Lebo has found it breeding recently at Hay Creek and Glen Morgan Lake. Rudy Keller reports that it nests in the brush along a power line cut on Topton Mountain.

Bart Smith and Matt Spence found singing males both at Schubert's Gap off Route 183 and at Water Street near Lake Ontelaunee on June 16, 1996.

Three sets of eggs in the Reading Public Museum collection were taken in Albany and Bethel townships between June 2 (1885) and June 15 (1907).

Although Poole found the Chestnut-sided Warbler a common summer resident in Berks in the South Mountains near Reading and during some years abundant along the Blue Mountain, for several years running it was unaccountably scarce during an entire season. He noted scarcities in Berks from 1941 to 1948 and again during 1958, 1959, and 1960.

Usually the Chestnut-sided Warbler is a fairly common migrant in spring but is somewhat less common in fall. It arrives on its breeding site during the first week of May, the early arrival date April 26 (1925 - Earl Poole).

After the nesting season it wanders widely, making it difficult to estimate fall migration dates. One of the earliest species to leave, it is often generally distributed by the last week in August and from then until mid-September is often one of the common migrants.

The fall migration dates at Hawk Mountain range from August 18 (1996) to October 10 (1947, 1990). On October 10, 1947, Maurice Broun counted 40 migrant Chestnut-sided Warblers.

Anna Kendall and Dean Kendall have seen Chestnut-sided Warblers in Leesport between August 2 (1992) and October 13 (1994).

Poole had an excellent view of an exceptionally late Chestnut-sided Warbler in the Reading Public Museum park November 20, 1943.

MAGNOLIA WARBLER *Dendroica magnolia*

Uncommon spring, common fall migrant

The Magnolia Warbler is not among the earlier warblers to arrive in spring but usually puts in its first appearance with the second wave. While there are a number of April records, it frequently does not reach Berks County until mid-May. The early spring arrival date is April 28 (1935 - Earl Poole). The late spring date for migrants is June 3 (1971 - Rudy Keller, a male and female in Pike Township).

Although Berks is south of the Magnolia Warbler's breeding range where it nests in hemlock forests in the higher mountains, Earl Poole believed scattered pairs sometimes nest in favorable situations at comparatively low elevations, such as Eckville in northern Berks (500 to 600 feet). The Eckville location typifies conditions that may be found at intervals along the entire Blue Mountain, where a few dense stands of second-growth hemlock are found at low elevations.

In such a growth, Poole found a Magnolia Warbler on July 22, 1923, and in the following year Byron Nunemacher, J. Hendel, and he found a family group of three in a grove of hemlocks and white pines near Mountain, Albany Township, on June 28 and 29. Nunemacher and Earl Rollman found a singing male two miles from there June 25, 1927.

Poole found a Magnolia Warbler on the northern side of the mountain on June 6, 1942, and Alex Nagy reported still another in the Pine Swamp near Eckville on June 14, 1957. On June 27, 1963, Bill Leeson heard two singing males at "The Slide" at Hawk Mountain.

During 1994, Kerry Grim observed a male Magnolia Warbler at Rattling Run which was present through July 29. However, he could not confirm whether nesting occurred.

The fall migration starts regularly in late August and is at full flood during September, with a few stragglers passing through during the first week or two in October. The range is August 6 (1992 - Harold and Joan Silagy at Blue Marsh Lake) to October 15 (1995 - Matt Spence.). An extremely late date is November 7 (1966 - Anna Kendall at Leesport).

High counts of migrant Magnolia Warblers at Hawk Mountain include over 75 on May 11, 1952 (Maurice Broun), and "hundreds" on September 11, 1948 (M.B.).

Two Magnolia Warblers are in the Levi Mengel collection at the Reading Public Museum: a male collected April 4, 1891, and a female secured June 13, 1888, both at Antietam.

CAPE MAY WARBLER *Dendroica tigrina*
Rare spring, common fall migrant

An irregular and often rare spring migrant, the Cape May Warbler is usually common in fall.

In spring it arrives in Berks County during the first week of May. April arrivals are very rare with an early date of April 28 (1990 - Kerry Grim at Hamburg; 1992 - Ken Lebo at Hay Creek). The late spring departure date is May 26 (1917 - Earl Poole).

On May 13, 1961, Earl Poole counted at least 40 Cape May Warblers during a half-mile stroll along a spruce-bordered road at Lake Ontelaunee.

According to Poole's records, the Cape May Warbler was common in spring in Berks County from about 1910 to about 1932, but has since become more irregular during that season. On the other hand, it has become increasingly common in fall, and its status during that season has changed from irregular up to 1937 to fairly regular and common with individuals remaining much later in the fall.

Rudy Keller notes that the Cape May Warbler was especially common in August and September of 1970 and 1971, a bit less so in the fall of 1972, and far less common in eastern Berks since. He saw more than 20 flycatching with 10 *Empidonax* flycatchers along a short stretch of hedgerow along a field in Pike Township September 4, 1971.

The bulk of the fall migration takes place during September and the first half of October. Exceptionally early fall arrival dates are at Hawk Mountain August 6, 1947, and August 15, 1952 (Maurice Broun).

The Cape May Warbler is often very common during fall at Hawk Mountain. Apparently, a vast majority of migrants follows the Kittatinny Ridge. On September 11, 1948, Maurice Broun reported "thousands passed forenoon." He counted at least 70 Cape May Warblers feasting on, and flitting out of, a mountain holly bush at the North Lookout on September 26, 1946 (Broun, 1949a:202).

There are a few records of the Cape May Warbler later than October 21. Poole had found it near Reading on that date on two occasions. In 1946 one remained until October 24, and another loitered about the Reading Public Museum park until November 20, 1943. Anna Kendall recorded one at Leesport October 26, 1971.

There are two winter records. Two Cape May Warblers remained about a feeding station at Green Hills Lake from January 12 until February 8, 1958 (E.P.). Jack Holcomb saw and photographed a female Cape May Warbler when it visited his feeder in the city of Reading between February 12 and March 5, 1995. He put out sliced grapes, but the bird didn't touch them. Instead it hopped around on the ground apparently picking at seeds. It appeared healthy and alert the whole time.

BLACK-THROATED BLUE WARBLER *Dendroica caerulescens*
Common spring and fall migrant

The Black-throated Blue Warbler is a fairly common migrant both in spring and fall.

Earl Poole found it more regular in spring, while in fall it may either be abundant, as in 1952, 1953, and 1954, or apparently altogether missing, as from 1933 to 1938.

Beginning in 1958, Poole noted an alarming reduction in the number of Black-throated Blue Warblers and of various other insectivorous birds, which he attributed, at least in part, to the widespread use of powerful insecticides in the northeastern Pennsylvania counties.

The winter home of this warbler is chiefly restricted to the West Indies, and it rarely reaches here before the first week in May, although there are a number of late April records. The earliest arrival date in Berks County is April 14 (1996 - Catherine Elwell). Maurice Broun's earliest date at Hawk Mountain is April 27 (1948).

A female Black-throated Blue Warbler specimen taken April 18, 1887, "near Reading" is in the Levi Mengel collection at the Reading Public Museum.

The last spring migrants may disappear anywhere from the second week of May until the end of that month, with occasional stragglers into June. Rudy Keller saw a male near Boyertown June 4, 1988.

Kerry Grim has found the Black-throated Blue Warbler in the Blue Mountains during summer, although in very low numbers. Prior to the 1990s, males would linger into early June at the Hamburg reservoir. The bird now can be found into July at the higher elevations of the reservoir and the Port Clinton fire tower and the lower elevations of Rattling Run and Shartlesville State Game Lands 110. It prefers hillsides with a mountain laurel and rhododendron understory. Grim has not been able to confirm any nesting.

The great majority of fall migrants passes through Berks in September, but a few are seen occasionally in late August and in October. Early fall Hawk Mountain records include August 15 (1995) and August 19 (1993 - Cathy Viverette). Matt Spence found a male Black-throated Blue Warbler at Lake Ontelaunee October 29, 1967, and Anna Kendall observed a Black-throated Blue Warbler with an injured wing at Leesport November 3, 1973.

YELLOW-RUMPED WARBLER *Dendroica coronata*
Common spring and fall migrant; uncommon winter visitor

Formerly called the Myrtle Warbler, the Yellow-rumped Warbler is common during the spring and fall migrations. There are records from Berks County for every month except June and July.

The Yellow-rumped Warbler often remains in sheltered spots where there is an abundance of food until midwinter, and occasional groups manage to survive Berks winters. It has appeared on the Reading Christmas Bird Count 57 of 86 years, 10 of the last 10 with a maximum of 85 on December 26, 1955. A peak of 69 was recorded on the Hamburg Christmas Bird Count January 2, 1983, and a high of 22 appeared during the Bernville Christmas Bird Count on January 5, 1986.

A few of these birds have been known to winter successfully, as did several small groups of three or four that were seen regularly around Reading through the winters of 1932-1933, 1938-1939, and 1955-1956 (Earl Poole).

On February 2, 1985, Kerry Grim found 20 Yellow-rumped Warblers in Virginia scrub pines in Hamburg.

As might be expected of a bird that is hardy enough to withstand our winters, the Yellow-rumped Warbler is one of the first of its family to arrive in spring when not known to have wintered.

Spring arrival dates are difficult to determine due to birds that have wintered successfully. However, by mid-April a definite movement is underway. Early dates when wintering birds were not observed are March 9 (1954 - Maurice Broun at Hawk Mountain) and April 4 (1925 - E.P.).

The late spring departure date is May 27 (1917 - E.P.).

During the early 1950s at Hawk Mountain, daily spring counts of up to over 300 were recorded, although today's counts nowhere approach these numbers, even for an entire season. Maurice Broun counted over 200 on May 11, 1952; over 300 May 4, 1953; and over 200 May 8, 1954. Jim Bednarz found over 30 in Eckville April 18, 1989. The spring of 1996 was an exception for recent counts of the Yellow-rumped Warbler. Grim counted 149 at State Game Lands 110 near Shartlesville on May 4.

The fall migration of the Yellow-rumped Warbler is a protracted affair, although by far the greater numbers are present during October, from year to year. Earl Poole has seen it as early as August 13 (1922), and Anna Kendall found it at Leesport August 19 (1978). Yet in other years it has not reached Berks County before October 20 (1918 - E.P.).

Fall departure dates are difficult to determine because of the laggards that remain until winter, but Poole considered the period between October 10 (1926, 1936) to November 27 (1932) to be definite departure dates. A recent single-day peak from Hawk Mountain is 35 on October 24, 1993.

Audubon's Warbler *Dendroica coronata auduboni*

Levi Mengel secured a specimen of Audubon's Warbler, a western subspecies of the Yellow-rumped Warbler, at Yost's Island in the Schuylkill River near Reading on October 14, 1888. Accidental in Pennsylvania, it breeds in the far West and winters south to Mexico and Guatemala.

BLACK-THROATED GRAY WARBLER *Dendroica nigrescens*
Accidental

Roy Ziegler identified an immature female Black-throated Gray Warbler that visited his feeding station in Bern Township from early December 1996 until February 13, 1997. The identity of this western vagrant was confirmed January 19, 1997, by Harold and Joan Silagy, Robert Cook, and Matt Spence. The bird was photographed (Robert Cook, Bill Uhrich) and seen by many observers.

BLACK-THROATED GREEN WARBLER *Dendroica virens*
Common spring and fall migrant; uncommon breeder

The Black-throated Green Warbler is a common spring and fall migrant and an uncommon breeding summer resident in mature stands of white pine and hemlock on the Blue Mountain of northern Berks County.

In spring, the Black-throated Green Warbler arrives in Berks anywhere from the last week in April to mid-May. An extremely early arrival date is April 12 (1992 - Matt Spence, Bart Smith at Peters Creek). The latest spring dates from areas where the species does not breed sometimes overlap the nesting season.

The Black-throated Green Warbler nests in mountain ravines at Shartlesville State Game Lands 110, Eckville State Game Lands 106, Rattling Run, Hawk Mountain, Hamburg reservoir, and at high elevations wherever there are mature hemlocks (Kerry Grim).

Levi Mengel found a nest containing three eggs in Bethel Township May 29, 1885.

During some years the fall migratory movement starts in late August, or it may not develop until September, although the Black-throated Green Warbler frequently is one of the most common warblers throughout the fall migration. A single-day high count during the migration at Hawk Mountain is over 100 on September 21, 1996 (K.G., Doug Wood).

An early fall arrival date south of nesting areas in the Blue Mountain is August 19 (1978 - Anna Kendall at Leesport). The migration is usually completed by early October, although late dates include November 6 (1995 - M.S. at Lake Ontelaunee), November 8 (1968 - Rudy Keller in Pike Township), November 9 (1994 - Dean Kendall at Leesport), and November 29 (1944 - Earl Poole).

BLACKBURNIAN WARBLER *Dendroica fusca*
Uncommon spring, rare fall migrant

This strikingly marked warbler is one of the gems of our native bird life. As a migrant, the Blackburnian Warbler is uncommon and irregular in spring and less frequent to rare in fall.

It is one of the species which, like the Cape May Warbler, passes through so rapidly in spring that it may easily be missed by observers who spend a limited time in the field.

In Berks County, the Blackburnian Warbler usually arrives during the second week of May, with an early date of April 25 (1925 - Earl Poole; 1961 - Maurice Broun at Hawk Mountain). Kerry Grim recorded nine at State Game Lands 110 in Shartlesville May 18, 1996. It departs in spring during the third week of May with a late date of May 31 (1924 - E.P.).

After the young are able to shift for themselves, both adults and young start to disperse over the surrounding country, appearing at Hawk Mountain as early as August 7 (1952 - Tommy Hanson). A single-day high count there is 25 on September 21, 1996. On August 20, 1963, Matt Spence found 10 migrating Blackburnian Warblers at Antietam Lake.

Most of the fall migrants pass through Berks in September, the late dates October 8 (1938 - E.P.) and October 9 (1993 - Cathy Viverette at Hawk Mountain).

YELLOW-THROATED WARBLER *Dendroica dominica*
Very rare

The Yellow-throated Warbler is a very rare visitor from the South and was regular in spring from 1978 to 1981 at Hay Creek, where Matt Spence found singing males in the high branches of sycamore trees as late as June 7 (1980).

In the spring of 1995, Ken Lebo recorded a Yellow-throated Warbler at Joanna Furnace on April 27 and one at Hay Creek April 30 and May 3. He found another May 7, 1996, in the sycamore trees at the Route 82 bridge in Birdsboro.

Other recent records include one near Lenhartsville May 7, 1984 (Catherine Elwell); at Baldy Hill, District Township, May 8, 1993 (C.E.); at Hay Creek May 10, 1970 (Robert Cook, Rudy Keller); and at Hawk Mountain May 17, 1981 (Bernie McCoy, Jim Brett).

David Berkheimer and Ralph Yerger each reported one on Mount Penn near Reading on May 12 and 20, 1939. Maurice Broun observed a Yellow-throated Warbler at Hawk Mountain May 4, 1947, and again on April 27, 1954. Alex Nagy recorded an adult male on May 7, 1960.

A specimen, originally labeled *D. d. dominica* but which Earl Poole proved on examination to be *D. d. albilora* - the Sycamore Warbler subspecies, in the Reading Public Museum collection was taken by Levi Mengel on Neversink Mountain September 26, 1892.

PINE WARBLER *Dendroica pinus*
Uncommon spring and rare fall migrant

The Pine Warbler shares the distinction with Yellow-rumped and Palm warblers as one of the first warblers to arrive in spring. The Pine Warbler is fairly hardy and has been found in winter in Berks County.

An uncommon migrant in spring and rare in the fall, the Pine Warbler arrives during the third week of April, but there are several March records.

Matt Spence found an extremely early Pine Warbler at Lake Ontelaunee March 10, 1985. Other March records include birds seen at Birdsboro March 19, 1989 (N. and C. Smith); at State Game Lands 182 in Greenwich Township March 21, 1982 (Catherine Elwell); in the pine plantations at Lake Ontelaunee March 24, 1995 (Ken Lebo); at Blue Marsh March 25, 1987 (Ed Barrell); in Pike Township March 28 to 30, 1967 (Rudy Keller); at a Plowville feeder March 28, 1992 (K.L.); and in Bern Township March 29, 1989 (Harold and Joan Silagy).

During late April 1924, there was an unprecedented flight of Pine Warblers in Berks County. From April 20 to 27, it was seen almost daily in several locations around Reading and especially in the pines on Mount Penn, where Harold Morris reported six on April 22 at the Hessian Camp (Earl Poole).

Its presence during the nesting season depends on habitats of fairly extensive stands of pine, either scrub, pitch, yellow, or red. There is one confirmed nesting record in Berks. Kerry Grim saw a female feeding fledged young in a row of Virginia pines near Shoemakersville July 6, 1985 (Brauning, 1992:325). At Green Hills Lake, a pair arrived April 2, 1995, and stayed all spring and summer, but Ken Lebo was unable to find a nest. One Pine Warbler was reported at Lake Ontelaunee from April 10 to July 16, 1994 (Kerry Grim, Matt Spence, K.L.).

Specimens in the Levi Mengel collection at the Reading Public Museum were taken at Tuckerton April 13, 1897; in Albany Township June 10, 1886; and in Bethel Township June 19, 1886.

During the fall migration, the Pine Warbler is rare, and there are very few records. Care must be taken with identification of fall migrants as immature Bay-breasted and Blackpoll warblers look similar. Anna Kendall's fall records at Leesport range from August 20 (1972) to October 26 (1994).

Earl Poole had only one fall record, October 12, 1923. Grim found three Pine Warblers at Shartlesville October 12, 1996.

Maurice Broun recorded it during the fall at Hawk Mountain October 14, 1935; September 11, 1936; September 23, 1947; September 19, 1957; and September 24, 1961. Broun and H. Axtell saw one October 24, 1948. Since 1983, it has been seen nearly every year at the North Lookout.

On December 18, 1957, Poole found one with a flock of Juncos in the Reading Public Museum park, and on January 16, 1958, one that looked precisely like the previous Pine Warbler turned up at his feeder in West Reading, approximately a half mile from the park.

The Pine Warbler was listed by John F. Hofmann in 1890.

PRAIRIE WARBLER *Dendroica discolor*

Uncommon spring migrant and breeder; very rare in fall

The Prairie Warbler is an uncommon spring migrant and a rare and very locally distributed summer resident, restricted to pine and scrub oak barrens, nurseries and Christmas tree plantations, or to abandoned fields. The early spring date is April 23 (1946 - Maurice Broun at Hawk Mountain).

However, the Prairie Warbler is common at Glen Morgan Lake. During 1995, Ken Lebo found it first arriving April 25, with at least seven pairs remaining through the summer in the scrubby, second-growth habitat. During the spring and summer of 1996, he recorded four pairs at the lake.

Rich Bonnett recorded two pairs nesting at a Christmas tree plantation next to French Creek State Park in June 1990. Kerry Grim found a territorial male in an Albany Township Christmas tree plantation June 26, 1994. There were also confirmed nesting records in southern Berks County during the *Atlas of Breeding Birds in Pennsylvania* survey from 1983 to 1989 (Brauning, 1992:327).

It was found during the nesting season at Five Points, about five miles east of Reading on June 13, 1949 (Sam Gundy), and also at Green Hills Lake, some five miles south of Reading from May 11 to June 14, 1958 (Robert Cook, Matt Spence).

Fall records of this warbler are rare, although it has been reported every year between 1989 and 1996, except 1990. The early date is August 19 (1993 - Rudy Keller in Pike Township). Anna Kendall's fall dates at Leesport range from August 23 (1980) to September 24 (1969). The late fall date is October 7 (1987 - Laurie Goodrich at Hawk Mountain's North Lookout).

Two specimens in the Reading Public Museum were taken by Levi Mengel in Albany Township April 30, 1886. He took a third there June 14, 1886.

PALM WARBLER *Dendroica palmarum*
Uncommon spring and fall migrant

One of the first warblers to arrive in Berks County in spring, the Palm Warbler appears in mid-April, sometimes much earlier. An early date is March 30 (1990 - Harold and Joan Silagy in Upper Bern Township). The late spring date is May 12 (1995 - Ken Lebo at Glen Morgan Lake).

Although the Palm Warbler is uncommon in spring, on April 13, 1989, Rich Bonnett watched a slowly moving wave of between 50 and 75 of these birds forage across the low ridge above the Schuylkill River and the old Union Canal near Routes 10 and 724. They were feeding on tiny flies that had recently hatched.

The Palm Warbler is also uncommon in fall. Dates range from August 25 (1994 - Cathy Viverette, three birds at Hawk Mountain) to November 16 (1993 - Catherine Elwell).

Winter records include the only Reading Christmas Bird Count occurrence December 23, 1962 (Matt Spence, Warren Faust). Matt Wlasniewski saw a Palm Warbler at Peters Creek January 27, 1991. One was recorded on the Bernville Christmas Bird Count January 1, 1992.

Although recent observers have not distinguished between the two races of the Palm Warbler that appear in Berks County- the Western Palm and the Yellow Palm warblers, Earl Poole describes their occurrence at length:

Since the two races of the Palm Warbler occur in Pennsylvania, and since each appears to follow a distinct migrational pattern, it may be advisable to treat them separately as far as possible, although many sight records are admittedly dubious, and in a goodly number of cases, observers do not attempt to specify the subspecies.

The Western Palm Warbler (*Dendroica p. palmarum*) is the common race to the west of the Allegheny Mountains, where it is a fairly common transient, less common in the spring than in the fall.... However, the Western Palm Warbler does occur in the eastern half of the state, where it has been taken on several occasions, and identified by a number of competent observers. Two specimens of this race in the Reading Public Museum

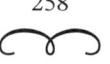

were taken at Greenawald [Albany Township] April 22, 1887 (Levi Mengel), and in the museum park May 5, 1932 (Sam Wishnieski).

The Western Palm Warbler arrives in this state later in spring than the Yellow Palm Warbler and passes through much earlier in the fall, although both subspecies have been reported in winter in the southeastern counties.

In the Reading region, in over forty years of observation, I have never seen the western race in spring earlier than April 22 (1943), and the eight-year average spring arrival date for this subspecies is May 4, while the Yellow Palm Warbler has arrived here as early as April 4 (1932); the 32-year average arrival date is April 15, or 19 days earlier than the western form.

In the fall the Western Palm Warbler arrives earlier. I have found it in Berks County as early as September 22 (1935) and the 12-year average arrival date is September 29, 16 days earlier than that for the Yellow Palm Warbler, which has not reached this locality before October 3, and for which the average fall arrival date is October 15. In this locality I have not seen the western subspecies later than October 7 (1944), while the eastern form remains with us until November 1 (1925, 1935). The western race also seems to occur in a different type of terrain while here and is seen in upland fields associated with the migrating sparrows, while the eastern form appears to prefer the vicinity of water.

The Yellow Palm Warbler (*D. p. hypochrysea*) is the common form east of the Allegheny Mountains and is generally fairly common in spring, but comparatively rare in fall. When not known to have wintered, as it sometimes does in the lower Delaware Valley, it often is the earliest of the warblers to arrive in spring. My earliest date at Reading is April 4 (1932).

This warbler was last seen in spring ... April 20 (1925) to May 14 (1917), the 32-year average departure date being April 28. Fall migration dates for the Reading area are from October 3 (1937) to November 1 (1925, 1935).

Poole believed that while well-marked adults of both subspecies can readily be distinguished, there is so much individual variation in some plumages that the identification of some specimens in collections is doubtful, and that of many individuals in the field is practically impossible.

BAY-BREASTED WARBLER *Dendroica castanea*
Rare spring, fairly common fall migrant

The Bay-breasted Warbler is a migrant of somewhat irregular occurrence.

It is one of the later warblers to pass through Berks County in spring. The earliest spring arrival date is April 30 (1995 - Ken Lebo at Hay Creek).

As a rule, male Bay-breasted Warblers are present in the greatest numbers during the third week in May with the females trailing by several days. A few remain until the end of May or early June.

Maurice Broun recorded a flock of over 60 Bay-breasted Warblers at Hawk Mountain May 25, 1950.

Late spring departure dates are June 4 (1972 - Rudy Keller in District Township), June 2 (1990 - Kerry Grim at State Game Lands 110 in Shartlesville), and June 1 (1924 - Earl Poole).

During the fall migration the Bay-breasted Warbler is more irregular than in spring, being common some years and rare or seemingly absent in others. Care must be taken with identification of fall migrants as immature Pine and Blackpoll warblers look very similar to the Bay-breasted.

Broun found an early Bay-breasted Warbler at Hawk Mountain August 7, 1957, while Tommy Hanson observed one there on August 10 and 14, 1952. The Bay-breasted usually passes through Berks County in mid-September. The late fall date is October 16 (1932 - E.P.).

BLACKPOLL WARBLER *Dendroica striata*
Common spring, uncommon fall migrant

A common migrant, the Blackpoll Warbler brings up the rear of the spring migration and is among the last of the warblers to leave in the fall.

During the latter half of May and through late September and the first half of October, it is often the most common of the warblers and is far more regular in its appearance here, both in spring and fall, than most of the other warblers. However, coming late in the spring and keeping well up in the dense foliage, it is far more often heard than seen.

Kerry Grim and Matt Spence have noticed a decrease in spring migrants during the past 15 years.

The early spring arrival date is May 1 (1948 - Earl Poole; 1970 - Rudy Keller in Pike Township; 1982 - Catherine Elwell in Greenwich Township). The latest spring departure date is June 13 (1926 - Anna and Mary Deeter).

There are very few August records of the Blackpoll Warbler. Anna Kendall has an early fall date of August 23 (1983) at Leesport. Tommy Hanson reported one at Hawk Mountain on August 27, 1951, and Earl Poole recorded one August 29, 1943. Maurice Broun found single Blackpoll Warblers at Hawk Mountain on August 30, 1949 and 1950.

The late fall date is November 10 (1977 - Anna Kendall at Leesport).

CERULEAN WARBLER *Dendroica cerulea*
Regular uncommon migrant; local breeder

An uncommon but regular migrant, the Cerulean Warbler usually reaches Berks County by the second week in May. An early date is April 30 (1980 - Seth Benz at Hawk Mountain).

It nests in a variety of habitats in Berks County, although not commonly. Kerry Grim has found the Cerulean Warbler to be territorial not only at lower elevations in the Blue Mountain, but also higher on the mountain such as at the Pinnacle (1,635 feet) and along the Lookout Trail at Hawk Mountain. Laurie Goodrich heard a singing male during June 1996 atop the ridge at Hawk Mountain.

A pair of Cerulean Warblers arrived by the Common Room at Hawk Mountain May 17, 1965. They built their nest 40 feet up in the crotch of a black birch, in precisely the spot used two years previously by a pair of Blue-gray Gnatcatchers. Eggs were laid, incubation proceeded, and then, on June 1, a severe windstorm destroyed the nest. The warblers were seen occasionally thereafter, posssibly nesting elsewhere in the area (Broun, 1966:11). Jim Brett found territorial males throughout the summers of 1977 to 1979 near the Common Room, where there had been June records from 1961 until 1981. There were no June records at Hawk Mountain from 1981 until the one in 1996, although Tom Leckey found one in State Game Lands 106 at Eckville on June 24, 1986.

Alex Nagy and Donald Heintzelman found a Cerulean Warbler at Rattling Run July 4, 1966.

During the *Atlas of Breeding Birds in Pennsylvania* survey from 1983 to 1989, the Cerulean Warbler was confirmed nesting in southern Berks and was rated as a probable breeder in eastern and northern Berks County (Brauning, 1992:329).

Before 1949, the Cerulean Warbler was rare and only known as a spring migrant. On May 8 of that year, Earl Poole noticed a female starting the construction of a nest along Hay Creek, near Birdsboro, while the male sang nearby. On May 14 the pair was flitting about the nest, which was apparently completed. The female was still setting on May 21, but Poole was unable to follow the nesting activities until June 23, when he collected the then empty nest for the Reading Public Museum. This occurrence represents the first recorded nesting of the Cerulean Warbler in eastern Pennsylvania (Poole, 1951d:35).

Poole discovered a second nest near the same area on May 26, 1951. The four young finally left on June 5. Each year until 1959 from one to three singing males had been noticed within a half mile of the same spot, and several other nests reported. The Cerulean Warbler has been a regular nester in the Hay Creek valley since. Rudy Keller and Joanne Kintner watched a female building a nest as the male sang nearby on May 13, 1995. Ken Lebo found three birds there June 29, 1996.

There are only five Cerulean Warbler records prior to 1947, all during the spring. Byron Nunemacher and Poole saw one in Hampden Park, Reading, on May 20, 1928. David Berkheimer found one at Hay Creek May 27, 1934, and he and Anna Deeter recorded one there from May 21 to 30, 1936. Nunemacher and Poole saw one at Hay Creek on May 25, 1937. Berkheimer and Nunemacher observed one on Mount Penn May 6 and 7, 1938.

The normal fall departure of the Cerulean Warbler takes place quite early. Dean Kendall's early fall date at Leesport is August 4 (1995), and Anna Kendall's late date there is August 31 (1993). Maurice Broun saw one at Hawk Mountain August 16, 1955. Poole had only one September record: September 14, 1952.

There is a specimen in the Levi Mengel collection at the Reading Public Museum taken near Reading June 6, 1888.

BLACK-AND-WHITE WARBLER *Mniotilta varia*
Common migrant; fairly common breeder

A common migrant and fairly common summer resident in all the more heavily wooded regions - such as the Hay Creek Valley, the Reading Hills, and the Blue Mountain, the Black-and-white Warbler is one of the earlier wood warblers to arrive in spring and usually appears in Berks County during the last 10 days of April. The early arrival date is April 15 (1985 - Laurie Goodrich at Hawk Mountain).

On May 1, 1955, Maurice Broun reported over 100 migrant Black-and-white Warblers at Hawk Mountain.

The Black-and-white Warbler is one of the ground-nesting species and may be found breeding wherever it finds suitable, large woodlands, particularly in well-watered ravines with a moderately heavy understory of shrubs and saplings. A set of eggs taken near Fleetwood June 2, 1903, is in the Reading Public Museum collection. Nesting densities at Hawk Mountain Sanctuary range from one to four pairs per 20 hectares. One hectare is equal to 10,000 square meters, or 2.47 acres.

This warbler appears at places distant from its nesting areas quite early in the summer, occasionally in July or early August, and its fall migration extends through August and September with individuals straggling through well into October. Earl Poole's late date is October 13 (1917). Anna Kendall recorded one at Leesport October 20, 1966.

Robert Schoenert identified an extraordinarily late Black-and-white Warbler at his feeder in Shillington from late November to December 22, 1996, for its only Reading Christmas Bird Count record. Schoenert sketched the bird and described its trunk-creeping behavior. Joan Silagy confirmed the identification.

AMERICAN REDSTART *Setophaga ruticilla*

Common migrant; uncommon breeder

During the spring migration, the American Redstart occurs throughout Berks County, arriving the beginning of May. However, Catherine Elwell saw one as early as April 18 (1994) at Landis Store.

Although far from uniformly distributed as a summer resident, it nests chiefly in rich woodlands, in bottomlands, and along the smaller streams.

Along Hay Creek during "Redstart years," Earl Poole found it to be the most common warbler. From there northward through Berks, it was common with several nests found in the Hessian Camp in the city of Reading, at Mohnton, Wyomissing, near Temple, and at Rittenhouse Gap.

During 1939 when the woodland was young due to timbering in the early part of the century, the American Redstart was a common nesting species along with the Chestnut-sided Warbler on the ridge top at Hawk Mountain Sanctuary. Now, the habitat has matured, and nesting numbers are lower. There was one territorial male during June 1996 near Schaumboch's.

In 1966, Dean Kendall found two nests at Rattling Run. On May 20, he observed a female carrying a bit of lining to a nest which was in a crotch of a vertically hanging grape vine 20 feet from the ground. There was a high canopy of deciduous trees, mostly tulip poplar, and a low understory of deciduous low trees and shrubs. On May 30 the nest was missing. He found a complete nest May 24 in a hemlock in the fork of a dead limb about 15 feet from the ground. The female was on the nest May 30. Currently, the Redstart no longer nests at Rattling Run.

According to the *Atlas of Breeding Birds in Pennsylvania* survey, 1983 to 1989, the Redstart was confirmed nesting in southern, eastern, and northern Berks County (Brauning, 1992:333). Ken Lebo has found it nesting in wooded areas of Hay Creek, Glen Morgan Lake, and Lake Ontelaunee. Kerry Grim has found nests in spotty locations in the Blue Mountain, mostly along edge habitats. It nests uncommonly at Shartlesville State Game Lands 110, including Auburn Lookout Road. Joan and Harold Silagy found male and female Redstarts at Blue Marsh June 14 and 15, 1996.

Levi Mengel collected a set of four eggs along the Wyomissing Creek May 27, 1893; a set of four eggs at Tuckerton May 27, 1899; and a set of three eggs in Brecknock Township June 16, 1890.

The American Redstart disperses from nesting areas about the middle of August and by the end of that month may appear almost anywhere, the migratory movement extending through September and occasionally into October. An early fall date away from nesting areas is July 25 (1983, 1985 - Anna Kendall at Leesport). Late dates include November 13 to 15 (1955 - Maurice Broun at Hawk Mountain) and November 20 (1955 - E.P.)

Anna Kendall had a high of 32 Redstart records at Leesport from August 6 to September 28, 1992.

Poole collected a specimen in Wyomissing on the extremely late date of December 1, 1934.

PROTHONOTARY WARBLER *Protonotaria citrea*

Very rare spring visitor

The Prothonotary Warbler is a very rare spring visitor of more southern distribution, which appeared to be gradually extending its breeding range northward during midcentury.

Specimen records from the Levi Mengel collection at the Reading Public Museum suggest that there was a somewhat similar invasion of Prothonotary Warblers during the closing years of the nineteenth century, followed by a period of comparative scarcity which lasted until about the mid-1940s. Mengel secured his specimens along the Tulpehocken Creek near Reading June 22, 1888; at Douglassville July 6, 1889; at Fritz's Island June 15, 1890; and along the Maiden Creek June 10, 1892.

The first Prothonotary Warbler record this century is of a male in full song discovered by Paul Martin in a wooded swamp near Gibraltar May 22, 1944. It was found at the same place on May 27 by Martin, Elwood Manning, and Earl Poole. This bird sang persistently in the area until June 4 but evidently could not attract a mate and eventually disappeared.

After that time until the late 1950s, the Prothonotary Warbler appeared in Berks County on seven occasions from April 24 (1954 - Alex Nagy in Albany Township) to September 29 (1958 - Earl Poole). In 1953, a Prothonotary Warbler appeared in the Reading Public Museum park, remaining from April 27 to May 1 (E.P.).

On May 19, 1957, a singing male was found at Moselem Station near the head of Lake Ontelaunee. By June 2 he had acquired a mate, and they were established in an old stump that projected from the water. On June 8 both birds were carrying food to the nest. On June 15 they continued to visit the nest, although less frequently, and by the following week the nest was deserted, and no birds were seen there (E.P.).

On May 16, 1961, one was seen in the rhododendrons near the North Lookout at Hawk Mountain by Mr. and Mrs. Franklin Jones (*fide* Maurice Broun).

There were no other records until Jack Holcomb, Rudy Keller, and about 60 others on a WEEU spring birdwalk found a male Prothonotary Warbler singing on the dark, mossy rocks in the stream below the Hopewell Lake dam May 2, 1970. The same group saw a female in the same location May 6, 1972.

Jim Brett and many observers saw a Prothonotary Warbler in the morning and the afternoon at the North Lookout at Hawk Mountain on September 16, 1974.

Other recent records include April 29, 1977 (Anna Kendall at Leesport) and May 13, 1985 (Matt Spence at the Reading Public Museum park). Harold and Joan Silagy reported an early fall bird in Bern Township August 27, 1991. Matt Spence recorded one at Hay Creek May 10, 1992.

Spence found two male Prothonotary Warblers during 1995, one singing at Hay Creek from April 24 to May 14 and another singing at Moselem May 14 and 15.

WORM-EATING WARBLER *Helmitheros vermivorus*

Fairly common but local breeder

A fairly common but local summer resident, the Worm-eating Warbler is uncommon or rare away from its nesting grounds. Anna Kendall has seen it only 12 times during 30 years of observations at Leesport.

It usually arrives during the first week in May, but there are a number of middle-and-late April records. Catherine Elwell and Richard Sharadin found one at Hawk Mountain April 14, 1973.

On March 28, 1939, Earl Poole had the amazing experience of seeing a Worm-eating Warbler in the Reading Public Museum park consorting with a small group of Myrtle Warblers and some Juncos, fully a month ahead of its normal arrival time. On April 25 of that year Poole saw

another one, or possibly the same individual, near the same place.

It is a fairly common nesting species in the Blue Mountain, although not nearly as common as the Common Yellowthroat or Ovenbird. The majority of nesting takes place on wooded hillsides with a thick mountain laurel and rhododendron understory.

Probably the highest population in northern Berks occurs along Rattling Run on the Berks - Schuylkill County line. Kerry Grim has found territories off the side of the Pinnacle at an elevation of nearly 1,600 feet and other cliff sides in the Blue Mountains. Singing males may be difficult to observe, but the bird is easy to see when it has young, popping up on a branch to protest intruders. Poole saw adults feeding young at Rattling Run on July 1 and 5, 1950.

It breeds rather commonly on the hillsides of the Hay Creek, Sixpenny Creek, and most of the gulleys of the South Mountain, as well as on the slopes of the Blue Mountain. Ken Lebo considers the Worm-eating Warbler a fairly common nester at Hay Creek, where he usually finds four to five pairs each season. Harold and Joan Silagy note that it breeds at Blue Marsh.

Fall records for this warbler are quite scarce as it apparently starts to migrate by mid-August. Poole had found it only twice after August 17, his latest Berks County observation September 3 (1917). Anna Kendall's fall range at Leesport is August 13 (1995) to September 9 (1987). The late date is September 15 (1994 - Cathy Viverette at Hawk Mountain; 1996 - Catherine Elwell at Baldy Hill, District Township).

OVENBIRD *Seiurus aurocapillus*

Common migrant and breeder

A common migrant and summer resident in woodlands throughout Berks County, the Ovenbird usually arrives during the last week in April. An early spring date is April 20 (1995 - Ken Lebo at Hay Creek).

The Ovenbird is by far the most common woodland warbler.

Kerry Grim has found nesting populations during the past 15 years to be stable, or at some places, increasing in northern Berks County. At upper elevations at the Hamburg reservoir, there were five territories during 1979. In 1993 at the same location there were 20 territories. There has been an increase in Ovenbirds on the Breeding Bird Censuses from 1982 to 1995.

Kerry Grim recorded the following Ovenbird numbers during the North America Migration Count on a 5.5 mile walk along the Northkill Gap at State Game Lands 110 in Shartlesville: 147 on May 8, 1993; 106 on May 14, 1994; and 153 on May 13, 1995.

Sets of eggs in the Reading Public Museum collection were taken between May 19 (1888) and June 15 (1886) although Earl Poole saw incomplete sets as late as June 16 (1917). Clutch sizes in the collected sets range from three to five eggs. Five sets contain Cowbird's eggs.

Research conducted at Hawk Mountain since 1988 on color-banded Ovenbirds suggests that these birds are most successful in large, continuous forests away from openings. Nest success in continuous forest is usually over 80 percent. In fragments or near openings, nest success is under 40 percent. Males are faithful to territories over the years unless unsuccessful at nesting or unless they nest near openings. Some males live for over seven years, returning to the same nesting territory each year. Predation, probably by mammals, is the main threat to the ground nests. Wandering males are often detected in small woodlots (under 20 hectares) but rarely attract mates. The overall male return rates average 54 percent (Laurie Goodrich).

Birds that have bred in Berks drift southward in late August, and migrants from farther north pass through the county chiefly during September, a few stragglers remaining until October.

There are three exceptionally late dates. Byron Nunemacher found a slightly wounded or crippled bird at Gibraltar on November 3, 1925. Earl Poole and Nunemacher saw a perfectly healthy looking Ovenbird at Moselem on December 23, 1934, for its only Reading Christmas Bird

Count record. Peter Saenger recorded one at his feeders in Henningsville from December 21, 1991, to January 10, 1992.

The Pennsylvania German names for the Ovenbird are "der Buschvoggel" and "der scheckich Buschvoggel," a name this species shares with the thrushes. William Rupp says that no special note seems to have been made of the bird's ringing call of "Teacher, teacher, teacher" (Rupp, 1946:210).

NORTHERN WATERTHRUSH *Seiurus noveboracensis*
Uncommon spring, irregular fall migrant

The Northern Waterthrush is a regular but uncommon migrant in spring, irregular in fall. Unlike the Louisiana Waterthrush, which is seldom seen away from its breeding habitat, the Northern Waterthrush may appear practically anywhere. However, it is secretive and is usually located by the male's distinctive song.

The Northern Waterthrush is unique in its peculiarly protracted migrations. Earl Poole noticed it as early as April 9 (1959) and as late as June 1 (1958). Kerry Grim's latest record is June 3 (1989 - in Tilden Township).

The fall migration is also a leisurely movement, with the first migrants appearing at places distant from the breeding areas early in August, sometimes loitering until mid-October or even later. Poole saw it in Berks County as early as July 26 (1922), and Anna Kendall recorded it at Leesport as late as October 3 (1966).

Because of the wide individual variation in the depth of the yellowish tone on the breast of different individuals of this species, it should be pointed out that a certain amount of error may occur in the identification of these waterthrushes.

There is a specimen in the Reading Public Museum collection taken by Levi Mengel July 5, 1880, labeled "Reading."

LOUISIANA WATERTHRUSH *Seiurus motacilla*
Uncommon breeder

The Louisiana Waterthrush is one of the earliest warblers to arrive in spring, often appearing in the vicinity of its nesting place as early as the first week in April. Elsewhere, the species is by no means common and is one of the wildest and shyest of our woodland birds, being heard far more often than seen.

This species is so local in Berks County that migration records are not representative. The early date is April 3 (1974 - Kenneth Grim, Lyle Layser in Tilden Township).

Throughout the ridges of the Blue Mountain, in the South Mountain, and the Piedmont region, it nests in varying abundance, although never actually common, wherever secluded, rapidly flowing streams are found. The Louisiana Waterthrush is a regular nester in the Hay Creek valley.

It nests at various places in the Blue Mountain. The mountain ravines at Shartlesville State Game Lands 110, Eckville State Game Lands 106, Rattling Run, Hawk Mountain Sanctuary, and the Hamburg reservoir are good locations as well as along streams at the base of the mountains.

Earl Poole saw it under conditions that indicated breeding at Vinemont, Hopewell, Plow Church, Hamburg, Eckville, Rattling Run, and Topton.

Rudy Keller has found the Louisiana Waterthrush nesting or at least on territory on the Oysterville Creek in District Township since he first covered the area in 1967. The bird's loud song and "Tick!" note make it easy to pick up. Between 1967 and 1996, Keller's earliest arrival date is April 8 (1970), but dates closer to mid-April have been more characteristic. The bird usually stops singing regularly in late June, and Keller often fails to find it after mid-July. His latest departure dates for these local birds is August 20 (1993). Keller has seen adult birds with between two and four young several times. On three occasions he saw them with only a fat Cowbird chick to show for their efforts and once saw them with a Cowbird and one of their own.

Dean Kendall found an early nest with five eggs May 21, 1966, at Rattling Run. Poole observed a family of young leaving the nest near Wernersville on June 4, 1921, and a pair feeding young recently out of the nest near Trap Rock June 9, 1917.

Levi Mengel took a set of three eggs at Fritz's Island May 19, 1888, and a set of four eggs in Caernarvon Township June 4, 1888.

The Louisiana Waterthrush disappears soon after the young are able to shift for themselves, as early as mid-July, and fall migration records are rare. The late date is September 1 (1983 - Anna Kendall at Leesport). Poole never saw it later than August 15 (1925) near Reading, and Tommy Hanson reported one at Hawk Mountain on August 20, 1951.

Kerry Grim has only one record (at Kaercher Creek Park August 4, 1981) of a Lousiana Waterthrush in nonbreeding habitat. Anna Kendall has 15 times as many Connecticut Warbler records at Leesport as Louisiana Waterthrush records, illustrating its rarity as a migrant.

Any nonsinging waterthrush must be studied carefully in order to differentiate the very similar Northern Waterthrush.

KENTUCKY WARBLER *Oporonis formosus*

Uncommon migrant; uncommon breeder.

As a breeding summer resident, the Kentucky Warbler has expanded its range during the second half of this century from the swampy lowlands of southern Berks County to the base of the Blue Mountain in the north. It is one of the most difficult birds to see because it stays hidden in the brush. Most identifications of this bird are made by its song.

Before 1950, Earl Poole considered the Kentucky Warbler a fairly common and regular breeder throughout the southern portions of Berks at Hopewell, Trap Rock, Sixpenny Creek, and Hay Creek, during some years extending to the neighborhood of Reading at Mount Penn, Neversink Mountain, and Mohnton. Harold Morris found a small colony of at least three pairs on Neversink Mountain in 1940.

According to the *Atlas of Breeding Birds in Pennsylvania*, the Kittatinny Ridge now represents the northern barrier in eastern Pennsylvania to the expansion of the Kentucky Warbler (Brauning, 1992:347). Poole believed that a male Kentucky Warbler killed by striking a television tower along Route 183 on the Berks-Schuylkill County line on June 7, 1953, was beyond its normal range.

A local nesting species which prefers moist, bottomland woods, the Kentucky Warbler has occupied the same territories recently at lower elevations in the Blue Mountain. Kerry Grim found adults feeding young at State Game Lands 106 at Eckville on June 23, 1982, and June 23, 1984; at the Hamburg reservoir July 30, 1981; and at State Game Lands 110 at Shartlesville June 27, 1993. A territorial male was recorded in Eckville throughout the breeding season in 1996.

In the dense understory of moist woods at the head of the Oysterville Creek in Pike and District townships, Rudy Keller has found one or two pairs of Kentucky Warblers during most years between 1968 and 1995. The earliest arrival date there is May 5. He saw adults with one to four fledged young from late June to early August several times over those years. At least twice he saw adults feeding mixed broods of Kentucky Warbler and Cowbird fledglings. This warbler usually leaves in late August or early September, Keller's latest date for these local birds September 14 (1991). He has also confirmed nesting on the Topton Mountain, Baldy Hill, and Trout Run reservoir near Boyertown in the 1980s and 1990s.

Mr. and Mrs. G. Henry Mengel found a nest with young in the Hay Creek valley June 14,

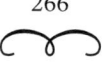

1924, and Paul Jensen and Poole found a nest with three eggs, doubtless an incomplete second set, along Hay Creek near Birdsboro on June 16, 1946. More recently, Ken Lebo found an adult Kentucky Warbler feeding three young at the Birdsboro reservoir June 29, 1996. The young were able to fly from branch to branch.

The Kentucky Warbler is one of the later warblers to reach Berks in spring and rarely arrives before the second week in May. April records are very rare, the earliest April 29 (1983 - Kerry Grim at Hamburg).

The male is in song when it arrives and sings persistently until the end of June, after which it becomes even more secretive and hard to find.

It withdraws from Berks County early in August. The early fall date is August 4 (1983 - Anna Kendall at Leesport) and the late date is October 13 (1993 - Catherine Elwell at Baldy Hill, South Mountain, District Township).

Levi Mengel took a specimen along the Tulpehocken Creek June 22, 1888.

CONNECTICUT WARBLER *Oporonis agilis*

Rare fall migrant

The Connecticut Warbler is an accidental migrant in spring and highly irregular in fall, appearing in some numbers during certain years but apparently absent or unreported in others.

It is one of the species that follows different migration routes in spring and fall. In the spring it passes up the Mississippi Valley, but in the fall it apparently migrates due east to the New England states and then follows the Atlantic coast southward. For this reason spring records are very scarce, although it has been reported during this season four times in Berks County.

Alex Nagy and Eric Bastin reported a singing male at Hawk Mountain on May 8 and 9, 1963. Dorothy Grim and Ethel Fink found a singing male near Hamburg on May 8, 1966, and one again near Hamburg the next year on May 1. Laurie Goodrich found one May 4, 1985, at Hawk Mountain's Visitor Center.

Earl Poole had never seen nor *thought* he saw this warbler in Pennsylvania in spring in more than a half century of active field work.

During the fall the Connecticut Warbler is rare in Berks, although the secretive habits of the bird, with its fondness for keeping close to the ground in dense weedy growth, often in marshy places, cause it to be overlooked unless it is especially searched for.

The bulk of the fall movement occurs in September, with a very few stragglers arriving in August and some remaining into October. Sightings range from August 23 (1980 - Anna Kendall at Leesport) to October 3 (1959 - Maurice Broun at Schaumbochs, Hawk Mountain; 1992 - Rudy Keller at Blue Marsh Lake; 1993 - R.K. at Pike Township). Matt Wlasniewski found one in Hamburg October 13, 1996.

Three were sighted at the North Lookout at Hawk Mountain September 21, 1996.

According to Poole, it was actually fairly common in 1922, at least 10 seen between August 29 and September 24.

Anna Kendall has more than 44 records of Connecticut Warblers at Leesport, all of them during fall. The arrival-departure range there is August 23 (1980) to October 2 (1971). During 1983, she had seven records between September 11 and September 28.

Fall identification between immature Connecticut Warblers and immature Mourning Warblers may be impossible at times. Kendall, who has more experience with these two birds than probably anyone else in Berks County, says that identification between the two species is not always possible. The Mourning Warbler migration is typically earlier than that of the Connecticut Warbler, but both may be present during the same time period.

Poole collected a specimen near Moselem Springs on September 2, 1925, and H. E.

Newkirk took another near Reading on September 25, 1928. One was killed by flying into a television tower on the Blue Mountain at Route 183 near Bethel on October 7, 1953. All three are in the Reading Public Museum.

Four spring specimens of the Connecticut Warbler taken by Levi Mengel in Berks are in the Reading Public Museum collection and are labeled Albany Township May 14, 1886; Lenhartsville May 8 and May 9, 1887; and near Reading May 6, 1892.

On May 15, 1916, Poole sent a list of the more interesting specimens out of the more than 1300 which he had examined from the Mengel collection to Dr. Witmer Stone at the Academy of Natural Sciences in Philadelphia. The list included the spring Connecticut Warblers (Academy of Natural Sciences Philadelphia: Stone Historical Manuscript 450 and collection 458 B and D). In 1930 and 1947, Poole writes that there were no spring records for the Connecticut Warbler, although he was certainly aware of the specimens. After 1930, he re-examined the collection and corrected the identification of several specimens, notably the Snowy Plover. He also questioned, for instance, whether the Seaside Sparrow specimen was labeled correctly because it was in a worn summer plumage but was dated April 30, 1887. Poole apparently chose neither to confirm nor question the labeling accuracy of the spring Connecticut Warbler specimens.

MOURNING WARBLER *Oporonis philadelphia*
Rare spring and fall migrant

The Mourning Warbler is a migrant, rare in spring and even more rare or possibly overlooked in the fall due to its secretive habits and the nature of its haunts, close to the ground in dense undergrowth.

In spring it brings up the rear of the warbler migration and is seldom seen anywhere before the middle of May. Observations earlier than May 15 are exceptional, the earliest May 9 (1943 - Earl Poole).

On rare occasions the Mourning Warbler appears in somewhat greater numbers than usual, as it apparently did in mid-May of 1943 (E.P.).

The spring migration of the Mourning Warbler is usually over by May 30, the latest spring date June 5 (1996 - Kerry Grim at State Game Lands 110).

The southward migration begins soon after the young are able to shift for themselves. The early fall date is July 20 (1985 - Anna Kendall at Leesport). Byron Nunemacher and Earl Poole saw a family group of four at Moselem Springs July 23, 1922.

During 1985, Anna Kendall recorded a high of nine Mourning Warblers between July 20 and September 5 at Leesport.

The late dates are October 12 (1947 - E.P., "This bird was carefully studied."), and October 13 (1968 - A.K. at Leesport).

During fall, very careful observation is necessary as immature Mourning and Connecticut warblers may be impossible to distinguish from one another.

By a curious coincidence, two Mourning Warblers were brought to the Reading Public Museum to be preserved on September 7, 1952. One had been found dead near New Holland, Lancaster County, and the other near Hawk Mountain.

Samuel Wishnieski took a specimen along the Wyomissing Creek May 18, 1933.

COMMON YELLOWTHROAT *Geothlypis trichas*
Common migrant and summer breeder

A common migrant and summer resident throughout Berks County, the Common Yellowthroat nests in marshy lowland thickets and in the scrub growth on mountain tops alike and is probably the commonest of the summer resident warblers.

It usually reaches Berks during the last few days in April or in the first week in May and is in full song upon its arrival, the earliest date April 21 (1995 - Ken Lebo at Geigertown).

Although thought of as a bird of swamps and marshes, the Common Yellowthroat is the most adaptable nesting warbler in a variety of habitats in the county. Probably the densest nesting population occurs on the mountain top at Shartlesville State Game Lands 110 between Forge Dam Road and the Sand Spring Trail. It is very common in blueberry thickets and in browse-cut areas maintained by the Pennsylvania Game Commission. During the fall of 1992, the game commission did some browse cutting on the game lands, and the following spring Common Yellowthroats quickly occupied the area. For the North America Migration Counts, Kerry Grim recorded the Common Yellowthroat in the browse cut area on the mountain top: 65 on May 8, 1993; 76 on May 14, 1994; and 69 on May 13, 1995.

Three sets of eggs in the Reading Public Museum collection were taken between May 22 (1887- at Pricetown) and July 21 (1914).

Earl Poole elaborates on the two races of this warbler:

"Of the two currently recognized races of the Common Yellowthroat that nest in Pennsylvania, the Northern Yellowthroat, *G. trichas brachidactyla*, breeds in an indefinite area in the higher mountainous regions, while the nominate race, *G. trichas trichas*, supposedly occupies the southeastern counties. Doubtless a large part of Piedmont and the Ridge and Valley sections form a broad belt of intergradation in which occur intermediates of varying degrees.

"Since Berks County apparently is in the area of intergradation between the two subspecies of Yellowthroat, breeding birds referable to both races have been taken locally. Most of these are clearly nearer to *trichas*, but one taken at Stouchsburg June 12, 1884, is much nearer *brachidactyla*; and another taken in Albany Township June 16, 1886, combines the characters of both races. Undoubtedly many of the northern birds (*brachidactyla*) pass through this area during the migrations."

The Common Yellowthroat may leave Berks County anywhere from September 20 (1945, 1946 - Earl Poole) to October 5 (1959 - E.P). Of numerous November records, the latest are November 20 (1961 - Maurice Broun at Hawk Mountain) and November 17 (1966 - Anna Kendall at Leesport).

Poole saw a Common Yellowthroat December 18, 1920. There are two Reading Christmas Bird Count records: December 27, 1936 (Harold Morris), and December 22, 1968. Matt Spence and Bart Smith recorded a Common Yellowthroat on the Elverson Christmas Bird Count December 26, 1993, near Twin Valley High School. Single birds were seen on the Bernville Christmas Bird Count January 3, 1993, and January 4, 1997.

Individual birds have been recorded during the Hamburg Christmas Bird Count December 26, 1983; December 17, 1988; December 28, 1991; December 27, 1992; and December 29, 1996.

HOODED WARBLER *Wilsonia citrina*
Rare migrant; fairly common breeder

Away from its breeding grounds, the Hooded Warbler is a rare or uncommon migrant. During 30 years of observations at Leesport, Anna Kendall has seen it during migration on only six occasions.

It apparently has always been a regular and rather common nesting species along the entire length of the Blue Mountain. Arrival dates at its nesting sites are seldom before the first week in May, the earliest April 24 (1994 - Ken Lebo at Hay Creek).

In ravines and damp spots along both sides of the Kittatinny Ridge in Berks and Schuylkill counties, the Hooded Warbler is a common frequenter of the laurel and rhododendron thickets, and during the nesting season its song is one of the characteristic sounds. It can be found in, but not restricted to, ravines at Shartlesville State Game Lands 110, Eckville State Game Lands 106, Rattling Run, Hawk Mountain Sanctuary, the Hamburg reservoir, and woodlands where there is an understory of mountain laurel and rhododendron. Sometimes found on the mountain tops, Hooded Warbler adults were feeding young at the Pinnacle July 16, 1987, at an elevation of 1,625 feet (Kerry Grim).

Earl Poole had frequently heard from six to 10 singing males in the course of a June morning's walk along the woodland trails of the Blue Mountain. Although he had not previously noticed it in the hills to the south of the Great Valley, in 1940 Poole discovered a few pairs nesting in the Hay Creek valley south of Birdsboro, and it has returned there in varying numbers. Ken Lebo has usually found two to three nesting pairs there each year during the 1990s.

On June 5, 1947, Poole found a nest with a full complement of eggs near the Birdsboro reservoir. On May 31, 1942, Paul Jensen reported a nest of Hooded Warblers containing four eggs on Neversink Mountain near Reading, and during subsequent years there have been several reports of the species being seen on Mount Penn during the nesting period, as well as on the hills above Fleetwood near Ludwig's Schoolhouse (E.P.).

Walter H. Leibelsperger and F. Bush found a nest containing four fresh eggs near Greenawald in Albany Township June 15, 1907.

During the *Atlas of Breeding Birds in Pennsylvania* survey from 1983 to 1989, Rudy Keller found the Hooded Warbler uncommon and scattered during the breeding season in eastern Berks County. He confirmed nesting twice in woodlands with a dense understory of blackberry and other deciduous shrubs. He also confirmed it nesting twice in Pike Township and on the Topton Mountain (Brauning, 1992:353).

As with many of Berks County's breeding warblers, the Hooded Warbler appears to scatter from its nesting areas quite early. A late date is October 8 (1972 - Anna Kendall at Leesport). Jim Brett and Tom Leckey found a male along a stream near Hawk Mountain Road in Albany Township on the exceptionally late date of November 13 (1995).

Levi Mengel collected specimens at Womelsdorf April 12, 1887; at Lenhartsville May 9, 1887; at Kutztown May 10, 1887; and at Oley June 21, 1886.

WILSON'S WARBLER *Wilsonia pusilla*
Uncommon migrant

The Wilson's Warbler is an uncommon migrant in spring and even more irregular in fall, inclined to feed in shrubbery and among the lower branches of trees. Nesting far to the north, it passes through in a leisurely manner and is among the later warblers to leave Berks County.

This is one species of warbler for which there are no April records, the earliest arrival May 1 (1943 - Earl Poole; 1989 - Catherine Elwell at State Game Lands 182 in Greenwich Township).

During backward seasons it has not appeared before May 22 (1917, 1920 - E.P.).

Rudy Keller found a male and a female in Pike Township June 3, 1971, and at Hawk Mountain, Maurice Broun had seen it as late as June 1 (1951).

The fall migration of the Wilson's Warbler is a rather protracted affair. An extremely early fall arrival record is an observation of a female by Broun at Hawk Mountain on August 15, 1938.

The bulk movement takes place in September, peaking during the third week. The late date is October 19 (1981 - Anna Kendall at Leesport).

Matt Spence and Warren Faust recorded an extremely late Wilson's Warbler December 26, 1971, on the Hamburg Christmas Bird Count.

Poole noted in 1964 that it was not recorded at all in the fall during 20 years out of 43, although it was decidedly common during a few seasons, as in 1939.

CANADA WARBLER *Wilsonia canadensis*
Common migrant, locally common breeder

The Canada Warbler is a common migrant and a locally common summer resident in wooded ravines and swampy woodlands, especially where dense growths of rhododendron and mountain laurel occur. It has been found in small numbers during the nesting season at elevations as low as 800 feet at Rattling Run, Northkill Gap above Shartlesville, and Eckville and occasionally, even lower.

Earl Poole found singing males at the Birdsboro reservoir on June 1, 1940, and on June 10, 1950, at an elevation of approximately 400 feet. The latter date is suspiciously late, although he was unable to find a nest or a female.

Wintering in the mountains of Peru and Ecuador, the Canada Warbler has a long journey before it reaches Berks County in spring. It usually arrives here in numbers during the first or second week in May, occasionally even later, the earliest date April 29 (1962 - Earl Poole).

The Canada Warbler is more local than any other nesting warbler species in Berks, restricted to the cool mountain ravines at Shartlesville State Game Lands 110, Rattling Run, and the Hamburg reservoir.

Poole found the Canada Warbler throughout June, apparently nesting in a number of locations along the Blue Mountain. It was probably the commonest species in the rhododendron thickets along Rattling Run, where he counted at least 12 singing males June 13, 1927.

The Canada Warbler goes about its nest building shortly after its arrival, and Poole saw adults feeding young at Rattling Run on the Berks-Schuylkill County line on June 17, 1951.

This warbler spends a remarkably short time in its breeding areas and starts to spread out over the surrounding country before starting on its southward journey early in August. Early dates include August 5 (1949 - Maurice Broun at Hawk Mountain); August 9 (1949 - M.B. at Hawk Mountain; 1970 - Rudy Keller in Pike Township); and August 10 (1970, 1979 - Anna Kendall at Leesport).

By late August the fall migration is apparently well under way and continues during the first, or occasionally, the second week in September.

The latest observation is October 16 (1971 - Anna Kendall at Leesport).

271

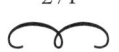

YELLOW-BREASTED CHAT *Icteria virens*

Rare migrant

The Yellow-breasted Chat population crashed in Berks County during the 1980s and has yet to recover. The Chat seems to need early successional habitat for nesting, and much of this has disappeared in Berks as the woodlands matured and scrub or shrubby meadows were eliminated.

Kerry Grim found summer residents at Eckville State Game Lands 106 until the mid-1980s (June 23, 1984), and the *Atlas of Breeding Birds in Pennsylvania* survey taken from 1983 to 1989 shows the Chat confirmed breeding in southern and eastern Berks with summer sightings scattered throughout the county, absent only in the northeast in the farm lands bordering Lehigh County (Brauning, 1992:357).

Now, it appears to be nearly extirpated as a breeding bird in Berks, and any sighting of a Chat in the county is notable. Tom Leckey found it nesting in Albany Township during 1994 and 1995. At Glen Morgan Lake, Ken Lebo sighted two Chats during the spring of 1995. They stayed until July 2. He found two Chats there again in 1996, both until July 4. He reported three there on June 23. Harold and Joan Silagy heard one singing in Bern Township June 11, 1996. Rich Bonnett found two on territory in an old field near the Daniel Boone Homestead in Amity Township in 1991.

The Yellow-breasted Chat rarely arrives before the first week in May and in some seasons does not appear until well into the third week in that month. Earl Poole recorded it only once in April, on April 29, 1956. Maurice Broun found one April 30, 1954, at Hawk Mountain. Poole's latest arrival date is May 19 (1917) during an unusually late spring.

For its nesting places the Chat selects dense thickets, the more impenetrable the better, whether in marshy places or on dry mountains where its song was often one of the characteristic sounds of the desolate, burned-over scrub.

A pair of Chats nested in brushy fields on a farm in Pike Township from 1985 to 1987. In 1987, the male arrived May 7. During all three years he would often sing at intervals at night in still, warm weather. The fields the birds nested in were impenetrable, but Rudy Keller was fortunate to see and study at some length a young bird in juvenal plumage as it perched in roadside bushes July 5, 1987. Both parents were "mewing" and "chucking" nearby.

Sam Gundy recalls that the Chat was a fairly common nester at Five Points in Exeter Township from 1946 to 1953. The males would sing all night around the approach of a full moon.

Thirty-three sets of eggs in the Levi Mengel collection at the Reading Public Museum were taken between May 20 (1888, 1896) and June 23 (1894). Clutch sizes in the collected sets range from three to five eggs. Two contain Cowbird's eggs.

During most years the Yellow-breasted Chat becomes silent around mid-July. It is rarely seen thereafter and evidently leaves for the south during August. Anna Kendall's early fall date at Leesport is August 14 (1977).

However, a few Chats can remain through the greater part of September, and Poole recorded it as late as September 25 during three years (1927, 1939, 1955). Kendall's late date at Leesport is October 21 (1967).

Since 1950 the Yellow-breasted Chat has been turning up at various points in southeastern Pennsylvania during the winter. On December 5, 1955, Conrad K. Roland captured a Chat that had been coming to his feeder near Kempton. Fearing that the bird would not survive the winter there, he kept it in his house until late the following spring when he released it.

There is one Reading Christmas Bird Count record: Dean Kendall found a Chat along

272

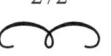

Kindt's Corner at Lake Ontelaunee on December 19, 1971. The Chat has been found twice on the Hamburg Christmas Bird Count, single birds December 30, 1990, and December 29, 1991. One was recorded on the Bernville Christmas Bird Count January 2, 1994.

Ralph W. Berky of Bally has noted that this bird of mysterious character and a strange assortment of calls may be classed with the mockers and called in Pennsylvania German "en Schpottvoggel" (Rupp, 1946:211).

SUMMER TANAGER *Piranga rubra*
Rare visitor

The Summer Tanager is a rare and irregular spring and fall visitor. Most records are of males that appear to have wandered beyond their normal range, which is to the south of Berks County, during the spring migration.

Earl Poole believed that two specimens taken by Levi Mengel in Albany Township June 17, 1886, and at Blue Marsh, June 5, 1887, seemed to indicate that the Summer Tanager may have bred in the county sometime during the last century. It was also listed by John F. Hofmann in 1890. Raymond Seibert saw a pair near Bethel in May 1931.

Other spring records include a male near the Birdsboro reservoir May 20, 1936 (David Berkheimer), and a male on Mount Penn May 18, 1952 (Charles Schaich, Earl Poole). Kerry Grim observed a male Summer Tanager in Hamburg May 11, 1980. He saw the bird at eye level from a distance of 15 feet. Jane Tobias reported a bird May 22, 1981.

Fall records at Hawk Mountain include sightings of female and immature Summer Tanagers. The early fall date from the North Lookout is September 5 (1942 - Maurice Broun), and the late date is September 24 (1935 - M.B.). Maurice Broun observed a female September 11, 1935, and an immature September 7, 1937. On September 15, 1938, Broun saw two female Summer Tanagers with three Scarlet Tanagers on top of a dead chestnut tree at the North Lookout. They stayed throughout the day.

SCARLET TANAGER *Piranga olivacea*
Common migrant; fairly common breeder

A common migrant and fairly common summer resident in woodlands throughout Berks County, the Scarlet Tanager usually nests in stands of oak or hemlock.

It returns from its wintering range in South America during the first week in May, the early date April 25 (1923 - Earl Poole).

Eight sets of eggs in the Levi Mengel collection at the Reading Public Museum were taken between June 7 (1887) and June 18 (1884). Clutch sizes in the collected sets range from two to four eggs. Mengel secured four birds, one male and three females, between June 20 (1887) and September 1 (1895) in the Pricetown Hills, near Reading, and at Neversink. He collected a male and female at Willow Creek June 15, 1895.

In contrast to the comparative regularity of the spring migration, the fall movement appears to be much more erratic, migrating birds passing through from late August through September. Maximum numbers are usually present during the third week of September, and stragglers appear well into October.

"Last seen" dates in Berks range from September 3 (1920 - E.P.) to October 19 (1955 - Maurice Broun at Hawk Mountain).

A late date at Hawk Mountain is October 26, 1966 (Bernard Theilen).

Maurice Broun noted that thousands of Scarlet Tanagers perished throughout the Northeast during the spring of 1956. The summer population at Hawk Mountain that year did not exceed more than six pairs.

Matt Spence has an unusual record of an orange Scarlet Tanager at Hawk Mountain on June 16, 1985.

The Pennsylvania German name for the Scarlet Tanager is "der Blutfink," the blood finch. Another name used in Berks is "der Flammvoggel," the flame bird (Rupp, 1936:219-220).

NORTHERN CARDINAL *Cardinalis cardinalis*
Common resident

Formerly a bird of more southern distribution, the Northern Cardinal has extended its range north during the last half century. In 1930, Earl Poole considered it a tolerably common resident, especially in the southern half of Berks County. It now breeds commonly throughout Berks.

The Cardinal is both an early and late nester. Poole saw a nest with three eggs at West Reading on April 11 (1958), and it routinely feeds young into late September.

The Cardinal's nest is placed fairly low in dense evergreens and ornamentals, in thickets, and in vines.

Four sets of eggs in the Reading Public Museum collection were taken between May 30 (1908) and June 20 (1887). Levi Mengel collected three of the sets in Bethel Township June 9, 1885; in Albany Township June 14, 1885; and in Bethel June 20, 1887. Each set contains four eggs.

Mengel collected both male and female Cardinals at Virginville June 2, 1889, and in Bethel Township June 30, 1885.

Most conspicuous in winter, the Cardinal has become one of the favorite visitors at feeding stations and can occur in flocks of 10 to 20 birds.

It has appeared on the Reading Christmas Bird Count 83 of 86 years, 10 of the last 10, with a maximum of 477 on December 18, 1994. The peak for the Hamburg Christmas Bird Count is 593 on December 30, 1990. The high for the Bernville count is 368 Cardinals on January 1, 1992.

"Der Rotvoggel," or "redbird," is the most common name in the Pennsylvania German for the Cardinal. "Der Kornkracker" is another name heard in Berks based on the English "corn cracker," a name applicable to any seed-eater or finch. William Rupp writes: "Several reliable observers have expressed the opinion that the Cardinal was not well known among the early Pennsylvania German people, but that its range has been expanding northward, and this accounts for the use of a name like 'corn cracker' and the more frequent use of the English name." Dr. Arthur D. Graeff is sure that he has heard several natives of western Berks use the name "der Guthaerr" for the Cardinal, even though this is the common name for the Blue Jay (Rupp, 1946:220-221).

ROSE-BREASTED GROSBEAK *Pheucticus ludovicianus*
Common migrant; uncommon nester

A regular and fairly common spring and fall migrant, the Rose-breasted Grosbeak is an uncommon, widespread nester throughout Berks County. Earl Poole noted that it appears to fluctuate in numbers, being comparatively common for several years running and quite uncommon for a like period.

Although strikingly marked, the Rose-breasted Grosbeak is not a conspicuous bird, staying within thickets and usually heard along edge habitats.

During the *Atlas of Breeding Birds in Pennsylvania* survey from 1983 to 1989, it was found nesting in southern, northern, and eastern Berks (Brauning, 1992:365).

Poole saw nests or found birds present during the nesting season in at least twelve areas in Berks County, mostly in the South Mountain region to the east and northeast of Reading but also along the Sixpenny and Hay creeks in the southern part of the county.

In 1951 a pair nested and successfully raised young in the Reading Public Museum park. The nest was about six feet above the ground in a *Lonicera* bush and was under observation from May 18 to June 7. On June 11 the female was seen feeding a bob-tailed fledgling that apparently had just left the nest.

The Rose-breasted Grosbeak usually nests along deciduous forest edges, especially in marshy places or near water. It also nests in parks and rural areas where tall shrubs or low trees furnish choice nesting sites, the nests being built from five to 20 feet from the ground.

Levi Mengel took a set of four eggs near Lenhartsville on June 16, 1887, and Walter Leibelsperger took several sets near Fleetwood, the latest June 20 (1906). Mengel collected birds in Albany Township June 5, 1889, and June 15, 1885, and in Bethel Township June 20, 1887.

Spring arrival dates are mostly in the first week of May, the earliest dates April 23 (1996 - Kenneth and Dorothy Grim at Hamburg) and April 27 (1957 - Earl Poole at Hawk Mountain, a female; 1995 - Catherine Elwell at District Township, five at a feeder).

There was a spring fallout at Hawk Mountain May 11, 1956. Maurice Broun recorded over 100 Rose-breasted Grosbeaks in a steady movement at the mountain. Over 50 stayed at his feeders until May 21.

The fall migration takes place during September with the maximum number present during the third week, although a few laggards remain into October. At Reading Poole last recorded the Rose-breasted Grosbeak from September 6 (1936) to October 25 (1959). Recent fall single-day peaks at Hawk Mountain include 35 birds on both September 21, 1996, and September 22, 1984.

Extremely late departure dates are November 19 (1932 - E.P. at Lake Ontelaunee) and November 22 and 23 (1951 - Maurice Broun at Eckville, two birds, *fide* J. Parsley).

A male Rose-breasted Grosbeak came to a feeding station maintained by Dr. F. E. Weatherby near Wernersville from December 3 to 16, 1961.

There is one Reading Christmas Bird Count record reported at Antietam Lake January 1, 1978, by Dr. George Kershner.

BLUE GROSBEAK *Guiraca caerulea*
Rare and irregular summer visitor

Formerly an accidental overshoot from the south, the Blue Grosbeak appears to have begun a range expansion north, but at present there are no confirmed nesting records in Berks County.

Until the mid-1980s, only five Blue Grosbeak sightings were recorded this century in Berks. G. Henry Mengel saw one in the Charles Evans Cemetery in May about 1925 but lost the exact date. Charles Schaich found one at Moselem September 9, 1956. Dorothy and Kenneth Grim and Lyle Layser sighted three that remained for nearly a week in Tilden Township beginning May 20, 1967. Grace Jones found one male migrating with Rose-breasted Grosbeaks along River Road in Reading May 5, 1970. Scott Shrieber and Jim Brett saw two immatures or young females on a snag at the North Lookout at Hawk Mountain September 2, 1978.

Since the 1980s, though, the Blue Grosbeak has become rare to uncommon, with sightings throughout Berks. May records from the 1980s include May 13, 1981 (Ira Weigley, Jr., a singing male at Blue Marsh); May 12, 1986 (Robert Cook, a singing male along Buck Hollow Road near

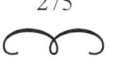

Geigertown); May 11, 1986 (Joan Silagy, a male in Bern Township); and May 9, 1988 (Catherine Elwell).

Of nine May records from the 1990s, the early date is May 1 (1996 - many observers at Hawk Mountain).

Two June records are of a singing male near Strausstown June 18, 1988 (Kerry Grim), and two females or immatures near Topton June 26, 1988 (Rudy Keller). There are 16 records between July 5 (1996) and September 30 (1996 - J.S. near Peacock Road at Blue Marsh). Females and immatures have been observed in August.

Singing males have been recorded through July. Ken Lebo found a singing male in a field July 30 and 31, 1994, at the intersection of Route 662 and Windsor Castle Road in Perry Township. It was seen by many observers. Rudy Keller found a mated pair on farmland near Albany July 5, 1996, but was unable to relocate them.

John F. Hofmann listed the Blue Grosbeak in 1890.

INDIGO BUNTING *Passerina cyanea*
Fairly common migrant and nester

A fairly common migrant and summer resident throughout Berks County, the Indigo Bunting nests in valleys and on mountain tops wherever it finds scrub growth, hedges, or thickets in which to hide its nest with taller trees or telephone wires nearby to serve as singing perches. It also occurs in parks and suburban areas.

In spring it rarely reaches Berks before the height of the migration during the second week in May although there are April records. Maurice Broun reported a male at Hawk Mountain, and Conrad Roland recorded one in Albany Township the same day: April 22, 1954. Laurie Goodrich saw an Indigo Bunting at a thistle feeder at Schaumboch's on Hawk Mountain April 23, 1985. Ken Lebo found one in Geigertown April 26, 1994.

Kerry Grim reported an unusual flock of over 100 Indigo Buntings May 22, 1976, at State Game Lands 106 near Hawk Mountain.

The Indigo Bunting nest is usually concealed in dense brush, weeds, or brier patches within a few feet of the ground. On August 24, 1920, Earl Poole found a nest containing three eggs in an undetermined state of incubation within a few miles of Reading. This was doubtless a late second or third nest.

As early as the last decade of the nineteenth century, 25 percent of the local Indigo Bunting nests were found to contain Cowbird's eggs. Of 29 sets of from one to five eggs in the Levi Mengel collection taken between May 21 (1897) and July 3 (1886), seven contain Cowbird's eggs.

Poole writes in 1964: "With the much greater abundance of Cowbirds today, the percentage is undoubtedly greater and must be a serious factor in reducing the population of one of our most attractive native birds, a delight both to the eye and ear, whose brave, spirited ditty is often the only bird song to be heard through the hot, humid days of midsummer."

The fall migration is well under way by the first week in September and is marked by an increase in the number of birds present. By the third week in September most Indigo Buntings have left, the late date October 13 (1960 - Earl Poole).

There is one winter record. Poole found an Indigo Bunting in first-winter plumage January 1, 1962, at Weiser Lake, also known as the "mine hole," in West Reading. The location is now a parking lot for the Reading Hospital.

Mengel collected seven Indigo Buntings, two males and five females, from May 15 (1884) to September 10 (1888) in Albany Township, Reading, Lenhartsville, Boyertown, West Reading, and along the Wyomissing Creek. He secured a male and female at Stouchsburg June 11, 1887. These specimens are in the Reading Public Museum collection.

The Pennsylvania Germans in Berks County know this bird as the "Indigo Voggel," a form based on the English name (Rupp, 1946:222).

PAINTED BUNTING *Passerina ciris*
Accidental

Earl Poole and Matt Spence found a male Painted Bunting in the Reading Public Museum park in a thicket 100 yards to the north of the museum May 13, 1961. The bird was under observation for several hours during the day and behaved much like an Indigo Bunting, spending most of the time on the ground feeding on dandelion heads and other low growth but flying into the bushes or lower branches of trees when approached too closely (Poole, 1962: 21-22).

A male Painted Bunting was seen off and on in Muhlenberg Township from October 1971 to mid-April 1972. Robert Cook and Dean Kelsey observed it April 12, 1972, behind the Clover Farms Dairy.

DICKCISSEL *Spiza americana*
Very rare and irregular vagrant

Formerly a common summer resident over large portions of the lowlands of eastern Pennsylvania during the nineteenth century, the Dickcissel had for many years been practically extirpated from the state. Currently in Berks County, it is a very rare and irregular vagrant from the Midwest.

Since about 1933, Earl Poole believed that the Dickcissel was attempting to return to the regions that were so long deserted, although he doubted whether it could ever regain even a small measure of its former abundance because of the earlier mowing of the grass, clover, and alfalfa fields.

There are no nesting records in Berks, but there are Dickcissel records from the spring and summer.

The first Dickcissel record this century is of a male singing at Lake Ontelaunee from July 26 to August 22, 1936, seen and heard by Earl Poole, Byron Nunemacher, and David Berkheimer. Conrad Roland observed birds in Albany Township May 5, 1937, and June 7, 1943. Maurice Broun found single Dickcissels dead beneath a television tower on the Blue Mountain near Bethel September 20, 1953, and September 22, 1954. These two specimens are in the Reading Public Museum collection. On September 29, 1954, Alex Nagy found one near Eckville, and on October 17, 1955, J. Arnett identified one at Maiden Creek Station at Lake Ontelaunee. From March 4 to April 16, 1958, one visited a Wyomissing feeder daily (E. Gage).

Poole found a singing male near Windsor Castle on May 30, 1959. It was definitely interested in a certain spot in an alfalfa field, to which it returned at intervals. It was still there on June 7, but the field was being mowed, and the bird disappeared. He saw one near Strausstown September 3, 1961. A male Dickcissel sang for most of June 1975 in an uncut hay field near Maxatawny but did not attract a mate (Rudy Keller).

Kerry Grim has spent many hours in the summers from the 1980s through the mid-1990s in northern Berks observing the grassland sparrows - the Vesper, Grasshopper, and Savannah - and has never heard a Dickcissel.

It wasn't reported in the county between 1988, a bird seen by Joan Silagy October 2 at the Route 183 hawk watch, and 1996, a bird seen and heard May 12 and 13 by Brian Martin along Deysher Road in Maxatawny Township. These were invasion years for the Dickcissel in Pennsylvania.

Fall records at Hawk Mountain include two birds that rested briefly on a hemlock below the North Lookout September 29, 1958 (Alex Nagy). Other records there are October 14, 1969; October 10 to 16, 1975; and September 20, 1979.

The Dickcissel has been recorded four times on the Reading Christmas Bird Count, single birds on December 22, 1963; December 24, 1967; December 21, 1969; and December 17, 1978. It has appeared on the Hamburg Christmas Bird Count twice: December 30, 1979, and December 17, 1988.

On December 30, 1979, and March 22, 1980, a male, believed to be the same bird, appeared at a feeder in Hamburg (Kerry Grim, Kenneth and Dorothy Grim). A male Dickcissel visited feeders in Hamburg January 23 and 30, 1983 (Kerry Grim, John and Marcia Bachman).

John F. Hofmann in 1890 listed the Dickcissel as occurring locally.

EASTERN TOWHEE *Pipilo erythrophthalmus*

Common migrant and nester

The Eastern Towhee is a common migrant and summer resident, nesting in thickets, brushy woodland, and scrub growth. Found in the river bottom lands and on mountain tops alike, it is one of the characteristic birds of recently lumbered and burned-over areas. This bird was known by two other names this century, the Red-eyed Towhee and the Rufous-sided Towhee.

It arrives around mid-April and leaves about the third week in October but is sometimes resident in well-sheltered spots. When not known or suspected to have wintered, the Towhee usually arrives in Berks County around mid-April, but individuals that probably have wintered nearby sometimes put in an appearance in March. Some of these early arrivals may actually be birds that have been overlooked during the winter, since wintering Towhees are extremely secretive and given to hiding in impenetrable tangles.

Some of the early arrival records may belong in this category, as in all probability were ones that Earl Poole saw at Birdsboro on February 4, 1951, and in Reading March 27, 1925. Towhees that have wintered near feeders include one at Leesport from January 6 to March 31, 1994 (Dean Kendall), and one at Hamburg January 10 to March 31, 1993 (Matt Wlasniewski).

Twenty-six sets of eggs in the Levi Mengel collection bear data from May 21 (1889) to June 19 (1887, 1888). Clutch sizes in these sets range from two to six eggs. The Eastern Towhee rears two broods.

The fall migratory movement becomes noticeable with Towhees appearing at unaccustomed places around the third week in September and continues into mid-October, but final departure dates vary greatly. Poole's "last seen" dates range from October 3 (1940) to December 1 (1937). As with the very early spring arrival dates for this species, December dates may pertain to birds that will attempt to winter.

The Eastern Towhee has appeared on the Reading Christmas Bird Count 35 of 86 years, five of the last 10, with a maximum of 56 on December 19, 1971. The peak for the Hamburg Christmas Bird Count is eight on January 2, 1971. On the Bernville count, a high count of six was made January 1, 1992. It was found on all three counts in 1996. As the Christmas count highs show, the Eastern Towhee was common during the winters of 1970-1971 and 1971-1972. Rudy Keller reports that seven birds were at two feeders in District Township until the end of January 1971, and one female in Pike Township was seen through March 1971.

"Der Schewink" is a common Pennsylvania German name for the Eastern Towhee based on its "chewink" call. "Der Joe Wink," used with the English spelling but given the dialect pronunciation, is a name that has occurred in lower Berks and upper Lehigh counties because "Wink" was a common family name in these areas. "Die Grundamschel," or "ground Robin," is a name used for this bird in Berks because it is always busy working on the ground beneath thickets and bushy undergrowth where it makes its home (Rupp, 1946:224).

AMERICAN TREE SPARROW *Spizella arborea*
Common migrant and winter visitor

The American Tree Sparrow is a common and generally distributed migrant and winter visitor, often associating with the Juncos in weedy fields and about the edges of woods and thickets. It is less abundant than the Junco, arrives later in the fall, and leaves earlier in the spring.

During occasional winters, the American Tree Sparrow is either very rare or absent in the depth of winter and is noticed chiefly as a migrant, occurring in November and early December and again in March and early April, which seem to be the months of the main migratory movements.

In Berks County, the American Tree Sparrow arrives anywhere from October 6 (1969 - Joan Silagy in the 18th Ward, Reading) to November 30 (1946 - Earl Poole).

During the winters of 1933–1934, 1943–1944, and 1947–1948, Earl Poole did not record it at all until the spring migration was under way in late March and April and suspects that during those years the bulk of the population wintered to the south of Berks.

The spring migratory movement is often noticeable during the second half of March, sometimes continuing until well into April. Last seen dates range from February 25 (1950 - E.P.) to April 24 (1926 - E.P.).

The late date at Hawk Mountain is April 13 (1960).

The Tree Sparrow, along with the Junco and Crow, has been found during every Reading Christmas Bird Count with a maximum of 1,647 in 1947. The high count for the Hamburg Christmas Bird Count is 1,467 on December 29, 1985. The peak for the Bernville count is 368 on January 1, 1992.

CHIPPING SPARROW *Spizella passerina*
Common migrant and summer nester

The Chipping Sparrow is a common migrant and breeding summer resident throughout Berks County as well as a rather rare and irregular winter resident, occasionally reported during the Christmas counts.

This familiar little sparrow has taken to suburban life and seems to be more common in close proximity to man-made environments than elsewhere. It is especially common about well-kept lawns planted with occasional ornamental evergreens or thorny shrubs in which it can hide its hair-lined nest. It is also frequently found in forests and plantations of various species of conifers, such as at Nolde Forest in Cumru Township and on Christmas tree farms, which doubtless formed its original habitat.

It arrives in Berks during the first week of April with an early date of March 26 (1994 - Matt Wlasniewski at Hamburg). A Chipping Sparrow that possibly wintered arrived in Leesport February 20, 1995, and stayed through the spring and summer (Dean Kendall).

The Chipping Sparrow's song is one of the characteristic sounds of the suburban areas which it frequents. By early May the neat cup-shaped nests are completed and the eggs laid.

Sets of eggs in the Levi Mengel collection were taken between May 16 (1885) and June 16 (1886). This is one of the species that is most frequently imposed upon by the Cowbird. Of 24 nests collected, 10 contain Cowbird's eggs. Clutch sizes from these sets range from three to five eggs.

In August and September after the nesting season, the Chipping Sparrow congregates in flocks, often in association with other sparrows, and moves south. Some high counts of flocking Chipping Sparrows have been recorded. Harold and Joan Silagy found almost 100 in Bern Township August 24, 1991.

It is most in evidence in late September and the first half of October and is usually gone by the end of that month. A late date is November 19 (1995 - Ken Lebo, M.W. at Glen Morgan Lake).

The Chipping Sparrow has shown an increased tendency to remain into the winter, but care must be taken in identification. The American Tree Sparrow is often misidentified in winter as the Chipping Sparrow.

Earl Poole found a Chipping Sparrow at the Hessian Camp in Reading on January 17, 1924. Matt Spence found one at a feeder at Maiden Creek Station near Lake Ontelaunee February 12, 1972.

The Chipping Sparrow was first recorded on the Reading Christmas Bird Count on December 22, 1957, when nine were seen. It has appeared on the count 12 times, once in the last 10 years. It has been recorded nine times on the Hamburg Christmas Bird Count, a high of 10 seen December 29, 1974, and three counted January 1, 1995, the only record in the last 10 years. The only Bernville count record is of a single bird January 4, 1997.

The Pennsylvania Germans call the Chipping Sparrow "es Zittche," based on its "chip" note. "Es Schpetzel" is a name as common as "Zittche," used for the Chipping Sparrow and any other small bird of the yard and garden (Rupp, 1946:226).

FIELD SPARROW *Spizella pusilla*

Common migrant and nester

A common migrant and summer resident in brushy fields and neglected areas throughout Berks County, the Field Sparrow is also fairly regular in winter.

It has remained in Berks up to the end of January but becomes rare in February. Harold and Joan Silagy saw one in Bern Township from February 8 to 24, 1994.

Because of the Field Sparrow's tendency to winter, spring migration dates are not easily determined, but what appear to be the earliest spring migrants usually arrive early in March (March 2, 1996 - Kerry Grim at a feeder in Hamburg).

During most years, however, the Field Sparrow does not become really common until April, when its sweet, plaintive song is one of the characteristic sounds. The Field Sparrow builds its nest on or near the ground, and full sets of eggs are laid from May to August, the later dates undoubtedly second broods.

Sets of eggs in the Levi Mengel collection were taken between May 15 (1887) and July 14 (1885, 1886). Clutch sizes in these sets range from three to five eggs. Of 33 nests collected in Berks in the 1880s, seven contain Cowbird's eggs, and the number of sparrows imposed upon by it must be much greater today with the greatly increased abundance of the Cowbird.

The Field Sparrow nested at Hawk Mountain Sanctuary in 1939, but there have been no summer records there since. Spring dates there range from March 27

(1948, 1949) to May 18. Fall dates are from August 12 to November 5.

After the prolonged nesting season, the little family groups often join with other species of native sparrows, and by October, the fall migration is well under way. This movement gradually tapers off until the end of that month, leaving the few tardy individuals that may attempt to winter.

The Field Sparrow has appeared on the Reading Christmas Bird Count 56 of 86 years, 10 of the last 10, with a maximum of 63 on December 27, 1970. It has been recorded every year on the Hamburg Christmas Bird Count with a peak of 107 December 29, 1984. The high for the Bernville count is 71 on January 3, 1988.

VESPER SPARROW *Pooecetes gramineus*
Uncommon migrant and summer nester

Declining from the loss of grass and hay fields, the Vesper Sparrow is an uncommon migrant and summer resident in the Great Valley between Reading and the Blue Mountain. Although appearing to adapt to alfalfa, it needs large, open fields to thrive.

A few stragglers remain at least until January 1, and some undoubtedly survive during mild winters, but definite observations are lacking between mid-January and the end of February.

The Vesper Sparrow is reported occasionally on Christmas counts. It has been recorded on the Reading Christmas Bird Count eight of 83 years, none of the last 10, with a maximum of eight on January 1, 1978. It hasn't been recorded on the Hamburg Christmas Bird Count since 1979, the peak count of 16 occurring January 2, 1971. Three Vesper Sparrows were tallied January 3, 1993, for the only Bernville count record.

The earliest actual spring arrival date appears to be March 9 (1960 - Earl Poole), the migration usually peaking by the end of March. Hawk Mountain Sanctuary spring records range from March 27 (1949) to April 16 (1948).

Kerry Grim, who has studied the grassland sparrows in northern Berks, writes that the Vesper Sparrow can be found not only in dry, open fields, but sometimes in trees bordering this habitat. Its song could be incorrectly identified as that of a Song Sparrow if it didn't start with two clear, slow notes. In flight, its outer white tail feathers are distinctive and are a better field mark than its chestnut shoulders.

Sets of eggs in the Reading Public Museum collection were taken from May 2 (1889) to June 22 (1888), although Earl Poole saw a nest with fresh eggs under a potato vine at Wyomissing as late as July 20 (1917). Clutch sizes in these sets range from two to six eggs. Of 23 sets in the Levi Mengel collection, five contain Cowbird's eggs.

The main fall migratory movement of the Vesper Sparrow takes place in late September and October, and the bird is last seen in Berks up to November 10 (1923), usually leaving by the third week in October, excluding the exceptional stragglers that remain into December.

The Pennsylvania Germans have no specific names for the grassland sparrows besides the general terms "Grundschpetzliche" and "Feldschpetzliche" (Rupp, 1946:224-225).

LARK BUNTING *Calamospiza melanocorys*

Accidental

Harold and Joan Silagy found a second-year Lark Bunting May 2, 1993, perched in a tree at State Game Lands 110 at Shartlesville near Bloody Spring Road. They viewed it for several minutes before it flew but were unable to relocate the bird. They were familiar with the Lark Bunting from previous trips to the West.

SAVANNAH SPARROW *Passerculus sandwichensis*

Fairly common migrant, local nester

The Savannah Sparrow is a fairly common migrant in open country. Definite nesting records are scarce.

Byron Nunemacher and Earl Poole found several pairs of Savannah Sparrows near the shores of Lake Ontelaunee on June 6, 1929, and on several later visits. On July 14, they noticed adults carrying green worms and decided that the nest could not be far away. While searching for it, they came upon one of the young, which was fully feathered but unable to fly more than a foot or two and mostly crept about in the meadow mouse runways (Poole, 1929a:550).

Savannah Sparrows returned to the same meadow during several subsequent summers and undoubtedly nested until 1940, by which time the habitat was altered and the birds did not return.

In 1953 Poole noticed several singing males in lightly grazed pastures in an area between Blandon and Kutztown. At least six singing males were found June 7 and 21 (Earl Poole, Byron Nunemacher, Anna Deeter). Checks on the area produced two to six pairs each year. Evidently Savannah Sparrows had nested here for many years since Levi Mengel collected adults in June in various locations in this valley in 1884, 1885, and 1887. That farm habitat still supports the Savannah Sparrow, according to records kept during the *Atlas of Breeding Birds in Pennsylvania* survey from 1983 to 1989 (Brauning, 1992:383).

One breeding record from southern Berks County is a nest with young discovered by Robert Cook July 21, 1951.

Between Windsor Castle and Lenhartsville and along Monument Road near Hamburg are good places for the grassland sparrows. On July 12, 1984, a flightless immature Savannah Sparrow walked across the road in Windsor Township, passing within 10 feet of Kerry Grim. Shortly thereafter, it was followed by an alarmed adult.

The Savannah Sparrow is easily overlooked by the uninitiated. It frequents the same type of broad, fairly level grass fields that attract the Bobolink, and, in some places, low-lying areas near water. Its song is weak and insect-like, the last note lower in pitch. It looks very much like a Song Sparrow but is slimmer and has a short, notched tail.

It usually arrives in Berks by the end of March, the early arrival date March 3 (1960 - Alex Nagy). The maximum number is usually present during mid-April, and during some years a few remain here until late May, late migrants being impossible to distinguish from the summer residents which remain to breed.

The main fall migratory movement occurs between mid-September and late October, but apparently is very irregular. On two occasions, Poole found the Savannah Sparrow fairly common in the valley to the north of Reading as early as September 1 (1920, 1929), but in other years he did not find it in numbers until October 26 (1930). Poole's last seen dates are as early as October 7 (1950) or as late as January 1 (1958).

The Savannah Sparrow has been recorded on the Reading Christmas Bird Count three of 86 years, once in the last 10, with a maximum of eight on December 17, 1995. It has appeared on the Hamburg Christmas Bird Count nine of 32 years with highs of six on December 30, 1979, and

January 2, 1983. The peak number on the Bernville count is eight on January 4, 1987.

Other January and February records include birds at Niantic in eastern Berks January 29, 1989 (Gary Freed); at Big Spring Farm near Robesonia February 18, 1993 (Ernie Schiefer, five); and in Albany Township February 28, 1993 (Kerry Grim).

"Ipswich" Sparrow *Passerculus sandwichensis princeps*
Hypothetical

Earl Poole felt certain that he saw an "Ipswich" Sparrow, a paler subspecies of the Savannah Sparrow, near Fleetwood on May 7, 1960 (Poole, 1964:69).

GRASSHOPPER SPARROW *Ammodramus savannarum*
Very local nester

The Grasshopper Sparrow is a regular migrant and fairly common but locally distributed summer resident in dry grass fields across northern Berks County.

It has arrived in spring as early as April 7 (1929 - Earl Poole), but most recent records are from early May of singing males on territory.

Since the detection of this secretive sparrow depends to a great extent on acute hearing, and since the birds are far more frequently heard than seen, records are scarce after the cessation of the song period. The latest date on which Poole heard the Grasshopper Sparrow sing is August 6 (1942). Kerry Grim's late date is August 18 (1984).

While working on the *Atlas of Breeding Birds in Pennsylvania* survey, Grim worked on two blocks near Hamburg for two-and-a-half hours June 23, 1985, and counted 15 Grasshopper Sparrows, 22 Vesper Sparrows, and 12 Savannah Sparrows.

Grim finds that the Grasshopper Sparrow occurs in the same habitat as the Savannah Sparrow. Its song is weak and insect-like but has many more notes than that of a Savannah Sparrow. It can be identified in flight by its slow, moth-like flight style. This sparrow is somewhat colonial, and at times many can be heard singing in one area.

The Grasshopper Sparrow has declined with habitat loss in the county, and where the habitat has remained stable, its insect prey has been reduced by spraying for spittle bugs in the alfalfa fields.

Because of the bird's secretive behavior, nesting confirmation is difficult. Grim has three records: an adult with fledged young in Windsor Township July 12, 1984, and July 3, 1985, and an adult carrying food for young in Tilden Township June 28, 1986.

Seven sets of eggs in the Reading Public Museum collection were taken from May 25 (1881, 1891) to July 2 (1900). Clutch sizes in these sets range from three to five eggs. One nest contains a Cowbird's egg.

An extremely late date is December 4 (1961 - E.P.), although this bird is usually gone by the first week in October.

HENSLOW'S SPARROW *Ammodramus henslowii*
Very rare

The Henslow's Sparrow is a very rare and local migrant and earlier this century was a summer resident of wide but spotty distribution in Berks County. There have been no county records since the early 1960s, both at Hawk Mountain.

Maurice Broun saw a Henslow's Sparrow at the North Lookout September 29, 1963, grounded by rain and fog in the early hours of the morning skulking around the rocks like a mouse. Maurice Broun and Alex Nagy found one grounded by fog near the Common Room May 9, 1961.

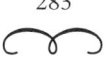

Apparently this sparrow is subject to extreme fluctuations in numbers and may appear in certain locations for a number of years, then suddenly vanish for no apparent reason.

Between 1934 and 1942, the Henslow's Sparrow was found throughout the nesting season in at least 10 separate locations in Berks, but annual checking of these same areas until the mid-1950s produced this species in only one area, near Geigertown, where one singing bird was found in 1950 (Earl Poole), and another July 14, 1953 (Robert Cook), but none since.

At various times this elusive sparrow had been reported present during the summer, usually under conditions that seemed to indicate nesting in Windsor Castle, Strausstown, Tuckerton, Lake Ontelaunee, Joanna, Geigertown, White Bear, and at Camp Joy just outside the Reading city limits, all between 1934 and 1950 (E.P.).

It inhabits poorly drained, sedgy meadows and weedy fields, but occasionally is found in high, dry upland fields as well. It seems to elude all but those who are on the alert for the insect-like "flee-sic," which serves as its song, but when found, this diminutive sparrow may be present in colonies of several pairs nesting within earshot of one another.

The Henslow's Sparrow was regarded as a very rare migrant prior to 1934, when Conrad Roland and Byron Nunemacher heard two in an old field along the edge of the Blue Mountain near Degler's Gap on June 23, 1934. Roland found a colony at Windsor Castle July 4, 1934.

Migration dates for this elusive little sparrow are remarkably scarce. Usually it is not observed until it is well established and in full song on its nesting grounds. An early spring date from Berks is April 28 (1941 - E.P.).

Once established in an acceptable breeding locality, whether nesting singly or in communities, the Henslow's Sparrow sings its brief but repetitious song right through the summer. Poole heard the song as late as September 13 (1936), the latest date which he found this species locally. The latest fall date from Eckville is November 8 (1950 - Maurice Broun).

Fall sight records of this species are not always reliable, since the young Grasshopper Sparrow has a streaked breast like the adult Henslow's.

It was listed by John F. Hofmann in 1890.

NELSON'S SHARP-TAILED SPARROW *Ammodramus nelsoni*
Accidental

The Nelson's Sharp-tailed Sparrow frequents a type of marsh habitat that is often inaccessible to the bird watcher. Extremely shy and secretive, it easily escapes observation and may occur more frequently than the records indicate.

The only opportunity that Earl Poole had to really study this sparrow in detail came on the chilly morning of October 18, 1924, when he found one sunning itself on a branch that projected above the marsh grass at Moselem. He had ample time to make a rather detailed sketch of this bird which was later compared with skins and identified at the time by Witmer Stone as Nelson's Sparrow, *Ammodramus caudacutus nelsoni*, then regarded as a subspecies of the Sharp-tailed Sparrow, as were most of the specimens actually taken in the state up to that time. The Nelson's Sharp-tailed Sparrow was elevated to full species status by the American Ornithologists' Union in 1995.

Poole had later observations of Nelson's Sharp-tailed Sparrows in marshes at the head of Lake Ontelaunee on June 3, 1930; September 27, 1931; September 28, 1932; and two on October 14, 1932. The marshes in which they were found have since been flooded.

There are no other records.

SEASIDE SPARROW *Ammodramus maritimus*
Accidental

A specimen in the Reading Public Museum collection is labeled "Fritz's Island, April 30, 1887— L. W. Mengel." Since this specimen is in worn, late-summer plumage, Earl Poole suspected that there was an error in labeling.

Anna and Mary Deeter saw one under favorable conditions at Lake Ontelaunee following a severe northeast storm on October 28, 1936.

FOX SPARROW *Passerella iliaca*
Fairly common migrant

The Fox Sparrow is a fairly common migrant, much more common some years than others, and usually more conspicuous in spring. Rare in winter, it is fairly regular and often remains up to late December or early January. Observations after mid-January are scarce.

This fine sparrow is one of the earliest migrants to reach Berks County in spring, sometimes appearing after the first mild spell in late February. An extremely early date is February 4 (1994 - Harold and Joan Silagy at Bernville). The earliest Hawk Mountain record is February 23 (1954 - Maurice Broun).

The Fox Sparrow reaches its maximum numbers around mid-March. Maurice Broun found over 150 Fox Sparrows, many in song, along the boundary of Hawk Mountain Sanctuary east of Schaumboch's March 30, 1947. Rudy Keller recorded 23 in Pike Township after a storm March 13, 1967. Many of these birds were also singing.

During favorable years it remains in numbers until early April and may stay as late as April 28 (1940 - Earl Poole). One exceptionally late record is a bird Earl Poole saw on May 11, 1950.

Most fall dates for the Fox Sparrow range from the beginning of November through December. An extremely early date is September 29 (1985 - Kathy Hall near River Road in Muhlenberg Township).

At Hawk Mountain, the Fox Sparrow arrives no earlier than October 10 (1963, 1992). Ten appeared at the North Lookout on October 30, 1992 (Cathy Viverette).

In most cases a Fox Sparrow seen later than December can be considered a straggler that will probably remain until severe winter weather arrives, or it may attempt to winter. There have been numerous reports of Fox Sparrows seen up to the first of January, mostly during the Christmas counts.

It has appeared on the Reading Christmas Bird Count 26 of 86 years, six of the last 10, with a maximum of nine on December 21, 1975. The peak for the Hamburg Christmas Bird Count is five on December 27, 1992. It has been recorded on that count 16 of 32 years. The only Bernville count record is three birds sighted January 1, 1992.

There are few definite records later than the first week in January. One or two remained at Birdsboro until January 23, 1926, but were not seen thereafter (E.P.). One wintered in the Reading Public Museum park and was seen frequently from December 30, 1929, to February 25, 1930, after which it became lost among the newly arrived migrants (E.P.). Harold Morris found one at Antietam on January 26, 1941. Keller observed one in Pike Township January 20 and 21, 1969. A

Fox Sparrow remained about a feeder in West Reading from December 21, 1969, to January 13, 1970 (E.P.). One was at the Hawk Mountain Sanctuary feeders February 27, 1990. Another visited a feeder in Plowville from December 1988 until March 1989 (Harold Lebo).

SONG SPARROW *Melospiza melodia*
Common resident

A common permanent resident over most of Berks County, the Song Sparrow is most abundant during the migrations in late February and March and again in late September through October, and least common in winter, when many of the breeding birds retire to the south. A few birds remain about springheads and sheltered thickets.

The Song Sparrow appears on the annual Christmas counts, and it is probable that many of the birds seen at this time manage to survive the average winter.

It has appeared on the Reading Christmas Bird Count 85 of 86 years with a maximum of 397 on December 20, 1992. It has been recorded on every Hamburg Christmas Bird Count with a peak of 635 on December 27, 1992, and on each Bernville count with a high of 502 on January 3, 1993.

The Song Sparrow, along with other sparrow species, was particularly abundant throughout Berks during 1992, as the Christmas counts show. On April 12, 1992, Kerry Grim found 100 migrants in two flocks at the Hamburg reservoir. Harold and Joan Silagy and Rudy Keller saw over 300 at Blue Marsh November 22 of that year.

In most areas the Song Sparrow is so inconspicuous during the winter that it is completely overlooked. Earl Poole writes: " It is only when the first mild, sunny days of February arrive and they commence to sing weakly, that they make their presence known. During rare 'warm' spells in January, they sometimes try out their voices, and it is then that we can appreciate what really fine little songsters they are."

There is a pronounced migratory movement in late February and early March. Maurice Broun recorded over 20 around Schaumboch's at Hawk Mountain on March 28, 1950.

Nest building does not begin until April. Probably three broods are raised each season. The earlier nests are usually placed on the ground, but later nests are elevated in tufts of weeds or in bushes.

Egg dates of sets in the Levi Mengel collection range from May 6 (1887) to July 8 (1887). Of 33 nests collected, seven contain Cowbird's eggs. Clutch sizes in these sets are from three to six eggs.

The Pennsylvania Germans call the Song Sparrow "es Grundschpetzel," or "ground sparrow," because it usually nests on the ground. "Der Friehyaahrsvoggel" is a general name for any arrival in early spring and specifically for this bird whose song is a sign of the coming spring (Rupp, 1946:228).

LINCOLN'S SPARROW *Melospiza lincolnii*
Very rare migrant

The Lincoln's Sparrow is a very rare migrant both in spring and fall and is accidental in winter.

This very secretive sparrow doubtlessly occurs more regularly than the records seem to indicate, since it is given to skulking under the cover of dense shrubbery and is difficult to flush. Fleeting glimpses are not satisfactory, since immature Swamp Sparrows and some fall Song Sparrows are sometimes misidentified as Lincoln's Sparrows. Unless the bird is well seen and all of its characteristics noted, sight records are often subject to suspicion.

Earl Poole found that a good small dog, such as a Cocker Spaniel, makes an excellent Lincoln's Sparrow finder, and can be depended upon to flush the birds to more exposed perches where an unobstructed view may be obtained.

When really well seen this sparrow is unmistakable. The squarish head, delicate bill, and fine markings are totally different from those of most other sparrows.

The Lincoln's Sparrow is usually noticed in mid-May on the days of the big warbler waves but is more likely to occur over a greater space of time during the fall migration, which covers the latter half of September and the first part of October.

Spring observations range between May 3 (1937 - Earl Poole) and May 24 (1950 - Maurice Broun at Hawk Mountain).

Specimens in the Reading Public Museum collection were taken in the museum park by Sam Wishnieski and Earl Poole May 13, 1932, and in Angelica by Wishnieski on May 14, 1933. Levi Mengel took a specimen in Albany Township April 17, 1886.

Kerry Grim found five Lincoln's Sparrows May 18, 1996, at State Game Lands 110 near Shartlesville.

Fall records run between September 4 (1954 - E.P.; 1989 - Anna Kendall at Leesport; Rudy Keller and Harold and Joan Silagy at the Route 183 Hawk Watch) and October 24 (1939 - E.P.), with a late date of November 14 (1993 - Matt Spence at Lake Ontelaunee). Fall records at Hawk Mountain range from September 9 (1951) to October 9 (1979).

The Lincoln's Sparrow will occasionally sing its wren-like song on migration. Kerry Grim has heard it sung softly, but the listener must be close to the bird to hear it. Matt Spence and Bart Smith heard one singing at Blue Marsh September 27, 1992.

The Lincoln's Sparrow has been recorded once on the Hamburg Christmas Bird Count, a single bird January 2, 1977 (Kenneth and Dorothy Grim). One appeared on the Bernville Christmas Bird Count January 1, 1992. There are no Reading Christmas Bird Count records.

There is one midwinter sighting. Robert Cook saw a Lincoln's Sparrow that was singing near Birdsboro February 6, 1948.

It was listed by John Hofmann in 1890.

SWAMP SPARROW *Melospiza georgiana*
Fairly common migrant and winter visitor

The Swamp Sparrow is a regular and fairly common spring and fall migrant in marshy areas. During the height of the migrations, individuals are often found in places that are by no means typical, such as along fence rows and in brushy hillsides at some distance from water.

This bird has been found in summer under conditions that suggest nesting in swamps and marshes of various sizes.

A local breeding colony was established in a marsh along the extreme southeastern boundary of the county near Elverson. Probably 12 or 15 pairs bred there each season from 1938 to 1941,

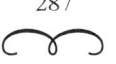

although Earl Poole knew of no nests or eggs being found. During the *Atlas of Breeding Birds in Pennsylvania* survey from 1983 to 1989, the Swamp Sparrrow was confirmed nesting near the same area and in northwestern Berks (Brauning, 1992:391).

Levi Mengel collected five sets of eggs between May 24 (1890) and June 21 (1884) along the Tulpehocken Creek, Blue Marsh, Caernarvon Township, and near Kutztown. Clutch sizes of the collected sets range from three to six eggs.

While not nearly as common as the Song Sparrow in winter, the Swamp Sparrow winters in varying numbers in suitable habitat. There are comparatively few definite records after early January, although Earl Poole found it present along strong, spring-fed streams near Peters Creek and Moselem throughout January and February during 13 of the 42 years which he covered the territory. He believed it doubtlessly would have been found present during other years if the marshes had been thoroughly combed.

The Swamp Sparrow has been recorded on the Reading Christmas Bird Count 53 of 86 years, 10 of the last 10, with a maximum of 21 on December 20, 1992. The peaks on the Hamburg Christmas Bird Count are 23 on December 29, 1991, and 22 on December 27, 1992. The high on the Bernville count is 31 on January 2, 1991.

Because of their widespread distribution in the state during both summer and winter, together with the nature of their haunts and shy and secretive habits, migrant Swamp Sparrows often are difficult to distinguish from wintering birds.

The spring migration usually begins in late March, reaches its peak in April, and often continues well into May.

When not known to have been present during the winter, the Swamp Sparrow has appeared in Berks as early as March 7 (1954 - E.P.) while the latest date on which it has been noticed locally, other than in probable nesting sites, is May 26 (1951 - E.P.).

Most Hawk Mountain records are in late April and May, but Maurice Broun banded one April 6, 1962. Fall records there are of single birds September 27, 1990; October 16, 1974; and October 18, 1950.

Both old and young appear to wander immediately after the conclusion of the breeding season. In 1935 the Swamp Sparrow appeared at Lake Ontelaunee on August 11 (E.P.).

WHITE-THROATED SPARROW *Zonotrichia albicollis*

Very common migrant and winter visitor

A very common migrant and regular but local winter visitor, the White-throated Sparrow has occurred in midsummer.

Ralph W. Berkey of Bally reported a nest observed near Landis Store May 17, 1938. Earl Poole heard and saw a singing male along the foot of the Blue Mountain east of Hamburg on June 23 and July 4, 1922. As this bird was in the same spot on both occasions, it is possible that it had a mate and nest nearby. Alex Nagy found a juvenal at Eckville in mid-July 1951.

Matt Spence heard one singing at Lake Ontelaunee on June 29, 1975.

Kerry Grim found a pair of White-throated Sparrows present at Rattling Run on the Berks County line as late as May 30, 1994. A pair was at the same location on June 18, 1995. The birds were very secretive and never sang. Grim was able to find them by their "teest" call, which was not loud and heard at close range. They foraged in dense shrubs and acted rather shyly.

The White-throated Sparrow invariably provides one of the conspicuous features of the spring and fall migrations. On favorable days it is likely to appear in towns, cemeteries, and backyards. Its sweet, tremulous song may be heard throughout late April and early May and again in late September and October.

In Berks, where this sparrow winters, it is often impossible to distinguish the migrants, but

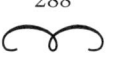

there is usually an increase in the numbers present some time after the first week of April. It remains common until mid-May.

Maurice Broun reported a large spring flight of White-throated Sparrows at Hawk Mountain in 1953, finding over 250 on May 3 and over 500 the next day.

Earl Poole noted its departure from May 7 (1925) to May 26 (1935).

The early fall arrival date from Hawk Mountain is September 3 (1949 - Maurice Broun, three juvenals), but it is usually common by the end of September.

The White-throated Sparrow winters regularly and often in numbers in sheltered locations over the lowland areas. It has appeared on the Reading Christmas Bird Count 78 of 86 years, 10 of the last 10, with a maximum of 1,550 on December 20, 1992. The peak for the Hamburg Christmas Bird Count is 1,695 on December 27, 1992. The high for the Bernville count is 1,339 on January 3, 1993.

As these Christmas count records show, the White-throated Sparrow, along with several other sparrow species, was abundant throughout the winter of 1992-1993.

A Pennsylvania German name heard in Berks for the White-throated Sparrow is "Weisshelsiche Schpetzlicher" (Rupp, 1946:227).

WHITE-CROWNED SPARROW *Zonotrichia leucophrys*
Uncommon migrant and winter visitor

The striking White-crowned Sparrow is chiefly an uncommon migrant and winter visitor, previously regarded as rare and erratic.

Ordinarily, this sparrow does not reach Berks County until the second week in May along with the big waves of warblers, but there are April observations: April 25 (1954 - Earl Poole) and April 28 (1956 - Maurice Broun at Hawk Mountain). Levi Mengel took a specimen April 22, 1887, in Greenawald, Albany Township. An extremely early record which may represent a wintering individual is one seen at Hawk Mountain March 14, 1973.

During the spring of 1917, the White-crowned Sparrow appeared in unusual numbers on May 17 and 18, and Earl Poole found the Reading City Park and nearby lawns "alive" with these birds, several of which he collected.

As a rule the White-crowned Sparrow passes through Berks quickly in the spring, but during exceptional years may linger for a week or two. The late date is May 30 (1994 - Kerry Grim at State Game Lands 110 in Shartlesville).

In the fall, it appears in what seems to be family groups with birds in the immature plumage predominating, the early date September 22 (1955 - M.B. at Schaumboch's).

The fall migration of White-crowned Sparrows reaches its height around the middle of October and often continues into the third week. Poole's latest observation in the Reading area is November 1 (1959).

The winter status of the White-crowned Sparrow has changed during the last 25 years. Previously, definite records after the first week in January were rare. David Berkheimer had two of these sparrows visiting his feeder at Limekiln from February 14 to March 23, 1958. Poole was able to personally verify the identification of these birds.

But now it has become regular in suitable habitat including hedgerows along corn fields, open fields, and in thickets of multiflora rose. White-crowns will appear in the same areas that support Tree Sparrows. Numbers can be found wintering in Marion Township, at Kaercher Creek Park in Windsor Township, Blue Marsh, and the Five Locks area along the Schuylkill River.

A flock of at least 35 White-crowned Sparrows wintered at Eckville below Hawk Mountain during the winter of 1963 - 1964. By January 11, Maurice Broun had banded over 25 of these birds. This flock remained in the same area until March 6, while a few were still there on March 24.

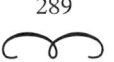

The White-crowned Sparrow first appeared on the Reading Christmas Bird Count in 1957 and has been recorded 36 years since, 10 of the last 10, with a maximum of 29 on December 17, 1995. The peak on the Hamburg Christmas Bird Count is 96 on December 29, 1996. The high for the Bernville count is 94 on December 30, 1995.

HARRIS' SPARROW *Zonotrichia querula*
Accidental

On February 10, 1967, an immature Harris' Sparrow visited a feeder maintained by Dr. David Berkheimer at Limekiln, six miles east of Reading. It remained until February 15. For several days around March 18, 1969, a mature Harris' Sparrow appeared at the same place (Earl Poole).

From April 29 to May 7, 1973, Anna Kendall found a Harris' Sparrow at her farm in Leesport. It was seen by many observers.

DARK-EYED JUNCO *Junco hyemalis*
Abundant winter visitor

The Dark-eyed Junco is an abundant winter visitor.

If the Junco nests anywhere in the Blue Mountain of northern Berks County, it has been overlooked, although there are a few summer records which may relate to casuals that have remained to the south of their normal range.

Samuel Guss found a pair at the Pinnacle in northern Berks County on June 27, 1936, and a lone male turned up in the Reading Public Museum park on July 11 and 12, 1957 (Earl Poole).

Betsy Lebow and Sue Guers found a singing male at the North Lookout at Hawk Mountain during June 1996. A singing male was sighted near the Visitor Center June 19, 1974. Alex Nagy recorded two Juncos at Hawk Mountain on July 23, 1966. Maurice Broun found one in the juvenal plumage along the side of the road below the orchard at Schaumboch's on August 2, 1951. It may have been an exceptionally early migrant, may have been hatched nearby, or may have been a wandering bird in post-nesting dispersal.

The Junco nests on the ground, sheltered by overhanging roots or grass, but in some situations the nest is hidden in the roots of upturned trees or in crevices of large tree trunks overhanging streams.

The first Junco usually appears in mid-to-late September, but sometimes much later. Earl Poole recorded the first fall arrivals as early as September 3 (1960 - at Hawk Mountain) or as late as October 27 (1956). T. V. Armentano, Robert Compton, and Donald Heintzelman found a group of four, one or two of which were young of the year, on The Pinnacle August 26, 1962. Anna Kendall's earliest fall record at Leesport is August 30 (1984).

The Junco, along with the Tree Sparrow and the Common Crow, has appeared on every Reading Christmas Bird Count with a maximum of 2,429 on December 22, 1985. The peak for the Hamburg Christmas Bird Count is 4,891 on December 30, 1990. The high for the Bernville count is 1,966 on January 4, 1987.

During January 1954, Broun recorded a high of over 80 Juncos wintering at his feeders at Schaumboch's. Many fed on donuts consistently.

In 1962, Broun received banding returns he considered extraordinary on two Juncos. An adult male he banded at Schaumboch's November 8, 1954, was recovered March 23, 1962, a bird at least 9 years old. An adult female banded November 12, 1955, was recovered February 20, 1962, reaching the age of at least 7-and-a-half years.

With the arrival of warm weather and the disappearance of the winter's accumulation of snow, the wintering Juncos seek the cooler northward-facing slopes and the shade of the evergreens as they start to drift northward.

During the first warm days in March males begin to sing. Poole recorded the last Juncos as early as April 6 (1919, 1941) and as late as May 8 (1920, 1932) in the Reading area. Maurice Broun's latest spring date at Hawk Mountain is May 15 (1952).

The Pennsylvania Germans refer to the Junco as "der Schneevoggel," or "snowbird." The appearance of this bird in the fall presages the coming of the winter's snows. This bird belongs to the "Schpotyaahrsveggel" and "Winterveggel" groups (Rupp, 1946:225).

Oregon Junco *Junco hyemalis oreganus*
Casual

The Oregon Junco, a subspecies of the Dark-eyed Junco, is distinguished by its dark hood, brown back, and pink sides.

Earl Poole identified an Oregon Junco in Pricetown on January 10, 1968. This is the first record for this subspecies in Berks County. Rudy Keller noted one, probably a female, at a feeder in District Township after a storm March 14, 1972. Matt Spence, Bart Smith, and Warren Faust found one at Lake Ontelaunee during the Reading Christmas Bird Count December 19, 1982.

There are two records at Hawk Mountain, both during 1995. On October 5, Arlene Koch found an Oregon Junco along the trail to the North Lookout. Laurie Goodrich identified one December 15 at the North Lookout.

It has appeared twice on the Hamburg Christmas Bird Count. One was recorded December 26, 1971, and Arlene Koch and Steve Smith found an Oregon Junco near Krumsville December 31, 1995.

LAPLAND LONGSPUR *Calcarius lapponicus*
Rare winter visitor

The Lapland Longspur is a rare, irregular winter visitor and migrant in spring and fall. It is exceedingly rare or undetected, possibly in some cases because the flocks of Horned Larks with which it associates are not carefully scrutinized. Older statements that it occurs only during severe winters or blizzard conditions do not hold today.

Earl Poole recorded the first Berks County bird near Fleetwood April 6, 1930. Most records are from the Great Valley to the north of Reading, although Arthur Sigman reported a Lapland Longspur near Morgantown December 20, 1942. This longspur has been recorded as early as October 29 (1938 - Maurice Broun) and as late as April 6 (1930 - Earl Poole).

Not more than five are usually seen at a time, and it is always associated with large flocks of Horned Larks and Snow Buntings. Linda Freedman, however, found eight Lapland Longspurs along Grim Road in Maxatawny Township on two occasions during the winter and spring of 1994, January 1 and March 27. On April 1, 1990, Matt Wlasniewski found two, one in breeding plumage, near the Fleetwood-Lyons Road.

The Lapland Longspur has appeared on the Reading Christmas Bird Count seven of 86 years, none of the last 10, with a maximum of 10 on December 21, 1980. It has been recorded during five years of the Hamburg Christmas Bird Count with a peak of four on January 1, 1968. A high of two was recorded on the Bernville count December 30, 1995.

SNOW BUNTING *Plectrophenax nivalis*
Uncommon and irregular winter visitor

An uncommon and irregular winter visitor, the Snow Bunting has appeared in Berks County in numbers ranging from single birds to the thousands.

The largest Snow Bunting invasion occurred in 1978. On February 6, Lyle Layser found a flock of several thousand Snow Buntings in a six-acre sorghum field along Hawk Mountain Road. Maurice Broun writes in the *Reading Eagle* of March 12:

"Arriving on the scene, we could hardly believe our eyes. We were greeted by a blizzard of birds. Snowbirds filled the sky; they perched briefly in bunches in small trees; they festooned the utility wires; they swirled back and forth and around and about - a dizzying overwhelming spectacle. Swirling masses of birds rushed past and overhead, the wind in their myriad wings, in a chorus of chirps and sweet musical twitterings....

"These great avian spectacles apparently began in late January or early February. A steady buildup took place and we probably saw the peak numbers in late February. The snowbirds begin drifting toward their boreal homelands during March."

Broun conservatively estimated that the flock of Snow Buntings numbered over 3,000 birds (Broun, 1979b:34-35).

Bob Cook recorded over 1,000 Snow Buntings near Fleetwood February 8, 1976.

On February 4, 1978, Joan Silagy saw 200 Snow Buntings near Fleetwood, and Catherine Elwell and Richard Sharadin counted over 150 near Moselem on February 5.

The Snow Bunting has also been observed on the bare rocks at the North Lookout at Hawk Mountain and flying over the Route 183 hawk watch. Broun comments: "From time to time through the years I have seen lone Snow Buntings flitting from rock to rock and seemingly quite at home on the lookout" (Broun, 1949a:204-205). Observations at that point range from October 23 (1967 - Maurice Broun, Alex Nagy) to December 8 (1990 - Jeanne Tinsman, eight birds).

Joan Silagy and Anne MacClay found one Snow Bunting November 24, 1990, at the pond near the Route 183 hawk watch.

In the broad Great Valley north of Reading, Earl Poole found it to be unaccountably scarce, although Horned Larks and Lapland Longspurs are fairly regular in the area. But Elwell saw 102 on January 22, 1984, along Kohler Road between Klinesville and Route 737 in Greenwich Township. Bernie and Pauline Morris found 50 along Grim Road in Maxatawny Township March 20, 1994.

The Snow Bunting has been seen from time to time along a bare, windswept part of the shore of Lake Ontelaunee between October 20 (1951 - J. Cadbury, Arnett, and Carson) and March 17 (1960 - Earl Poole). By the latter date, the males were in their striking black and white breeding plumage. Silagy has found the Snow Bunting along the beach of Blue Marsh Lake, counting 13 on November 29, 1992.

In 1949 Arthur Sigman found a lone Snow Bunting at Morgantown as early as October 11. His latest date there is February 25 (1935).

The latest date for the Snow Bunting in Berks County is March 21 (1993 - Matt Spence, three near the Fleetwood-Lyons Road).

The Snow Bunting has appeared on the Reading Christmas Bird Count nine of 86 years, once in the last 10, with a maximum of 31 on December 21, 1980. The peak for the Hamburg Christmas Bird Count is 246 on January 1, 1970. The high for the Bernville count is 153 on January 1, 1990.

Ten specimens in the Reading Public Museum collection taken by Levi Mengel on Mount Penn, Neversink Mountain, and Fritz's Island range from November 13 (1890) to February 8 (1887).

John F. Hofmann listed it as occurring locally in 1890.

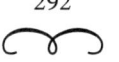

BOBOLINK *Dolichonyx oryzivorus*
Fairly common migrant; rare local nester

A fairly common migrant, the Bobolink can be found nesting locally in Berks County grass and alfalfa fields.

During the mid-to-late-1980s, Kerry Grim found the Bobolink nesting in fields near Hawk Mountain, and through the 1990s, there were summer birds regularly in the valley between Eckville and Wanamaker. Rudy Keller found females feeding young in early July 1996 in an uncut hay field along Mountain Road near Eckville. Recently, the Bobolink has been found breeding along Monument Road east of Hamburg.

In parts of Berks County such as Douglassville, Fleetwood, Walnuttown, and Shartlesville, Earl Poole found the Bobolink regular but very local, occurring in the valleys where broad meadows and upland fields of tall grass exist. Poole found at Lake Ontelaunee a colony that was apparently well established in 1929 and for several years after, although there are no recent records for it there. The last record at Lake Ontelaunee is May 14, 1994 (Matt Spence).

A colony of Bobolinks and Eastern Meadowlarks discovered in May 1988 on Douglass Drive near Boyertown and visited intermittently through the years was still active in 1995, according to Keller. The birds nested in a timothy-orchard grass field that was left uncut until early fall.

The nesting population of Bobolinks in Berks is limited by modern farming practices. Early cutting of fields tends to destroy the nests.

Wintering in central South America, the Bobolink is one of the species which generally arrive en masse in spring, usually during the first week of May, the early arrival dates April 26 (1992 - Harold and Joan Silagy, ten near Robesonia) and May 1 (1932 - Earl Poole). The recent high count during the spring migration is 100 on May 20, 1979, in Tilden Township (Kerry Grim, Kenneth and Dorothy Grim).

After the young leave the nest in late July or early August, the Bobolink, now mostly in the less familiar "reedbird" plumage, wanders over the countryside, visiting weedy fields and marshes. Maurice Broun counted 80 at Hawk Mountain September 2, 1948.

The main migratory movement continues through September and is usually over by the end of that month, but small flocks often remain into October. The late date is October 4 (1931 - E.P.).

The Pennsylvania Germans call the Bobolink "der Riedvoggel," or reedbird, based on the English name for the bird in its fall and winter plumage (Rupp, 1946:214-215).

RED-WINGED BLACKBIRD *Agelaius phoeniceus*
Very common migrant and nester

A very common migrant and summer resident, the Red-winged Blackbird occurs in nearly every small swamp or marsh and even in upland meadows. In spring and fall the migrating flocks pass over the county at random.

In the Lake Ontelaunee area, small bands of Red-winged Blackbirds have remained up to the last week in December. In 1940, a small band remained until January 7, and in 1938, another flock of 30 remained until January 8, and one was found in the same region until February 3 (Earl Poole).

In spring the Red-winged Blackbird is very erratic in its time of arrival. The first migrants have appeared as early as February 2 (1963 - Maurice Broun at Hawk Mountain) and as late as March 28 (1920 - E.P.).

Thirty-two sets of eggs in the Reading Public Museum collection were taken in the county from May 8 (1884) to June 14 (1890). Clutch sizes in these sets range from three to six eggs.

As soon as the first broods of young leave the nest, they begin to flock, and by the latter part of June, the family groups have combined into flocks of considerable size which continue to

grow as they forage over the marshes and grain fields.

In Berks County, the local population seems to dwindle toward the end of August. Numbers increase in October, when migrant flocks pass through the region and continue to straggle past at irregular intervals through November, with a few bands sometimes appearing well into December.

On November 8, 1948, Maurice Broun counted 11,100 Red-winged Blackbirds in 15 flocks passing over Hawk Mountain. Recent peak counts include 2,343 on November 10, 1995, and 1,300 on November 2, 1996, although flocks have not been counted regularly there.

The Red-winged Blackbird has appeared on the Reading Christmas Bird Count 40 of 86 years, seven of the last 10, with a maximum of 640 on December 16, 1979. A peak of 148 was counted on the Hamburg Christmas Bird Count December 30, 1979. A high of 50 was found on the Bernville count December 30, 1995.

"Der Schtaar" is a general Pennsylvania German name for all the blackbirds, including the Red-winged. Another name heard in Berks County is "der rotfliggelich Schtaar" (Rupp, 1946:216).

EASTERN MEADOWLARK *Sturnella magna*

Locally uncommon nester

The Eastern Meadowlark is a locally uncommon summer resident in farming country in northern Berks County, occurring rarely in winter in Marion Township, the Fleetwood-Kutztown area, and the Oley Valley. Meadowlark populations are affected by farming practices, its nests destroyed by the early cutting of hay. Habitat changes with the loss of farm land have also diminished its numbers.

It is no longer as commonly found as when Earl Poole last wrote about the bird in the mid-1960s. He notes that there was a local shift in the Meadowlark population from the higher land to the valleys during late February or early March. For this reason it was often difficult to distinguish bona fide spring arrivals from the birds that have been close at hand all winter, but suddenly make their presence known during the first sunny days of late winter by bursting into song.

Poole writes in 1964 that there is usually a noticeable increase in the Meadowlark population in Berks County somewhere between February 24 and March 15, with the average bulk spring appearance about March 9.

The Meadowlark's nest is notoriously hard to find, as it is usually sunk in the ground and carefully concealed from above. Levi Mengel collected complete sets of eggs in Berks County from May 15 (1884) to June 24 (1894). Clutch sizes in these sets range from four to six eggs.

The Eastern Meadowlark has been recorded during the fall migration at Hawk Mountain, the early date October 4 (1967, 1991) and the late date November 1 (1947 - Maurice Broun). The high count is 18 on October 30, 1953 (M.B.).

It has appeared on the Reading Christmas Bird Count 52 of 86 years, twice in the last 10, with a maximum of 183 on December 27, 1970. The decline of the Eastern Meadowlark in Berks County is reflected in the Reading count statistics. From 1967 to 1981, one to 183 birds with a total of 496 were seen 14 of those 15 years. From 1982 to 1996, one to 15 birds with a total of 24 were seen during three of those 15 years.

The peak for the Hamburg Christmas Bird Count is 136 on January 1, 1971. On the Bernville count, a high of 74 was recorded January 3, 1993.

The Pennsylvania German name for the Meadowlark is "die Laerrich" (Rupp, 1946:215).

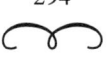

WESTERN MEADOWLARK *Sturnella neglecta*
Accidental

Matt Spence found a Western Meadowlark singing in Albany Township June 11, 1972. He was previously familiar with the bird in the West.

YELLOW-HEADED BLACKBIRD *Xanthocephalus xanthocephalus*
Accidental western vagrant

A female Yellow-headed Blackbird flew over Hawk Mountain on November 6, 1962, along with over 50 Red-winged Blackbirds for the first Berks County record this century. The bird flew low within 50 feet (Meritt, 1964:38-39).

Maurice Broun saw two fly low over the North Lookout toward the northwest on November 19, 1965.

Allen Metz found a Yellow-headed Blackbird November 18, 1981, at Hawk Mountain near Drehersville, Schuylkill County, following an eight-inch snowstorm (*fide* Jim Brett).

A female visited a feeder maintained by Jack and Ellen Weirich in Hamburg April 26, 1975 (Kenneth and Dorothy Grim).

One female remained at a feeder near Kirbyville from April 29 to May 5, 1984 (*fide* Matt Spence).

Robert Cook observed two male Yellow-headed Blackbirds in Morgantown from March 28 to April 12, 1988. They were photographed by Barbara Haas.

John F. Hofmann listed the Yellow-headed Blackbird in 1890.

RUSTY BLACKBIRD *Euphagus carolinus*
Fairly common spring migrant; irregular in fall

A fairly common migrant at marshes and along streams in spring, the Rusty Blackbird is irregular in fall and an occasional winter visitor.

Earl Poole found the Rusty Blackbird present during five winters: a pair at Carsonia from January 23 to February 1, 1921; one at Charming Forge on February 19, 1929; four at Lake Ontelaunee on December 27, 1936, and January 1, 1937; and 14 at Moselem on January 13, 1957. More recently, Anna Kendall recorded one at her Leesport feeder from January 1 to 30, 1992, and Matt Spence found nine Rusty Blackbirds February 2, 1995, at the Earl L. Poole Preserve in Alsace Township.

The spring migration of the Rusty Blackbird is protracted and irregular. The first migrants may not appear until well into April. Usually, however, the bulk movement takes place during the latter part of March and is over by the third week in April, with a few lingering in May. Kerry Grim found a spring high count of 50 at Hamburg on April 11, 1982.

The early spring date is March 9 (1939 - Maurice Broun) and the late spring record is May 21 (1921 - Earl Poole).

Since the Rusty Blackbird nests well to the north of Berks County, there are no summer records. It reappears late in September with the greater majority of the birds passing through in October. The early fall date is September 16 (1991 - 56 birds at Hawk Mountain).

Poole considered the Rusty Blackbird to be quite irregular in fall, rather common some years and then apparently absent for several years running.

Matt Spence, Matt Wlasniewski, and Ken Lebo recorded 300 Rusty Blackbirds at Peters Creek October 29 and 30, 1995. The count peaked at 590 on November 3 (Matt Spence).

At Hawk Mountain, the late date is November 23 (1946 - M.B.) with high counts of 150 on November 6, 1962 (M.B.), and October 26, 1993.

The fall migration period apparently is of much shorter duration than that of spring. Late migrants cannot always be distinguished from potential wintering birds.

The Rusty Blackbird has appeared on the Reading Christmas Bird Count 17 of 86 years, once in the last 10, with a maximum of 152 on December 15, 1974. The peak on the Hamburg Christmas Bird Count is 45 on December 29, 1984. The high for the Bernville count is 27 on January 1, 1989.

BREWER'S BLACKBIRD *Euphagus cyanocephalus*

Rare migrant

The Brewer's Blackbird, a western species, undoubtedly occurs in the large mixed flocks of blackbirds that pass over Berks County each spring and fall. Given good light conditions and a close approach, it can be identified by anyone familiar with the characters that distinguish this bird from its relative, the Rusty Blackbird.

The Rusty Blackbird is found in wet areas while the Brewer's is found in fields, farms, and feed lots. The bird's glossy coloration helps to separate the Brewer's from the Rusty while its shorter tail and smaller overall size separate it from the Common Grackle.

Maurice Broun recorded two females for the first Berks County sighting of the Brewer's Blackbird on September 29, 1954, near Eckville. On the same day, Alex Nagy found a Dickcissel at the same spot.

On October 6, 1955, Broun, Nagy, and Conrad Roland saw a single male at Nagy's Pond in Eckville. On October 19, Walter Booth and Broun saw six among a mob of noisy crows at the North Lookout. The same evening, 20 Brewer's Blackbirds were seen at Nagy's Pond. On October 22, Broun recorded two males and one female at the North Lookout.

During the fall of 1956, Earl Poole had two satisfactory views of male Brewer's Blackbirds: one in a large flock of Red-winged and Rusty blackbirds, Cowbirds, and Grackles at Moselem on October 14 and one at Pikeville on October 28.

On March 16, 1958, Poole saw one under excellent light conditions at Green Hills Lake and several others in a large, mixed flock of Grackles and Red-winged Blackbirds in a newly plowed field near Leesport on April 7 of the same year.

Broun recorded a male flying past the North Lookout December 2, 1960.

More recently, Kerry Grim found one male Brewer's Blackbird April 23, 1985, along Lowland Road in Tilden Township.

There is one Bernville Christmas Bird Count record. Joan Silagy recorded a Brewer's Blackbird at a steer feeder near a barn in Marion Township in a flock of other blackbirds and Starlings on January 1, 1990.

COMMON GRACKLE *Quiscalus quiscula*

Abundant, but diminishing

An abundant migrant and summer resident, the Common Grackle also winters in variable numbers as hundreds, or even thousands, have been found roosting with various other species of "blackbirds" and Starlings throughout entire winters.

A fall roost in an evergreen plantation in District Township attracted thousands of Grackles during the late 1960s and early 1970s. The birds would be gone by the first hard freeze. On

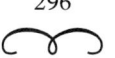

September 7, 1968, between 10,000 and 15,000 Grackles and 5,000 Robins roosted there (Rudy Keller).

During the Reading Christmas Bird Count December 21, 1975, over 23,000 Grackles occupied a roost on the Penn State Berks Campus near Broadcasting Road. The Common Grackle appeared on the Reading count 44 of 86 years, four of the last 10. From 1956 to 1987, the Grackle was recorded on every count. On the Hamburg Christmas Bird Count, the Common Grackle was consistently recorded every year until the early 1980s, then irregularly since. The peak for the Hamburg count is 4,000 on December 26, 1971. The high for the Bernville Count is 130 on January 4, 1997.

A roost existed in the pines on the Antietam watershed near Reading during the winters of 1936–1937 to 1940–1941. Approximately 500 Grackles occupied this roost with about 25,000 Starlings and a considerable number of Cowbirds and Red-winged Blackbirds. After the spring of 1941, this roost was abandoned.

During severe winters there is a partial withdrawal of Grackles, but a few return upon the slightest moderation of weather conditions, often toward the end of January.

Earl Poole in 1964 discussed the two forms of the Common Grackle which appear in Berks County: "The relationship and distribution of the two forms of Grackles found in Pennsylvania are not well understood, beyond the fact that the birds nesting to the west and north of the Allegheny divide are generally Bronzed Grackles (*Q. q. versicolor*), while those nesting to the south and east are of the race currently known as Stone's Grackles (*Q. q. stonei*)... Examples of *versicolor* have been taken during the breeding season in northern Berks. ...The assertion that wintering birds in this section are likely to be 'Bronzed Grackles' has never been proven. All those found at the Antietam wintering roost were 'Purple Grackles' (*Q. q. stonei*)."

On April 14, 1932, Poole pointed out a Bronzed Grackle on the Reading Public Museum grounds to Sam Wishnieski, who collected it for the museum. The American Ornithologists' Union *Check-list of North American Birds* (1983) treats them as one species because of their "random and essentially complete interbreeding."

The Common Grackle is a widespread nester throughout Berks County. Sets of eggs in the Reading Public Museum were taken between April 26 (1906) and June 16 (1893). The clutch sizes of the sets taken range from four to six eggs.

The single-day peak for migrating Grackles at Hawk Mountain is 3,240 on November 12, 1989 (John Bachman). Maurice Broun regarded the Grackle as an abundant migrant with Red-winged Blackbirds in huge flocks from the north in late October and early November.

As a summer resident, however, the Grackle was rather rare at Hawk Mountain until July 1, 1961. Broun writes: "Grackles, daily, almost any hour, almost anywhere at any level in the woods - most astonishing ornithological development on the mountain in recent years. Prior to 1958 we never saw Grackles except as migrants in spring and summer. HORDES, early July."

During the emergence of the 17-year cicada (*Magicicada septendecim*) in 1962 from June 26 to early July, Broun found over 2,000 Grackles all through the woods feeding on the cicadas. During the same time period in 1996 after another emergence of the 17-year cicada, hundreds of Grackles roamed the forest daily feeding on these insects at Hawk Mountain.

Several names for the Common Grackle appear among the Pennsylvania Germans. The general name, "die Schtaare," is used in the plural because these birds, like the Red-winged Blackbirds and Starlings, travel in great flocks. "Die schwatze Schtaare" is a name that distinguishes it from the Red-winged Blackbird, and "die grosse Schtaare" distinguishes it from the smaller Starling. "Die grosse schwatze Schtaare" is the ultimate name for this large bird. The name "die langfliggeliche Schtaare" means long-winged blackbird. The Pennsylvania Germans in Berks County also call this bird "die Welschkarn Schtaare" because it pulls up the corn in the fields and damages the ripening ears (Rupp, 1946:218).

BROWN-HEADED COWBIRD *Molothrus ater*
Common migrant and breeder

The Brown-headed Cowbird is common to abundant as a migrant and is becoming increasingly common as a breeding species. It winters in variable numbers.

The Cowbird is doubtless an alarmingly important factor in reducing the population of many of the small, insectivorous birds, since it appears to be increasing in numbers from year to year. Most of the flycatchers, vireos, warblers, and finches are victimized. As the population of Cowbirds increases in proportion to the species imposed upon, the problem becomes increasingly serious.

According to recent research conducted in northern Berks County, Cowbird nest parasitism on Wood Thrush nests range from 13 percent in small woodland patches to 5 percent in contiguous forests (Hoover, 1992b).

The Cowbird has been found wintering in roosts of considerable size. During the winters of 1936-1937 to 1938-1939, at least 1,000 roosted with Starlings and Grackles in the pines at Antietam a few miles east of Reading, and larger flocks have been reported roosting during subsequent years near Fleetwood.

It is also found in winter around steer feed lots and open dairy barns.

Earl Poole knew this bird to winter seven years out of 40, and when not wintering it appears anywhere from January 29 (1949) to March 29 (1931), generally during the third week of March. Poole's departure dates for Cowbirds not wintering are from September 23 (1927) to November 20 (1949), averaging the third week in October.

The Cowbird has appeared on the Reading Christmas Bird Count 44 of 86 years, eight of the last 10, with a peak of 15,500 at Penn State Berks Campus December 19, 1976. The peak for the Hamburg Christmas Bird Count is 5,200 on December 26, 1971. The high for the Bernville count is 340 on January 1, 1992.

Maurice Broun banded an adult male Cowbird on May 9, 1958. The bird was trapped on May 9, 1959, near Lawrenceville, on the Pennsylvania - New York border, 110 air-miles to the northwest, and released. On May 8, 1964, Broun retrapped the bird at Hawk Mountain, six years after he banded it (Broun, 1965:9-10).

To test its homing abilities, Broun trapped and banded an adult male Cowbird and sent it to Philadelphia with a visiting group of Boy Scouts. The scouts left at 5 p.m. April 23, 1961, and released it in Philadelphia, assuming they kept their oath. Broun retrapped the bird at 11:10 a.m. the next morning. It apparently traveled the 63 air-miles back to Hawk Mountain overnight.

Flocks of Cowbirds are observed flying past Hawk Mountain during the fall, but the counters do not record them regularly. Some high counts there include 193 on November 4, 1996, and 112 on October 15, 1995.

Eggs have been found locally in nests collected of the following species during the late nineteenth century: Field Sparrow (21), Chipping Sparrow (16), Song Sparrow (10), Indigo

Bunting (eight), Eastern Phoebe (five), Cliff Swallow (four), Vesper Sparrow (four), Wood Pewee, Goldfinch, Orchard Oriole, and Barn Swallow (two each). These sets are in the Levi Mengel collection at the Reading Public Museum.

The Pennsylvania Germans name the Cowbird "der Kihschtaar" because it follows the cattle in the pasture to feed on insects (Rupp, 1946:218).

ORCHARD ORIOLE *Icterus spurius*

Locally fairly common

A fairly common migrant and local summer resident, the Orchard Oriole appears to be increasing in Berks County. Earl Poole regarded it as uncommon and local in 1964, a condition he attributed to the increased use of highly toxic sprays.

Not a deep woods bird, the Orchard Oriole nests in the mature orchards and among shade trees and fence rows. This splendid songster is generally restricted to the neighborhood of villages and rural districts during the breeding season, but during migration may appear almost anywhere.

It is a bird more often heard before seen, and a good percentage of the singing males are second-year birds. The Orchard Oriole nests commonly at Blue Marsh, the Red Bridge at the Tulpehocken Creek, Maiden Creek Station at Lake Ontelaunee, and along the Maiden and Sacony creeks.

Unfortunately its stay here is brief and is limited to about three months of the year, the balance being spent in its winter quarters from Mexico to northern South America.

The Orchard Oriole usually reaches Berks during the first week in May. Arrival dates are from April 27 (1995 - Ken Lebo, two at Joanna) to May 19 (1945 - Earl Poole). Six records from Hawk Mountain are from May 1 (1954 - Maurice Broun) to May 17 (1959 - M.B.).

Eight sets of eggs in the Reading Public Museum collection have been found between May 21 (1889) and June 8 (1890). The clutch size of the collected sets is four eggs. One nest contains one Cowbird's egg while another contains two.

On August 3, 1995, Jason Horn saw a female Orchard Oriole feeding two young and the young of a Cowbird at Water Street near Lake Ontelaunee.

Rudy Keller reported the unusual occurrence of a second-year male feeding recently fledged young in Albany Township July 7, 1996.

The Orchard Oriole becomes remarkably shy and secretive at the conclusion of its song period in mid-July and is one of the earliest departing migrants, being decidedly rare even in August. Departure dates in Berks County are from August 1 (1926) to August 29 (1922).

The Pennsylvania German name for the Orchard Oriole is "die schwarz Goldamschel," based on the male's darker plumage which shows much black and chestnut as compared with the orange, yellow, and black plumage of the Baltimore Oriole (Rupp, 1946:217).

BALTIMORE ORIOLE *Icterus galbula*

Common breeder

Brilliant and assertive in manner and voice, the Baltimore Oriole is a common and well-known summer resident in suburban areas and farming regions. It seems most at home among sycamores, silver maples, weeping willows, and other shade trees with pendant branches from which it suspends its purse-like nest.

It seldom reaches Berks County before May or during the last few days in April, and usually leaves in August. During the migrations, the Baltimore Oriole may appear almost anywhere.

The early spring arrival date is April 19 (1987 - Catherine Elwell at State Game Lands 182 in Greenwich Township) with the average arrival occurring during the first week of May.

Eight sets of eggs in the Levi Mengel collection were taken between May 28 (1888) and June 7 (1887). The clutch sizes of these sets range from three to five eggs. One nest contains a Cowbird's egg.

Maurice Broun at Hawk Mountain noted that over 30 Baltimore Orioles in various plumages devoured donuts at his feeders throughout the day on May 8, 1965. Numbers from six to 28 came to the feeders every day that year between June 25 to July 30, diminishing in August.

The Baltimore Oriole begins to drift southward by the middle of August, and there are days, usually around the third week of that month, when it is much in evidence. By the end of August the majority has gone, leaving a few stragglers into the first week in September or later.

In recent years there have been a few exceptionally early and late observations, some of the latter extending into January. As a matter of fact, February and March are the only months for which there are no records. Most of the winter occurrences have been in apple orchards, in which the Orioles subsist on the frozen fruits, but occasional birds have learned to come to the feeders that are provided by bird-conscious people.

G. Henry Mengel reported an individual near Mohnton late in December 1916. The bird was feeding on the frozen apples that remained on the trees. Baltimore Orioles remained in Birdsboro December 29, 1954, through January 16, 1955 (Arthur Sigman, Earl Poole) and at Geigertown January 16, 1955 (many observers, E.P.). Doris and Gerald Steffy reported a Baltimore Oriole at their feeder in Pennside January 5, 1972.

The Baltimore Oriole has appeared on the Reading Christmas Bird Count 10 of 86 years, all single birds. It was last recorded December 20, 1987. One was found on the Hamburg Christmas Bird Count December 30, 1990.

From observations in Berks County, Earl Poole believed that the Baltimore Oriole, like many other species, passes through definite fluctuations in abundance. It was comparatively common in Berks from 1916 to 1925. Then there was a period of comparative scarcity until 1935, followed by a few years of increasing numbers which lasted until 1940. Then came another period of local scarcity until 1955, since which time it has again appeared in slightly greater numbers.

"Die Goldamschel" is a popular Pennsylvania German name for the Baltimore Oriole based on the German "Goldamsel," the name for the European "golden Oriole" (Rupp, 1946:217).

BULLOCK'S ORIOLE *Icterus bullockii*

Accidental

One Bullock's Oriole, a western bird formerly a subspecies of the Baltimore Oriole but now considered a distinct species, frequented the feeder of Norman and Nancy Reifsnyder near Mount Pleasant in Bern Township from January 8 to 18, 1994. The bird was also seen by Harold and Joan Silagy, and a photograph was taken.

The bird fed on suet and seeds mixed with peanut butter.

PINE GROSBEAK *Pinicola enucleator*
Rare and irregular winter visitor

The irregular visits of the Pine Grosbeak appear to be governed by the failure of the food supply in its usual winter habitat rather than by any seasonal urge to migrate. When in Berks County, it feeds on a wide variety of fruits, seeds, and buds. It seems particularly fond of the berries of the Japanese honeysuckle and mountain ash, but also eats sumac and frozen apples; the seeds of larch, hemlock, and various pines; and the buds of hickory and maple.

During some winters the Pine Grosbeak does not appear until midwinter and remains for a short period of time, while in other seasons it may appear in October and remain until March.

Extensive incursions of the Pine Grosbeak have occurred throughout much of eastern Pennsylvania during the winters of 1929-1930, 1951-1952, 1954-1955, 1957-1958, 1961-1962, and 1968-1969.

The earliest arrival date this century is one seen and heard at Hawk Mountain from October 26 to 29, 1957 (Earl Poole, many observers). It is rarely seen after February, but a surprisingly late date from Reading is May 1 (1960 - Joseph Malek, two birds).

Between November 6 and December 12, 1951, 194 Pine Grosbeaks were counted from the North Lookout at Hawk Mountain. Flights occurred from October 26 to December 12, 1957, with a high of 33 on November 10. Up to 25 were counted from November 7 until well into December 1961 (Maurice Broun).

The largest number seen at Hawk Mountain on a single day is 208 on November 21, 1968. The flight that fall built from nine birds on November 19 and 70 on November 20. Sightings continued through January 30, 1969.

Numbers of Pine Grosbeaks appeared elsewhere in the county during the winter of 1968-1969. From November 19, 1968, to February 20, 1969, Pine Grosbeaks inhabited evergreen plantations in District and Pike townships, reaching a high of 30 on November 26. The birds fed on spruce buds and white ash seeds (Rudy Keller). Harold Lebo had one bird at his feeder in Plowville January 8. At a pine plantation at Scott's Run Lake from January 12 to 19, Joan and Harold Silagy counted a total of 30 Pine Grosbeaks in two flocks.

After 1968, the number of sightings at Hawk Mountain and the number of birds seen have diminished. On December 8, 1985, Mark Blauer watched a female Pine Grosbeak clear a mountain ash of berries in one-and-a-half hours at the lookout. The most recent observation is of a flock of 25 birds Jim Brett sighted November 12, 1987, on a blustery day that brought a record 14 Golden Eagles past the North Lookout (Goodrich, 1988:33).

On February 5, 1978, Catherine Elwell found 31 Pine Grosbeaks two miles north of Kutztown.

Matt Spence counted 25 near the twin churches near Molltown December 31, 1961.

The Pine Grosbeak has appeared on the Reading Christmas Bird Count nine of 86 years, none in the last 10, with a maximum of 28 on January 1, 1978. There are four records on the Hamburg Christmas Bird Count, the peak of 88 on December 29, 1968.

On the southern slope of Mount Penn, just east of Reading, is the site of the Hessian Camp of the Revolutionary War period. For many years this tract supported a dense tangle of scrub pine, greenbrier, and Japanese honeysuckle. This spot was formerly the favorite resort of the Pine Grosbeak and the Red and White-winged crossbills whenever they appeared in the region. Earl Poole regarded this area as a typical winter habitat. This bird was there or at nearby Antietam gorge for varying periods in the winters of 1919-1920, 1921-1922, 1929-1930, 1936-1937, 1945-1946, 1951-1952, and 1961-1962.

Much of this area has been converted into a suburban development, and the bands of Pine Grosbeaks that frequented it in former years no longer do so. However, the area should still be checked for occasional visitors.

Levi Mengel secured specimens now in the Reading Public Museum collection in Bethel Township March 5, 1886; in Maidencreek Township December 19,1886; and at Yost's Island October 14, 1888.

Samuel Wishnieski collected a specimen at High's Woods south of Reading along the Schuylkill River near Poplar Neck on January 1, 1930.

PURPLE FINCH *Carpodacus purpureus*
Uncommon migrant and winter visitor

The comings and goings of the Purple Finch defy all efforts at generalization, but there has been a dramatic decline in numbers occurring in Berks County during the past 10 years.

Earl Poole found it to be a regular and common spring and fall migrant. Occasionally, about one year in 10, it was apparently absent or very rare for an entire season, as it was in 1920-1921, 1944-1945, 1947-1948, and 1956-1957.

Currently, the Purple Finch is an uncommon migrant and winter visitor. The status of this bird over the past 20 years is illustrated by the Reading Christmas Bird Count. From 1976 to 1985, there are 10 records of from 30 to 522 birds with a total of 1,331 reported in those 10 years. From 1986 to 1995, there are 10 records of from one to 24 birds with a total of 60 in those 10 years.

The Purple Finch has appeared on the Reading Christmas Bird Count 60 of 86 years, 10 of the last 10, with a maximum of 522 on December 19, 1982. The peak for the Hamburg Christmas Bird Count is 600 on January 2, 1983. The numbers are below 10 on the last eight years of the count against the average of over 20 previously. The high for the Bernville count is 19 on January 1, 1989.

In spring, Matt Spence found the Purple Finch to be regular in mid-May up to 1986, but since then he has no mid-May records. Catherine Elwell has recorded high counts of Purple Finches at her feeders near Huff's Church: 52 on April 18, 1991, and 45 on April 18, 1992.

The Purple Finch first appears in fall anywhere from August 23 (1929, 1957) to December 24 (1950), usually by the first week in October.

Recent single-day high counts at Hawk Mountain are 75 on October 15, 1983, and 53 on October 6, 1993. Birds have been recorded flying past the North Lookout between August 25 (1949 - Maurice Broun, one bird) and December 2 (1996).

During the spring of 1956, Maurice Broun experienced an unprecedented influx of Purple Finches at Schaumboch's, Hawk Mountain. On March 23, 30 appeared at his feeders. Then from two birds on April 10, the numbers increased to 300 on May 12. He banded 439 Purple Finches that spring. The next year during the spring of 1957, not one Purple Finch visited the feeders, but in September and October 1957, a season high count of over 980 was recorded at the North Lookout. A season low of 15 was recorded during the fall of 1992.

Departure dates in spring range from April 14 (1954) to May 31 (1924). At this season it usually is most common during the last week in April and up to the middle of May.

Levi Mengel collected a male in Albany Township March 5, 1886; a male near Reading April 29, 1890; and a female at Virginville May 21, 1889. These specimens are in the Reading Public Museum collection.

HOUSE FINCH *Carpodacus mexicanus*
Very common

This attractive finch, originally native to the far West, was introduced on Long Island in 1940. Pet store dealers released them when they discovered they were in violation of federal law for selling the finches as cage birds. The House Finch then established itself at a number of points in the vicinity of New York City (Bull, 1964:427-428).

By the winter of 1959-1960 these finches apparently had become generally distributed as winter visitors in the Philadelphia area.

By the following winter the House Finch had evidently increased and appeared at additional areas throughout the region. On November 5, 1961, two visited a feeder at Jacksonwald for the first Berks County record of this bird, and others appeared at other points around Reading (Earl Poole).

The first Hawk Mountain record is of a male House Finch that visited Maurice Broun's feeders at Schaumboch's January 16 to March 9, 1965.

In 1969 two pairs nested at Mifflin Park near Shillington, and one pair brought young off the nest on April 28. On April 10, 1970, Earl Poole was shown a nest which contained three eggs in the top of a yew in West Reading.

Poole writes in 1964: "It is to be hoped that this bright and attractive western songster will continue to increase and learn to compete with those unattractive and aggressive introductions, the European Starling and House Sparrow, that now fill the avian vacuum in and about our towns and cities."

In the following years, the House Finch populations increased until leveling off in the mid-1990s. During the winter of 1993-1994, an outbreak of an eye infection among House Finches that gathered at feeders diminished their numbers.

The House Finch has appeared on the Reading Christmas Bird Count 33 of 86 years, first recorded in 1964 and every year thereafter with a maximum of 1,908 on December 19, 1993. The peak for the Hamburg Christmas Bird Count is 2,524 on December 28, 1986. It first appeared on the Hamburg count in 1967. The high for the Bernville count is 1,609 on January 1, 1992.

RED CROSSBILL *Loxia curvirostra*
Rare and irregular winter visitor

A rare and irregular winter visitor, the Red Crossbill has occurred in Berks County as early as August and as late as June.

On August 3, 1969, Robert Cook and Matt Spence found a male and female Red Crossbill at the dam breast at Lake Ontelaunee. Alex Nagy and Bernard Theilan observed two immature males near the Common Room at Hawk Mountain in the hemlocks August 8, 1966. These are the earliest Berks records.

During the winter, the Red Crossbill usually travels in flocks of from three to 30 or 35, but occasionally during the major invasions of former years it was reported to have "fairly swarmed." During the invasion of 1960-1961, Nagy reported 140 Red Crossbills in three flocks at Hawk Mountain on March 20, 1961. On October 29, 1969, 115 were seen from the North Lookout. The total for that fall was 225.

The Red Crossbill feeds chiefly on the seeds of the hemlock and various species of pine and spruce, its bill being admirably specialized for their extraction. It also has been seen feeding on seeds of the ash and sunflower and the seeds, buds, and blossoms of apple trees. Earl Poole watched one eating the seeds of a great ragweed.

The Red Crossbill extended across practically the entire state in the winters of 1906-1907, 1922-1923, 1940-1941, 1952-1953, 1960-1961, and 1969-1970 with a number of lesser flights in

between. The last significant flight season at Hawk Mountain occurred during the fall of 1975 when 42 were recorded.

From February 13 to April 5, 1964, Matt Spence saw up to 17 Red Crossbills feeding in the red pines at Reading High School. Rudy Keller found 40 Red Crossbills feeding on the seeds of European larches in District Township November 10, 1972.

Most of the crossbills have retreated to the northern coniferous forests by the end of March. On rare occasions a few have been noticed well into April. But during the spring of 1970, the Red Crossbill extended its stay in Berks throughout the month of June. Keller recorded 10 in District Township for a short time in midmorning on May 22. Cook saw eight at Hay Creek on May 31. Keller found seven birds June 19 in the woods of District Township and heard one singing near his home June 20, the latest Berks record.

Prior to 1897 or 1898, crossbills were said to have been quite abundant in the Hessian Camp section of Mount Penn, and several local people made a lucrative business of trapping and selling them for cage birds. According to Albert Mittower and Harry Wickel, a male bird was captured and placed in a cage, which was so constructed that the decoy occupied a central compartment surrounded by a number of others accessible to the outside. These could be sprung by cords in the hands of the trapper. As many as 200 birds are said to have been captured in this manner in the space of a day or two (Poole, 1930).

Levi Mengel collected a Red Crossbill at Lenhartsville on April 16, 1886, that appears to be *L. c. pusilla*, the Newfoundland race. He collected another specimen November 19, 1886, at the Hessian Camp.

The Red Crossbill has occurred on the Reading Christmas Bird Count once, eight birds on December 21, 1969. There are two Hamburg Christmas Bird Count records: four during the invasion year on January 1, 1970, and three on January 2, 1977.

WHITE-WINGED CROSSBILL *Loxia leucoptera*
Very rare and irregular winter visitor

The White-winged Crossbill is a very rare and irregular winter visitor from the north. During some of the notable invasions, it was fairly common in favored areas for limited periods. At such times it often did not appear until mid-January or February and remained for a few weeks only.

The White-winged Crossbill has occurred in Berks County between August 15 and April 23. Alex Nagy recorded one immature male at Hawk Mountain August 15 and 16, 1977 (*American Birds*, 32(2):188). Matt Spence found one at Lake Ontelaunee April 23, 1972. Nagy observed four along Hawk Mountain Road April 22, 1966.

Extensive invasions of the White-winged Crossbill, sometimes associated with Red Crossbills, have been recorded in the winters of 1922-1923, 1963-1964, and in 1969-1970.

In addition to these more or less general invasions, there are many scattered records usually in January and February. There have been more reports of this bird since 1950 than during the first half century.

Usually this crossbill is seen in small groups of from two to six individuals, but during the more extensive invasions, flocks of up to a hundred or more have gathered where there was an abundance of food. During January and February 1923, when White-winged Crossbills occurred generally throughout the state, a flock of well over 100 spent the week from January 20 to 26 in a stand of hemlocks below Antietam Lake. On the latter date Earl Poole collected three birds out of this flock and found them much emaciated. These are now in the Reading Public Museum collection. Crossbills remained at Antietam until February 18.

During the fall of 1963 at Hawk Mountain, White-winged Crossbill numbers increased beginning October 17 when one was seen and when 20 were recorded on October 22 and 26. The peak flight occurred on November 24 when 200 flew past the North Lookout. The bird was seen almost daily through December in small flocks.

In the winter of 1969-1970 at Hawk Mountain, the White-winged Crossbill was recorded from September 18, 1969, to February 26, 1970, with a peak flight of over 50 at the North Lookout on October 28.

Kerry Grim counted 40 White-winged Crossbills at the entrance to Hawk Mountain November 14, 1981, and Jim Brett recorded 28 at the North Lookout November 12, 1981.

The White-winged Crossbill has appeared on the Reading Christmas Bird Count two of 86 years: 26 on December 22, 1963, and 15 on January 1, 1978. Single birds were found on the Hamburg Christmas Bird Count on January 2, 1966; December 29, 1968; and December 28, 1975.

John F. Hofmann listed the White-winged Crossbill in 1890.

COMMON REDPOLL *Carduelis flammea*
Rare and irregular winter visitor

The Common Redpoll is a rare and erratic winter visitor, generally occurring and occasionally common during severe winters.

While in Berks County, the Common Redpoll feeds largely on the seeds of alder, various species of birch, and on weed seeds of various sorts but seems particularly fond of the evening primrose. It also appears at feeders for thistle and sunflower seeds.

Most of the recorded observations are in February and March.

The early date is November 2 (1993 - John Puschack, one bird) at Hawk Mountain. There are several other November records there: Alex Nagy saw two at the entrance November 7, 1959; one appeared at the feeders November 12 and 14, 1980 (Seth Benz); Maurice Broun saw two November 17, 1959; there were six on November 15, 1993; and one flew by the North Lookout November 21, 1995.

Matt Spence found two at Lake Ontelaunee November 3, 1959.

Most of the larger flocks have broken up by mid-March, and by the end of that month the pairs or smaller groups have left for the north, leaving a few stragglers into April. Dean Kendall has seen the Common Redpoll at his feeders in Leesport as late as April 8 (1994 - seven birds). The late date at Hawk Mountain is March 31 (1970 - Alex Nagy).

From December 31, 1916, to March 16, 1917, large flocks up to 500 in number were reported in Berks County. Large groups were also reported from February 8 to March 14, 1920, and from January 26 to March 1, 1936.

Small groups were noted on the following dates: March 10, 1923; March 10, 1928; March 26, 1939; and a flock of 75 at Dengler Hill on January 30, 1944.

A major invasion of the Common Redpoll occurred in 1947. On February 1, Earl Poole saw a flock of at least 250 that had been frequenting a weed-grown field near Eckville. Broun first recorded seven at Schaumboch's at Hawk Mountain with 85 Pine Siskins on January 6. The Redpolls numbered up to 300 throughout the winter until March 9. Broun writes:

"Redpolls - very rare in our region - spent the winter of 1947 with us. I first saw the dainty little finches at the Lookout on a brilliant day in early January. A major event, and a very exciting one! It had been ten years since I had seen any of these gregarious wanderers from the Far North. Some 300 redpolls were swarming among the birches, feeding on the catkins, and with them were a score of siskins and a few goldfinches. The next day, and almost every morning thereafter, until March 9th, they flocked about the house, usually late in the forenoon. Each morning's visit brought fresh excitement. On a Sunday morning in late January, I tramped through our woods, avoiding the glare-ice road, to enjoy a ten-mile hike in the valley, hoping to see large numbers of birds. Imagine my delight upon returning to the house at noon to find far more birds than I had seen on my long walk. Redpolls covered two apple trees; they swarmed in the road, gleaning grit from the coal-ashes; they fluttered on the ice-encrusted snow, picking up the seeds of the birches; and, most surprising, at least fifty of the hardy little birds were bathing and wading in the icy water of the tiny brook by the house. The temperature was 38 degrees. The bathers then flew up to the apple trees and shook and flashed their feathers, chattering contentedly in low tones" (Broun, 1949a:131-132).

A similar visitation occurred in February 1953, followed by others of somewhat less magnitude in 1956 and 1958. Other major invasions reached Berks during January, February, and March 1960 and 1966. Other invasion years include 1969, 1970, 1972, 1978, 1982, 1986, 1987, 1993, and 1994.

There have been a number of minor flights of these birds in intervening years, although there have been periods of from four to eight years when none or very few were seen.

In 1972, Rudy Keller recorded Common Redpolls in District Township beginning January 5. Numbers peaked at 50 on March 23.

From January 10 through March 17, 1978, Common Redpolls were common at Hawk Mountain. The first bird appeared at the feeders January 10 and numbers swelled to over 15 by mid-February and "many, many" on February 20. On February 12, 1978, Kerry Grim found 70 Redpolls at the Hamburg reservoir.

During the winter of 1987, "hundreds" of Redpolls occurred at Hawk Mountain, "so many they pushed each other off the feeders" (Laurie Goodrich). The birds were there from January to March with a count of over 50 on March 21. Harold and Joan Silagy had between eight and 40 Redpolls at their feeders in Bern Township between February 4 and March 21.

In 1994, between 50 and 100 were coming to the Hawk Mountain feeders beginning January 27. The Silagys had up to 50 in Bern Township until March 27, and Kendall had up to 30 until the late date of April 8, when seven were at his feeder.

The Common Redpoll has appeared on the Reading Christmas Bird Count five of 86 years, once in the last 10, with a maximum of 90 on December 20, 1981. It was first recorded on the count in 1969, two birds on December 21. The Common Redpoll has been seen on 10 of 32 Hamburg Christmas Bird Counts with a peak of 143 on January 1, 1970. The only Bernville count record is two on January 1, 1990.

Levi Mengel collected a Greater Redpoll *Acanthis flammea rostrata*, a subspecies of the Common Redpoll, on Mount Penn January 17, 1888. It is now in the Reading Public Museum collection. This more northern race is larger, darker, more heavily streaked with a thicker bill.

Six Common Redpolls taken by Mengel between November 30 (1887) and March 8 (1886) are in the museum collection.

HOARY REDPOLL *Carduelis hornemanni*
Accidental winter visitor

Maurice Broun identified and obtained satisfactory photographs of a quartet of Hoary Redpolls which appeared at the Hawk Mountain Sanctuary following a blizzard from March 18 to 23, 1956 (Broun, 1958:23). Broun writes in his notes: "1956 - March 18 Swirling snow all day. At 3 p.m. saw a pale-colored [Hoary] Redpoll working on lilac seeds. A half-hour later, three pale-colored [Hoary] Redpolls, all females, feeding in black birch opposite house. Watched a long time, with and without binoculars within 17 feet. Some time after they disappeared, about 4 o'clock, Alex [Nagy] and I saw and heard a male [Hoary] Redpoll alight briefly in birch and smokehouse apple tree by kitchen window. The females studied carefully and each very white, especially on underparts which were clear on breasts and lower abdomen. Unable to see rumps well." During the birds' second visit, a flock of 30 or more Common Redpolls appeared, but the four Hoary Redpolls did not mix with them. The Hoary Redpolls returned on each afternoon, usually after 2:30. On March 22 at 5 p.m., Broun found the birds a mile to the north of Schaumboch's.

Broun reported two others in a flock of over 175 Common Redpolls near Drehersville February 3, 1960. Earl Poole saw at least one in a large flock of Redpolls near Fleetwood on February 26, 1960. The paler coloration and extensive whitish rump stood out in marked contrast with the others.

From February 6 to 10, 1981, Jim Brett recorded a Hoary Redpoll among 100 Common Redpolls at the Hawk Mountain feeders.

In January and February 1987, one frequented the feeders at Hawk Mountain with hundreds of Common Redpolls. Matt Spence photographed the bird February 8. On March 14, 1987, Joan Silagy recorded a Hoary Redpoll at her feeders in Bern Township. One appeared at the North Lookout at Hawk Mountain November 22, 1987.

Peter Saenger and John Muddeman found a female Hoary Redpoll at Saenger's feeders near Henningsville February 18, 1996. Ken Lebo photographed the bird.

Because of plumage variations between the two birds, it is extremely difficult to separate Hoary and Common redpolls in the field, and any sight record must be accepted with caution.

PINE SISKIN *Carduelis pinus*
Irregular migrant and winter visitor

The Pine Siskin is an irregular migrant and winter visitor and has been found nesting in Berks County on several occasions.

Its erratic wanderings at all seasons seem to defy all efforts at description. In Berks County, Earl Poole found it present during eight full months out of the year, but had no local records between May 16 (1955) and September 17 (1935). In 43 years of observation between 1921 and 1964, he described it as a winter visitor during 10 winters, chiefly a spring migrant during 13 years, a fall migrant during 15 years, and was altogether absent or not detected during the entire year for 10 years in that period. Only once, during the winter of 1922-1923, did he find the Pine Siskin consistently in the county through the winter from its arrival on October 22 to its departure on May 14, following.

More recently, the Pine Siskin has nested in Berks. In May 1978, a pair raised three young in the back yard of Ronald Cocroft in Greenfields. On June 18, 1978, Kerry Grim and Kenneth and Dorothy Grim saw a Pine Siskin in their yard in Hamburg feeding one young. On June 25, two adults and four young returned. On July 4, an immature Pine Siskin fed at their thistle feeder. They did not see the Siskins after that date.

In 1988, Rudy Keller found a pair nesting in a white pine in District Township. The birds were present until June 8; however, they raised a single Cowbird.

Kerry Grim has several other late spring and summer records in Hamburg, but there was no indication of nesting. On June 1, 1986, he briefly saw a Pine Siskin in his yard, and on July 8, 1988, one was calling from a tree.

The Pine Siskin is by no means confined to conifers for its food supply. The seeds of the black birch, hemlock, sweet gum, alder, goldenrod, and several other common weeds appear to attract it. It also favors thistle feeders.

An albino Pine Siskin was seen at the North Lookout at Hawk Mountain in early November 1963 (Maurice Broun). The single-day high count there is 425 on October 26, 1989. That fall, 2,669 Pine Siskins were tallied.

The late spring date at Hawk Mountain is May 21 (1964). Maurice Broun remarks about the abundance of Pine Siskins during the winter of 1964: "But the Siskins stole the show. The dainty sprites swarmed at our smorgasbord (walnut screenings, sunflower seeds, suet, donuts), fascinating all our visitors. Utterly fearless, the Siskins would flutter about me, accept food from my outstretched hand. They were pure delight; and they made the winter and spring for us" (Broun, 1965:9-10).

Broun trapped and banded 550 Siskins during the winter of 1964. Two were previously banded. One he trapped on February 13 had been banded March 16, 1963, at Washington Crossing State Park, and the other trapped on April 15 had been banded two months earlier at Murray Hill, New Jersey.

The Pine Siskin has appeared on the Reading Christmas Bird Count 41 of 86 years, once in the last 10, with a maximum of 1,014 on January 1, 1978. The peak for the Hamburg Count is 492 on December 27, 1987, the only year the totals exceeded 200 birds. The high for the Bernville Count is 35 on January 3, 1988.

During the winters of 1959-60, 1969-1970, 1971-1972, 1977-1978, 1987-1988, and 1989-1990, the Pine Siskin appeared in unusual numbers throughout the entire county.

AMERICAN GOLDFINCH *Carduelis tristis*
Common resident

The American Goldfinch is the bird the Pennsylvania Germans refer to as "der Dischdelfink," or "thistle finch," from the German "Distelfink" for the European Goldfinch. It is so named because it likes to feed on this seed-bearing plant and use the thistledown to line its nest.

It is a common permanent resident, but Earl Poole found it occasionally scarce in winter. However, with the increase of bird feeding in recent years, the Goldfinch is much more regular.

Poole writes in 1964: "There is a spectacular increase in the number and activities of Goldfinches, usually during the last week in April into early May, when the elms are in blossom. At this time, brilliant in their fresh spring plumage, they troop through the country in droves, singing and chattering with the utmost abandon. Doubtless these are mostly transients which pass on to the north."

The latest of our native species to nest, it breeds commonly, but somewhat locally, throughout Berks County. Levi Mengel collected a Goldfinch nest near Tuckerton on July 1, 1895. He remarked: "First egg laid, May 19 (1895), last May 24. Nest collected after full brood had been hatched and raised." If there has not been a mistake, this is an unusually early nesting record.

The latest nesting record is of an adult feeding young out of the nest at Peters Creek October 11, 1969 (Matt Spence).

Two of nine sets of eggs, the latest dated June 10 (1888), in the Mengel collection contain Cowbird's eggs. The clutch sizes in the collection range from three to five eggs.

At Hawk Mountain, the American Goldfinch was not well monitored prior to 1984. The early date for fall migrants there is August 18 (1988), and the late date is December 10 (1996). The peak count from the North Lookout is 126 on November 4, 1995. The season high count is 854 in 1992.

The American Goldfinch has appeared on the Reading Christmas Bird Count 80 of 86 years, 10 of the last 10, with a maximum of 455 on December 22, 1968. The peak for the Hamburg Christmas Bird Count is 708 on December 29, 1974. Numbers on that count usually run between 200 to 400. The high for the Bernville count is 151 on January 4, 1987.

Other Pennsylvania German names include "der Zelaatvoggel," or "salad bird," because it likes to feed on the seed-bearing lettuce plants and "der wild Kanaeri," or "wild canary," because of its appearance and song (Rupp, 1946:222).

EVENING GROSBEAK *Coccothraustes vespertinus*
Erratic winter visitor

Practically unknown in the East prior to the winter of 1889–1890, the Evening Grosbeak became an increasingly common, if somewhat irregular, winter visitor during midcentury, but numbers declined beginning in the early 1970s until presently it is rare and irregular. This bird is native to the far Northwest.

During the years between the big invasions of 1889–1890 and 1941–1942, records were few in number and at long intervals, most of the observations single birds or small groups. After the winter of 1941–1942 the Evening Grosbeak appeared much more frequently. Again in 1945–1946 flocks of considerable size remained in Berks County until May. Sam Gundy recorded 25 in Kutztown from May 3 to 13.

In 1949–1950 there was an invasion on a smaller scale, and in 1951–1952 a much larger one occurred, Maurice Broun counting 163 for the fall at Hawk Mountain between October 14 and November 22. That winter he had Evening Grosbeaks at his feeders for exactly 19 weeks from January 12 to May 24. He banded 206 of them and estimated that a total of 450 visited. He had four foreign station banding recoveries that year: an adult female January 12, 1952, banded at Hartford, Connecticut, March 18, 1950; an adult female February 25, 1952, banded at Old Deerfield, Massachusetts, April 14, 1950; an adult male March 18, 1952, banded at Hardwick, Massachusetts, January 22, 1950; and an adult female April 22, 1952, banded at Storrs, Connecticut, February 5, 1950.

Broun noticed in 1952 that the flocks were very nervous during January and February, arriving at the feeders around 6:40 a.m. and staying until 11:30 a.m. That schedule changed in the spring. On May 12, 42 were at the feeders from daybreak to late in the afternoon, one pair staying until 5 p.m. The grosbeaks remained that year until May 24.

In January 1956 Broun entertained well over 500 Evening Grosbeaks at his Hawk Mountain feeding station with a total of at least 1,500 during the 22-week stay. Of these, he banded 1,079. Two females spent the summer through July 19 and at intervals thereafter.

The following winter, 1956–1957, was not a grosbeak year, but in 1957-1958 the grosbeaks arrived early. Broun had 20 at his feeder at Hawk Mountain on October 5, and large flocks remained throughout much of the winter. Of 110 at his feeder on November 25, one was a banding return, an adult female he banded January 14, 1956. Nine remained at Hawk Mountain until May 17, and two until May 18, when they evidently left, although a lone male returned on June 12, 13, and 14.

A female Evening Grosbeak Broun banded on February 15, 1958, was retrapped near Binghamton, New York, on May 3, 1958. It was later found dead on Martha's Vineyard on April 12, 1959 (Broun, 1960). Broun noted that of 900 Evening Grosbeaks banded at Hawk Mountain that year, several were recovered from distant points, including north-central Tennessee, and there were also five exchange visitors from a banding program at University Park (Broun, 1959).

In 1962 following another extensive visitation of these birds, two remained at Hawk Mountain until May 27. Numbers increased to over 500 in January, of which Broun banded 386.

He banded 1,124 by the end of February.

Evening Grosbeak visits declined during the last 25 years. The last big year for Evening Grosbeak flights was the winter of 1972 and the following fall. Rudy Keller observed grosbeaks at his feeders in District Township and recorded a high of 125 on January 7, 1972, with spring migrants daily through mid-April. Flocks appeared from May 3 to 14. The following fall, he saw one on October 11 and several flocks a day to mid-November, reaching a high of over 100 on November 17.

Reading Christmas Bird Count records reflect the declining trend. In 1971, 233 were counted, and in 1972, 169 were found. That was the last year that numbers exceeded 100 on the count. It has appeared on the Reading count 31 of 86 years, three of the last 10, with a maximum of 250 on December 22, 1963. The peak for the Hamburg Christmas Bird Count is 500 on December 29, 1985. It has been recorded during only three of the last eight years. The high for the Bernville count is 12 on December 30, 1995.

Some recent peak flights at Hawk Mountain include 51 on November 4, 1987; 12 on November 14, 1988; 15 on November 8, 1989; 75 on November 18, 1990; 23 on November 2, 1993; and 82 on November 6, 1995.

Earl Poole writes: "While the natural food of the Evening Grosbeaks consists of the seeds of the box elder, various other maples, ash, sumac, and dried and frozen fruits, they are inordinately fond of sunflower seeds, which they devour with evident relish, returning year after year to feeding stations where this delicacy is supplied."

HOUSE SPARROW *Passer domesticus*
Locally abundant resident

This abundant and well-known bird, formerly called the English Sparrow and introduced into the United States from Europe during the second half of the nineteenth century, has for many years been thoroughly naturalized and established in all parts of Berks County. It is at home in the city, villages, and farms, but is also seen from time to time in fairly remote places as the records suggest some dispersal or wandering.

It is comparatively rare or absent from the heavily forested areas, except where permanent human habitations and livestock exist. Rarely seen at Hawk Mountain, it is an irregular visitor in spring, usually in April, and rare in fall. Maurice Broun noted a high of 30 on September 29, 1953. The first nesting he recorded occurred during the spring of 1954, when three young were raised in a nest box. The House Sparrow was last recorded at Hawk Mountain in 1980.

It is not now, however, as generally distributed as it was earlier this century, since the automobile replaced the horse and the county became more suburbanized. Competition for nesting territories from the House Finch also may have contributed to its decline.

The first record of a nest in Berks County is one that Levi Mengel collected May 27, 1888, at 739 Penn Street, Reading. The nest contained seven eggs. Six other sets of eggs in the Reading Public Museum collection were taken between May 13 (1889) and June 2 (1894). Clutch sizes in these sets number from five to seven eggs.

The House Sparrow has appeared on the Reading Christmas Bird Count 63 of 86 years, 10 of the last 10, with a maximum of 2,903 on December 15, 1974. There was debate earlier this century whether to include the bird on the count due to its introduced status, so it was not counted from 1911 to 1920 and from 1922 to 1933. The peak for the Hamburg Christmas Bird Count is 2,983 on January 2, 1983. The high for the Bernville Count is 1,723 on January 3, 1988.

The Pennsylvania Germans call the House Sparrow "die Schpatz," and in Berks the names "Schparlinge" or "Schbarlinge" have been used. The dialect names are derived from the German words for the sparrow (Rupp, 1946:212-213).

SUPPLEMENTARY LIST

Eared Grebe *Podiceps nigricollis*
Hypothetical

George S. Scoufalos reported sighting an Eared Grebe, a western species, at the southeastern corner of Lake Ontelaunee March 28, 1982. The grebe was in winter plumage and in the company of three Red-necked Grebes - two in winter plumage and one in intermediate plumage, and two Horned Grebes - one in winter plumage and one in intermediate plumage.

Wilson's Storm-Petrel *Oceanites oceanicus*
Hypothetical

Although reasonably certain that he correctly identified these birds, Earl Poole believed two Wilson's Storm-Petrels occurring with the influx of Leach's Storm-Petrels on August 24, 1933, had better be regarded as doubtful (Poole, 1935:24).

White Pelican *Pelecanus erythrorhynchos*
Hypothetical

Walter H. Leibelsperger reported a White Pelican on a dam at Moselem Springs about 1892.

Magnificent Frigatebird *Fregata magnificens*
Hypothetical

Jim Brett reported a possible Magnificent Frigatebird flying southwest over the ridge past Hemlock Heights while observing from the North Lookout at Hawk Mountain Sanctuary on September 15, 1994.

Black Swan *Cygnus atratus*
Escape

Many observers reported a Black Swan at Lake Ontelaunee from April 19 to November 8, 1992. Kerry Grim observed one at Kaercher Creek Park in Windsor Township September 23, 1995.

Graylag Goose *Anser anser*
Escape

One Graylag Goose remained at Lake Ontelaunee from April 15 to December 2, 1973, and was seen by many observers.

Bar-headed Goose *Anser indicus*
Escape

Harold and Joan Silagy found a Bar-headed Goose at Blue Marsh Lake on March 4, 1980.

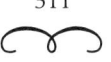

Barnacle Goose *Branta leucopsis*
Hypothetical

Charles Schaich, Paul Martin, and Warren Kalbach saw a bird they believed to be a Barnacle Goose on October 15, 1950, at Lake Ontelaunee. The next month on November 19, Matt Spence and B. Bressler saw what might have been the same bird at the same location.

Egyptian Goose *Alopochen aegypticus*
Escape

Matt Spence observed an Egyptian Goose at Lake Ontelaunee on October 9, 1965. A second bird was recorded there from July 6 to 28, 1968, by many observers.

Muscovy Duck *Cairina moschata*
Escape

Matt Spence found one female Muscovy Duck with young on the Maiden Creek July 28, 1985.

Mandarin Duck *Aix galericulata*
Escape

Matt Spence saw a Mandarin Duck at the Reading Public Museum park during February 1987. Kerry Grim and Matt Wlasnieski observed a male at Shartlesville from April 6 to May 19, 1996.

Ruddy Shelduck *Tadorna ferruginea*
Escape

Rudy Keller found a Ruddy Shelduck on a pond near Oley on the Reading Christmas Bird Count December 18, 1983.

Red-crested Pochard *Nett rufina*
Escape

Harold and Joan Silagy found a Red-crested Pochard on the Tulpehocken Creek April 22, 1990. Matt Spence noted what may have been the same male bird at the Reading Public Museum park June 4 to 6, 1990.

Harlequin Duck *Histrionicus histrionicus*
Hypothetical

John F. Hofmann listed the Harlequin Duck as occurring in Berks County. In the late 1950s or early 1960s, there was a report of one seen by two observers near the dam at Lake Ontelaunee.

Eagle *Haliaeetus sp.*
Hypothetical

What could have been a White-tailed Eagle, *H. albicilla*, or a Steller's Sea-Eagle, *H.*

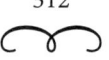

pelagicus, was seen and photographed by Jim Brett and a number of other observers at the North Lookout of Hawk Mountain on October 9, 1986. After looking at the photographs, Kenneth Parkes of the Carnegie Museum felt that the bird was an immature White-tailed Eagle.

Tawny Eagle *Aquila rapax*
Escape

  Jim Brett, Harold Axtell, Joe Taylor, Richard Sharadin, and Joan Silagy observed a Tawny Eagle with falconer's jesses flying over Hawk Mountain November 8, 1974.

Gray Partridge *Perdix perdix*
Introduced

  The Gray Partridge has been liberated on several occasions, apparently some time in the early 1920s near Bally and Bechtelsville and in 1925 and 1928 at several points in the county. None of these introductions thrived.

  One was found dead near Pricetown in March 1925, and Earl Poole flushed a covey near Fox Lake on January 10, 1926. Fox Lake was flooded when the Blue Marsh Lake project was completed in 1976.

Chukar *Alectoris chukar*
Introduced

  In the late 1950s, a Chukar was brought to the Reading Public Museum after it was captured on a farm near Fleetwood. Earl Poole writes in 1964 that there were Berks County records as late as 1963. On August 5, 1989, one was recorded at Hawk Mountain, and on May 14, 1994, Rudy Keller saw a Chukar that escaped from the collection of a local exotic fowl fancier in Pike Township.

Red-legged Partridge *Alectoris rufa*
Escape

  Laurie Goodrich identified a Red-legged Partridge on the trail to the North Lookout at Hawk Mountain on April 21, 1988.

Silver Pheasant *Lophura nycthemera*
Introduced

  Several of these supposedly hardy pheasants were released near Hamburg by P. J. Glessner around 1927. One was shot near Krumsville on November 1, 1932, and another was seen near the same place (Poole, 1964:68).

Golden Pheasant *Chrysolophus pictus*
Introduced

  This brightly colored pheasant is sometimes raised in aviaries and pheasant farms from which individuals occasionally escape. Maurice Broun reported a cock Golden Pheasant on the Hawk Mountain Sanctuary on November 5, 1950. Helen and Earl Poole saw a male along the edge of a woodland near Jacksonwald on June 16, 1963 (Poole, 1964:68).

Black-necked Stilt *Himantopus mexicanus*
Hypothetical

William R. Fink reported seeing a Black-necked Stilt standing in a mud puddle May 6, 1992, on a department store parking lot off Fourth Street in Hamburg.

Long-billed Curlew *Numenius americanus*
Hypothetical

Mr. D. Frank Keller, of Reading, said it had been taken in Berks County (Warren, 1890:96).

Earl Poole believed, however, since Warren did not mention the Whimbrel or Hudsonian Curlew in his report, there may be some reason to question this statement, especially since some long-billed female specimens of the Whimbrel in his collection, taken on the Virginia coast, have been misidentified as this species.

Long-billed Dowitcher *Limnodromus scolopaceus*
Hypothetical

Although the Long-billed Dowitcher, a western bird, undoubtedly has occurred in Berks County, the difficulty of separating it from the Short-billed Dowitcher makes sight records unreliable. Therefore, it remains on the hypothetical list.

Earl Poole thought he saw a Long-billed Dowitcher at Lake Ontelaunee September 8, 1964.

Rick Wiltraut observed a Long-billed Dowitcher July 23, 1994, at the Water Street mud flats at Lake Ontelaunee.

Parasitic Jaeger *Stercorarius parasiticus*
Hypothetical

Ruth Olson and Charles Kidder reported a Parasitic Jaeger October 29, 1963, flying past the North Lookout at Hawk Mountain.

Kidder writes: "We each had a good, unobstructed view in good light in our binoculars for almost a minute. The bird was over the Kettle all the time, about at the horizon, flying a little north of west, approaching us but not directly toward us - kind of quartering, flapping (not sailing) all the time. We got two good views of its upper parts and two good views of its lower parts. It suddenly plummeted straight down, and we lost sight of it.

"The head and neck were much too long for a Peregrine (first impression) and tail much too pointed for a Peregrine. Ruth Olson had seen them in Iceland that summer as well as the summer before. She saw the flash of white in the upper wing surface."

California Gull *Larus californicus*
Hypothetical

Larry Lewis found a California Gull at Blue Marsh Lake December 4, 1992. He saw it again near Strausstown on December 5 and 6 and at Blue Marsh on December 9. Dean Kendall observed a bird he believed to be a first-winter California Gull at Blue Marsh Lake on December 9. He wrote an extensive description of the bird and noted that in nearly every respect it could be separated from nearby first-winter Herring Gulls.

Thayer's Gull *Larus thayeri*
Hypothetical

Dean Kendall saw a bird he considered "a real good candidate" for a Thayer's Gull in first-winter plumage at Blue Marsh Lake November 14 and 15, 1992. Among the details he noted in a lengthy description were its smaller size than a Herring Gull; its shorter, thinner, black bill; and its uniformly pale underwings.

Gull-billed Tern *Sterna nilotica*
Hypothetical

John F. Hofmann listed the Gull-billed Tern in 1890.

Royal Tern *Sterna maxima*
Hypothetical

On August 13, 1955, during the late stage of Hurricane Connie, which blew many unusual southern sea-birds inland, Earl Poole saw a tern that he believed must have been of this species on Lake Ontelaunee, but the terrific wind prevented his obtaining a thoroughly satisfactory view.

Henry B. Graves recorded the capture of a specimen in Berks County in September 1879 (Warren, 1890:19).

Arctic Tern *Sterna paradisaea*
Hypothetical

D. Frank Keller reported the Arctic Tern as an accidental visitor in Berks County (Warren, 1890:21).

Passenger Pigeon *Ectopistes migratorius*
Extinct

Prior to 1880 or 1881 the Passenger Pigeons resorted for several weeks each fall to the southwestern side of Neversink Mountain, where the roosting multitudes spread from the site of the Highland House to the old Tuberculosis Sanitarium. During flights the local gunners would take up a position on the open slopes of the mountain below and fire until their guns became hot. A large rock in the Schuylkill River, known as Pigeon Rock, was so named from the fact that the pigeons resorted to it to bathe and drink (From conversations Earl Poole had with Adam Leader and Richard Lawrence).

Pigeon Rock, visible in the Schuylkill River from Route 422, is now regularly covered with paint and graffiti by high school students.

A female Passenger Pigeon taken in Albany Township April 6, 1878, by John F. Hofmann is in the Reading Public Museum collection. Two eggs are also in the collection: No. C1504; Dr. Murray Weidman - "Northern Berks County, 1877; These eggs while hunting with artist Fred Spay were collected. He gave them to [Levi] Mengel about 1890."

The Pennsylvania German name for the Passenger Pigeon is "die wilde Dauwe." William Rupp writes:

"This is the one and only name given for this extinct species by those who know and remember. ...The singular form of the dialect name is rarely heard, for a person rarely spoke of 'en wildi Daub' or 'die wild Daub.' In this case it was 'die wilde Dauwe,' for no other name could encompass the enormity of this singular phenomenon on the early American scene. It was here when the fathers arrived on these shores. It shook the earth for a while and then, thanks to man's greed, it was gone. Here is a name to be reckoned with: 'Die wilde Dauwe!'" (Rupp, 1946:126)

Ringed Turtle-Dove *Streptopelia risoria*
Feral

Kerry Grim reported seeing a Ringed Turtle-Dove in Hamburg in the 1980s. During the Hamburg Christmas Bird Count, two were counted in 1982, one in 1986, and one during the count week in 1988. One was reported on the Reading Christmas Bird Count December 18, 1988.

Budgerigar *Melopsittacus undulatus*
Escape

In the early 1970s, one Budgerigar survived the entire winter at a feeder on North 11th Street in Reading (Matt Spence).

Rose-ringed Parakeet *Psittacula krameri*
Escape

A Rose-ringed Parakeet flew by the North Lookout of Hawk Mountain Sanctuary on September 28, 1986, and was seen by Phil Haas, Mark Blauer, Kerry Grim, and Laurie Goodrich.

Burrowing Owl *Athene cunicularia*
Hypothetical

A mounted Burrowing Owl is in the collection of Dr. Stanley Brunner on display at the Pennsylvania Dutch Folk Culture Museum in Lenhartsville. There is no data accompanying the specimen, but in newspaper interviews Brunner stated that all the birds in his collection were taken by him during the early part of the century in northern Berks County.

The Burrowing Owl breeds in Florida and in western North America. The western bird is migratory, and there are records from New York, Massachusetts, and New Hampshire during the late nineteenth and early twentieth centuries.

One bird caught alive when it flew through a window in New York City on August 8, 1875, was suspected of being an escaped cage bird (Griscom, 1923:387). Specimens were also taken in Newburyport, Massachusetts, on May 15, 1875, and in Dover, New Hampshire, on February 20, 1922 (Forbush, 1927: 238-239).

Three-toed Woodpecker *Picoides tridactylus*
Hypothetical

On November 11, 1981, Ronnie Hooper and Lee Perzanowski reported seeing a Three-toed Woodpecker at the North Lookout at Hawk Mountain Sanctuary. Mrs. Joseph Seifert reported one at Bernhart's Dam in Muhlenberg Township January 7, 1970.

Gray Jay *Perisoreus canadensis*
Hypothetical

Warren Kalbach and Charles Schaich reported a Gray Jay present at Stony Creek Mills near Reading from May 21 to July 12, 1960. Schaich later examined skins of this species in the Reading Public Museum and writes: "The general mousiness of its coloration is in agreement with my observation. Even the dirty-white of the forehead and under-parts check...The bird acted 'dopey' - that is, not active, and flew away slowly."

Having spent some time in the field with these observers, Earl Poole was inclined to give credence to this report, as unlikely as the occurrence of this species at that season may seem.

316

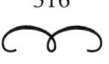

Black-billed Magpie *Pica pica*
Escape

Richard Harlow in 1953 mentioned having seen one near Maxatawny in northern Berks County, and there are other records of Magpies having been seen in several eastern states. Some of these are known to have been released in New Jersey and Vermont (Griscom and Snyder, 1955:258).

Kirtland's Warbler *Dendroica kirtlandii*
Hypothetical

Katrina Knight reported observing a Kirtland's Warbler at Egelman's Park on Mount Penn at 8:20 a.m. September 5, 1996. She viewed it under overcast skies at a distance of 10 to 15 feet for about 15 minutes as it moved among several bushes and small trees. She noted bright yellow underparts with distinct black streaking on the sides and gray or brown back, wings and tail. It had two indistinct white wing bars and dark head with distinct, broken white eye rings. There was no noticeable white in the tail and no yellow on the rump. The bird jerked its tail every few minutes. It was larger than the Canada Warblers that were passing through the same area.

Black-headed Grosbeak *Pheucticus melanocephalus*
Hypothetical

Walter W. Kelly reported a male Black-headed Grosbeak in breeding plumage visited his feeder near Reading April 26 and 27, 1976 (*American Birds*. 30(4):822).

Yellow-fronted Canary *Serinus mozambicus*
Escape

Arlene Koch and Steven Smith found a Yellow-fronted Canary at a bird feeder in Klinesville during the Hamburg Christmas Bird Count December 26, 1993. It had been there for about a week. Frank Haas photographed the bird (Koch, 1994:129-130).

Clay-colored Sparrow *Spizella pallida*
Hypothetical

Earl Poole found a "probable" Clay-colored Sparrow, a western bird, October 20, 1964, at Lake Ontelaunee.

White-winged Junco *Junco hyemalis aikeni*
Hypothetical

On February 11, 1958, Anna Kendall of Leesport reported a White-winged Junco, a subspecies of the Dark-eyed Junco, at her feeder.

Red-crested Cardinal *Paroaria coronata*
Escape

Matt Spence and Warren Faust saw a Red-crested Cardinal at a feeder in Hyde Park April 4, 1969.

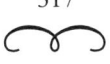

Java Sparrow *Padda oryzivora*
Escape

  Alex Nagy and David Karraker found a Java Sparrow at Hawk Mountain Sanctuary on October 5, 1954.

Cut-throat Finch *Amadina fasciata*
Escape

  A Cut-throat Finch perched on a dead hemlock at the North Lookout at Hawk Mountain Sanctuary on August 26, 1988, and was seen by Laurie Goodrich, Tony Bledsoe, and Bruce Williams.

Pin-tailed Whyda *Vidua macroura*
Escape

  A Pin-tailed Whyda was observed at a feeder near Reading from early November to December 27, 1970, and was confirmed by William Miller.

A COMPREHENSIVE BIBLIOGRAPHY OF BERKS COUNTY BIRD LIFE

Allen, P. E., Laurie J. Goodrich, and Keith L. Bildstein. 1995. Hawk Mountain's Million-bird Database. *Birding*, 27(1):24-32.

_____. 1996. Within-and-among-year Effects of Cold Fronts on Migrating Raptors at Hawk Mountain, Pennsylvania, 1934-1991. *Auk*, 113:329-338.

American Ornithologists' Union. 1957. *Check-list of North American Birds*. Fifth Edition. Baltimore, Maryland:Port City Press, Inc.

_____. 1983. *Check-list of North American Birds*. Sixth Edition. Lawrence, Kansas: Allen Press, Inc.

_____. 1985. Thirty-fifth Supplement to the American Ornithologists' Union *Check-List of North American Birds*. Auk 102:680-686.

_____. 1987. Thirty-sixth Supplement to the American Ornithologists' Union *Check-List of North American Birds*. Auk 104:591-596.

_____. 1989. Thirty-seventh Supplement to the American Ornithologists' Union *Check-list of North American Birds*. Auk 106:532-538.

_____. 1991. Thirty-eighth Supplement to the American Ornithologists' Union *Check-list of North American Birds*. Auk 108:750-754.

_____. 1993. Thirty-ninth Supplement to the American Ornithologists' Union *Check-list of North American Birds*. Auk 110:675-682.

_____. 1995. Fortieth Supplement to the American Ornithologists' Union *Check-list of North American Birds*. Auk 112:819-830.

Anonymous. 1941. *Peace at Hawk Mountain Sanctuary*. Hawk Mountain Sanctuary Association, Publication No. 3.

_____. 1951. Focusing Public Opinion on Hawk Shooting. *Atlantic Naturalist*, 7(1).

_____. 1963. Hawk Mountain Sanctuary for Predatory Birds. *Internal Affairs*, 31(8): 16-18.

_____. 1966. Birdman Quits at Hawk Mountain. *Internal Affairs*, 34(5):22.

_____. 1973. Three Records Set at Hawk Mountain. *Pennsylvania Game News*, 44(7):11.

_____. 1975. Summary of Hawk Migration. *News Letter 47*. Hawk Mountain Sanctuary Association, Kempton, Pa.

_____. 1976. Summary of Hawk Migration. *News Letter 48*. Hawk Mountain Sanctuary Association, Kempton, Pa.

_____. 1977. Summary of Hawk Migration. *News Letter 49*. Hawk Mountain Sanctuary Association, Kempton, Pa.

_____. 1978. The Migration. *Hawk Mountain News*, 50:21-24.

_____. 1979. The Migration Hawk Mountain 1978. *Hawk Mountain News*, 50 [*sic* 51]:30-34.

_____. 1981. Summary of Hawk Migration. *Hawk Mountain News*, 55:21-28.

_____. 1992. American Kestrel Studies Provide Useful Baseline Information. *Wildlife Activist*, 16:9.

_____. 1996. Mountain Friends: The Chemistry of Julian Hill. *Hawk Mountain News*, 84:31.

Andres, B., Seth Benz, and Stanley Senner. 1984a. Oak-Maple Slope Forest (Thirty-sixth winter bird population study - Hawk Mountain). *American Birds*, 38:38.

_____. 1984b. Oak-Maple Ridge-top Forest (Thirty-sixth winter bird population study - Hawk Mountain). *American Birds*, 38:38.

_____. 1984c. Oak-Maple Ridge-top Forest (Forty-seventh breeding bird census - Hawk Mountain). *American Birds*, 38:72.

_____. 1984d. Oak-Maple Slope Forest. (Forty-seventh breeding bird census - Hawk Mountain). *American Birds*, 38:72.

Apanius, V. 1991. *Blood Parasitism, Immunity, and Reproduction in American Kestrels (*Falco sparverius*)*. Unpublished Ph.D dissertation. The University of Pennsylvania, Philadelphia, Pennsylvania.

Apanius, V., and C. E. Kirkpatrick. 1988. Preliminary Report of *Haemoproteus tinnunculi* Infection in a Breeding Population of American Kestrels (*Falco sparverius*). *Journal of Wildlife Diseases*, 24:150-153.

Arbib Jr., Robert S. 1957. The New York State Standard of Abundance, Frequency, and Seasonal Occurrence. *Audubon Field Notes*, 11(1):63-64.

Ardia, D., and K. L. Bildstein. Sex-related Differences in Habitat Selection in Wintering American Kestrels. *Animal Behavior*. In press.

Atkinson, Eric C., Laurie J. Goodrich, and Keith L. Bildstein. 1996. A Temporal Guide to Autumn Raptor Migration at Hawk Mountain Sanctuary, Pennsylvania. *Pennsylvania Birds*, 10(3):134-137.

Baird Ornithological Club. 1923. Bird-Lore's Twenty-third Christmas Census: Reading. *Bird-Lore*, 25:25.

_____. 1925. Bird-Lore's Twenty-fifth Christmas Census: Reading. *Bird-Lore*, 27:40-41.

_____. 1926. Bird-Lore's Twenty-sixth Christmas Census: Reading. *Bird-Lore*, 28:31.

_____. 1927. Bird-Lore's Twenty-seventh Christmas Census: Reading. *Bird-Lore*, 29:28-29.

_____. 1928. Bird-Lore's Twenty-eighth Christmas Census: Reading. *Bird-Lore*, 30:42.

_____. 1929. Bird-Lore's Twenty-ninth Christmas Census: Reading. *Bird-Lore*, 31:37.

_____. 1930. Bird-Lore's Thirtieth Christmas Census: Reading. *Bird-Lore*, 32:37.

_____. 1931. Bird-Lore's Thirty-first Christmas Census: Reading. *Bird-Lore*, 33:44.

_____. 1932. Bird-Lore's Thirty-second Christmas Census: Reading. *Bird-Lore*, 34:46-47.

_____. 1933. Bird-Lore's Thirty-third Christmas Census: Reading. *Bird-Lore*, 35:28.

_____. 1934. Bird-Lore's Thirty-fourth Christmas Census: Reading. *Bird-Lore*, 36:34.

_____. 1935. Bird-Lore's Thirty-fifth Christmas Census: Reading. *Bird-Lore*, 37:48.

_____. 1936. Bird-Lore's Thirty-sixth Christmas Census: Reading. *Bird-Lore*, 38:56.

_____. 1937. Bird-Lore's Thirty-seventh Christmas Census: Reading. *Bird-Lore*, 39:43.

_____. 1938. Bird-Lore's Thirty-eighth Christmas Census: Reading. *Bird-Lore*, 40:39.

_____. 1939. Bird-Lore's Thirty-ninth Christmas Bird Census: Reading. *Bird-Lore*, 41:20-21.

_____. 1940. Bird-Lore's Fortieth Christmas Bird Census: Reading. *Bird-Lore*, 42:87.

_____. 1941. Forty-first Christmas Bird Census. *Audubon* (Supplement), 43:96.

_____. 1947. Forty-seventh Christmas Bird Count: Reading. *Audubon Field Notes*, 1:51-52.

_____. 1948. Forty-eighth Christmas Bird Count: Reading. *Audubon Field Notes*, 2:54.

_____. 1949. Forty-ninth Christmas Bird Count: Reading. *Audubon Field Notes*, 3:68.

_____. 1950. Fiftieth Christmas Bird Count: Reading. *Audubon Field Notes*, 4:82.

_____. 1951. Fifty-first Christmas Bird Count: Reading. *Audubon Field Notes*, 5:80.

_____. 1952. Fifty-second Christmas Bird Count: Reading. Earl Poole, compiler. *Audubon Field Notes*, 6:80.

_____. 1953. Fifty-third Christmas Bird Count: Reading. Kenneth Dearolf, compiler. *Audubon Field Notes*, 7:84.

_____. 1954. Fifty-fourth Christmas Bird Count: Reading. Earl Poole, compiler. *Audubon Field Notes*, 8:95.

_____. 1955. Fifty-fifth Christmas Bird Count: Reading. *Audubon Field Notes*, 9:109.

_____. 1956. Fifty-sixth Christmas Bird Count: Reading. D. Burger, compiler. *Audubon Field Notes*, 10:95.
_____. 1957. Fifty-seventh Christmas Bird Count: Reading. Donald Burger, compiler. *Audubon Field Notes*, 11:111.
_____. 1958. Fifty-eighth Christmas Bird Count: Reading. Catherine Feick, compiler. *Audubon Field Notes*, 12:111.
_____. 1959. Fifty-ninth Christmas Bird Count: Reading. Matthew Spence, compiler. *Audubon Field Notes*, 13:122.
_____. 1960. Sixtieth Christmas Bird Count: Reading. Emma Gage, compiler. *Audubon Field Notes*, 14:134.
_____. 1961. Sixty-first Christmas Bird Count: Reading. Matthew Spence, compiler. *Audubon Field Notes*, 15:142.
_____. 1962. Sixty-second Christmas Bird Count: Reading. Matthew Spence, compiler. *Audubon Field Notes*, 16:133-134.
_____. 1963. Sixty-third Christmas Bird Count: Reading. Matthew Spence, compiler. *Audubon Field Notes*, 17:129-130.
_____. 1964. Sixty-fourth Christmas Bird Count: Reading. Matthew Spence, compiler. *Audubon Field Notes*, 18:141.
_____. 1965. Sixty-fifth Christmas Bird Count: Reading. Matthew Spence, compiler. *Audubon Field Notes*, 19:150.
_____. 1966. Sixty-sixth Christmas Bird Count: Reading. Matthew Spence, compiler. *Audubon Field Notes*, 20:168.
_____. 1967. Sixty-seventh Christmas Bird Count: Reading. Matthew Spence, compiler. *Audubon Field Notes*, 21:157-158.
_____. 1968. Sixty-eighth Christmas Bird Count: Reading. Matthew Spence, compiler. *Audubon Field Notes*, 22:176.
_____. 1969. Sixty-ninth Christmas Bird Count: Reading. Matthew Spence, compiler. *Audubon Field Notes*, 23:200.
_____. 1970. Seventieth Christmas Bird Count: Reading. Matthew Spence, compiler. *Audubon Field Notes*, 24:197-198.
_____. 1971. Seventy-first Christmas Bird Count: Reading. Matthew Spence, compiler. *American Birds*, 25:234-235.
_____. 1972. Seventy-second Christmas Bird Count: Reading. Matthew Spence, compiler. *American Birds*, 26:250.
_____. 1973. Seventy-third Christmas Bird Count: Reading. Matthew Spence, compiler. *American Birds*, 27:251-252.
_____. 1974. Seventy-fourth Christmas Bird Count: Reading. Matthew Spence, compiler. *American Birds*, 28:262.
_____. 1975. Seventy-fifth Audubon Christmas Bird Count: Reading. Matthew Spence, compiler. *American Birds*, 29:286.
_____. 1976. Seventy-sixth Audubon Christmas Bird Count: Reading. Matthew Spence, compiler. *American Birds*, 30:293-294.
_____. 1977. Seventy-seventh Audubon Christmas Bird Count: Reading. Matthew Spence, compiler. *American Birds*, 31:545-546.
_____. 1978. Seventy-eighth Audubon Christmas Bird Count: Reading. Matthew Spence, compiler. *American Birds*, 32:557-558.
_____. 1979. Seventy-ninth Audubon Christmas Bird Count: Reading. Matthew Spence, compiler. *American Birds*, 33:434.
_____. 1980. Eightieth Audubon Christmas Bird Count: Reading. Matthew Spence, compiler. *American Birds*, 34:436-437.
_____. 1981. Eighty-first Audubon Christmas Bird Count: Reading. Matthew Spence, compiler. *American Birds*, 35:472.
_____. 1982. Eighty-second Audubon Christmas Bird Count: Reading. Matthew Spence, compiler. *American Birds*, 36:500.
_____. 1983. Eighty-third Audubon Christmas Bird Count: Reading. Matthew Spence, compiler. *American Birds*, 37:507-508.
_____. 1984. Eighty-fourth Audubon Christmas Bird Count: Reading. Matthew Spence, compiler. *American Birds*, 38:534-535.
_____. 1985. Eighty-fifth Christmas Bird Count: Reading. Matthew Spence, compiler. *American Birds*, 39:522.
_____. 1986a. Eighty-sixth Christmas Bird Count: Reading. Matthew Spence, compiler. *American Birds*, 40:714-715.
_____. 1986b. Eighty-sixth Christmas Bird Count: Bernville. Ernest and Terence Schiefer, compilers. *American Birds*, 40:704.
_____. 1987a. Eighty-seventh Christmas Bird Count: Reading. Matthew Spence, compiler. *American Birds*, 41:763; 765-780.
_____. 1987b. Eighty-seventh Christmas Bird Count: Bernville. Terence Schiefer, compiler. *American Birds*, 41:759;765-780.
_____. 1988a. Eighty-eighth Christmas Bird Count: Reading. Matthew Spence, compiler. *American Birds*, 42:721-722.
_____. 1988b. Eighty-eighth Christmas Bird Count: Bernville. Michael and Janet Slater, compilers. *American Birds*, 42:708.
_____. 1989a. Eighty-ninth Christmas Bird Count: Reading. Matthew Spence, compiler. *American Birds*, 43:764-765.
_____. 1989b. Eighty-ninth Christmas Bird Count: Bernville. Michael Slater, compiler. *American Birds*, 43:751-752.
_____. 1990a. Ninetieth Christmas Bird Count: Reading. Matthew Spence, compiler. *American Birds*, 44:669.
_____. 1990b. Ninetieth Christmas Bird Count: Bernville. Michael Slater, compiler. *American Birds*, 44:658-659.
_____. 1991a. Ninety-first Christmas Bird Count: Reading. Matthew Spence, compiler. *American Birds*, 45:676.
_____. 1991b. Ninety-first Christmas Bird Count: Bernville. Michael Slater, compiler. *American Birds*, 45:666.
_____. 1992a. Ninety-second Christmas Bird Count: Reading. Matthew Spence, compiler. *American Birds*, 46:668-669.
_____. 1992b. Ninety-second Christmas Bird Count: Bernville. Michael Slater, compiler. *American Birds*, 46:657-658
_____. 1993a. Ninety-third Christmas Bird Count: Reading. Matthew Spence, compiler. *American Birds*, 47:635.
_____. 1993b. Ninety-third Christmas Bird Count: Bernville. Michael Slater, compiler. *American Birds*, 47:624.
_____. 1994a. Ninety-fourth Christmas Bird Count: Reading. Matthew Spence, compiler. *Field Notes*, 48:512-513.
_____. 1994b. Ninety-fourth Christmas Bird Count: Bernville. Ed Barrell, compiler. *Field Notes*, 48:501-502.
_____. 1995a. Ninety-fifth Christmas Bird Count: Reading. Matthew Spence, compiler. *Field Notes*, 49:482.
_____. 1995b. Ninety-fifth Christmas Bird Count: Bernville. Ed Barrell, compiler. *Field Notes*, 49:471.
_____. 1996a. Ninety-sixth Christmas Bird Count: Reading. Matthew Spence, compiler. *Field Notes*, 50:510.
_____. 1996b. Ninety-sixth Christmas Bird Count: Bernville. Ed Barrell, compiler. *Field Notes*, 50:498.
Baird Ornithological Club and Hawk Mountain Sanctuary. 1966. Sixty-sixth Christmas Bird Count: Hamburg. Warren Faust, compiler. *Audubon Field Notes*, 20:163.
_____. 1967. Sixty-seventh Christmas Bird Count: Hamburg. Warren Faust, compiler. *Audubon Field Notes*, 21:153.
_____. 1968. Sixty-eighth Christmas Bird Count: Hamburg. Warren Faust, compiler. *Audubon Field Notes*, 22:170.
_____. 1969. Sixty-ninth Christmas Bird Count: Hamburg. Warren Faust, compiler. *Audubon Field Notes*, 23:194.
_____. 1970. Seventieth Christmas Bird Count: Hamburg. Warren Faust, compiler. *Audubon Field Notes*, 24:190-191.
_____. 1971. Seventy-first Christmas Bird Count: Hamburg. Warren Faust, compiler. *American Birds*, 25:227.
_____. 1972. Seventy-second Christmas Bird Count: Hamburg. Warren Faust, compiler. *American Birds*, 26:244-245.
_____. 1973. Seventy-third Christmas Bird Count: Hamburg. Warren Faust, compiler. *American Birds*, 27:246.
_____. 1974. Seventy-fourth Christmas Bird Count: Hamburg. Warren Faust, compiler. *American Birds*, 28:256.
_____. 1975. Seventy-fifth Audubon Christmas Bird Count: Hamburg. Warren Faust, compiler. *American Birds*, 29:280.
_____. 1976. Seventy-sixth Audubon Christmas Bird Count: Hamburg. Warren Faust, compiler. *American Birds*, 30:288.
_____. 1977. Seventy-seventh Audubon Christmas Bird Count: Hamburg. Warren Faust, compiler. *American Birds*, 31:539-540.
_____. 1978. Seventy-eighth Audubon Christmas Bird Count: Hamburg. Warren Faust, compiler. *American Birds*, 32:552.
_____. 1979. Seventy-ninth Audubon Christmas Bird Count: Hamburg. Warren Faust, compiler. *American Birds*, 33:430.
_____. 1980. Eightieth Audubon Christmas Bird Count: Hamburg. Warren Faust, compiler. *American Birds*, 34:433.

_____. 1981. Eighty-first Audubon Christmas Bird Count: Hamburg. Warren Faust, compiler. *American Birds*, 35:468.

_____. 1982. Eighty-second Audubon Christmas Bird Count: Hamburg. Warren Faust, compiler. *American Birds*, 36:495-496.

_____. 1983. Eighty-third Audubon Christmas Bird Count: Hamburg. Warren Faust, compiler. *American Birds*, 37:503.

Barnard, Phoebe. 1989. Faecal Bacteria in Unhatched Eggs of Box-Nesting Kestrels (*Falco sparverius*). International Conference of Birds of Prey Technical Publication No. 10:135-139.

Beck, Herbert H. 1924. The Pennsylvania German Names for Birds. *Auk*, 41: 288-295.

Bednarz, James C. 1989. [Review of] Return of the Falcons. *Science*, 244:233-234.

_____. 1990a. [Review of] Flight Strategies of Migrating Hawks. *Auk*, 107:801-802.

_____. 1990b. 53 Years of Migration Data Analyzed and Published. *Hawk Mountain News*, 73:32-37.

_____. 1992a. Red-shouldered Hawk. Pages 102-103 in *Atlas of Breeding Birds in Pennsylvania*, edited by Daniel W. Brauning. Pittsburgh: University of Pittsburgh Press.

_____. 1992b. Red-tailed Hawk. Pages 106-107 in *Atlas of Breeding Birds in Pennsylvania*, edited by Daniel W. Brauning. Pittsburgh: University of Pittsburgh Press.

Bednarz, James C., and Paul Kerlinger. 1989. Monitoring Hawk Populations by Counting Migrants. Pages 3280342 in *Proceedings of the Northeast Raptor Management Symposium and Workshop*, edited by B. G. Pendleton. Washington, D.C.: National Wildlife Federation.

Bednarz, James C., Daniel Klem, Laurie J. Goodrich, and Stanley E. Senner. 1990. Migration Counts at Hawk Mountain, Pennsylvania, As Indicators of Population Trends, 1934-1984. *Auk*, 107:96-107.

Benz, Seth. 1980a. Migration 1979. *Hawk Mountain News*, 53:42-53.

_____. 1980b. Northern Appalachians. *Hawk Migration Studies*, 5(2):20-22.

_____. 1981a. Northern Appalachians. *Hawk Migration Studies*, 6(1):15-16.

_____. 1981b. Northern Appalachians. *Hawk Migration Studies*, 6(2):20-22.

_____. 1982a. Migration: A New Emphasis. *Hawk Mountain News*, 57:20-27.

_____. 1982b. Northern Appalachians. *Hawk Migration Studies*, 7(1):17.

_____. 1982c. Northern Appalachians. *Hawk Migration Studies*, 7(2):23-24.

_____. 1983a. The Fall Season: Migration Report. *Hawk Mountain News*, 59:14-21.

_____. 1983b. Northern Appalachians. *Hawk Migration Studies*, 8(1):14.

_____. 1983c. Northern Appalachians. *Hawk Migration Studies*, 8(2):21-24.

_____. 1984a. The Fall Season Migration Report. *Hawk Mountain News*, 61:27-35.

_____. 1984b. Northern Appalachians. *Hawk Migration Studies*, 9(2):23-27.

Benz, Seth, and David DeReamus. 1984. Northern Appalachians. *Hawk Migration Studies*, 9(1);17-19.

_____. 1985. Northern Appalachians. *Hawk Migration Studies*, 10(1):25.

Berks County Planning Commission. December 1991. *Berks County Comprehensive Plan Revision*. Reading.

_____. January 1994. *Berks County Open Space and Recreation Plan*. Reading.

Bildstein, Keith L. 1992. Causes and Consequences of Reversed Sexual Size Dimorphism in Raptors: the Head Start Hypothesis. *Journal of Raptor Research*, 26:115-123.

_____. 1993a. Field Notes: Count Data Come of Age. *Hawk Mountain News*, 78:35-36.

_____. 1993b. Field Notes: Deja Vu All Over Again? *Hawk Mountain News*, 79:26-27.

_____. 1995a. Redtail 0877-17127. *Hawk Mountain News*, 83:22-23.

_____. 1995b. [Review of] Trends in Geographic Variation of Cooper's Hawk and Northern Goshawk in North America: A Multivariate Analysis by C. White. *Wilson Bulletin*, 107:770-771.

_____. 1996a. A Promise Kept. *Hawk Mountain News*, 84:22-23.

_____. 1996b. *Adopt-a-Kestrel-Box News*. Newsletter of Hawk Mountain Sanctuary.

_____. 1997a. Sixty Years of Science at Hawk Mountain Sanctuary. *Buteo* (Journal of the Czech Republic Working Group on Protection of Birds of Prey and Owls). In press.

_____. 1997b. Field Notes: Circular Argument. *Hawk Mountain News*, 86:22-23.

_____. Linking Raptor Migration Science to Mainstream Ecology and Conservation: An Ambitious Agenda for the 21st Century. In *Proceedings of the World Working Group for Birds of Prey and Owls Conference, Badajoz, Spain*. WWGBP, Berlin, Germany. In press.

_____. [Review of] How Birds Migrate by P. Kerlinger. *Wilson Bulletin*. In Press.

_____. [Review of] The Northern Goshawk: Ecology and Management, edited by W. M. Bock, M. L. Morrison, and M. H. Reiser. *Wilson Bulletin*. In press.

Bildstein, Keith L., James J. Brett, Laurie J. Goodrich, and Cathy B. Viverette. 1993. Shooting Galleries. *American Birds*, 47:38-43.

_____. 1995. Hawks Aloft Worldwide: Networking to Protect the World's Migrating Birds of Prey and Their Migratory Habitats. In *Nature Conservation: The Role of Networks* (D. Saunders, ed.) Surrey Beatty and Sons Pty Ltd, Chipping Norton, New South Wales, Australia.

Bildstein, K. L. and M. W. Collopy. Geographic Variation in the Hunting Behaviour of Northern Harriers in North America: Ecological and Conservation Implications for the Genus Circus in *Ecology and Conservation of Harriers*. London, England: Hawk and Owl Trust. In press.

Bildstein, K. L., W. Schelsky, J. Zalles, and S. Ellis. Conservation Status of Tropical Raptors. *Journal of Raptor Research*. In press.

Bildstein, K. L. and J. I. Zalles. editors. 1995. *Raptor Migration Watch-site Manual*. Hawk Mountain Sanctuary Association, Kempton, Pennsylvania.

Bird, David. 1996. Those Remarkable K-Birds. *Hawk Mountain News*, 84:18-21.

Blauer, Mark. 1996. Northern Appalachian Region. *Hawk Migration Studies*, 22(1):73-96.

Blew, Jan H. 1990a. Conventional Dairy Farm. (Kempton Area Breeding Bird Census - 1989). *Journal of Field Ornithology*, 61(Supplement):82-83.

_____. 1990b. Organic Pasture - Grain Farm. (Maxatawny Township Breeding Bird Census - 1989). *Journal of Field Ornithology*, 61(Supplement):83-84.

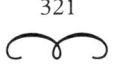

Bohall Wood, P., C. Viverette, L. Goodrich, M. Pokras, and C. Tibbott. 1996. Environmental Contaminant Levels in Sharp-shinned Hawks from the Eastern United States. *Journal of Raptor Research*, 30:136-144.

Bonta, Marcia. 1993. Appalachian Trails: The Leaves of Autumn. *Hawk Mountain News*, 79:22-24.

Boyer, Dean A. 1989. Nine Bluebirds in One Box! *Sialia*, 11(1):15-16.

Brauning, Daniel W., ed. 1992. *Atlas of Breeding Birds in Pennsylvania*. Pittsburgh: Pittsburgh University Press.

Brett, James J. 1974. The Mountain Year. *Hawk Mountain News Letter No. 46*, Hawk Mountain Sanctuary Association, Kempton, Pa. pp. 6-38.

_____. 1981. The School in the Clouds, Continued. *Hawk Mountain News*, 56:4-11.

_____. 1982. Curator's Report. *Hawk Mountain News*, 57:3-18.

_____. 1983. Curator's Report: The Mountain Year. *Hawk Mountain News*, 59:3-9.

_____. 1984a American Conservation's "Glorious Joan of Arc." *Hawk Mountain News*, 62:4-14.

_____. 1984b. The First Years on the Mountain: Maurice Broun's Journals. *Hawk Mountain News*, 62:20-28.

_____. 1984c. Red Letter Days. *Hawk Mountain News, 62*:53-57.

_____. 1984d. Mountain Journey. *Pennsylvania Game News*, 55(10):3-11.

_____. 1984e. Curator's Report: The Mountain Year. *Hawk Mountain News*, 61:3-18.

_____. 1986a. *The Mountain and the Migration*. Ithaca, N.Y.: Cornell University Press.

_____. 1985b. The Slide: An Historic Site. *Hawk Mountain News*, 64:14-15.

_____. 1986a. Curator's Report. *Hawk Mountain News*, 65:3-16.

_____. 1986b. Education and the Lookout. *Hawk Mountain News*, 66:16-19.

_____. 1987. Curator's Report. *Hawk Mountain News*, 67:3-13.

_____. 1988. Curator's Report: The Mountain Year. *Hawk Mountain News*, 69:3-17.

_____. 1989. Curator's Report: The Mountain Year. *Hawk Mountain News*, 71:3-17.

_____. 1990a. Curator's Report. *Hawk Mountain News*, 73:8-16.

_____. 1990b. From the Mountain. *Eyas*, 13(1):15-18.

_____. 1991a. *The Mountain and the Migration (revised and expanded edition)*. Ithaca, N.Y.: Cornell University Press.

_____. 1991b. From Karisimbe to Kittatinny. *Hawk Mountain News*, 75:22-31.

_____. 1992a. Mountain Year: Of Raptors and Reverence. *Hawk Mountain News*, 76:20-31.

_____. 1992b. Mountain Year: Rainbows of Winter. *Hawk Mountain News*, 77:11-21.

_____. 1993a. Mountain Year: Morning Dawns Softly. *Hawk Mountain News*. 78:18-27.

_____. 1993b. Mountain Year: Under the Owl Moon. *Hawk Mountain News*, 79:11-21.

_____. 1993c. Birder's Guide to Hawk Mountain. *Wildbird*, 7(10):58-63.

_____. 1994a. Mountain Year: Season of Silk Rain. *Hawk Mountain News*, 80:20-31.

_____. 1994b. Mountain Year: Winter into Spring. *Hawk Mountain News*, 81:10-19.

_____. 1995a. Mountain Year: Perfect Scents. *Hawk Mountain News*, 82:22-31.

_____. 1995b. Mountain Year: Full Circle. *Hawk Mountain News*, 83:12-17.

Brett, James J. and Keith L. Bildstein. 1993. Pages 367-370 in *An International Scheme for Monitoring Raptor Populations at Migration Sites*, E. T. Wilson, editor. Proceedings of the Eighth Pan African Ornithological Congress, Musee Royal de Afrique Centrale, Tervuren, Belgium.

Brett, James J., Tom and Mickie Mutchler, and Michael Harwood. 1987. Alexander Charles Nagy 1924 - 1986. *Hawk Mountain News*, 67:14-17.

Brett, James J. and Alex C. Nagy. 1973. *Feathers in the Wind: The Mountain and the Migration.* Kutztown, Pa.: Kutztown Publishing Co.

Brett, James J. and Stephan B. Oresman. 1990. Michael Harwood: 1984-1989. *Hawk Mountain News*, 73:4-7.

Briggs, S. A. 1957. Safer Passage for Hawks in Pennsylvania. *Atlantic Naturalist*, 12(6):293-296.

Bright, Stanley and Earl Poole. 1924. Bird-Lore's Twenty-fourth Christmas Census: Reading. *Bird-Lore*, 26:30.

Brock, Frederic H., Bernard L. Morris, and Richard E. Wiltraut. 1984. *Birds of the Lehigh Valley Area*. Emmaus, Pa.: Lehigh Valley Audubon Society.

Broley, Charles, L. 1947. Migration and Nesting of Florida Bald Eagles. *Wilson Bulletin*, 59:3-20.

_____. 1952. *Eagle Man*. New York: Pellegrini and Cudahy.

Brooks, Maurice. 1965. *The Appalachians*. Boston: Houghton Mifflin.

Broun, Maurice. 1934 to 1966. Unpublished field journals. Archived at Muhlenberg College, Allentown, Pa.

_____. 1935a. The Hawk Migration During the Fall of 1934, Along the Kittatinny Ridge in Pennsylvania. *Auk*, 52: 233-247.

_____. 1935b. Ravens in the Kittatinny Ridge of Pennsylvania. *Auk*, 52:311.

_____. 1935c. Pennsylvania Sanctuary for Birds of Prey. *Bulletin of the Massachusetts Audubon Society*, 18(9):3-7.

_____. 1936a. Three Seasons at Hawk Mountain. *Publication No. 61*. Emergency Conservation Committee.

_____. 1936b. Hawk Mountain Sanctuary. *Nature Magazine*, 27:367-368.

_____. 1936c. Hawk Mountain Sanctuary - Season of 1935. Emergency Conservation Committee Report for 1935: Forward into Battle, pp. 7-11.

_____. 1936d. The First Hawk Sanctuary - Season of 1935. *Bulletin of the Massachusetts Audubon Society*, 19(9):5-9.

_____. 1937. Hawk Mountain. *Frontiers*, October:8-11.

_____. 1939. Fall Migration of Hawks at Hawk Mountain, Pennsylvania, 1934-1938. *Auk*, 56:429-441.

_____. 1940. *News Letter to Members No. 3*. Hawk Mountain Sanctuary Association, Kempton, Pa.

_____. 1941a. Migration of Blue Jays. *Auk*, 58:262.

_____. 1941b. Notes from Hawk Mountain Sanctuary. *Auk*, 58:267-268.

_____. 1941c. Hawk Mountain Sanctuary. *Fauna*, 3:83-85.

_____. 1946a. *News Letter to Members No. 14*. Hawk Mountain Sanctuary Association, Kempton, Pa.

_____. 1946b. Report of the Curator. *News Letter to Members No. 15*. Hawk Mountain Sanctuary Association, Kempton.

_____. 1947a. Hawk Mountain Sanctuary Autumn News from the Curator October, November and December, 1946. *News Letter to Members No. 16*. Hawk Mountain Sanctuary Association, Kempton, Pa.

_____. 1947b. Golden Eagle Captures Red-shouldered Hawk. *Auk*, 64(2):317-318.

_____. 1948. Hawk Mountain Sanctuary/The Curator's Bird Report for 1947. *News Letter to Members No. 17.* Hawk Mountain Sanctuary Association, Kempton, Pa.

_____. 1949a. *Hawks Aloft: the Story of Hawk Mountain.* New York: Dodd, Mead.

_____. 1949b. Curator's Report 1948. *News Letter to Members No. 18.* Hawk Mountain Sanctuary Association, Kempton, Pa.

_____. 1950. The Curator's Report. *News Letter to Members No. 19.* Hawk Mountain Sanctuary Association, Kempton.

_____. 1951a. The Curator's Report. *News Letter to Members No. 20.* Hawk Mountain Sanctuary Association, Kempton.

_____. 1951b. Hawks and the Weather. *Atlantic Naturalist*, 6:105-112.

_____. 1952. The Curator's Report. *News Letter to Members No. 21.* Hawk Mountain Sanctuary Association, Kempton.

_____. 1953. The Curator's Report. *News Letter to Members No. 22.* Hawk Mountain Sanctuary Association, Kempton.

_____. 1954. The Curator's Report. *News Letter to Members No. 23.* Hawk Mountain Sanctuary Association, Kempton.

_____. 1955. The Curator's Report. *News Letter to Members No. 24.* Hawk Mountain Sanctuary Association, Kempton.

_____. 1956a. The Curator's Report. *News Letter to Members No. 25.* Hawk Mountain Sanctuary Association, Kempton.

_____. 1956b. Pennsylvania's Bloody Ridges. *Nature Magazine*, 49:288-292.

_____. 1957. The Curator's Report. *News Letter to Members No. 26.* Hawk Mountain Sanctuary Association, Kempton.

_____. 1958a. The Curator's Report. *News Letter to Members No. 27.* Hawk Mountain Sanctuary Association, Kempton.

_____. 1958b. Hawk Mountain Sanctuary Deer-Hunting Regulations. *News Letter to Members No. 28.* Hawk Mountain Sanctuary Association, Kempton, Pa.

_____. 1958c. Homing Cowbirds at Hawk Mountain. *EBBA News*, 22(20):27-28.

_____. 1959. The Curator's Report. *News Letter to Members No. 29.* Hawk Mountain Sanctuary Association, Kempton.

_____. 1960a. Curator's Report - 1959. *News Letter to Members No. 30.* Hawk Mountain Sanctuary Association, Kempton, Pa.

_____. 1960b. Hoary Redpolls at Hawk Mountain. *Cassinia*, 43:23.

_____. 1961. Curator's Report - 1960. *News Letter to Members No. 31.* Hawk Mountain Sanctuary Association, Kempton.

_____. 1962. Curator's Report - 1961. *News Letter to Members No. 32.* Hawk Mountain Sanctuary Association, Kempton.

_____. 1963a. *Hawk Migrations and the Weather.* Hawk Mountain Sanctuary Association, Kempton, Pa.

_____. 1963b. Curator's Report - Highlights of 1962. *News Letter to Members No. 34.* Hawk Mountain Sanctuary Association, Kempton, Pa.

_____. 1964. Curator's Report - 1963. *News Letter to Members No. 35.* Hawk Mountain Sanctuary Association, Kempton.

_____. 1965. Curator's Report - 1964. *News Letter to Members No. 36.* Hawk Mountain Sanctuary Association, Kempton.

_____. 1966a. Curator's Report - 1965. *News Letter to Members No. 37.* Hawk Mountain Sanctuary Association, Kempton, Pa.

_____. 1966b. What Future for Birds of Prey? *Audubon Magazine*, 68:330-334, 341-342.

_____. 1966c. Baltimore Orioles at Hawk Mountain, Pa. *EBBA*, 29(1):6-7.

_____. 1968. Notes on a Brewer's Blackbird in Pennsylvania. *Cassinia*, 50:58.

_____. 1973. Earl L. Poole. *Cassinia*, 54:22-24.

_____. 1975. A Send-off On the Adventure. Pages 162-165 in *Proceedings of the North American Hawk Migration Conference, Syracuse, New York, April 18-21, 1974.* Hawk Migration Association of North America, Washington, Connecticut.

_____. 1979a. Cliff Swallows at Lake Ontelaunee. *Cassinia*, 57:47.

_____. 1979b. Of Snow-birds and Sorghum. *Cassinia*, 57:34-35.

_____. 1979c. The Importance of Being Sober/Are We Suffering from Diplopia? *Osprey*, 2(1):2-3.

Broun, Maurice and Benjamin V. Goodwin. 1943. Flight Speeds of Hawks and Crows. *Auk*, 60:487-492.

Bull, John. 1964. *Birds of the New York Area.* New York: Harper and Row.

Bulletin of the Baird Ornithological Club. 1939 to 1948. Reading Public Museum and Art Gallery.

_____. 1974. *Birds of New York State.* Garden City, New York: Doubleday/Natural History Press.

Bunn, A., W. Klein, and K. L. Bildstein. 1995. Time-of-day Effects on the Numbers and Behavior of Non-breeding Raptors Seen on Roadside Surveys in Eastern Pennsylvania. *Journal of Field Ornithology*, 66:544-552.

Carson, Rachel. 1962. *Silent Spring.* Boston, Mass.: Houghton Mifflin.

Collins, Jr., Henry H. 1933. *Hawk Slaughter at Drehersville.* The Hawk and Owl Society Bulletin No. 3:10-18.

_____. 1935. A Hawk Sanctuary, Pennsylvania Mountain is First Refuge. *Nature Magazine*, 25:84-86.

Commonwealth of Pennsylvania. 1992. *Nolde Forest Environmental Education Center Resource Management Plan.* Harrisburg Pa.: Department of Environmental Resources, Bureau of State Parks.

_____. 1996. *French Creek State Park Resource Management Plan.* Harrisburg, Pa.: Department of Conservation and Natural Resources, Bureau of State Parks.

Conway, Albert E. 1992. In Memoriam: Maurice Broun, 1906-1979. *Auk*, 109(4):908.

Crocoll, S. T. 1994. Red-Shouldered Hawk (*Buteo lineatus*). In *The Birds of North America*, No. 218 (A. Poole and F. Gill, eds.) The Academy of Natural Sciences, Philadelphia, PA, and the American Ornithologists' Union, Washington, D.C.

Daub, B. C. 1996a. Oak-Maple Ridge-top Forest (Hawk Mountain Winter Bird Population Study -1995). *Journal of Field Ornithology*, 67(Supplement):12.

_____. 1996b. Oak-Maple Slope Forest (Hawk Mountain Winter Bird Population Study - 1995). *Journal of Field Ornithology*, 67(Supplement):12-13.

Deeter, Anna P. and Mary E. 1917. Bird-Lore's Seventeenth Christmas Census: Reading. *Bird-Lore*, 19:23.

_____. 1918. Bird-Lore's Eighteenth Christmas Census: Reading. *Bird-Lore*, 20:38.

DeReamus, David. 1987. Northern Appalachians. *Hawk Migration Studies*, 12(1):30-32.

_____. 1988. Northern Appalachians. *Hawk Migration Studies*, 13(2):34-36.

_____. 1989. Northern Appalachians. *Hawk Migration Studies*, 14(2):68.

_____. 1990. Northern Appalachians. *Hawk Migration Studies*, 15(2):107-109.

_____. 1991. Northern Appalachians. *Hawk Migration Studies*, 16(2):42-44.

_____. 1993. Northern Appalachians. *Hawk Migration Studies*, 18(2):49-50.

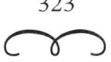

_____. 1994. Northern Appalachians. *Hawk Migration Studies*, 19(2):36-37.

_____. 1995. Northern Appalachian Region. *Hawk Migration Studies*, 20(2):45-47.

DeReamus, David and Henry Durrae. 1986. Northern Appalachians. *Hawk Migration Studies*, 11(1):24-25.

_____. 1986. Northern Appalachians. *Hawk Migration Studies*, 11(2):24-27.

The Distelfink. 1949 to 1997. Newsletter of the Baird Ornithological Club.

Dunne, Pete, David Sibley, and Clay Sutton. 1988. *Hawks in Flight.* Boston: Houghton Mifflin Co.

Durrae, Henry. 1985. Northern Appalachians. *Hawk Migration Studies*, 10(2):21.

Eakright, A., D. Jie, L. Goodrich, and C. Viverette. 1996. Oak-Maple Ridge-top Forest (Hawk Mountain Breeding Bird Census - 1995). *Journal of Field Ornithology*, 67(Supplement):47.

Edge, C. N. 1939. Hawk Mountain Sanctuary Association First Annual Report.

Edge, Rosalie. 1935. "Hawk Mountain" Sanctuary. *Emergency Conservation Committee Report for 1934: Fighting the Good Fight.* pp. 9-12.

_____. 1936a. Hawk Mountain. *Emergency Conservation Committee Report for 1935: Forward into Battle.* pp. 2-3.

_____. 1936b. The World's First Hawk Sanctuary. *International Journal of Animal Protection.* May:14-16.

_____. 1937. Hawk Mountain Sanctuary. *Emergency Conservation Committee Report for 1936: Facing Conservation Facts.* pp. 6-7.

_____. 1938. Hawk Mountain Sanctuary. *Emergency Conservation Committee Report for 1937: The Advance of Conservation.* pp. 5-7.

_____. 1939a. The Protection of the Birds of Prey. *Emergency Conservation Committe Report for 1938: Conservation - Come and Get It!* pp. 11-14.

_____. 1939b. *News Letter to Members No. 1.* Hawk Mountain Sanctuary Association, Kempton, Pa.

_____. 1939c. *News Letter to Members No. 2.* Hawk Mountain Sanctuary Associaton, Kempton, Pa.

_____. 1940a. Parital Protection for the Bald Eagle. In *Conservation and Defense; Notes, News and Comments.* Annual Report of the ECC for the Year 1940. Publication No. 84:8.

_____. 1940b. *News Letter to Members No. 4.* Hawk Mountain Sanctuary Association, Kempton, Pa.

_____. 1940c. *News Letter to Members No. 5.* Hawk Mountain Sanctuary Association, Kempton, Pa.

_____. 1942. *News Letter to Members No. 8.* Hawk Mountain Sanctuary Association, Kempton, Pa.

_____. 1943. *News Letter to Members No. 11.* Hawk Mountain Sanctuary Association, Kempton, Pa.

_____. 1945a. *Eagles in Wonderland.* Hawk Mountain Sanctuary Association, New York, N.Y.

_____. 1945b. *News Letter to Members No. 13.* Hawk Mountain Sanctuary Association, Kempton, Pa.

_____. 1956. *News Letter to Members No. 25.* Hawk Mountain Sanctuary Association, Kempton, Pa.

_____. 1962. Hawk Mountain. *Plants and Gardens*, 18:31-32.

Edge, Rosalie, and Ellsworth D. Lumley. 1940. Common Hawks of North America. *Emergency Conservation Committee Publication No. 81.*

Emergency Conservation Committee. 1935. Save the Bald Eagle. *Emergency Conservation Committee Publication No. 44.*

Environmental Information Center. February 1974. *An Environmental Profile of Reading and Berks County.* Reading: Albright College.

Fales, G. B. 1980. Hawk Mountain: A Very Special Refuge. *Bird Watcher's Digest*, 3(10):44-47.

Fingerhood, Edward D. 1984. Gyrfalcon Records in Pennsylvania: Part Two. *Cassinia*, 60:41-46.

_____. 1992. History of Pennsylvania Ornithology. Pages 35-39 in *Atlas of Breeding Birds in Pennsylvania*, edited by Daniel W. Brauning. Pittsburgh: Pittsburgh University Press.

Fingerhood, Edward D. and Sidney Lipschutz. 1982. Gyrfalcon (*Falco rusticolus*) Records in Pennsylvania. *Cassinia*, 59:68-76.

Fish, Allen. 1992. Bridging the Golden Gate and Hawk Mountain, Pennsylvania. *Pacific Raptor Report*, [Fall issue]:2-4.

Forbush, Edward H. 1927. *Birds of Massachusetts and Other New England States.* Vol. 2. Massachusetts Department of Agriculture. Norwood, Mass.: Norwood Press.

Ford, Paula. 1995. *Birder's Guide to Pennsylvania.* Houston, Texas: Gulf Publishing Co.

Frey, Edward S. 1943. *Centennial Check-list of the Birds of Cumberland County, Pennsylvania, and Her Borders., 1840 1943.* A Review of Local Observations Including and Since Spencer F. Baird. Published privately, Lemoyne, Pa.

Gabrielson, I. N., H. A. Hochbaum, R. A. McCabe, D. A. Munro, R. Pough, and C. Cottam. 1962. Report to the American Ornithologists' Union by the Committee on Bird Protection, 1961. *Auk*, 79(3):463-478.

Geffen, Alice M. 1978. *A Birdwatcher's Guide to the Eastern United States.* Woodbury, N.Y.: Barron's.

Genoways, Hugh H. and Fred J. Brenner. 1985. Species of Special Concern in Pennsylvania. Special Number 11. Carnegie Museum of Natural History, Pittsburgh, Pa.

George, J. L. 1989. Bald Eagle Kills Sharp-shinned Hawk. *Journal of Raptor Research*, 23:55-56.

Goodrich, Laurie J. 1985. The 1985 Spring Migration. *Hawk Mountain News*, 64:23-25.

_____. 1986a. The Fall Season. *Hawk Mountain News*, 65:24-36.

_____. 1986b. Breeding Birds. *Hawk Mountain News*, 66:25-31.

_____. 1987. The Fall Season. *Hawk Mountain News*, 67:24-36.

_____. 1988. The Fall Season Migration Report. *Hawk Mountain News.* 69:28-42.

_____. 1989a. The Fall Season: Migration Report. *Hawk Mountain News*, 71:26-39.

_____. 1989b. Oak-Maple Slope Forest (Hawk Mountain Breeding Bird Census - 1988). *Journal of Field Ornithology*, 60(Supplement):31.

_____. 1989c. Oak-Maple Ridge-top Forest (Hawk Mountain Breeding Bird Census - 1988). *Journal of Field Ornithology*, 60(Supplement):31-32.

_____. 1989d. Oak-Maple Slope Forest (Hawk Mountain Winter Bird Population Study - 1988). *Journal of Field Ornithology*, 60(Supplement):9-10.

_____. 1990a. The 1989 Fall Season: Migration Report. *Hawk Mountain News*, 73:18-31.

_____. 1990b. Oak-Maple Slope Forest (Hawk Mountain Breeding Bird Census - 1989). *Journal of Field Ornithology*, 61(Supplement):44.

_____. 1991a. Oak-Maple Ridge-top Forest (Hawk Mountain Breeding Bird Census - 1990). *Journal of Field Ornithology*, 62(Supplement):46.

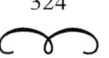

_____. 1991b. Oak-Maple Slope Forest (Hawk Mountain Breeding Bird Census - 1990). *Journal of Field Ornithology*, 62(Supplement):46-47.

_____. 1991c. Fall 1990: The Migration. *Hawk Mountain News*, 75:8-21.

_____. 1992a. Oak-Maple Ridge-top Forest (Hawk Mountain Breeding Bird Census - 1991). *Journal of Field Ornithology*, 62(Supplement):61.

_____. 1992b. Oak-Maple Slope forest (Hawk Mountain Breeding Bird Census - 1991). *Journal of Field Ornithology*, 62(Supplement):61.

_____. 1992c. A Case for Doing Nothing. *New Jersey Audubon*, Spring 1992:20-21.

_____. 1992d. Northern Harrier. Pages 94-95 in *Atlas of Breeding Birds in Pennsylvania*, edited by Daniel W. Brauning. Pittsburgh: University of Pittsburgh Press.

_____. 1992e. Sharp-shinned Hawk. Pages 96-97 in *Atlas of Breeding Birds in Pennsylvania*, edited by Daniel W. Brauning. Pittsburgh: University of Pittsburgh Press.

_____. 1992f. Cooper's Hawk. Pages 98-99 in *Atlas of Breeding Birds in Pennsylvania*, edited by Daniel W. Brauning. Pittsburgh: University of Pittsburgh Press.

_____. 1992g. Fall 1991: The Migration. *Hawk Mountain News*, 76:5-15.

_____. 1992h. Field Notes: Songbird Research; Hawk Mountain's Kestrels. *Hawk Mountain News*, 77:28-29.

_____. 1993. Migration Report: One Million and Counting. *Hawk Mountain News*, 78:7-17.

_____. 1995. Migration Report: The Raptor Circle. *Hawk Mountain News*, 82:6-17.

_____. 1996. A Hawk Watcher's Fall. *Hawk Mountain News*, 84:8-17.

_____. 1997. Migration Report: Wayward Winds of Fall. *Hawk Mountain News*, 86:8-17.

Goodrich, Laurie J. and Keith L. Bildstein, 1995. Forest Fragmentation and Bird Habitats, Hawk Shooting, and Peregrine Falcon. Pages 287-288, 343, and 514-515 in *Conservation and Environmentalism: An Encyclopedia*, R. Paehlke, editor. Garland, New York, N.Y.

Goodrich, Laurie J., James J. Brett, Cathy B. Viverette, and Keith L. Bildstein. 1994. An Invitation to Join Hawks Aloft Worldwide: Hawk Mountain's Raptor Migration Atlas Project. *Journal of Hawk Migration Studies*, 19(2):7-10.

Goodrich, L. J., S. C. Crocoll, and S. E. Senner. 1996. Broad-winged Hawk (*Buteo platypterus*) in *The Birds of North America*, No. 218 (A. Poole and F. Gill, eds.). The Academy of Natural Sciences, Philadelphia, PA, and the American Ornithologists' Union, Washington, D.C.

Goodrich, Laurie J. and Stanley E. Senner. 1988. Recent Trends of Wintering Great Horned Owls (*Bubo virginianus*), Red-tailed Hawks (*Buteo jamaicensis*), and Two of Their Avian Prey in Pennsylvania. *Journal of the Pennsylvania Academy of Sciences*, 62:131-137.

Goodrich, Laurie J., Cathy B. Viverette, Stanley E. Senner, and Keith L. Bildstein. Long-term Use of Breeding Bird Census Plots to Monitor Populations of Neotropical Migrants Breeding in Deciduous Forest in Eastern Pennsylvania, USA. In *Measuring and Monitoring Forest Biodiversity*. Washington, D.C.: Smithsonian Institution Press. In press.

Graham Jr., Frank. 1971. Of Muskrats and Birdwatchers. Pages 268-272 in *Man's Dominion: The Story of Conservation in America*. M. Evans and Co.

_____. 1984. Battle of Hawk Mountain. *Audubon*, 86(5):28-31.

_____. 1991. *The Audubon Ark: A History of the National Audubon Society*. Knopf.

Greenawalt, June. 1982. From the Window at Headquarters. *Hawk Mountain News*, 57:18-19.

_____. 1983. The Window at Headquarters. *Hawk Mountain News*, 59:9-10.

Grim, Kerry A. 1987. A Sabine's Gull in Schuylkill County. *Pennsylvania Birds*, 1(3):74.

_____. 1991. State Game Lands 110 Site Guide, Berks County. *Pennsylvania Birds*, 5(2):68-69.

_____. 1992. Letter to the Editor (Winter Wren breeding). *Pennsylvania Birds*, 5(4):146.

_____. 1994. Letter to the Editor (Ovenbird abundance). *Pennsylvania Birds*, 8(2):62.

Griscom, Ludlow. 1923. *Birds of the New York City Region*. New York: American Museum of Natural History.

Griscom, Ludlow, and Dorothy E. Snyder. 1955. *Birds of Massachusetts*. Salem, Mass.: Peabody Museum.

Gross, Alfred O. and Edna G. 1912. Bird-Lore's Twelfth Christmas Census: Reading. *Bird-Lore*, 14:29.

_____. 1913. Bird-Lore's Thirteenth Christmas Census: Reading. *Bird-Lore*, 15:30.

_____. 1914. Bird-Lore's Fourteenth Christmas Census: Reading. *Bird-Lore*, 16:38

Guers, S. and L. Goodrich. Oak-Maple Ridge-top Forest (Breeding Bird Census - 1996). *Journal of Field Ornithology*. In press.

_____. Oak-Maple Slope Forest (Breeding Bird Census - 1996). *Journal of Field Ornithology*,. In press.

Haas, Franklin C. 1975. Say's Phoebe in Pennsylvania. *Cassinia*, 55:39.

Haas, Franklin and Barbara. 1995. Birds of note - April through June 1995. *Pennsylvania Birds*, 9(2):87.

Hake, Theodore. 1955. Hurricane Birds in Pennsylvania. *Atlantic Naturalist*, 11:77-79.

Harding, John J. and Justin J. 1980. *Birding the Delaware Valley Region*. Philadelphia: Temple University Press.

Harlow, Richard C. 1918. Notes on the Breeding Birds of Pennsylvania and New Jersey. *Auk*, 35:18-29; 136-147.

Harrison, G. H. 1976. *Roger Tory Peterson's Dozen Birding Hot Spots*. New York: Simon and Schuster.

Harwood, Michael. 1973. *The View From Hawk Mountain*. New York: Charles Scribner's Sons..

_____. 1979. Broun Aloft on Kittatinny: First Curator of Hawk Mountain Takes Sanctuary One Ridge Away. *Defenders*, October 1979: 254-260.

_____. 1980. New Directions for Hawkwatching. *Journal of the Hawk Migration Association of North America*, 2(1):1-4.

_____. 1989. Giants of the Past: Maurice Broun. *American Birds*, 43(1):242-247.

Harwood, Michael, and Alexander C. Nagy. 1977. Assessing the Hawk Counts at Hawk Mountain. Pages 69-75 in J. C. Ogden, editor. *Transactions of the North American Osprey Research Conference* (National Park Service Transactions and Proceedings Series No. 2). U.S. Department of the Interior, Washington, D.C.

Haugh, John R. 1970. A Study of Hawk Migration and Weather in Eastern North America. Ph.D. dissertation. Cornell University, Ithaca, N.Y. 240 pp.

_____. 1972. A Study of Hawk Migration in Eastern North America. *Search*, 2(16):1-60.

Hawk Mountain Sanctuary. 1984. Eighty-fourth Audubon Christmas Bird Count: Hamburg. Jim Brett, compiler. *American Birds*, 38:529-520.

_____. 1985. Eighty-fifth Christmas Bird Count: Hamburg. Jim Brett and Laurie Goodrich, compilers. *American Birds*, 39:522.

_____. 1986. Eighty-sixth Christmas Bird Count: Hamburg. Jim Brett and Laurie Goodrich, compilers. *American Birds*, 40:709.

_____. 1987. Eighty-seventh Christmas Bird Count: Hamburg. Jim Brett and Laurie Goodrich, compilers. *American Birds*, 41:761; 765-780.

_____. 1988. Eighty-eighth Christmas Bird Count: Hamburg. Jim Brett and Laurie Goodrich, compilers. *American Birds*, 42:713-714.

_____. 1989. Eighty-ninth Christmas Bird Count: Hamburg. Laurie Goodrich, compiler. *American Birds*, 43:757.

_____. 1990. Ninetieth Christmas Bird Count: Hamburg. Laurie Goodrich, compiler. *American Birds*, 44:663.

_____. 1991. Ninety-first Christmas Bird Count: Hamburg. Laurie Goodrich, compiler. *American Birds*, 45:670.

_____. 1992. Ninety-second Christmas Bird Count: Hamburg. Laurie Goodrich, compiler. *American Birds*, 46:662.

_____. 1993. Ninety-third Christmas Bird Count: Hamburg. Laurie Goodrich and Cathy Viverette, compilers. *American Birds*, 47:629.

_____. 1994. Ninety-fourth Christmas Bird Count: Hamburg. Laurie Goodrich, compiler. *Field Notes*, 48:506.

_____. 1995. Ninety-fifth Christmas Bird Count: Hamburg. Laurie Goodrich, compiler. *Field Notes*, 49:475-476.

_____. 1996. Ninety-sixth Christmas Bird Count: Hamburg. Laurie Goodrich, compiler. *Field Notes*, 50:503.

Heintzelman, Donald S. 1960. Further Comments on the Hawk Mountain Petrel. *Linnaean News-Letter*, 14(6)

_____. 1961. Kermadec Petrel in Pennsylvania. *Wilson Bulletin*, 73:262-267.

_____. 1962. An Unusual Sparrow Hawk Tail. *Bird-Banding*, 33:204-205.

_____. 1963a. Mockingbird Mimics a Sparrow Hawk. *Linnaean News-Letter*, 17(2).

_____. 1963b. Cedar Waxwings Feed on Winged Ants. *Cassinia*, 48:37.

_____. 1964a. Spring and Summer Sparrow Hawk Food Habits. *Wilson Bulletin*. 76: 323-330.

_____. 1964b Note on Olive-sided Flycatcher Feeding Habits. *Cassinia*, 48:37.

_____. 1966a. Cannibalism at a Broad-winged Hawk Nest. *Auk*, 83(2): 307.

_____. 1966b. Observations and Comments on the Aerial Capture of Prey by the Sparrow Hawk. *Linnaean News-Letter*, 20(6&7).

_____. 1968. *Empidonax hammondii* in Pennsylvania. *Auk*, 85(3): 512.

_____. 1969. The Black Vulture in Pennsylvania. *Pennsylvania Game News*, 40(5):17-19.

_____. 1970a. Wings Over Hawk Mountain. *National Wildlife*, 8(5):22-27.

_____. 1970b. Autumn Hawk Watch. *Frontiers*, 35(1):16-21.

_____. 1970c. Speculation on DDT and Altered Osprey Migrations. *Raptor Research News*, 4:120-124.

_____. 1971. Observations on the Role of Nest Box Sanitation in Affecting Egg Hatchability of Wild Sparrow Hawks in Eastern Pennsylvania. *Raptor Research News,* 5(3):100.

_____. 1972. *A Guide to Northeastern Hawk Watching.* Privately published, Lambertville, N.J.

_____. 1972b. Speculation on the Possible Origin of some Sharp-shinned and Red-tailed Hawk Flights along the Kittatinny Ridge - Autumn 1971. *Science Notes No. 10.* New Jersey State Museum, Trenton, N.J.

_____. 1975. *Autumn Hawk Flights: The Migrations in Eastern North America.* New Brunswick, N.J.: Rutgers University Press.

_____. 1976. *A Guide to Eastern Hawk Watching.* University Park: Pennsylvania State University Press.

_____. 1979a. *A Guide to Hawk Watching in North America.* University Park: Pennsylvania State University.

_____. 1979b. *Hawks and Owls of North America.* New York: Universe Books.

_____. 1982. Variations in Utilization of the Kittatinny Ridge in Eastern Pennsylvania in Autumn by Migrating Golden Eagles and Bald Eagles (1968-1981). *American Hawkwatcher*, 3:1-4.

_____. 1983a. Variations in Numbers of, and Influence of Intersecting Diversion-Lines Upon, Ospreys Migrating Along the Kittatinny Ridge in Eastern Pennsylvania. *American Hawkwatcher*, 6:1-4.

_____. 1983b. An Interdisciplinary Comparison of Recreational Hawk Watching in Eastern Pennsylvania with Recreational Whale Watching in California. *American Hawkwatcher*, 7:1-4.

_____. 1984a. National Birds of Prey Conservation Week: America's Potential New Raptor Conservation Tool. *Eyas*, 7(1):8.

_____. 1984b. *Guide to Owl Watching in North America.* Piscataway, N.J.: Winchester Press.

_____. 1986. *The Migrations of Hawks.* Bloomington, Ind.: Indiana University Press.

Heintzelman, Donald S., and Robert MacClay. 1971. An Extraordinary Autumn Migration of White-breasted Nuthatches. *Wilson Bulletin*, 83:129-131.

Heintzelman, Donald S. and Alexander C. Nagy. 1968. Clutch Sizes, Hatchability Rates, and Sex Ratios of Sparrow Hawks in Eastern Pennsylvania. *Wilson Bulletin*, 80: 306-311.

Heizmann, Louis J. 1961. From Lyceum to Museum: Scientific Societies in Reading and Berks County. *Historical Review of Berks County*, 26(4):106-131.

Heller, Jonathan. 1992. Looking for Gulls in Berks County (Nine Species of Gulls). *Pennsylvania Birds*, 6(1):12.

_____. 1995. Kites and More. *Pennsylvania Birds*, 9(2):65.

Herber, Elmer C. 1956. Spencer Baird. *Historical Review of Berks County*, 21(3):66-72.

Hergesheimer, Florence, Mary E. Deeter, and Anna P. Deeter. 1924. Bird-Lore's Twenty-fourth Christmas Census: Reading. *Bird-Lore*, 26:30.

Hickey, Joseph J. 1943. *A Guide to Bird Watching.* New York: Oxford University Press.

Hill, Julian W. 1985. Reminiscences of Hawk Mountain. *Delmarva Ornithologist*, 18:3-9.

Hilton Jr., Bill. 1996. Appalachian Trails: Humming Along the Trails. *Hawk Mountain News*, 85:20-21.

_____. 1997. Appalachian Trails: A Bird in the Hand. *Hawk Mountain News*, 86:24-25.

Hoover, Jeffrey P. 1992a. *Nesting Success of Wood Thrush in a Fragmented Forest.* Unpublished master's thesis. Pennsylvania State University, University Park, Pennsylvania.

_____. 1992b. Wood Thrush in a Fragmented Pennsylvania Forest. *Keystone Wild Notes*. Newsletter of the Wild Resource Conservation Fund, Fall.

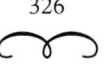

Hoover, J. and M. C. Brittingham. 1993. Regional Variation in Cowbird Parasitism of Wood Thrushes. *Wilson Bulletin*, 105:228-238.

Hoover, J. P., M. C. Brittingham, and L. J. Goodrich. 1994. Effect of Forest Patch Size on Nesting Success of Wood Thrushes. *Auk*, 112:146-155.

Ingram, Linda M. 1994. Oak-Maple-Poplar Hollow. (Nolde Forest Breeding Bird Survey - 1993). *Journal of Field Ornithology*, 65(Supplement):61.

_____. 1995. Oak-Maple-Poplar Hollow. (Nolde Forest Breeding Bird Survey - 1994). *Journal of Field Ornithology*, 66(Supplement):55.

_____. 1996. Oak-Maple-Poplar Hollow. (Nolde Forest Breeding Bird Survey - 1995). *Journal of Field Ornithology*, 67(Supplement):47.

Jie, D., A. Eakright, L. Goodrich, and C. Viverette. Oak-Maple Slope Forest (Hawk Mountain Breeding Bird Census - 1995). *Journal of Field Ornithology*, 67(Supplement)47.

Keller, Rudolph C. 1988a. County Reports April - June 1988. *Pennsylvania Birds*, 2(2):59-60.

_____. 1988b. County Reports July - September 1988. *Pennsylvania Birds*, 2(3):97-98.

_____. 1988c. County Reports October to December 1988. *Pennsylvania Birds*, 2(4):138.

_____. 1989a. County Reports January - March 1989. *Pennsylvania Birds*, 3(1):25.

_____. 1989b. County Reports April - June 1989. *Pennsylvania Birds*, 3(2):61-62.

_____. 1989c. County Reports July - September 1989. *Pennsylvania Birds*, 3(3):100.

_____. 1989d. County Reports October - December 1989. *Pennsylvania Birds*, 3(4):137.

_____. 1990a. County Reports January - March 1990. *Pennsylvania Birds*, 4(1):19-20.

_____. 1990b. County Reports April - June 1990. *Pennsylvania Birds*, 4(2):59.

_____. 1990c. County Reports July - September 1990. *Pennsylvania Birds*, 4(3):106.

_____. 1991a. County Reports October - December 1990. *Pennsylvania Birds*, 4(4):148.

_____. 1991b. County Reports January - March 1991. *Pennsylvania Birds*, 5(1):31.

_____. 1991c. Second Record of Iceland Gull (*Larus glaucoides*) for Berks County. *Pennsylvania Birds*, 5(1):23.

_____. 1991d. Second Record of Black-legged Kittiwake (*Larus tridactyla*) for Berks County. *Pennsylvania Birds*, 5(1):23.

_____. 1991e. County Reports April - June 1991. *Pennsylvania Birds*, 5(2):78.

_____. 1991f. County Reports July - September 1991. *Pennsylvania Birds*, 5(3):123-124.

_____. 1992a. County Reports October - December 1991. *Pennsylvania Birds*, 5(4):165.

_____. 1992b. County Reports January - March 1992. *Pennsylvania Birds*, 6(1):29.

_____. 1992c. County Reports April - June 1992. *Pennsylvania Birds*, 6(2):70-71.

_____. 1992d. County Reports July - September 1992. *Pennsylvania Birds*, 6(3):116-126.

_____. 1993a. County Reports October - December 1992. *Pennsylvania Birds*, 6(4):169-178.

_____. 1993b. County Reports January - March 1993. *Pennsylvania Birds*, 7(1):24-31.

_____. 1993c. Notes from the Field April - June 1993. *Pennsylvania Birds*, 7(2):61.

_____. 1993d. Notes from the Field July - September 1993. *Pennsylvania Birds*, 7(3):96.

_____. 1993e. Conventional Dairy Farm. (Kempton Area Breeding Bird Census - 1992). *Journal of Field Ornithology*, 64(Supplement):114.

_____. 1994a. Notes from the Field October - December 1993. *Pennsylvania Birds*, 7(4):155.

_____. 1994b. Notes from the Field January - March 1994. *Pennsylvania Birds*, 8(1):36.

_____. 1994c. Notes from the Field April - June 1994. *Pennsylvania Birds*, 8(2):99.

_____. 1994d. Notes from the Field July - September 1994. *Pennsylvania Birds*, 8(3):158.

_____. 1994e. Conventional Dairy Farm. (Kempton Area Breeding Bird Census - 1993). *Journal of Field Ornithology*, 65(Supplement):126-127.

_____. 1995a. Notes from the Field October - December 1994. *Pennsylvania Birds*, 8(4):223.

_____. 1995b. Local Notes January - March 1995. *Pennsylvania Birds*, 9(1):31.

_____. 1995c. Local Notes April - June 1995. *Pennsylvania Birds*, 9(2):89-90.

_____. 1995d. Local Notes July - September 1995. *Pennsylvania Birds*, 9(3):145.

_____. 1995e. Conventional Dairy Farm. (Kempton Area Breeding Bird Census - 1994). *Journal of Field Ornithology*, 66(Supplement):117.

_____. 1996a. Local Notes October - December 1995. *Pennsylvania Birds*, 9(4):211.

_____. 1996b. Local Notes January - March 1996. *Pennsylvania Birds*, 10(1):16.

_____. 1996c. Local Notes April - June 1996. *Pennsylvania Birds*, 10(2):97.

_____. 1996d. Local Notes July - September 1996. *Pennsylvania Birds*, 10(3):161.

_____. 1996e. Conventional Dairy Farm. (Kempton Area Breeding Bird Census - 1995). *Journal of Field Ornithology*, 67(Supplement):90.

_____. 1997. Local Notes October - December 1996. *Pennsylvania Birds*, 10(4):223.

Kerlinger, Paul and James Brett. 1995. Hawk Mountain Sanctuary: A Case Study of Birder Visitation and Birding Economics at a Private Refuge. Pages 271-280 in *Wildlife and Recreationists: Coexistence Through Management and Research*. Washington, D.C.: Island Press.

Koch, Arlene. 1994. The Less than Lesser Goldfinch. *Pennsylvania Birds*, 7(4):129-130.

Kwater, Ed. 1992. Pennsylvania's First Mew Gull with Notes on Its Racial Identification. *Pennsylvania Birds*, 6(1):8-9.

Large, J. Warren. 1927. Bird-Lore's Twenty-seventh Christmas Census: Reading. *Bird-Lore*, 29:28.

_____. 1928. Bird-Lore's Twenty-eighth Christmas Census: Reading. *Bird-Lore*, 30:42.

_____. 1929. Bird-Lore's Twenty-ninth Christmas Census: Reading. *Bird-Lore*, 31:37-38.

_____. 1931. Bird-Lore's Thirty-first Christmas Census: Reading. *Bird-Lore*, 33:44.

_____. 1932. Bird-Lore's Thirty-second Christmas Census: Reading. *Bird-Lore*, 34:46.

Laura, Thomas. 1992. Northern Appalachians. *Hawk Migration Studies*, 18(1):40-50.

Lawrence, S. and B. Gross. 1984. *The Audubon Society Field Guide to the Natural Places of the Mid - Atlantic States: Inland*. New York: Pantheon Books.

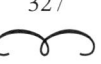

Lebo, Kenneth. 1996. Carr's Recreation Park, New Morgan, Berks County. *Pennsylvania Birds*, 10(3):143-144.

Leckey, T., S. Nord, and S. Benz. 1983a. Oak-Maple Ridge-top Forest (Forty-sixth Breeding Bird Census). *American Birds*, 37:55.

Leckey, Thomas, Steven Nord, and Deborah Keller. 1982. Breeding Bird Survey. *Hawk Mountain News*, 57:28-29.

_____. 1983b. Oak-Maple Slope Forest (Forty-sixth Breeding Bird Census). *American Birds*, 37:55.

Lenhart, Cynthia. 1992. Is History Repeating Itself? *Hawk Mountain News*, 76:3-4.

_____. 1996. Other Side of the Mountain: Taking Stock. *Hawk Mountain News*, 85:1-2.

Maransky, B., L. Goodrich, and K. Bildstein. 1997. Seasonal Shifts in the Effects of Weather on the Visible Migration of Red-tailed Hawks at Hawk Mountain, Pennsylvania, 1992-1994. *Wilson Bulletin*, 109:246-252.

McDowell, R. T. 1948. *Pennsylvania Birds of Prey*. Pennsylvania Game Commission, Harrisburg, Pa.

Mengel, G. Henry. 1912. Bird-Lore's Twelfth Christmas Census: Reading. *Bird-Lore*, 14:29.

_____. 1914. Bird-Lore's Fourteenth Christmas Census: Reading. *Bird-Lore*, 16:38.

_____. 1915. Bird-Lore's Fifteenth Christmas Census: Reading. *Bird-Lore*, 17:34.

_____. 1916. Bird-Lore's Sixteenth Christmas Census: Reading. *Bird-Lore*, 18:28.

_____. 1917. Bird-Lore's Seventeenth Christmas Census: Reading. *Bird-Lore*, 19:23.

_____. 1918. Bird-Lore's Eighteenth Christmas Census: Reading. *Bird-Lore*, 20:38.

_____. 1919. Bird-Lore's Nineteenth Christmas Census: Reading. *Bird-Lore*, 21:36.

_____. 1920. Bird-Lore's Twentieth Christmas Census: Reading. *Bird-Lore*, 22:30.

_____. 1921. Bird-Lore's Twenty-first Christmas Census: Reading. *Bird-Lore*, 23(1):17.

_____. 1922. Bird-Lore's Twenty-second Christmas Census: Reading. *Bird-Lore*, 24(1):23.

_____. 1924. Bird-Lore's Twenty-fourth Christmas Census: Reading. *Bird-Lore*, 26(1):30.

Mengel, G. Henry and J. Warren Large. 1928. Bird-Lore's Twenty-eighth Christmas Census: Reading. *Bird-Lore*, 30(1):42.

Mengel, Levi W. 1937. Spencer F. Baird 1823-1887. *Historical Review of Berks County*. 3(1):25-26.

Meritt, James K. 1964. Yellow-headed Blackbird at Hawk Mountain. *Cassinia*, 47:38-39.

Morgan, G. R. 1995. *Identifying Nest Predators of Forest Songbirds and Quantifying Predation Rates*. Unpublished master's thesis. Pennsylvania State University, University Park, Pennsylvania.

Morton, R. 1982. Spring Migration at Hawk Mountain. *Hawk Mountain News*, 58:7-10.

_____. 1983. Spring Migration at Hawk Mountain. *Hawk Mountain News*, 60:10-12.

Muhlenberg, J. Peter. 1993. Dr. Earl Lincoln Poole... A Man of Excellence and Versatility 1891-1972. *The Historical Review of Berks County*, LVIII(4): 173-177.

Mutchler, T. 1971. *Surgical Treatment by Pinning of Longbone Fractures on Raptors*. Hawk Mountain Sanctuary Association, Kempton, Pennsylvania.

Nagy, Alexander C. 1962. Biography of a Farm. *Plants and Gardens*, 18(2):31-32.

_____. 1963. Population Density of Sparrow Hawks in Eastern Pennsylvania. *Wilson Bulletin*, 75(1):93.

_____. 1966. Curator's Report. *News Letter No. 38*. Hawk Mountain Sanctuary Association, Kempton, Pa.

_____. 1967. Curator's Report - 1966. *News Letter to Members No. 39*. Hawk Mountain Sanctuary Association, Kempton.

_____. 1968. Curator's Report. *News Letter to Members No. 40*. Hawk Mountain Sanctuary Association, Kempton, Pa.

_____. 1970. Curator's Report. *News Letter to Members No. 42*. Hawk Mountain Sanctuary Association, Kempton, Pa.

_____. 1972. 1971 Curator's Report. *News Letter to Members No. 44*. Hawk Mountain Sanctuary Association, Kempton.

_____. 1973. 1972 Curator's Report. *News Letter to Members No. 45*. Hawk Mountain Sanctuary Association, Kempton.

_____. 1975. Hawk Mountain Osprey Project. Pages 147-150 in M. Harwood, editor. *Proceedings of the North American Hawk Migration Conference 1974*. Washington, Connecticut.

_____. 1976. Northern Appalachians. *Hawk Migration Studies*, 1(2):11-14.

_____. 1977a. Population Trend Indices Based on 40 Years of Autumn Counts at Hawk Mountain Sanctuary in Northeastern Pennsylvania. Pages 243-253 *in* R.D. Chancellor, editor. *World Conference on Birds of Prey, Report of Proceedings, Vienna 1975*. International Council for Bird Preservation, Cambridge, England.

_____. 1977b. Northern Appalachians. *Hawk Migration Studies*, 2(1):7-8.

_____. 1977c. Northern Appalachians. *Hawk Migration Studies*, 2(2):12-16.

_____. 1978a. Northern Appalachians. *Hawk Migration Studies*, 3(1):9-10.

_____. 1978b. Northern Appalachians. *Hawk Migration Studies*, 3(2):22-25.

_____. 1979a. Northern Appalachians. *Hawk Migration Studies*, 4(1):12-13.

_____. 1979b. Northern Appalachians. *Hawk Migration Studies*, 4(2):29-33.

_____. 1979c. Miracle Day. *Hawk Mountain News*, 50 [*sic*, 51]:25-29.

_____. 1980. Northern Appalachians. *Hawk Migration Studies*, 5(1):11.

_____. 1984. Labor Day Bald Eagles. *Hawk Mountain News*, 62:37-41.

Negro, J. J., K. L. Bildstein, and D. M. Bird. 1995. Effects of Food Deprivation and Handling Stress on Fault-bar Formation in Nestling American Kestrels (*Falco sparverius*). *Ardea*, 82:262-267.

Noojibail, G. 1995. A Relationship Between Songbird Breeding Success, Small Mammal Abundance and Fragmented Forests in Eastern Pennsylvania. *The Meadowlark* (Journal of Illinois Ornithology) 4:7-11.

Oehser, Paul H. 1966. Spencer Fullerton Baird. *Historical Review of Berks County*, 31(3):86-88; 108.

Peterson, Roger T. 1947. *A Field Guide to the Birds*. (Second revised and enlarged edition). Boston: Houghton Mifflin Co.

_____. 1948. The Sky is Their Highway. Pages 152-163 in *Birds Over America*. New York: Grosset and Dunlap.

_____. 1966. Tribute to Maurice and Irma Broun. *News Letter to Members No. 38*. Hawk Mountain Sanctuary Association, Kempton, Pa.

_____. 1985. Hawk Mountain Celebrates it Fiftieth Anniversary. *Bird Watcher's Digest*, 7(3):83-92.

_____. 1996. A Short History of Hawk Mountain. *Bird Watcher's Digest*, 18(5):16-28.

Pettingill Jr., Olin Sewall. 1977. *A Guide to Bird Finding East of the Mississippi*. (second edition). New York: Oxford University Press.

Poole, Alan. 1996. Thinking Like An Osprey. *Hawk Mountain News*, 85:5-8.

Poole, Earl L. No Date. *Enter Hawk - Exit Mouse.* Hawk Mountain Sanctuary Association, Kempton, Pa.

_____. 1922 to 1972. Unpublished field journals. Archived at the Academy of Natural Sciences, Philadelphia.

_____. 1925. A Graphic Method of Recording Flight. *Auk*, 42:209-216.

_____. 1929a. Savannah Sparrow Nesting Near Reading, Pennsylvania. *Auk*, 46:550.

_____. 1929b. Northern Phalarope in Pennsylvania. *Auk*, 46:108.

_____. 1929c. Ducks and Other Water Birds on the Reading, Pa., Reservoir. *Auk*, 46:534.

_____. 1930a. *The Bird Life of Berks County, Pennsylvania.* Reading Public Museum Bulletin No. 12.

_____. 1930b. Winter Nesting of the Barn Owl. *Auk*, 47:84.

_____. 1930c. Holboell's Grebes in Pennsylvania. *Auk*, 47:241.

_____. 1930d. The Fall Migration of Water Birds and Others at Reading, Pennsylvania. *Auk*, 47:427.

_____. 1931. Breeding of the Blue-winged Teal in Pennsylvania. *Auk*, 48:110.

_____. 1932. Some Recent Records from Reading, Pennsylvania. *Auk*, 49(2):233-235.

_____. 1933a. A Pennsylvania Specimen of the White Gyrfalcon. *Auk*, 50:97-98.

_____. 1933b. Water Birds Observed at Reading, Pa. *Auk*, 50:230.

_____. 1934a. The Hawk Migration Along the Kittatinny Ridge in Pennsylvania. *Auk*, 51:17-20.

_____. 1934b. An Influx of Leach's Petrels. *Auk*, 51:74.

_____. 1934c. Rare Birds at Lake Ontelaunee, Reading, Pa. *Auk*, 51:94.

_____. 1935. Water Birds on an Inland Reservoir. *Cassinia*, 29:21-34.

_____. 1938. Weights and Wing Areas in North American Birds. *Auk*, 55:511-517.

_____. 1940. Recent Records from Lake Ontelaunee, Pennsylvania. *Auk*, 57:577.

_____. 1947 and 1954. *A Half Century of Bird Life in Berks County.* (and Supplement). Reading Public Museum Bulletin No. 19.

_____. 1951a. Hutchins's Goose at Lake Ontelaunee, Berks County, Pa. *Cassinia*, 38:33-34.

_____. 1951b. Blue Geese at Lake Ontelaunee, Berks Co., Pa. *Cassinia*, 38:34.

_____. 1951c. Brunnich's Murre in Berks County, Pa. *Cassinia*, 38:34.

_____. 1951d. First Nesting of the Cerulean Warbler in Eastern Pennsylvania. *Cassinia*, 38:35.

_____. 1956. [Review of] North American Birds of Prey. *Auk*, 73:297.

_____. 1957. Lake Ontelaunee Records. *Cassinia*, 41:29.

_____. 1958. Recent Records of the Black-backed Three-toed Woodpecker in Berks County. *Cassinia*, 42:22-23.

_____. 1959. Lake Ontelaunee Records. *Cassinia*, 43:21.

_____. 1960. Lake Ontelaunee Records. *Cassinia*, 44:19.

_____. 1961. Herbert H. Beck. *Cassinia*, 45:19.

_____. 1962. Painted Bunting at Reading. *Cassinia*, 46:21-22.

_____. 1964. *Pennsylvania Birds - An Annotated List.* Narberth, Pa.: Livingston Publishing Co.

_____. 1965. White Ibis in Berks County. *Cassinia*, 48:37-38.

_____. *Pennsylvania Birds.* Unpublished manuscript, mid-1960s. Archived at the Academy of Natural Sciences, Philadelphia.

_____. 1971. Herbert Heubman Beck. *Auk*, 88:710-711.

Poole, Earl L. and Wendell Kern. 1920. Bird-Lore's Twentieth Christmas Census: Reading. *Bird-Lore*, 22:30.

Porneluzi, P., J. Bednarz, L. Goodrich, J. Hoover, and N. Zawada. 1993. Reproductive Performance of Territorial Ovenbirds Occupying Forest Fragments and a Contiguous Forest in Pennsylvania. *Conservation Biology*, 7:618-622.

Pough, Richard H. 1932. Wholesale Killing of Hawks in Pennsylvania. *Bird-Lore*, 34(6):429.

_____. 1936a. A Glider Highway. *Bird-Lore*, Sept. Oct.:317-321.

_____. 1936b. Pennsylvania and the Hawk Problem. *Pennsylvania Game News*, 7(4):8, 23.

_____. 1984. Recollections of a Pioneer. *Hawk Mountain News*, 62:15-18.

Powers, L., M. Pokras, K. Rio, C. Viverette, and L. Goodrich. 1994. Hematology and Occurrence of Hemoparasites in Migrating Sharp-shinned Hawks (*Accipiter striatus*) During Fall Migration. *Journal of Raptor Research*, 28:178-185.

Pulcinella, Nick. 1995. Official List of the Birds of Pennsylvania. *Pennsylvania Birds*, 9(3):118-123.

_____. 1996. Hurricane Fran's Fallout. *Pennsylvania Birds*, 10(3):138-142.

Raptor Research Foundation. 1986. Raptor Conservation in the Next 50 Years. *Raptor Research Report No. 5.*

Rich, David, Harold Morrin, and Jonathan Heller. 1992. First Pennsylvania Record of Mew Gull, Berks County. *Pennsylvania Birds*, 6(1):7.

Robbins, C. S. 1975. A History of North American Hawk Watching. Pages 29-40 in *Proceedings of the North American Hawk Migration Conference.*

Roberts, P. M. 1984. Why Count Hawks? A Continental Perspective. *Hawk Mountain News*, 62:46-51.

Robson, J. E. 1958. Hawk Mountain. *Falconer*, 3(5):159-160.

Rohrbaugh, R. 1994. *Effects of Microclimate, Mircrohabitat, and Macrohabitat on Nest-box Use and Nesting Success of American Kestrels in Eastern Pennsylvania.* Unpublished master's thesis. Pennsylvania State University, University Park, Pennsylvania.

_____. 1995. Effects of Microclimate, Mircrohabitat, and Macrohabitat on Nest-box Use and Nesting Success of American Kestrels in Eastern Pennsylvania. *Wingspan* (Raptor Research Foundation), 4(1):16 abstract only.

Rohrbaugh, R. W. and R. H. Yahner. 1991. Nest-box Use and Reproductive Success of American Kestrels in Southeastern Pennsylvania. *Journal of Raptor Research*, 25(4):159.

Rosenfield, R. N. and J. Bielefeldt. 1993. Cooper's Hawk (*Accipiter cooperii*). In The Birds of North America, No. 75 (A. Poole and F. Gill, eds.). Philadelphia: The Academy of Natural Sciences; Washington, D.C.: The American Ornithologists' Union.

Rupp, William J. 1946. *Bird Names and Bird Lore Among the Pennsylvania Germans.* Norristown, Pa.: The Pennsylvania German Society Vol. LII.

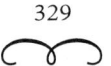

Saenger, Peter G. 1984. Territorial Dispute Between Female American Kestrels. *Journal of Field Ornithology*, 55(3):387-388.

Santner, Steven J., Daniel W. Brauning, Glenna P. Schwalbe, and Paul W. Schwalbe. 1992. *Annotated List of the Birds of Pennsylvania*. Ornithological Technical Committee, Pennsylvania Biological Survey Contribution No. 4.

Schneck, Marcus. 1992. Bald Eagles Soaring in the Eye of a Storm. *Hawk Mountain News*, 77:7-9.

Senner, Stanley E. 1984a. The Model Hawk Law - 1934 to 1972. *Hawk Mountain News*, 62:29-36.

_____. 1984b. Why Count Hawks? A Hawk Mountain Perspective. *Hawk Mountain News*, 62:42-45.

_____. 1989. Hawk Mountain Sanctuary Association, Pennsylvania. *American Birds*, 43:248-253.

_____. 1990. Oak-Maple Ridge-top Forest (Hawk Mountain Breeding Bird Census - 1989). *Journal of Field Ornithology*, 61(Supplement):44-45.

Senner, Stanley E. and James C. Bednarz. 1989. Oak-maple Ridge-top Forest (Hawk Mountain Winter Bird Population Study - 1988). *Journal of Field Ornithology*, 60(Supplement):10.

Senner, Stanley E. and James J. Brett. 1989. A Proposal to Create a Registry of Sites of International Importance to Raptors, Especially on Migration. Pages 33-37 in B. Meyburg and R. D. Chancellor, editors. *Raptors in the Modern World*. World Working Group for Birds of Prey, Berlin, London, and Paris.

Senner, Stanley E. and M. R. Fuller. 1989. Status and Conservation of North American Raptors Migrating to the Neotropics. Pages 53-58 in B. Meyburg and R. D. Chancellor, editors. *Raptors in the Modern World*. World Working Group for Birds of Prey, Berlin, London, and Paris.

Senner, Stanley E. and Laurie J. Goodrich. 1992. Broad-winged Hawk. Pages 104-105 in *Atlas of Breeding Birds in Pennsylvania*, edited by Daniel W. Brauning. Pittsburgh: University of Pittsburgh Press.

Sharadin, Richard. 1972. 1971 Hawk Migrations. *News Letter to Members No. 44*. Hawk Mountain Sanctuary Association, Kempton, Pa.

_____. 1973. 1972 Hawk Migration. *News Letter to Members No. 45*. Hawk Mountain Sanctuary Association, Kempton.

_____. 1974. Migration 1973. *News Letter to Members No. 46*. Hawk Mountain Sanctuary Association, Kempton, Pa.

Shelley, E. and S. Benz. 1985. Observations of Aerial Hunting, Food Carrying and Crop Size of Migrant Raptors. Pages 299-301 in I. Newton and R. D. Chancellor, editors. *Conservation Studies on Raptors*. International Council for Bird Preservation, Cambridge, England.

Sielman, M.S., L. A. Sheriff, and T. C. William. 1981. Nocturnal Migration at Hawk Mountain, Pennsylvania. *American Birds*, 35:906-909.

Slater, Michael. 1987a. County Reports January - March 1987. *Pennsylvania Birds*, 1(1):8.

_____. 1987b. County Reports April - June 1987. *Pennsylvania Birds*, 1(2):42-43.

_____. 1987c. County Reports July - September 1987. *Pennsylvania Birds*, 1(3):79-80.

_____. 1987d. County Reports October - December 1987. *Pennsylvania Birds*, 1(4):121-123.

_____. 1988. County Reports January - March 1988. *Pennsylvania Birds*, 2(1):19-20.

Smith, Stephen. 1987. Northern Appalachians. *Hawk Migration Studies*, 12(2):27-33.

Smith, Gregory. 1988. Northern Appalachians. *Hawk Migration Studies*, 14(1):43-45.

_____. 1990. Northern Appalachians. *Hawk Migration Studies*, 16(1):52-58.

_____. 1991. Northern Appalachians. *Hawk Migration Studies*, 16[sic 17](1):64-69.

Spence, Matthew J. 1991. Site Guide: Lake Ontelaunee Berks County. *Pennsylvania Birds*, 5(1):13-15.

Spofford, W. R. 1969. Hawk Mountain Counts as Population Indices in Northeastern America. Pages 323-332 in J. J. Hickey, editor. *Peregrine Falcon Populations*. Madison, Wisconsin: University of Wisconsin Press.

Sprunt, Alexander IV. 1969. Population Trends of the Bald Eagle in North America. In J.J. Hickey, editor, *Peregrine Falcon Populations*. Madison, Wisconsin: University of Wisconsin Press.

Stone, Witmer. 1894. *The Birds of Eastern Pennsylvania and New Jersey*. Delaware Valley Ornithological Club, Philadelphia, Pa.

_____. 1930. Poole on Birds of Berks County, Pa. *Auk*, 46:108.

_____. 1937. *Bird Studies at Old Cape May*. 2 Volumes. Delaware Valley Ornithological Club, Philadelphia, Pa.

Stotz, N. G. and Laurie J. Goodrich. 1989. Sexual Differences in Timing of American Kestrel Migration at Hawk Mountain Sanctuary, PA. *Journal of Raptor Research*, 23(4):167-171.

Sutton, George M. 1927. The Invasion of Goshawks and Snow Owls during the Winter of 1926-1927. *Cardinal*, 2:35-41.

_____. 1928a. *An Introduction to the Birds of Pennsylvania*. Harrisburg: J. Horace McFarland Co.

_____. 1928b. Notes on a Collection of Hawks from Schuylkill County, Pennsylvania. *Wilson Bulletin*, 40:84-89, 193-194.

_____. 1928c. Abundance of the Golden Eagle in Pennsylvania in 1927-1928. *Auk*, 45:375.

_____. 1929. How Can the Bird-Lover Help to Save the Hawks and Owls? *Auk*, 46:190-195.

_____. 1931. The Status of the Goshawk in Pennsylvania. *Wilson Bulletin*, 43(2):108-113.

Taylor, Robert L. 1948. Profiles: Oh Hawk of Mercy! *New Yorker*, April 17:31.

Thorpe, Steven. 1996. Northern Appalachian Region. *Hawk Migration Studies*, 21(2):47-48.

Todd, W. E. Clyde. 1966. [Review of] Pennsylvania Birds. An Annotated List by Earl L. Poole. *Auk*, 83:320-321.

Tordoff, Harrison B. 1995. Return of the Peregrine. *Hawk Mountain News*, 83:7-11.

Turnbull, W. P. 1869. *The Birds of East Pennsylvania and New Jersey*. Philadelphia, Pa.: Henry Grambo & Co.

Viverette, Cathy B. 1993a. Oak-Maple Ridge-top Forest (Hawk Mountain Breeding Bird Census - 1992). *Journal of Field Ornithology*, 64(Supplement)53-54.

_____. 1993b. Oak-Maple Slope Forest (Hawk Mountain Breeding Bird Census - 1992). *Journal of Field Ornithology*, 64(Supplement):54.

_____. 1994a. The Game of Hawkwatching. *Hawk Mountain News*, 80:9-19.

_____. 1994b. Oak-Maple Ridge-top Forest (Hawk Mountain Breeding Bird Census - 1993). *Journal of Field Ornithology*, 65(Supplement):61-62.

_____. 1994c. Oak-Maple Slope Forest. (Hawk Mountain Breeding Bird Census - 1993). *Journal of Field Ornithology*, 65(Supplement):62.

_____. 1995a. Oak-Maple Slope Forest (Hawk Mountain Breeding Bird Census - 1994). *Journal of Field Ornithology*, 66(Supplement):56.

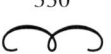

_____. 1995b. Oak-Maple Ridge-top Forest (Hawk Mountain Breeding Bird Census - 1994). *Journal of Field Ornithology*, 66(Supplement):55-56.

Viverette, Cathy B., Laurie J. Goodrich, and M. Pokras. 1994. Levels of DDE in Eastern Flyway Populations of Migrating Sharp-shinned Hawks and the Question of Recent Declines in Numbers Sighted. *Journal of Hawk Migration Studies*, 20(1):5-7.

Viverette, C. B., L. Goodrich, P. Kerlinger, P. Wood, and M. Pokras. 1994. Sharp-shinned Hawk Counts at Hawk Mountain, PA, and Cape May, NJ: An Indicator of Population Declines or a Change in Geographic Distributions? *Journal of Raptor Research*, 28(1):66-67.

Viverette, Cathy, S. Struve, Laurie J. Goodrich, and Keith L. Bildstein. 1996. Decreases in Migrating Sharp-shinned Hawks (*Accipiter striatus*) at Traditional Raptor Migration Watch Sites in Eastern North America. *Auk*, 113:32-40.

Wakely, James S. and Lillian D. Wakely. 1983. *Birds of Pennsylvania*. Harrisburg: Pennsylvania Game Commission.

Warren, B. H. 1890. *Report on the Birds of Pennsylvania*. Second edition. Harrisburg: State Board of Agriculture.

Weidensaul, Scott. 1992a. Ghosts Return to Penn's Woods. *Hawk Mountain News*, 76:16-19.

_____. 1992b. *Seasonal Guide to the Natural Year - Mid-Atlantic*. Golden, Colorado: Fulcrum Publishing.

_____. 1992c. Appalachian Trails: Travelers on the Ridge. *Hawk Mountain News*, 77:23-26.

_____. 1993. Golden Eagles: Enigmas of the East. *Hawk Mountain News*, 79:7-9.

_____. 1994a. *Mountains of the Heart: A Natural History of the Appalachians*. Golden, Colo.: Fulcrum.

_____. 1994b. In Flight: Hawk of Empty Skies. *Hawk Mountain News*, 81:7-9.

_____. 1995. In Flight - Broadwings: Living on the Wind. *Hawk Mountain News*, 82:18-21.

_____. 1997. In Flight: Beauties (In the Eye of the Beholder). *Hawk Mountain News*, 86:18-21.

Wetzel, Frederick W. 1969. The Hawk Season. *News Letter to Members No. 41*. Hawk Mountain Sanctuary Association, Kempton, Pa.

_____. 1970. 1969 Hawk Migration. *News Letter to Members No. 42*. Hawk Mountain Sanctuary Association, Kempton.

_____. 1971. 1970 Hawk Migration. *News Letter to Members No. 43*. Hawk Mountain Sanctuary Association, Kempton.

Wiehn, J. and E. Korpimaki. Plumage Characteristics and Reproductive Fitness in American Kestrels. *Journal of Avian Biology*. In press.

Wiehn, J., E. Korpimaki, and K. L. Bildstein. Plumage Characteristics and Blood Parasites in American Kestrels. *Ethology*. In press.

Willimont, Lori A., Stanley E. Senner, and Laurie J. Goodrich. 1988. Fall Migration of Ruby-throated Hummingbirds in the Northeastern United States. *Wilson Bulletin*, 100(3):482-488.

Wiltraut, Rick. 1994. A Ruddy Turnbark and a Ruddy Rototiller. *Pennsylvania Birds*, 8(3):144.

Wink, Judy, Stanley E. Senner, and Laurie J. Goodrich. 1987. Food Habits of Great Horned Owls in Pennsylvania. *Journal of the Pennsylvania Academy of Science*, 61:133-137.

Wink, Judy, Laurie Goodrich, and Stanley Senner. 1988. Research Results: Raptors and Their Prey. *Hawk Mountain News*, 70:25-30.

Wlasniewski, Matthew. 1992. First Pennsylvania Record of Ancient Murrelet in Berks County. *Pennsylvania Birds*, 6(4):143.

Wright, Minturn. 1994. 60 years of Conservation. *Hawk Mountain News*, 80:1-3.

Wood, Merrill. 1979. *Birds of Pennsylvania: When and Where to Find Them*. Rev. ed. State College, Pa.: Pennsylvania State University.

Zalles, Jorge and Keith Bildstein. 1996. Spreading Our Wings: Hawks Aloft Worldwide. *Hawk Mountain News*, 85:10-18.

Zaslowsky, Diane. 1994. In Profile: Rosalie Edge. *Hawk Mountain News*, 81:20-23.

Index to the Common Names